THE
CRICKETERS' WHO'S WHO
1988

compiled and edited by
IAIN SPROAT

WILLOW BOOKS
Collins
8 Grafton Street, London W1
1988

THE CRICKETERS'
WHO'S WHO
1988

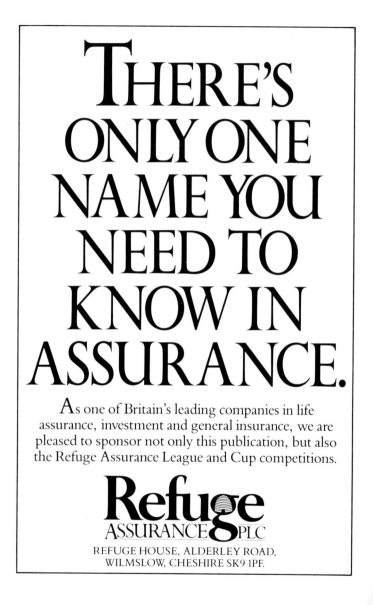

Willow Books
William Collins Sons & Co. Ltd
London · Glasgow · Sydney · Auckland
Toronto · Johannesburg

First published in Great Britain in 1988 by
William Collins Sons & Co. Ltd, 8 Grafton Street,
London W1X 3LA in association with The
Cricketers' Who's Who Limited
© Iain Sproat 1988

British Library Cataloguing in Publication Data
The Cricketers' who's who – 9th ed.
1. Cricket players – Biography
I. Sproat, Iain
796.35'8'0922   GV915.A1
ISBN 0-00-218286-6 hardback
ISBN 0-00-218285-8 paperback

Cover photographs of
David Capel and David Lawrence
by Adrian Murrell/Allsport

Portraits by Bill Smith

Typeset by Rowland Phototypesetting Ltd
Bury St Edmunds, Suffolk
Printed and bound in Great Britain by
Butler and Tanner Ltd, Frome, Somerset

PREFACE

THIS YEAR I have added several new elements to the *Cricketers' Who's Who*, now in its ninth successive season. First, I have given a bowler's strike rate, which is how many balls he has to bowl, on average, before he takes a wicket. Like all statistics, this one has to be set very much in context: nonetheless, there are some interesting comparisons thrown up. I have also included the county first-class batting and bowling averages as a long list; that is to say, not just as a place against an individual player's name. Having all the players listed together thus – as well as individually, in their own entries when included with the year's visiting tourists and University players – again throws up some interesting thoughts about those with high averages who never get chosen for England, and those with low averages who consistently do (or, at least, some do). I have also included the league tables for the County Championship and the Refuge Assurance Sunday League, and the winners and runners-up of the Benson & Hedges and NatWest trophies.

The cricketers listed in this volume include those who played for their county at least once last season, either in the County Championship, Refuge Assurance League, Benson & Hedges or NatWest matches. The statistics are accurate up to the end of the last English season – with one exception: it has proved impossible to guarantee the accuracy of the statistics of certain matches, classified as first-class, in India and Pakistan. However, Test match figures in those countries have been included. Figures about 50 wickets and 1000 runs, etc. in a season refer to matches in England only. First-class figures do not include figures for Test matches which are listed separately. One-day 50s and 100s are for English domestic competitions plus all Internationals, home and abroad.

The following abbreviations apply: * means not out; RAL means Refuge Assurance League; and B & H means Benson & Hedges. The figures for batting and bowling averages refer to the full first-class list (including the year's visiting tourists and University players) for 1987, followed in brackets by the 1986 figures. Inclusion in the batting averages depends on a minimum of eight innings, and an average of at least 10 runs; a bowler has had to have taken at least 10 wickets in at least 10 innings. The same qualification has been used for compiling the bowlers' strike rate.

Readers will notice certain occasional differences in the way the same kind of information is presented. This is because I have usually tried to follow the way in which the cricketers themselves have provided the relevant information.

A book of this complexity and detail has to be prepared several months in advance of the cricket season, and occasionally there are recent changes in a player's circumstances which cannot be included in time. For example, Colin Metson did not decide to join Glamorgan for the 1987 season until the Spring of that year, and so he appeared in the 1987 *Cricketers' Who's Who* as being still on the Middlesex staff. Many other examples of facts and statistics which can quickly become outdated in the period between the actual compilation of the book and its publication, months later, will spring to the reader's mind, and I ask him or her to make the necessary commonsense allowance and adjustments.

I am indebted to Mr Les Hatton for his splendidly professional work in the collection of statistics, and to Mr Bill Smith, FRPS, who personally took most of the photographs. I should also like to thank Mr Ralph Dellor and Mr James Vyvyan for their help in the production of this book.

Above all I am grateful for the cricketers themselves without whose support this book could not have been compiled.

Iain Sproat
January 1988

FOREWORD

V. G. RAMSDEN
Chairman, Refuge Assurance p.l.c.

I AM DELIGHTED that two solid institutions, Refuge Assurance p.l.c. and the classic game of cricket, now combine together.

This is the second season of our sponsorship of the Refuge Assurance League.

It sees the introduction of both the Refuge Assurance Cup, a knockout competition between the four teams finishing top of the Refuge Assurance League table, and our sponsorship of this book, an essential package for every cricket enthusiast.

I hope you relish the excitement of the season and enjoy the interesting reading this book presents.

ABRAHAMS, J.　　　　　Lancashire

Full Name: John Abrahams
Role: Left-hand bat, off-break bowler
Born: 21 July 1952, Cape Town, South Africa
Height: 5' 7" **Weight:** 10st 8lbs
Nickname: Abey
County debut: 1973
County cap: 1982
Benefit: 1988
1000 runs in a season: 4
1st-Class 50s scored: 53
1st-Class 100s scored: 13
1st-Class 200s scored: 1
One-Day 50s: 17
One-Day 100s: 1
Place in batting averages: 54th
av. 37.50 (1986 45th av. 40.35)
1st-Class catches 1987: 5
(career 160)
Parents: Cecil John and Cynthia Jean
Wife and date of marriage: Debbie, 5 April 1986
Family links with cricket: Father was professional with Milnrow and Radcliffe in Central Lancashire League. Brothers Basil and Peter have both pro'd in the Leagues for Uppermill CC and Heyside CC
Education: Moorhouse County Primary School; Heywood Grammar School (later became Heywood Senior High School)
Qualifications: 9 O-levels, 1 A-level, Senior Coaching Certificate
Jobs outside cricket: Shop manager and representative, Beaverwise Plant Hire, Oldham; coaching community groups through GMYA
Overseas teams played for: Player-coach for Mowbray CC, Tasmania 1980–81; Western Creek CC, Canberra 1983–84, 1984–85
Cricketers particularly learnt from: David Lloyd, Clive Lloyd
Cricketers particularly admired: Clive Lloyd, Mike Brearley
Other sports played: Badminton, golf
Other sports followed: Watching rugby union on TV. Almost all sports
Injuries 1987: 'Run insufficientus (not scoring enough runs!)'
Relaxations: Music and reading
Extras: Has lived in UK since 1962. Substitute for England in place of Brian Rose in Fifth Test against West Indies at Headingley in August 1980. 'Would very much like to be a physiotherapist when I retire.' Gold award winner in 1984 B & H final. Captain 1984 and 1985
Opinions on cricket: 'The game's getting harder!'

Best batting performance: 201* Lancashire v Warwickshire, Nuneaton 1984
Best bowling performance: 3-27 Lancashire v Worcestershire, Old Trafford 1981

LAST SEASON: BATTING

	I.	N.O.	R.	H.S.	AV.
TEST					
1ST-CLASS	15	1	525	140*	37.50
INT					
RAL	7	0	67	24	9.57
NAT.W.					
B & H	4	1	54	31*	18.00

LAST SEASON: BOWLING

	O.	M.	R.	W.	AV.
TEST					
1ST-CLASS	23	6	65	2	32.50
INT					
RAL	5	0	19	2	9.50
NAT.W.					
B & H	8	2	32	2	16.00

CAREER: BATTING

	I.	N.O.	R.	H.S.	AV.
TEST					
1ST-CLASS	386	52	10001	201*	29.94
INT					
RAL	122	23	2442	103*	24.66
NAT.W.	24	3	491	67*	23.38
B & H	31	6	627	66*	25.08

CAREER: BOWLING

	O.	M.	R.	W.	AV.
TEST					
1ST-CLASS	948.1	201	2811	56	50.19
INT					
RAL	86.2	6	439	13	33.76
NAT.W.	44	6	176	5	35.20
B & H	39	4	166	4	41.50

AFFORD, J. A.   Nottinghamshire

Full Name: John Andrew Afford
Role: Right-hand bat, slow left-arm bowler
Born: 12 May 1964, Crowland, Nr. Peterborough
Height: 6′ 2″ **Weight:** 13st
Nickname: Aff
County debut: 1984
1st-Class 5 w. in innings: 4
1st-Class 10 w. in match: 1
Place in bowling averages: 52nd av. 28.03 (1986 67th av. 32.33)
Strike rate 1987: 63.84 (career 66.21)
1st-Class catches 1987: 1 (career 8)
Parents: Jill
Marital status: Single
Family links with cricket: 'Uncle played for school 2nd XI!'
Education: Spalding Grammar School; Stamford College for Further Education
Qualifications: 5 O-levels, NCA Coaching Certificate
Cricketing superstitions or habits: 'Do not change gear if doing well during a game. Try not to go for too many sixes early on in a spell!'

Overseas teams played for: Upper Hutt CC, New Zealand 1985–87
Cricketers particularly learnt from: David Johnson at Bourne CC and everyone at Nottinghamshire, especially Eddie Hemmings
Cricketers particularly admired: Richard Hadlee, Bishan Bedi, Derek Underwood
Other sports followed: 'Will give anything a whirl, but nothing too serious. Able to watch most things – just can't fathom out people's fascination for horse racing.' Supports Peterborough United FC
Relaxations: Listening to music, playing bass guitar, and 'a few quiet ones in the TBI'.
Injuries 1987: 'Slipped disc in lower back caused me to miss last two months of the season.'
Best batting performance: 16 Nottinghamshire v Surrey, Trent Bridge 1987
Best bowling performance: 6-81 Nottinghamshire v Kent, Trent Bridge 1986

LAST SEASON: BATTING

	I.	N.O.	R.	H.S.	AV.
TEST					
1ST-CLASS	10	6	23	16	5.75
INT					
RAL					
NAT.W.					
B & H					

CAREER: BATTING

	I.	N.O.	R.	H.S.	AV.
TEST					
1ST-CLASS	23	13	44	16	4.40
INT					
RAL					
NAT.W.					
B & H					

LAST SEASON: BOWLING

	O.	M.	R.	W.	AV.
TEST					
1ST-CLASS	276.4	87	729	26	28.03
INT					
RAL					
NAT.W.					
B & H	8	0	55	0	–

CAREER: BOWLING

	O.	M.	R.	W.	AV.
TEST					
1ST-CLASS	882.5	256	2517	80	31.46
INT					
RAL	8	1	27	1	27.00
NAT.W.					
B & H	8	0	55	0	–

---

1. Which legendary England fast bowler used to comfort his victims as they passed him by on their way to the pavilion by saying: 'Best one I've bowled this year, sir!'?

2. Which former first-class cricketer, who made a century in his first game for Cambridge, was last year revealed as a member of M.I.5?

AGNEW, J. P.   Leicestershire

Full Name: Jonathan Philip Agnew
Role: Right-hand bat, right-arm
fast bowler, outfielder
Born: 4 April 1960, Macclesfield,
Cheshire
Height: 6′ 4″ **Weight:** 12st 6lbs
Nickname: Spiro (after former US
Vice-President Spiro Agnew),
Rambo
County debut: 1978
County cap: 1984
Test debut: 1984
No. of Tests: 3
No. of One-Day Internationals: 3
50 wickets in a season: 4
1st-Class 50s scored: 2
1st-Class 5 w. in innings: 21
1st-Class 10 w. in match: 4
Place in batting averages:
201st av. 16.82 (1986 222nd av. 12.92)
Place in bowling averages: 25th av. 24.26 (1986 49th av. 27.78)
Strike rate 1987: 46.15 (career 50.87)
1st-Class catches 1987: 1 (career 29)
Parents: Philip and Margaret
Wife and date of marriage: Beverley, 8 October 1983
Children: Jennifer, 31 October 1985
Family links with cricket: First cousin, Mary Duggan, Captain of England's
Women's XI in 1960s. Father very keen cricketer
Education: Taverham Hall Prep School; Uppingham School
Qualifications: 9 O-levels, 2 A-levels in German and English
Jobs outside cricket: Cricket Coach. Spent 1981–82 off-season coaching at
Sindia High School, Zimbabwe. Production control at T. L. Bennett's
Windows Ltd. Sports producer at BBC Radio Leicester
Off-season 1987–88: Freelance journalist with BBC Radio Leicester
Cricketing superstitions or habits: 'I never use a bowling marker so am never
popular with groundsmen! Don't whiten boots.'
Overseas tours: Young England to Australia, 1978–79; Leicestershire CCC to
Zimbabwe, 1981; England to India and Australia, 1984–85; England B to Sri
Lanka, 1986
Overseas teams played for: Whitbread scholarship, playing for Essendon CC,
Melbourne, 1978, 1980; Alexandra CC, Harare, Zimbabwe, 1981–82; Cen-
tral Cumberland District Cricket Club, Sydney, 1982–83

Cricketers particularly learnt from: Ken Higgs, Frank Tyson, Peter Willey, Ken Shuttleworth
Cricketers particularly admired: Imran Khan, Wayne Larkins
Other sports played: Hockey, golf
Relaxations: Music (all kinds). Playing piano and tuba. Coaching cricket. 'I became very interested in game viewing in Zimbabwe. I spent days driving around to study and photograph – particularly elephants. Watching "Only Fools and Horses", "Minder", and "Blackadder".'
Extras: Played for Surrey 2nd XI 1976–77. Leicestershire CCC Player of the Year 1987. One of *Wisden*'s Cricketers of the Year 1987
Opinions on cricket: 'It would be absolutely absurd and pointless to play four-day matches on uncovered wickets.'
Best batting performance: 90 Leicestershire v Yorkshire, Scarborough 1987
Best bowling performance: 9-70 Leicestershire v Kent, Leicester 1985

LAST SEASON: BATTING

	I.	N.O.	R.	H.S.	AV.
TEST					
1ST-CLASS	27	4	387	90	16.82
INT					
RAL	5	4	27	23*	27.00
NAT.W.	2	2	13	8*	
B & H	3	0	25	20	8.33

CAREER: BATTING

	I.	N.O.	R.	H.S.	AV.
TEST	4	3	10	5	10.00
1ST-CLASS	142	25	1301	90	11.11
INT	1	1	2	2*	–
RAL	15	9	58	23*	9.66
NAT.W.	5	4	27	8*	27.00
B & H	10	2	56	23*	7.00

LAST SEASON: BOWLING

	O.	M.	R.	W.	AV.
TEST					
1ST-CLASS	777	144	2451	101	24.26
INT					
RAL	74.4	1	349	11	31.72
NAT.W.	46	6	214	6	35.66
B & H	31	6	105	7	15.00

CAREER: BOWLING

	O.	M.	R.	W.	AV.
TEST	92	22	373	4	93.25
1ST-CLASS	3672.4	702	12227	440	27.78
INT	21	0	120	3	40.00
RAL	291.2	11	1428	43	33.20
NAT.W.	113	18	419	14	29.92
B & H	206.2	32	772	33	23.39

3. At which Test ground is the Vulture Street End?

4. At which ground is the Swan River End?

5. Which English batsmen scored their first Test century in the Second Test v Australia at Perth in November 1986, and who missed it by only 4 runs?

ALIKHAN, R. K.   Sussex

Full Name: Rehan Kebal Alikhan
Role: Right-hand bat
Born: 28 December 1962, London
Height: 6′ 1½″ **Weight:** 13st
Nickname: Prince, Oily, Pretty
Polly, Munch
County debut: 1986
1st-Class 50s scored: 12
One-Day 50s: 2
Place in batting averages: 162nd
av. 21.48 (1986 73rd av. 35.12)
1st-Class catches 1987: 9
(career 26)
Parents: Akbar and Farida
Marital status: Single
Education: King's College School,
Wimbledon

Qualifications: 2 A-levels, 8 O-levels
Jobs outside cricket: Insurance Broker
Cricketing superstitions or habits: 'I never bat with a cap on.'
Overseas tours: King's College School, Wimbledon to Holland 1978 and 1980;
Surrey Schools U-19 to Australia 1979–80; Club Cricket Conference to
Kenya 1985
Overseas teams played for: Mosman Middle Harbour District CC 1982–83
and 1983–84
Cricketers particularly learnt from: Imran Khan, Paul Parker, Monty Lynch
Cricketers particularly admired: Zaheer Abbas, Imran Khan, Viv Richards,
Greg Chappell
Off-season 1987–88: Playing cricket in Pakistan

LAST SEASON: BATTING

	I.	N.O.	R.	H.S.	AV.
TEST					
1ST-CLASS	34	3	666	78	21.48
INT					
RAL	6	1	62	23	12.40
NAT.W.	2	0	55	37	27.50
B & H	3	0	137	71	45.66

LAST SEASON: BOWLING

	O.	M.	R.	W.	AV.
TEST					
1ST-CLASS	0.1	0	4	0	–
INT					
RAL	1	0	5	0	–
NAT.W.					
B & H					

CAREER: BATTING

	I.	N.O.	R.	H.S.	AV.
TEST					
1ST-CLASS	84	8	1921	78	25.27
INT					
RAL	7	1	72	23	12.00
NAT.W.	7	1	116	41	19.33
B & H	3	0	137	71	45.66

CAREER: BOWLING

	O.	M.	R.	W.	AV.
TEST					
1ST-CLASS	20.1	1	98	1	98.00
INT					
RAL	1	0	5	0	–
NAT.W.					
B & H					

Other sports played: Squash, soccer, rugby
Other sports followed: American football, Aussie rules, hockey, golf, tennis
Relaxations: Reading, music, theatre, watching sport
Best batting performance: 78 Sussex v Glamorgan, Hove 1987

ALLEYNE, M. W. Gloucestershire

Full Name: Mark Wayne Alleyne
Role: Right-hand bat, medium
pace bowler, cover fielder
Born: 23 May 1968, Tottenham
Height: 5′ 10½″ **Weight:** 12st 2lbs
Nickname: Boo-Boo
County debut: 1986
1st-Class 50s scored: 6
1st-Class 100s scored: 1
Place in batting averages: 128th
av. 27.30 (1986 102nd av. 30.54)
Place in bowling averages: 141st
av. 64.45
Strike rate 1987: 94.18 (career 95.81)
1st-Class catches 1987: 7
(career 12)
Parents: Euclid Clevis and
Hyacinth Cordeilla
Marital status: Single
Family links with cricket: Brother played for Gloucestershire 2nd XI and Middlesex YCs. Father played club cricket in Barbados and England
Education: Harrison College, Barbados and Cardinal Pole School, E London
Qualifications: 6 O-levels, NCA senior coaching award
Off-season 1987–88: Playing in Melbourne
Overseas tours: South of England YC to Bermuda; England YC to Sri Lanka 1987; Gloucestershire CC to Sri Lanka 1987
Cricketers particularly learnt from: Seymour Nurse (former coach)
Cricketers particularly admired: Gordon Greenidge, Viv Richards
Other sports played: Basketball
Other sports followed: Football, snooker
Relaxations: Watching films and sport; listening to music
Extras: Youngest player to score a century for Gloucestershire
Best batting performance: 116* Gloucestershire v Sussex, Bristol 1986
Best bowling performance: 4-128 Gloucestershire v Warwickshire, Edgbaston 1987

LAST SEASON: BATTING

	I.	N.O.	R.	H.S.	AV.
TEST					
1ST-CLASS	30	7	628	82	27.30
INT					
RAL	12	6	105	23*	17.50
NAT.W.	4	2	9	9*	4.50
B & H	4	0	53	36	13.25

LAST SEASON: BOWLING

	O.	M.	R.	W.	AV.
TEST					
1ST-CLASS	172.4	35	709	11	64.45
INT					
RAL	80	2	396	16	24.75
NAT.W.	14	1	48	1	48.00
B & H	17	0	75	4	18.75

CAREER: BATTING

	I.	N.O.	R.	H.S.	AV.
TEST					
1ST-CLASS	48	12	1021	116*	28.36
INT					
RAL	14	6	152	46	19.00
NAT.W.	4	2	9	9*	4.50
B & H	4	0	53	36	13.25

CAREER: BOWLING

	O.	M.	R.	W.	AV.
TEST					
1ST-CLASS	175.4	35	724	11	65.81
INT					
RAL	80	2	396	16	24.75
NAT.W.	14	1	48	1	48.00
B & H	17	0	75	4	18.75

ALLOTT, P. J. W.   Lancashire

Full Name: Paul John Walter Allott
Role: Right-hand bat, right-arm fast-medium bowler
Born: 14 September 1956, Altrincham, Cheshire
Height: 6' 4" **Weight:** 14st
County debut: 1978
County cap: 1981
Test debut: 1981
No. of Tests: 13
No. of One-Day Internationals: 13
50 wickets in a season: 4
1st-Class 50s scored: 9
1st-Class 5 w. in innings: 24
Place in batting averages: 122nd av. 27.86 (1986 129th av. 27.28)
Place in bowling averages: 9th av. 20.71 (1986 29th av. 24.48)
Strike rate 1987: 54.54 (career 58.30)
1st-Class catches 1987: 24 (career 59)
Parents: John Norman and Lillian Patricia
Wife and date of marriage: Helen, 27 October 1979
Family links with cricket: Father was dedicated club cricketer for 20 years with Ashley CC and is now active with Bowdon CC (Cheshire County League) as a selector, administrator and junior organiser
Education: Altrincham Grammar School; Bede College, Durham
Qualifications: Qualified teacher; cricket coach

15

Jobs outside cricket: Teacher; cricket coach for Manchester Education Committee; coach in Tasmania for Tasmanian Cricket Association
Overseas tours: With England to India 1981–82; India and Australia 1984–85; International XI to Jamaica 1982–83
Cricketers particularly learnt from: Dennis Lillee, Steve Murrills
Other sports played: Golf, football, squash, rugby, tennis
Relaxations: Playing golf, watching all sports, listening to music, eating out, photography
Extras: Played as goalkeeper for Cheshire schoolboys. Took part in 10th wicket record partnership for England with Bob Willis, 70 v India, at Lord's, June 1982. Wears contact lenses. Forced by injury to return early from Indian tour in 1984–85
Best batting performance: 88 Lancashire v Hampshire, Southampton 1987
Best bowling performance: 8-48 Lancashire v Northamptonshire, Northampton 1981

LAST SEASON: BATTING

	I.	N.O.	R.	H.S.	AV.
TEST					
1ST-CLASS	27	4	641	88	27.86
INT					
RAL	4	2	64	34	32.00
NAT.W.					
B & H	1	0	18	18	18.00

CAREER: BATTING

	I.	N.O.	R.	H.S.	AV.
TEST	18	3	213	52*	14.20
1ST-CLASS	177	47	2442	88	18.78
INT	6	1	15	8	3.00
RAL	43	22	347	34	16.52
NAT.W.	8	3	40	19*	8.00
B & H	16	5	110	23*	10.00

LAST SEASON: BOWLING

	O.	M.	R.	W.	AV.
TEST					
1ST-CLASS	535.2	166	1222	59	20.71
INT					
RAL	67.3	5	326	7	46.57
NAT.W.					
B & H	22	4	68	4	17.00

CAREER: BOWLING

	O.	M.	R.	W.	AV.
TEST	370.5	75	1084	26	41.69
1ST-CLASS	4594.5	1276	11848	485	24.42
INT	136.3	19	552	15	36.80
RAL	652.5	60	2632	104	25.30
NAT.W.	178.4	36	535	34	15.73
B & H	317.1	53	1012	43	23.53

6. Which current Australian cricketer likes to bat and bowl with his sleeves buttoned down, shirt buttoned almost to the neck, collar turned up, wearing a cap?

7. Which great batsman said of which great bowler that it was hard enough to play a ball from him when you didn't know which way it was meant to turn, but almost impossible when the bowler didn't know either?

AMISS, D. L. Warwickshire

Full Name: Dennis Leslie Amiss
Role: Right-hand bat, slow left-arm chinaman bowler, slip fielder
Born: 7 April 1943, Harborne, Birmingham
Height: 5′ 11″ **Weight:** 13st
Nickname: Sacka
County debut: 1960
County cap: 1965
Benefit: 1975 (£34,947)
Testimonial: 1985 (when part of proceeds went to schools' cricket in Warwickshire)
Test debut: 1966
No. of Tests: 50
No. of One-Day Internationals: 18
1000 runs in a season: 23
1st-Class 50s scored: 213
1st-Class 100s scored: 99
1st-Class 200s scored: 3
One-day 50s: 74
One-day 100s: 13
Place in batting averages: 107th av. 30.23 (1986 64th av. 37.17)
1st-Class catches 1987: 8 (career 418)
Wife: Jill
Children: Paul, Becca
Family links with cricket: Father, A. F. Amiss, played good club cricket
Jobs outside cricket: Director of Officescape Ltd (office interior space planning and design consultancy)

LAST SEASON: BATTING

	I.	N.O.	R.	H.S.	AV.
TEST					
1ST-CLASS	46	3	1300	123	30.23
INT					
RAL	9	1	179	53	22.37
NAT.W.	3	0	89	40	29.66
B & H	3	1	80	49*	40.00

CAREER: BATTING

	I.	N.O.	R.	H.S.	AV.
TEST	88	10	3612	262*	46.30
1ST-CLASS	1051	116	39811	232*	42.57
INT	18	0	859	137	47.72
RAL	239	20	7040	117*	32.14
NAT.W.	55	5	1950	135	39.00
B & H	67	7	1257	100*	28.56

LAST SEASON: BOWLING

	O.	M.	R.	W.	AV.
TEST					
1ST-CLASS					
INT					
RAL					
NAT.W.					
B & H					

CAREER: BOWLING

	O.	M.	R.	W.	AV.
TEST					
1ST-CLASS	213.1	32	718	18	39.88
INT					
RAL	3	0	23	1	23.00
NAT.W.	12.1	0	67	0	–
B & H	0.2	0	4	0	–

Overseas tours: Pakistan 1966–67; India, Pakistan and Sri Lanka 1972–73; West Indies 1973–74; Australia and New Zealand 1974–75; India, Sri Lanka and Australia 1976–77; South Africa (Rebel tour) 1982
Overseas teams played for: World Series Cricket 1978–79
Other sports played: Golf, tennis
Other sports followed: Soccer, rugby
Relaxations: Bridge, gardening
Extras: Scored two centuries in one match, 155* and 112 v Worcestershire at Birmingham 1978. Slipped a disc at 17 playing football and the injury means he still has to take precautionary exercise every day. Banned from Test cricket for three years for playing for England Rebels in South Africa, 1982. Retired at end of 1987 season
Best batting performance: 262* England v West Indies, Kingston 1973–74
Best bowling performance: 3-21 Warwickshire v Middlesex, Lord's 1970

ANDERSON, I. S. Derbyshire

Full Name: Iain Stuart Anderson
Role: Right-hand opening bat, off-break bowler
Born: 24 April 1960, Derby
Height: 6' 0" **Weight:** 11st 2lbs
Nickname: Tommy, Tom
County debut: 1978
County cap: 1985
1000 runs in a season: 1
1st-Class 50s scored: 26
1st-Class 100s scored: 2
One-Day 50s: 5
One-Day 100s: 1
Place in batting averages: 163rd
av. 21.42 (1986 180th av. 20.40)
1st-Class catches 1987: 6
(career 106)
Parents: May and Norman
Wife and date of marriage: Linda,
28 September 1985
Family links with cricket: Father and brother (Kenny) played club cricket
Education: Dovecliff Grammar School; Wulfric School, Burton
Qualifications: 8 O-levels, 3 A-levels, Preliminary Coaching Certificate
Overseas tours: England Young Cricketers to Australia 1979
Overseas teams played for: Bergvliet, Cape Town, 1979–80 and 1980–81; Kew, Melbourne, 1982; Ellerslie, Auckland, 1982; Boland, South Africa, 1983–84

Other sports played: Soccer, squash
Relaxations: Eating, listening to music, sleeping
Best batting performance: 112 Derbyshire v Kent, Chesterfield 1983
Best bowling performance: 4-35 Derbyshire v Australia, Derby 1981

LAST SEASON: BATTING

	I.	N.O.	R.	H.S.	AV.
TEST					
1ST-CLASS	21	2	407	87*	21.42
INT					
RAL	11	3	210	41*	26.25
NAT.W.	3	2	80	54*	80.00
B & H	4	1	43	28*	14.33

LAST SEASON: BOWLING

	O.	M.	R.	W.	AV.
TEST					
1ST-CLASS	24.4	6	66	2	33.00
INT					
RAL					
NAT.W.					
B & H					

CAREER: BATTING

	I.	N.O.	R.	H.S.	AV.
TEST					
1ST-CLASS	225	27	4726	112	23.86
INT					
RAL	53	7	1079	64	23.45
NAT.W.	9	2	299	134	42.71
B & H	10	1	192	42	21.33

CAREER: BOWLING

	O.	M.	R.	W.	AV.
TEST					
1ST-CLASS	380.3	73	1356	22	61.63
INT					
RAL	7.1	2	28	2	14.00
NAT.W.					
B & H					

ANDREW, S. J. W.   Hampshire

Full Name: Stephen Jon Walter Andrew
Role: Right-hand bat, right-arm medium bowler
Born: 27 January 1966, London
Height: 6′ 3″ **Weight:** 13st
Nickname: Rip
County debut: 1984
1st-Class 5 w. in innings: 3
Place in bowling averages: 14th av. 21.29 (1986 61st av. 29.92)
Strike rate 1987: 39.52 (career 52.65)
1st-Class catches 1987: 1 (career 10)
Parents: Jon Trevor and Victoria Julia Maud
Marital status: Single
Education: Hordle House Prep. School; Milton Abbey Public School
Qualifications: 3 O-levels
Overseas teams played for: Pirates CC, Durban, South Africa, 1983–84; South African Police CC, 1984
Overseas tours: Young England to West Indies 1985
Cricketers particularly learnt from: Peter Sainsbury, Malcolm Marshall

Cricketers particularly admired: Dennis Lillee, Malcolm Marshall
Other sports played: Squash, golf
Other sports followed: Interested in most sports
Relaxations: Listening to music
Extras: Youngest bowler to have opened bowling for Hampshire
Best batting performance: 7 Hampshire v Kent, Southampton 1986
Best bowling performance: 7-92 Hampshire v Gloucestershire, Southampton 1987

LAST SEASON: BATTING

	I.	N.O.	R.	H.S.	AV.
TEST					
1ST-CLASS	2	1	7	4*	7.00
INT					
RAL					
NAT.W.	1	1	0	0*	
B & H	1	1	0	0*	

CAREER: BATTING

	I.	N.O.	R.	H.S.	AV.
TEST					
1ST-CLASS	18	11	43	7	6.14
INT					
RAL					
NAT.W.	1	1	0	0*	
B & H	2	2	1	1*	

LAST SEASON: BOWLING

	O.	M.	R.	W.	AV.
TEST					
1ST-CLASS	316.1	61	1022	48	21.29
INT					
RAL	13	1	68	1	68.00
NAT.W.	16	1	88	2	44.00
B & H	16	3	58	5	11.60

CAREER: BOWLING

	O.	M.	R.	W.	AV.
TEST					
1ST-CLASS	903.5	189	2963	103	28.76
INT					
RAL	75.3	1	372	7	53.14
NAT.W.	26	2	116	3	38.66
B & H	34	4	118	11	10.72

ASIF DIN, M. Warwickshire

Full Name: Mohamed Asif Din
Role: Right-hand bat, leg-break bowler
Born: 21 September 1960, Kampala, Uganda
Height: 5′ 10″ **Weight:** 10st
Nickname: Gunga and many others
County debut: 1981
County cap: 1987
1000 runs in a season: 1
1st-Class 50s scored: 20
1st-Class 100s scored: 3
1st-Class 5 w. in innings: 1
One-Day 50s: 7
One-Day 100s: 1
Place in batting averages: 89th av. 33.00 (1986 90th av. 32.83)
1st-Class catches 1987: 12 (career 62)

Parents: Jamiz and Mumtaz
Marital status: Married
Family links with cricket: Brothers Khalid and Abid play in Birmingham League
Education: Ladywood Comprehensive School, Birmingham
Qualifications: CSEs and O-levels
Jobs outside cricket: Argos Distributors Limited
Cricketing superstitions: 'Mixing my batting gloves around every time.'
Overseas tours: MCC to East Africa 1981; MCC to Bangladesh 1980–81; Dennis Amiss XI to Barbados 1985
Overseas teams played for: Rugby Union CC, Bathurst, New South Wales, 1984–85; Blayney CC, Blayney, New South Wales, 1985–86
Cricketers particularly admired: Zaheer Abbas, Majid Khan
Off-season 1987–88: Working at Argos
Other sports played: Squash, badminton, golf, snooker
Other sports followed: American football, basketball
Relaxations: Staying in
Opinions on cricket: 'Too much cricket. Would like to see 16 four-day matches.'
Best batting performance: 115* Warwickshire v Gloucestershire, Edgbaston 1987
Best bowling performance: 5-100 Warwickshire v Glamorgan, Edgbaston 1982

LAST SEASON: BATTING

	I.	N.O.	R.	H.S.	AV.
TEST					
1ST-CLASS	36	4	1056	115*	33.00
INT					
RAL	10	2	209	46*	26.12
NAT.W.	3	1	39	25*	19.50
B & H	1	0	2	2	2.00

LAST SEASON: BOWLING

	O.	M.	R.	W.	AV.
TEST					
1ST-CLASS	59	9	251	5	50.20
INT					
RAL					
NAT.W.					
B & H					

CAREER: BATTING

	I.	N.O.	R.	H.S.	AV.
TEST					
1ST-CLASS	186	31	4412	115*	28.46
INT					
RAL	75	13	1571	108*	25.33
NAT.W.	13	4	221	45	24.55
B & H	18	3	352	61	23.46

CAREER: BOWLING

	O.	M.	R.	W.	AV.
TEST					
1ST-CLASS	617.5	108	2512	44	57.09
INT					
RAL	15.3	1	90	3	30.00
NAT.W.	1.1	0	5	1	5.00
B & H	2	0	20	0	–

8. Which current Test player has the first name of Augustine?

9. Who headed the England Test batting averages in Australia, 1986–87?

ASLETT, D. G.   Kent

Full Name: Derek George Aslett
Role: Right-hand bat, leg-break bowler
Born: 12 February 1958, Dover
Height: 6′ **Weight:** 12st
Nickname: Spacko and variations
County debut: 1981
County cap: 1983
1000 runs in a season: 2
1st-Class 50s scored: 26
1st-Class 100s scored: 11
1st-Class 200s scored: 1
One-Day 50s: 9
One-Day 100s: 2
Place in batting averages: 104th
av. 30.28 (1986 172nd av. 22.47)
1st-Class catches 1987: 13
(career 82)

Parents: George and Jean
Wife and date of marriage: Bernadine, 17 November 1984
Family links with cricket: Father played club cricket for Dover
Education: Dover Grammar School; Leicester University
Qualifications: BA (Hons) History
Jobs outside cricket: Postman, orderly, window cleaner for Jim Day International
Overseas teams played for: West Perth CC 1981 and 1982, Bayswater CC 1983–84 on Whitbread Scholarship
Cricketers particularly learnt from: Father, Nigel Sutton, Andy Froude, Graham Mart, and senior Kent players

LAST SEASON: BATTING

	I.	N.O.	R.	H.S.	AV.
TEST					
1ST-CLASS	40	8	969	101*	30.28
INT					
RAL	13	5	354	122*	44.25
NAT.W.	2	0	51	32	25.50
B & H	4	0	123	56	30.75

LAST SEASON: BOWLING

	O.	M.	R.	W.	AV.
TEST					
1ST-CLASS	74.1	8	335	2	167.50
INT					
RAL					
NAT.W.					
B & H					

CAREER: BATTING

	I.	N.O.	R.	H.S.	AV.
TEST					
1ST-CLASS	199	20	6128	221*	34.23
INT					
RAL	58	7	1451	122*	28.45
NAT.W.	14	0	325	67	23.21
B & H	15	1	385	56	27.50

CAREER: BOWLING

	O.	M.	R.	W.	AV.
TEST					
1ST-CLASS	266.1	28	1253	17	73.70
INT					
RAL					
NAT.W.	0.5	0	0	1	0.00
B & H					

Cricketers particularly admired: Mark Benson, Bob Woolmer, C. B. Fry
Other sports played: Rugby, hurling, tennis, diving
Relaxations: Reading, yoga, music
Extras: Scored 146 on debut v Hampshire, 1981. Scored 168 and 119 in same match v Derbyshire, 1983. Wears spectacles. Released by Kent at end of 1987 season
Best batting performance: 221* Kent v Sri Lanka, Canterbury 1984
Best bowling performance: 4-119 Kent v Sussex, Hove 1982

ATHERTON, M. A.   Lancashire

Full Name: Michael Andrew Atherton
Role: Right-hand bat, leg-break bowler
Born: 23 March 1968, Manchester
Height: 6′ **Weight:** 12st
Nickname: Athers
County debut: 1987
1000 runs in a season: 1
1st-Class 50s scored: 4
1st-Class 100s scored: 2
One-Day 50s: 1
Place in batting averages: 50th av. 38.48
1st-Class catches 1987: 7 (career 7)
Parents: Alan and Wendy
Marital status: Single
Family links with cricket:
Father and brother both play
club cricket in Lancashire and Cheshire Leagues
Education: The Manchester Grammar School; Downing College, Cambridge
Qualifications: 10 O-levels, 3 A-levels
Off-season 1987–88: Student at Cambridge University
Cricketing superstitions or habits: Always put left pad on first
Overseas tours: NCA to Bermuda 1985; Young England to Sri Lanka 1987
Cricketers particularly learnt from: Father, Graham Saville (Cambridge coach), and all staff at Lancashire CC
Cricketers particularly admired: Gordon Greenidge, Malcolm Marshall, Abdul Qadir
Other sports played: Football, golf, squash
Other sports followed: Most sports except horse racing
Opinions on cricket: 'Over-rate fines should be abolished.'

Best batting performance: 110 MCC v Yorkshire, Scarborough 1987
Best bowling performance: 3-72 Lancashire v Nottinghamshire, Old Trafford 1987

LAST SEASON: BATTING

	I.	N.O.	R.	H.S.	AV.
TEST					
1ST-CLASS	35	4	1193	110	38.48
INT					
RAL	3	0	25	22	8.33
NAT.W.					
B & H	3	0	87	57	29.00

CAREER: BATTING

	I.	N.O.	R.	H.S.	AV.
TEST					
1ST-CLASS	35	4	1193	110	38.48
INT					
RAL	3	0	25	22	8.33
NAT.W.					
B & H	3	0	87	57	29.00

LAST SEASON: BOWLING

	O.	M.	R.	W.	AV.
TEST					
1ST-CLASS	162.5	16	544	9	60.44
INT					
RAL					
NAT.W.					
B & H	2	0	22	0	–

CAREER: BOWLING

	O.	M.	R.	W.	AV.
TEST					
1ST-CLASS	162.5	16	544	9	60.44
INT					
RAL					
NAT.W.					
B & H	2	0	22	0	–

ATHEY, C. W. J. Gloucestershire

Full Name: Charles William Jeffrey Athey
Role: Right-hand bat, right-arm medium bowler
Born: 27 September 1957, Middlesbrough
Height: 5′ 10″ **Weight:** 12st 3lbs
Nickname: Bumper, Wingnut, Ath
County debut: 1976 (Yorkshire), 1984 (Gloucestershire)
County cap: 1980 (Yorkshire), 1985 (Gloucestershire)
Test debut: 1980
No. of Tests: 17
No. of One-Day Internationals: 20
1000 runs in a season: 6
1st-Class 50s scored: 63
1st-Class 100s scored: 28
One-Day 50s: 47
One-Day 100s: 6
Place in batting averages: 22nd av. 44.65 (1986 42nd av. 41.10)
1st-Class catches 1987: 14 (career 257 + 2 stumpings)
Parents: Peter and Maree
Wife and date of marriage: Janet Linda, 9 October 1982

24

Family links with cricket: 'Father played league cricket in North Yorkshire and South Durham League for 29 years, 25 of them with Middlesbrough. President of Middlesbrough CC since 1975. Brother-in-law Colin Cook played for Middlesex, other brother-in-law (Martin) plays in Thames Valley League. Father-in-law deeply involved in Middlesex Youth cricket.'

Education: Linthorpe Junior School; Stainsby Secondary School; Acklam Hall High School

Qualifications: 4 O-levels, some CSEs, National Cricket Association Coaching Certificate

Jobs outside cricket: Barman, building labourer, sports shop assistant

Overseas tours: D. H. Robins' XI to Canada 1976; South America 1979; Australasia 1980; England U-19 to West Indies 1976; England to West Indies 1981; Barbican XI to Gulf States 1983; England B to Sri Lanka 1985–86; England to Australia 1986–87; World Cup, Pakistan, Australia and New Zealand 1987–88

Overseas teams played for: Manly Warringah, Sydney, Australia, 1977–78, 1978–79, 1979–80; Balmain, Sydney, 1980–81; Schoeman Park, Bloemfontein, South Africa, 1981–82; Papatoetoe, Auckland, New Zealand, 1983–84

Cricketers particularly learnt from: Doug Padgett

Cricketers particularly admired: Gordon Greenidge, Malcolm Marshall, Chris Smith

Off-season 1987–88: On tour with England

Other sports played: Squash, tennis, soccer

Other sports followed: Most sports

Relaxations: Music, good films, good food

Extras: Played for Teeside County Schools U-16s at age 12. Made debut in 1972 North Yorkshire and South Durham League. Played for Yorkshire Colts 1974. Played for North of England Young Cricketers XI v West Indies Young Cricketers at Old Trafford in 1974. Played football for Middlesbrough Schools U-16 XI 1972–74. Played for Middlesbrough Juniors 1974–75. Offered but declined apprenticeship terms with Middlesbrough FC. Captained North Riding U-19 XI 1975–76. Has Union Jack tattoo on left shoulder

LAST SEASON: BATTING

	I.	N.O.	R.	H.S.	AV.
TEST	6	1	186	123	37.20
1ST-CLASS	28	4	1109	160	46.20
INT	3	0	39	33	13.00
RAL	12	0	336	70	28.00
NAT.W.	4	1	130	79	43.33
B & H	5	0	327	95	65.40

LAST SEASON: BOWLING

	O.	M.	R.	W.	AV.
TEST					
1ST-CLASS	56.4	5	199	4	49.75
INT					
RAL					
NAT.W.					
B & H					

CAREER: BATTING

	I.	N.O.	R.	H.S.	AV.
TEST	30	1	722	123	24.89
1ST-CLASS	420	39	12736	184	33.42
INT	20	1	607	142*	31.94
RAL	138	12	4375	121*	34.72
NAT.W.	26	4	826	115	37.54
B & H	43	6	1218	95	32.91

CAREER: BOWLING

	O.	M.	R.	W.	AV.
TEST					
1ST-CLASS	494	88	1661	37	44.89
INT					
RAL	95.4	1	545	21	25.95
NAT.W.	19.1	1	106	1	106.00
B & H	56.4	4	242	12	20.16

Opinions on cricket: 'Tighten up on "qualifying for England" rules; too many overseas players. Must have covered pitches for county games as long as Tests are played on covered pitches.'
Best batting performance: 184 England B v Sri Lanka XI, Galle 1985–86
Best bowling performance: 3-3 Gloucestershire v Hampshire, Bristol 1985

ATKINSON, J. C. M. Somerset

Full Name: Jonathon Colin Mark Atkinson
Role: Right-hand bat, right-arm medium bowler
Born: 10 July 1968, Butleigh
Height: 6′ 3″ **Weight:** 14st
Nickname: Sprog, Ako, Aki
County debut: 1985
1st-Class 50s scored: 1
Parents: Colin (C. R. M.) and Shirley
Marital status: Single
Family links with cricket: Father Captain of Somerset CCC 1965–67; President of Somerset CCC. Also played for Northumberland and Durham. On TCCB.
Education: Millfield School; Cambridge University
Qualifications: 11 O-levels, 3 A-levels
Off-season 1987–88: At Cambridge University
Overseas tours: Millfield School to Barbados 1986

LAST SEASON: BATTING

	I.	N.O.	R.	H.S.	AV.
TEST					
1ST-CLASS					
INT					
RAL	1	0	0		0.00
NAT.W.					
B & H					

LAST SEASON: BOWLING

	O.	M.	R.	W.	AV.
TEST					
1ST-CLASS					
INT					
RAL					
NAT.W.					
B & H					

CAREER: BATTING

	I.	N.O.	R.	H.S.	AV.
TEST					
1ST-CLASS	11	3	238	79	29.75
INT					
RAL	1	0	0		0.00
NAT.W.					
B & H					

CAREER: BOWLING

	O.	M.	R.	W.	AV.
TEST					
1ST-CLASS	99	16	382	4	95.50
INT					
RAL					
NAT.W.	6	2	16	1	16.00
B & H					

Cricketers particularly learnt from: Father, Gerry Wilson (Millfield pro.), Martin Crowe, Peter Robinson (Somerset CC coach)
Cricketers particularly admired: Vivian Richards and Ian Botham for their competitive natures, Imran Khan, Dennis Lillee, Richard Hadlee
Other sports played: Rugby, hockey, basketball, golf
Relaxations: Socialising
Injuries 1987: Badly cut finger, bruised foot, and shoulder
Opinions on cricket: 'I think it's upsetting that politics should interfere with cricket re South Africa with so much talent in that country. I found the politics of a cricket dressing-room sometimes volatile and juvenile, but most of all interesting.'
Best batting performance: 79 Somerset v Northamptonshire, Weston 1985
Best bowling performance: 2-80 Somerset v India, Taunton 1986

AUSTIN, I. D. Lancashire

Full Name: Ian David Austin
Role: Left-hand bat, right-arm medium bowler
Born: 30 May 1966, Haslingden, Lancashire
Height: 5′ 10″ **Weight:** 14st 7lbs
Nickname: Oscar, Bully
County debut: 1986
One-Day 50s: 1
Parents: Jack and Ursula
Marital status: Single
Family links with cricket: Father opened batting for Haslingden CC
Education: Haslingden High School
Qualifications: NCA coach
Jobs outside cricket: Carpet fitter and cabinet maker

Off-season 1987–88: Playing in Australia
Overseas tours: NCA North U-19 to Bermuda 1985; Lancashire CCC to Jamaica 1987
Overseas teams played for: Morochydore, Queensland 1987
Cricketers particularly learnt from: Hartley Alleyne, Robby Bentley
Cricketers particularly admired: Ian Botham, Collis King, Mudassar Nazar
Other sports played: Football, snooker, golf
Injuries 1987: Strained hamstring
Relaxations: Listening to music, playing snooker, reading

Extras: Holds amateur Lancashire League record for highest individual score for amateur since limited overs (149*)

Opinions on cricket: 'I think the game would benefit from playing four-day county games. It would cut down the number of games played and save the clubs money in the long run, making results more possible and therefore more enjoyable to watch.'

Best batting performance: 37 Lancashire v Derbyshire, Derby 1987

Best bowling performance: 3-28 Lancashire v Kent, Liverpool 1987

LAST SEASON: BATTING

	I.	N.O.	R.	H.S.	AV.
TEST					
1ST-CLASS	1	0	37	37	37.00
INT					
RAL	5	1	30	14	7.50
NAT.W.	1	0	10	10	10.00
B & H	2	0	82	80	41.00

LAST SEASON: BOWLING

	O.	M.	R.	W.	AV.
TEST					
1ST-CLASS	33.5	7	64	3	21.33
INT					
RAL	44	0	257	3	85.66
NAT.W.	12	1	50	0	–
B & H	22	3	85	1	85.00

CAREER: BATTING

	I.	N.O.	R.	H.S.	AV.
TEST					
1ST-CLASS	1	0	37	37	37.00
INT					
RAL	6	1	34	14	6.80
NAT.W.	1	0	10	10	10.00
B & H	2	0	82	80	41.00

CAREER: BOWLING

	O.	M.	R.	W.	AV.
TEST					
1ST-CLASS	33.5	7	64	3	21.33
INT					
RAL	52	1	282	3	94.00
NAT.W.	12	1	50	0	–
B & H	22	3	85	1	85.00

AYLING, J. R. Hampshire

Full Name: Jonathon Richard Ayling
Role: Right-hand bat, right-arm
medium bowler
Born: 13 June 1967, Portsmouth
Height: 6' 4½" **Weight:** 13st 7lbs
Nickname: Victor
County debut: 1987
Parents: Christopher Jeremy and Mary
Marital status: Single
Education: Portsmouth Grammar
School, Hampshire
Qualifications: 8 O-levels, 1 A-level
Off-season 1987–88:
Playing and coaching in
Cape Town, South Africa
Overseas teams played for:
Pinelands CC, Cape Town 1986–87,
1987–88

Cricketers particularly learnt from: John Rice, Robin and Chris Smith, Jimmy Gray, Peter Sainsbury

Cricketers particularly admired: Barry Richards, Gordon Greenidge, Richard Hadlee, Malcolm Marshall

Other sports played: Snooker, squash, tennis

Other sports followed: Soccer, rugby, golf, tennis, athletics

Relaxations: Fell walking in Lake District, reading, listening to music, evenings out with friends

Opinions on cricket: 'I feel that there is too much first-class cricket played during the English season, and that consequently players' performances will not always be at their best. Regarding the situation in South Africa, it is terribly sad that their cricket, and sport in general, has been missed for so long. To deny a player such as Graeme Pollock the opportunity to play official international cricket is extremely unfair. It seems a pity that politicians interfere with sport, and armchair critics frown on cricketing links with South Africa. Club tours and individual players can only improve race-relations. The ethics of sport and sportsmen on the whole are more creditable than those of the politicians. Given the chance, I would abolish leg-byes which keep the game moving, but have introduced a recognised "technique" for accumulating runs. I also believe if playing surfaces are to be left uncovered so too should the bowlers run-ups.'

LAST SEASON: BATTING

	I.	N.O.	R.	H.S.	AV.
TEST					
1ST-CLASS					
INT					
RAL	1	0	15	15	15.00
NAT.W.					
B & H					

LAST SEASON: BOWLING

	O.	M.	R.	W.	AV.
TEST					
1ST-CLASS					
INT					
RAL	16	0	67	3	22.33
NAT.W.					
B & H					

CAREER: BATTING

	I.	N.O.	R.	H.S.	AV.
TEST					
1ST-CLASS					
INT					
RAL	1	0	15	15	15.00
NAT.W.					
B & H					

CAREER: BOWLING

	O.	M.	R.	W.	AV.
TEST					
1ST-CLASS					
INT					
RAL	16	0	67	3	22.33
NAT.W.					
B & H					

10. Who headed the Australian Test batting averages in Australia, 1986–87?

11. Who headed the England Test bowling averages in Australia, 1986–87?

12. Who got the most Test wickets for England in Australia, 1986–87?

13. What was odd about Gooch's two innings in the Fifth Test v West Indies in April 1986?

AYMES, A. N. Hampshire

Full Name: Adrian Nigel Aymes
Role: Right-hand bat,
wicket-keeper
Born: 4 June 1964, Southampton
Height: 6′ **Weight:** 13st
Nickname: Ady, Virus
County debut: 1987
1st-Class 50s scored: 1
1st-Class catches 1987: 1 (career 1)
Parents: Michael and Barbara
Marital status: Single
Education: Shirley Middle;
Bellemoor Secondary; Hill College
Qualifications: 3 O-levels, 1 A-level
Jobs outside cricket:
Sport shop salesman, labourer
Off-season 1987–88:
Working for a builder

Cricketing superstitions or habits:
Tap four corners of the batting crease
Cricketers particularly admired: Bob Taylor
Other sports played: Football, tennis
Other sports followed: Like watching most sports
Injuries 1987: Groin strain
Relaxations: Watching video films, keeping fit
Extras: Half century on debut v Surrey
Best batting performance: 58 Hampshire v Surrey, Southampton 1987

LAST SEASON: BATTING

	I.	N.O.	R.	H.S.	AV.
TEST					
1ST-CLASS	1	0	58	58	58.00
INT					
RAL					
NAT.W.					
B & H					

CAREER: BATTING

	I.	N.O.	R.	H.S.	AV.
TEST					
1ST-CLASS	1	0	58	58	58.00
INT					
RAL					
NAT.W.					
B & H					

---

14. What was remarkable about Peter Roebuck's 82 for Somerset v
    Hampshire in the Refuge Assurance League game on 23 August
    1987?

BABINGTON, A. M.   Sussex

Full Name: Andrew Mark
Babington
Role: Left-hand bat, right-arm
fast-medium bowler
Born: 22 July 1963, London
Height: 6′ 2″ **Weight:** 12st 12lbs
Nickname: Hagar, Reggie, Shilts,
Mongo
County debut: 1986
Place in bowling averages: 125th
av. 42.76 (1986 18th av. 23.20)
Strike rate 1987: 70.90 (career 61.00)
1st-Class catches 1987: 3 (career 7)
Parents: Roy and Maureen
Marital status: Single
Family links with cricket: Father
played club cricket
Education: Reigate Grammar
School; Borough Road PE
College

Qualifications: 5 O-levels,
2 A-levels; Member of Institute of Legal Executives
Jobs outside cricket: Work for my father's and other firms of solicitors
Cricketing superstitions or habits: Always put my kit on in the same order
Overseas tours: Surrey Schools Cricket Association to Australia 1980
Cricketers particularly learnt from: Bob Cottam, Kevin Gibbs, John Snow,
John Goodey
Cricketers particularly admired: Dennis Lillee, John Snow, Andy Roberts
Other sports played: Football, squash, golf

LAST SEASON: BATTING

	I.	N.O.	R.	H.S.	AV.
TEST					
1ST-CLASS	15	8	58	16	8.28
INT					
RAL	3	1	1	1	0.50
NAT.W.					
B & H	1	0	1	1	1.00

CAREER: BATTING

	I.	N.O.	R.	H.S.	AV.
TEST					
1ST-CLASS	18	9	59	16	6.55
INT					
RAL	4	1	1	1	0.33
NAT.W.	1	1	4	4*	–
B & H	1	0	1	1	1.00

LAST SEASON: BOWLING

	O.	M.	R.	W.	AV.
TEST					
1ST-CLASS	248.1	44	898	21	42.76
INT					
RAL	63	2	326	8	40.75
NAT.W.	22	0	109	2	54.50
B & H	25	3	118	7	16.85

CAREER: BOWLING

	O.	M.	R.	W.	AV.
TEST					
1ST-CLASS	366	60	1246	36	34.61
INT					
RAL	82	4	426	9	47.33
NAT.W.	35	0	163	6	27.16
B & H	25	3	118	7	16.85

Other sports followed: Motor racing, boxing
Relaxations: Eating out, social drinking with friends, playing golf, reading, listening to music
Extras: 'Took a hat-trick against Gloucestershire (Bainbridge, Curran, Lloyds), my 2nd, 3rd and 4th championship wickets in my 3rd championship game, 1986.'
Opinions on cricket: 'Players should be able to do their job, i.e. play cricket, in any part of the world without recriminations, if they choose to play abroad. Counties should have only one overseas player.'
Best batting performance: 16 Sussex v Middlesex, Lord's 1987
Best bowling performance: 4-18 Sussex v Gloucestershire, Bristol 1986

BAILEY, R. J.   Northamptonshire

Full Name: Robert John Bailey
Role: Right-hand bat, off-break bowler
Born: 28 October 1963, Biddulph, Stoke-on-Trent
Height: 6' 3" **Weight:** 14st
Nickname: Bailers
County debut: 1982
County cap: 1985
No. of One-Day Internationals: 2
1000 runs in a season: 4
1st-Class 50s scored: 29
1st-Class 100s scored: 10
1st-Class 200s scored: 2
One-Day 50s: 16
One-Day 100s: 4
Place in batting averages: 56th
av. 37.47 (1986 6th av. 56.32)
1st-Class catches 1987: 18
(career 67)
Parents: John and Marie
Wife and date of marriage: Rachel, 11 April 1987
Family links with cricket: Father played in North Staffordshire League for 30 years for Knypersley and Minor Counties cricket for Staffordshire as wicket-keeper
Education: Biddulph High School
Qualifications: 6 CSEs, 1 O-level
Jobs outside cricket: Worked for three winters in electrical trade
Off-season 1987–88: Playing for Gosnells CC in Perth

Overseas tours: England to Sharjah 1985 and 1987 for Rothmans One-Day International tournament

Overseas teams played for: Rhodes University, Grahamstown, 1982–83; Witenhage CC, South Africa, 1983–84, 1984–85; Fitzroy CC, Melbourne 1985–86

Cricketers particularly learnt from: My father, Stan Crump

Other sports played: Badminton, football, golf

Other sports followed: 'Like to see Port Vale and Stoke City doing well.'

Relaxations: Listening to music

Extras: Played for Young England v Young Australia, 1983. Scored two hundreds in match v Middlesex 2nd XI 1984

Best batting performance: 224* Northamptonshire v Glamorgan, Swansea 1986

Best bowling performance: 3-33 Northamptonshire v Cambridge University, Cambridge 1983

LAST SEASON: BATTING

	I.	N.O.	R.	H.S.	AV.
TEST					
1ST-CLASS	42	8	1274	158	37.47
INT					
RAL	11	1	368	125*	36.80
NAT.W.	5	1	121	44	30.25
B & H	7	0	286	134	40.85

CAREER: BATTING

	I.	N.O.	R.	H.S.	AV.
TEST					
1ST-CLASS	176	33	5898	224*	41.24
INT	2	1	52	41*	52.00
RAL	58	9	1828	125*	37.30
NAT.W.	13	4	307	56*	34.11
B & H	19	1	765	134	42.50

LAST SEASON: BOWLING

	O.	M.	R.	W.	AV.
TEST					
1ST-CLASS	18	7	41	1	41.00
INT					
RAL	5	0	33	3	11.00
NAT.W.					
B & H					

CAREER: BOWLING

	O.	M.	R.	W.	AV.
TEST					
1ST-CLASS	72.5	25	184	7	26.28
INT	6	0	25	0	–
RAL	10	0	82	3	27.33
NAT.W.	2	0	16	1	16.00
B & H	7	3	22	1	22.00

15. When Abdul Qadir of Pakistan left the field through injury, playing for the Rest of the World v M.C.C. in the Bicentenary Test, who took his place?

16. What was unusual about Sunil Gavaskar's 35th Test century?

17. What legendary cricket commentator returned to commentate on the M.C.C. v Rest of the World Bicentenary Test, for the first time in almost 25 years?

18. Who took the most ever wickets in a Test series?

BAINBRIDGE, P. Gloucestershire

Full Name: Philip Bainbridge
Role: Right-hand bat, right-arm medium bowler
Born: 16 April 1958, Stoke-on-Trent
Height: 5′ 10″ **Weight:** 11st 13lbs
Nickname: Bains, Robbo
County debut: 1977
County cap: 1981
1000 runs in a season: 6
1st-Class 50s scored: 53
1st-Class 100s scored: 14
1st-Class 5 w. in innings: 6
One-Day 50s: 11
One-Day 100s: 1
Place in batting averages: 69th av. 35.15 (1986 128th av. 27.30)
Place in bowling averages: 105th av. 37.26 (1986 46th av. 27.55)

Strike rate 1987: 50.94 (career 69.53)
1st-Class catches 1987: 9 (career 93)
Parents: Leonard George and Lilian Rose
Wife and date of marriage: Barbara, 22 September 1979
Children: Neil, 11 January 1984; Laura, 15 January 1985
Family links with cricket: Cousin, Stephen Wilkinson, played for Somerset 1969–72
Education: Hanley High School; Stoke-on-Trent Sixth Form College; Borough Road College of Education
Qualifications: 9 O-levels, 2 A-levels, BEd, MCC Coaching Certificate
Jobs outside cricket: PE Lecturer, Marketing Executive Gloucs CCC
Off-season 1987–88: Working in the marketing department of Gloucs CCC
Overseas tours: Holland with NCA North of England Youth team 1976; Barbados, Trinidad and Tobago with British Colleges 1978; Barbados with Gloucestershire CCC 1980; Pakistan for two Zaheer Abbas benefit matches 1983; Zimbabwe with English Counties XI 1985; Barbados with David Graveney Benefit Tour 1986; Sri Lanka with Gloucestershire 1987; Zimbabwe with Gloucestershire CCC 1988
Cricketers particularly learnt from: All senior players at Gloucestershire – and county coach
Cricketers particularly admired: Mike Procter
Other sports played: Football, rugby, squash, golf
Injuries 1987: Missed month with knee trouble, and missed month with ruptured ligaments in the back of right hand

Relaxations: Photography, wine-making, beer-making, listening to music, 'walking in the country with my Golden Retriever dog and my wife, entertaining my children.'

Extras: Played for four 2nd XIs in 1976 – Gloucestershire, Derbyshire, Northamptonshire and Warwickshire. Played for Young England v Australia 1977. Won Commercial Union U-23 Batsman of the Year 1981. Scored first century for Stoke-on-Trent aged 14. Produced a cricket calendar for 1987 with photographer David Munden. Provided engraved glass trophies for our beneficiary, David Graveney. Vice-captain of Gloucestershire CCC

Opinions on cricket: 'We play too much cricket; the game should be restructured in some way. Should return to covered wickets. The 1987 experiment with uncovered wickets – particularly with covered run-ups – was a complete failure.'

Best batting performance: 151* Gloucestershire v Derbyshire, Derby 1985

Best bowling performance: 8-53 Gloucestershire v Somerset, Bristol 1986

LAST SEASON: BATTING

	I.	N.O.	R.	H.S.	AV.
TEST					
1ST-CLASS	25	6	668	151	35.15
INT					
RAL	12	6	180	38*	30.00
NAT.W.	3	0	24	18	8.00
B & H	5	1	140	59	35.00

LAST SEASON: BOWLING

	O.	M.	R.	W.	AV.
TEST					
1ST-CLASS	288.4	62	927	34	27.26
INT					
RAL	82.3	3	395	20	19.75
NAT.W.	30	2	152	3	50.66
B & H	55	3	235	5	47.00

CAREER: BATTING

	I.	N.O.	R.	H.S.	AV.
TEST					
1ST-CLASS	325	53	8957	151*	32.93
INT					
RAL	105	21	1613	106*	19.20
NAT.W.	16	2	427	75	30.50
B & H	30	8	597	80	27.13

CAREER: BOWLING

	O.	M.	R.	W.	AV.
TEST					
1ST-CLASS	2549.4	591	7654	220	34.79
INT					
RAL	689.4	21	3486	119	29.29
NAT.W.	169	19	605	21	28.80
B & H	257.3	26	949	29	32.72

19. What record did Ian Botham break in Pakistan's first innings v England at The Oval in August 1987?

20. What was Pakistan's record-breaking first innings total v England in the Fifth Test at The Oval in 1987?

BAIRSTOW, D. L.   Yorkshire

Full Name: David Leslie Bairstow
Role: Right-hand bat, wicket-keeper, occasional medium pacer
Born: 1 September 1951, Bradford
Height: 5' 10" **Weight:** 14st 7lbs
Nickname: Bluey
County debut: 1970
County cap: 1973
Benefit: 1982 (£56,913)
Test debut: 1979
No. of Tests: 4
No. of One-Day Internationals: 21
1000 runs in a season: 3
1st-Class 50s scored: 69
1st-Class 100s scored: 9
One-Day 50s: 16
One-Day 100s: 1
Place in batting averages: 82nd
av. 33.45 (1986 127th av. 27.44)
Marital status: Divorced
Children: Andrew David, Claire Louise
Family links with cricket: Father, Lesley, played cricket for Laisterdyke
Education: Hanson Grammar School, Bradford
Qualifications: O and A-levels
Jobs outside cricket: Sales representative
Cricketing superstitions or habits: 'I will pat the ground three times or fiddle with my gloves three times. It is ridiculous but I do not want to stop it. I was in a pub a couple of days before the Leeds Test, and a lad I had never seen before gave me a medallion, and told me to keep it in my pocket for luck. Many people would have forgotten completely, but that medallion went into the pocket of my flannels, and stayed there for the whole match.'
Overseas tours: Australia 1978–79 and 1979–80; West Indies 1981
Overseas teams played for: Griqualand West 1966–67 and 1977–78
Cricketers particularly learnt from: Laurie Bennett, maths and sports master at school; Mike Fearnley
Relaxations: Gardening
Other sports played: Golf
Extras: Turned down an offer to play for Bradford City FC. Played for MCC Schools at Lord's in 1970. First Yorkshire wicket-keeper to get 1000 runs in a season (1982) since Arthur Wood in 1935. Set Yorkshire record of seven catches v Derbyshire at Scarborough, 1982. 133 consecutive John Player League matches. His 145 for Yorkshire v Middlesex is the highest score by a Yorkshire wicket-keeper. Allowed to take an A-level at 6 am at school in

order to make Yorkshire debut. Published *A Yorkshire Diary – a year of crisis* 1984. Captain 1984–86

Best batting performance: 145 Yorkshire v Middlesex, Scarborough 1980
Best bowling performance: 3-25 Yorkshire v MCC, Scarborough 1987

LAST SEASON: BATTING

	I.	N.O.	R.	H.S.	AV.
TEST					
1ST-CLASS	23	1	736	128	33.45
INT					
RAL	13	1	353	66*	29.41
NAT.W.	2	0	32	28	16.00
B & H	4	0	105	45	26.25

CAREER: BATTING

	I.	N.O.	R.	H.S.	AV.
TEST	7	1	125	59	20.83
1ST-CLASS	594	112	12914	145	26.79
INT	20	6	206	23*	14.71
RAL	204	46	3369	83*	21.32
NAT.W.	26	5	456	92	21.71
B & H	51	9	782	103*	18.61

LAST SEASON: BOWLING

	O.	M.	R.	W.	AV.
TEST					
1ST-CLASS	13	1	54	3	18.00
INT					
RAL					
NAT.W.					
B & H					

CAREER: BOWLING

	O.	M.	R.	W.	AV.
TEST					
1ST-CLASS	97	19	308	9	34.22
INT					
RAL					
NAT.W.					
B & H	3	0	17	0	–

LAST SEASON: WICKET KEEPING

	C.	ST.
TEST		
1ST-CLASS	31	5
INT		
RAL	16	1
NAT.W.	4	–
B & H	14	–

CAREER: WICKET KEEPING

	C.	ST.
TEST	12	1
1ST-CLASS	876	136
INT	17	4
RAL	212	20
NAT.W.	33	3
B & H	109	5

21. Who made the top score in Pakistan's first innings in the Fifth Test at The Oval v England in 1987, and what was the score?

22. What England Test cricketer went on a diet last season and lost a stone in three weeks?

23. Which former England Test captain last year published the official history of the M.C.C. as part of its 200th birthday celebrations?

BAKKER, P.-J.   Hampshire

Full Name: Paul-Jan Bakker
Role: Right-hand bat, right-arm
medium pace bowler
Born: 19 August 1957,
Vlaardingen, Holland
Height: 6′ **Weight:** 14st
Nickname: Nip, Grandad, Peech,
Daisy, Dutchie, BHOF
County debut: 1986
No. of One-Day Internationals: 17
for Holland
1st-Class 5 w. in innings: 1
Parents: Hubertus Antonius
Bakker and Wilhelmina Hendrika
Bakker-Goos
Marital status: Single
Family links with cricket: Father is
the scorer for the first team of my

club in The Hague, and has been scorer of Hague CC for 13 years
Education: I^e VCL and Hugo de Groot College, The Hague, Holland
Qualifications: 'We have a different school system but finished my HAVO
schooling.' Ski-instructor
Cricketing superstitions or habits: 'I need coffee before a game, and always
wear a T-shirt and short-sleeved sweater.'
Overseas tours: South Africa 1978 with Klaas Vervelde XI; since 1974 toured
England almost every summer with touring sides; since 1983 invited to play
for the Dutch 'MCC', the Flamingo Touring Club
Overseas teams played for: Green Point CC, Cape Town 1981–86; Flamingo

LAST SEASON: BATTING

	I.	N.O.	R.	H.S.	AV.
TEST					
1ST-CLASS	1	0	0		0.00
INT					
RAL					
NAT.W.					
B & H					

LAST SEASON: BOWLING

	O.	M.	R.	W.	AV.
TEST					
1ST-CLASS	92.5	23	249	12	20.75
INT					
RAL	21.4	0	101	5	20.20
NAT.W.					
B & H					

CAREER: BATTING

	I.	N.O.	R.	H.S.	AV.
TEST					
1ST-CLASS	3	1	6	3*	3.00
INT					
RAL					
NAT.W.					
B & H					

CAREER: BOWLING

	O.	M.	R.	W.	AV.
TEST					
1ST-CLASS	159.4	43	469	18	26.05
INT					
RAL	34.4	0	167	7	23.85
NAT.W.					
B & H	11	5	19	2	9.50

Touring Club, Kent and Essex 1983; Holland, Gloucester, Essex and MCC 1984 and ICC trophy 1986
Cricketers particularly learnt from: Laddy Outschoorn, Hylton Ackerman
Cricketers particularly admired: Michael Holding, Malcolm Marshall
Jobs outside cricket: Ski-instructor, public relations officer
Off-season 1987–88: Touring Perth and New Zealand with Holland XI
Other sports played: 'I ski, play a bit of golf and like to drive fast.'
Other sports followed: Grand Prix motor racing, tennis, football, golf and most other sports
Relaxations: Social visits to pubs, bars and restaurants; films and newspapers
Extras: First ever Dutch player to play professional cricket
Opinions on cricket: 'A great game.'
Injuries 1987: 'Nothing serious enough to have a day off.'
Best batting performance: 3* Hampshire v Gloucestershire, Bournemouth 1986
Best bowling performance: 7-31 Hampshire v Kent, Bournemouth 1987

BAPTISTE, E. A. E.   Kent

Full Name: Eldine Ashworth Elderfield Baptiste
Role: Right-hand bat, right-arm fast-medium bowler
Born: 12 March 1960, Liberta, Antigua
Height: 6′ **Weight:** 12st
Nickname: Soca, Bapo
County debut: 1981
County cap: 1983
Test debut: 1983–84
No. of Tests: 9
No. of One-Day Internationals: 29
50 wickets in a season: 3
1st-Class 50s scored: 21
1st-Class 100s scored: 3
1st-Class 5 w. in innings: 12
1st-Class 10 w. in match: 1
One-Day 50s: 5
Place in batting averages: 140th av. 25.85 (1986 78th av. 34.12)
Place in bowling averages: 47th av. 26.69
Strike rate 1987: 55.66 (career 48.88)
1st-Class catches 1987: 6 (career 60)
Parents: Gertrude and Samuel

Children: Forbes, Javed
Family links with cricket: Father played for Liberta 1940–48. Brother, Rowan, played for Liberta at school level
Education: Liberta Primary; All Saints Secondary School
Qualification: Coach
Jobs outside cricket: Sports officer in the Sports Department of the Ministry of Education. 'Chauffeur to Derek Aslett!'
Off-season 1987–1988: Touring with West Indies
Cricketing superstitions or habits: The numbers 49 and 13. Puts left pad on first
Overseas tours: With Leeward Youths to Barbados 1978; to Australia, St Lucia, St Kitts, St Thomas and Montserrat with Antigua National team in 1979; to England with Antigua Youth 1979; with West Indies to India 1983, England 1984, Australia 1984–85
Overseas teams played for: Geelong CC, Australia, 1985–86; Leeward Islands 1981–86
Cricketers particularly learnt from: Guy Yearwood, Viv Richards, Andy Roberts, Malcolm Marshall, Graham Milkmart
Cricketers particularly admired: Derek Aslett, Mark Benson, Chris Tavaré
Other sports played: Football, tennis, Aussie rules football
Other sports followed: Boxing, athletics, golf, baseball, basketball
Injuries 1987: Groin injury
Opinion on cricket: 'Neutral umpires in Test matches. The idea of the four-day game for county games is long overdue.'
Relaxations: Watching movies, music – especially calypso, soul and reggae – and meeting people
Extras: Awarded Viv Richards Schools Cricket Trophy for the Most Outstanding Cricketer 1979. Sportsman of the Year in Antigua 1979. Released by Kent at end of 1987 season
Best batting performance: 136* Kent v Yorkshire, Sheffield 1983
Best bowling performance: 8-76 Kent v Warwickshire, Edgbaston 1987

LAST SEASON: BATTING

	I.	N.O.	R.	H.S.	AV.
TEST					
1ST-CLASS	23	3	517	95	25.85
INT					
RAL	9	2	113	56	16.14
NAT.W.	1	0	14	14	14.00
B & H	5	3	52	21	26.00

CAREER: BATTING

	I.	N.O.	R.	H.S.	AV.
TEST	10	1	224	87*	24.88
1ST-CLASS	178	27	4240	136*	28.07
INT	10	2	119	28*	14.87
RAL	52	6	802	60	17.43
NAT.W.	10	1	78	22	8.66
B & H	17	5	200	43*	16.66

LAST SEASON: BOWLING

	O.	M.	R.	W.	AV.
TEST					
1ST-CLASS	519.3	117	1495	45	26.69
INT					
RAL	63.1	1	308	11	28.00
NAT.W.	12	3	39	0	–
B & H	46	7	140	4	35.00

CAREER: BOWLING

	O.	M.	R.	W.	AV.
TEST	204	55	486	15	32.40
1ST-CLASS	2805.1	619	8943	344	25.99
INT	246	17	989	27	36.63
RAL	413.3	15	1889	73	25.87
NAT.W.	127	21	424	14	30.28
B & H	175	20	644	22	29.27

BARNETT, K. J.   Derbyshire

Full Name: Kim John Barnett
Role: Right-hand bat, leg-break or
seam bowler, cover fielder
Born: 17 July 1960, Stoke-on-Trent
Height: 6′ 1″ **Weight:** 13st
Nickname: Wristy
County debut: 1979
County cap: 1982
1000 runs in a season: 5
1st-Class 50s scored: 57
1st-Class 100s scored: 20
1st-Class 5 w. in innings: 1
One-Day 50s: 20
One-Day 100s: 4
Place in batting averages: 63rd
av. 36.64 (1986 65th av. 36.76)
Place in bowling averages: 3rd
av. 17.30
Strike rate 1987: 40.76 (career
83.50)
1st-Class catches 1987: 12 (career 133)
Parents: Derek and Doreen
Wife and date of marriage: Nancy, 30 September 1984
Children: Rebecca, 13 September 1986
Education: Leek High School, Staffs
Qualifications: 7 O-levels
Jobs outside cricket: Bank clerk, National Westminster Bank 1978
Overseas tours: With England Schools to India 1977; Young England to

LAST SEASON: BATTING

	I.	N.O.	R.	H.S.	AV.
TEST					
1ST-CLASS	40	1	1429	130	36.64
INT					
RAL	14	0	387	82	27.64
NAT.W.	3	0	110	53	36.66
B & H	4	0	186	115	46.50

CAREER: BATTING

	I.	N.O.	R.	H.S.	AV.
TEST					
1ST-CLASS	343	30	10844	144	34.64
INT					
RAL	121	20	3286	131*	32.53
NAT.W.	18	2	585	88	36.56
B & H	32	1	721	115	23.25

LAST SEASON: BOWLING

	O.	M.	R.	W.	AV.
TEST					
1ST-CLASS	88.2	27	225	13	17.30
INT					
RAL					
NAT.W.					
B & H					

CAREER: BOWLING

	O.	M.	R.	W.	AV.
TEST					
1ST-CLASS	821.1	168	2812	59	47.66
INT					
RAL	42.3	2	278	7	39.71
NAT.W.	29.4	5	107	11	9.72
B & H	9	2	33	2	16.50

Australia 1978–79; Derrick Robins XI to New Zealand and Australia 1979–80; England B to Sri Lanka 1986 (vice-captain)
Overseas teams played for: Boland, South Africa, 1982–83, 1984–85
Cricketers particularly learnt from: Eddie Barlow
Off-season 1987–88: Coaching in South Africa
Other sports played: Football (has played soccer semi-professionally for Cheshire League side, Leek Town FC), tennis, squash
Other sports followed: Horse racing
Relaxations: Watching racing on TV, reading, eating
Extras: Played for Northants 2nd XI when aged 15. Played one Minor County match for Staffordshire; also for Warwickshire 2nd XI. Became youngest captain of a first-class county when appointed in 1983
Opinions on cricket: 'Would like to see the introduction of four-day cricket to the County Championship with each team played only once. Also one overseas player per side as soon as possible.'
Best batting performance: 144 Derbyshire v Middlesex, Derby 1984
Best bowling performance: 6-115 Derbyshire v Yorkshire, Bradford 1985

BARTLETT, R. J.   Somerset

Full Name: Richard James Bartlett
Role: Right-hand bat
Born: 8 October 1966, Ash Priors, Somerset
Height: 5' 9"
County debut: 1986
1st-Class 100s scored: 1
One-day 50s: 1
Place in batting averages: —
(1986 32nd av. 43.85)
1st-Class catches 1987: 0 (career 4)
Education: Taunton School; Swansea University
Other sports played: Represented Somerset at U-21 hockey
Extras: First Somerset player to score a century on first-class debut since Harold

Gimblett. Won Gray-Nicholls Trophy 1985 as most improved schools cricketer. Represented England Schools and England Young Cricketers
Best batting performance: 117* Somerset v Oxford University, Oxford 1986

LAST SEASON: BATTING

	I.	N.O.	R.	H.S.	AV.
TEST					
1ST-CLASS	1	0	0		0.00
INT					
RAL	1	0	23	23	23.00
NAT.W.	1	0	56	56	56.00
B & H					

CAREER: BATTING

	I.	N.O.	R.	H.S.	AV.
TEST					
1ST-CLASS	10	2	307	117*	38.37
INT					
RAL	1	0	23	23	23.00
NAT.W.	1	0	56	56	56.00
B & H	2	0	4	4	2.00

BARWICK, S. R. Glamorgan

Full Name: Stephen Royston Barwick
Role: Right-hand bat, right-arm medium bowler
Born: 6 September 1960, Neath
Height: 6′ 2″ **Weight:** 13st 2lbs
Nickname: Baz
County debut: 1981
County cap: 1987
50 wickets in a season: 1
1st-Class 5 w. in innings: 5
Place in bowling averages: 108th av. 38.27 (1986 89th av. 37.07)
Strike rate 1987: 77.00 (career 68.06)
1st-Class catches 1987: 1 (career 22)
Parents: Margaret and Roy
Marital status: Single
Family links with cricket: 'My Uncle David played for Glamorgan 2nd XI.'

LAST SEASON: BATTING

	I.	N.O.	R.	H.S.	AV.
TEST					
1ST-CLASS	30	10	150	21*	7.50
INT					
RAL	6	3	22	14	7.33
NAT.W.	1	0	5	5	5.00
B & H	2	1	9	8*	9

CAREER: BATTING

	I.	N.O.	R.	H.S.	AV.
TEST					
1ST-CLASS	101	40	522	29	8.55
INT					
RAL	20	12	79	29*	9.87
NAT.W.	5	2	18	6	6.00
B & H	12	7	49	18	9.80

LAST SEASON: BOWLING

	O.	M.	R.	W.	AV.
TEST					
1ST-CLASS	603.1	122	1797	47	38.27
INT					
RAL	97	7	457	17	26.88
NAT.W.	17	7	35	3	11.66
B & H	41	5	171	4	42.75

CAREER: BOWLING

	O.	M.	R.	W.	AV.
TEST					
1ST-CLASS	2371.4	534	7084	209	33.88
INT					
RAL	375.1	24	1707	50	34.14
NAT.W.	63.2	16	166	13	12.76
B & H	147.1	21	537	23	23.34

Education: Cwrt Sart Comprehensive School; Dwr-y-Felin Comprehensive School
Qualifications: 'Commerce, human biology, mathematics, English.'
Jobs outside cricket: Ex-steel worker
Other sports played: Badminton, squash, table tennis, football
Other sports followed: Watching Swansea City FC
Extras: Made debut on 25 April 1981 v Oxford University, and took 4 wickets in 1st innings
Best batting performance: 29 Glamorgan v Somerset, Cardiff 1985
Best bowling performance: 8-42 Glamorgan v Worcestershire, Worcester 1983

BASE, S. J. Glamorgan

Full Name: Simon John Base
Role: Right-hand bat, right-arm medium bowler
Born: 2 January 1960, Maidstone
Height: 6′ 2″ **Weight:** 13st 5lbs
Nickname: Basey
County debut: 1986
1st-Class 5 w. in innings: 2
Place in batting averages: 236th av. 12.70
Place in bowling averages: 19th av. 23.57 (1986 87th av. 36.85)
Strike rate 1987: 43.53 (career 52.11)
1st-Class catches 1987: 1 (career 4)
Parents: Christine and Peter
Marital status: Single
Education: Fish Hoek Primary School, Fish Hoek High School, Cape Town, South Africa
Qualifications: High School, School Certificate. Refrigeration and air conditioning technician
Jobs outside cricket: Hall-Thermotank in South Africa as a technician and S.A. Sea Products. G.S.P.K. Electronics in North Yorkshire, England
Overseas teams played for: Western Province B 1982–83
Cricketers particularly learnt from: Stuart Leary, Graham Gooch, Kevin Lyons, Martin Stovold
Cricketers particularly admired: Stuart Leary, Graham Gooch
Other sports played: Football, golf, windsurfing
Other sports followed: Golf, tennis, snooker

Relaxations: Windsurfing and golf. Reading science fiction, watching films and music
Best batting performance: 38 Glamorgan v Gloucestershire, Swansea 1987
Best bowling performance: 5-67 Glamorgan v Surrey, The Oval 1987

LAST SEASON: BATTING

	I.	N.O.	R.	H.S.	AV.
TEST					
1ST-CLASS	14	4	127	38	12.70
INT					
RAL	4	0	36	19	9.00
NAT.W.	1	0	4	4	4.00
B & H	1	0	12	12	12.00

LAST SEASON: BOWLING

	O.	M.	R.	W.	AV.
TEST					
1ST-CLASS	203.1	38	660	28	23.57
INT					
RAL	24	0	149	2	74.50
NAT.W.	3	0	12	0	–
B & H	9	0	43	1	43.00

CAREER: BATTING

	I.	N.O.	R.	H.S.	AV.
TEST					
1ST-CLASS	27	9	182	38	10.11
INT					
RAL	5	0	37	19	7.40
NAT.W.	2	0	6	4	3.00
B & H	3	1	20	12	10.00

CAREER: BOWLING

	O.	M.	R.	W.	AV.
TEST					
1ST-CLASS	469	96	1495	54	27.68
INT					
RAL	49	0	271	7	38.71
NAT.W.	15	0	61	2	30.50
B & H	28	1	147	3	49.00

BEARDSHALL, M.   Derbyshire

Full name: Mark Beardshall
Role: Right-hand bat, right-arm medium-fast bowler, short-leg fielder
Born: 10 January 1962, Barnsley
Height: 6′ 0″ **Weight:** 13st
Nickname: Budgie, Birdseed
County debut: 1987
Place in bowling averages: 135th av. 47.66
Strike rate 1987: 79.16 (career 79.16)
1st-Class catches 1987: 2 (career 2)
Parents: Bill and Eileen
Wife and date of marriage: Joy Lesley, 21 September 1985
Education: Holgate School, Barnsley
Qualifications: 2 O-levels, Preliminary coaching certificate
Jobs outside cricket: Miner, coal face electrician
Off-season 1987–88: Half a mile underground at Darfield Main Colliery, Barnsley

Cricketing superstitions or habits: Right pad on first
Overseas tours: Wombwell Cricket Lovers' Society old boys tour to Lancashire 1986
Cricketers particularly learnt from: Steve Oldham
Cricketers particularly admired: Dennis Lillee, Ian Botham, Geoff Boycott
Other sports played: Football, snooker, squash
Other sports followed: Football, all TV sports, female mud wrestling
Relaxations: Watching or playing sport, music and videos
Extras: Assistant Secretary Wombwell Cricket Lovers' Society
Best batting performance: 25 Derbyshire v Gloucestershire, Bristol 1987
Best bowling pereformance: 4-68 Derbyshire v Kent, Canterbury 1987

LAST SEASON: BATTING

	I.	N.O.	R.	H.S.	AV.
TEST					
1ST-CLASS	8	3	47	25	9.40
INT					
RAL	1	0	7	7	7.00
NAT.W.					
B & H					

LAST SEASON: BOWLING

	O.	M.	R.	W.	AV.
TEST					
1ST-CLASS	158.2	21	572	12	47.66
INT					
RAL	8	1	23	0	
NAT.W.					
B & H					

CAREER: BATTING

	I.	N.O.	R.	H.S.	AV.
TEST					
1ST-CLASS	8	3	47	25	9.40
INT					
RAL	1	0	7	7	7.00
NAT.W.					
B & H					

CAREER: BOWLING

	O.	M.	R.	W.	AV.
TEST					
1ST-CLASS	158.2	21	572	12	47.66
INT					
RAL	8	1	23	0	
NAT.W.					
B & H					

24. How tall was Don Bradman? 5' 6¾", 5' 11⅞", or 6' 1½"?
25. In the M.C.C. Bicentenary Test, who kept wicket for the Rest of the World when Dujon had to retire injured?
26. What was unusual, even unique, about Qadir's field for Greenidge in the M.C.C. Bicentenary Test?

BENJAMIN, W. K. M.   Leicestershire

Full name: Winston Keithroy
Matthew Benjamin
Role: Right-hand bat, right-arm
fast bowler
Born: 31 December 1964, All
Saints, Antigua
County debut: 1986
No. of One-Day Internationals: 11
1st-Class 50s scored: 3
1st-Class 10 w. in match: 1
1st-Class 5 w. in innings: 7
Place in batting averages: —
(1986 44th av. 40.40)
Place in bowling averages: 96th
av. 35.00 (1986 75th av. 33.50)
Strike rate 1987: 82.93
(career 59.41)
1st-Class catches 1987: 5 (career 16)
Education: All Saints School
Overseas teams played for: Leeward Islands since 1985
Extras: Played Minor Counties cricket for Cheshire since 1985. Appeared for
Rest of the World XI v D. B. Close's XI at Scarborough 1985
Best batting performance: 95* Leicestershire v India, Leicester 1986
Best bowling performance: 6-33 Leicestershire v Nottinghamshire, Leicester
1986

LAST SEASON: BATTING

	I.	N.O.	R.	H.S.	AV.
TEST					
1ST-CLASS	9	1	69	30	8.62
INT					
RAL	5	0	37	14	7.40
NAT.W.	1	1	2	2*	–
B & H	3	0	37	21	12.33

CAREER: BATTING

	I.	N.O.	R.	H.S.	AV.
TEST					
1ST-CLASS	48	15	781	95*	23.66
INT	7	1	23	8	3.83
RAL	15	4	125	19*	11.36
NAT.W.	2	1	7	5	7.00
B & H	6	2	60	21	15.00

LAST SEASON: BOWLING

	O.	M.	R.	W.	AV.
TEST					
1ST-CLASS	207.2	54	525	15	35.00
INT					
RAL	27	0	129	2	64.50
NAT.W.	24	4	80	4	20.00
B & H	37	3	144	8	18.00

CAREER: BOWLING

	O.	M.	R.	W.	AV.
TEST					
1ST-CLASS	1010	215	2968	102	29.09
INT	93.1	11	310	12	25.83
RAL	122.1	5	537	19	28.26
NAT.W.	45	6	131	7	18.71
B & H	78.4	11	271	19	14.26

BENSON, M. R.   Kent

Full Name: Mark Richard Benson
Role: Left-hand bat, off-break
bowler
Born: 6 July 1958, Shoreham,
Sussex
Height: 5′ 10″ **Weight:** 12st 7lbs
Nickname: Benny
County debut: 1980
County cap: 1981
Test debut: 1986
No. of Tests: 1
No. of One-Day Internationals: 1
1000 runs in a season: 6
1st-Class 50s scored: 57
1st-Class 100s scored: 22
One-Day 50s: 25
One-Day 100s: 2
Place in batting averages: 24th
av. 44.23 (1986 52nd av. 39.48)

1st-Class catches 1987: 17 (career 77)
Parents: Frank and Judy
Wife and date of marriage: Sarah, 20 September 1986
Family links with cricket: Father played for Ghana
Education: Sutton Valence School
Qualifications: O- and A-levels and 1 S-level. Qualified tennis coach
Jobs outside cricket: Marketing assistant with Shell UK Oil; Financial adviser
Cricketing superstitions or habits: Left pad on first
Overseas teams played for: Balfour Guild CC, 1979–80; Johannesburg
Municipals, 1980–81; Port Adelaide CC, 1981–82

LAST SEASON: BATTING

	I.	N.O.	R.	H.S.	AV.
TEST					
1ST-CLASS	39	0	1725	131	44.23
INT					
RAL	12	0	399	92	33.25
NAT.W.	2	0	22	20	11.00
B & H	6	1	284	107*	56.80

LAST SEASON: BOWLING

	O.	M.	R.	W.	AV.
TEST					
1ST-CLASS	2	0	8	0	–
INT					
RAL					
NAT.W.					
B & H					

CAREER: BATTING

	I.	N.O.	R.	H.S.	AV.
TEST	2	0	51	30	25.50
1ST-CLASS	261	20	9476	162	39.31
INT					
RAL	82	1	2380	97	29.38
NAT.W.	19	1	721	113*	40.05
B & H	32	6	873	107*	33.57

CAREER: BOWLING

	O.	M.	R.	W.	AV.
TEST					
1ST-CLASS	42.2	1	273	3	91.00
INT					
RAL					
NAT.W.					
B & H					

Cricketers particularly learnt from: Derek Aslett, Bob Woolmer
Cricketers particularly admired: Malcolm Marshall, Neal Radford, Ian Botham
Off-season 1987–88: Working for Stanford Benson & Co.
Other sports played: Golf, table tennis, windsurfing
Other sports followed: Rugby, horse racing
Relaxations: Windsurfing
Extras: Scored 1000 runs in first full season. Record for most runs in career and season at Sutton Valence School
Opinions on cricket: 'We play too much cricket, thus breeding mediocrity.'
Best batting performance: 162 Kent v Hampshire, Southampton 1985
Best bowling performance: 2-55 Kent v Surrey, Dartford 1986

BERRY, P. J. Yorkshire

Full Name: Philip John Berry
Role: Right-hand bat, off-break bowler
Born: 28 December 1966, Saltburn, Cleveland
Height: 6′ **Weight:** 11st 7lbs
Nickname: 'Chuck, Goose, Bill and anymore they can think of.'
County debut: 1986
1st-Class catches 1987: 2 (career 4)
Parents: John and Beryl
Marital status: Engaged to Judith
Family links with cricket: Brother plays for Saltburn in North Yorkshire and South Durham Cricket League
Education: Saltscar Comprehensive; Longlands College of Further Education
Qualifications: 1 O-level, City and Guilds passes in Recreational Management

Jobs outside cricket: Worked for Redcar Racecourse Co as a groundsman
Cricketing superstitions or habits: Put left pad on first. Try to change in same place in a changing room if I have done well from that place before. Wear same kit as day before if successful
Overseas tours: NCA North U-19 to Bermuda in July 1985 for the International Youth Tournament
Cricketers particularly learnt from: 'Steve Oldham, Doug Padgett and Brian Bainbridge, who taught me everything about the game, when I joined Middlesbrough.'

Cricketers particularly admired: Brian Bainbridge for showing keeness at 55 years old, turning out for Middlesbrough 1st Team every week

Off-season 1987–88: Working on Redcar racecourse and keeping fit for coming season

Other sports played: Snooker, football, swimming

Other sports followed: Rugby union, Middlesbrough FC, American Football

Injuries 1987: Strained stomach muscle, missing one game

Relaxations: Reading, snooker, rugby, listening to music

Extras: Played for young Young England in the Final Test against Sri Lanka at Trent Bridge which England won by 6 wkts to win series 1–0

Best batting performance: 4* Yorkshire v Northamptonshire, Scarborough 1986

Best bowling performance: 1-10 Yorkshire v Northamptonshire, Scarborough 1986

LAST SEASON: BATTING

	I.	N.O.	R.	H.S.	AV.
TEST					
1ST-CLASS					
INT					
RAL					
NAT.W.					
B & H					

LAST SEASON: BOWLING

	O.	M.	R.	W.	AV.
TEST					
1ST-CLASS	14	3	55	1	55.00
INT					
RAL					
NAT.W.					
B & H					

CAREER: BATTING

	I.	N.O.	R.	H.S.	AV.
TEST					
1ST-CLASS	1	1	4	4*	–
INT					
RAL					
NAT.W.					
B & H					

CAREER: BOWLING

	O.	M.	R.	W.	AV.
TEST					
fiST-CLASS	53	16	138	2	69.00
INT					
RAL					
NAT.W.					
B & H					

27. Who bowled the most overs in county cricket in 1987, and how many?

28. How many players changed counties between the 1986 and 1987 seasons: 16, 21 or 29?

BICKNELL, D. J. Surrey

Full Name: Darren John Bicknell
Role: Opening bat, short-leg fielder
Born: 24 June 1967, Guildford
Height: 6′ 4″ **Weight:** 13½st
Nickname: Denzil, Razor
County debut: 1987
1st-Class 50s scored: 4
1st-Class 100s scored: 1
Place in batting averages: 68th av. 35.29
1st-Class catches 1987: 5 (career 5)
Parents: Vic and Valerie
Marital status: Single
Family links with cricket: Brother plays for Surrey, father is a qualified umpire; little brother Stuart plays for Guildford CC

Education: Robert Haining County Secondary, Mychett, Hampshire
Qualifications: 2 O-levels, 5 CSEs, City and Guilds qualification in Recreation Administration and Sports Studies
Jobs outside cricket: Sports centre lifeguard
Off-season 1987–88: Enjoying club cricket in Melbourne
Cricketing superstitions or habits: 'If I score runs in a particular shirt, pair of trousers or pair of boots, I try to bat in the same gear next time.'
Overseas teams played for: Cobury CC, Melbourne 1987–88
Cricketers particularly learnt from: David Smith, Geoff Arnold
Cricketers particularly admired: Geoff Boycott, Mike Gatting
Other sports played: Football, golf, snooker
Other sports followed: Aldershot FC
Relaxations: Listening to music, playing golf, eating out
Extras: Supporters Young Player of the Year 1987
Opinions on cricket: 'Standard of pitches should be improved to have more pace and bounce as this would suit all players – fast bowlers, spinners and

LAST SEASON: BATTING	I.	N.O.	R.	H.S.	AV.
TEST					
1ST-CLASS	20	3	600	105	35.29
INT					
RAL					
NAT.W.					
B & H	1	0	17	17	17.00

CAREER: BATTING	I.	N.O.	R.	H.S.	AV.
TEST					
1ST-CLASS	20	3	600	105	35.29
INT					
RAL					
NAT.W.					
B & H	1	0	17	17	17.00

batsmen. Also more effort should be made to play 2nd XI games on first-class grounds.'
Best batting performance: 105 Surrey v Hampshire, The Oval 1987

BICKNELL, M. P. Surrey

Full Name: Martin Paul Bicknell
Role: Right-hand bat, right-arm fast medium bowler
Born: 14 January 1969, Guildford
Height: 6′ 3½″ **Weight:** 13½st
Nickname: Bickers, Spandau
County debut: 1986
1st-Class 5 w. in innings: 2
Place in batting averages: 117th av. 15.42
Place in bowling averages: 21st av. 23.73 (1986 11th av. 22.22)
Strike rate 1987: 51.90 (career 48.63)
1st-Class catches 1987: 5 (career 9)
Parents: Vic and Valerie
Marital status: Single
Family links with cricket: Brother Darren plays for Surrey. Father is qualified umpire. Younger brother Stuart plays for Guildford Colts
Education: Robert Haining County Secondary, Mychett, Hampshire
Qualifications: 2 O-levels, 5 CSEs
Cricketing superstitions or habits: 'Left pad on first, not that it helps!'
Overseas tours: Surrey Young Cricketers to Australia 1985–86; Young England to Sri Lanka 1987
Overseas teams played for: Suburbs, New Zealand 1987–88
Cricketers particularly learnt from: Geoff Arnold, Mickey Stewart
Cricketers particularly admired: Richard Hadlee, Dennis Lillee, Ian Botham
Off-season 1987–88: Club cricket in New Zealand. Playing in the Youth World Cup in Australia
Other sports played: Football, golf
Other sports followed: Anything except horse racing
Injuries 1987: Bruised heel for two weeks, back strain for one week
Relaxations: Watching greyhound racing, music
Extras: Youngest player to play for Surrey since David Smith. On County debut first two overs were maidens. Scored four successive ducks in June!! Played in successful series win for Young England against Sri Lanka. Finished

11th in National Bowling Averages. 1986 won Supporters Young Player of the Year, also George Brittain Young Player of the Year

Opinions on cricket: 'Championship should be 16 four-day games. Too many boring captains; there is nothing to lose by going for a result. Go back to covered wickets; when it rained last season all we ended up with were slow wickets which in some cases prevented a result.'

Best batting performance: 18 Surrey v Somerset, The Oval 1987
Best bowling performance: 6-63 Surrey v Somerset, The Oval 1987

LAST SEASON: BATTING

	I.	N.O.	R.	H.S.	AV.
TEST					
1ST-CLASS	14	7	108	18	15.42
INT					
RAL	3	3	15	12*	
NAT.W.	1	0	0		0.00
B & H	1	1	1	1*	

CAREER: BATTING

	I.	N.O.	R.	H.S.	AV.
TEST					
1ST-CLASS	24	9	129	18	8.60
INT					
RAL	5	4	28	13	28.00
NAT.W.	4	2	5	2*	2.50
B & H	1	1	1	1*	–

LAST SEASON: BOWLING

	O.	M.	R.	W.	AV.
TEST					
1ST-CLASS	363.2	94	997	42	23.73
INT					
RAL	79	3	339	6	56.50
NAT.W.	24	4	71	0	–
B & H	25	4	72	7	10.28

CAREER: BOWLING

	O.	M.	R.	W.	AV.
TEST					
1ST-CLASS	559.2	137	1597	69	23.14
INT					
RAL	114	4	477	10	47.70
NAT.W.	61	10	176	5	35.20
B & H	25	4	72	7	10.28

BIRCH, J. D.　　　Nottinghamshire

Full Name: John Dennis Birch
Role: Right-hand bat, right-arm medium bowler, slip fielder
Born: 18 June 1955, Nottingham
Height: 6′ 1″ **Weight:** 13st
Nickname: Bonk, Denzil
County debut: 1973
County cap: 1981
1000 runs in a season: 2
1st-Class 50s scored: 49
1st-Class 100s scored: 5
1st-Class 5 w. in innings: 1
One-Day 50s: 15
Place in batting averages: 98th av. 31.51 (1986 77th av. 34.19)
1st-Class catches 1987: 10 (career: 168)
Parents: Bill and Mavis

Wife and date of marriage: Linda, 15 May 1980

Children: Nathalie and Daniel (twins), 31 January 1981

Family links with cricket: Father was a local cricketer

Education: William Crane Bilateral School

Qualifications: O-levels and CSEs

Jobs outside cricket: Runs a small building firm with a friend and brothers; player-manager, Arnold Town FC; coaching director at Nottingham Cricket Centre

Off-season 1987–88: Doing jobs above

Cricketing superstitions or habits: Left pad on first

Cricketers particularly learnt from: Clive Rice, Richard Hadlee

Cricketers particularly admired: Clive Rice, Richard Hadlee, Geoffrey Boycott

Other sports played: Soccer, golf, snooker all sports

Other sports followed: Watching any other sports

Injuries 1987: Medial ligament

Relaxations: 'Gardening, fishing and the odd pint of good beer.'

Extras: 'Would like to thank Frank Woodhead for giving me the chance to play for Notts and all who have helped me at the club.'

Opinions: 'To play night cricket in coloured gear. South Africa to play Test cricket. England to become the best Test side.'

Best batting performance: 125 Nottinghamshire v Leicestershire, Trent Bridge 1982

Best bowling performance: 6-64 Nottinghamshire v Hampshire, Bournemouth 1975

LAST SEASON: BATTING

	I.	N.O.	R.	H.S.	AV.
TEST					
1ST-CLASS	32	3	914	82	31.51
INT					
RAL	5	2	56	20*	18.66
NAT.W.	4	0	84	28	21.00
B & H	2	1	29	26*	29.00

CAREER: BATTING

	I.	N.O.	R.	H.S.	AV.
TEST					
1ST-CLASS	335	55	7897	125	28.20
INT					
RAL	126	30	2459	92	25.61
NAT.W.	17	2	217	32	14.46
B & H	38	8	665	85	22.16

LAST SEASON: BOWLING

	O.	M.	R.	W.	AV.
TEST					
1ST-CLASS	38.2	8	140	4	35.00
INT					
RAL					
NAT.W.					
B & H					

CAREER: BOWLING

	O.	M.	R.	W.	AV.
TEST					
1ST-CLASS	544.1	80	2067	43	48.06
INT					
RAL	152	12	719	20	35.95
NAT.W.	14	1	73	1	73.00
B & H	59	7	237	8	29.62

BLAKEY, R. J.   Yorkshire

Full Name: Richard John Blakey
Role: Right-hand bat, occasional
wicket-keeper, right-arm medium
bowler
Born: 15 January 1967, Huddersfield
Height: 5′ 9″ **Weight:** 11st 6lbs
Nickname: Dick, Mutley, CO, TB, TJ
County debut: 1985
County cap: 1987
1st-Class 50s scored: 9
1st-Class 100s scored: 3
1st-Class 200s scored: 1
One-Day 50s: 2
Place in batting averages: 33rd
av. 41.30)
1st-Class catches 1987: 28 (career 45)
Parents: Brian and Pauline
Marital status: Single
Family links with cricket: Father
played local cricket

Education: Woodhouse Primary; Rastrick Grammar School
Qualifications: 4 O-levels, NCA Coaching Certificate
Overseas tours: Young England to West Indies 1985; Yorkshire CCC to Saint
Lucia 1987
Overseas teams played for: Waverley CC, Melbourne 1985–86, 1986–87
Cricketers particularly learnt from: My father Brian, Doug Padgett, Steve
Oldham, Martyn Moxon and all Yorkshire's capped players
Cricketers particularly admired: Ian Botham, Martyn Moxon
Off-season 1987–88: In Melbourne playing and coaching

LAST SEASON: BATTING

	I.	N.O.	R.	H.S.	AV.
TEST					
1ST-CLASS	38	5	1363	204*	41.30
INT					
RAL					
NAT.W.	3	1	18	14	9.00
B & H	6	2	155	58	38.75

LAST SEASON: BOWLING

	O.	M.	R.	W.	AV.
TEST					
1ST-CLASS					
INT					
RAL					
NAT.W.					
B & H					

CAREER: BATTING

	I.	N.O.	R.	H.S.	AV.
TEST					
1ST-CLASS	69	7	2119	204*	34.17
INT					
RAL	1	0	3	3	3.00
NAT.W.	3	1	18	14	9.00
B & H	6	2	155	58	38.75

CAREER: BOWLING

	O.	M.	R.	W.	AV.
TEST					
1ST-CLASS	10.3	1	68	1	68.00
INT					
RAL					
NAT.W.					
B & H					

Other sports played: Golf, squash, snooker
Other sports followed: Football, most other sports but not ice skating
Relaxations: Music and watching Leeds United FC
Extras: Made record 2nd XI score – 273* v Northamptonshire 1986
Opinions on cricket: 'In our climate I would like to see 16 four-day matches. With three-day fixtures you seem to spend the first 2½ days jockeying for position, using declaration bowlers, forfeits etc, in order to try to manufacture a result. If you are to have uncovered wickets, the bowlers run-ups should be uncovered too.'
Best batting performance: 204* Yorkshire v Gloucestershire, Leeds 1987
Best bowling performance: 1-68 Yorkshire v Nottinghamshire, Sheffield 1986

BOON, T. J. Leicestershire

Full Name: Timothy James Boon
Role: Right-hand bat,
right-arm medium bowler
Born: 1 November 1961,
Doncaster, South Yorkshire
Height: 5′ 11½″ **Weight:** 12st 3lbs
Nickname: Ted Moon, Cod
County debut: 1980
County cap: 1986
1000 runs in a season: 3
1st-Class 50s scored: 23
1st-Class 100s scored: 5
One-Day 50s: 2
Place in batting averages: 30th
av. 42.04 (1986 56th av. 38.57)
1st-Class catches 1987: 14 (career 45)
Parents: Jeffrey and Elizabeth
Marital status: Single
Family links with cricket: Father
played club cricket
Education: Mill Lane Primary; Edlington Comprehensive. Three months at Doncaster Art School
Qualifications: 1 A-level, 6 O-levels. Coaching qualifications
Jobs outside cricket: Worked with Leicester Dyers, 1986–1987
Off-season 1987–88: Selling promotional leisure-wear, and touring Sri Lanka
Cricketing superstitions or habits: 'Constantly changing.'
Overseas tours: Toured the Caribbean with England Young Cricketers 1980, as captain; Leicestershire CCC to Zimbabwe 1981
Overseas teams played for: Old Hararians, Zimbabwe, 1980–81; Ceylon CC, Colombo, 1981–82; Pirates CC, Durban, 1982–83, 1984–85

Cricketers particularly learnt from: The late Mike Fearnley, Ken Higgs, Chris Balderstone, Peter Willey
Cricketers particularly admired: 'Those who make the most of their ability.'
Other sports played: 'Enjoy playing and watching all sports.'
Injuries 1987: Broken bone in left hand, so missed five weeks
Relaxations: Sleeping, barbecue in garden, dining out
Extras: Captain England Young Cricketers Tour West Indies 1980; Captain England Young Cricketers v Indian Young Cricketers 1981; Most Promising Schoolboy Cricketer 1979. Missed 1985 season due to broken leg sustained in a car crash in South Africa the previous winter. Had sixteen inch nail removed in October 1986
Best batting performance: 144 Leicestershire v Gloucestershire, Leicester 1984
Best bowling performance: 3-40 Leicestershire v Yorkshire, Leicester 1986

LAST SEASON: BATTING

	I.	N.O.	R.	H.S.	AV.
TEST					
1ST-CLASS	26	2	1009	94	42.04
INT					
RAL	7	0	137	61	19.57
NAT.W.	1	0	17	17	17.00
B & H	3	1	60	58*	30.00

CAREER: BATTING

	I.	N.O.	R.	H.S.	AV.
TEST					
1ST-CLASS	162	24	4395	144	31.84
INT					
RAL	50	9	812	61	19.80
NAT.W.	6	3	72	22*	24.00
B & H	8	3	155	58*	31.00

LAST SEASON: BOWLING

	O.	M.	R.	W.	AV.
TEST					
1ST-CLASS	3	0	22	0	–
INT					
RAL					
NAT.W.					
B & H					

CAREER: BOWLING

	O.	M.	R.	W.	AV.
TEST					
1ST-CLASS	49.3	7	249	5	49.80
INT					
RAL	2	0	14	0	–
NAT.W.	1	0	2	0	–
B & H					

29. True or false: Test captains Woodfull, Bradman, Goddard, Kardar and Cowdrey always batted first if they won the toss?

BORDER, A. R.   Essex

Full Name: Allan Robert Border
Role: Left-hand bat, slow
left-arm bowler
Born: 27 July 1955, Cremorne,
Sydney
Height: 5′ 9″
Nickname: AB, Herby
(from Herbaceous)
County debut: 1977 (Gloucestershire),
1986 (Essex)
County cap: 1986 (Essex)
Test debut: 1978–79
No. of Tests: 89
No. of One-Day Internationals: 151
1000 runs in a season: 2
1st-Class 50s scored: 83
1st-Class 100s scored: 47
1st-Class 200s scored: 1
One-Day 50s: 28
One-Day 100s: 3
Place in batting averages: — (1986 13th av. 49.46)
1st-Class catches 1987: 0 (career 199)
Wife and date of marriage: Jane, 12 April 1980
Children: Dene and Nicole
Family links with cricket: Father-in-law, president of Mosman CC
Education: Mosman Primary; North Sydney Technical School; North Sydney Boys High
Jobs outside cricket: Clerk; working in motor-trade, mainly of a promotional nature, for Ron McConnell (who brought me to Queensland)
Off-season 1987–88: Playing for Australia in World Cup and on tour
Overseas tours: With Australia to England for World Cup, 1979, and for tour in 1980, 1981, 1985; West Indies 1983–84; New Zealand 1981–82, 1986; India 1979–80, 1986, Pakistan 1979–80, 1982–83; Sri Lanka 1982–83; to India and Pakistan for World Cup 1987
Overseas teams played for: New South Wales 1976–80; Queensland 1980–86
Cricketers admired: Gary Sobers, Barry Knight, Mark Williamson (elder half-brother)
Other sports played: Baseball (when younger), golf
Opinion on cricket: 'I have always regarded Headingly as a sub-standard Test wicket. The unpredictable nature of it makes team selection and captaincy a bit of a nightmare. Overseas tours have been too long. I'd strongly favour reducing future tours to three months. I also advocate less cricket and oppose players' wives coming on tour.'

Extras: Played for Gloucestershire 2nd XI in 1977 and one match for Gloucestershire 1st XI that year. Captained North Sydney High. Made A-grade debut for Mosman at 16. Third highest run-scorer in Australian Test cricket (at end of 1987). Captained Australia World Cup-winning side 1987. Has appeared in more one-day internationals than any other player in the world. Captain of Queensland since 1983–84; captain of Australia since 1985. Played for East Lancashire in Lancashire League 1978, scoring 1100 odd runs, a club record. Also took about 50 wickets with medium-pace slingers, as opposed to the normal slow left-arm. Joined Essex on 2-year contract in 1986. Published autobiography in 1986

Best batting performance: 200 New South Wales v Queensland, Brisbane 1979–80

Best bowling performance: 4-61 Queensland v New South Wales, Sydney 1980–81

LAST SEASON: BATTING

	I.	N.O.	R.	H.S.	AV.
TEST					
1ST-CLASS	3	0	111	57	37.00
INT					
RAL					
NAT.W.	1	1	46	46*	–
B & H					

LAST SEASON: BOWLING

	O.	M.	R.	W.	AV.
TEST					
1ST-CLASS					
INT					
RAL					
NAT.W.	0.4	0	1	1	1.00
B & H					

CAREER: BATTING

	I.	N.O.	R.	H.S.	AV.
TEST	157	26	6917	196	52.80
1ST-CLASS	198	25	9336	200	53.96
INT	142	20	3952	127*	32.39
RAL	13	1	330	75	27.50
NAT.W.	3	1	75	46*	37.50
B & H	5	0	81	31	16.20

CAREER: BOWLING

	O.	M.	R.	W.	AV.
TEST	49 231.3	18 64	699	16	43.68
1ST-CLASS	243.6 283.1	35 64	1456	44	33.09
INT	171	6	814	23	35.39
RAL	5	0	26	3	8.66
NAT.W.	2.4	0	12	1	12.00
B & H					

---

30. Which England captain said: 'You should sometimes think of putting the other side in to bat, and then not do it'?

31. What were the approximate takings at the M.C.C. Bicentenary Test: £125,000, £700,000, or £1,250,000?

BORE, M. K.　　　　　Nottinghamshire

Full Name: Michael Kenneth Bore
Born: 2 June 1947, Hull
Height: 5′ 10″ **Weight:** 14st
Nickname: Nod
County debut: 1969 (Yorkshire),
1979 (Nottinghamshire)
County cap: 1980 (Nottinghamshire)
1st-Class 5 w. in innings: 9
1st-Class catches 1987: 1 (career 51)
Parents: Kenneth and Cicely
Wife and date of marriage: Ann,
30 September 1972
Children: Christopher Mark, 17 July
1977; Suzanne, 23 July 1979
Family links with cricket: Father
played a good level of local amateur
league cricket
Education: Maybury High School
Qualifications: NCA Advanced Coach
Jobs outside cricket: Full-time coach with Nottinghamshire CC
Off-season 1987–88: Coaching children and club players, running courses and
seminars at college and university level
Superstitions or habits: Always put right pad on first. When not captain,
prefer to follow wicket-keeper on to field
Overseas tours: Gibraltar with Yorkshire CCC, 1976–77
Cricketers particularly learnt from: 'Most I've played with and against.'
Cricketers particularly admired: Richard Hadlee, Jimmy Binks
Other sports played: Badminton, squash, snooker, golf (badly)
Other sports followed: Football, Rugby League

LAST SEASON: BATTING

	I.	N.O.	R.	H.S.	AV.
TEST					
1ST-CLASS	5	1	13	7	3.25
INT					
RAL					
NAT.W.					
B & H					

LAST SEASON: BOWLING

	O.	M.	R.	W.	AV.
TEST					
1ST-CLASS	148.2	58	344	13	26.46
INT					
RAL	28	0	90	2	45.00
NAT.W.					
B & H					

CAREER: BATTING

	I.	N.O.	R.	H.S.	AV.
TEST					
1ST-CLASS	156	52	869	37*	8.35
INT					
RAL	32	14	129	28*	7.16
NAT.W.	7	4	9	4*	3.00
B & H	10	7	27	7*	9.00

CAREER: BOWLING

	O.	M.	R.	W.	AV.
TEST					
1ST-CLASS	4600.1	1559	11202	372	30.11
INT					
RAL	768	81	3052	96	31.79
NAT.W.	109.2	19	327	11	29.72
B & H	259.4	59	736	29	25.38

Injuries 1987: Old age!

Relaxations: Family, gardening, driving, watching out for younger cricketers at Sunday matches

Extras: Having just retired from first-class cricket in the last few years, was reinstated for 1987 season

Opinions on cricket: 'Reservations on four-day cricket. More time should be spent by the TCCB into looking into better quality pitches and facilities for 2nd XI cricket, and to help the counties with more funding, especially covering the cost of first-class umpires standing in 2nd XI games.'

Best batting performance: 37* Yorkshire v Nottinghamshire, Bradford 1973

Best bowling performance: 8-89 Nottinghamshire v Kent, Folkestone 1979

BOTHAM, I. T. Worcestershire

Full Name: Ian Terrence Botham
Role: Right-hand bat, right-arm fast-medium bowler, slip fielder
Born: 24 November 1955, Heswall, Cheshire
Height: 6' 2" **Weight:** 15st 5lbs
Nickname: Guy, Both, Beefy
County debut: 1974 (Somerset), 1987 (Worcestershire)
County cap: 1976 (Somerset), 1987 (Worcestershire)
Benefit: 1984 (£90,822)
Test debut: 1977
No. of Tests: 94
No. of One-Day Internationals: 95
1000 runs in a season: 4
50 wickets in a season: 7
1st-Class 50s scored: 74
1st-Class 100s scored: 33
1st-Class 200s scored: 2
1st-Class 5 w. in innings: 53
1st-Class 10 w. in match: 7
One-Day 50s: 54
One-Day 100s: 7
Place in batting averages: 108th av. 29.90 (1986 19th av. 47.94)
Place in bowling averages: 121st av. 42.04 (1986 102nd av. 41.72)
Strike rate 1987: 74.28 (career 68.24)
1st-Class catches 1987: 10 (career 281)
Parents: Les and Marie
Wife and date of marriage: Kathryn, 31 January 1976

Children: Liam James, 26 August 1977; Sarah Lianne, 3 February 1979; Rebecca Kate, 13 November 1985

Family links with cricket: Father played for Navy and Fleet Air Arm; mother played for VAD nursing staff

Education: Millford Junior School; Buckler's Mead Secondary School, Yeovil

Overseas tours: Pakistan and New Zealand 1977–78; Australia 1978–79; Australia and India, 1979–80; West Indies 1981 as captain; India 1981–82; Australia and New Zealand 1982–83; West Indies 1986

Cricketers particularly learnt from: Brian Close

Cricketers particularly admired: Viv Richards, David Gower, Allan Border

Off-season 1987–88: Playing for Queensland

Other sports played: Captained school soccer team, and has played for Scunthorpe United, making debut as striker v Bournemouth in March 1980. Offered terms by Crystal Palace. Now plays for Yeovil Town. U-16 Somerset champion, badminton doubles

Relaxations: Golf, shooting, fishing (salmon and trout). Has learned to fly

Extras: Captain of England 1980–81. Took five Australian wickets in his first day of Test Match cricket aged 21. Played for County 2nd XI 1971. On MCC staff 1972–73. Played for county in last two John Player League matches 1973. Subject of 'This is Your Life' television programme in November 1981. Was Best Man at Viv Richards' wedding in March 1981 in Antigua. Voted BBC TV Sportsview Sporting Personality of 1981. Having a go at baseball in Los Angeles in September 1981 easily exceeded the striking rate of established American baseball stars: he complained that Americans could not pitch the ball fast enough. Scored fastest 100 of 1982 and 1985 seasons. Scored 200 in 272 minutes for England v India at The Oval, 9 July 1982, third fastest Test double century by an Englishman, after Walter Hammond (240 mins v New Zealand in 1932) and Denis Compton (245 mins v Pakistan in 1954). Crashed two £12,000 sports cars at 100 mph in same afternoon in May 1982. Among the books he chose to take to a desert island was Jack Fingleton's book on the great Australian cricketer *The Immortal Victor Trumper*. Published books include *High, Wide and Handsome*, an account of his record-breaking 1985 season and *It Sort of Clicks*, in collaboration with his former Somerset colleague Peter Roebuck. First cricketer since W. G. Grace to have painting commissioned by National Portrait Gallery. Captain of Somerset 1984–85. Holds record for having scored 1000 runs and taken 100 wickets in fewest Test matches. First player to score a century and take 8 wickets in an innings in a Test Match, v Pakistan at Lord's in 1978. Most sixes in a first-class season and most instances of 5 wickets in a Test innings (both 1985). Leading wicket-taker in Test cricket. Left Somerset at the beginning of 1987 to join Worcestershire after Somerset had decided not to renew the contracts of Richards and Garner

Opinions on cricket: 'Too many people live in the past.'

Best batting performance: 228 Somerset v Gloucestershire, Taunton 1980

Best bowling performance: 8-34 England v Pakistan, Lord's 1978

LAST SEASON: BATTING

	I.	N.O.	R.	H.S.	AV.
TEST	8	1	232	51*	33.14
1ST-CLASS	14	1	366	126*	28.15
INT	3	1	30	24	15.00
RAL	11	1	578	125*	57.80
NAT.W.	2	0	101	101	50.50
B & H	4	0	28	18	7.00

LAST SEASON: BOWLING

	O.	M.	R.	W.	AV.
TEST	134.3	30	433	7	61.85
1ST-CLASS	125.3	17	450	14	32.14
INT	29	3	103	0	–
RAL	69.3	6	295	19	15.52
NAT.W.	12	0	29	1	29.00
B & H	48.4	8	148	7	21.14

CAREER: BATTING

	I.	N.O.	R.	H.S.	AV.
TEST	150	5	5057	208	34.87
1ST-CLASS	336	32	10701	228	35.20
INT	86	11	1693	72	22.57
RAL	135	22	3763	175*	33.30
NAT.W.	30	6	926	101	38.58
B & H	52	7	1067	126*	23.71

CAREER: BOWLING

	O.	M.	R.	W.	AV.
TEST	259.4 3120.5	42 705	10392	373	27.86
1ST-CLASS	190.3 7370.1	43 1689	15668	602	26.02
INT	38.7 794.4	2 93	3398	116	29.29
RAL	468.4	59	4259	190	22.41
NAT.W.	353.3	56	1191	42	28.35
B & H	604	116	2038	95	21.45

BOWLER, P. D.   Derbyshire

Full Name: Peter Duncan Bowler
Role: Right-hand opening bat,
off-spinner
Born: 30 July 1963, Plymouth,
Australia
Height: 6′ 2″ **Weight:** 13st
Nickname: Skippy
County debut: 1986
1st-Class 50s scored: 1
1st-Class 100s scored: 1
One-Day 50s: 1
Place in batting averages: —
(1986 150th av. 24.90)
1st-Class catches 1987: 0 (career 2)
Parents: Peter and Etta
Marital status: Engaged to Julie
Education: Daramalan College,
Canberra, Australia
Qualifications: Australia Yr 12 Certificate
Overseas teams played for: Manly CC 1982; Westbury CC 1983–87
Cricketers particularly learnt from: Rob Jeffery, Bill Carracher, Gus Valence
Cricketers particularly admired: Greg Chappell, Richard Hadlee, Dennis
Lillee
Off-season 1987–88: Playing in Australia
Other sports played: Rugby union

Relaxations: Music, reading, newspapers. Playing sports other than cricket. Relaxing with family
Extras: First Leicestershire player to score a first-class hundred on debut (100 not out v Hampshire 1986). Moved to Derbyshire at end of 1987 season
Best batting performance: 100* Leicestershire v Hampshire, Leicester 1986

LAST SEASON: BATTING

	I.	N.O.	R.	H.S.	AV.
TEST					
1ST-CLASS					
INT					
RAL	1	0	7	7	7.00
NAT.W.					
B & H					

CAREER: BATTING

	I.	N.O.	R.	H.S.	AV.
TEST					
1ST-CLASS	14	1	264	100*	20.30
INT					
RAL	11	1	171	55	17.10
NAT.W.					
B & H					

BOYD-MOSS, R. J.   Northamptonshire

Full Name: Robin James Boyd-Moss
Role: Right-hand bat, slow left-arm bowler
Born: 16 December 1959, Hatton, Sri Lanka
Height: 5' 10½" **Weight:** 12st 9lbs
Nickname: Mossy, Mouse
County debut: 1980
County cap: 1984
1000 runs in a season: 3
1st-Class 50s scored: 42
1st-Class 100s scored: 13
1st-Class 5 w. in innings: 1
One-Day 50s: 8
Place in batting averages: 133rd av. 26.75 (1986 101st av. 30.56)
1st-Class catches 1987: 3 (career 61)
Parents: Michael and Shelagh

Wife and date of marriage: Deborah, 21 December 1985
Education: Bedford School; Cambridge University
Qualifications: 3 A-levels, BA in Land Economy, Certificate of Education (Cantab)
Off-season 1987–88: Coaching in Kenya
Cricketing superstitions or habits: Puts left pad on first
Cricketers particularly learnt from: Allan Lamb
Other sports played: Rugby union (played centre for Cambridge v Oxford in 100th Varsity Match and was a Double Blue), golf, squash

Injuries 1987: Broken thumb
Relaxations: Fishing
Best batting performance: 155 Northamptonshire v Lincolnshire, Northampton 1986
Best bowling performance: 5-27 Cambridge University v Oxford University, Lord's 1983

LAST SEASON: BATTING

	I.	N.O.	R.	H.S.	AV.
TEST					
1ST-CLASS	13	1	321	77	26.75
INT					
RAL	1	0	39	39	39.00
NAT.W.					
B & H	1	0	4	4	4.00

CAREER: BATTING

	I.	N.O.	R.	H.S.	AV.
TEST					
1ST-CLASS	257	20	7171	155	30.25
INT					
RAL	51	6	1049	99	23.31
NAT.W.	6	2	179	88*	44.75
B & H	21	1	364	58	18.20

LAST SEASON: BOWLING

	O.	M.	R.	W.	AV.
TEST					
1ST-CLASS	34	13	87	1	87.00
INT					
RAL	4	0	26	0	–
NAT.W.					
B & H					

CAREER: BOWLING

	O.	M.	R.	W.	AV.
TEST					
1ST-CLASS	651.5	156	2198	51	43.09
INT					
RAL	5	0	37	0	–
NAT.W.	12	1	47	3	15.66
B & H	12	1	49	0	–

BRIERS, N. E. Leicestershire

Full Name: Nigel Edwin Briers
Role: Right-hand bat, right-arm medium bowler, cover fielder
Born: 15 January 1955, Leicester
Height: 6′ 0″ **Weight:** 12st 5lbs
Nickname: Kudu
County debut: 1971 (aged 16 yrs 104 days)
County cap: 1981
1000 runs in a season: 4
1st-Class 50s scored: 42
1st-Class 100s scored: 11
1st-Class 200s scored: 1
One-Day 50s: 28
One-Day 100s: 3
Place in batting averages: 21st av. 44.89
1st-Class catches 1987: 11 (career 86)
Parents: Leonard Arthur Roger and Eveline

Wife and date of marriage: Suzanne Mary Tudor, 3 September 1977
Children: Michael Edward Tudor, 25 March 1983; Andrew James Tudor, 30 June 1986
Family links with cricket: Father was captain and wicket-keeper of Narborough and Littlethorpe Cricket Club, first division of Leicestershire League, for 15 years. Mother was scorer for team. Father was Captain of South Leicestershire Representative XI and played for the Royal Marines in the same team as Trevor Bailey. Cousin, Norman Briers, played for Leicestershire once in 1967
Education: Lutterworth Grammar School; Borough Road College
Qualifications: Qualified teacher (Certificate of Education), BEd Hons, MCC Advanced Coach
Jobs outside cricket: Lecturer in Physical Education at Leicester Polytechnic
Off-season 1987–88: Teaching PE and history at Ludgrove School
Overseas tours: Derrick Robins' XI to South America, 1979; MCC to Far East, 1981; Leicestershire CCC to Zimbabwe, 1981
Best batting performance: 201* Leicestershire v Warwickshire, Edgbaston 1983
Best bowling performance: 4-29 Leicestershire v Derbyshire, Leicester 1985

LAST SEASON: BATTING

	I.	N.O.	R.	H.S.	AV.
TEST					
1ST-CLASS	32	4	1257	104	44.89
INT					
RAL	10	2	256	79	32.00
NAT.W.	4	0	61	32	15.25
B & H					

LAST SEASON: BOWLING

	O.	M.	R.	W.	AV.
TEST					
1ST-CLASS	7	1	18	0	
INT					
RAL					
NAT.W.					
B & H					

CAREER: BATTING

	I.	N.O.	R.	H.S.	AV.
TEST					
1ST-CLASS	333	35	8728	201*	29.28
INT					
RAL	122	19	3599	119*	34.94
NAT.W.	21	2	352	59	18.52
B & H	29	2	436	71*	16.14

CAREER: BOWLING

	O.	M.	R.	W.	AV.
TEST					
1ST-CLASS	338.5	70	988	32	30.87
INT					
RAL	80.2	5	384	10	38.40
NAT.W.	14	0	75	6	12.50
B & H	55	3	266	3	88.60

32. When did Derek Underwood play his first and last first-class matches in Kent?

BROAD, B. C. Nottinghamshire

Full Name: Brian Christopher Broad

Role: Left-hand bat, right-arm medium bowler

Born: 29 September 1957, Bristol

Height: 6′ 4″ **Weight:** 14st 7lbs

Nickname: Walter, Broadie, Whoda (by Mike Gatting, as in 'Whoda thought of you')

County debut: 1979 (Gloucestershire), 1984 (Nottinghamshire)

County cap: 1981 (Gloucestershire), 1984 (Nottinghamshire)

Test debut: 1984

No. of Tests: 14

No. of One-Day Internationals: 20

1000 runs in a season: 6

1st-Class 50s scored: 67

1st-Class 100s scored: 21

One-Day 50s: 38

One-Day 100s: 3

Place in batting averages: 92nd av. 32.18 (1986 49th av. 39.82)

1st-Class catches 1987: 15 (career 110)

Parents: Nancy and Kenneth

Wife and date of marriage: Carole Ann, 14 July 1979

Children: Gemma Joanne, 14 January 1984; Stuart Christopher John, 24 June 1986

Education: Colston's School, Bristol; St Paul's College, Cheltenham

Qualifications: 5 O-levels, NCA advanced coach

Family links with cricket: Father and grandfather both played local cricket. Father member of Gloucestershire Committee until retired

Cricketing superstitions or habits: Puts left pad on first

Overseas tours: Gloucestershire CCC to Malawi 1978 and Barbados 1980; British Colleges to Trinidad and Barbados 1979; English Counties to Zimbabwe, 1985; International XI to Jamaica, 1985; England to West Indies 1986; World Cup, Pakistan, New Zealand and Australia 1987–88

Overseas teams played for: Somerville CC, Melbourne, 1979–80, Takapuna CC, Auckland 1982–83, 1983–84, Orange Free State 1985–86 (Captain)

Cricketers particularly learnt from: Reg Sinfield, Sadiq Mohammed, John Sullivan

Cricketers particularly admired: Graham Gooch, Richard Hadlee, Clive Rice

Off-season 1987–88: Touring with England
Other sports played: Played Rugby for English Colleges, Bristol United, St Paul's College, and Clifton
Relaxations: 'Playing any sport, spending time with my family.'
Extras: Struck down by osteomyelitis at age 15. First played adult cricket for Downend CC, where W. G. Grace learnt to play; then Long Ashton CC; Gloucestershire U-19s; Gloucestershire Young Cricketers'; NAYC v MCC Schools. Played with Allan Border in Gloucestershire 2nd XI. Played with Tim Robinson in 1977 for NAYC v Young Australians. Published autobiography *Home Thoughts from Abroad* in 1987. Hit three centuries in a row in Test series v Australia, 1986–87. Uses a bat weighing 3lbs. Considers Hadlee a better all-rounder than Botham
Opinions on cricket: 'I would have loved playing as an amateur. I am an unashamed traditionalist.'
Best batting performance: 171 Nottinghamshire v Derbyshire, Derby 1985
Best bowling performance: 2-14 Gloucestershire v West Indies, Bristol 1980

LAST SEASON: BATTING

	I.	N.O.	R.	H.S.	AV.
TEST	7	0	193	55	27.57
1ST-CLASS	19	4	515	80	34.33
INT	3	0	166	99	55.33
RAL	8	2	289	76*	48.16
NAT.W.	5	0	236	67	47.20
B & H	2	0	89	83	44.50

CAREER: BATTING

	I.	N.O.	R.	H.S.	AV.
TEST	25	2	961	162	41.78
1ST-CLASS	323	25	10723	171	35.98
INT	20	0	891	97	44.55
RAL	100	5	3059	104*	32.20
NAT.W.	21	0	791	98	37.66
B & H	35	2	889	122	16.93

LAST SEASON: BOWLING

	O.	M.	R.	W.	AV.
TEST					
1ST-CLASS					
INT					
RAL					
NAT.W.					
B & H					

CAREER: BOWLING

	O.	M.	R.	W.	AV.
TEST					
1ST-CLASS	265.5	60	1002	16	52.81
INT					
RAL	111.3	4	602	19	31.68
NAT.W.					
B & H	50.4	2	282	5	56.40

33. True or false: Derek Underwood was the youngest player to take 100 wickets in a season in his first season?

34. Of which England player did Peter Roebuck write: 'More of a rusty tractor than a new Maestro'?

BROWN, G. E. — Surrey

Full Name: Graham Elliott Brown
Role: Right-hand bat, wicket-keeper
Born: 11 October 1966, Balham
Height: 5′ 7″ **Weight:** 9½st
Nickname: Browny, Stumper, Pipsqueek
County debut: 1986
Parents: Alan and Dorothy
Wife and date of marriage: Pamela, January 1987
Family links with cricket: Father and uncles avid watchers
Education: Spencer Park School, Wandsworth; South London College, West Norwood
Qualifications: 6 CSEs, 3 O-levels
Jobs outside cricket: Postman, sports coach, insurance broker
Cricketing superstitions or habits: Left keeping pad on first; left inner glove on first; being first out onto the middle to get new ball off umpire
Overseas tours: London Schools U-16s to Jamaica 1983
Cricketers particularly learnt from: Jack Richards, Ray Jackson, Ron Brown
Cricketers particularly admired: Jack Richards
Off-season 1987–88: Working at an insurance brokers
Other sports played: Football, athletics
Relaxations: Reading, travelling, listening to music, photography
Extras: Released by Surrey at end of 1987 season
Best batting performance: 13* Surrey v Pakistanis, The Oval 1987

LAST SEASON: BATTING

	I.	N.O.	R.	H.S.	AV.
TEST					
1ST-CLASS	7	6	47	13*	47.00
INT					
RAL					
NAT.W.					
B & H					

LAST SEASON: WICKET KEEPING

	C.	ST.			
TEST					
1ST-CLASS	9	–			
INT					
RAL					
NAT.W.					
B & H					

CAREER: BATTING

	I.	N.O.	R.	H.S.	AV.
TEST					
1ST-CLASS	9	8	49	13*	49.00
INT					
RAL					
NAT.W.					
B & H					

CAREER: WICKET KEEPING

	C.	ST.			
TEST					
1ST-CLASS	13	1			
INT					
RAL					
NAT.W.					
B & H					

BROWN, K. R.   Middlesex

Full Name: Keith Robert Brown
Role: Right-hand bat, wicket-keeper
Born: 18 March 1963, Edmonton
Height: 5' 11" **Weight:** 13st 7lbs
Nickname: Browny, Gloves, Scarface, Pigsy
County debut: 1984
1st-Class 50s scored: 8
1st-Class 100s scored: 1
One-Day 50s: 1
Place in batting averages: 126th
av. 27.57 (1986 138th av. 26.40)
1st-Class catches 1987: 15 (career 32)
Parents: Kenneth William and
Margaret Sonia
Wife and date of marriage: Marie,
3 November 1984
Children: Zachary, 24 February 1987
Family links with cricket: Brother Gary was on Middlesex staff for 3 years.
Father is qualified umpire and played club cricket
Education: Chance Boys' School, Enfield
Qualifications: French O-level; Junior and Senior Cricket Coach
Jobs outside cricket: Plasterer, light engineering, painter, decorator
Cricketing superstitions or habits: Nelson 111. Wear same gear if successful
Overseas tours: NCA to Denmark 1981. Pre-season trips with Middlesex to
La Manga 1985 and 86
Cricketers particularly learnt from: Father and Don Bennett, Clive Radley
Cricketers particularly admired: Clive Radley

LAST SEASON: BATTING

	I.	N.O.	R.	H.S.	AV.
TEST					
1ST-CLASS	24	3	579	70	27.57
INT					
RAL	8	4	210	50*	52.50
NAT.W.	1	0	24	24	24.00
B & H					

LAST SEASON: BOWLING

	O.	M.	R.	W.	AV.
TEST					
1ST-CLASS	13	1	54	3	18.00
INT					
RAL	1	0	1	0	—
NAT.W.					
B & H					

CAREER: BATTING

	I.	N.O.	R.	H.S.	AV.
TEST					
1ST-CLASS	52	7	1250	102	27.77
INT					
RAL	13	4	278	50*	30.88
NAT.W.	1	0	24	24	24.00
B & H					

CAREER: BOWLING

	O.	M.	R.	W.	AV.
TEST					
1ST-CLASS	14.4	2	64	3	21.33
INT					
RAL	1	0	1	0	—
NAT.W.					
B & H					

Off-season 1987–88: Keeping fit and moving house
Other sports played: Rugby, tennis, snooker
Other sports followed: All of them, especially boxing and football
Relaxations: Exercising Golden Retriever Wesley, looking after baby Zachary – not relaxing but enjoyable
Extras: Had promising boxing career but gave it up in order to concentrate on cricket. Picked to play rugby for Essex
Opinions on cricket: 'Four-day cricket may benefit county players with a view to representing their country.'
Best batting performance: 102 Middlesex v Australia, Lord's 1985
Best bowling performance: 2-7 Middlsex v Gloucestershire, Bristol 1987

BROWN, S. J.　　　Northamptonshire

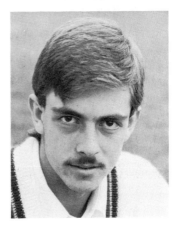

Full Name: Simon John Brown
Role: Right-hand bat, left-arm medium pace bowler
Born: 29 June 1969, Cleadon Village, Sunderland
Height: 6′ 3″ **Weight:** 12st
Nickname: Chubby
County debut: 1987
1st-Class catches 1987: 1 (career 1)
Parents: Ernie and Doreen
Marital status: Single
Education: Boldon Comprehensive, Tyne & Wear
Qualifications: 5 O-levels 5 CSE's
Jobs outside cricket: Sales assistant, part-time groundsman
Off-season 1987–88: Working as a sales promoter
Cricketers particularly learnt from: Alec Coxon
Cricketers particularly admired: John Lever, Denis Lillee, Richard Hadlee
Other sports played: Basketball, football, tennis, golf, snooker, squash
Other sports followed: Basketball, snooker
Injuries 1987: Missed a lot of season with torn side muscles
Relaxations: Fishing, cycling, playing snooker
Extras: Offered basketball scholarship in America. Also professional terms with Sunderland FC. Took wicket with first ball in Sunday League
Best batting performance: 20 Northamptonshire v Leicestershire, Leicester 1987

Best bowling performance: 3-67 Northamptonshire v Pakistanis, Milton Keynes 1987

LAST SEASON: BATTING

	I.	N.O.	R.	H.S.	AV.
TEST					
1ST-CLASS	5	3	25	20	12.50
INT					
RAL					
NAT.W.					
B & H					

LAST SEASON: BOWLING

	O.	M.	R.	W.	AV.
TEST					
1ST-CLASS	82	23	216	9	24.00
INT					
RAL	11	1	64	2	32.00
NAT.W.					
B & H					

CAREER: BATTING

	I.	N.O.	R.	H.S.	AV.
TEST					
1ST-CLASS	5	3	25	20	12.50
INT					
RAL					
NAT.W.					
B & H					

CAREER: BOWLING

	O.	M.	R.	W.	AV.
TEST					
1ST-CLASS	82	23	216	9	24.00
INT					
RAL	11	1	64	2	32.00
NAT.W.					
B & H					

BULLEN, C. K. Surrey

Full Name: Christopher Keith Bullen
Role: Right-hand bat, off-break bowler, slip fielder
Born: 5 November 1962, Clapham
Height: 6′ 5″ **Weight:** 14st 7lbs
Nickname: CB, Jasper, Bullo, Roadrunner, Steeley
County debut: 1985
1st-Class 50s scored: 2
1st-Class 5 w. in innings: 1
Place in batting averages: 138th av. 25.90
Place in bowling averages: 48th av. 26.85
Strike rate 1987: 64.47 (career 68.52)
1st-Class catches 1987: 14 (career 16)
Parents: Keith Thomas and Joan
Marital status: Single
Family links with cricket: 'Parents are enthusiastic cricket watchers. Father claims he played cricket at a high standard, but there's no evidence!'
Education: Glenbrook Primary; Chaucer Middle; Rutlish School

Qualifications: 6 O-levels

Jobs outside cricket: Labourer, car washer, packer

Off-season 1987–88: Working on my game at home and playing rugby for Old Rutlishians

Cricketing superstitions or habits: Always put left things on first, i.e. socks, shoes, batting gloves. Always brush hair before going out to field

Overseas tours: Surrey Schools U-19 to Australia 1980–81

Overseas teams played for: Claremont Cottesloe, Perth, 1984–85, 1985–86

Cricketers particularly learnt from: Mickey Stewart, Geoff Arnold, Chris Waller

Cricketers particularly admired: Pat Pocock, Jim Laker

Other sports played: Golf, rugby

Other sports followed: Soccer, American football, Aussie rules

Injuries 1987: Premature greyness!

Relaxations: Listening to music, leisurely walk after a golf ball

Extras: Spends free time playing club cricket for Wimbledon. Captain of Surrey U-25 side which won Warwick Trophy in 1986. Once a night-watchman in B & H semi-final

Opinions: 'Four-day county games. English registration is given too freely. 2nd XI matches should be played under same conditions as first-class games. More should be done by clubs to look after their players during the winter, especially those staying in this country.'

Best batting performance: 65 Surrey v Pakistanis, The Oval 1987

Best bowling performance: 6-19 Surrey v Middlesex, Lord's, 1987

LAST SEASON: BATTING

	I.	N.O.	R.	H.S.	AV.
TEST					
1ST-CLASS	13	3	259	65	25.90
INT					
RAL	7	3	73	25	18.25
NAT.W.	1	1	1	1*	–
B & H	1	0	33	33	33.00

LAST SEASON: BOWLING

	O.	M.	R.	W.	AV.
TEST					
1ST-CLASS	225.4	71	564	21	26.85
INT					
RAL	81.3	4	404	14	28.85
NAT.W.	24	5	74	1	74.00
B & H	55	5	180	5	36.00

CAREER: BATTING

	I.	N.O.	R.	H.S.	AV.
TEST					
1ST-CLASS	17	3	312	65	22.28
INT					
RAL	12	5	93	25	13.28
NAT.W.	1	1	1	1*	–
B & H	1	0	33	33	33.00

CAREER: BOWLING

	O.	M.	R.	W.	AV.
TEST					
1ST-CLASS	262.4	82	668	23	29.04
INT					
RAL	119.3	9	520	18	28.88
NAT.W.	24	5	74	1	74.00
B & H	55	5	180	5	36.00

BURNS, N. D.   Somerset

Full Name: Neil David Burns
Role: Left-hand bat,
wicket-keeper
Born: 19 September 1965,
Chelmsford
Height: 5' 10" **Weight:** 11½st
Nickname: Burnsie, Ernie
County debut: 1986 (Essex),
1987 (Somerset)
County cap: 1987 (Somerset)
1st-Class 50s scored: 4
1st-Class 100s scored: 1
One-Day 50s: 1
Place in batting averages: 136th
av. 26.03
Parents: Roy and Marie
Wife and date of marriage: Anne,
26 September 1987

Family links with cricket: Father
Roy played club cricket for Finchley
CC; brother Ian captained Essex U-19 and plays for Chelmsford CC and
Stock Exchange CC
Education: Mildmay Junior and Moulsham High School
Qualifications: 5 O-levels, Advanced Cricket Coach
Jobs outside cricket: Worked in a sports shop one winter
Off-season 1987–88: Playing and coaching in Cape Town
Cricketing superstitions or habits: Must go through a particular warm-up and
practice before every day's play. Always keep wicket in a cap
Overseas tours: Young England to West Indies 1985
Overseas teams played for: Northerns-Goonwood CC (Cape Town) 1984–85,
1985–86; Western Province B in Sach Castle Bowl 1985–86
Cricketers particularly learnt from: Ray East, Graham Saville, Alan Knott,
Robin Jackman, Martin Crowe
Cricketers particularly admired: Alan Knott, Bob Taylor, Rod Marsh,
Graham Gooch, Martin Crowe, John Lever
Other sports followed: Most sports particularly soccer and West Ham United
FC
Relaxations: Relaxing at home, music, theatre, watching and playing sport,
TV, sleeping
Extras: Former schoolboy footballer with Spurs and Orient FC. Joined
Somerset in 1987 on two-year contract to further career after spending four
years at Essex. Once took 8 stumpings in match v Kent 2nd XI at Dartford

1984. Essex Young Player of Year 1984. Trained with West Ham United FC. Joined Somerset in 1987. Scored maiden 1st-class century against old county at Chelmsford

Opinions on cricket: 'Should be a regular overseas tour in the winter of an England U-25 or B team to bridge gap between young England and the full side. More should be done by clubs to encourage players to work for the club in winter months in some promotional capacity. Bowlers run-ups should be uncovered, if pitches are. 16 four-day matches for 1st-class games. 2nd XI competition to be 16 three-day games playing each county once with venues switching alternate seasons. Better quality pitches at 2nd XI level and one 1st-class umpire to stand to raise umpiring level. All grounds should have top quality grass practice pitches available.'

Best batting performance: 100* Somerset v Essex, Chelmsford 1987

LAST SEASON: BATTING

	I.	N.O.	R.	H.S.	AV.
TEST					
1ST-CLASS	35	7	729	100*	26.03
INT					
RAL	11	2	75	29	8.33
NAT.W.	1	0	17	17	17.00
B & H	4	3	145	51	145.00

LAST SEASON: WICKET KEEPING

	C.	ST.		
TEST				
1ST-CLASS	44	6		
INT				
RAL	13	3		
NAT.W.	1	1		
B & H	6	1		

CAREER: BATTING

	I.	N.O.	R.	H.S.	AV.
TEST					
1ST-CLASS	43	7	813	100*	22.58
INT					
RAL	11	2	75	29	8.33
NAT.W.	1	0	17	17	17.00
B & H	4	3	145	51	145.00

CAREER: WICKET KEEPING

	C.	ST.		
TEST				
1ST-CLASS	54	8		
INT				
RAL	13	3		
NAT.W.	1	1		
B & H	6	1		

35. Which county-cricketer-turned-umpire once allowed an over to run for eleven true balls?

36. Who is the only man to have played rugby for Scotland and cricket for South Africa?

BURROWS, D. A.　　　Gloucestershire

Full Name: Dean Andrew Burrows
Role: Right-hand bat, right-arm
fast bowler
Born: 20 June 1966, Easington,
Co Durham
Height: 6' 4" **Weight:** 14st
Nickname: Deano, Nugget (by
Bill Athey), Top Porridge Gun
County debut: 1984
Parents: Michael Alec John
(deceased) and Barbara Michelle
Marital status: Single
Family links with cricket: Brother
Nicholas plays club cricket. Father
also was very interested in the game
Education: Shotton Hall School,
Peterlee, Co Durham
Qualifications: 5 O-levels
Overseas tours: Gloucestershire
CCC to Barbados

Overseas teams played for: Fraser Technical CC, Hamilton, New Zealand
1986–87
Other sports followed: Most sports except anything involving horses
Off-season 1987–88: Working in England
Cricketers particularly learnt from: Dennis Lillee, Keith Tomlins, Derek
Moreland, Les King
Cricketers particularly admired: Dennis Lillee, Michael Holding, Rakesh
Shakla
Other sports played: Soccer, swimming, some tennis. Will try anything

LAST SEASON: BATTING

	I.	N.O.	R.	H.S.	AV.
TEST					
1ST-CLASS					
INT					
RAL					
NAT.W.					
B & H					

LAST SEASON: BOWLING

	O.	M.	R.	W.	AV.
TEST					
1ST-CLASS	9	0	27	0	
INT					
RAL					
NAT.W.					
B & H					

CAREER: BATTING

	I.	N.O.	R.	H.S.	AV.
TEST					
1ST-CLASS	1	0	0		0.00
INT					
RAL	2	2	1	1*	–
NAT.W.					
B & H					

CAREER: BOWLING

	O.	M.	R.	W.	AV.
TEST					
1ST-CLASS	24	0	103	0	–
INT					
RAL	13	0	70	2	35.00
NAT.W.					
B & H					

Injuries 1987: Missed 4 months with disc trouble in back
Relaxations: Watching films, videos, music, food
Extras: Represented Durham County in the Minor Counties when 17. Released at end of 1987 season – 'found this out from dressing-room attendant'
Opinions on cricket: 'Fines system should be returned. More rest days during season. 2nd XI matches are generally inferior and provide bad cricket.'

BUTCHER, A. R. Glamorgan

Full Name: Alan Raymond Butcher
Role: Left-hand bat, slow left-arm or medium pace bowler
Born: 7 January 1954, Croydon
Height: 5′ 8″ **Weight:** 11st 7lbs
Nickname: Butch, Budgie
County debut: 1972 (Surrey), 1987 (Glamorgan)
County cap: 1975 (Surrey), 1987 (Glamorgan)
Benefit: 1985 (Surrey)
Test debut: 1979
No. of Tests: 1
No. of One-Day Internationals: 1
1000 runs in a season: 8
1st-Class 50s scored: 73
1st-Class 100s scored: 32
1st-Class 200s scored: 1
1st-Class 5 w. in innings: 1
One-Day 50s: 41
One-Day 100s: 4
Place in batting averages: 41st av. 40.36 (1986 142nd av. 25.36)
1st-Class catches 1987: 6 (career 138)
Parents: Raymond and Jackie
Wife and date of marriage: Elaine, 27 September 1972
Children: Mark, Gary, Lisa
Family links with cricket: Brother, Martin, played for MCC Young Professionals. Brother, Ian, plays for Leicestershire CC
Education: Heath Clark Grammar School
Qualifications: 5 O-levels, 1 A-level
Jobs outside cricket: Football coach, PE master
Other sports played: Football
Relaxations: Most sport, rock music, reading

Extras: Scored a century before lunch v Glamorgan at The Oval, 1980. Released by county at end of 1986 season. Joined Glamorgan in 1987
Best batting performance: 216* Surrey v Cambridge University, Cambridge 1980
Best bowling performance: 6-48 Surrey v Hampshire, Guildford 1972

LAST SEASON: BATTING

	I.	N.O.	R.	H.S.	AV.
TEST					
1ST-CLASS	27	2	1009	135*	40.36
INT					
RAL	8	1	114	40	16.28
NAT.W.					
B & H	4	0	108	65	27.00

LAST SEASON: BOWLING

	O.	M.	R.	W.	AV.
TEST					
1ST-CLASS	21	1	52	3	17.33
INT					
RAL					
NAT.W.					
B & H					

CAREER: BATTING

	I.	N.O.	R.	H.S.	AV.
TEST	2	0	34	20	17.00
1ST-CLASS	515	45	15709	216*	33.42
INT			14	14	14.00
RAL	172	18	4347	113*	28.22
NAT.W.	25	3	615	86*	27.95
B & H	55	4	1311	80	25.70

CAREER: BOWLING

	O.	M.	R.	W.	AV.
TEST	2	0	9	0	
1ST-CLASS	1536.2	317	4851	129	37.60
INT					
RAL	323.2	22	1420	36	39.44
NAT.W.	67.2	10	249	5	49.80
B & H	168.3	30	507	24	21.12

BUTCHER, I. P. Leicestershire

Full Name: Ian Paul Butcher
Role: Right-hand bat, slip fielder
Born: 1 July 1962, Farnborough, Kent
Height: 6′ 0″ **Weight:** 14st
Nickname: Butch, Dog
County debut: 1980
County cap: 1984
1000 runs in a season: 2
1st-Class 50s scored: 20
1st-Class 100s scored: 9
One-Day 50s: 7
One-Day 100s: 2
Place in batting averages: 78th
av. 33.91 (1986 210th av. 15.16)
1st-Class catches 1987: 5 (career 77)
Parents: Raymond and Jackie
Wife and date of marriage: Marie, 12 March 1983
Children: Marie
Family links with cricket: Brother, Alan, Glamorgan CCC and England. Brother, Martin, MCC Young Professionals

Education: John Ruskin High School
Qualifications: Preliminary Coaching Certificate
Jobs outside cricket: Football coach, Cumnor House School, South Croydon. Asst Sports Director, Leicester University
Off-season 1987–88: Working at Leicester University as assistant director of sport and playing football
Cricketing superstitions or habits: 'I have many . . . If I score runs I like to do everything (if possible) the same, the following day. I always wear a sweatband on left wrist while batting.'
Overseas tours: England Young Cricketers to West Indies 1980
Cricketers particularly learnt from: Brian Davison, Graham Gooch, Chris Balderstone, Paddy Clift
Other sports played: Football, golf. 'I'll try my hand at anything!'
Relaxations: Sleeping, good beer, good food, music, TV
Extras: Made his debut for Leicestershire CCC in the John Player League v Surrey 1979. Scored century on championship debut at Grace Road
Best batting performance: 139 Leicestershire v Nottinghamshire, Leicester 1983
Best bowling performance: 1-2 Leicestershire v Essex, Chelmsford 1983

LAST SEASON: BATTING

	I.	N.O.	R.	H.S.	AV.
TEST					
1ST-CLASS	12	0	407	88	33.91
INT					
RAL	3	0	85	66	28.33
NAT.W.	1	0	2	2	2.00
B & H	4	0	100	80	25.00

LAST SEASON: BOWLING

	O.	M.	R.	W.	AV.
TEST					
1ST-CLASS	2	0	4	0	–
INT					
RAL					
NAT.W.					
B & H					

CAREER: BATTING

	I.	N.O.	R.	H.S.	AV.
TEST					
1ST-CLASS	153	9	4432	139	30.77
INT					
RAL	50	3	928	71	19.74
NAT.W.	7	0	172	81	24.57
B & H	18	1	647	103*	38.05

CAREER: BOWLING

	O.	M.	R.	W.	AV.
TEST					
1ST-CLASS	10	2	28	1	28.00
INT					
RAL	1	0	4	0	–
NAT.W.	0.3	0	6	1	6.00
B & H					

37. Who was captain of India in the 1987 World Cup?

38. Who was vice-captain of India in the 1987 World Cup?

BUTCHER, R. O.   Middlesex

Full Name: Roland Orlando
Butcher
Role: Right-hand bat, right-arm
medium bowler
Born: 14 October 1953, East Point,
St Philip, Barbados
Height: 5′ 7″ **Weight:** 12st
Nickname: Butch
County debut: 1974
County cap: 1979
Test debut: 1980–81
No. of Tests: 3
No. of One-Day Internationals: 3
1000 runs in a season: 4
1st-Class 50s scored: 60
1st-Class 100s scored: 15
One-Day 50s: 21
One-Day 100s: 1
Place in batting averages: 125th

av. 27.61 (1986 99th av. 30.78)
1st-Class catches 1987: 15 (career 259 + 1 stumping)
Parents: Robert and Doreen
Wife: Cheryl Denise
Children: Paul Nicholas Roland, 2 January 1979; Michelle Denise, 11
November 1982
Family links with cricket: Cousin is Basil Butcher, of Guyana and West Indies
Qualifications: Advanced Cricket Coaching Certificate, Football Association
Preliminary Coaching Certificate
Jobs outside cricket: Football coach, insurance salesman

LAST SEASON: BATTING

	I.	N.O.	R.	H.S.	AV.
TEST					
1ST-CLASS	22	1	580	118	27.61
INT					
RAL	8	2	136	42*	22.66
NAT.W.	1	1	16	16*	–
B & H	4	1	77	50	25.66

LAST SEASON: BOWLING

	O.	M.	R.	W.	AV.
TEST					
1ST-CLASS	2.3	1	9	0	–
INT					
RAL					
NAT.W.					
B & H					

CAREER: BATTING

	I.	N.O.	R.	H.S.	AV.
TEST	5	0	71	32	14.20
1ST-CLASS	370	36	10552	197	31.59
INT	3	0	58	52	19.33
RAL	133	13	2637	59	21.97
NAT.W.	22	4	335	59	18.61
B & H	26	3	532	85	23.13

CAREER: BOWLING

	O.	M.	R.	W.	AV.
TEST					
1ST-CLASS	48.1	10	180	4	45.00
INT					
RAL	1.2	0	5	0	–
NAT.W.	2	0	18	1	18.00
B & H					

Overseas teams played for: Barbados in 1974–75 Shell Shield Competition
Other sports played: Football
Relaxations: Television, horse racing, cinema
Extras: Arrived in England aged 13. Played semi-professional soccer for Biggleswade and Stevenage. Does work for Inter-Action Group in deprived areas of London. A devout member of the Anglican church
Best batting performance: 197 Middlesex v Yorkshire, Lord's 1982
Best bowling performance: 2-37 Middlesex v Gloucestershire, Cheltenham 1986

CANN, M. J.   Glamorgan

Full Name: Michael James Cann
Role: Left-hand bat, off-break bowler
Born: 4 July 1965, Cardiff
Height: 5' 9" **Weight:** 11½st
Nickname: Tin, Canny, Three Noses
County debut: 1986
1st-Class catches 1987: 0 (career 1)
Parents: Leslie and Catherine
Marital status: Single
Education: St Illtyos College, Cardiff; Swansea University
Qualifications: 10 O-levels, 3 A-levels, Degree in Biochemistry, Senior NCA coach
Cricketers particularly learnt from: Tom Cartwright, Alan Jones, Tony Cordle
Cricketers particularly admired: Barry Lloyd
Cricketing superstitions or habits: 'I don't have any. I don't consider cricket to be a game of luck!'
Other sports played: Squash, cards, snooker
Other sports followed: Football (Cardiff City)
Injuries 1987: Ankle ligaments
Relaxations: Contract bridge, general socialising, going out for meals, reading cricket books
Extras: Represented Combined Universities in B & H Cup
Opinions on cricket: 'Uncovered wickets make the game a lottery. I find it a disgrace that overseas players and foreigners can play county cricket registered as English.'

Best batting performance: 16* Glamorgan v Essex, Chelmsford 1986
16* Glamorgan v Northamptonshire, Swansea 1987
Best bowling performance: 1-48 Glamorgan v Northamptonshire, Swansea 1987

LAST SEASON: BATTING

	I.	N.O.	R.	H.S.	AV.
TEST					
1ST-CLASS	2	2	24	16*	
INT					
RAL					
NAT.W.					
B & H					

LAST SEASON: BOWLING

	O.	M.	R.	W.	AV.
TEST					
!ST-CLASS	23.5	3	110	1	110.00
INT					
RAL					
NAT.W.					
B & H					

CAREER: BATTING

	I.	N.O.	R.	H.S.	AV.
TEST					
1ST-CLASS	3	3	40	16*	–
INT					
RAL					
NAT.W.					
B & H					

CAREER: BOWLING

	O.	M.	R.	W.	AV.
TEST					
!ST-CLASS	24.5	4	110	1	110.00
INT					
RAL					
NAT.W.					
B & H					

CAPEL, D. J.   Northamptonshire

Full Name: David John Capel
Role: Right-hand bat, right-arm fast medium bowler, all-rounder
Born: 6 July 1963, Northampton
Height: 6' **Weight:** 12st 6lbs
Nickname: Capes
County debut: 1981
County cap: 1986
Test debut: 1987
No. of Tests: 1
No. of One-Day Internationals: 3
50 wickets in a season: 2
1st-Class 50s scored: 22
1st-Class 100s scored: 4
1st-Class 5 w. in innings: 9
One-Day 50s: 8
Place in batting averages: 153rd av. 23.66 (1986 108th av. 29.41)
Place in bowling averages: 45th av. 26.33 (1986 68th av. 32.44)
Strike rate 1987: 52.62 (career 59.59)
1st-Class catches 1987: 10 (career 63)

Parents: John and Angela Janet
Wife and date of marriage: Debbie, 21 September 1985
Family links with cricket: Father played in local league and brother Andrew in County League
Education: Roade Primary and Roade Comprehensive School
Qualifications: 3 O-levels, 5 CSEs, NCA Coaching Certificate
Jobs outside cricket: Hand-made surgical shoemaker (when 16–17)
Overseas tours: Dubai with *The Cricketer* XI, 1983; England to Sharjah 1986; England to Pakistan, New Zealand and Australia 1987–88
Overseas teams played for: Latrobe, Tasmania, 1982–83; Westview CC, Port Elizabeth, 1983–84–85; Grey School and Eastern Province, 1985–86
Cricketers particularly learnt from: Brian Reynolds (coach) and many others
Cricketers particularly admired: Barry Richards, Richard Hadlee, Ian Botham, Clive Rice, Kepler Wessels
Off-season 1987–88: Touring with England
Cricket superstitions or habits: 'I tend to change in most of the same places in grounds on the circuit.'
Other sports played: Golf
Injuries 1987: Leg-strain in upper thigh in August; right-side of back in September
Relaxations: Enjoys swimming and eating out at restaurants
Extras: Played for Young England 1982
Opinions on cricket: 'Personally I feel that there is probably a little too much cricket played during a first-class English season. Particularly for the bowler, there is too little time to recover between games. I feel that a side should play two or three first-class matches, then rest a few days, especially now that high pressure one-day games are on the fixture list.'
Best batting performance: 134 Eastern Province v Western Province, Port Elizabeth 1986–87
Best bowling performance: 7-62 Northamptonshire v Lancashire, Lytham 1985

LAST SEASON: BATTING

	I.	N.O.	R.	H.S.	AV.
TEST	2	0	81	53	40.50
1ST-CLASS	28	3	558	91*	22.32
INT					
RAL	10	1	235	77*	26.11
NAT.W.	5	3	183	48	91.50
B & H	6	0	171	97	28.50

LAST SEASON: BOWLING

	O.	M.	R.	W.	AV.
TEST	18	1	64	0	–
1ST-CLASS	446.5	86	1332	53	25.13
INT					
RAL	65.1	5	244	4	61.00
NAT.W.	43.3	10	143	4	35.75
B & H	76	9	302	13	23.23

CAREER: BATTING

	I.	N.O.	R.	H.S.	AV.
TEST	2	0	81	53	40.50
1ST-CLASS	191	34	4320	134	27.51
INT	3	0	27	17	9.00
RAL	62	15	1229	79	26.14
NAT.W.	13	6	289	48	41.28
B & H	19	4	365	97	24.33

CAREER: BOWLING

	O.	M.	R.	W.	AV.
TEST	18	1	64	0	–
1ST-CLASS	2038.1	385	6709	207	32.41
INT	25	0	111	4	27.75
RAL	297.1	12	1409	48	29.35
NAT.W.	77.3	12	281	8	35.12
B & H	165	24	587	25	23.48

CARR, J. D.   Middlesex

Full Name: John Donald Carr
Role: Right-hand bat, off-break bowler, slip fielder
Born: 15 June 1963, St John's Wood
Height: 6′ **Weight:** 12st
Nickname: Carsy
County debut: 1983
County cap: 1987
1000 runs in a season: 1
1st-Class 50s scored: 16
1st-Class 100s scored: 7
1st-Class 5 w. in innings: 3
One-Day 50s: 4
Place in batting averages: 32nd av 41.64 (1986 79th av. 34.00)
1st-Class catches 1987: 10 (career 41)
Parents: Donald and Stella
Marital status: Single
Family links with cricket: Father, D. B. Carr, was secretary of TCCB and played for Oxford University, Derbyshire and England, captaining all three at some stage
Education: The Hall School, Repton School and Oxford University (Worcester College)
Qualifications: BA Hons (Philosophy, Politics and Economics)
Jobs outside cricket: Taught one term at St George's School, Windsor. Worked briefly at DHSS in Oxford
Overseas tours: Australia with Repton Pilgrims 1982–83; La Manga with Hertfordshire 1983; Australia and Hong Kong with Oxbridge 1985–86
Overseas teams played for: Sydney University, 1986; Western Creek, Canberra, 1986–87
Cricketers particularly admired: Viv Richards, Ian Botham, Michael Holding, Graeme Hick
Off-season 1987–88: Working in London
Other sports played: Eton fives, golf, squash, soccer
Other sports followed: 'I like watching any sport played well.'
Relaxations: TV and cinema, listening to pop music, eating good food
Opinions on cricket: 'There should be some small reward for drawing as opposed to losing a Championship game. Perhaps two points. The difference between "win" bonus points and "draw" bonus points would still be great enough to encourage positive and adventurous cricket.'
Extras: Played for Oxford in Varsity Match 1984. Secretary of University in

1984. Came on as substitute fielder for Middlesex in the 1983 Benson and Hedges Cup Final, holding a vital catch to help his side defeat Essex. Received special clearance to play in the match having previously appeared for Combined Universities in the same competition

Best batting performance: 156 Middlesex v Essex, Lord's 1987
Best bowling performance: 6-61 Middlesex v Gloucestershire, Lord's 1985

LAST SEASON: BATTING

	I.	N.O.	R.	H.S.	AV.
TEST					
1ST-CLASS	41	4	1541	156	41.64
INT					
RAL	11	0	280	84	25.45
NAT.W.	2	0	27	14	13.50
B & H	1	0	5	5	5.00

LAST SEASON: BOWLING

	O.	M.	R.	W.	AV.
TEST					
1ST-CLASS	37	7	131	2	65.50
INT					
RAL	2.2	0	10	1	10.00
NAT.W.					
B & H	2	0	9	0	–

CAREER: BATTING

	I.	N.O.	R.	H.S.	AV.
TEST					
1ST-CLASS	107	12	3332	156	35.07
INT					
RAL	22	4	470	84	26.11
NAT.W.	2	0	27	14	13.50
B & H	10	1	274	67	30.44

CAREER: BOWLING

	O.	M.	R.	W.	AV.
TEST					
1ST-CLASS	892.3	232	2392	51	46.90
INT					
RAL	23.2	1	113	4	28.25
NAT.W.					
B & H	81.2	9	327	7	46.71

CARRICK, P. Yorkshire

Full Name: Phillip Carrick
Role: Right-hand bat, slow left-arm bowler, slip fielder
Born: 16 July 1952, Leeds
Height: 6' 0" **Weight:** 14st
Nickname: Fergie
County debut: 1970
County cap: 1976
Benefit: 1985
50 wickets in a season: 8
1st-Class 50s scored: 28
1st-Class 100s scored: 3
1st-Class 5 w. in innings: 36
1st-Class 10 w. in match: 5
One-Day 50s: 2
Place in batting averages: 197th av. 17.44 (1986 154th av. 24.50)
Place in bowling averages: 40th av. 25.94 (1986 109th av. 43.05)
Strike rate 1987: 67.22 (career 71.85)
1st-Class catches 1987: 8 (career 167)

Parents: Arthur (deceased) and Ivy
Wife and date of marriage: Elspeth, 2 April 1977
Children: Emma Elizabeth, 6 May 1980; Phillipa Louse, 11 January 1982
Family links with cricket: Father and brother useful league players
Education: Bramley CS, Intake CS, Park Lane College of Further Education
Qualifications: 2 O-levels, 8 CSEs, NCA Coaching Certificate
Jobs outside cricket: Company Director in promotional business, coach
Cricketing superstitions or habits: Left pad on first
Overseas tours: Derrick Robins XI to South Africa 1975–76; Far East 1977
Overseas teams played for: Eastern Province in 1976–77 Currie Cup Competition; Northern Transvaal 1982–83
Cricketers particularly learnt from: Geoff Boycott, Ray Illingworth, Mike Fearnley
Off-season 1987–88: Working at my business
Other sports played: Golf
Other sports followed: Rugby, most sports
Extras: Appointed Yorkshire captain for 1987. Led them to victory in the B & H Cup in first season as captain
Best batting performance: 131* Yorkshire v Northamptonshire 1980
Best bowling performance: 8-33 Yorkshire v Cambridge University, Cambridge 1973

LAST SEASON: BATTING

	I.	N.O.	R.	H.S.	AV.
TEST					
1ST-CLASS	29	2	471	61	17.44
INT					
RAL	9	1	66	19	8.25
NAT.W.	2	0	24	14	12.00
B & H	4	0	21	10	5.25

LAST SEASON: BOWLING

	O.	M.	R.	W.	AV.
TEST					
1ST-CLASS	575.4	198	1323	51	25.94
INT					
RAL	59	2	344	9	38.22
NAT.W.	24	9	55	1	55.00
B & H	69	11	184	3	61.33

CAREER: BATTING

	I.	N.O.	R.	H.S.	AV.
TEST					
1ST-CLASS	422	76	7512	131*	21.71
INT					
RAL	98	28	945	43*	13.50
NAT.W.	17	2	230	68	15.33
B & H	26	4	251	53	11.40

CAREER: BOWLING

	O.	M.	R.	W.	AV.
TEST					
1ST-CLASS	9700	3118	24154	810	29.81
INT					
RAL	674	29	3062	95	32.23
NAT.W.	170.5	39	444	15	29.60
B & H	341.3	49	1112	31	35.87

39. Who was vice-captain of Pakistan in the 1987 World Cup?
40. Who was captain of New Zealand in the 1987 World Cup?

CHADWICK, M. R.   Lancashire

Full Name: Mark Robert Chadwick
Role: Right-hand bat, off-break
bowler
Born: 9 February 1963, Rochdale
Height: 6′ 1″ **Weight:** 13st
Nickname: Chad
County debut: 1983
1st-Class 50s scored: 5
1st-Class 100s scored: 1
One-Day 50s: 1
Place in batting averages: — (1986
158th av. 23.50)
1st-Class catches 1987: 1 (career 15)
Parents: Robert and Kathleen
Family links with cricket: 'Father
club cricketer and now umpires in
Lancashire League. Mother washes
all my kit and is very good critic
but knows nothing about the game.'

Education: Moorhouse County Primary School, Milnrow; Roch Valley High
School, Milnrow
Qualifications: 2 O-levels
Jobs outside cricket: Storeman for diesel engine firm, window cleaner
Cricketing superstitions or habits: 'Trying not to make a habit of fielding at
short leg.'
Overseas tours: Lancashire CCC to Barbados, 1984
Cricketers particularly learnt from: Picked up lots of helpful tips from all the
staff at Lancashire CC

LAST SEASON: BATTING

	I.	N.O.	R.	H.S.	AV.
TEST					
1ST-CLASS	3	0	53	38	17.66
INT					
RAL					
NAT.W.					
B & H					

LAST SEASON: BOWLING

	O.	M.	R.	W.	AV.
TEST					
1ST-CLASS					
INT					
RAL					
NAT.W.					
B & H					

CAREER: BATTING

	I.	N.O.	R.	H.S.	AV.
TEST					
1ST-CLASS	56	1	1197	132	21.76
INT					
RAL	3	0	16	10	5.33
NAT.W.	1	0	43	43	43.00
B & H	1	0	87	87	87.00

CAREER: BOWLING

	O.	M.	R.	W.	AV.
TEST					
1ST-CLASS	7	0	71	0	–
INT					
RAL					
NAT.W.					
B & H					

Cricketers particularly admired: Geoffrey Boycott for powers of concentration while at the crease, Viv Richards for domination of bowlers
Other sports played: Football, table tennis, badminton, golf
Other sports followed: Very keen rugby league fan
Relaxations: Listening to music
Extras: Central Lancashire League record run scorer for amateur. 1267 runs for Milnrow CC in 1983, beating the previous record of 1205 from 1915. Won gold award in first B & H match (1984 semi-final).
Best batting performance: 132 Lancashire v Somerset, Old Trafford 1985

CHILDS, J. H. Essex

Full Name: John Henry Childs
Role: Left-hand bat, slow left-arm orthodox bowler
Born: 15 August 1951, Plymouth
Height: 6' 0" **Weight:** 12st 6lbs
Nickname: Charlie
County debut: 1975 (Gloucestershire), 1985 (Essex)
County cap: 1977 (Gloucestershire), 1986 (Essex)
Testimonial: 1985
50 wickets in a season: 3
1st-Class 5 w. in innings: 26
1st-Class 10 w. in match: 5
Place in batting averages: 237th av. 12.55 (1986 218th av. 13.37)
Place in bowling averages: 88th av. 33.18 (1986 3rd av. 16.28)
Strike rate 1987: 77.75 (career 68.38)
1st-Class catches 1987: 6 (career 74)
Parents: Sydney and Barbara (both deceased)
Wife and date of marriage: Jane Anne, 11 November 1978
Children: Lee Robert, 28 November 1980; Scott Alexander, 21 August 1984
Education: Audley Park Secondary Modern, Torquay
Qualifications: Advanced Cricket Coach
Jobs outside cricket: Signwriter
Overseas tours: Zambia, 1977; Barbados, 1983
Cricketers particularly admired: Gary Sobers, Mike Procter
Other sports played: Most ball games
Relaxations: Watching rugby, decorating at home, walking on moors and beaches, enjoying my family

Extras: Played for Devon 1973–74. Released by Gloucestershire at end of 1984 and joined Essex
Best batting performance: 34* Gloucestershire v Nottinghamshire, Cheltenham 1982
Best bowling performance: 9-56 Gloucestershire v Somerset, Bristol 1981

LAST SEASON: BATTING

	I.	N.O.	R.	H.S.	AV.
TEST					
1ST-CLASS	22	13	113	26	12.55
INT					
RAL	1	0	10	10	10.00
NAT.W.					
B & H					

LAST SEASON: BOWLING

	O.	M.	R.	W.	AV.
TEST					
1ST-CLASS	479.3	143	1228	37	33.18
INT					
RAL	5	0	33	0	–
NAT.W.					
B & H					

CAREER: BATTING

	I.	N.O.	R.	H.S.	AV.
TEST					
1ST-CLASS	200	93	879	34*	8.21
INT					
RAL	19	10	84	16*	9.33
NAT.W.	4	3	22	14*	22.00
B & H	7	5	25	10	12.50

CAREER: BOWLING

	O.	M.	R.	W.	AV.
TEST					
1ST-CLASS	6291.2	1855	16673	552	30.20
INT					
RAL	323.1	17	1477	39	37.87
NAT.W.	60	12	180	7	25.71
B & H	156	35	466	14	33.29

CLARKE, S. T. Surrey

Full Name: Sylvester Theophilus Clarke
Role: Right-hand bat, right-arm fast bowler, gulley fielder
Born: 11 December 1955, Lead Vale, Christchurch, Barbados
Height: 6′ 2″ **Weight:** 15st
Nickname: Silvers
County debut: 1979
County cap: 1980
Benefit: 1987
Test debut: 1977–78
No. of Tests: 11
No. of One-Day Internationals: 10
50 wickets in a season: 5
1st-Class 50s scored: 4
1st-Class 100s scored: 1
1st-Class 5 w. in innings: 52
1st-Class 10 w. in match: 8
Place in batting averages: — (1986 197th av. 17.33
Place in bowling averages: 4th av. 17.31 (1986 4th av. 16.79)

Strike rate 1987: 40.89 (career 46.49)
1st-Class catches 1987: 8 (career 118)
Parents: Marjorie and Ashton
Children: Desiree, 8 December 1974; Dawn, 18 August 1976; Shelly, 2 July 1978
Family links with cricket: Half-brother Damien is professional at Todmorden CC
Education: St Bartholomew Boys' School
Jobs outside cricket: Carpenter
Overseas tours: West Indies to India and Sri Lanka, 1978–79. Pakistan 1980–81, Australia 1981, Rebel West Indian XI to South Africa 1982–83 and 1983–84
Overseas teams played for: Local club in Barbados Cricket League; Transvaal
Cricketers particularly learnt from: Vanburn Holder
Other sports played: Football
Other sports followed: Tennis
Relaxations: 'Music and parties.'
Extras: Made fastest century of the 1981 season in 62 mins v Glamorgan. Took Championship hat-trick in 1980 season v Nottinghamshire
Best batting performance: 100* Surrey v Glamorgan, Swansea 1981
Best bowling performance: 8-62 Surrey v Northamptonshire, The Oval 1987

LAST SEASON: BATTING

	I.	N.O.	R.	H.S.	AV.
TEST					
1ST-CLASS	15	1	131	44	9.35
INT					
RAL	2	1	19	15	19.00
NAT.W.	1	0	5	5	5.00
B & H	1	0	1	1	1.00

CAREER: BATTING

	I.	N.O.	R.	H.S.	AV.
TEST	16	5	176	35*	15.64
1ST-CLASS	214	36	2653	100*	14.90
INT	8	2	60	20	10.00
RAL	48	12	455	34*	12.63
NAT.W.	12	4	164	45*	20.50
B & H	24	4	173	39	8.65

LAST SEASON: BOWLING

	O.	M.	R.	W.	AV.
TEST					
1ST-CLASS	456.4	124	1160	67	17.31
INT					
RAL	47	2	186	5	37.20
NAT.W.	24	4	61	4	15.25
B & H	55	10	196	10	19.60

CAREER: BOWLING

	O.	M.	R.	W.	AV.
TEST	412.5	79	1171	42	27.88
1ST-CLASS	5979.4	1567	15243	783	19.46
INT	87.2	13	245	13	18.85
RAL	518.3	46	2044	82	24.92
NAT.W.	213.2	54	493	29	17.00
B & H	381.4	83	1062	63	16.85

41. Who was vice-captain of New Zealand in the 1987 World Cup?
42. Who was captain of Sri Lanka in the 1987 World Cup?

CLIFT, P. B.   Leicestershire

Full Name: Patrick Bernard Clift
Role: Right-hand bat, right-arm medium bowler
Born: 14 July 1953, Salisbury, Rhodesia
Height: 6′ 1″ **Weight:** 14st
Nickname: Paddy, Paddles
County debut: 1975
County cap: 1976
50 wickets in a season: 6
1st-Class 50s scored: 31
1st-Class 100s scored: 2
1st-Class 5 w. in innings: 25
1st-Class 10 w. in match: 2
One-Day 50s: 4
Place in batting averages: 95th av. 32.00 (1986 152nd av. 24.66)
Place in bowling averages: 27th av. 24.32 (1986 12th av. 22.26)
Strike rate 1987: 65.70 (career 59.25)
1st-Class catches 1987: 8 (career 160)

Parents: George Neville and Ivy Susan
Wife and date of marriage: Penelope Anne, 18 May 1978
Children: Robert William Patrick, 16 September 1982; Josephine Anne, 10 May 1984
Education: St Michael's; Hartmann House, St George's College
Qualifications: 1 O-level
Jobs outside cricket: Accounting, insurance
Overseas tours: Rhodesia Ridgebacks to UK 1974

LAST SEASON: BATTING

	I.	N.O.	R.	H.S.	AV.
TEST					
1ST-CLASS	22	3	608	88	32.00
INT					
RAL	7	2	104	41	20.80
NAT.W.	3	0	34	20	11.33
B & H					

LAST SEASON: BOWLING

	O.	M.	R.	W.	AV.
TEST					
1ST-CLASS	405.1	114	900	37	24.32
INT					
RAL	57.4	2	245	11	22.27
NAT.W.	48	5	171	5	34.20
B & H					

CAREER: BATTING

	I.	N.O.	R.	H.S.	AV.
TEST					
1ST-CLASS	436	90	8279	106*	23.92
INT					
RAL	92	29	1267	51*	20.11
NAT.W.	19	5	278	48*	19.85
B & H	25	5	389	91	19.45

CAREER: BOWLING

	O.	M.	R.	W.	AV.
TEST					
1ST-CLASS	8423.4	2229	21136	853	24.77
INT					
RAL	920.1	66	3806	169	22.52
NAT.W.	219.3	25	784	24	32.66
B & H	370.4	51	1255	47	26.70

Overseas teams played for: Rhodesia, Natal
Cricketers particularly learnt from: Robin Jackman, Mike Procter, Duncan Fletcher, Jack Birkenshaw, Roger Tolchard, Ken Higgs, Jim Cornford (school coach at St George's College)
Other sports played: Squash, golf, tennis, jogging
Relaxations: Stamp collecting, reading, listening to records
Extras: Debut for Rhodesia 1971–72. Took 8-17 in opening match in 1976 season v MCC. Performed hat-trick in 1976 at Grace Road v Yorkshire. Suffered from injury in 1981 and 1982 seasons. Holds record Rhodesian 7th wicket partnership of 174 with Howie Gardiner v Western Province, and record 9th wicket partnership of 154 with Robin Jackman v Eastern Province, both in Currie Cup Competition, South Africa
Best batting performance: 106 Leicestershire v Essex, Chelmsford 1985
Best bowling performance: 8-17 Leicestershire v MCC, Lord's 1976

CLINTON, G. S. Surrey

Full Name: Graham Selvey Clinton
Role: Left-hand bat, right-arm medium bowler
Born: 5 May 1953, Sidcup
Nickname: Clint
County debut: 1974 (Kent), 1979 (Surrey)
County cap: 1980 (Surrey)
1000 runs in a season: 5
1st-Class 50s scored: 56
1st-Class 100s scored: 15
One-Day 50s: 23
One-Day 100s: 3
Place in batting averages: 106th av. 30.28 (1986 87th av. 33.12)
1st-Class catches 1987: 6 (career 75)
Family links with cricket: Younger brothers Neil and Tony regular members of Blackheath CC
Education: Chislehurst and Sidcup Grammar School
Overseas tours: England Young Cricketers to West Indies 1972
Extras: Formerly played for Kent, where he made his debut 1974. Left after 1978 season to join Surrey. Renowned as a dressing-room wit and as being one of the most injury-prone cricketers. At age 11, he played for Kemnal Manor, Kent. Later played club cricket for Sidcup and for Blackheath
Best batting performance: 192 Surrey v Yorkshire, The Oval 1984
Best bowling performance: 2-8 Kent v Pakistan, Canterbury 1978

LAST SEASON: BATTING

	I.	N.O.	R.	H.S.	AV.
TEST					
1ST-CLASS	30	2	848	93	30.28
INT					
RAL	6	0	208	52	34.66
NAT.W.	2	0	62	34	31.00
B & H	4	0	221	71	55.25

LAST SEASON: BOWLING

	O.	M.	R.	W.	AV.
TEST					
1ST-CLASS					
INT					
RAL					
NAT.W.					
B & H					

CAREER: BATTING

	I.	N.O.	R.	H.S.	AV.
TEST					
1ST-CLASS	349	41	9902	192	32.14
INT					
RAL	66	9	1878	105*	32.94
NAT.W.	19	1	588	146	32.66
B & H	37	1	1197	106*	33.25

CAREER: BOWLING

	O.	M.	R.	. W.	AV.
TEST					
1ST-CLASS	26	2	185	4	46.25
INT					
RAL					
NAT.W.	4	2	2	0	–
B & H	1.2	0	10	0	–

COBB, R. A.   Leicestershire

Full Name: Russell Alan Cobb
Role: Right-hand bat, slow
left-arm bowler, short-leg
fielder
Born: 18 May 1961, Leicester
Height: 5′ 11″ **Weight:** 11st 7lbs
Nickname: Cobby
County debut: 1980
County cap: 1986
1000 runs in a season: 1
1st-Class 50s scored: 20
One-Day 50s: 1
Place in batting averages: 116th
av. 29.14 (1986 118th av. 28.23)
1st-Class catches 1987: 9
(career 55)
Parents: Alan and Betty
Wife and date of marriage: Sharon,
30 March 1985
Family links with cricket: Father a club cricketer. Godfather, Maurice
Hallam, former Leicestershire captain
Education: Woodbank School, Leicester, Trent College, Nottingham
Qualifications: 7 O-levels, NCA Advanced Coaching Certificate
Jobs outside cricket: Clerk for British Shoe Corporation, Leicester. Worked
on promotion for Leicestershire CCC
Cricketing superstitions or habits: 'Always put my left pad on first. Must wear
some sort of headgear.'
Off-season 1987–88: Playing and coaching abroad

Overseas tours: Young England to Australia 1979; Young England to West Indies 1980; Leicestershire to Zimbabwe 1981

Overseas teams played for: Glenelg, Adelaide, South Australia, 1980–81; Teachers Training College, Pretoria, 1983–84, 1984–85

Cricketers particularly learnt from: Jack Birkenshaw, Ken Higgs, Chris Balderstone

Cricketers particularly admired: 'All who have played top class cricket for a number of years.'

Other sports played: Squash, badminton

Other sports followed: Most sports, particularly rugby

Relaxations: 'A little gardening, walking, eating out – good for my back.'

Best batting performance: 91 Leicestershire v Northamptonshire, Leicester 1986

LAST SEASON: BATTING

	I.	N.O.	R.	H.S.	AV.
TEST					
1ST-CLASS	26	5	612	88	29.14
INT					
RAL					
NAT.W.	3	1	83	66*	41.50
B & H					

CAREER: BATTING

	I.	N.O.	R.	H.S.	AV.
TEST					
1ST-CLASS	158	13	3640	91	25.10
INT					
RAL	6	4	60	24	30.00
NAT.W.	6	1	140	66*	28.00
B & H	2	0	26	22	13.00

43. Who was captain of West Indies in the 1987 World Cup?

44. Who was captain of Zimbabwe in the 1987 World Cup?

45. Who was dropped by England in 1987 and then scored four centuries in a row?

CONNOR, C. A.   Hampshire

Full Name: Cardigan Adolphus Connor
Role: Right-hand bat, right-arm fast-medium bowler
Born: 24 March 1961, West End, Anguilla
Height: 5′ 10″ **Weight:** 11st 6lbs
Nickname: 'Christy, Cardy and many more.'
County debut: 1984
1st-Class 5 w. in innings: 2
Place in bowling averages: 87th av. 33.15 (1986 71st av. 32.97)
Strike rate 1987: 74.43 (career 69.07)
1st-Class catches 1987: 7 (career 26)
Parents: Ethleen Snagg
Marital status: Single
Education: Valley Secondary School, Anguilla; Langley College
Qualifications: Engineer
Jobs outside cricket: Timko Engineering, Slough Trading Estate
Cricketing superstitions or habits: Never change before the end of the day's play
Overseas tours: Hampshire CCC tour of Hong Kong, Singapore, New Zealand and Australia 1983
Overseas teams played for: Merriweather CC, Newcastle, Australia, 1983–84 and 1984–85; West End CC, Anguilla, 1973–76
Cricketers particularly learnt from: Tim Tremlett

LAST SEASON: BATTING

	I.	N.O.	R.	H.S.	AV.
TEST					
1ST-CLASS	9	5	31	11*	7.75
INT					
RAL	4	4	5	5*	–
NAT.W.					
B & H	1	1	0	0*	–

CAREER: BATTING

	I.	N.O.	R.	H.S.	AV.
TEST					
1ST-CLASS	54	23	202	36	6.51
INT					
RAL	7	7	7	5*	–
NAT.W.	2	1	8	5	8.00
B & H	3	2	4	4*	4.00

LAST SEASON: BOWLING

	O.	M.	R.	W.	AV.
TEST					
1ST-CLASS	397	87	1061	32	33.15
INT					
RAL	95.2	7	403	17	23.70
NAT.W.					
B & H	30	3	147	1	147.00

CAREER: BOWLING

	O.	M.	R.	W.	AV.
TEST					
1ST-CLASS	2049.2	456	6093	178	34.23
INT					
RAL	408.4	21	1808	74	24.43
NAT.W.	71.5	10	231	8	28.87
B & H	110.1	10	448	17	26.35

Cricketers particularly admired: Viv Richards, Andy Roberts, Richard Hadlee
Other sports played: Most other sports
Other sports followed: Football, boxing, tennis
Relaxations: Music, wine bars, meeting people
Extras: Played for Buckinghamshire in Minor Counties before joining Hampshire. First Anguillan-born player to appear in the County Championship
Best batting performance: 36 Hampshire v Northamptonshire, Northampton 1985
Best bowling performance: 7-37 Hampshire v Kent, Bournemouth 1984

COOK, G.   Northamptonshire

Full Name: Geoffrey Cook
Role: Right-hand bat, slow
left-arm bowler, occasional
wicket-keeper
Born: 9 October 1951,
Middlesbrough, Yorkshire
Height: 6′ 0″ **Weight:** 12st 10lbs
Nickname: Geoff
County debut: 1971
County cap: 1975
Benefit: 1985
Test debut: 1981–82
No. of Tests: 7
No. of One-Day Internationals: 6
1000 runs in a season: 11
1st-Class 50s scored: 104
1st-Class 100s scored: 31
One-Day 50s: 44
One-Day 100s: 4
Place in batting averages: 105th av. 30.28 (1986 39th av. 41.69)
1st-Class catches 1987: 15 (career 399 + 3 stumpings)
Parents: Harry and Helen
Wife and date of marriage: Judith, 22 November 1975
Children: Anna, 21 May 1980
Family links with cricket: Father and brother, David, very keen club cricketers. 'Father was virtually "Mr Cricket" in Middlesbrough cricket in the 1960s being secretary, president and chairman of various leagues at one time or another.'
Education: Middlesbrough High School
Qualifications: 6 O-levels, 1 A-level
Jobs outside cricket: Has taught at Spratton Hall Prep. School

Overseas tours: England to India 1981–82 and Australia 1982–83
Overseas teams played for: Eastern Province, 1978–81
Cricketers particularly learnt from: Wayne Larkins
Cricketers particularly admired: Clive Rice
Other sports played: 'All sports when given opportunity.' Football with Wellingborough in the Southern League
Relaxations: Walking, reading, crosswords
Extras: 'Great believer in organised recreation for young people. Would enjoy time and scope to carry my beliefs through.' Captain since 1981. Chairman of the Cricketers' Association
Best batting performance: 183 Northamptonshire v Lancashire, Northampton 1986
Best bowling performance: 3-47 England XI v South Australia, Adelaide 1982–83

LAST SEASON: BATTING

	I.	N.O.	R.	H.S.	AV.
TEST					
1ST-CLASS	41	9	969	111*	30.28
INT					
RAL	9	2	81	16	11.57
NAT.W.	5	0	142	51	28.40
B & H	7	0	234	108	33.42

LAST SEASON: BOWLING

	O.	M.	R.	W.	AV.
TEST					
1ST-CLASS	10.1	2	71	0	–
INT					
RAL					
NAT.W.					
B & H					

CAREER: BATTING

	I.	N.O.	R.	H.S.	AV.
TEST	13	0	203	66	15.61
1ST-CLASS	702	60	20763	183	32.34
INT	6	0	106	32	17.66
RAL	203	19	4355	98	23.66
NAT.W.	38	1	1414	130	38.21
B & H	61	4	1591	108	27.91

CAREER: BOWLING

	O.	M.	R.	W.	AV.
TEST	7	3	27	0	–
1ST-CLASS	191.2	38	757	15	50.46
INT					
RAL	1	0	6	0	–
NAT.W.					
B & H					

46. What have Winston Davis, David Ripley, and Alan Walker in common?

47. Who was vice-captain of England in the 1987 World Cup?

COOK, N. G. B. Northamptonshire

Full Name: Nicholas Grant
Billson Cook
Role: Right-hand bat, slow
left-arm bowler, backward
short-leg fielder
Born: 17 June 1956, Leicester
Height: 6′ 0″ **Weight:** 12st 8lbs
Nickname: Beast, Rag'ead
County debut: 1978 (Leicestershire),
1986 (Northamptonshire)
County cap: 1982 (Leicestershire),
1987 (Northamptonshire)
Test debut: 1983
No. of Tests: 9

No. of One-Day Internationals: 1
50 wickets in a season: 5
1st-Class 50s scored: 4
1st-Class 5 w. in innings: 23
1st-Class 10 w. in match: 3
Place in batting averages: 204th
av. 16.61 (1986 212th av. 14.62)
Place in bowling averages: 62nd av. 29.14 (1986 60th av. 29.53)
Strike rate 1987: 78.37 (career 66.27)
1st-Class catches 1987: 13 (career 136)
Parents: Peter and Cynthia
Wife and date of marriage: Janet Elizabeth, 3 November 1979
Family links with cricket: Father played club cricket
Education: Stokes Croft Junior; Lutterworth High; Lutterworth Upper
Qualifications: 7 O-levels, 1 A-level, Advanced Cricket Coach
Jobs outside cricket: Has worked for Leicestershire CCC on promotions, organising lotteries, sponsored walks, general fund-raising projects. Also coaching
Overseas tours: Whitbread Scholarship to Perth, Australia, 1980–81; Far East tour with MCC to Bangkok, Singapore, Hong Kong, 1981; Australia and New Zealand with Derrick Robins XI, 1980; Zimbabwe with Leicestershire CCC, 1981; Dubai with Barbican XI 1982; America with MCC 1982–83; Kuwait with MCC 1983; New Zealand and Pakistan with England 1983–84; Sri Lanka with England B, 1986; Pakistan with England, 1987; MCC to Bermuda, 1987
Overseas teams played for: Claremont-Cottesloe CC, Perth, 1980–81
Cricketers particularly learnt from: Jack Birkenshaw, Roger Tolchard
Other sports followed: Soccer, rugby, horse racing
Off-season 1987–88: Touring with England in Pakistan

Relaxations: Crosswords, watching horse racing and football (especially Leicester City), reading (especially Wilbur Smith), good comedy programmes, good food

Extras: Played for ESCA 1975. Played for Young England v Young West Indies 1975. Played for MCC v Middlesex at start of 1981 season. Played for England B Team v Pakistan, August 1982. Left Leicestershire to join Northamptonshire for 1986 season

Opinions on cricket: 'Overseas players should be limited to one per county team. Loopholes in TCCB rules should be tightened up to prevent overseas players becoming "English". To play for England you should be brought up and educated in England and have at least a father who has been through the same process.'

Best batting performance: 75 Leicestershire v Somerset, Taunton 1980

Best bowling performance: 7-63 Leicestershire v Somerset, Taunton 1982

LAST SEASON: BATTING

	I.	N.O.	R.	H.S.	AV.
TEST					
1ST-CLASS	25	7	299	64	16.61
INT					
RAL	4	2	14	12	7.00
NAT.W.	1	0	4	4	4.00
B & H	4	1	35	21	11.66

LAST SEASON: BOWLING

	O.	M.	R.	W.	AV.
TEST					
1ST-CLASS	705.2	228	1574	54	29.14
INT					
RAL	72	6	352	11	32.00
NAT.W.	55	11	162	8	20.25
B & H	71	2	329	6	54.83

CAREER: BATTING

	I.	N.O.	R.	H.S.	AV.
TEST	15	1	101	26	7.21
1ST-CLASS	218	62	2072	75	13.28
INT					
RAL	22	10	108	13*	9.00
NAT.W.	2	0	17	13	8.50
B & H	9	3	97	23	16.16

CAREER: BOWLING

	O.	M.	R.	W.	AV.
TEST	498.2	162	1212	40	30.30
1ST-CLASS	6228.2	2017	16631	569	29.22
INT	8	0	34	1	34.00
RAL	353.2	26	1555	53	29.33
NAT.W.	97	19	331	12	27.58
B & H	186	20	718	12	59.08

48. Which England opening batsman who retired last season did not score a County Championship century until after he had played for England?

49. How many first-class wickets did Dennis Amiss take in his 28-year career: 0, 18, or 51?

COOPER, K. E.   Nottinghamshire

Full Name: Kevin Edwin Cooper
Role: Left-hand bat, right-arm
fast-medium bowler
Born: 27 December 1957,
Sutton-in-Ashfield
Height: 6′ 1″ **Weight:** 12st 4lbs
Nickname: Henry
County debut: 1976
County cap: 1980
50 wickets in a season: 5
1st-Class 5 w. in innings: 15
Place in batting averages: — (1986
220th av. 13.12)
Place in bowling averages: 37th
av. 25.80 (1986 26th av. 23.86)
Strike rate 1987: 63.40 (career 61.00)
1st-Class catches 1987: 1 (career 62)
Parents: Gerald Edwin and Margaret

Wife and date of marriage: Linda
Carol, 14 February 1981
Children: Kelly Louise, 8 April 1982; Tara Amy, 22 November 1984
Family links with cricket: Father played local cricket
Jobs outside cricket: Warehouseman and maintenance man, public relations
officer in free trade department of local brewery
Overseas tours: Australasia with Derrick Robins U-23 XI 1979–80
Cricketers particularly admired: John Snow
Other sports played: Football, golf, shooting
Injuries 1987: Pulled muscle and groin strain
Relaxations: Golf, clay pigeon shooting

LAST SEASON: BATTING

	I.	N.O.	R.	H.S.	AV.
TEST					
1ST-CLASS	6	1	22	17	4.40
INT					
RAL	1	1	0	0*	–
NAT.W.					
B & H	1	1	4	4*	–

LAST SEASON: BOWLING

	O.	M.	R.	W.	AV.
TEST					
1ST-CLASS	158.3	50	387	15	25.80
INT					
RAL	27	2	89	3	29.66
NAT.W.	10	4	9	3	3.00
B & H	12	2	43	3	14.33

CAREER: BATTING

	I.	N.O.	R.	H.S.	AV.
TEST					
1ST-CLASS	192	46	1379	46	9.44
INT					
RAL	36	12	116	31	4.83
NAT.W.	5	1	29	11	7.25
B & H	14	9	66	25*	13.20

CAREER: BOWLING

	O.	M.	R.	W.	AV.
TEST					
1ST-CLASS	4982	1379	13280	490	27.10
INT					
RAL	749	51	3357	98	34.25
NAT.W.	193.2	47	523	26	20.11
B & H	401.4	77	1412	45	31.37

Extras: In 1974, playing for Hucknall Ramblers CC, took 10 wickets for 6 runs in one innings against Sutton College in the Mansfield and District League
Best batting performance: 46 Nottinghamshire v Middlesex, Trent Bridge 1985
Best bowling performance: 8-44 Nottinghamshire v Middlesex, Lord's 1984

COTTEY, P. A. Glamorgan

Full Name: Phillip Anthony Cottey
Role: Right-hand bat
Born: 2 June 1966, Swansea
Height: 5′ 5″ **Weight:** 9st 10lbs
County debut: 1986
Nickname: Colts
1st-Class catches 1987: 2 (career 4)
Parents: Bernard John and Ruth
Marital status: Single
Family links with cricket: Father played for Swansea CC
Education: Bishopston Comprehensive School
Jobs outside cricket: Played professional soccer for Swansea City until 1985
Overseas teams played for: Penrith DCC 1986–1987

Cricketers particularly learnt from: Alan Jones, Tom Cartwright, John Hopkins
Cricketers particularly admired: Alan Jones, Ian Botham, Viv Richards
Other sports played: Soccer, golf, squash
Relaxations: Golf, cycling, running
Extras: Left school at 16 to play for Swansea City FC for three years as a professional. Captained Welsh Youth Soccer XI (3 caps). Played in Football League
Opinions on cricket: 'Far too many 2nd XI fixtures are played on club

LAST SEASON: BATTING

	I.	N.O.	R.	H.S.	AV.
TEST					
1ST-CLASS	10	1	161	42*	17.88
INT					
RAL	3	0	12	10	4.00
NAT.W.					
B & H					

CAREER: BATTING

	I.	N.O.	R.	H.S.	AV.
TEST					
1ST-CLASS	15	2	185	42*	14.23
INT					
RAL	6	0	17	10	2.83
NAT.W.					
B & H					

grounds, with no nets and covering facilities. I think that it is of great benefit for young players to play on 1st-class and Test Match grounds. I also think that it is unfair to leave wickets uncovered whilst allowing bowlers' run-ups to be covered. If uncovered wickets were introduced to help spin bowlers then covered run-ups are going to encourage the faster bowlers to bowl on rain-affected wickets. To ease travelling throughout the summer and encourage batsmen to occupy the crease longer, I think four-day cricket would be a great improvement to the County Championship.'

Best batting performance: 42* Glamorgan v Derbyshire, Chesterfield 1987

COVERDALE, S. P.   Northamptonshire

Full Name: Stephen Peter Coverdale
Role: Right-hand bat, wicket-keeper
Born: 20 November 1954, York
Height: 5′ 11″ **Weight:** 13st
Nickname: Sec
County debut: 1973 (Yorkshire) 1987 (Northamptonshire)
1st-Class 50s scored: 7
One-Day 50s: 1
Parents: John Peter and Margaret Ann
Wife and date of marriage: Jane, 2 July 1977
Children: Paul Stephen, 24 July 1983; Duncan Philip, 14 February 1986
Education: St Peter's School, York; Emmanuel College, Cambridge
Qualifications: 10 O-levels, 4 A-levels, 1 S-level, MA(Cantab) LLB. Qualified solicitor
Jobs outside cricket: Solicitor. Worked with BBC for two-and-a-half years as sports editor for Radio Leeds
Off-season 1987–88: Secretary/manager of Northampton's ground hire
Cricketing superstitions or habits: Sit in same place if we are doing well
Overseas tours: Sheffield Cricket Lovers to Bermuda, 1973; MCC to East and Central Africa, 1981; MCC to Holland and Denmark, 1983
Cricketers particularly learnt from: Phil Carrick, Ray Illingworth, Geoff Cook and all at Northamptonshire
Cricketers particularly admired: For sheer profesionalism Geoffrey Boycott and Richard Hadlee
Other sports played: Golf, squash, football – when there's time

Other sports followed: All sports
Relaxations: Work – totally absorbed in the job (and there's no time for anything else)
Extras: Youngest county secretary; played for Yorkshire 1973–1982
Opinions on cricket: 'It is a great privilege to be involved in the greatest of all games, at a time when the image and public profile of cricket is so good. It is the responsibility of us all to maintain and enhance the game's popularity.'
Best batting performance: 85 Cambridge University v Somerset, Cambridge 1976

CAREER: BATTING

	I.	N.O.	R.	H.S.	AV.
TEST					
1ST-CLASS	75	6	1245	85	18.04
INT					
RAL	3	2	18	17*	18.00
NAT.W.					
B & H	9	0	124	79	13.77

CAREER: WICKET KEEPING

	C.	ST.			
TEST					
1ST-CLASS	41	10			
INT					
RAL	3	–			
NAT.W.					
B & H	6	–			

COWANS, N. G.   Middlesex

Full Name: Norman George Cowans
Role: Right-hand bat, right-arm fast bowler
Born: 17 April 1961, Enfield St Mary, Jamaica
Height: 6' 3" **Weight:** 14st
Nickname: Flash
County debut: 1980
County cap: 1984
Test debut: 1982–83
No. of Tests: 19
No. of One-Day Internationals: 23
50 wickets in a season: 3
1st-Class 50s scored: 1
1st-Class 5 w. in innings: 18
Place in batting averages: —
(1986 206th av. 15.92)
Place in bowling averages: 5th
av. 18.78 (1986 25th av. 23.79)
Strike rate 1987: 40.17 (career 45.66)
1st-Class catches 1987: 3 (career 45)
Parents: Gloria and Ivan
Marital status: Single

Education: Park High Secondary, Stanmore, Middlesex
Qualifications: Qualified coach
Jobs outside cricket: Squash and real tennis professional. Glassblower with Whitefriars hand-made glass
Overseas tours: Young England to Australia 1979; Middlesex to Zimbabwe 1980; *The Cricketer* to Dubai 1981; England to Australia and New Zealand 1982–83 and New Zealand and Pakistan 1983–84; International tour to Jamaica 1983; India and Australia with England 1984–85; England B to Sri Lanka 1986
Overseas teams played for: Claremont-Cottesloe CC, Perth, Australia
Cricketers particularly learnt from: Dennis Lillee, Wayne Daniel, Michael Holding. 'The aggression of Lillee, the power of Daniel, and the smoothness of Holding.'
Other sports played: Basketball, squash, table tennis, swimming, tennis, real tennis
Other sports followed: Football (Arsenal FC)
Injuries 1987: Hernia kept him out of early season
Relaxations: Dancing, reading, being with friends, listening to reggae music
Extras: Two Young England Tests, one One-Day Youth International. Has won athletics championships in sprinting and javelin throwing
Best batting performance: 66 Middlesex v Surrey, Lord's 1984
Best bowling performance: 6-31 Middlesex v Leicestershire, Leicester 1985

LAST SEASON: BATTING

	I.	N.O.	R.	H.S.	AV.
TEST					
1ST-CLASS	16	4	87	24	7.25
INT					
RAL					
NAT.W.					
B & H					

LAST SEASON: BOWLING

	O.	M.	R.	W.	AV.
TEST					
1ST-CLASS	341.3	78	958	51	18.78
INT					
RAL	35	6	98	10	9.80
NAT.W.					
B & H					

CAREER: BATTING

	I.	N.O.	R.	H.S.	AV.
TEST	29	7	175	36	7.96
1ST-CLASS	108	22	797	66	9.26
INT	8	3	13	4*	2.60
RAL	13	6	78	20	11.14
NAT.W.	10	2	33	12*	4.12
B & H	5	2	16	6	5.33

CAREER: BOWLING

	O.	M.	R.	W.	AV.
TEST	575.2	113	2003	51	39.27
1ST-CLASS	2499.3	509	7871	353	22.29
INT	213.4	17	913	23	39.70
RAL	281.2	18	1166	45	25.91
NAT.W.	147	23	497	22	22.59
B & H	149.2	21	481	29	16.58

50. Who was vice-captain of Australia in the 1987 World Cup?

51. What was the name of Pakistan's manager on their 1987 tour of England?

COWDREY, C. S.   Kent

Full Name: Christopher Stuart
Cowdrey
Role: Right-hand bat, right-arm
medium bowler
Born: 20 October 1957,
Farnborough, Kent
Height: 6' 0" **Weight:** 13½st
Nickname: Cow, Woody
County debut: 1977
County cap: 1979
Test debut: 1984
No. of Tests: 5
No. of One-Day Internationals: 3
1000 runs in a season: 3
1st-Class 50s scored: 41
1st-Class 100s scored: 14
1st-Class 5 w. innings: 1
One-Day 50s: 32
One-Day 100s: 2
Place in batting averages: 102nd av. 30.90 (1986 112th av. 29.10)
Place in bowling averages: 130th av. 45.84 (1986 76th av. 33.51)
Strike rate 1987: 87.84 (career 71.35)
1st-Class catches 1987: 21 (career 226)
Parents: Michael Colin and Penelope Susan
Marital status: Single
Family links with cricket: Grandfather, Stuart Chiesman, on Kent Committee, 12 years as Chairman. Pavilion on Kent's ground at Canterbury named after him. Father played for Kent and England, brother made Kent debut 1984
Education: Wellesley House, Broadstairs; Tonbridge School
Jobs outside cricket: Employed by Fred Rumsey
Overseas tours: Captained Young England to West Indies, 1976; with Derrick Robins XI to Far East, South America and Australasia, 1979–80; India and Australia with England, 1984–85
Overseas teams played for: Avendale CC, Cape Town, 1983–84; Cumberland CC, Sydney, 1978–79 and 1982–83
Cricketers particularly learnt from: Asif Iqbal, Allan Lamb, Clive Radley
Cricketers particularly admired: David Gower
Other sports played: Golf, tennis, backgammon
Other sports followed: All sports
Injuries 1987: Achilles tendon
Relaxations: Dining at Silks Restaurant with Richard Scott and taking Blaise Craven's money at backgammon

Extras: Played for Kent 2nd XI at age 15. Vice-captain 1984. Captain 1985
Best batting performance: 159 Kent v Surrey, Canterbury 1985
Best bowling performance: 5-69 Kent v Hampshire, Canterbury 1986

LAST SEASON: BATTING

	I.	N.O.	R.	H.S.	AV.
TEST					
1ST-CLASS	37	6	958	135	30.90
INT					
RAL	14	3	472	77	42.30
NAT.W.	2	1	82	48	82.00
B & H	6	0	258	87	43.00

LAST SEASON: BOWLING

	O.	M.	R.	W.	AV.
TEST					
1ST-CLASS	278.1	64	871	19	45.84
INT					
RAL	71	0	342	19	18.00
NAT.W.	12	3	40	1	40.00
B & H	58.4	6	256	11	23.27

CAREER: BATTING

	I.	N.O.	R.	H.S.	AV.
TEST	6	1	96	38	19.20
1ST-CLASS	345	49	9188	159	31.04
INT	3	1	51	46*	25.50
RAL	136	19	2961	95	25.30
NAT.W.	25	5	689	122*	34.95
B & H	44	6	1209	114	31.81

CAREER: BOWLING

	O.	M.	R.	W.	AV.
TEST	61	2	288	4	72.00
1ST-CLASS	1653	311	5461	139	39.28
INT	8.4	0	55	2	27.50
RAL	477.3	5	2266	83	27.30
NAT.W.	138	16	510	21	24.28
B & H	223.4	9	1004	26	38.61

COWDREY, G. R.   Kent

Full Name: Graham Robert Cowdrey
Role: Right-hand bat, right-arm medium bowler, cover fielder
Born: 27 June 1964, Farnborough, Kent
Height: 5′ 10″ **Weight:** 13st
Nickname: Van, Cow
County debut: 1984
1st-Class 50s scored: 8
One-Day 50s: 4
Place in batting averages: 100th av. 31.28 (1986 200th av. 17.00)
1st-Class catches 1987: 4 (career 20)
Parents: Michael Colin and Penelope Susan
Marital status: Single
Family links with cricket: Father played for England and Kent. Brother captain of Kent
Education: Wellesley House, Broadstairs; Tonbridge School; Durham University
Qualifications: 8 O-levels, 3 A-levels, University entrance
Off-season 1987–88: In Sydney

Cricketing superstitions or habits: Say a prayer at the top of the steps before batting. Have to run every day
Overseas tours: Australia with Tonbridge School in 1980; Christians in Sport India tour, 1985–86
Overseas teams played for: Avendale CC, Cape Town, 1983–84; Mosman CC, Sydney, 1985–86
Cricketers particularly learnt from: Mark Benson, Chris Tavaré, Bob Woolmer, Roy Pienaar, Father
Cricketers particularly admired: Richard Hadlee, Chris Cowdrey, Richard Ellison
Other sports played: Most sports, particularly golf, rackets, snooker, tennis
Other sports followed: Rugby union
Injuries 1987: 'Broken jaw (from Michael Holding) kept me out for five weeks.'
Opinions on cricket: 'Too much travel and staying in hotels. Fitness is an increasingly important part of the game.'
Extras: Played for Young England and Australia. 1000 runs for Kent 2nd XI first season on staff, captain of Kent 2nd XI in 1984. Very interested in psychology of cricket. Broke 2nd XI record with 1300 runs in 26 innings in 1985. 'Kent running adviser Colin Tomlin helped me get fit after broken jaw. I owe a lot to Colin and his family.'
Best batting performance: 75 Kent v Northamptonshire, Canterbury 1986
Best bowling performance: 1-17 Kent v Glamorgan, Maidstone 1986

LAST SEASON: BATTING

	I.	N.O.	R.	H.S.	AV.
TEST					
1ST-CLASS	8	1	219	68	31.28
INT					
RAL	8	0	84	43	10.50
NAT.W.	2	1	27	18*	27.00
B & H	6	0	169	69	28.16

CAREER: BATTING

	I.	N.O.	R.	H.S.	AV.
TEST					
1ST-CLASS	44	4	893	75	22.32
INT					
RAL	24	3	374	48	17.80
NAT.W.	3	1	49	22	24.50
B & H	12	1	401	69	36.45

LAST SEASON: BOWLING

	O.	M.	R.	W.	AV.
TEST					
1ST-CLASS	8	2	43	0	–
INT					
RAL	22	1	113	9	12.55
NAT.W.	5	2	15	0	–
B & H	4	0	18	0	–

CAREER: BOWLING

	O.	M.	R.	W.	AV.
TEST					
1ST-CLASS	25	5	92	2	46.00
INT					
RAL	22	1	113	9	12.55
NAT.W.	16	4	45	1	45.00
B & H	4	0	18	0	–

52. Who captained Pakistan on their 1987 tour of England?
53. What, according to *Spycatcher* author Peter Wright, closed down M.I.5 each year?

COWLEY, N. G. — Hampshire

Full Name: Nigel Geoffrey Cowley
Role: Right-hand bat, off-break bowler
Born: 1 March 1953, Shaftesbury, Dorset
Height: 5′ 7″ **Weight:** 12st 5lbs
Nickname: Dougall
County debut: 1974
County cap: 1978
Benefit: 1988
1000 runs in a season: 1
50 wickets in a season: 5
1st-Class 50s scored: 29
1st-Class 100s scored: 2
1st-Class 5 w. in innings: 5
One-Day 50s: 5
Place in batting averages: 178th av. 19.70 (1986 140th av. 25.71)
Place in bowling averages: 94th av. 34.45 (1986 36th av. 26.50)
Strike rate 1987: 75.05 (career 72.08)
1st-Class catches 1987: 5 (career 95)
Parents: Geoffrey and Betty
Wife: Susan
Children: Mark and Darren
Family links with cricket: Father played good club cricket, two sons play for Hampshire U-13 and U-11 teams
Education: Mere Dutchy Manor, Mere, Wiltshire
Overseas tours: Sri Lanka 1977; West Indies 1980

LAST SEASON: BATTING

	I.	N.O.	R.	H.S.	AV.
TEST					
1ST-CLASS	12	2	197	96	19.70
INT					
RAL	7	1	79	35*	13.16
NAT.W.	1	0	16	16	16.00
B & H	4	0	47	27	11.75

CAREER: BATTING

	I.	N.O.	R.	H.S.	AV.
TEST					
1ST-CLASS	349	55	6537	109*	22.23
INT					
RAL	130	27	1969	74	19.11
NAT.W.	21	3	331	63*	18.38
B & H	39	3	487	59	13.52

LAST SEASON: BOWLING

	O.	M.	R.	W.	AV.
TEST					
1ST-CLASS	250.1	57	689	20	34.45
INT					
RAL	68	2	321	15	21.40
NAT.W.	12	1	48	1	48.00
B & H	40	1	164	1	164.00

CAREER: BOWLING

	O.	M.	R.	W.	AV.
TEST					
1ST-CLASS	4941	1290	13540	412	32.86
INT					
RAL	881.4	47	4211	143	29.44
NAT.W.	224.1	32	660	26	25.38
B & H	341.3	49	1137	26	43.73

Overseas teams played for: Paarl CC, Cape Town, 1981–83
Cricketers particularly learnt from: Peter Sainsbury
Other sports played: Golf (9 handicap)
Extras: In charge of pre-season and match day training
Best batting performance: 109* Hampshire v Somerset, Taunton 1977
Best bowling performance: 6-48 Hampshire v Leicestershire, Southampton 1982

CROWE, M. D. Somerset

Full Name: Mark David Crowe
Role: Right-hand bat, slip fielder
Born: 22 September 1962, Auckland, New Zealand
Height: 6′ 1½″ **Weight:** 14st
Nickname: Hogan
County debut: 1984
County cap: 1984
Test debut: 1981–82
No. of Tests: 36
No. of One-Day Internationals: 59
1000 runs in a season: 2
1st-Class 50s scored: 52
1st-Class 100s scored: 37
1st-Class 200s scored: 2
1st-Class 5 w. in innings: 4
One-Day 50s: 20
One-Day 100s: 3
Place in batting averages: 1st av. 67.79
1st-Class catches 1987: 15 (career 160)
Parents: David William and Audrey Sybil
Marital status: Single
Family links with cricket: Father played 1st-class cricket for Canterbury and Wellington. Brother Jeff Captain of New Zealand
Education: Auckland Grammar School
Off-season 1987–88: Touring with New Zealand
Qualifications: School Certificate, advanced Coaching Certificate
Overseas tours: New Zealand to Australia 1982, 1984, 1985; to England 1983, 1986; to Sri Lanka 1984, 1985, 1987; to Pakistan 1984, 1987; to West Indies 1985
Overseas teams played for: Auckland 1979–83 ; Central Districts 1984–87
Cricketers particularly learnt from: Greg Chappell, Richard Hadlee
Cricketers particularly admired: Greg Chappell, Richard Hadlee

Other sports played: Golf, tennis
Other sports followed: All Blacks, top golf
Injuries 1987: Broken thumb in right hand
Best batting performance: 242* New Zealanders v South Australia, Adelaide 1985–86
Best bowling performance: 5-18 Central Districts v Auckland, Auckland 1983–84

LAST SEASON: BATTING

	I.	N.O.	R.	H.S.	AV.
TEST					
1ST-CLASS	29	5	1627	206*	67.79
INT					
RAL	12	1	382	82	34.72
NAT.W.	1	0	2	2	2.00
B & H	5	1	241	155*	60.25

LAST SEASON: BOWLING

	O.	M.	R.	W.	AV.
TEST					
1ST-CLASS	33	8	100	0	–
INT					
RAL	4	0	24	0	–
NAT.W.					
B & H	40	0	186	5	37.20

CAREER: BATTING

	I.	N.O.	R.	H.S.	AV.
TEST	59	6	2162	188	40.79
1ST-CLASS	190	33	9438	242*	60.11
INT	56	6	1640	105*	32.80
RAL	27	1	839	82	32.26
NAT.W.	4	0	143	114	35.75
B & H	10	2	393	155*	49.12

CAREER: BOWLING

	O.	M.	R.	W.	AV.
TEST	206.3	46	607	13	46.69
1ST-CLASS			3077	102	30.16
INT	183	11	781	25	31.24
RAL	84	3	426	10	42.60
NAT.W.	30	6	75	6	12.50
B & H	89	3	368	15	24.53

CURRAN, K. M.　　　Gloucestershire

Full Name: Kevin Malcolm Curran
Role: Right-hand bat, right-arm fast-medium bowler
Born: 7 September 1959, Rusape, Zimbabwe
Height: 6′ 2″ Weight: 13st 9lbs
Nickname: KC
County debut: 1985
County cap: 1985
No. of One-Day Internationals: 6
1000 runs in a season: 2
50 wickets in a season: 1
1st-Class 50s scored: 19
1st-Class 100s scored: 7
1st-Class 5 w. in innings: 2
One-Day 50s: 12
Place in batting averages: 28th av. 42.29 (1986 33rd av. 43.64)
1st-Class catches 1987: 12 (career 55)
Parents: Kevin Patrick and Sylvia

Marital status: Single
Family links with cricket: Father played for Rhodesia 1949–53
Education: Marandelias High School
Qualifications: 6 O-levels, 2 M-levels
Jobs outside cricket: Tobacco buyer/farmer
Off-season 1987–88: Resting completely from cricket
Overseas tours: Sri Lanka 1982; World Cup 1983 with Zimbabwe; World XI to West Indies, 1985; World Cup 1987
Cricket superstitions or habits: 111, 222, 333 on the scoreboard while batting
Overseas teams played for: Harare SC, Zimbabwe 1981–85
Cricketers particularly learnt from: Brian Davison, Duncan Fletcher
Cricketers particularly admired: Mike Procter, Graeme Pollock, Barry Richards, John Traicos
Other sports played: Rugby, squash, tennis
Injuries 1987: 'Back injury prevented me bowling for most of the season.'
Relaxations: 'Both deep-sea and fresh-water fishing. Hunting for guinea-fowl, partridge and spring hares. Music, movies and good restaurants with stimulating company. Running and gym.'
Extras: 'The introduction of the four-day game sounds like a good idea. If the counties produced result wickets, far more quick English bowlers would be produced. It would also encourage the batsmen to play a few more shots, and get the game moving forward. We owe it to our sponsors and the cricketing public to play more attractive cricket. County cricketers would have to play more for a team, and would be involved in more result games. There would be no selfish players, who are content with occupying the crease for the whole day and scoring runs basically for their averages at the end of the season (i.e. 100 runs in 100 overs).'
Best batting performance: 119 Gloucestershire v Kent, Cheltenham 1987
Best bowling performance: 5-35 Gloucestershire v Australians, Bristol 1985

LAST SEASON: BATTING

	I.	N.O.	R.	H.S.	AV.
TEST					
1ST-CLASS	33	6	1142	119	42.29
INT					
RAL	13	4	409	69*	45.44
NAT.W.	4	0	24	22	6.00
B & H	4	1	140	57	46.66

CAREER: BATTING

	I.	N.O.	R.	H.S.	AV.
TEST					
1ST-CLASS	139	23	3927	119	33.85
INT	6	0	212	73	35.33
RAL	42	10	1154	71*	36.06
NAT.W.	9	0	164	38	18.22
B & H	10	3	324	57	46.28

LAST SEASON: BOWLING

	O.	M.	R.	W.	AV.
TEST					
1ST-CLASS	48	5	203	2	101.50
INT					
RAL	24	2	92	6	15.33
NAT.W.	21	2	69	1	69.00
B & H	47.2	4	202	5	40.40

CAREER: BOWLING

	O.	M.	R.	W.	AV.
TEST					
1ST-CLASS	940.5	196	3005	116	25.90
INT	88.2	3	274	5	54.80
RAL	126.5	8	606	33	18.36
NAT.W.	55	12	146	7	20.85
B & H	91.1	8	371	13	28.53

CURTIS, T. S.   Worcestershire

Full Name: Timothy Stephen Curtis
Role: Right-hand bat, leg-break
bowler
Born: 15 January 1960, Chislehurst,
Kent
Height: 5′ 11″ **Weight:** 12st 5lbs
Nickname: TC, Duracell,
Professor
County debut: 1979
County cap: 1984
1000 runs in a season: 4
1st-Class 50s scored: 43
1st-Class 100s: 10
One-Day 50s: 22
One-Day 100s: 1
Place in batting averages: 16th
av. 47.08 (1986 11th av. 49.93)

1st-Class catches 1987: 10 (career 62)
Parents: Bruce and Betty
Wife and date of marriage: Philippa, 21 September 1985
Family links with cricket: Father played good club cricket in Bristol and
Stafford
Education: The Royal Grammar School, Worcester; Durham University;
Cambridge University
Qualifications: 12 O-levels, 4 A-levels, BA (Hons) English, postgraduate
certificate in Education in English and Games
Overseas tours: NCA U-19 tour of Canada 1979
Cricketers particularly learnt from: Glenn Turner
Off-season 1987–88: Teaching

LAST SEASON: BATTING

	I.	N.O.	R.	H.S.	AV.
TEST					
1ST-CLASS	40	6	1601	138*	47.08
INT					
RAL	16	3	617	86	47.46
NAT.W.	2	0	89	79	44.50
B & H	5	1	221	78	55.25

LAST SEASON: BOWLING

	O.	M.	R.	W.	AV.
TEST					
1ST-CLASS	19	2	94	2	47.00
INT					
RAL					
NAT.W.	2	0	9	1	9.00
B & H					

CAREER: BATTING

	I.	N.O.	R.	H.S.	AV.
TEST					
1ST-CLASS	229	32	7273	153	36.91
INT					
RAL	61	12	1814	102	37.02
NAT.W.	13	2	522	94	47.45
B & H	19	2	577	78	33.94

CAREER: BOWLING

	O.	M.	R.	W.	AV.
TEST					
1ST-CLASS	73.3	11	288	6	48.00
INT					
RAL					
NAT.W.	2	0	9	1	9.00
B & H					

Other sports played: Rugby, tennis, squash, golf
Extras: Captained Durham University to a UAU Championship. According to Ian Botham, he is 'extremely unlucky not to have been chosen for England yet'.
Opinions on cricket: '16 four-day matches would seem to be the best combination for Championship cricket, with one-day competitions taking place at the weekends. This would reduce the amount of cricket played and place a greater emphasis on the quality of the cricket. It would also avoid the lottery which I feel uncovered wickets would produce.'
Best batting performance: 153 Worcestershire v Somerset, Worcester 1986
Best bowling performance: 2-58 Cambridge University v Nottinghamshire, Cambridge 1983

DANIEL, W. W.   Middlesex

Full Name: Wayne Wendell Daniel
Role: Right-hand bat, right-arm fast bowler
Born: 16 January 1956, St Philip, Barbados
Nickname: Diamond
County debut: 1977
County cap: 1977
Benefit: 1985
Test debut: 1975–76
No. of Tests: 10
No. of One-Day Internationals: 18
50 wickets in a season: 10
1st-Class 50s scored: 2
1st-Class 5 w. in innings: 31
1st-Class 10 w. in innings: 7
Place in batting averages: — (1986 216th av. 14.00)
Place in bowling averages: 114th av. 39.84 (1986 15th av. 22.37)
Strike rate 1987: 65.28 (career 46.20)
1st-Class catches 1987: 5 (career 63)
Marital status: Single
Relaxations: Enjoys listening to soul music
Extras: Toured England with West Indies Schoolboys team 1974. Played for Middlesex 2nd XI 1975. Debut for Barbados 1975–76. Toured with West Indies to England 1976. Spent 1979–80 off-season in Barbados playing island cricket. Best bowling record for B & H competition in 1978 with 7 for 12 v Minor Counties East at Ipswich

Best batting performance: 53* Barbados v Jamaica, Bridgetown 1979–80
53* Middlesex v Yorkshire, Lord's 1981
Best bowling performance: 9-61 Middlesex v Glamorgan, Swansea 1982

LAST SEASON: BATTING

	I.	N.O.	R.	H.S.	AV.
TEST					
1ST-CLASS	12	8	31	9*	7.75
INT					
RAL	2	1	12	9	12.00
NAT.W.	1	1	3	3*	–
B & H	1	0	17	17	17.00

LAST SEASON: BOWLING

	O.	M.	R.	W.	AV.
TEST					
1ST-CLASS	348.1	47	1275	32	39.84
INT					
RAL	35.3	1	148	6	24.66
NAT.W.	19.3	4	53	5	10.60
B & H	16	0	88	0	–

CAREER: BATTING

	I.	N.O.	R.	H.S.	AV.
TEST	11	4	46	11	6.57
1ST-CLASS	228	102	1505	53*	11.94
INT	5	4	49	16*	49.00
RAL	40	16	105	14	4.37
NAT.W.	18	10	42	14	5.25
B & H	18	5	73	20*	5.61

CAREER: BOWLING

	O.	M.	R.	W.	AV.
TEST	292	61	910	36	25.28
1ST-CLASS	6369.2	1231	18543	829	22.36
INT	152	17	595	23	25.87
RAL	831.3	77	3057	163	18.75
NAT.W.	360	62	1033	70	14.75
B & H	434	71	1370	82	16.70

DAVIS, M. R. Somerset

Full Name: Mark Richard Davis
Role: Left-hand bat, left-arm
fast-medium bowler, outfielder
Born: 26 February 1962, Kilve,
Somerset
Height: 5′ 11½″ **Weight:** 13st
Nickname: Pooch
County debut: 1982
50 wickets in a season: 1
1st-Class 50s scored: 1
1st-Class 5 w. in innings: 4
1st-Class 10 w. in match: 1
Place in batting averages: — (1986
207th av. 15.75)
Place in bowling averages: 132nd
av. 45.90 (1986 125th av. 57.36)
Strike rate 1987: 83.90 (career 63.36)
1st-Class catches 1987: 4 (career 29)
Parents: Penelope and Robert Ernest
Charles
Wife: Elizabeth Rebecca

Family links with cricket: 'Father and relatives all play for my local club side,
Kilve.'

Education: Kilve Primary School; Williton First and Middle School; West Somerset School; Bridgwater College
Qualifications: 4 O-levels, NCA Senior Coaching Award
Jobs outside cricket: Self employed in building trade
Overseas tours: Zimbabwe with English Counties XI
Cricketers particularly admired: Ian Botham, Martin Crowe, Viv Richards, Joel Garner
Other sports played: Squash
Other sports followed: Football
Relaxations: 'Playing skittles in my local.'
Opinions on cricket: 'Four-day matches (or three-day matches on uncovered pitches). More positive result wickets required from batsmen captains.'
Best batting performance: 60* Somerset v Glamorgan, Taunton 1984
Best bowling performance: 7-55 Somerset v Northamptonshire, Northampton 1984

LAST SEASON: BATTING

	I.	N.O.	R.	H.S.	AV.
TEST					
1ST-CLASS	8	1	57	23*	8.14
INT					
RAL					
NAT.W.					
B & H	2	0	7	4	3.50

CAREER: BATTING

	I.	N.O.	R.	H.S.	AV.
TEST					
1ST-CLASS	79	24	803	60*	14.60
INT					
RAL	13	6	54	11	7.71
NAT.W.	2	1	6	6	6.00
B & H	9	0	74	28	8.22

LAST SEASON: BOWLING

	O.	M.	R.	W.	AV.
TEST					
1ST-CLASS	153.5	25	505	11	45.90
INT					
RAL	13	0	50	1	50.00
NAT.W.					
B & H	21	1	85	2	42.50

CAREER: BOWLING

	O.	M.	R.	W.	AV.
TEST					
1ST-CLASS	1573.3	277	5308	149	35.62
INT					
RAL	243.4	10	1046	29	36.06
NAT.W.	34	6	132	2	66.00
B & H	138	20	489	16	30.56

54. Who was the Cricket Writers' Young Cricketer of the Year in 1987?

55. Which county cricketer who represented Great Britain in the Olympics at fencing retired at the end of last season?

DAVIS, R. P.   Kent

Full Name: Richard Peter Davis
Role: Slow left-arm bowler,
gully fielder
Born: 18 March 1966, Westgate
Height: 6′ 4″ **Weight:** 14st 7lbs
Nickname: Dickie, Doughnut
County debut: 1986
Place in bowling averages: 134th
av. 47.30
Strike rate 1987: 91.80 (career 79.81)
1st-Class catches 1987: 5 (career 6)
Parents: Brian and Silvia
Marital status: Single
Family links with cricket: Father
played local club cricket and
is an NCA coach
Education: King Ethelberts School,
Birchington; Thanet Technical
College, Broadstairs

Qualifications: 8 CSEs
Jobs outside cricket: Carpenter
Overseas tours: Kent Schools CA U-17s Canadian tour 1983
Overseas team played for: Hutt District CC, New Zealand 1986–87, 1987–88
Cricketers particularly learnt from: Derek Underwood, Eldine Baptiste
Cricketers particularly admired: Derek Underwood
Off-season 1987–88: In New Zealand
Other sports played: Golf, football, badminton
Other sports followed: American football, motor racing
Relaxations: Reading, sport, TV

LAST SEASON: BATTING

	I.	N.O.	R.	H.S.	AV.
TEST					
1ST-CLASS	9	4	43	21*	8.60
INT					
RAL	3	2	14	7*	14.00
NAT.W.					
B & H					

LAST SEASON: BOWLING

	O.	M.	R.	W.	AV.
TEST					
1ST-CLASS	153	35	473	10	47.30
INT					
RAL	59	3	297	9	33.00
NAT.W.					
B & H					

CAREER: BATTING

	I.	N.O.	R.	H.S.	AV.
TEST					
1ST-CLASS	10	5	43	21*	8.60
INT					
RAL	3	2	14	7*	14.00
NAT.W.					
B & H					

CAREER: BOWLING

	O.	M.	R.	W.	AV.
TEST					
1ST-CLASS	212.5	57	594	16	37.12
INT					
RAL	59	3	297	9	33.00
NAT.W.					
B & H					

Opinions on cricket: 'I would like to see wickets re-covered, and the tracks hard and brown, encouraging quick bowlers and spinners.'
Best batting performance: 21* Kent v Warwickshire, Edgbaston 1987
Best bowling performance: 3-38 Kent v Warwickshire, Folkestone 1986

DAVIS, W. W.   Northamptonshire

Full Name: Winston Walter Davis
Role: Right-hand bat, right-arm fast bowler
Born: 18 September 1958, St Vincent, Windward Islands
County debut: 1982 (Glamorgan), 1987 (Northamptonshire)
County cap: 1987 (Northamptonshire)
Test debut: 1982–83
No. of Tests: 11
No. of One-Day Internationals: 32
50 wickets in a season: 3
1st-Class 50s scored: 5
1st-Class 5 w. in innings: 19
1st-Class 10 w. in match: 4
Place in batting averages: 125th av. 14.30
Place in bowling averages: 50th av. 27.22
Strike rate 1987: 50.67 (career 60.84)

LAST SEASON: BATTING

	I.	N.O.	R.	H.S.	AV.
TEST					
1ST-CLASS	18	5	186	25*	14.30
INT					
RAL					
NAT.W.	1	1	14	14*	–
B & H	5	3	42	15*	21.00

CAREER: BATTING

	I.	N.O.	R.	H.S.	AV.
TEST	12	4	157	77	19.62
1ST-CLASS	133	43	1188	77	13.20
INT	3	3	15	8*	–
RAL	4	2	10	5	5.00
NAT.W.	5	3	22	14*	11.00
B & H	8	3	56	15*	11.20

LAST SEASON: BOWLING

	O.	M.	R.	W.	AV.
TEST					
1ST-CLASS	591.1	100	1906	70	27.22
INT					
RAL					
NAT.W.	37	4	129	5	25.80
B & H	73	7	289	10	28.90

CAREER: BOWLING

	O.	M.	R.	W.	AV.
TEST	350	43	1082	32	33.81
1ST-CLASS	3675.4	450	10216	365	27.98
INT	291.3	29	1023	33	31.00
RAL	156.4	14	649	30	21.63
NAT.W.	79.5	12	258	9	28.66
B & H	111.2	12	438	19	23.05

1st-Class catches 1987: 7 (career 40)
Overseas tours: Young West Indies to Zimbabwe, 1981–82; West Indies to India 1983–84
Overseas teams played for: Windward Islands, Combined Islands
Best batting performance: 77 West Indies v England, Old Trafford 1984
Best bowling performance: 7-70 Glamorgan v Nottinghamshire, Ebbw Vale 1983

DEFREITAS, P. A. J.　　Leicestershire

Full Name: Phillip Anthony Jason DeFreitas
Role: Right-hand bat, right-arm fast-medium bowler, cover fielder
Born: 18 February 1966, Dominica
Height: 6′ **Weight:** 12st
Nickname: Daffy
County debut: 1985
County cap: 1986
Test debut: 1986–87
No. of Tests: 5
No. of One-Day Internationals: 19
50 wickets in a season: 2
1st-Class 50s scored: 5
1st-Class 100s scored: 1
1st-Class 5 w. in innings: 10
1st-Class 10 w. in match: 1
One-Day 50s: 1
Place in batting averages: 179th av. 19.61 (1986 167th av. 23.03)
Place in bowling averages: 39th av. 25.89 (1986 16th av. 23.09)

LAST SEASON: BATTING

	I.	N.O.	R.	H.S.	AV.
TEST	1	0	11	11	11.00
1ST-CLASS	22	2	401	74	20.05
INT	2	0	36	33	18.00
RAL	7	1	80	31	13.33
NAT.W.	3	1	54	33	27.00
B & H	3	0	27	14	9.00

CAREER: BATTING

	I.	N.O.	R.	H.S.	AV.
TEST	6	1	88	40	17.60
1ST-CLASS	69	8	1216	106	19.93
INT	13	6	128	33	18.28
RAL	24	5	232	32	12.21
NAT.W.	4	1	123	69	41.00
B & H	6	2	49	14	12.25

LAST SEASON: BOWLING

	O.	M.	R.	W.	AV.
TEST	12	4	36	1	36.00
1ST-CLASS	465.3	103	1414	55	25.70
INT	33	6	110	1	110.00
RAL	53.2	1	290	7	41.42
NAT.W.	34.5	8	120	8	15.00
B & H	36	4	110	3	36.66

CAREER: BOWLING

	O.	M.	R.	W.	AV.
TEST	153.4	28	482	10	48.20
1ST-CLASS	1540.4	298	4596	189	24.31
INT	184.1	24	621	25	24.84
RAL	211.3	10	1048	45	23.28
NAT.W.	61.3	14	212	11	19.27
B & H	87	13	258	8	32.25

Strike rate 1987: 51.16 (career 51.08)
1st-Class catches 1987: 9 (career 18)
Parents: Sybil and Martin
Marital status: Single
Family links with cricket: Father played in the Windward Islands. All six brothers play
Education: Willesden High School
Qualifications: 2 CSEs
Overseas tours: Young England to West Indies 1985; England to Australia 1986–87; World Cup, Pakistan, Australia and New Zealand 1987–88
Overseas teams played for: Port Adelaide CC 1985–86
Cricketers particularly learnt from: Don Wilson, Ken Higgs, Paddy Clift, Peter Willey and several others
Off-season 1987–88: On tour with England
Other sports played: Football and golf
Opinions on cricket: 'Fines on over rates to be abolished. 2nd XI wickets ought to be much better.'
Best batting performance: 106 Leicestershire v Kent, Canterbury 1986
Best bowling performance: 7-44 Leicestershire v Essex, Southend 1986

DENNIS, S. J. Yorkshire

Full Name: Simon John Dennis
Role: Right-hand bat, left-arm fast-medium bowler
Born: 18 October 1960, Scarborough
Height: 6′ 1″ **Weight:** 13st
Nickname: Donkey
County debut: 1980
County cap: 1983
50 wickets in a season: 1
1st-Class 50s scored: 1
1st-Class 5 w. in innings: 5
Place in batting averages: — (1986 239th av. 10.25)
Place in bowling averages: — (1986 64th av. 30.65)
1st-Class catches 1987: 0 (career 19)
Parents: Margaret and Geoff
Marital status: Single

Family links with cricket: Father captained Scarborough for many years. Uncle, Frank Dennis, played for Yorkshire 1928–33. Uncle, Sir Leonard Hutton, played for Yorkshire and England

Education: Northstead County Primary School; Scarborough College
Qualifications: 7 O-levels, 1 A-level, City and Guilds Computer Literacy
Jobs outside cricket: Assistant groundsman at Scarborough CC. Furniture salesman. Worked for a Scarborough printing firm. Currently working for G. A. Pinder & Sons Ltd in sales department
Cricketing superstitions or habits: 'If I have a good day I try to do everything the same the next day before the game.'
Overseas tours: ESCA to India, 1978–79; Young England to Australia, 1980; MCC to East and Central Africa, 1981; MCC to America, 1982; Sheffield Cricket Lovers to Gibraltar, 1983
Overseas teams played for: Orange Free State 1982–83; Durban Collegians 1985–86
Cricketers particularly learnt from: Doug Padgett, Don Wilson, Ray Illingworth
Cricketers particularly admired: Dennis Lillee, John Lever
Off-season 1987–88: Working for G. A. Pinder & Sons Ltd
Other sports played: Rugby, hockey, squash, golf, soccer
Relaxations: Car maintenance, wine- and beer-making. Photography and real ale. Home computer, video games. 'Also terrible snooker player.'
Extras: On debut for Yorkshire v Somerset, at Weston 1980, got Gavaskar as his first wicket
Best batting performance: 53* Yorkshire v Nottinghamshire, Trent Bridge 1984
Best bowling performance: 5-35 Yorkshire v Somerset, Sheffield 1981

LAST SEASON: BATTING

	I.	N.O.	R.	H.S.	AV.
TEST					
1ST-CLASS	2	0	5	4	2.50
INT					
RAL					
NAT.W.					
B & H					

LAST SEASON: BOWLING

	O.	M.	R.	W.	AV.
TEST					
1ST-CLASS	47	8	168	2	84.00
INT					
RAL	3	0	16	0	
NAT.W.					
B & H	11	2	36	0	–

CAREER: BATTING

	I.	N.O.	R.	H.S.	AV.
TEST					
1ST-CLASS	66	25	406	53*	9.90
INT					
RAL	19	11	87	16*	10.87
NAT.W.	2	0	14	14	7.00
B & H					

CAREER: BOWLING

	O.	M.	R.	W.	AV.
TEST					
1ST-CLASS	1808	357	5799	186	31.17
INT					
RAL	261	14	1188	27	44.00
NAT.W.	52.2	8	202	6	33.66
B & H	87	15	327	7	46.71

56. Who won the Benson & Hedges Cup in 1987?

57. Which county was runner-up in both the Benson & Hedges and NatWest competitions?

DERRICK, J.   Glamorgan

Full Name: John Derrick
Role: Right-hand bat, right-arm
medium bowler
Born: 15 January 1963, Aberdare,
South Wales
Height: 6′ 2″ **Weight:** 15st
Nickname: JD, Bo
County debut: 1983
1st-Class 50s scored: 9
1st-Class 5 w. in innings: 1
Place in batting averages: 176th
av. 19.90 (1986 71st av. 35.56)
Place in bowling averages: 78th
av. 31.29 (1986 100th av. 40.77)
Strike rate 1987: 56.73 (career 73.44)
1st-Class catches 1986: 7 (career 22)
Parents: John Raymond and
Megan Irene

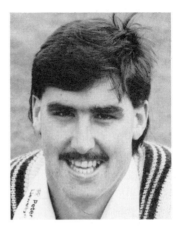

Wife and date of marriage: Anne
Irene, 20 April 1985
Children: Liam Kyle, 3 April 1987
Family links with cricket: Father and brother play club cricket for Aberdare
Education: Glynhafod and Blaengwawr Primary Schools; Blaengwawr Comprehensive School
Qualifications: School Certificate
Jobs outside cricket: Coaching cricket
Overseas teams played for: Toombul CC, Brisbane, 1982–85; Te Puke CC & Bay of Plenty Red Team New Zealand 1985–86; Northern Districts 1986–87
Cricketers particularly learnt from: Tom Cartwright, Don Wilson, Andy

LAST SEASON: BATTING

	I.	N.O.	R.	H.S.	AV.
TEST					
1ST-CLASS	27	7	398	57	19.90
INT					
RAL	10	3	54	21*	7.71
NAT.W.	1	1	2	2*	–
B & H	1	1	2	2*	–

LAST SEASON: BOWLING

	O.	M.	R.	W.	AV.
TEST					
1ST-CLASS	321.3	70	1064	34	31.29
INT					
RAL	62	0	316	10	31.60
NAT.W.					
B & H	10	2	39	0	–

CAREER: BATTING

	I.	N.O.	R.	H.S.	AV.
TEST					
1ST-CLASS	86	27	1530	78*	25.93
INT					
RAL	34	11	296	26	12.86
NAT.W.	2	1	6	4	6.00
B & H	7	2	83	42	16.60

CAREER: BOWLING

	O.	M.	R.	W.	AV.
TEST					
1ST-CLASS	954.5	188	3139	78	40.24
INT					
RAL	272.3	3	1415	38	37.23
NAT.W.	28.3	6	62	6	10.33
B & H	62	7	231	5	46.20

Wagner and senior Glamorgan players, Lance Cairns and Andy Roberts in New Zealand
Cricketers particularly admired: Geoff Boycott, John Snow, Dennis Lillee
Off-season 1987–88: Coaching cricket in New Zealand
Other sports played: Soccer, squash, golf – 'give anything a try'
Other sports followed: Rugby, Chelsea FC
Relaxations: Swimming, TV, music, cooking
Injuries 1987: Hit on head at Lord's. Shin splints for last two weeks of season
Extras: Spent three years on MCC groundstaff 1980–82. Coached at Lord's in winter of 1981. Captained Welsh Schools U-11s on tour to Lancashire and Cheshire. Took 9 for 9 off 9 overs v Lancashire and 6 for 6 off 6 overs v Cheshire
Opinions on cricket: 'Review the points system, i.e. perhaps points for first innings win. Looking forward to four-day Championship games.'
Best batting performance: 78* Glamorgan v Derbyshire, Abergavenny 1986
Best bowling performance: 5-50 Glamorgan v Hampshire, Swansea 1987

DILLEY, G. R. Worcestershire

Full Name: Graham Roy Dilley
Role: Left-hand bat, right-arm fast bowler
Born: 18 May 1959, Dartford
Height: 6' 4" **Weight:** 15st
Nickname: Picca
County debut: 1977 (Kent), 1987 (Worcestershire)
County cap: 1980 (Kent), 1987 (Worcestershire)
Test debut: 1979–80
No. of Tests: 30
No. of One-Day Internationals: 34
50 wickets in a season: 5
1st-Class 50s scored: 4
1st-Class 5 w. in innings: 18
1st-Class 10 w. in match: 2
Place in batting averages: 252nd av. 10.00 (1986 224th av. 12.11)
Place in bowling averages: 17th av. 23.34 (1986 33rd av. 25.93)
Strike rate 1987: 45.51 (career 54.63)
1st-Class catches 1987: 2 (career 65)
Parents: Geoff and Jean
Wife and date of marriage: Helen, 6 November 1980

Family links with cricket: Father and grandfather both played local cricket. Wife is former Kent colleague Graham Johnson's sister
Education: Dartford West Secondary School
Qualifications: 3 O-levels
Jobs outside cricket: Diamond setter
Overseas tours: With England to Australia 1979–80, West Indies 1981, India 1981–82, New Zealand and Pakistan 1983–84, Australia 1986–87, World Cup, Pakistan, New Zealand and Australia 1987–88
Cricketers particularly learnt from: Dennis Lillee, John Snow
Off-season 1987–88: Touring with England
Other sports played: Golf, squash, badminton
Relaxations: Music
Extras: Got sacked from his first job with a Hatton Garden diamond firm after taking time off to play for Kent 2nd XI. Suffered from glandular fever at end of 1980 season, causing him to miss Centenary Test. Voted Young Cricketer of the Year 1980 by Cricket Writers' Club. Missed 1984 season after suffering back injury on 1983–84 tour. Joined Worcestershire in 1987
Best batting performance: 81 Kent v Northamptonshire, Northampton 1979
Best bowling performance: 7-63 Natal v Transvaal, Johannesburg 1985–86

LAST SEASON: BATTING

	I.	N.O.	R.	H.S.	AV.
TEST	5	2	20	17	6.66
1ST-CLASS	4	1	40	29	13.33
INT	1	1	0	0*	–
RAL	1	0	0		0.00
NAT.W.	1	0	25	25	25.00
B & H	1	0	4	4	4.00

LAST SEASON: BOWLING

	O.	M.	R.	W.	AV.
TEST	133.3	26	388	14	27.71
1ST-CLASS	132	26	429	21	20.42
INT	20	5	79	2	39.50
RAL	44	2	233	8	29.12
NAT.W.	17	3	51	2	25.50
B & H	47	10	127	7	18.14

CAREER: BATTING

	I.	N.O.	R.	H.S.	AV.
TEST	42	13	391	56	13.48
1ST-CLASS	146	50	1352	81	14.08
INT	18	8	114	31*	11.40
RAL	27	8	252	33	13.26
NAT.W.	11	3	102	25	14.57
B & H	23	7	129	37*	8.06

CAREER: BOWLING

	O.	M.	R.	W.	AV.
TEST	986.1	202	2972	99	30.02
1ST-CLASS	3120.5	671	9447	352	26.83
INT	318.3	33	1182	45	26.26
RAL	424.2	31	1740	71	24.50
NAT.W.	146.4	24	444	23	19.30
B & H	336.5	45	1113	54	20.61

58. Who was Gladstone Small's best man at his wedding in 1987?
59. Which former England player is now Sussex coach?
60. Who scored the most, and second most, runs in the Refuge Assurance Sunday League in 1987?

D'OLIVEIRA, D. B.   Worcestershire

Full Name: Damian Basil
D'Oliveira
Role: Right-hand bat, off-break
bowler, fields anywhere 'except
short leg'
Born: 19 October 1960, Cape
Town, South Africa
Height: 5' 8" **Weight:** 11st 8lbs
Nickname: Dolly
County debut: 1982
County cap: 1985
1000 runs in a season: 3
1st-Class 50s scored: 25
1st-Class 100s scored: 6
One-Day 50s: 8
One-Day 100s: 1
Place in batting averages: 81st

av. 33.51 (1986 117th av. 28.78)
1st-Class catches 1987: 25 (career 93)
Parents: Basil and Naomi
Wife and date of marriage: Tracey, 26 September 1983
Children: Marcus Damian, 27 April 1986
Family links with cricket: Father played for Worcestershire and England
Education: St George's RC Primary School; Blessed Edward Oldcorne
Secondary School
Qualifications: 3 O-levels, 5 CSEs
Overseas tours: English Counties XI to Zimbabwe 1985
Overseas teams played for: West Perth CC, Western Australia, 1979–80;
Christchurch Shirley 1982–83 and 1983–84 on a Whitbread scholarship

LAST SEASON: BATTING

	I.	N.O.	R.	H.S.	AV.
TEST					
1ST-CLASS	37	4	1106	131*	33.51
INT					
RAL	12	2	281	56	28.10
NAT.W.	2	0	28	19	14.00
B & H	4	1	128	59	42.66

LAST SEASON: BOWLING

	O.	M.	R.	W.	AV.
TEST					
1ST-CLASS	31.2	5	147	3	49.00
INT					
RAL					
NAT.W.	8	0	33	1	33.00
B & H					

CAREER: BATTING

	I.	N.O.	R.	H.S.	AV.
TEST					
1ST-CLASS	204	15	5304	146*	28.06
INT					
RAL	71	5	1381	103	20.92
NAT.W.	13	1	326	99	27.16
B & H	21	3	434	66	24.11

CAREER: BOWLING

	O.	M.	R.	W.	AV.
TEST					
1ST-CLASS	257.1	49	923	23	40.13
INT					
RAL	39	2	232	7	33.14
NAT.W.	36	5	122	6	20.33
B & H	38	4	148	5	29.60

Cricketers particularly admired: Greg Chappell, Viv Richards, Dennis Lillee, Malcolm Marshall, Richard Hadlee
Other sports played: Football
Other sports followed: Most others, but not horse racing
Relaxations: Watching films, TV and eating out
Best batting performance: 146* Worcestershire v Gloucestershire, Cheltenham 1986
Best bowling performance: 2-17 Worcestershire v Gloucestershire, Cheltenham 1986

DONALD, A. A. Warwickshire

Full Name: Allan Anthony Donald
Role: Right-hand bat, right-arm fast-medium bowler
Born: 20 October 1966, Bloemfontein, South Africa
Height: 6′ 3″ **Weight:** 13½st
County debut: 1987
1st-Class 5 w. in innings: 6
1st-Class 10 w. in match: 1
Place in batting averages: 211th av. 15.85
Place in bowling averages: 41st av. 25.94
Strike rate 1987: 46.10
1st-Class catches 1987: 1 (career 4)
Parents: Stuart and Francina
Marital status: Single
Education: Grey College High School and Technical High School, Bloemfontein
Qualifications: Matriculation
Off-season 1987–88: Playing cricket
Cricketing superstitions or habits: Love bowling to left-handers
Overseas teams played for: Orange Free State, South Africa
Cricketers particularly learnt from: Chris Broad, Vanburn Holder, Alvin Kallicharran
Cricketers particularly admired: Ian Botham, Imran Khan
Other sports played: Rugby
Other sports followed: Rugby, football
Injuries 1987: Back and knee
Relaxations: Playing tennis, listening to music

Extras: Played for a South Africa XI v an Australian XI in one 5-day Test and three One-Day Internationals, 1986–87
Opinions on cricket: 'There should not be politics in world sport.'
Best batting performance: 37* Warwickshire v Sussex, Nuneaton 1987
Best bowling performance: 8-37 Orange Free State v Transvaal, Johannesburg 1986–87

LAST SEASON: BATTING

	I.	N.O.	R.	H.S.	AV.
TEST					
1ST-CLASS	10	3	111	37*	15.85
INT					
RAL	4	2	23	13*	11.50
NAT.W.					
B & H	1	0	0		0.00

LAST SEASON: BOWLING

	O.	M.	R.	W.	AV.
TEST					
1ST-CLASS	301.4	36	1012	39	25.94
INT					
RAL	40	5	163	10	16.30
NAT.W.	29.2	4	88	10	8.80
B & H	23.2	3	91	7	13.00

CAREER: BATTING

	I.	N.O.	R.	H.S.	AV.
TEST					
1ST-CLASS	32	14	220	37*	12.22
INT					
RAL	4	2	23	13*	11.50
NAT.W.					
B & H	1	0	0		0.00

CAREER: BOWLING

	O.	M.	R.	W.	AV.
TEST					
1ST-CLASS	835.3	126	2632	107	24.59
INT					
RAL	40	5	163	10	16.30
NAT.W.	29.2	4	88	10	8.80
B & H	23.2	3	91	7	13.00

DOUGHTY, R. J. Surrey

Full Name: Richard John Doughty
Role: Right-hand bat, right-arm fast-medium bowler
Born: 17 November 1960, Bridlington, Yorkshire
Height: 6′ **Weight:** 12½st
Nickname: Dick
County debut: 1981 (Gloucestershire), 1985 (Surrey)
1st-Class 50s scored: 2
1st-Class 5 w. in innings: 2
One-Day 50s: 1
Place in batting averages: 168th av. 22.76 (1986 159th av. 23.90)
Place in bowling averages: 78th av. 34.50 (1986 19th av. 25.50)
1st-Class catches 1987: 2 (career 24)
Parents: Mary and Trevor
Wife and date of marriage: Elizabeth, 2 April 1982
Education: Scarborough College, Yorkshire

Qualifications: 3 O-levels, 4 CSEs
Jobs outside cricket: Ski technician
Cricketing superstitions or habits: Putting left boot on first; changing chewing gum every hour when in the field
Overseas tours: 'The Leg Trap tour of South Africa 1981, a Canadian team for which I guested.'
Cricketers particularly learnt from: Don Wilson, Geoff Arnold, Trevor Jesty
Cricketers particularly admired: Richard Hadlee, Malcolm Marshall
Off-season 1987–88: Preparing for 1988 season
Other sports played: Golf, rugby, skiing, tennis, fishing
Other sports followed: Motor racing, athletics, American football, soccer
Relaxations: Music, eating, watching TV, films, painting and cooking
Extras: 'After being released by Gloucestershire at the end of the 1984 season, I discovered in February 1985 that I had become a diabetic. With help and encouragement from my wife and friends I persisted in trying to carry on playing cricket and eventually won a place with Surrey. I hope this will encourage other diabetics to live a full life and an active sporting one.'
Best batting performance: 65 Surrey v Derbyshire, Derby 1985
Best bowling performance: 6-33 Surrey v Warwickshire, The Oval 1985

LAST SEASON: BATTING

	I.	N.O.	R.	H.S.	AV.
TEST					
1ST-CLASS	2	0	5	5	2.50
INT					
RAL	1	0	18	18	18.00
NAT.W.					
B & H					

LAST SEASON: BOWLING

	O.	M.	R.	W.	AV.
TEST					
1ST-CLASS	26	3	76	0	–
INT					
RAL	6	0	35	1	35.00
NAT.W.					
B & H					

CAREER: BATTING

	I.	N.O.	R.	H.S.	AV.
TEST					
1ST-CLASS	52	11	845	65	20.60
INT					
RAL	25	8	272	50*	16.00
NAT.W.	1	1	5	5*	–
B & H	7	0	122	31	17.42

CAREER: BOWLING

	O.	M.	R.	W.	AV.
TEST					
1ST-CLASS	815.5	129	2986	89	33.55
INT					
RAL	205.3	3	1132	21	53.90
NAT.W.	15	2	60	2	30.00
B & H	77	8	359	6	59.83

61. How many Championship matches were played in 1987: 166, 204, or 286?

62. What percentage of Championship games were drawn in 1987: 40%, 60%, or 80%?

63. Who, according to Middlesex's Simon Hughes, has the deepest voice in county cricket?

DOWNTON, P. R.   Middlesex

Full Name: Paul Rupert Downton
Role: Right-hand bat, wicket-keeper
Born: 4 April 1957, Farnborough, Kent
Height: 5′ 10″ **Weight:** 12st 4lbs
Nickname: Nobby
County debut: 1977 (Kent), 1980 (Middlesex)
County cap: 1979 (Kent), 1981 (Middlesex)
Test debut: 1980–81
No. of Tests: 27
No. of One-Day Internationals: 17
1000 runs in a season: 1
1st-Class 50s scored: 34
1st-Class 100s scored: 4
One-Day 50s: 7
Place in batting averages: 57th
av. 37.33 (1986 62nd av. 37.70)
Parents: George Charles and Jill Elizabeth
Wife and date of marriage: Alison, 19 October 1985
Family links with cricket: Father kept wicket for Kent 1948–49
Education: Sevenoaks School; Exeter University
Qualifications: 9 O-levels, 3 A-levels; Law degree (LLB); NCA Coaching Certificate
Jobs outside cricket: Stockbroker
Overseas tours: England Young Cricketers to West Indies, 1976; England to Pakistan and New Zealand, 1977; West Indies 1980–81 and 1986; India and Australia 1984–85

LAST SEASON: BATTING

	I.	N.O.	R.	H.S.	AV.
TEST					
1ST-CLASS	39	9	1120	103*	37.33
INT					
RAL	11	2	140	30	15.55
NAT.W.	1	0	3	3	3.00
B & H	3	1	150	80*	75.00

LAST SEASON: WICKET KEEPING

	C.	ST.	
TEST			
1ST-CLASS	57	8	
INT			
RAL	7	–	
NAT.W.	1	1	
B & H	2	1	

CAREER: BATTING

	I.	N.O.	R.	H.S.	AV.
TEST	43	7	701	74	19.47
1ST-CLASS	274	57	5607	126*	25.83
INT	14	4	193	44*	19.30
RAL	80	25	1192	70	21.67
NAT.W.	19	2	300	62	17.64
B & H	27	10	453	80*	26.64

CAREER: WICKET KEEPING

	C.	ST.	
TEST	61	5	
1ST-CLASS	473	69	
INT	12	2	
RAL	103	29	
NAT.W.	32	5	
B & H	34	9	

Overseas teams played for: Sandgate, Redcliffe 1981–82; Stellenbosch University 1983–84
Cricketers particularly learnt from: Father, Alan Knott, Clive Radley
Cricketers particularly admired: Alan Knott, Rod Marsh
Off-season 1987–88: Working for James Capel (stockbrokers) and playing for England in World Cup
Other sports played: Rugby (played in England U-19 squad 1975 and Exeter University 1st XV), golf, tennis
Other sports followed: American football
Relaxations: Reading
Extras: Made debut for Kent CCC in 1977, gaining cap in 1979. Played for Kent 2nd XI at age 16. Joined Middlesex in 1980
Opinions on cricket: 'We play too much cricket which inevitably leads to a dilution in quality. Each game should be a big game, but the system rarely allows that.'
Best batting performance: 126* Middlesex v Oxford University, Oxford 1986

EAST, D. E. Essex

Full Name: David Edward East
Role: Right-hand bat, wicket-keeper
Born: 27 July 1959, Clapton
Height: 5′ 10″ **Weight:** 12st 10lbs
Nickname: 'Various insults, but Ethel seems popular and Easty.'
County debut: 1981
County cap: 1982
1st-Class 50s scored: 13
1st-Class 100s scored: 3
Place in batting averages: 215th av. 15.48 (1986 181st av. 20.27)
Parents: Edward William and Joan Lillian
Wife and date of marriage: Jeanette Anne, 14 September 1984
Children: Matthew Davis Leonard, 8 November 1986
Family links with cricket: Father played club cricket for Hadley CC, an Essex touring side
Education: Millfields Primary; Hackney Downs School; University of East Anglia
Qualifications: BSc Hons in Biological Sciences. Advanced Cricket Coach
Jobs outside cricket: Has worked for shipping, insurance and finance brokers,

cricket coaching and now cricket administration. Cricket consultant to Pony Sports (UK) Ltd

Off-season 1987–88: Running the County Benefit season for 1988
Overseas teams played for: Avendale CC, Cape Town, 1984–85
Cricketing superstitions or habits: 'The number 111. Never take wicket-keeping pads off between sessions unless raining hard!'
Cricketers particularly learnt from: Alan Knott
Other sports played: Hockey, 'poor squash'
Other sports followed: Interested in most but loathes horse racing
Relaxations: Playing the piano, listening to various types of music, video, spending time at home; cooking (especially curry and Chinese)
Extras: Spent 1980 season with Northamptonshire 2nd XI. Played for Essex 2nd XI at 16. Gordon's Gin Wicket-keeper of the Year 1983. World record holder for most catches in an innings in first-class cricket, 8, on my birthday in 1985
Cricketing opinions: 'I believe that the "bad light" law is far too ambiguous and that it is interpreted badly by a great number of umpires, particularly when tail-end batsmen are subjected to fast, often short-pitched, bowling.'
Best batting performance: 131 Essex v Gloucestershire, Southend 1985

LAST SEASON: BATTING

	I.	N.O.	R.	H.S.	AV.
TEST					
1ST-CLASS	32	3	449	73	15.48
INT					
RAL	10	2	99	35	12.37
NAT.W.	2	1	13	13	13.00
B & H	3	0	36	32	12.00

LAST SEASON: WICKET KEEPING

	C.	ST.		
TEST				
1ST-CLASS	57	4		
INT				
RAL	5	2		
NAT.W.	6	–		
B & H	4	–		

CAREER: BATTING

	I.	N.O.	R.	H.S.	AV.
TEST					
1ST-CLASS	222	30	3882	131	20.21
INT					
RAL	48	16	389	43	12.15
NAT.W.	15	5	122	28	12.20
B & H	19	4	217	33	14.46

CAREER: WICKET KEEPING

	C.	ST.		
TEST				
1ST-CLASS	418	47		
INT				
RAL	78	14		
NAT.W.	27	3		
B & H	42	–		

EDMONDS, P. H.   Middlesex

Full Name: Phillippe Henri Edmonds
Role: Right-hand bat, slow left-arm bowler, 'self-confessed all-rounder'
Born: 8 March 1951, Lusaka
Height: 6' 2" **Weight:** 'Post Cambridge Diet', 14½st
Nickname: Goat, Henry, Rommel, Duke
County debut: 1971
County cap: 1974
Benefit: 1983 (£80,000)
Test debut: 1975
No. of Tests: 51
No. of One-Day Internationals: 29
50 wickets in a season: 11
1st-Class 50s scored: 22
1st-Class 100s scored: 3
1st-Class 5 w. in innings: 47
1st-Class 10 w. in match: 9
One-Day 50s: 2
Place in batting averages: 200th av. 17.33 (1986 213th av. 14.42)
Place in bowling averages: 91st av. 34.18 (1986 56th av. 29.23)
Strike rate 1987: 90.34 (career 69.09)
1st-Class catches 1987: 3 (career 342)
Wife: Frances
Education: Gilbert Rennie High School, Lusaka; Skinner's School, Tunbridge Wells; Cranbrook School; Cambridge University
Qualifications: MA Hons. Cantab.
Injuries 1987: 'Psychosomatic pains in the neck!'
Jobs outside cricket: 'Aspiring tycoon.'
Off-season 1987–88: 'Making enough money to pay the fines I accumulate during the playing season.'
Overseas tours: Pakistan and New Zealand 1977–78; Australia 1978–79; India and Australia 1984–85; West Indies 1986
Overseas teams played for: Eastern Province in 1975–76 Currie Cup
Other sports played: Rugby for Cambridge but missed blue. Squash
Relaxations: 'Read *Financial Times* avidly at breakfast.' Crosswords. Frances Edmonds: 'An interest if not a relaxation.'
Extras: Cambridge cricket blue 1971–72–73. Captain 1973. Vice-captain of Middlesex, 1980

Opinions on cricket: 'i. Too much of it. ii. Amateur when it should be professional, and professional when it should be amateur.'
Best batting performance: 142 Middlesex v Glamorgan, Swansea 1984
Best bowling performance: 8-53 Middlesex v Hampshire, Bournemouth 1984

LAST SEASON: BATTING

	I.	N.O.	R.	H.S.	AV.
TEST	7	4	66	24*	22.00
1ST-CLASS	11	2	142	32	15.77
INT					
RAL					
NAT.W.	1	0	0		0.00
B & H	2	0	27	14	13.50

LAST SEASON: BOWLING

	O.	M.	R.	W.	AV.
TEST	92.3	36	219	4	54.75
1ST-CLASS	389.2	124	875	28	31.25
INT					
RAL					
NAT.W.	22	3	76	2	38.00
B & H	11	1	27	1	27.00

CAREER: BATTING

	I.	N.O.	R.	H.S.	AV.
TEST	65	15	875	64	17.50
1ST-CLASS	430	76	6776	142	19.14
INT	18	7	116	20	10.54
RAL	115	29	1283	52	14.91
NAT.W.	28	9	368	63*	19.36
B & H	41	9	533	44*	16.65

CAREER: BOWLING

	O.	M.	R.	W.	AV.
TEST	199 1739.2	48 565	4273	125	34.18
1ST-CLASS	287 11914.2	72 3688	27660	1117	24.76
INT	28 218.2	1 18	965	26	37.11
RAL	972	74	4064	175	23.22
NAT.W.	408.2	66	1245	45	27.66
B & H	674.1	85	1457	66	22.07

ELLCOCK, R. M. Worcestershire

Full Name: Ricardo McDonald Ellcock
Role: Right-hand bat, right-arm fast bowler
Born: 17 June 1965, Barbados
Height: 5' 11" **Weight:** 13st
Nickname: Ricky
County debut: 1982
1st-Class catches 1987: 0 (career: 4)
Parents: Everson McDonald (deceased) and Ione Marian
Marital status: Single
Education: Welches Mixed School, Combermere, Barbados; Malvern College, England
Qualifications: 6 O-levels
Overseas tours: Around West Indies with Barbados
Overseas teams played for:
Combined Schools, Barbados, 1980; Carlton and Barbados
Cricketers particularly learnt from: Malcolm Marshall

132

Cricketers particularly admired: Alvin Kallicharran, Michael Holding
Other sports played: Table tennis, basketball
Other sports followed: Soccer, motor racing
Relaxations: Movies, music, TV
Best batting performance: 45* Worcestershire v Essex, Worcester 1984
Best bowling performance: 4-34 Worcestershire v Glamorgan, Worcester 1984

LAST SEASON: BATTING

	I.	N.O.	R.	H.S.	AV.
TEST					
1ST-CLASS					
INT					
RAL					
NAT.W.					
B & H					

LAST SEASON: BOWLING

	O.	M.	R.	W.	AV.
TEST					
1ST-CLASS	10	0	69	1	69.00
INT					
RAL					
NAT.W.					
B & H					

CAREER: BATTING

	I.	N.O.	R.	H.S.	AV.
TEST					
1ST-CLASS	36	10	344	45*	13.23
INT					
RAL	5	2	6	5*	2.00
NAT.W.	1	0	6	6	6.00
B & H	2	1	16	12	16.00

CAREER: BOWLING

	O.	M.	R.	W.	AV.
TEST					
1ST-CLASS	603.4	82	2197	68	32.30
INT					
RAL	61.3	4	235	13	18.07
NAT.W.	10	2	49	3	16.33
B & H	25	4	98	3	32.66

EMBUREY, J. E.   Middlesex

Full Name: John Ernest Emburey
Role: Right-hand bat, off-break bowler, slip or gully fielder
Born: 20 August 1952, Peckham
Height: 6' 2" **Weight:** 13st 12lbs
Nickname: Embers, Ernie, Knuckles
County debut: 1973
County cap: 1977
Benefit: 1986
Test debut: 1978
No. of Tests: 46
No. of One-Day Internationals: 36
50 wickets in a season: 9
1st-Class 50s scored: 28
1st-Class 100s scored: 2
1st-Class 5 w. in innings: 51
1st-Class 10 w. in match: 8
One-Day 50s: 1
Place in batting averages: 91st av. 32.27 (1986 190th av. 18.63)

Place in bowling averages: 106th av. 37.45 (1986 13th av. 22.35)
Strike rate 1987: 79.45 (career 67.80)
1st-Class catches 1987: 9 (career 277)
Parents: John and Rose
Wife and date of marriage: Susie, 20 September 1980
Children: Clare, 1 March 1983; Chloe, 31 October 1985
Family links with cricket: Brother, Stephen, represented London Schools Colts in 1977
Education: Peckham Manor Secondary School
Qualifications: O-levels, Advanced Cricket Coaching Certificate
Jobs outside cricket: 'No other jobs. Have been abroad coaching most years.'
Off-season 1987–88: Touring with England
Overseas tours: With England to Australia 1978–79 and 1979–80 (following injury to Geoff Miller), West Indies 1981 and 1986, India 1981–82; World Cup, Pakistan, Australia and New Zealand 1987–88
Overseas teams played for: St Kilda CC, Melbourne, 1979–80, 1984–85; Prahran, Melbourne, 1977–78; Western Province 1982–83, 1983–84
Cricketers particularly learnt from: 'All.'
Cricketers particularly admired: Ken Barrington
Other sports: Golf, squash
Relaxations: Reading
Extras: Played for Surrey Young Cricketers 1969–70. Middlesex vice-captain since 1983. Banned from Test cricket for three years after playing for England Rebels in South Africa. Hit 6 sixes in 7 balls for Western Province v Eastern Province 1983–84 (52* in 22 balls)
Best batting performance: 133 Middlesex v Essex, Chelmsford 1983
Best bowling performance: 7-36 Middlesex v Cambridge University, Cambridge 1977

LAST SEASON: BATTING

	I.	N.O.	R.	H.S.	AV.
TEST	5	0	162	58	32.40
1ST-CLASS	21	4	548	74	32.23
INT	2	0	41	25	20.50
RAL	5	2	57	26*	19.00
NAT.W.	1	0	11	11	11.00
B & H	3	0	17	14	5.66

LAST SEASON: BOWLING

	O.	M.	R.	W.	AV.
TEST	107	21	222	0	–
1ST-CLASS	463.3	131	1089	35	31.11
INT	33	4	118	3	39.33
RAL	49	1	235	13	18.07
NAT.W.	24	7	72	3	24.00
B & H	20.5	1	99	0	–

CAREER: BATTING

	I.	N.O.	R.	H.S.	AV.
TEST	68	14	1027	75	19.01
1ST-CLASS	327	68	5765	133	32.25
INT	27	7	295	34	14.75
RAL	106	37	1130	49	16.37
NAT.W.	20	6	292	36*	20.85
B & H	33	11	440	50	20.00

CAREER: BOWLING

	O.	M.	R.	W.	AV.
TEST	144.4 1763.2	49 529	3855	115	33.52
1ST-CLASS	155.1 9403.5	39 2828	21370	904	23.63
INT	344.1	29	1356	42	32.28
RAL	1056.5	93	4450	207	21.49
NAT.W.	362	64	939	34	27.61
B & H	411.4	73	1150	39	29.48

EVANS, K. P.   Nottinghamshire

Full Name: Kevin Paul Evans
Role: Right-hand bat, right-arm
medium bowler, slip fielder
Born: 10 September 1963, Calverton,
Nottingham
Height: 6′ 2″ **Weight:** 13st
Nickname: Ghost
County debut: 1984
1st-Class catches 1987: 0 (career 5)
Parents: Eric and Eileen
Marital status: Engaged
Family links with cricket: Brother
Russell taken onto Nottinghamshire
staff in 1985. Father played local
cricket
Education: William Lee Primary;
Colonel Frank Seely Comprehensive,
Calverton
Qualifications: 9 O-levels, 3 A-levels
Jobs outside cricket: Bank work
Off-season 1987–88: Labouring
Cricketing superstitions and habits: Left pad on first
Cricketers particularly learnt from: Mike Hendrick, Mike Bore, Bob White
Cricketers particularly admired: Richard Hadlee
Other sports played: Football, tennis, badminton, squash
Injuries 1987: 'Shoulder problem, and sore heel which prevented me bowling
for four weeks.'
Relaxations: Listening to music, reading
Opinions on cricket: 'Review of the Championship points system. Maybe give

LAST SEASON: BATTING

	I.	N.O.	R.	H.S.	AV.
TEST					
1ST-CLASS	1	0	21	21	21.00
INT					
RAL					
NAT.W.					
B & H					

LAST SEASON: BOWLING

	O.	M.	R.	W.	AV.
TEST					
1ST-CLASS	29.3	2	102	5	20.40
INT					
RAL	8	0	31	1	31.00
NAT.W.					
B & H					

CAREER: BATTING

	I.	N.O.	R.	H.S.	AV.
TEST					
1ST-CLASS	11	0	108	42	9.81
INT					
RAL	10	3	130	28	18.57
NAT.W.	3	0	19	10	6.33
B & H	2	1	22	20	22.00

CAREER: BOWLING

	O.	M.	R.	W.	AV.
TEST					
1ST-CLASS	158.5	26	562	9	62.44
INT					
RAL	89	2	538	14	38.42
NAT.W.	36	8	94	6	15.66
B & H	11	0	47	1	47.00

points to the team with a first innings lead so that the Championship is not decided totally on declarations and weather.'

Best batting performance: 42 Nottinghamshire v Cambridge University, Trent Bridge 1984

Best bowling performance: 3-65 Nottinghamshire v Pakistanis, Trent Bridge 1987

EVANS, R. J.   Nottinghamshire

Full Name: Russell John Evans
Role: Right-hand bat, occasional off-spin bowler, gully or slip fielder
Born: 1 October 1965, Calverton, Nottingham
Height: 6' **Weight:** 11st 11lbs
Nickname: Brains, GC, Rubber-head (by John Birch only)
1st-Class catches 1987: 1 (career 1)
Parents: Eric and Eileen
Marital status: Single
Family links with cricket: Brother Kevin on Nottinghamshire staff. Father played local cricket
Education: Colonel Frank Seely Comprehensive, Calverton
Qualifications: 8 O-levels, 3 A-levels
Jobs outside cricket: Driving jobs, warehouse work

Cricketing superstitions and habits: Left pad on first
Overseas teams played for: Papakura, New Zealand 1986–87

LAST SEASON: BATTING

	I.	N.O.	R.	H.S.	AV.
TEST					
1ST-CLASS	2	0	4	4	2.00
INT					
RAL	2	1	17	15*	17.00
NAT.W.					
B & H					

LAST SEASON: BOWLING

	O.	M.	R.	W.	AV.
TEST					
1ST-CLASS	2	0	10	0	–
INT					
RAL					
NAT.W.					
B & H					

CAREER: BATTING

	I.	N.O.	R.	H.S.	AV.
TEST					
1ST-CLASS	2	0	4	4	2.00
INT					
RAL	4	1	48	20	16.00
NAT.W.					
B & H					

CAREER: BOWLING

	O.	M.	R.	W.	AV.
TEST					
1ST-CLASS	2	0	10	0	–
INT					
RAL					
NAT.W.					
B & H					

Cricketers particularly learnt from: Mike Bore, Tim Robinson, Clive Rice
Cricketers particularly admired: Richard Hadlee, Clive Rice, Graham Gooch, Ian Botham
Other sports played: Football, tennis, squash, swimming
Other sports followed: Football, International rugby
Relaxations: Music, crosswords, watching videos
Injuries 1987: Transverse fracture of right thumb in mid July, did not play again for the rest of the season
Opinions on cricket: 'Bonus points should be altered for four-day cricket. There should be no limit of overs to gain bonus points. Playing a limited number of four-day games and the rest three-day games makes it difficult as it depends upon who you play. There will be more chance of a result in four-day cricket so if you get drawn against the weaker counties for the four-day game you can pick up points more easily.'
Best batting performance: 4 Nottinghamshire v Pakistanis, Trent Bridge 1987

FAIRBROTHER, N. H.   Lancashire

Full Name: Neil Harvey Fairbrother
Role: Left-hand bat, left-arm medium bowler
Born: 9 September 1963, Warrington, Cheshire
Height: 5′ 8″ **Weight:** 11st
Nicknames: Harvey, Farnsbarns, Little Ted
County debut: 1982
County cap: 1985
Test debut: 1987
No. of Tests: 1
No. of One-Day Internationals: 3
1000 runs in a season: 4
1st-Class 50s scored: 36
1st-Class 100s scored: 10
One-Day 50s: 12
One-Day 100s: 2
Place in batting averages: 29th av. 42.25 (1986 15th av. 48.68)
1st-Class catches 1987: 17 (career 67)
Parents: Leslie Robert and Barbara
Marital status: Single
Family links with cricket: Father and two uncles played local league cricket
Education: St Margaret's Church of England School, Oxford; Lymn Grammar School

Qualifications: 5 O-levels
Off-season 1987–88: Touring with England
Overseas tours: Denmark 1980 with North of England U-19; England to Sharjah 1987; World Cup, Pakistan, Australia and New Zealand 1987–88
Overseas teams played for: Eastern Suburbs CC, Canberra, Australia 1985–86
Cricketers particularly learnt from: 'All the senior players at Old Trafford have been a great help, particularly Messrs Fowler and Allott.'
Cricketers particularly admired: Clive Lloyd, Allan Border
Other sports played: Rugby, squash
Other sports followed: Football, rugby union, rugby league
Injuries 1987: Sprained ankle
Relaxations: Music and playing sport
Extras: 'I was named after the Australian cricketer Neil Harvey, who was my mum's favourite cricketer.' Three Tests and two U-19 one-day internationals v Young Australians 1983. Made full Test debut v Pakistan at Old Trafford 1987
Best batting performance: 164* Lancashire v Hampshire, Liverpool 1985
Best bowling performance: 2-91 Lancashire v Nottinghamshire, Old Trafford 1987

LAST SEASON: BATTING

	I.	N.O.	R.	H.S.	AV.
TEST	1	0	0		0.00
1ST-CLASS	29	6	1014	109*	44.08
INT					
RAL	10	2	440	102*	55.50
NAT.W.	1	0	87	87	87.00
B & H	3	0	106	54	35.33

LAST SEASON: BOWLING

	O.	M.	R.	W.	AV.
TEST					
1ST-CLASS	22	2	111	2	55.50
INT					
RAL					
NAT.W.					
B & H					

CAREER: BATTING

	I.	N.O.	R.	H.S.	AV.
TEST	1	0	0		0.00
1ST-CLASS	166	24	5586	164*	39.33
INT	3	0	52	32	17.33
RAL	54	11	1384	102*	32.18
NAT.W.	10	2	419	93*	52.37
B & H	16	4	388	54	32.33

CAREER: BOWLING

	O.	M.	R.	W.	AV.
TEST					
1ST-CLASS	78.1	21	255	4	63.75
INT					
RAL	2	0	15	0	–
NAT.W.	3	0	16	0	–
B & H					

64. Who was tipped as a second W. G. Grace, then lost an arm in the First World War, and became a great umpire?

65. What have Greenidge, Gooch, Gatting and Gavaskar got in common, apart from the letter 'G'?

66. What did Maynard of Glamorgan and Carr of Middlesex both do on 1 August 1987?

FALKNER, N. J. Surrey

Full Name: Nicholas James
Falkner
Role: Right-hand bat, right-arm
seamer, cover or mid-wicket
fielder
Born: 30 September 1962, Redhill
Height: 5′ 10½″ **Weight:** 12st 3lbs
Nickname: Beefy, Vulture, Falksy
County debut: 1984
1st-Class 50s scored: 2
1st-Class 100s scored: 2
One-Day 50s: 2
Place in batting averages: –
(1986 72nd av. 25.43)
1st-Class catches 1987: 3 (career 10)
Parents: John and Barbara
Family links with cricket:
Father plays club cricket for
Chipstead and Coulsdon

Education: Yardley Court; Reigate Grammar School
Wife and date of marriage: Jacqueline Patricia, 19 March 1988
Qualifications: 5 O-levels
Jobs outside cricket: Assistant buyer for Balfour Beatty Int Construction;
worked in insurance company
Off-season 1987–88: Working for NatWest Bank, Redhill
Cricketing superstitions or habits: Left pad on first. One of the last to leave
changing room
Overseas tours: Captained Surrey Schools to Australia 1980–81

LAST SEASON: BATTING

	I.	N.O.	R.	H.S.	AV.
TEST					
1ST-CLASS	5	0	66	29	13.20
INT					
RAL	1	0	52	52	52.00
NAT.W.					
B & H	3	1	59	58	29.50

CAREER: BATTING

	I.	N.O.	R.	H.S.	AV.
TEST					
1ST-CLASS	24	3	734	102	34.95
INT					
RAL	4	0	151	52	37.75
NAT.W.	2	0	36	36	18.00
B & H	4	1	61	58	20.33

LAST SEASON: BOWLING

	O.	M.	R.	W.	AV.
TEST					
1ST-CLASS					
INT					
RAL					
NAT.W.					

CAREER: BOWLING

	O.	M.	R.	W.	AV.
TEST					
1ST-CLASS	4	1	9	1	9.00
INT					
RAL					
NAT.W.					
B & H					

Overseas teams played for: Perth Cricket Club 1982–83, 1985–86; University Cricket Club, Perth 1986–87

Cricketers particularly learnt from: Les Smithers, Father ('Always give me sound advice')

Cricketers particularly admired: Ian Botham, John Goddey

Other sports played: Squash, golf, rugby

Other sports followed: All sports

Injuries 1987: Badly bruised ankle sustained in early season; also slight strain in back

Relaxations: Reading, playing chess, sleeping, pottering around in the garden

Extras: Scored a century on first team debut for Surrey, 101* v Cambridge University. 'I have taken only *one* first-class wicket, namely a Test captain – Imran Khan!'

Opinions on cricket: 'When the 110 overs are complete that should be it for the day even if all 110 overs are complete by 6.15 pm. Four-day games are a must. Every county would then play each other once only – a much fairer system. Only one overseas player per county staff!'

Best batting performance: 102 Surrey v Middlesex, Lord's 1986

Best bowling performance: 1-3 Surrey v Sussex, Guildford 1986

FARBRACE, P.   Kent

Full Name: Paul Farbrace
Role: Right-hand bat, wicket-keeper
Born: 7 July 1967, Ash, nr Canterbury
Height: 5′ 10″ **Weight:** 11st 7lbs
Nickname: Farby, Ugly
County debut: 1987
1st-Class 50s scored: 1
Parents: David and Betty
Wife and date of marriage: Elizabeth Jane, 27 July 1985
Children: Jemma Elizabeth, 30 March 1985
Family links with cricket: Father played village cricket, as do my two brothers – Ian plays for a Cardiff side in South Wales and Colin plays for Ash. Dad and eldest brothers both keep wicket
Education: Geoffrey Chaucer School, Canterbury

Qualifications: 2 O-levels, 6 CSEs, NCA Cricket Coaching Certificate and NCA Senior Coaching Award
Jobs outside cricket: Working for HM Customs and Excise
Off-season 1987–88: Working for HM Customs and Excise at Dover Eastern Docks
Cricketing superstitions or habits: 'Always arrive at ground very early, then lay all my kit out. Follow captain onto field, then on to collect ball off the umpire. Fiddle with pads, trousers and then gloves when keeping, in sequence before every ball. Too many to mention when batting.'
Overseas tours: Kent Schools U-17 XI to Canada 1983
Cricketers particularly learnt from: Alan Knott, Derek Underwood, Bob Woolmer, Colin Page
Cricketers particularly admired: Alan Knott, Derek Underwood
Other sports played: Football, golf, rugby, basketball
Other sports followed: All sports except horse racing
Injuries 1987: 'Back spasm forced me not to keep for one day of a three-day game.'
Relaxations: 'Reading and spending as much time with my wife and daughter.'
Extras: Played County Schools football, had England Schools U-18 trial, attracted attention from Notts County, then had extended trials with Coventry City when seventeen as a goalkeeper
Opinions on cricket: 'I would like to see wickets uncovered but also leave the bowlers' run-ups uncovered as well. More spinners would have to be used, making the keeper's job a little more interesting. I think that players should not put umpires under too much pressure, forcing them into making bad decisions. In particular, 2nd XI umpires who may not be quite as good as first-class umpires, are put under too much pressure by continual shouting by bowlers and close fielders. We all complain from time to time about decisions that go against us, but I'm sure we could help ourselves by being easier on the umpires.'
Best batting performance: 75* Kent v Yorkshire, Canterbury 1987

LAST SEASON: BATTING

	I.	N.O.	R.	H.S.	AV.
TEST					
1ST-CLASS	7	3	134	75*	33.50
INT					
RAL					
NAT.W.	1	0	4	4	4.00
B & H					

LAST SEASON: WICKET KEEPING

	C.	ST.		
TEST				
1ST-CLASS	11	–		
INT				
RAL				
NAT.W.	3	–		
B & H				

CAREER: BATTING

	I.	N.O.	R.	H.S.	AV.
TEST					
1ST-CLASS	7	3	134	75*	33.50
INT					
RAL					
NAT.W.	1	0	4	4	4.00
B & H					

CAREER: WICKET KEEPING

	C.	ST.		
TEST				
1ST-CLASS	11	–		
INT				
RAL				
NAT.W.	3	–		
B & H				

FELTHAM, M. A.   Surrey

Full Name: Mark Andrew Feltham
Role: Right-hand bat, right-arm
fast-medium bowler
Born: 26 June 1963, London
Height: 6' 2" **Weight:** 13st 10bs
Nickname: Felts, Felpsy, Boff or
Douglas
County debut: 1983
1st-Class 50s scored: 1
1st-Class 5 w. in innings: 2
Place in batting averages: 124th
av. 14.33 (1986 137th av. 26.33)
Place in bowling averages: 69th
av. 30.05 (1986 63rd av. 30.03)
Strike rate 1987: 61.85 (career 57.40)
1st-Class catches 1987: 6 (career 12)
Parents: Leonard William and
Patricia Louise
Marital status: Engaged to Debi

Family links with cricket: Mother involved in Ken Barrington Cricket Centre
Appeal; brother plays for Surrey Young Cricketers and League cricket
Education: Roehampton Church School; Tiffin Boys' School
Qualifications: 7 O-levels; Advanced Cricket Coach
Cricketing superstitions or habits: 'Left pad on before right. Have favourite
trousers, shirt etc, to bat in.'
Overseas tours: Australia, 1980, with Surrey Cricket Association U-19s;
Barbados, 1981, with MCC Young Professionals
Overseas teams played for: Glenwood High School Old Boys, Durban,
1984–85
Cricketers particularly learnt from: Sylvester Clarke, Pat Pocock, Mickey
Stewart, Geoff Arnold, Trevor Jesty
Cricketers particularly admired: Ian Botham, David Gower, Graham
Gooch, Sylvester Clarke, Gordon Greenidge
Other sports played: Football, snooker
Relaxations: Listening to music, crosswords – 'although only in *Sun* and *Star*!'
Extras: Played for England Schools at U-15 and U-19 levels. On the MCC
Young Professionals Staff 1981 and 1982
Opinions on cricket: 'With the 1988 first-class programme involving more days
cricket, it seems to me that the authorities are trying to get more and more
each year from the modern players. Why we couldn't have gone straight to 16
four-day games seems strange to me. Players should be allowed to play and
and earn a living wherever they wish without being put under pressure by

politicians. There are so many hypocrises on this subject it is disgraceful.'

Best batting performance: 76 Surrey v Gloucestershire, The Oval 1986
Best bowling performance: 5-62 Surrey v Warwickshire, Edgbaston 1984

LAST SEASON: BATTING

	I.	N.O.	R.	H.S.	AV.
TEST					
1ST-CLASS	12	3	129	39	14.33
INT					
RAL	6	1	35	17	7.00
NAT.W.	1	0	8	8	8.00
B & H	1	0	21	21	21.00

CAREER: BATTING

	I.	N.O.	R.	H.S.	AV.
TEST					
1ST-CLASS	43	13	607	76	20.23
INT					
RAL	24	10	179	37	12.78
NAT.W.	4	0	25	12	6.25
B & H	7	3	72	22*	18.00

LAST SEASON: BOWLING

	O.	M.	R.	W.	AV.
TEST					
1ST-CLASS	412.2	101	1202	40	30.05
INT					
RAL	68	1	315	9	35.00
NAT.W.	9	1	46	0	–
B & H	42	4	159	7	22.71

CAREER: BOWLING

	O.	M.	R.	W.	AV.
TEST					
1ST-CLASS	956.4	208	3113	100	31.13
INT					
RAL	230.2	8	1239	33	37.54
NAT.W.	44	8	164	5	32.80
B & H	112.2	13	461	14	32.92

FELTON, N. A. Somerset

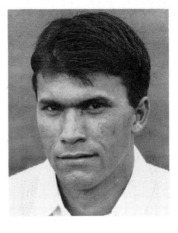

Full Name: Nigel Alfred Felton
Role: Left-hand bat
Born: 24 October 1960,
Guildford
Height: 5′ 7″ **Weight:** 10st 7lbs
Nickname: Will, Twiglets
County debut: 1982
1000 runs in a season: 2
1st-Class 50s scored: 24
1st-Class 100s scored: 7
One-Day 50s: 7
Place in batting averages: 134th
av. 26.68 (1986 103rd av. 30.29)
1st-Class catches 1987: 18 (career 39)
Parents: Ralph and Enid
Marital status: Single
Family links with cricket:
Father played club cricket
Education: Hawes Down Secondary
School, West Wickham, Kent; Millfield School, Street, Somerset; Loughborough University
Qualifications: 6 O-levels, 2 A-levels, BSc(Hons), Cert of Education PE/ Sports Sciences, qualified teacher

Jobs outside cricket: Teaching, digging holes, working with Somerset CCC marketing dept
Cricketing superstitions or habits: Always put right pad on first
Overseas tours: English Schools to India 1976–77; Young England to Australia 1978; Scorpions CC to Sierra Leone 1987
Overseas teams played for: Waneroro CC, Perth, Western Australia 1985–86
Other sports followed: Most ball games
Other sports played: Most winter sports
Relaxations: Music, reading, relaxing at home
Extras: Joined Somerset in July 1981. Played a season for Kent in 1980 after leaving Millfield and before going to Loughborough. Left Kent at pre-season training 1981, due to the size of the staff. Joined Somerset at end of first year at Loughborough
Opinions on cricket: 'In favour of four-day cricket.'
Best batting performance: 173* Somerset v Kent, Taunton 1983

LAST SEASON: BATTING

	I.	N.O.	R.	H.S.	AV.
TEST					
1ST-CLASS	41	0	1094	110	26.68
INT					
RAL	9	1	141	42	17.62
NAT.W.	1	0	8	8	8.00
B & H	5	0	61	31	12.20

LAST SEASON: BOWLING

	O.	M.	R.	W.	AV.
TEST					
1ST-CLASS					
INT					
RAL					
NAT.W.					
B & H					

CAREER: BATTING

	I.	N.O.	R.	H.S.	AV.
TEST					
1ST-CLASS	153	5	4267	173*	28.83
INT					
RAL	36	5	765	96	24.67
NAT.W.	8	2	303	87	50.50
B & H	7	0	64	31	9.14

CAREER: BOWLING

	O.	M.	R.	W.	AV.
TEST					
1ST-CLASS	1.1	0	7	0	–
INT					
RAL	1	0	7	0	–
NAT.W.					
B & H					

67. Which Australian player, who died in 1987, scored 99 in his first Test?

68. Who was runner up in the Britannic Assurance County Championship in 1987?

69. Who was runner up in the Refuge Assurance Sunday League in 1987?

FERRIS, G. J. F.　　　Leicestershire

Full Name: George John Fitzgerald Ferris
Role: Right-hand bat, right-arm fast bowler
Born: 18 October 1964, Urlings Village, Antigua
Height: 6' 3" **Weight:** 14st
Nickname: Ferro, Slugo
County debut: 1983
1st-Class 5 w. in innings: 7
1st-Class 10 w. in match: 1
Place in batting averages: 248th av. 10.33
Place in bowling averages: 15th av. 21.98
Strike rate 1987: 41.44 (career 47.20)
1st-Class catches 1987: 0 (career 9)
Children: Imran J., 12 November 1984
Education: Jenning's Secondary
Jobs outside cricket: Physical education teacher
Off-season 1987–88: Coaching and playing in Shell Shield
Overseas tours: With Young West Indies to Zimbabwe 1983
Overseas teams played for: Leeward Islands; Matabeleland
Cricketers particularly learnt from: Andy Roberts (neighbour in Antigua), Ken Higgs
Cricketers particularly admired: Michael Holding, Malcolm Marshall
Other sports played: Soccer, tennis
Other sports followed: Soccer, tennis, American basketball
Relaxations: Listening to music

LAST SEASON: BATTING

	I.	N.O.	R.	H.S.	AV.
TEST					
1ST-CLASS	13	4	93	25	10.33
INT					
RAL	1	0	0		0.00
NAT.W.	2	1	2	2*	2.00
B & H					

LAST SEASON: BOWLING

	O.	M.	R.	W.	AV.
TEST					
1ST-CLASS	359.1	69	1143	52	21.98
INT					
RAL	29	0	134	4	33.50
NAT.W.	19	2	90	3	30.00
B & H					

CAREER: BATTING

	I.	N.O.	R.	H.S.	AV.
TEST					
1ST-CLASS	58	26	351	26	10.96
INT					
RAL	4	2	15	9*	7.50
NAT.W.	2	1	2	2*	2.00
B & H	1	1	0	0*	–

CAREER: BOWLING

	O.	M.	R.	W.	AV.
TEST					
1ST-CLASS	1369	253	4544	174	26.11
INT					
RAL	91.5	3	412	13	31.69
NAT.W.	34	3	148	3	49.33
B & H	40	3	209	6	34.83

Best batting performance: 26 Leeward Islands v Guyana, Nevis 1982–83
Best bowling performance: 7-42 Leicestershire v Glamorgan, Hinckley 1983

FIELD-BUSS, M. Essex

Full Name: Michael Field-Buss
Role: Right-hand bat, off-break
bowler
Born: 23 September 1964, Malta
Height: 5′ 10″ **Weight:** 11st
Nickname: Mouse
County debut: 1987
Parents: Monica and Gwyn
Marital status: Single
Family links with cricket:
Father played local cricket
with Ilford RAFA
Education: Wanstead High School
Qualifications: Qualified coach
Jobs outside cricket: Warehouseman
Off-season 1987–88: Playing club
cricket in Melbourne, Australia for
Werribee CC

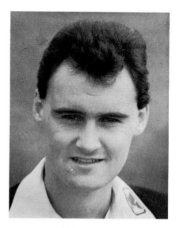

Cricketing superstitions or habits:
Left pad on first. Try not to knock-up too much before game. Never watch too
much cricket before going into bat.
Overseas teams played for: Werribee CC, 1986–87
Cricketers particularly learnt from: Bill Morris (coach at Ilford Cricket
School during my early years), Ray East, David Acfield, Geoff Miller
Cricketers particularly admired: Graham Gooch (makes batting look easy),
John Emburey
Other sports played: Football
Other sports followed: Watching Leyton Orient FC ('although I support
Arsenal')
Relaxations: Listening to music
Best batting performance: 34* Essex v Middlesex, Lords 1987

LAST SEASON: BATTING

	I.	N.O.	R.	H.S.	AV.
TEST					
1ST-CLASS	4	1	56	34*	18.66
INT					
RAL					
NAT.W.					
B & H					

CAREER: BATTING

	I.	N.O.	R.	H.S.	AV.
TEST					
1ST-CLASS	4	1	56	34*	18.66
INT					
RAL					
NAT.W.					
B & H					

FINNEY, R. J.   Derbyshire

Full Name: Roger John Finney
Role: Right-hand bat, left-arm
slow bowler
Born: 2 August 1960, Darley Dale,
Derbyshire
Height: 6′ 1″ **Weight:** 12st 10lbs
Nickname: Albert
County debut: 1982
County cap: 1985
50 wickets in a season: 2
1st-Class 50s scored: 13
1st-Class 5 w. in innings: 8
One-Day 50s: 1
Place in batting averages: 149th
av. 24.51 (1986 166th av. 23.08)
Place in bowling averages: 75th
av. 31.07 (1986 92nd av. 37.75)
Strike rate 1987: 61.18 (career 57.41)
1st-Class catches 1987: 11 (career 26)
Parents: Roy and Janet
Wife and date of marriage: Carol, 21 September 1985
Children: Ryan Anthony Edward, 28 April 1987
Family links with cricket: Father played and captained local side for many years
Education: Lady Manners School, Bakewell
Qualifications: O-levels
Jobs outside cricket: Production clerk and sports salesman
Off-season 1987–88: 'Developing my business'
Cricketing superstitions or habits: Left pad on first

LAST SEASON: BATTING

	I.	N.O.	R.	H.S.	AV.
TEST					
1ST-CLASS	36	5	760	77	24.51
INT					
RAL	7	2	54	14	10.80
NAT.W.	1	0	40	40	40.00
B & H	2	0	8	6	4.00

CAREER: BATTING

	I.	N.O.	R.	H.S.	AV.
TEST					
1ST-CLASS	163	27	2714	82	19.95
INT					
RAL	44	12	523	50*	16.34
NAT.W.	3	1	59	40	29.50
B & H	11	2	160	46	17.77

LAST SEASON: BOWLING

	O.	M.	R.	W.	AV.
TEST					
1ST-CLASS	275.2	57	839	27	31.07
INT					
RAL	13.4	0	65	0	
NAT.W.	2	0	17	0	
B & H	16	1	66	1	66.00

CAREER: BOWLING

	O.	M.	R.	W.	AV.
TEST					
1ST-CLASS	1923.2	376	6129	201	30.49
INT					
RAL	322.3	18	1589	49	32.42
NAT.W.	40	7	128	4	32.00
B & H	118.5	14	460	15	30.66

Overseas teams played for: Alexandrians, Pietermaritzburg, South Africa, 1980–82, 1984–85
Cricketers particularly learnt from: Phil Russell (Derbyshire coach), Don Wilson (head coach at Lord's)
Other sports played: Rugby, football, golf
Relaxations: 'Music, movies, good beer, eating at a good restaurant.'
Injuries 1987: 'A back injury from 1986 forced me to change from medium pace to left-arm spin.'
Extras: Before joining Derbyshire, spent two years with the MCC Young Professionals
Best batting performance: 82 Derbyshire v Gloucestershire, Derby 1985
Best bowling performance: 7-54 Derbyshire v Leicestershire, Leicester 1986

FITTON, J. D.   Lancashire

Full Name: John Dexter Fitton
Role: Left-hand bat, right-arm spin bowler
Born: 24 August 1965, Rochdale
Height: 5' 10" **Weight:** 12st
Nickname: Ted, Bert, Lord
County debut: 1987
Parents: Derek and Jean
Marital status: Single
Family links with cricket: Father dedicated cricketer for 20 years with Littleboro in Central Lancashire League and Robinsons in North Manchester League
Education: Redbrook and Auder Hill Upper School
Qualifications: 2 O-levels, Diploma in Business Studies
Jobs outside cricket: Worked for three years as an Export Administrator at a steel springs works
Off-season 1987–88: In Christchurch, New Zealand
Cricket superstitions or habits: 'Always clean my teeth prior to the start of a match.'
Cricketers particularly learnt from: Dad, Paul Rocca (Rochdale coach), John Abrahams
Cricketers particularly admired: David Gower, Clive Lloyd, Richard Hadlee, Neil Fairbrother
Other sports played: Football, golf, badminton
Other sports followed: Manchester City FC, greyhound racing at Oldham

Relaxations: Listening to music, watching comedy films and shows
Extras: Youngest player to take 50 wickets and score 500 runs for Rochdale in the Central Lancashire League. Scored 1000 runs a season for three seasons running in the same league
Best batting performance: 3 Lancashire v Hampshire, Southampton 1987
Best bowling performance: 1-23 Lancashire v Hampshire, Southampton 1987

LAST SEASON: BATTING

	I.	N.O.	R.	H.S.	AV.
TEST					
1ST-CLASS	1	0	3	3	3.00
INT					
RAL	1	0	0		0.00
NAT.W.					
B & H					

LAST SEASON: BOWLING

	O.	M.	R.	W.	AV.
TEST					
1ST-CLASS	7	0	23	1	23.00
INT					
RAL	8	0	25	1	25.00
NAT.W.					
B & H					

CAREER: BATTING

	I.	N.O.	R.	H.S.	AV.
TEST					
1ST-CLASS	1	0	3	3	3.00
INT					
RAL	1	0	0		0.00
NAT.W.					
B & H					

CAREER: BOWLING

	O.	M.	R.	W.	AV.
TEST					
1ST-CLASS	7	0	23	1	23.00
INT					
RAL	8	0	25	1	25.00
NAT.W.					
B & H					

FLETCHER, K. W. R.   Essex

Full Name: Keith William Robert Fletcher
Role: Right-hand bat, leg-break bowler
Born: 20 May 1944, Worcester
Height: 5' 10" **Weight:** 10st 7lbs
Nickname: Gnome, Fletch
County debut: 1962
County cap: 1963
Benefit: 1973
Testimonial: 1982
Test debut: 1968
No. of Tests: 59
No. of One-Day Internationals: 24
1000 runs in a season: 20
1st-Class 50s scored: 220
1st-Class 100s scored: 61
1st-class 200s scored: 2
1st-Class 5 w. in innings: 1
One-Day 50s: 62

One-Day 100s: 2
Place in batting averages: 117th av. 28.90 (1986 84th av. 33.45)
1st-Class catches 1987: 12 (career 634)
Parents: Joseph and Doris
Wife and date of marriage: Susan Elizabeth, 22 March 1969
Children: Tamara Jane, 2 August 1970; Sara Jane, 19 December 1972
Jobs outside cricket: Has worked as oil representative
Overseas tours: Pakistan 1966–67; Ceylon and Pakistan 1968–69; Australia and New Zealand 1970–71 and 1974–75; India, Sri Lanka and Pakistan 1972–73; West Indies 1973–74; India, Sri Lanka and Australia 1976–77; India and Sri Lanka 1981–82 as captain
Other sports played: Golf, fishing, shooting partridge – 'my second favourite sport after cricket.'
Relaxations: Gardening
Extras: Played for Essex at age of 17. Captained Essex from 1974 and led county to first County Championship in 1979, second in 1983 and third in 1984. Also Benson & Hedges Cup in 1979 and John Player Special League in 1981, 1984 and 1985. Won NatWest Trophy in 1985 to become first captain to win all four domestic competitions. Scored two centuries in a match, 111 and 102* v Nottinghamshire, at Nottingham in 1976. Awarded OBE in 1985 New Year's Honours list. Gave up captaincy at end of 1985 season, but frequently stood in for Graham Gooch to lead Essex in 1986 Championship-winning season. Appointed Essex captain again for 1988
Best batting performance: 228* Essex v Sussex, Hastings 1968
Best bowling performance: 5-41 Essex v Middlesex, Colchester 1979

LAST SEASON: BATTING

	I.	N.O.	R.	H.S.	AV.
TEST					
1ST-CLASS	35	3	925	121	28.90
INT					
RAL	8	0	98	52	12.25
NAT.W.	3	0	79	49	26.33
B & H	4	1	70	39	23.33

CAREER: BATTING

	I.	N.O.	R.	H.S.	AV.
TEST	96	14	3272	216	39.90
1ST-CLASS	1057	153	34090	228*	37.71
INT	22	3	757	131	39.84
RAL	228	38	5622	99*	29.58
NAT.W.	44	4	1036	97	25.90
B & H	74	14	2023	101*	33.71

LAST SEASON: BOWLING

	O.	M.	R.	W.	AV.
TEST					
1ST-CLASS	2	0	9	0	–
INT					
RAL					
NAT.W.					
B & H					

CAREER: BOWLING

	O.	M.	R.	W.	AV.
TEST	20 20.5	1 5	193	2	96.50
1ST-CLASS	64.3 367.3	6 52	2103	49	42.91
INT					
RAL	2.5	0	37	1	37.00
NAT.W.	10.3	1	43	2	21.50
B & H	4.4	0	30	1	30.00

FLETCHER, S. D. Yorkshire

Full Name: Stuart David Fletcher
Role: Right-hand bat, right-arm
medium bowler
Born: 8 June 1964, Keighley
Height: 5′ 10″ **Weight:** 12st
Nickname: Fletch, Godber, Norman
Stanley, Dr Death, Ghostie
County debut: 1983
1st-Class 5 w. in innings: 1
Place in batting averages:
249th av. 10.16
Place in bowling averages: 55th
av. 28.21 (1986 101st av. 41.06)
Strike rate 1987: 51.96 (career 67.81)
1st-Class catches 1987: 3 (career 9)
Parents: Brough and Norma Hilda
Family links with cricket:
Father played league cricket
Education: Woodhouse Primary;
Reins Wood Secondary
Qualifications: O-level English and Woodwork; City and Guilds in coach-building
Jobs outside cricket: Coachbuilder at Reliance Commercial Vehicles Ltd.
Worked at Ben Shaw's Pop Merchants
Overseas tours: Holland 1983 with National Cricket Association U-19s
Cricketers particularly learnt from: Father, Phil Carrick, Steve Oldham
Cricketers particularly admired: Ian Botham, Arnie Sidebottom
Other sports played: Snooker, golf, football
Other sports followed: Watches Leeds United FC

LAST SEASON: BATTING

	I.	N.O.	R.	H.S.	AV.
TEST					
1ST-CLASS	12	6	61	15	10.16
INT					
RAL	4	3	7	6	7.00
NAT.W.	1	0	0		0.00
B & H	1	0	1	1	1.00

LAST SEASON: BOWLING

	O.	M.	R.	W.	AV.
TEST					
1ST-CLASS	277.1	55	903	32	28.21
INT					
RAL	82	5	416	18	23.11
NAT.W.	21	2	68	1	68.00
B & H	68.1	6	258	15	17.20

CAREER: BATTING

	I.	N.O.	R.	H.S.	AV.
TEST					
1ST-CLASS	41	19	365	28*	16.59
INT					
RAL	9	6	21	8	7.00
NAT.W.	3	2	3	2*	3.00
B & H	2	1	1	1	1.00

CAREER: BOWLING

	O.	M.	R.	W.	AV.
TEST					
1ST-CLASS	1254.4	227	4086	111	36.81
INT					
RAL	274.4	9	1456	46	31.65
NAT.W.	80	11	265	10	26.50
B & H	131.4	7	549	19	28.89

Relaxations: Watching TV, snooker and golf
Extras: Played in the Yorkshire U-19s who were the first Yorkshire side to win the Cambridge and Oxford Festival, 1983
Best batting performance: 28* Yorkshire v Kent, Tunbridge Wells 1984
Best bowling performance: 5-90 Yorkshire v Middlesex, Leeds 1986

FOLLEY, I.   Lancashire

Full Name: Ian Folley
Role: Right-hand bat, slow left-arm bowler, 'night-watchman and Mendo's bag packer'
Born: 9 January 1963
Height: 5' 9½" **Weight:** 11st
Nickname: Thatch, Vicar, Reverend
County debut: 1982
County cap: 1987
1st-Class 50s scored: 1
1st-Class 5 w. in innings: 8
1st-Class 10 w. in match: 1
Place in batting averages: 223rd av. 14.79
Place in bowling averages: 31st av. 25.20 (1986 84th av. 36.06)
Strike rate 1987: 61.06 (career 68.43)
1st-Class catches 1987: 18 (career 51)
Parents: James and Constance
Wife and date of marriage: Julie, 27 September 1986
Education: Mansfield High School, Nelson; Colne College
Qualifications: 5 O-levels, Business Studies diploma
Off-season 1987–88: In Tasmania
Cricketers particularly learnt from: D. Bloodworth
Cricketers particularly admired: Clive Lloyd, Ian Botham
Overseas tours: Barbados 1982 with Lancashire; Denmark 1981 with NCA
Other sports played: Golf, squash, football
Other sports followed: 'I'm a bad watcher.'
Extras: Represented Lancashire Schools U-15s and U-19s as captain. Represented Lancashire Federation 1979–81. Played for England U-19 v India U-19 in three 'Tests' in 1981. Young England v West Indies (three 'Tests') and two One-Day 'Internationals'. Debut for Lancashire v Cambridge University at Fenners. In 1984 changed from left-arm medium pace to slow left-arm bowler
Relaxations: Listening to Caribbean music, driving ('except taking Simmo')

Best batting performance: 69 Lancashire v Yorkshire, Old Trafford 1985
Best bowling performance: 7-15 Lancashire v Warwickshire, Southport 1987

LAST SEASON: BATTING

	I.	N.O.	R.	H.S.	AV.
TEST					
1ST-CLASS	31	7	355	38	14.79
INT					
RAL	3	1	23	19	11.50
NAT.W.					
B & H					

LAST SEASON: BOWLING

	O.	M.	R.	W.	AV.
TEST					
1ST-CLASS	753.1	240	1865	74	25.20
INT					
RAL	20	1	115	4	28.75
NAT.W.					
B & H					

CAREER: BATTING

	I.	N.O.	R.	H.S.	AV.
TEST					
1ST-CLASS	131	34	1249	69	12.87
INT					
RAL	10	6	56	19	14.00
NAT.W.	2	1	4	3*	4.00
B & H	5	5	21	11*	–

CAREER: BOWLING

	O.	M.	R.	W.	AV.
TEST					
1ST-CLASS	2452.1	677	6536	215	30.40
INT					
RAL	144	5	703	14	50.21
NAT.W.	39.3	4	114	7	16.28
B & H	84	17	215	14	15.36

FOSTER, D. J.   Somerset

Full Name: Daren Joseph Foster
Role: Right-hand bat, right-arm fast medium bowler
Born: 14 March 1966, London
Height: 5' 8" **Weight:** 10st
Nickname: DJ
County debut: 1986
Place in bowling averages: 107th av. 37.69
Strike rate 1987: 51.61 (career 53.92)
1st-Class catches 1987: 3 (career 3)
Parents: Vivian and Sadie
Children: Marcella and Daren
Education: Somerset School; Southgate Technical College
Qualifications: 2 O-levels, 1 CSE, City and Guilds Clerical Studies
Off-season 1987–88: Training
Cricketers particularly learnt from:
Malcolm Marshall, Hallam Moseley
Cricketers particularly admired: Malcolm Marshall, Michael Holding, Gary Sobers, Joel Garner, Viv Richards, Ian Botham
Other sports played: Football, basketball, badminton
Other sports followed: American football, athletics
Relaxations: 'Music, pretty girls.'

Extras: Appeared for Middlesex and Surrey 2nd XI's in 1985
Best batting performance: 16 Somerset v Hampshire, Weston-super-Mare 1987
Best bowling performance: 4-56 Somerset v Glamorgan, Weston-super-Mare 1987

LAST SEASON: BATTING

	I.	N.O.	R.	H.S.	AV.
TEST					
1ST-CLASS	3	1	25	16	12.50
INT					
RAL	1	1	3	3*	–
NAT.W.					
B & H					

LAST SEASON: BOWLING

	O.	M.	R.	W.	AV.
TEST					
1ST-CLASS	111.5	10	490	13	37.69
INT					
RAL	20	1	90	0	–
NAT.W.					
B & H					

CAREER: BATTING

	I.	N.O.	R.	H.S.	AV.
TEST					
1ST-CLASS	4	1	25	16	8.33
INT					
RAL	1	1	3	3*	–
NAT.W.					
B & H					

CAREER: BOWLING

	O.	M.	R.	W.	AV.
TEST					
1ST-CLASS	116.5	10	519	13	39.92
INT					
RAL	21	1	90	0	–
NAT.W.					
B & H					

FOSTER, N. A. Essex

Full Name: Neil Alan Foster
Role: Right-hand bat, right-arm fast-medium bowler, outfielder
Born: 6 May 1962, Colchester
Height: 6′ 4″ **Weight:** 12st 12lbs
Nickname: Fozzy
County debut: 1980
County cap: 1983
Test debut: 1983
No. of Tests: 19
No. of One-Day Internationals: 34
50 wickets in a season: 5
1st-Class 50s scored: 5
1st-Class 5 w. in innings: 27
1st-Class 10 w. in match: 4
One-Day 50s: 4
Place in batting averages: 175th
av. 19.95 (1986 185th av. 19.91)
Place in bowling averages: 16th
av. 22.00 (1986 14th av. 22.37)
Strike rate 1987: 47.08 (career 38.41)
1st-Class catches 1987: 5 (career 51)

Parents: Jean and Alan
Wife and date of marriage: Romany, 21 September 1985
Family links with cricket: Father and brother both play local cricket
Education: Broomgrove Infant & Junior Schools; Philip Morant Comprehensive, Colchester
Qualifications: 9 O-levels, 1 A-level, NCA Coaching Award
Jobs outside cricket: Played semi-pro football for some years
Off-season 1987–88: Touring with England
Overseas tours: NCA tour of Canada 1978; Young England XI tour of West Indies 1980; England tour of New Zealand and Pakistan 1983–84, India and Australia 1984–85, West Indies 1986; World Cup, Pakistan, Australia and New Zealand 1987–88
Overseas teams played for: Glenorchy (Tasmania) 1981–82 on Whitbread Scholarship
Cricketers particularly learnt from: All Essex players
Cricketers particularly admired: Dennis Lillee, Richard Hadlee
Other sports played: Nearly any sport. Has had football trials with Colchester and Ipswich. Golf. 'Nothing horsey.'
Injuries 1987: Back and ankle strain
Relaxations: 'My Boxer dog – Bertie; kennel name: Tropical Burlington Bertie.'
Extras: Was summoned from school at short notice to play for Essex v Kent at Ilford to open bowling. First ball went for 4 wides, but he went on to dismiss Woolmer, Tavaré and Ealham for 51 runs in 15 overs. Played for Young England v Young India 1981
Opinions on cricket: 'I'm fed up seeing all the critics always complaining about our performances. This does not just apply to cricket but all our sports with national sides. Those critics build people up to knock them down and I find it incredible that they get paid to do just that. It's about time we gave people a fair chance and showed them some loyalty.'
Best batting performance: 74* England v Queensland, Brisbane 1986–87
Best bowling performance: 8-107 England v Pakistan, Leeds 1987

LAST SEASON: BATTING

	I.	N.O.	R.	H.S.	AV.
TEST	6	0	93	29	15.50
1ST-CLASS	17	2	326	49*	21.73
INT	2	1	19	14*	19.00
RAL	5	3	99	35*	49.50
NAT.W.	3	1	71	26	35.50
B & H	3	2	76	37*	76.00

CAREER: BATTING

	I.	N.O.	R.	H.S.	AV.
TEST	27	3	220	29	9.16
1ST-CLASS	121	32	1938	74*	21.77
INT	17	6	96	24	8.72
RAL	18	6	201	38	16.75
NAT.W.	7	1	100	26	16.66
B & H	11	5	126	37*	21.00

LAST SEASON: BOWLING

	O.	M.	R.	W.	AV.
TEST	137.2	36	339	15	22.60
1ST-CLASS	537.3	111	1553	71	21.87
INT	33	2	90	7	12.85
RAL	48.5	4	254	11	23.09
NAT.W.	28	6	73	5	14.60
B & H	38.2	4	114	8	14.25

CAREER: BOWLING

	O.	M.	R.	W.	AV.
TEST	641.1	141	1819	54	33.68
1ST-CLASS	2637.2	619	9969	432	23.07
INT	301	18	1242	36	34.50
RAL	256.1	17	1198	51	23.49
NAT.W.	140.2	26	390	25	15.60
B & H	244.3	21	903	46	19.63

FOWLER, G.   Lancashire

Full Name: Graeme Fowler
Role: Left-hand opening bat,
cover fielder, occasional wicket-
keeper
Born: 20 April 1957, Accrington
Height: 5′ 9″ **Weight:** 'Near 11st'
Nickname: Fow, Fox, Foxy
County debut: 1979
County cap: 1981
Test debut: 1982
No. of Tests: 21
No. of One-Day Internationals: 26
1000 runs in a season: 6
1st-Class 50s scored: 62
1st-Class 100s scored: 23
1st-Class 200s scored: 2
One-Day 50s: 24
One-Day 100s: 5

Place in batting averages: 15th
av. 47.36 (1986 55th av. 38.76)
1st-Class catches 1987: 12 (career 84 + 5 stumpings)
Education: Accrington Grammar School; Bede College, Durham University
Wife: Stephanie
Jobs outside cricket: Qualified teacher, swimming teacher, Advanced Cricket Coach
Overseas tours: England to Australia and New Zealand 1982–83; New Zealand and Pakistan 1983–84; India and Australia 1984–85
Overseas teams played for: Scarborough, Perth, Western Australia; Tasmania, 1981–82

LAST SEASON: BATTING

	I.	N.O.	R.	H.S.	AV.
TEST					
1ST-CLASS	43	5	1800	169*	47.36
INT					
RAL	11	2	391	100*	43.44
NAT.W.	1	0	9	9	9.00
B & H	4	0	21	16	5.25

CAREER: BATTING

	I.	N.O.	R.	H.S.	AV.
TEST	37	0	1307	201	35.32
1ST-CLASS	261	16	9359	226	38.20
INT	26	2	744	81*	31.00
RAL	94	7	2557	112	29.39
NAT.W.	17	0	530	122	31.17
B & H	35	1	811	97	23.85

LAST SEASON: BOWLING

	O.	M.	R.	W.	AV.
TEST					
1ST-CLASS	13.3	3	43	3	14.33
INT					
RAL					
NAT.W.					

CAREER: BOWLING

	O.	M.	R.	W.	AV.
TEST	3	1	11	0	–
1ST-CLASS	36.5	5	160	7	22.85
INT					
RAL	1	0	1	0	–
NAT.W.					

Extras: At 15 he was the youngest opener in the Lancashire League. Scored two consecutive centuries v Warwickshire in July 1982 with aid of a runner. Never played cricket until he was 12. Played for Accrington and Rawtenstall in Lancashire League. In 1975 and 1976 played for ESCA, NAYC, and MCC Schools and Young England

Best batting performance: 226 Lancashire v Kent, Maidstone 1984

Best bowling performance: 2-34 Lancashire v Warwickshire, Old Trafford 1986

FRASER, A. R. C. Middlesex

Full Name: Angus Robert Charles Fraser

Role: Right-hand bat, right-arm fast-medium bowler, outfielder

Born: 8 August 1965, Billinge, Lancashire

Height: 6′ 6″ **Weight:** 15st 7lbs

Nickname: Gus, Gnat, Jacques Cousteau ('due to a bad round of golf in La Manga'), Boots, Plod

County debut: 1984

Place in batting averages: 240th av. 11.88

Place in bowling averages: 92nd av. 34.22

Strike rate 1987: 77.47 (career 57.26)

1st-Class catches 1987: 4 (career 4)

Parents: Don and Irene

Marital status: Single

Family links with cricket: Father keen follower of cricket; brother Alastair on Middlesex staff

Education: Gayton High School, Harrow; Orange High School, Edgware

Qualifications: 7 O-levels, coaching certificate

Jobs outside cricket: Worked at Makro in North Acton 1984–85; labouring for Norwest Holst Construction Ltd 1986–87

Off-season 1987–88: Coaching and playing in New Zealand

Cricketing superstitions or habits: 'Zorro in the slip area.'

Overseas tours: Barbados with Thames Valley Gentlemen 1985; La Manga with Middlesex 1985 and 1986

Overseas teams played for: Plimmerton CC, Wellington 1985–86

Cricketers particularly learnt from: Don Bennett, Don Wilson, Clive Desmond, Norman Jacobs

Cricketers particularly admired: Dennis Lillee, Richard Hadlee

Other sports played: Rugby, golf, football
Relaxations: Playing other sports, watching Liverpool FC, driving
Extras: Took 3 wickets in 4 balls v Glamorgan in 1985
Opinions on cricket: 'England should play whom they like, whether it be players or other countries, and not be told what to do by other cricket-playing countries.'
Best batting performance: 38 Middlesex v Kent, Canterbury 1987
Best bowling performance: 4-48 Middlesex v Cambridge University, Cambridge 1985

LAST SEASON: BATTING

	I.	N.O.	R.	H.S.	AV.
TEST					
1ST-CLASS	22	5	202	38	11.88
INT					
RAL	4	1	14	6*	4.66
NAT.W.					
B & H	1	0	4	4	4.00

LAST SEASON: BOWLING

	O.	M.	R.	W.	AV.
TEST					
1ST-CLASS	568.1	143	1506	44	34.22
INT					
RAL	69	6	294	3	98.00
NAT.W.	12	5	24	1	24.00
B & H	11	1	37	0	–

CAREER: BATTING

	I.	N.O.	R.	H.S.	AV.
TEST					
1ST-CLASS	30	6	244	38	10.16
INT					
RAL	11	4	40	9*	5.71
NAT.W.					
B & H	3	0	6	4	2.00

CAREER: BOWLING

	O.	M.	R.	W.	AV.
TEST					
1ST-CLASS	601.2	195	2119	63	33.63
INT					
RAL	168	10	731	17	43.00
NAT.W.	12	5	24	1	24.00
B & H	60	5	206	3	68.66

FRASER-DARLING, D. Nottinghamshire

Full Name: David Fraser-Darling
Role: Right-hand bat, right-arm
fast-medium bowler
Born: 30 September 1963, Sheffield
Height: 6′ 5″ **Weight:** 14st 7lbs
Nickname: Meat, Axe, Lazer, Beefy
County debut: 1984
1st-Class 50s scored: 1
1st-Class 5 w. in innings: 1
1st-Class catches 1987: 1 (career 9)
Parents: Alasdair and Mary
Marital status: Single
Education: Edinburgh University
Qualifications: 7 O-levels, 3 A-levels,
Junior Cricket Coach
Jobs outside cricket: Coaching
Off-season 1987–88:
Coaching and playing in New Zealand

Cricketing superstitions or habits: Left sock, shoe, pad, etc on first
Overseas teams played for: Upper Hutt CC, Wellington, New Zealand 1987–88
Cricketers particularly learnt from: Mike Hendrick, David Stanley, Tony Dyer and all at Nottinghamshire
Cricketers particularly admired: Mike Hendrick, Richard Hadlee, Geoff Boycott
Other sports played: Football, rugby, golf – 'of a low standard'
Other sports followed: Rugby, horse racing, American football
Injuries 1987: Shoulder and shin strains
Relaxations: Eating out in poor restaurants, TV, films
Extras: Played rugby for Scotland U-19 v England, Wales and Ireland 1981
Best batting performance: 61 Nottinghamshire v Northamptonshire, Northampton 1986
Best bowling performance: 5-84 Nottinghamshire v Northamptonshire, Northampton 1986

LAST SEASON: BATTING

	I.	N.O.	R.	H.S.	AV.
TEST					
1ST-CLASS	3	1	49	33	24.50
INT					
RAL	2	0	11	11	5.50
NAT.W.					
B & H					

LAST SEASON: BOWLING

	O.	M.	R.	W.	AV.
TEST					
1ST-CLASS	46	6	242	2	121.00
INT					
RAL	10	1	46	3	15.33
NAT.W.					
B & H	3	0	12	0	–

CAREER: BATTING

	I.	N.O.	R.	H.S.	AV.
TEST					
1ST-CLASS	11	2	224	61	24.88
INT					
RAL	6	1	31	11	6.20
NAT.W.					
B & H					

CAREER: BOWLING

	O.	M.	R.	W.	AV.
TEST					
1ST-CLASS	214	34	846	17	49.76
INT					
RAL	53	4	272	12	22.66
NAT.W.					
B & H	3	0	12	0	–

70. Who was the only player in the M.C.C. Bicentenary Test whose name began with 'G' not to make a century?

71. Which Essex cricketer played soccer for England in the 1966 World Cup?

72. Who was the most recent man to be capped by England at both cricket and rugger?

73. Who captained England at both cricket and soccer?

FRENCH, B. N.　　Nottinghamshire

Full Name: Bruce Nicholas French
Role: Right-hand bat, wicket-keeper
Born: 13 August 1959, Warsop,
Nottinghamshire
Height: 5' 8" **Weight:** 10st
Nickname: Frog
County debut: 1976
County cap: 1980
Test debut: 1986
No. of Tests: 9
No. of One-Day Internationals: 7
1st-Class 50s scored: 18
Place in batting averages: 173rd
av. 20.27 (1986 184th av. 20.05)
Parents: Maurice and Betty
Wife and date of marriage:
Ellen Rose, 9 March 1978
Children: Charles Daniel,
31 August 1978; Catherine Ellen,
28 December 1980

Family links with cricket: Brothers, Neil, David, Charlie, Joe, play for Welbeck CC. Father, Treasurer Welbeck CC
Education: Meden School, Warsop
Qualifications: O-level and CSE
Jobs outside cricket: Warehouseman, window cleaner, bricklayer's labourer
Off-season 1987–88: On tour with England
Overseas tours: England to India and Sri Lanka 1984–85; West Indies 1985–86; Australia 1986–87; World Cup, Pakistan, Australia and New Zealand 1987–88

LAST SEASON: BATTING

	I.	N.O.	R.	H.S.	AV.
TEST	5	1	103	59	25.75
1ST-CLASS	15	1	262	70	18.71
INT					
RAL	4	0	20	9	5.00
NAT.W.	4	0	42	35	10.50
B & H	3	1	3	2*	1.50

CAREER: BATTING

	I.	N.O.	R.	H.S.	AV.
TEST	12	3	158	59	17.55
1ST-CLASS	299	58	4495	98	18.65
INT	5	2	25	9*	8.33
RAL	64	21	579	37	13.46
NAT.W.	18	5	291	49	22.38
B & H	29	6	219	48*	9.52

LAST SEASON: WICKET KEEPING

	C.	ST.			
TEST	4	–			
1ST-CLASS	41	4			
INT					
RAL	6	–			
NAT.W.	4	1			
B & H	4	–			

CAREER: WICKET KEEPING

	C.	ST.			
TEST	16	–			
1ST-CLASS	543	60			
INT	8	2			
RAL	75	12			
NAT.W.	28	4			
B & H	40	8			

Cricketing superstitions or habits: Right pad on before left when keeping wicket
Cricketers particularly learnt from: Bob Taylor, Clive Rice
Other sports played: Rock climbing, fell walking and all aspects of mountaineering
Relaxations: Reading, pipe smoking and drinking Theakston's Ale
Extras: Youngest player to play for Nottinghamshire, aged 16 years 10 months. Equalled Nottinghamshire record for dismissals in match with 10 (7ct 3st), and dismissals in innings with 6 catches. New Nottinghamshire record for dismissals in a season with 87 (75ct 12st). Wicket-Keeper of the Year 1984
Best batting performance: 98 Nottinghamshire v Lancashire, Trent Bridge 1984

GATTING, M. W.   Middlesex

Full Name: Michael William Gatting
Role: Right-hand bat, right-arm medium bowler, slip fielder
Born: 6 June 1957, Kingsbury, Middlesex
Height: 5′ 10″ **Weight:** 14st
Nickname: Gatt
County debut: 1975
County cap: 1977
Benefit: 1988
Test debut: 1977–78
No. of Tests: 58
No. of One-Day Internationals: 63
1000 runs in a season: 9
1st-Class 50s scored: 96
1st-Class 100s scored: 44
1st-Class 200s scored: 3
1st-Class 5 w. in innings: 2
One-Day 50s: 40
One-Day 100s: 5
Place in batting averages: 4th av. 60.96 (1986 8th av. 54.55)
1st-Class catches 1987: 13 (career 278)
Parents: Bill and Vera
Wife and date of marriage: Elaine, September 1980
Children: Andrew, 21 January 1983; James, 11 July 1986
Family links with cricket: Father used to play club cricket
Education: Wykeham Primary School; John Kelly Boys' High School
Off-season 1987–88: Touring with England

Overseas tours: Toured West Indies with England Young Cricketers 1979–80; with England in West Indies 1981 and 1986; India 1981–82; New Zealand and Pakistan 1983–84; World Cup, Pakistan, Australia and New Zealand 1987–88

Overseas teams played for: Club cricket in Sydney, Australia 1979–80

Cricketers particularly admired: Gary Sobers

Other sports: Football, tennis, swimming, golf, squash

Other sports followed: Soccer (Spurs) and snooker

Relaxations: Reading (Tolkien), crosswords

Extras: Played for England Young Cricketers 1974. Young Cricketer of the Year 1981. Captain of Middlesex since 1983. Captain of England since 1986. Author of *Limited Overs* and *Triumph in Australia*

Best batting performance: 258 Middlesex v Somerset, Bath 1984

Best bowling performance: 5-34 Middlesex v Glamorgan, Swansea 1982

LAST SEASON: BATTING

	I.	N.O.	R.	H.S.	AV.
TEST	8	1	445	150*	63.57
1ST-CLASS	21	1	1201	196	60.05
INT	2	1	43	41	43.00
RAL	6	1	238	96*	47.60
NAT.W.	2	1	118	73	118.00
B & H	3	0	42	31	14.00

LAST SEASON: BOWLING

	O.	M.	R.	W.	AV.
TEST	22	5	40	0	–
1ST-CLASS	51	10	169	5	33.80
INT					
RAL	19.4	0	108	1	108.00
NAT.W.	6	0	33	0	–
B & H	12.1	1	55	2	27.50

CAREER: BATTING

	I.	N.O.	R.	H.S.	AV.
TEST	100	13	3563	207	40.95
1ST-CLASS	377	58	15523	258	48.66
INT	60	14	1241	115*	26.97
RAL	124	14	3281	109	29.82
NAT.W.	36	9	1128	118*	41.77
B & H	51	15	1696	143*	47.11

CAREER: BOWLING

	O.	M.	R.	W.	AV.
TEST	101	24	256	2	128.00
1ST-CLASS	19.7 1231.2	3 293	3384	136	24.88
INT	61.2	14	320	10	32.00
RAL	413.5	12	2040	71	28.73
NAT.W.	142.3	21	536	16	33.50
B & H	190.5	15	762	37	20.59

74. What was unusual about the late England and Yorkshire player W. E. (Bill) Bowes' signature?

75. Which England player has a Union Jack tattooed on his left shoulder?

76. What is the nickname of Mike Watkinson of Lancashire?

77. What were the most northerly and southerly grounds in the 1987 World Cup?

GIFFORD, N. Warwickshire

Full Name: Norman Gifford
Role: Left-hand bat, slow left-arm
bowler
Born: 30 March 1940, Ulverston,
Cumbria
Height: 5′ 10″ **Weight:** 13st 7lbs
Nickname: Giff
County debut: 1960 (Worcestershire),
1983 (Warwickshire)
County cap: 1961 (Worcestershire),
1983 (Warwickshire)
Benefit: 1974 (£11,047)
Testimonial: 1981
Test debut: 1964
No. of Tests: 15

No. of One-Day Internationals: 2
50 wickets in a season: 22
1st-Class 50s scored: 3
1st-Class 5 w. in innings: 93
1st-Class 10 w. in match: 14
Place in batting averages: 251st av. 10.07
Place in bowling averages: 77th av. 31.13 (1986 27th av. 23.88)
Strike-rate 1987: 75.50 (career 61.77)
1st-Class catches 1987: 1 (career 316)
Family links with cricket: Father played amateur cricket and football, and was
also cricket umpire
Qualifications: City & Guilds
Jobs outside cricket: Estimator, industrial decorating

LAST SEASON: BATTING

	I.	N.O.	R.	H.S.	AV.
TEST					
1ST-CLASS	25	12	131	36	10.07
INT					
RAL	1	1	6	6*	
NAT.W.					
B & H	1	0	0		0.00

LAST SEASON: BOWLING

	O.	M.	R.	W.	AV.
TEST					
1ST-CLASS	453	136	1121	36	31.13
INT					
RAL	58.3	1	271	7	38.71
NAT.W.	28	7	60	6	10.00
B & H	26	1	94	4	23.50

CAREER: BATTING

	I.	N.O.	R.	H.S.	AV.
TEST	20	9	179	25*	16.27
1ST-CLASS	760	244	6764	89	13.10
INT	1	0	0		0.00
RAL	137	60	950	32*	12.33
NAT.W.	33	7	221	38	8.50
B & H	42	14	300	33	10.71

CAREER: BOWLING

	O.	M.	R.	W.	AV.
TEST	146.4	14			
	514	17	1026	33	31.09
1ST-CLASS	20263.2	6847	46729	2004	23.31
INT	20	1	50	4	25.00
RAL	1630.4	96	7357	275	26.75
NAT.W.	479	104	1388	60	23.13
B & H	703.3	102	2373	87	27.27

Cricketers particularly learnt from: Charles Hallows (Worcestershire coach)
Overseas tours: Rest of World to Australia 1971–72; India, Pakistan and Sri Lanka 1972–73; Sharjah 1985 as captain
Other sports: Football, golf
Relaxations: Horse racing
Extras: Was awarded MBE in 1979. Played in one match for Rest of World v Australia 1972. Suffers badly from the sun on overseas tours. Took 100 wickets in a season four times. Uncle, Harry Gifford, played rugby union for England. Released by Worcestershire at end of 1982 season. Debut 1960, cap 1961, captain 1971–80. England selector, and assistant manager of England side on tour. Warwickshire captain 1985–87
Best batting performance: 89 Worcestershire v Oxford University, Oxford 1963
Best bowling performance: 8-28 Worcestershire v Yorkshire, Sheffield 1968

GILL, P. Leicestershire

Full Name: Paul Gill
Role: Right-hand bat,
wicket-keeper
Born: 31 May 1963, Greenfield,
Manchester
Height: 5′ 7″
County debut: 1986
Education: Saddleworth and
Grange Schools
Extras: Has played in 2nd XI
since 1983
Best batting performance: 17
Leicestershire v Essex,
Southend 1986

LAST SEASON: BATTING

	I.	N.O.	R.	H.S.	AV.
TEST					
1ST-CLASS					
INT					
RAL	1	1	0	0*	–
NAT.W.					
B & H					

LAST SEASON: WICKET KEEPING

	C.	ST.			
TEST					
1ST-CLASS					
INT					
RAL	1	–			
NAT.W.					
B & H					

CAREER: BATTING

	I.	N.O.	R.	H.S.	AV.
TEST					
1ST-CLASS	11	4	68	17	9.71
INT					
RAL	3	2	5	3	5.00
NAT.W.					
B & H					

CAREER: WICKET KEEPING

	C.	ST.			
TEST					
1ST-CLASS	24	–			
INT					
RAL	2	–			
NAT.W.					
B & H					

GLADWIN, C. Essex

Full Name: Christopher Gladwin
Role: Left-hand bat, right-arm
medium bowler, first slip or
cover fielder
Born: 10 May 1962, East Ham
Height: 6′ 2″ **Weight:** 14st
Nickname: Gladares, Guvnor
County debut: 1982
County cap: 1984
1000 runs in a season: 1
1st-Class 50s scored: 17
1st-Class 100s scored: 1
One-Day 50s: 3
Place in batting averages: 159th
av. 22.60 (1986 221st av. 13.00)
1st-Class catches 1987: 5 (career 31)
Parents: Edna and Ron
Wife and date of marriage: Julia,
20 September 1986
Family links with cricket: Father and brother played club cricket
Education: Brampton Junior and Landon Crescent
Qualifications: 5 CSEs
Jobs outside cricket: Pipe fitter, qualified cricket coach
Overseas tours: England Schoolboys to West Indies 1977
Cricketers particularly learnt from: Graham Gooch, Keith Fletcher, Allan
Border
Other sports played: Football, snooker, athletics, table tennis, basketball,
golf

Other sports followed: Snooker, football
Best batting performance: 162 Essex v Cambridge University, Cambridge 1984

LAST SEASON: BATTING

	I.	N.O.	R.	H.S.	AV.
TEST					
1ST-CLASS	17	2	339	77	22.60
INT					
RAL	2	0	43	37	21.50
NAT.W.					
B & H	4	0	27	24	6.75

LAST SEASON: BOWLING

	O.	M.	R.	W.	AV.
TEST					
1ST-CLASS					
INT					
RAL					
NAT.W.					
B & H					

CAREER: BATTING

	I.	N.O.	R.	H.S.	AV.
TEST					
1ST-CLASS	114	7	2953	162	27.59
INT					
RAL	30	1	580	75	20.00
NAT.W.	4	0	26	15	6.50
B & H	11	0	205	41	18.63

CAREER: BOWLING

	O.	M.	R.	W.	AV.
TEST					
1ST-CLASS	21	1	71	0	–
INT					
RAL					
NAT.W.					
B & H					

GOLDSMITH, S. C. Derbyshire

Full Name: Steven Clive Goldsmith
Role: Right-hand bat, right-arm medium or off-break bowler, cover fielder
Born: 19 December 1964, Ashford, Kent
Height: 5′ 10½″ **Weight:** 12st 7lbs
Nickname: Goldy
County debut: 1987 (Kent)
1st-Class catches 1987: 1 (career 1)
Parents: Tony and Daphne
Marital status: Engaged
Family links with cricket:
Father played for Folkestone, captaining them for a few years
Education: Simon Langton Grammar School, Canterbury
Qualifications: 8 O-levels, NCA Coaching Award
Jobs outside cricket: Bar Steward, waiter, undertaker's assistant
Off-season 1987–88: Coaching
Cricketing superstitions or habits: 'I always buckle my pads on the same way and smoke a fair bit as well as biting my nails down to the elbows.'

Overseas tours: ESCA U-19 to Zimbabwe 1982–83; UK Upsetters to Trinidad and Tobago 1985
Overseas teams played for: Essendon, Melbourne 1984
Cricketers particularly learnt from: Colin Page, Chris Tavaré, Simon Hinks
Cricketers particularly admired: Chris Tavaré, David Gower, Eldine Baptiste
Other sports played: Hockey, golf, snooker – 'and anything else where a ball moves'
Other sports followed: All sports
Injuries 1987: Back injury due to chipped lower vertebrae
Relaxations: Golf, serious drinking, comedy on TV, Van Morrison's music, Tony Hancock, Richard Pryor
Extras: Spent four years on Kent staff. Only wicket in first-class cricket was David Gower's. Released at end of 1987 season. Joined Derbyshire for 1988
Cricketing opinions: 'With the introduction of uncovered wickets, the bowlers' run-ups should also be uncovered. Four-day cricket would be a good idea but should be confined to say half the matches at the end of the season. All professional cricketers should be made to take an NCA Coaching Award.'
Best batting performance: 25 Kent v Leicestershire, Canterbury 1987
Best bowling performance: 1-37 Kent v Leicestershire, Canterbury 1987

LAST SEASON: BATTING

	I.	N.O.	R.	H.S.	AV.
TEST					
1ST-CLASS	4	0	49	25	12.25
INT					
RAL	2	1	43	43*	43.00
NAT.W.					
B & H					

CAREER: BATTING

	I.	N.O.	R.	H.S.	AV.
TEST					
1ST-CLASS	4	0	49	25	12.50
INT					
RAL	3	1	49	43*	24.50
NAT.W.					
B & H					

LAST SEASON: BOWLING

	O.	M.	R.	W.	AV.
TEST					
1ST-CLASS	6	0	37	1	37.00
INT					
RAL					
NAT.W.					
B & H					

CAREER: BOWLING

	O.	M.	R.	W.	AV.
TEST					
1ST-CLASS	6	0	37	1	37.00
INT					
RAL					
NAT.W.					
B & H					

78. Who was the leading run-scorer in county cricket in 1987, and how many runs did he score?

GOOCH, G. A.   Essex

Full Name: Graham Alan Gooch
Role: Right-hand bat, right-arm
medium bowler
Born: 23 July 1953, Leytonstone
Height: 6′ 0″ **Weight:** 13st
Nickname: Zap, Goochie
County debut: 1973
County cap: 1975
Benefit: 1985 (£153,906)
Test debut: 1975
No. of Tests: 59
No. of One-Day Internationals: 52
1000 runs in a season: 11
1st-Class 50s scored: 121
1st-Class 100s scored: 56
1st-Class 200s scored: 4
1st-Class 5 w. in innings: 3
One-Day 50s: 73
One-Day 100s: 19
Place in batting averages: 48th av. 38.88 (1986 60th av. 38.15)
Place in bowling averages: 85th av. 32.71
Strike rate 1987: 71.57 (career 72.35)
1st-Class catches 1987: 20 (career 348)
Parents: Alfred and Rose
Wife and date of marriage: Brenda, 23 October 1976
Children: Hannah, Megan, Sally
Family links with cricket: Father played local cricket for East Ham Corinthians. Second cousin, Graham Saville, played for Essex CCC and is now NCA coach for Eastern England
Education: Norlington Junior High School, Leytonstone
Qualifications: Four-year apprenticeship in toolmaking
Jobs outside cricket: Toolmaker
Off-season 1987–88: Touring with England
Overseas tours: West Indies with England Young Cricketers 1972; England to Australia 1978–79 and 1979–80; West Indies 1981 and 1986; India 1981–82; World Cup, Pakistan and New Zealand 1987–88
Overseas teams played for: Perth CC, Western Australia; Western Province, South Africa
Cricketers particularly admired: Bob Taylor, a model sportsman; Mike Procter for his enthusiasm; Barry Richards for his ability
Other sports played: Squash, soccer, golf. Trains in off-season with West Ham United FC
Relaxations: 'Relaxing at home.'

Extras: Published *Batting* in 1980. Wrote a diary of 1981 cricket year. Autobiography *Out of the Wilderness* published by Collins in 1985. Hit a century before lunch v Leicester, 28 June 1981. Kept wicket for England v India in 2nd innings at Madras, 1982. Captained English rebel team in South Africa, 1982 and was banned from Test cricket for three years. Hit a hole in one at Tollygunge Golf Club during England's tour in India, 1981–82. Bowled both right and left handed in a Test match (v India at Calcutta, imitating Dilip Doshi). Shared in second wicket record partnership for county, 321 with K. S. McEwan v Northamptonshire, at Ilford in 1978. Holds record (jointly) for Essex for catches in match (6) and innings (5) v Gloucestershire, 1982. Appointed Essex captain 1986. Resigned captaincy at end of 1987 season
Best batting performance: 227 Essex v Derbyshire, Chesterfield 1984
Best bowling performance: 7-14 Essex v Worcestershire, Ilford 1982

LAST SEASON: BATTING

	I.	N.O.	R.	H.S.	AV.
TEST					
1ST-CLASS	41	6	1361	171	38.88
INT	1	0	9	9	9.00
RAL	10	1	258	70*	28.66
NAT.W.	3	0	112	76	37.33
B & H	4	1	69	53*	23.00

LAST SEASON: BOWLING

	O.	M.	R.	W.	AV.
TEST					
1ST-CLASS	250.3	64	687	21	32.71
INT	3	0	12	0	–
RAL	60.1	3	268	6	44.66
NAT.W.	28	2	76	2	38.00
B & H	29	5	95	5	19.00

CAREER: BATTING

	I.	N.O.	R.	H.S.	AV.
TEST	105	4	3746	196	37.08
1ST-CLASS	512	47	20450	227	43.97
INT	51	3	1792	129*	37.33
RAL	175	15	5063	176	31.64
NAT.W.	33	1	1338	133	41.81
B & H	69	5	3007	198*	46.98

CAREER: BOWLING

	O.	M.	R.	W.	AV.
TEST	6 228.3	1 66	546	13	42.00
1ST-CLASS	1 2174.1	0 544	5917	187	31.64
INT	174.5	10	837	19	44.05
RAL	670.2	35	2997	109	27.49
NAT.W.	219.1	30	659	21	31.38
B & H	378.5	41	1238	44	28.13

79. Who was the leading wicket-taker in county cricket in 1987, and how many wickets did he take?

GOULD, I. J.　　　　　　　　　Sussex

Full Name: Ian James Gould
Role: Left-hand bat, wicket-keeper
Born: 19 August 1957, Taplow, Bucks
Height: 5′ 8″ **Weight:** 11st 10lbs
Nickname: Gunner
County debut: 1975 (Middlesex), 1981 (Sussex)
County cap: 1977 (Middlesex), 1981 (Sussex)
No. of One-Day Internationals: 18
1000 runs in a season: 1
1st-Class 50s scored: 32
1st-Class 100s scored: 3
One-Day 50s scored: 14
Place in batting averages: 88th av. 33.00 (1986 93rd av. 32.55)
Parents: Doreen and George
Wife: Jo
Children: Gemma Louise, 30 June 1984
Education: Westgate School
Jobs outside cricket: Barman

LAST SEASON: BATTING

	I.	N.O.	R.	H.S.	AV.
TEST					
1ST-CLASS	29	5	792	111	33.00
INT					
RAL	11	2	287	74	31.88
NAT.W.	1	0	15	15	15.00
B & H	4	1	94	65	31.33

CAREER: BATTING

	I.	N.O.	R.	H.S.	AV.
TEST					
1ST-CLASS	323	53	6776	128	25.09
INT	14	2	155	42	12.91
RAL	132	22	2074	74	18.85
NAT.W.	21	2	398	88	20.94
B & H	42	7	630	72	18.00

LAST SEASON: WICKET KEEPING

	C.	ST.
TEST		
1ST-CLASS	23	–
INT		
RAL	8	–
NAT.W.	–	–
B & H	2	2

LAST SEASON: BOWLING

	O.	M.	R.	W.	AV.
TEST					
1ST-CLASS	1	0	1	0	
INT					
RAL					
NAT.W.					
B & H	0.2	0	0	1	0.00

CAREER: BOWLING

	O.	M.	R.	W.	AV.
TEST					
1ST-CLASS	40	2	221	2	110.50
INT					
RAL					
NAT.W.					
B & H	0.2	0	0	1	0.00

CAREER: WICKET KEEPING

	C.	ST.
TEST		
1ST-CLASS	476	67
INT	15	3
RAL	128	21
NAT.W.	25	7
B & H	48	5

Overseas tours: West Indies with England Young Cricketers 1976; with England in Australia and New Zealand 1982–83
Overseas teams played for: Auckland, 1980
Other sports played: Amateur footballer for Slough Town FC at full-back; golf, swimming
Relaxations: Spending time with the family
Extras: Made debut for Middlesex in 1975, gaining cap in 1977. Was offered contract for 1981 by Middlesex but chose to join Sussex. Vice-captain in 1985. Took over captaincy during 1986 and officially appointed for 1987. Resigned captaincy at end of 1987 season
Best batting performance: 128 Middlesex v Worcestershire, Worcester 1978
Best bowling performance: 2-67 Sussex v Derbyshire, Eastbourne 1986

GOWER, D. I. Leicestershire

Full Name: David Ivon Gower
Role: Left-hand bat, off-break bowler
Born: 1 April 1957, Tunbridge Wells
Height: 5' 11¾" **Weight:** 11st 11lbs
Nickname: Stoat, Lubo
County debut: 1975
County cap: 1977
Benefit: 1987
Test debut: 1978
No. of Tests: 96
No. of One-Day Internationals: 102
1000 runs in a season: 7
1st-Class 50s scored: 100
1st-Class 100s scored: 36
1st-Class 200s scored: 2
One-Day 50s: 40
One-Day 100s: 17
Place in batting averages: 23rd av. 44.33 (1986 51st av. 39.52)
1st-Class catches 1987: 5 (career 193 + 1 stumping)
Parents: Richard Hallam and Sylvia Mary
Marital status: Single
Family links with cricket: Father was club cricketer
Education: Marlborough House School; King's School, Canterbury; University College, London (did not complete law course)
Qualifications: 8 O-levels, 3 A-levels
Jobs outside cricket: Worked at Bostik Ltd

Off-season 1987–88: 'On the Cresta Run or in bed.'

Cricketing superstitions or habits: 'They change every time they go wrong.'

Overseas tours: Toured South Africa with English Schools XI 1974–75 and West Indies with England Young Cricketers 1976; Derrick Robins XI to Canada 1976 and to Far East 1977; with England to Australia 1978–79 and 1979–80, West Indies 1980–1, India 1981–82, Australia and New Zealand 1982–83, New Zealand 1983–84, India and Australia 1984–85, West Indies 1986

Overseas teams played for: Claremont-Cottesloe, Perth, Australia, 1977–78

Cricketers particularly learnt from: 'Ray Illingworth and Jack Birkenshaw, amongst many others whose advice has come my way.'

Cricketers particularly admired: Graeme Pollock and many others

Other sports played: Golf, squash, water and snow skiing. Rode in a British bobsled at Cervinia (Italy) in 1985, diving

Other sports followed: Rugby, bob-sledding

Relaxations: Music, photographs, beaches, vintage port and crosswords

Extras: Played for King's Canterbury 1st XI for three years. Has written *Anyone for Cricket* jointly with Bob Taylor about the 1978–79 Australian tour. Also *With Time to Spare*, an autobiography published in 1980. Published *Heroes and Contemporaries* (Collins) 1983, *A Right Ambition* (Collins) 1986. Writes regular column for *Wisden Cricket Monthly*. England captain 1984–86; Leicestershire captain 1984–86. Declared himself not available for England tour 1987–88. Reappointed Leicestershire captain for 1988

Best batting performance: 215 England v Australia, Edgbaston 1985

Best bowling performance: 3-47 Leicestershire v Essex, Leicester 1977

LAST SEASON: BATTING

	I.	N.O.	R.	H.S.	AV.
TEST	8	0	236	61	29.50
1ST-CLASS	23	4	961	125	50.57
INT	3	1	50	24	25.00
RAL	9	0	319	94	35.44
NAT.W.	4	0	214	79	53.50
B & H	4	1	49	38*	16.33

LAST SEASON: BOWLING

	O.	M.	R.	W.	AV.
TEST					
1ST-CLASS	1	0	9	0	–
INT					
RAL					
NAT.W.					
B & H					

CAREER: BATTING

	I.	N.O.	R.	H.S.	AV.
TEST	164	12	6789	215	44.66
1ST-CLASS	344	34	11783	187	38.00
INT	99	8	2905	158	31.92
RAL	119	19	3900	135*	39.00
NAT.W.	29	4	1265	156	50.60
B & H	45	5	1070	114*	26.75

CAREER: BOWLING

	O.	M.	R.	W.	AV.
TEST	6	1	20	1	20.00
1ST-CLASS	37.1	4	203	3	67.66
INT	0.5	0	14	0	–
RAL					
NAT.W.	1.3	0	12	0	–
B & H					

GRAVENEY, D. A.　　Gloucestershire

Full Name: David Anthony
Graveney
Role: Right-hand bat, slow
left-arm bowler
Born: 2 January 1953, Bristol
Height: 6′ 4″ **Weight:** 14st
Nickname: Gravity, Grav
County debut: 1972
County cap: 1976
Benefit: 1986
50 wickets in a season: 4
1st-Class 50s scored: 15
1st-Class 100s scored: 2
1st-Class 5 w. in innings: 29
1st-Class 10 w. in match: 4
One-Day 50s: 1
Place in batting averages: —
(1986 238th av. 10.44)
Place in bowling averages: 70th

av. 30.25 (1986 74th av. 33.30)
Strike rate 1987: 76.32 (career 67.27)
1st-Class catches 1987: 8 (career 179)
Parents: Ken and Jeanne (deceased)
Wife and date of marriage: Julie, 23 September 1978
Children: Adam, 13 October 1982
Family links with cricket: Son of J. K. Graveney, captain of Gloucestershire,
who took 10 wickets for 66 runs v Derbyshire at Chesterfield in 1949, and
nephew of Tom Graveney of Gloucestershire, Worcestershire and England.
Brother, John, selected for English Public Schools v English Schools at Lord's

LAST SEASON: BATTING

	I.	N.O.	R.	H.S.	AV.
TEST					
1ST-CLASS	17	3	139	30	9.92
INT					
RAL	6	2	43	23*	10.75
NAT.W.	1	1	5	5*	—
B & H	3	2	13	11	13.00

CAREER: BATTING

	I.	N.O.	R.	H.S.	AV.
TEST					
1ST-CLASS	427	120	5605	119	18.25
INT					
RAL	127	46	1264	56*	15.60
NAT.W.	24	9	270	44	18.00
B & H	38	11	392	49*	14.51

LAST SEASON: BOWLING

	O.	M.	R.	W.	AV.
TEST					
1ST-CLASS	356.1	112	847	28	30.25
INT					
RAL	43	2	199	0	—
NAT.W.	48	4	146	9	16.22
B & H	45	1	168	2	84.00

CAREER: BOWLING

	O.	M.	R.	W.	AV.
TEST					
1ST-CLASS	7803.5	2338	20118	696	28.90
INT					
RAL	897.1	50	4191	124	33.79
NAT.W.	303.5	45	994	42	23.66
B & H	398.5	37	1440	46	31.30

Education: Millfield School, Somerset
Jobs outside cricket: Company director. Accountant
Other sports played: Golf, soccer, squash
Relaxations: 'Playing sport, TV and cinema. Relaxing at a good pub.'
Extras: Treasurer of the County Cricketers' Association. Captain of Gloucestershire since 1981
Best batting performance: 119 Gloucestershire v Oxford University, Oxford 1980
Best bowling performance: 8-85 Gloucestershire v Nottinghamshire, Cheltenham 1974

GRAY, A. H. Surrey

Full Name: Anthony Hollis Gray
Role: Right-hand bat, right-arm fast bowler
Born: 23 May 1963, Belmont, Port of Spain, Trinidad
Height: 6' 6" **Weight:** 15st
Nickname: Big Man
County debut: 1985
County cap: 1985
Test debut: 1986–87
No. of Tests: 5
No. of One-Day Internationals: 19
50 wickets in a season: 2
1st-Class 50s scored: 1
1st-Class 5 w. in innings: 16
1st-Class 10 w. in match: 3
Place in batting averages: 232nd av. 13.40
Place in bowling averages: 2nd av. 15.58 (1986 6th av. 18.94)
Strike rate 1987: 36.36 (career 58.65)
1st-Class catches 1987: 4 (career 28)
Parents: Anthony and Merle
Education: Marlick Ser. Comprehensive; St Augustine Ser. Comprehensive
Qualifications: 3 O-levels, 1 CXC
Cricketing superstitions or habits: Always bat with cap on
Cricketers particularly learnt from: Alf Gover
Cricketers particularly admired: Viv Richards, Mike Holding
Other sports played: Football, basketball, table tennis
Other sports followed: Football
Relaxations: Watching sports, watching movies, music, going to the parks

174

Extras: The only son in a family of five. Trinidad and Tobago Player of the Year 1985. Surrey CC Supporters' Association Player of the Year 1985. Hat-trick v Yorkshire 1985
Best batting performance: 54* Trinidad v Leeward Islands, Bissetirre 1985–86
Best bowling performance: 8-40 Surrey v Yorkshire, Sheffield 1985

LAST SEASON: BATTING

	I.	N.O.	R.	H.S.	AV.
TEST					
1ST-CLASS	8	3	67	35	13.40
INT					
RAL	3	1	54	24	27.00
NAT.W.					
B & H					

CAREER: BATTING

	I.	N.O.	R.	H.S.	AV.
TEST	8	2	48	12*	8.00
1ST-CLASS	63	12	569	54*	11.15
INT	8	4	43	10*	10.75
RAL	11	6	115	24*	23.00
NAT.W.	1	0	3	3	3.00
B & H					

LAST SEASON: BOWLING

	O.	M.	R.	W.	AV.
TEST					
1ST-CLASS	291.1	59	748	48	15.58
INT					
RAL	39	2	199	2	99.50
NAT.W.					
B & H					

CAREER: BOWLING

	O.	M.	R.	W.	AV.
TEST	148	37	377	22	17.13
1ST-CLASS	2608.4	319	5488	260	21.10
INT	154.4	16	540	31	17.41
RAL	165	5	712	35	20.34
NAT.W.	23	3	89	5	17.80
B & H	11	1	33	0	–

GREEN, A. M. Sussex

Full Name: Allan Michael Green
Role: Right-hand bat, off-break bowler, short-leg fielder
Born: 28 May 1960, Pulborough
Height: 5' 10" **Weight:** 11st
Nickname: Gilbert, Greenie, Wedgey
County debut: 1980
County cap: 1985
1000 runs in a season: 2
1st-Class 50s scored: 30
1st-Class 100s scored: 9
One-Day 50s: 12
One-Day 100s: 1
Place in batting averages: 151st av. 24.14 (1986 96th av. 31.23)
1st-Class catches 1987: 9 (career 72)
Parents: Sheila Cynthia and Basil Michael
Wife and date of marriage: Kerry Louise, 19 September 1986

Family links with cricket: Father played for Findon CC 'as a fielder'
Education: Knoll School, Hove; Brighton Sixth Form College
Qualifications: 5 O-levels
Jobs outside cricket: Sports shop assistant, labourer
Cricketing superstitions or habits: 'Strap left pad on first and like to bat in same clothes, smell permitting.'
Overseas tours: *The Cricketer* tour to Dubai 1983
Overseas teams played for: Orange Free State, South Africa 1985–87
Cricketers particularly learnt from: Ian Thomson, Chris Waller, Roger Marshall, Tony Buss, Alvin Kallicharran
Other sports played: Golf, snooker, football
Relaxations: 'Sleeping, going to concerts, eating, drinking and watching it rain!'
Opinions on cricket: 'Should play 16 four-day championship matches.'
Best batting performance: 179 Sussex v Glamorgan, Cardiff 1986
Best bowling performance: 4-59 Orange Free State v Northern Transvaal, Bloemfontein 1985–86

LAST SEASON: BATTING

	I.	N.O.	R.	H.S.	AV.
TEST					
1ST-CLASS	36	2	821	115	24.14
INT					
RAL	9	0	239	62	26.55
NAT.W.	2	0	168	84	84.00
B & H	3	0	46	32	15.33

CAREER: BATTING

	I.	N.O.	R.	H.S.	AV.
TEST					
1ST-CLASS	255	15	7095	179	29.56
INT					
RAL	44	3	1159	83	28.26
NAT.W.	12	0	503	102	41.91
B & H	15	0	314	50	20.93

LAST SEASON: BOWLING

	O.	M.	R.	W.	AV.
TEST					
1ST-CLASS	38	7	130	4	32.50
INT					
RAL					
NAT.W.	0.3	0	2	0	–
B & H					

CAREER: BOWLING

	O.	M.	R.	W.	AV.
TEST					
1ST-CLASS	492.5	79	1689	36	46.91
INT					
RAL	1	0	7	0	–
NAT.W.	1.3	0	9	0	–
B & H	6	2	26	1	26.00

80. How many England batsmen of 1987 appeared in the top ten scores of 1987?

GREENE, V. S.　　　Gloucestershire

Full Name: Victor Sylvester Greene
Role: Right-hand bat, right arm
fast-medium bowler
Born: 24 September 1960, Barbados
Nickname: Vibert
County debut: 1987
1st-Class 50s scored: 1
1st-Class 5 w. in innings: 2
Place in batting averages:
135th av. 26.57
Place in bowling averages:
56th av. 28.24
Strike rate 1987: 49.00 (career 44.12)
1st-Class catches 1987: 4
(career 6)
Overseas tours: Barbados 1985–86
Best batting performance:
62* Gloucestershire v
Leicestershire, Cheltenham 1987

Best bowling performance: 7-96 Gloucestershire v Nottinghamshire, Trent
Bridge 1987

LAST SEASON: BATTING

	I.	N.O.	R.	H.S.	AV.
TEST					
1ST-CLASS	11	4	186	62*	26.57
INT					
RAL					
NAT.W.					
B & H					

CAREER: BATTING

	I.	N.O.	R.	H.S.	AV.
TEST					
1ST-CLASS	21	7	281	62*	20.07
INT					
RAL					
NAT.W.					
B & H					

LAST SEASON: BOWLING

	O.	M.	R.	W.	AV.
TEST					
1ST-CLASS	236.5	32	819	29	28.24
INT					
RAL	12	1	47	2	23.50
NAT.W.					
B & H					

CAREER: BOWLING

	O.	M.	R.	W.	AV.
TEST					
1ST-CLASS	478	83	1463	65	22.50
INT					
RAL	12	1	47	2	23.50
NAT.W.					
B & H					

GREENFIELD, K.   Sussex

Full Name: Keith Greenfield
Role: Right-hand bat, right arm
medium bowler
Born: 6 December 1968, Brighton
Height: 6′ **Weight:** 12st 1lb
Nickname: Missakeith ('I play
and miss a few times'), Flash
County debut: 1987
1st-Class catches 1987: 2
(career 2)
Parents: Leslie Ernest and Sheila
Marital status: Single
Education: Coldean Primary
and Middle; Falmer High School
Qualifications: 2 O-levels,
Business and Finance B Tec
First Certificate, Sports
Leaders Award, Computer
Literacy Certificate
Jobs outside cricket: Employed on groundstaff at Hove during winter
Off-season 1987–88: Working at Hove and coaching at Sussex Schools
Cricketing superstitions or habits: 'Always put my batting shoes on last when
padding up.'
Overseas tours: Sussex U-16s to Guernsey 1985
Cricketers particularly learnt from: Chris Waller, Stuart Storey, Jim Parks,
Ian Thompson
Cricketers particularly admired: Paul Parker, Derek Randall, Ian Botham
Other sports played: Snooker, football, swimming, golf, tennis
Relaxations: 'Listening to music, watching films and TV, going out with
friends and enjoying myself.'
Extras: First YTS person at Sussex CCC to turn professional
Opinions on cricket: 'I'll keep them to myself.'
Best batting performance: 18 Sussex v Lancashire, Lytham 1987

LAST SEASON: BATTING

	I.	N.O.	R.	H.S.	AV.
TEST					
1ST-CLASS	4	0	34	18	8.50
INT					
RAL	1	1	8	8*	–
NAT.W.					
B & H					

CAREER: BATTING

	I.	N.O.	R.	H.S.	AV.
TEST					
1ST-CLASS	4	0	34	18	8.50
INT					
RAL	1	1	8	8*	–
NAT.W.					
B & H					

GREENIDGE, C. G.   Hampshire

Full Name: Cuthbert Gordon Greenidge
Role: Right-hand bat, right-arm medium bowler
Born: 1 May 1951, St Peter, Barbados
County debut: 1970
County cap: 1972
Benefit: 1983 (£28,648)
Test debut: 1974–75
No. of Tests: 77
No. of One-Day Internationals: 87
1000 runs in a season: 15
1st-Class 50s scored: 165
1st-Class 100s scored: 68
1st-Class 200s scored: 10
1st-Class 5 w. in innings: 1
One-Day 50s: 76
One-Day 100s: 29
Place in batting averages: 11th av. 49.94 (1986 1st av. 67.83)
1st-Class catches 1987: 21 (career: 471)
Wife and date of marriage: Anita, September 1977
Children: Carl, 1978
Family links with cricket: Wife is cousin of West Indian and Leicestershire fast bowler Andy Roberts
Education: Black Bess School; St Peter's Boys' School; Sutton Secondary School, Reading
Qualifications: Studied accountancy and book-keeping
Jobs outside cricket: Working for Sutton's Seeds, Reading; Dimplex, Southampton
Overseas tours: Toured with West Indies to India, Sri Lanka and Pakistan 1974–75; Australia 1975–76; England 1976, 1980 and 1984; Australia 1979–80; Pakistan 1980; Australia 1981–82; India 1983; Australia 1984–85
Overseas teams played for: Barbados
Other sports played: Soccer, rugby, golf
Extras: Could have played for either England or West Indies. Persuaded to join Hampshire by John Arlott after playing for Berkshire U-19s. Scored two centuries in one match (134 and 101) for West Indies v England at Manchester 1976, and v Kent at Bournemouth (136 and 120) in 1978. Shared in partnership of 285 for second wicket with D. R. Turner v Minor Counties South at Amersham in 1973, being the record partnership for all one-day competitions. Awarded MBE in 1985

Best batting performance: 273* D. H. Robins' XI v Pakistan, Eastbourne 1974
Best bowling performance: 5-49 Hampshire v Surrey, Southampton 1971

LAST SEASON: BATTING

	I.	N.O.	R.	H.S.	AV.
TEST					
1ST-CLASS	18	0	899	163	49.94
INT					
RAL	6	0	299	172	49.83
NAT.W.	2	0	22	22	11.00
B & H	5	0	242	133	48.40

LAST SEASON: BOWLING

	O.	M.	R.	W.	AV.
TEST					
1ST-CLASS					
INT					
RAL					
NAT.W.					
B & H					

CAREER: BATTING

	I.	N.O.	R.	H.S.	AV.
TEST	128	14	5509	223	48.32
1ST-CLASS	652	53	27290	273*	45.55
INT	87	8	3652	115`	46.22
RAL	180	12	6348	172	37.78
NAT.W.	33	1	1284	177	40.12
B & H	58	3	2157	173*	39.21

CAREER: BOWLING

	O.	M.	R.	W.	AV.
TEST	4.2	3	4	0	—
1ST-CLASS	155.5	37	468	17	27.53
INT	10	0	45	1	45.00
RAL	18	0	89	1	89.00
NAT.W.	1	0	5	0	—
B & H	12.1	1	57	0	—

GREIG, I. A. Surrey

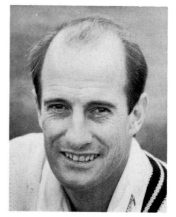

Full Name: Ian Alexander Greig
Role: Right-hand bat, right-arm medium bowler, slip fielder
Born: 8 December 1955, Queenstown, South Africa
Height: 6′ **Weight:** 12st
Nickname: Washies, Greigy
County debut: 1980 (Sussex), 1987 (Surrey)
County cap: 1981 (Sussex), 1987 (Surrey)
Test debut: 1982
No. of Tests: 2
1st-Class 50s scored: 23
1st-Class 100s scored: 5
1st-Class 5 w. in innings: 8
1st-Class 10 w. in match: 2
One-Day 50s: 2
Place in batting averages: 103rd av. 30.58
Place in bowling averages: 99th av. 35.91
Strike rate 1987: 70.91 (career 57.36)
1st-Class catches 1987: 17 (career 105)
Parents: Sandy and Joyce

180

Wife and date of marriage: Cheryl, 8 January 1983

Children: Michelle, 17 December 1984; Andrew, 20 January 1987

Family links with cricket: Brother of Tony, former captain of Sussex and England; brother-in-law Phillip Hodson played for Cambridge University and Yorkshire

Education: Queens College, Queenstown; Downing College, Cambridge

Qualifications: MA Law (Cantab)

Cricketing superstitions or habits: Left pad on first

Overseas tours: Combined Universities to Australia 1979–80

Overseas teams played for: Border, South Africa 1974–75; Griqualand West, South Africa 1975–76

Cricketers particularly learnt from: Geoff Arnold

Cricketers particularly admired: Garth le Roux, Richard Hadlee

Other sports played: Rugby Union, fishing

Other sports followed: Football

Relaxations: Relaxing with family, barbecues

Cricketing opinions: 'It is hoped that the forthcoming four-day matches are a success in order that we may, as soon as 1989, get into 16 four-day matches which will surely be a benefit to English cricket fortunes *provided* that the wickets are fully covered.'

Best batting performance: 147* Sussex v Oxford University, Oxford 1983

Best bowling performance: 7-43 Sussex v Cambridge University, Cambridge 1981

LAST SEASON: BATTING

	I.	N.O.	R.	H.S.	AV.
TEST					
1ST-CLASS	35	6	887	104*	30.58
INT					
RAL	10	2	171	41*	21.37
NAT.W.	1	0	13	13	13.00
B & H	4	0	19	10	4.75

LAST SEASON: BOWLING

	O.	M.	R.	W.	AV.
TEST					
1ST-CLASS	413.4	86	1257	35	35.91
INT					
RAL	81	1	488	19	25.68
NAT.W.	17.5	0	62	4	15.50
B & H	23.1	1	133	6	22.16

CAREER: BATTING

	I.	N.O.	R.	H.S.	AV.
TEST	4	0	26	14	6.50
1ST-CLASS	213	29	4864	147*	57.90
INT					
RAL	69	15	1155	48	21.38
NAT.W.	10	0	197	82	19.20
B & H	37	3	501	51	14.73

CAREER: BOWLING

	O.	M.	R.	W.	AV.
TEST	31.2	6	114	4	28.50
1ST-CLASS	3181	664	9886	332	29.77
INT					
RAL	488.1	16	2528	81	31.20
NAT.W.	103.4	11	349	16	21.81
B & H	312	29	1216	44	27.63

---

81. Who was top of the 1987 first-class batting averages?

82. Who was the top-placed Englishman in the 1987 first-class batting averages?

HADLEE, R. J.　Nottinghamshire

Full Name: Richard John Hadlee
Role: Left-hand bat, right-arm fast bowler
Born: 3 July 1951, Christchurch, New Zealand
Height: 6′ 1″ **Weight:** 11st 9 lbs
Nickname: Paddles
County debut: 1978
County cap: 1978
Benefit: 1986
Test debut: 1972–73
No. of Tests: 70
No. of One-Day Internationals: 94
1000 runs in a season: 2
50 wickets in a season: 9
1st-Class 50s scored: 56
1st-Class 100s scored: 13
1st-Class 200s scored: 1
1st-Class 5 w. in innings: 91
1st-Class 10 w. in match: 15
One-Day 50s: 13
One-Day 100s: 1
Place in batting averages: 7th av. 52.90 (1986 10th av. 50.81)
Place in bowling averages: 1st av. 12.64 (1986 2nd av. 15.98)
Strike rate 1987: 36.55 (career 36.06)
1st-Class catches 1987: 16 (career 191)
Parents: Walter Arnold and Lillius Agnes
Wife and date of marriage: Karen Ann, 24 August 1973
Family links with cricket: Father played for New Zealand 1937–49, captaining New Zealand on tour of UK 1949. Brother, Dayle, played for New Zealand 1969–78. Brother Barry played for Canterbury. His father, Walter, has succeeded Gordon Burgess (father of former New Zealand Test captain, Mark) as president of the New Zealand Cricket Council
Jobs outside cricket: Trainee manager, Woolworth's 1970; Dept. trainee manager, Bing Harris Sargood 1973; Sales manager, Shawn Sports, 1975. Employed by New Zealand CC; managed by International Management Group, contracted to Leopard Breweries and Armoured Security Services
Overseas tours: With New Zealand to England 1973, 1978, 1983, 1986; Australia 1973–74, 1980–81, 1986; India, Pakistan 1976; World Cup in UK 1975, 1979, 1983
Overseas teams played for: Canterbury, New Zealand, 1971–; Tasmania 1979–80; World XI v Australia 1979, World Series Cricket
Cricketers particularly learnt from: 'My brother, Dayle; Dennis Lillee – I

admire his approach to the game: competitive, inspires his team, great bowler.'

Cricketers particularly admired: Viv Richards, Gary Sobers, Greg Chappell, Abdul Qadir

Other sports played: Golf. Played goalkeeper for Rangers and for Woolston in New Zealand Southern League, 'but I never took it seriously'

Other sports followed: Soccer, rugby, tennis, golf, snooker, etc.

Relaxations: 'Watching movies, music, writing weekly newspaper columns.'

Extras: Awarded MBE 1980. Hat-trick v Central Districts 1972 at Nelson. Only bowler to take 100 wickets in 1981 season. Top of English bowling averages 1980, 1981, 1982 and 1984. New Zealand Personality of the Year 1978 and nominated in final six on five occasions. New Zealand Bowler of the Year 1978–84. Has written autobiography *Hadlee*. Author of *Hadlee on Cricket, Hadlee's Humour* and *Hadlee Hits Out*. New Zealand records: (1) Most wickets in Test cricket. (2) Most numbers of 5 wickets in a Test innings. (3) Most wickets in a Test innings, and in a Test match, 15 for 123. (4) Best bowling in a Test match, 9-52 v Australia, 1985–86. (5) Most number of 10 wickets in a Test match, three times. (6) First New Zealand player to take Test double of 100 wickets and 1000 runs. In 1984 did 'double' of 1000 runs and 100 wickets in first-class cricket – first time achieved since F. J. Titmus in 1967. Retired from Notts at end of 1987 season

Best batting performance: 210* Nottinghamshire v Middlesex, Lord's 1984

Best bowling performance: 9-52 New Zealand v Australia, Brisbane 1985–86

LAST SEASON: BATTING

	I.	N.O.	R.	H.S.	AV.
TEST					
1ST-CLASS	28	7	1111	133*	52.90
INT					
RAL	9	1	157	36*	19.62
NAT.W.	4	1	118	70*	39.33
B & H	2	0	28	28	14.00

LAST SEASON: BOWLING

	O.	M.	R.	W.	AV.
TEST					
1ST-CLASS	591	189	1227	97	12.64
INT					
RAL	84	6	303	11	27.54
NAT.W.	47.5	8	121	6	20.16
B & H	16	2	53	0	–

CAREER: BATTING

	I.	N.O.	R.	H.S.	AV.
TEST	111	16	2622	151*	27.60
1ST-CLASS	333	71	8727	210*	33.30
INT	80	12	1310	79	19.26
RAL	82	21	1618	100*	26.52
NAT.W.	17	3	412	70*	29.42
B & H	37	9	920	70	32.85

CAREER: BOWLING

	O.	M.	R.	W.	AV.
TEST	577.2 2245.3	68 578	7976	355	22.46
1ST-CLASS	1009 3959.3	163 1173	16854	1029	16.37
INT	277.1 461.5	57 103	2702	128	21.10
RAL	683.2	73	2532	125	20.25
NAT.W.	197.2	47	480	32	15.00
B & H	412.4	85	1144	74	15.45

HARDEN, R. J. Somerset

Full Name: Richard John Harden
Role: Right-hand bat, left-arm
medium bowler
Born: 16 August 1965, Bridgwater
Height: 6′ 0″ **Weight:** 13st 3lbs
Nickname: Rich
County debut: 1985
1000 runs in a season: 1
1st-Class 50s scored: 9
1st-Class 100s scored: 3
One-Day 50s: 4
Place in batting averages: 154th
av. 23.66 (1986 88th av. 33.12)
1st-Class catches 1987: 9
(career 30)
Parents: Chris and Ann
Marital status: Single
Family links with cricket: Grand-

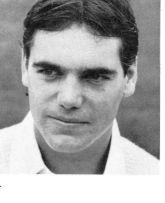

father played club cricket for Bridgwater
Education: Kings College, Taunton
Qualifications: 8 O-levels, 2 A-levels. Coaching award
Jobs outside cricket: Insurance clerk
Off-season 1987–88: Playing in New Zealand
Cricketing superstitions or habits: Right pad on first
Overseas teams played for: New Plymouth Old Boys, 1984–85, 1985–86
Cricketers particularly learnt from: Roy Marshall
Cricketers particularly admired: Viv Richards, David Gower
Other sports played: Squash, 'struggling golfer'

LAST SEASON: BATTING

	I.	N.O.	R.	H.S.	AV.
TEST					
1ST-CLASS	30	6	568	59	23.66
INT					
RAL	14	3	382	73	34.72
NAT.W.					
B & H	4	0	74	35	18.50

LAST SEASON: BOWLING

	O.	M.	R.	W.	AV.
TEST					
1ST-CLASS	2	0	8	0	—
INT					
RAL					
NAT.W.					
B & H					

CAREER: BATTING

	I.	N.O.	R.	H.S.	AV.
TEST					
1ST-CLASS	83	14	2027	108	29.37
INT					
RAL	31	6	666	73	26.64
NAT.W.	1	0	17	17	17.00
B & H	9	0	129	35	14.33

CAREER: BOWLING

	O.	M.	R.	W.	AV.
TEST					
1ST-CLASS	68.3	10	249	6	41.50
INT					
RAL	0.1	0	0	0	—
NAT.W.					
B & H					

Relaxations: Listening to music, eating good food, playing snooker or pool, drinking in good wine bars

Opinions on cricket: 'It's a batsman's point of view, but if wickets are uncovered, bowlers run-ups should be uncovered as well.'

Best batting performance: 108 Somerset v Sussex, Taunton 1986

Best bowling performance: 2-24 Somerset v Hampshire, Taunton 1986

HARDIE, B. R.   Essex

Full Name: Brian Ross Hardie
Role: Right-hand bat, right-arm medium bowler, bat/pad fielder
Born: 14 January 1950, Stenhousemuir
Height: 5' 10" **Weight:** 12st 7lbs
Nickname: Lager
County debut: 1973
County cap: 1974
Benefit: 1983 (£48,486)
1000 runs in a season: 11
1st-Class 50s scored: 81
1st-Class 100s scored: 23
One-Day 50s: 35
One-Day 100s: 6
Place in batting averages: 70th av. 35.12 (1986 107th av. 29.43)
1st-Class catches 1987: 22 (career 304)
Parents: James Millar and Elspet
Wife and date of marriage: Fiona, 28 October 1977
Family links with cricket: Father and brother, Keith, played for Scotland
Education: Stenhousemuir Primary School; Larbert High School
Qualifications: 7 O-levels, 3 H-levels, NCA Advanced Cricket Coach
Jobs outside cricket: Computer operator, bank clerk, shipping clerk
Off-season 1987–88: Cricket manager in Auckland, New Zealand
Overseas teams played for: Two seasons in New Zealand club cricket 1980–81 and 1981–82
Cricketers particularly learnt from: 'Everyone has something to offer.'
Other sports played: Football, golf
Relaxations: Sport
Extras: Played for Stenhousemuir in East of Scotland League. Debut for Scotland 1970. Scored two centuries for Scotland v MCC at Aberdeen in 1971, but not then regarded as first-class match. Man of the Match in 1985 NatWest Final

Best batting performance: 162 Essex v Warwickshire, Edgbaston 1975
162 Essex v Somerset, Southend 1985
Best bowling performance: 2-39 Essex v Glamorgan, Ilford 1979

LAST SEASON: BATTING

	I.	N.O.	R.	H.S.	AV.
TEST					
1ST-CLASS	43	4	1370	143	35.12
INT					
RAL	12	2	356	102*	35.60
NAT.W.	3	0	89	56	29.66
B & H	4	1	125	70*	41.66

CAREER: BATTING

	I.	N.O.	R.	H.S.	AV.
TEST					
1ST-CLASS	544	67	16206	162	33.97
INT					
RAL	179	17	4316	109	26.64
NAT.W.	30	0	1017	110	33.90
B & H	63	15	1456	119*	30.33

LAST SEASON: BOWLING

	O.	M.	R.	W.	AV.
TEST					
1ST-CLASS	13	1	65	0	–
INT					
RAL					
NAT.W.					
B & H					

CAREER: BOWLING

	O.	M.	R.	W.	AV.
TEST					
1ST-CLASS	46	3	238	3	79.33
INT					
RAL	4.5	0	24	1	24.00
NAT.W.	8	1	16	1	16.00
B & H					

HARDY, J. J. E.   Somerset

Full Name: Jonathan James Ean Hardy
Role: Left-hand bat
Born: 2 October 1960, Nakuru, Kenya
Height: 6′ 3″ **Weight:** 13½st
Nickname: JJ
County debut: 1984 (Hampshire), 1986 (Somerset)
County cap: 1987 (Somerset)
1000 runs in a season: 1
1st-Class 50s scored: 22
1st-Class 100s scored: 2
One-Day 50s: 5
Place in batting averages: 118th av. 28.65 (1986 106th av. 29.75)
1st-Class catches 1987: 8 (career 33)
Parents: Ray and Petasue
Marital status: Single
Family links with cricket: Father played for Yorkshire Schools; related to Nottinghamshire Gunn's
Education: Pembroke House, Gilgil, Kenya; Canford School, Dorset
Qualifications: 10 O-levels, 3 A-levels (English, Economics, Geography)

Off-season 1987–88: Captaining Cape Town CC, South African national club champions
Overseas teams played for: Pirates, Durban 1981–85; Paarl CC 1985–86
Cricketers particularly admired: Graeme Pollock, Greg Chappell, Malcolm Marshall
Other sports played: Hockey (captain Dorset U-19), rugby, squash
Relaxations: Photography, walking
Extras: Suffered from bilharzia, a tropical parasitic disease from 1980 to February 1986. Left Hampshire to join Somerset for 1986 season
Opinions on cricket: 'Would like to see an increasing role in Championship cricket for spinners and No.6 batsmen and a decreased one for continued finishes and attempts at under-prepared pitches.'
Best batting performance: 119 Somerset v Gloucestershire, Taunton 1987

LAST SEASON: BATTING

	I.	N.O.	R.	H.S.	AV.
TEST					
1ST-CLASS	40	2	1089	119	28.65
INT					
RAL	14	4	418	94*	41.80
NAT.W.	1	0	4	4	4.00
B & H	5	0	101	35	20.20

CAREER: BATTING

	I.	N.O.	R.	H.S.	AV.
TEST					
1ST-CLASS	114	12	3207	119	31.44
INT					
RAL	34	7	687	94*	25.44
NAT.W.	5	1	78	53	19.50
B & H	10	0	163	35	16.30

HARMAN, M. D. Kent

Full Name: Mark David Harman
Role: Right-hand bat, right-arm off-spinner, 1st slip fielder
Born: 30 June 1964, Aylesbury
Height: 5′ 11″ **Weight:** 11st 12lbs
Nickname: Harmony, Basil
County debut: 1986
Place in batting averages: 213th av. 15.66
1st-Class catches 1987: 6 (career 7)
Parents: Michael and Barbara
Marital status: Single
Family links with cricket: Father played club cricket
Education: Frome College; Loughborough University
Qualifications: 9 O-levels, 3 A-levels, BSc(First-Class Honours) Degree in Financial Management; cricket coaching awards

Jobs outside cricket: Chartered Accountancy

Off-season 1987–88: Getting fit for 1988 season

Cricketing superstitions or habits: Always put socks on before shoes. 'I like to do a thorough series of stretching exercises before the day's play.'

Cricketers particularly learnt from: Peter Robinson among many others at Somerset CCC

Cricketers particularly admired: Viv Richards, Vic Marks, Martin Crowe, Steve Waugh, Richard Hadlee, Roger Harper

Other sports played: Soccer, golf, swimming, squash

Other sports followed: All sports through TV, media etc

Relaxations: Reading, sleeping, walking in the country, listening to music (not all at the same time)

Extras: Nearly run-out from first delivery in first-class cricket! Left Somerset at the end of 1987 season to join Kent to further my career, as first-team opportunities at Somerset were limited due to presence of Vic Marks in the side.'

Opinions on cricket: '1) Uncovered wickets as an aid to the development of spin bowling, when combined with covered run-ups, are completely ineffective as shown in the 1987 season. 2) Hopefully the four-day games played in 1988 will prove successful so that a full four-day programme can be developed for 1989 and onwards. Four-day cricket should enable the development of some areas of the game that are neglected in three-day and one-day matches.'

Best batting performance: 41 Somerset v Kent, Bath 1987

Best bowling performance: 2-38 Somerset v Hampshire, Weston-super-Mare 1987

LAST SEASON: BATTING

	I.	N.O.	R.	H.S.	AV.
TEST					
1ST-CLASS	8	2	94	41	15.66
INT					
RAL	1	0	2	2	2.00
NAT.W.	1	0	0		0.00
B & H					

CAREER: BATTING

	I.	N.O.	R.	H.S.	AV.
TEST					
1ST-CLASS	13	4	121	41	13.44
INT					
RAL	1	0	2	2	2.00
NAT.W.	1	0	0		0.00
B & H					

LAST SEASON: BOWLING

	O.	M.	R.	W.	AV.
TEST					
1ST-CLASS	131	35	369	7	52.71
INT					
RAL	8	0	53	0	–
NAT.W.	12	1	38	1	38.00
B & H					

CAREER: BOWLING

	O.	M.	R.	W.	AV.
TEST					
1ST-CLASS	191.3	47	518	8	64.75
INT					
RAL	8	0	53	0	–
NAT.W.	12	1	38	1	38.00
B & H					

HARPER, R. A.   Northamptonshire

Full Name: Roger Andrew Harper
Role: Right-hand bat, off-break bowler, slip fielder, all-rounder
Born: 19 March 1963, Georgetown, Guyana
Height: 6′ 5″ **Weight:** 14st 7lbs
Nickname: Juice ('I'm tee-total')
County debut: 1985
Test debut: 1983–84
No. of Tests: 19
No. of One-Day Internationals: 48
50 wickets in a season: 2
1st-Class 50s scored: 14
1st-Class 100s scored: 5
1st-Class 200s scored: 1
1st-Class 5 w. in innings: 17
1st-Class 10 w. in match: 2
One-Day 50s: 4
Place in batting averages: 14th
av. 48.25 (1986 69th av. 35.88)
Place in bowling averages: 80th av. 31.52 (1986 45th av. 27.41)
Strike rate 1987: 73.14 (career 59.02)
1st-Class catches 1987: 7 (career 149)
Parents: Henry and Lynette
Wife and date of marriage: Shevan, 26 September 1987
Family links with cricket: Brother Mark plays for Guyana and for Young West Indies in 1976
Education: Queen's College High School, Georgetown
Qualifications: 7 O-levels
Overseas tours: West Indies to India 1983, England 1984, Australia 1984–85, Pakistan 1985, World Cup 1987
Overseas teams played for: Guyana 1980–
Cricketers particularly learnt from: Brother Mark, Clive Lloyd
Cricketers particularly admired: Clive Lloyd, Gary Sobers
Off-season 1987–88: Touring with West Indies
Other sports played: Tennis, table tennis
Other sports followed: Tennis, athletics, boxing
Injuries 1987: Cut above right eye on last day of season
Relaxations: Movies, music, good novels
Extras: Captain West Indies Youth XI on tour of England in 1982. County vice-captain 1986
Opinions on cricket: 'Four-day cricket will be good for the game in England. It

will help to prepare players for Tests. And it should reduce the number of manufactured finishes.'

Best batting performance: 234 Northamptonshire v Gloucestershire, Northampton 1986

Best bowling performance: 6-57 West Indies v England, Old Trafford 1984

LAST SEASON: BATTING

	I.	N.O.	R.	H.S.	AV.
TEST					
1ST-CLASS	9	5	193	127*	48.25
INT					
RAL	10	2	252	65*	31.50
NAT.W.	1	1	4	4*	–
B & H					

LAST SEASON: BOWLING

	O.	M.	R.	W.	AV.
TEST					
1ST-CLASS	256	56	662	21	31.52
INT					
RAL	79	5	362	15	24.13
NAT.W.	12	3	40	3	13.33
B & H					

CAREER: BATTING

	I.	N.O.	R.	H.S.	AV.
TEST	25	3	352	60	16.00
1ST-CLASS	143	22	3876	234	32.03
INT	26	11	286	45*	19.06
RAL	33	9	668	65*	27.88
NAT.W.	3	1	5	4*	2.50
B & H	5	0	118	56	23.60

CAREER: BOWLING

	O.	M.	R.	W.	AV.
TEST	499.5	143	1090	40	27.25
1ST-CLASS	3345	866	9179	340	26.99
INT	418	24	1646	49	33.59
RAL	276	15	1186	40	29.65
NAT.W.	32	7	109	4	27.25
B & H	76	17	217	7	31.00

HARTLEY, P. J. Yorkshire

Full Name: Peter John Hartley
Role: Right-hand bat, right-arm fast-medium bowler
Born: 18 April 1960, Keighley
Height: 6′ 0″ **Weight:** 13st 4lbs
Nickname: Daisy
County debut: 1982 (Warwickshire), 1985 (Yorkshire)
County cap: 1987 (Yorkshire)
1st-Class 50s scored: 4
1st-Class 5 w. in innings: 3
Place in batting averages: 189th av. 18.26 (1986 80th av. 33.92)
Place in bowling averages: 103rd av. 36.72 (1986 38th av. 26.70)
Strike rate 1987: 61.27 (career 58.62)
1st-Class catches 1987: 7 (career 17)
Parents: Thomas and Molly
Wife and date of marriage: Sharon, 12 March 1988
Family links with cricket: Father played village cricket

Education: Greenhead Grammar School; Bradford College
Qualifications: City & Guilds in Textiles
Jobs outside cricket: Textile supervisor
Overseas teams played for: Hamilton, Melville, New Zealand, 1983–84; Adelaide CC, 1985–86
Cricketers particularly learnt from: Phil Carrick, Steve Oldham, Mike Page
Cricketers particularly admired: Dennis Lillee, Richard Hadlee, Gordon Greenidge
Other sports played: Golf, tennis, football
Other sports followed: Bradford City FC
Relaxations: Any sport, music
Best batting performance: 87* Yorkshire v Essex, Chelmsford 1986
Best bowling performance: 6-68 Yorkshire v Nottinghamshire, Sheffield 1986

LAST SEASON: BATTING

	I.	N.O.	R.	H.S.	AV.
TEST					
1ST-CLASS	26	7	347	49	18.26
INT					
RAL	9	5	48	17*	12.00
NAT.W.	2	1	18	11	18.00
B & H	3	2	9	7*	9.00

LAST SEASON: BOWLING

	O.	M.	R.	W.	AV.
TEST					
1ST-CLASS	480	88	1726	47	36.72
INT					
RAL	90.4	0	470	15	31.33
NAT.W.	23	0	73	6	12.16
B & H	77	8	274	14	19.57

CAREER: BATTING

	I.	N.O.	R.	H.S.	AV.
TEST					
1ST-CLASS	59	15	990	87*	22.50
INT					
RAL	18	7	110	35	10.00
NAT.W.	3	1	41	23	20.50
B & H	5	3	38	29*	19.00

CAREER: BOWLING

	O.	M.	R.	W.	AV.
TEST					
1ST-CLASS	1192	190	4281	122	35.09
INT					
RAL	187.4	4	889	30	29.63
NAT.W.	47	4	169	12	14.08
B & H	118	9	459	22	20.86

83. Who came top of the first-class bowling averages in 1987?

84. Which Englishman came nearest the top of the first-class bowling averages in 1987?

85. Which wicket-keeper took most dismissals in first-class games in 1987, and how many?

86. Which England cricketer has the nickname 'Knuckles'?

HARTLEY, S. N.   *Yorkshire*

Full Name: Stuart Neil Hartley
Role: Right-hand bat, right-arm
medium bowler, outfielder
Born: 18 March 1956, Shipley,
West Yorkshire
Height: 5' 11½" **Weight:** 12st 3lbs
Nickname: Tommy
County debut: 1978
County cap: 1981
1st-Class 50s scored: 25
1st-Class 100s scored: 4
One-Day 50s: 13
Place in batting averages: 186th
av. 18.62 (1986 123rd av. 28.03)
1st-Class catches 1987: 5 (career 54)
Parents: Marjorie and Horace
Marital status: Divorced
Family links with cricket:

Father played league cricket
Education: Beckfoot Grammar School, Bingley; Cannington High, Perth,
Western Australia
Qualifications: 8 O-levels, 3 A-levels; exam passes in insurance
Jobs outside cricket: Trained insurance underwriter; National Sales Execu-
tive for R.B.S. (Financial Services) Ltd
Off-season 1987–88: Working as financial consultant
Overseas tours: Captained North of England NCA team to Holland 1975 and
Gibraltar 1981
Overseas teams played for: Orange Free State, 1981–82

LAST SEASON: BATTING

	I.	N.O.	R.	H.S.	AV.
TEST					
1ST-CLASS	18	2	298	63	18.62
INT					
RAL	13	6	281	83*	40.14
NAT.W.					
B & H	1	0	7	7	7.00

CAREER: BATTING

	I.	N.O.	R.	H.S.	AV.
TEST					
1ST-CLASS	212	27	4607	114	24.90
INT					
RAL	103	21	1846	83*	22.51
NAT.W.	10	0	239	69	23.90
B & H	20	5	408	65*	27.20

LAST SEASON: BOWLING

	O.	M.	R.	W.	AV.
TEST					
1ST-CLASS	12	2	50	2	25.00
INT					
RAL	22	0	135	3	45.00
NAT.W.					
B & H	5	0	25	1	25.00

CAREER: BOWLING

	O.	M.	R.	W.	AV.
TEST					
1ST-CLASS	592	108	2157	48	44.93
INT					
RAL	226.3	3	1328	40	33.20
NAT.W.	26	2	102	1	102.00
B & H	86	3	336	13	25.84

Cricketers particularly learnt from: Doug Padgett and Mike Fearnley – Yorkshire CCC coaching staff
Cricketers particularly admired: Imran Khan, Clive Rice
Other sports played: Golf
Extras: 'Started to play cricket in Perth, Western Australia, where I lived for 2½ years, 1967–69. I would like to live in Perth in the future.' Amateur football with Bradford City 1970–75. Rugby Union with Bingley RUFC. Has been acting captain of Yorkshire
Best batting performance: 114 Yorkshire v Gloucestershire, Bradford 1982
Best bowling performance: 4-51 Yorkshire v Surrey, The Oval 1985

HAYHURST, A. N. Lancashire

Full Name: Andrew Neil Hayhurst
Role: Right-hand bat, right-arm medium bowler
Born: 23 November 1962, Davyhulme, Manchester
Height: 6′ 0″ **Weight:** 13st
Nickname: Barney, Ritchie Cunningham
County debut: 1985
One-Day 50s: 1
Place in batting averages: —
(1986 237th av. 11.14)
Place in bowling averages: —
(1986 108th av. 42.90)
1st-Class catches 1987: 1 (career 3)
Parents: William and Margaret
Marital status: Single
Family links with cricket: Father played club cricket
Education: St Mark's Primary School; Worsley Wardley High; Eccles College; Carnegie College, Leeds
Qualifications: 8 O-levels, 3 A-levels, BA(Hons) Human Movement
Jobs outside cricket: Lecturing in winter 1985–86 and 1986–87
Off-season 1987–88: Playing and coaching in Launceston, Tasmania
Cricketers particularly learnt from: Father and Geoff Ogden (Worsley CC)
Cricketers particularly admired: Geoff Boycott, Ian Botham, Viv Richards
Other sports played: Football, golf – all sports
Relaxations: Watching all sports, good food, good company
Extras: Scored a record 197 runs whilst playing for North of England v South, Southampton 1982. Represented NAYC v MCC 1982. Holds record number

of runs for Lancashire Cricket Fed. U-19 (av. 105.00), 1982. Holds record number of runs in Manchester & District Cricket Association League, whilst playing for Worsley CC in 1984: 1193 runs (av. 70.17). Represented Greater Manchester U-19 County at football 1981–82

Opinions on cricket: '2nd XI cricket should be played on better pitches if that cricket is to be a successful grounding for future 1st XI players.'

Best batting performance: 80 Lancashire v Jamaica, Sabina Park 1987

Best bowling performance: 4-27 Lancashire v Middlesex, Old Trafford 1987

LAST SEASON: BATTING

	I.	N.O.	R.	H.S.	AV.
TEST					
1ST-CLASS	5	1	45	30*	11.25
INT					
RAL	6	2	125	61	31.25
NAT.W.	1	0	16	16	16.00
B & H	1	0	1	1	1.00

LAST SEASON: BOWLING

	O.	M.	R.	W.	AV.
TEST					
1ST-CLASS	111.4	20	350	9	38.88
INT					
RAL	39.3	4	172	4	43.00
NAT.W.	12	0	52	1	52.00
B & H	11	1	50	4	12.50

CAREER: BATTING

	I.	N.O.	R.	H.S.	AV.
TEST					
1ST-CLASS	22	1	317	80	15.09
INT					
RAL	12	4	202	61	25.25
NAT.W.	4	0	75	49	18.75
B & H	1	0	1	1	1.00

CAREER: BOWLING

	O.	M.	R.	W.	AV.
TEST					
1ST-CLASS	250.5	38	863	25	34.52
INT					
RAL	105.3	5	486	8	60.75
NAT.W.	52.5	3	212	7	30.28
B & H	11	1	50	4	12.50

HEGG, W. K.   Lancashire

Full Name: Warren Kevin Hegg
Role: Right-hand bat, wicket-keeper
Born: 23 February 1968, Radcliffe, Lancashire
Height: 5' 10" **Weight:** 11st 5lbs
Nickname: Chucky, Chutch
County debut: 1986
1st-Class 100s scored: 1
Place in batting averages: 161st av. 21.87
Parents: Kevin and Glenda
Marital status: Single
Family links with cricket: Father played in local leagues, as does brother Martin
Education: Unsworth High School; Stand College, Whitefield
Qualifications: 5 O-levels, 7 CSEs; qualified coach

Jobs outside cricket: Groundsman at Old Trafford; worked at warehouse (involved in textiles)

Off-season 1987–88: Playing for Sheffield CC, Tasmania

Cricketing superstitions or habits: Left pad on first. Always wear a cap when keeping wicket

Overseas tours: North of England U-19 to Bermuda 1985; England Young Cricketers to Sri Lanka

Cricketers particularly learnt from: Father Kevin and Jim Kenyon (old pro), Clive Lloyd

Cricketers particularly admired: Ian Botham, Bob Taylor, Alan Knott

Other sports played: County football, golf, tennis

Other sports followed: Football, golf

Relaxations: Watching TV, sleeping, walking dog, fishing

Extras: First player to make County debut from Lytham CC. Holds Lancashire Schools U-19 record for most dismissals in a match – 6 (previous holder Graeme Fowler). Youngest player to score a 100 for Lancashire for 30 years, 130 v Northants in fourth 1st-class game

Opinions on cricket: 'Over-rate fines should be abolished. Tea sessions should be ten minutes longer.'

Best batting performance: 130 Lancashire v Northamptonshire, Northampton 1987

LAST SEASON: BATTING

	I.	N.O.	R.	H.S.	AV.
TEST					
1ST-CLASS	20	4	350	130	21.87
INT					
RAL	3	1	12	6*	6.00
NAT.W.					
B & H					

LAST SEASON: WICKET KEEPING

	C.	ST.			
TEST					
1ST-CLASS	24	11			
INT					
RAL	9	2			
NAT.W.					
B & H					

CAREER: BATTING

	I.	N.O.	R.	H.S.	AV.
TEST					
1ST-CLASS	24	4	369	130	18.45
INT					
RAL	3	1	12	6*	6.00
NAT.W.					
B & H					

CAREER: WICKET KEEPING

	C.	ST.			
TEST					
1ST-CLASS	27	14			
INT					
RAL	9	2			
NAT.W.					
B & H					

87. For which Test team did E. D. A. St J. McMorris open the batting, and how many Tests did he play?

HEMMINGS, E. E.   Nottinghamshire

Full Name: Edward Ernest
Hemmings
Role: Right-hand bat, off-break
bowler
Born: 20 February 1949,
Leamington Spa, Warwickshire
Height: 5' 10" **Weight:** 13st
Nickname: Eddie
County debut: 1966 (Warwickshire),
1979 (Nottinghamshire)
County cap: 1974 (Warwickshire),
1980 (Nottinghamshire)
Benefit: 1987
Test debut: 1982
No. of Tests: 5
No. of One-Day Internationals: 5
50 wickets in a season: 12
1st-Class 50s scored: 22
1st-Class 100s scored: 1
1st-Class 5 w. in innings: 58
1st-Class 10 w. in match: 13
One-Day 50s: 1
Place in batting averages: 171st av. 20.47 (1986 195th av. 17.36)
Place in bowling averages: 24th av. 24.07 (1986 57th av. 29.23)
Strike rate 1987: 59.50 (career 64.84)
1st-Class catches 1987: 5 (career 169)
Parents: Edward and Dorothy Phyliss
Wife and date of marriage: Christine Mary, 23 October 1971
Children: Thomas Edward, 26 July 1977; James Oliver, 9 September 1979
Family links with cricket: Father and father's father played Minor Counties
and League cricket
Education: Campion School, Leamington Spa
Off-season 1987–88: Touring with England
Overseas tours: Derrick Robins XI tour to South Africa 1975; International
XI tour to Pakistan 1981; England to Australia and New Zealand 1982–83;
World Cup 1987
Cricketers particularly learnt from: John Jameson
Cricketers particularly admired: Tim Robinson
Other sport played: Golf
Relaxations: 'Watching football at any level – especially junior. Dining out
with my wife.'
Extras: Debut for Warwickshire 1966, cap 1974. No longer wears glasses,
plays in contact lenses. Started his career as a medium-pacer, and was thought

of as a successor to Tom Cartwright. 'I was even known as "Tommy's Ghost" around Edgbaston.' Suffers from asthma. Took a hat-trick for Warwickshire in 1977 but had to wait four years to receive the inscribed match ball, when he had moved to Nottinghamshire. Hit first century – 127* v Yorkshire at Worksop, July 1982 – after 16 years in first-class game

Best batting performance: 127* Nottinghamshire v Yorkshire, Worksop 1982
Best bowling performance: 10-175 International XI v West Indies XI, Kingston 1982–83

LAST SEASON: BATTING

	I.	N.O.	R.	H.S.	AV.
TEST					
1ST-CLASS	27	8	389	75	20.47
INT					
RAL	7	3	42	29*	10.50
NAT.W.	4	3	23	19*	23.00
B & H	3	0	39	26	13.00

LAST SEASON: BOWLING

	O.	M.	R.	W.	AV.
TEST					
1ST-CLASS	872.4	294	2119	88	24.07
INT					
RAL	69	7	298	7	42.57
NAT.W.	49	6	159	9	17.66
B & H	35	4	123	3	41.00

CAREER: BATTING

	I.	N.O.	R.	H.S.	AV.
TEST	10	1	198	95	22.00
1ST-CLASS	498	111	7666	127*	19.80
INT	2	0	4	2	2.00
RAL	145	41	1405	44*	13.50
NAT.W.	26	9	230	31*	13.52
B & H	39	11	424	61*	15.14

CAREER: BOWLING

	O.	M.	R.	W.	AV.
TEST	244.4	71	558	12	46.50
1ST-CLASS	12163	3465	32433	1136	28.55
INT	41.5	4	175	5	35.00
RAL	1409	95	6535	229	29.43
NAT.W.	377.1	62	1229	37	33.21
B & H	629.4	83	1962	57	34.42

HESELTINE, P. A. W.　　　　　Sussex

Full Name: Peter Anthony William Heseltine
Role: Right-hand bat, off-break bowler
Born: 5 April 1965, Barnsley
Height: 5' 10" **Weight:** 10st 10lbs
Nickname: Gonzo, Yorkie, Woodstock, Rigger, Streisand, Manilow
County debut: 1987
Place in batting averages: 244th av. 11.46
Place in bowling averages: 131st av. 45.85
Strike rate 1987: 42.18 (career 42.18)
1st-Class catches 1987: 3 (career 3)
Parents: Colin James and Georgina Mae

Marital status: Single
Family links with cricket: Brother Philip gained Oxford Blue 1983
Education: Queen Elizabeth Grammar School, Wakefield; King's College, London
Qualifications: 9 O-levels, 3 A-levels
Jobs outside cricket: Ice-cream man, baker, labourer, quarryman, local government officer
Off-season 1987–88: Playing grade cricket in Canberra, Australia
Cricketers particularly learnt from: Steve Oldham, Paul Parker, brother Philip
Cricketers particularly admired: John Emburey, Richard Hadlee, David Gower, Derek Randall
Other sports played: Golf, football
Other sports followed: Barnsley FC when possible and all other sports
Relaxations: Listening to all kinds of music, fly-fishing, watching television
Best batting performance: 26 Sussex v Kent, Dartford 1987
Best bowling performance: 3-33 Sussex v Nottinghamshire, Eastbourne 1987

LAST SEASON: BATTING

	I.	N.O.	R.	H.S.	AV.
TEST					
1ST-CLASS	18	3	172	26	11.46
INT					
RAL	1	1	6	6*	–
NAT.W.					
B & H					

LAST SEASON: BOWLING

	O.	M.	R.	W.	AV.
TEST					
1ST-CLASS	316.2	76	963	21	45.85
INT					
RAL	6	0	34	1	34.00
NAT.W.					
B & H	2	0	12	2	6.00

CAREER: BATTING

	I.	N.O.	R.	H.S.	AV.
TEST					
1ST-CLASS	18	3	172	26	11.46
INT					
RAL	1	1	6	6*	–
NAT.W.					
B & H					

CAREER: BOWLING

	O.	M.	R.	W.	AV.
TEST					
1ST-CLASS	316.2	76	963	21	45.85
INT					
RAL	6	0	34	1	34.00
NAT.W.					
B & H	2	0	12	2	6.00

88. Who won the first ever Test Match, and who played it, and when?

HICK, G. A. — Worcestershire

Full Name: Graeme Ashley Hick
Role: Right-hand bat, off-break bowler, slip and gully fielder
Born: 23 May 1966, Salisbury, Rhodesia
Height: 6′ 3″ **Weight:** 14½st
Nickname: Hicky, Hickery
County debut: 1984
County cap: 1986
1000 runs in a season: 3
1st-Class 50s scored: 24
1st-Class 100s scored: 17
1st-Class 200s scored: 3
One-Day 50s: 18
One-Day 100s: 3
Place in batting averages: 8th av. 52.19 (1986 3rd av. 64.64)
Place in bowling averages: 120th av. 41.68
Strike rate 1987: 74.48 (career 85.56)
1st-Class catches 1987: 13 (career 75)
Parents: John and Eve
Marital status: Single
Family links with cricket: Father connected with cricket administration since 1972 and in 1984 elected to Zimbabwe Cricket Union Board of Control
Education: Banket Primary; Prince Edward Boys' High School, Zimbabwe
Qualifications: 4 O-levels, NCA coaching award
Jobs outside cricket: Zimbabwe Cricket Union coach
Off-season 1987–88: Playing for Northern Districts, New Zealand
Cricketing superstitions or habits: Left pad on first
Overseas tours: Zimbabwe XI 1983 World Cup; Zimbabwe v Sri Lanka in Sri Lanka; Zimbabwe U-23 Triangular Tournament to Zambia; Zimbabwe to UK 1985
Overseas teams played for: Old Harrarians, Zimbabwe, since 1982
Cricketers particularly learnt from: David Houghton, Basil D'Oliveira, Father
Cricketers particularly admired: Duncan Fletcher (Zimbabwe captain) for approach and understanding of the game
Other sports played: Golf, tennis, squash, indoor hockey
Other sports followed: Follows Liverpool FC
Relaxations: Watching movies, television, listening to music
Extras: Youngest player participating in 1983 Prudential World Cup (aged 17); youngest player to represent Zimbabwe. Scored 1234 runs in 1984

Birmingham League season; scored 964 runs in 1984 2nd XI for Worcestershire; scored 185 in Birmingham League – highest score since the War; scored 11 centuries (including six in a row) in both above competitions. Has decided to qualify for England

Opinions on cricket: 'A little more time between games for players to get together and discuss coming games and relax. It may give better performances on the field.'

Best batting performance: 230 Zimbabwe v Oxford University, Oxford 1985
Best bowling performance: 4-31 Worcestershire v Lancashire, Old Trafford 1987

LAST SEASON: BATTING

	I.	N.O.	R.	H.S.	AV.
TEST					
1ST-CLASS	38	2	1879	173	52.19
INT					
RAL	16	6	599	88	59.90
NAT.W.	2	1	227	172*	227.00
B & H	5	1	265	88	66.25

LAST SEASON: BOWLING

	O.	M.	R.	W.	AV.
TEST					
1ST-CLASS	310.2	62	1042	25	41.68
INT					
RAL	69.1	1	334	10	33.40
NAT.W.					
B & H	8	0	30	0	–

CAREER: BATTING

	I.	N.O.	R.	H.S.	AV.
TEST					
1ST-CLASS	129	13	6141	230	52.93
INT					
RAL	40	8	1311	90	40.96
NAT.W.	6	2	264	172*	66.00
B & H	11	2	610	103*	67.77

CAREER: BOWLING

	O.	M.	R.	W.	AV.
TEST					
1ST-CLASS	656	129	2203	46	47.89
INT					
RAL	93.1	1	470	15	31.33
NAT.W.	10	1	25	1	25.00
B & H	20	1	77	3	25.66

HINKS, S. G.   Kent

Full Name: Simon Graham Hinks
Role: Left-hand bat, bat/pad fielder
Born: 12 October 1960, Northfleet, Kent
Height: 6' 2" **Weight:** 13st 7lbs
Nickname: Hinksy
County debut: 1982
County cap: 1985
1000 runs in a season: 1
1st-Class 50s scored: 13
1st-Class 100s scored: 5
One-Day 50s: 8
Place in batting averages: 94th av. 32.00 (1986 139th av. 26.00)
1st-Class catches 1987: 18 (career 62)
Parents: Mary and Graham
Marital status: Single
Family links with cricket: Father

captained Gravesend CC and is now chairman. Brother Joanathan plays for
Gravesend and Kent U-19s

Education: Dover Road Infant and Junior Schools, Northfleet; St George's
C of E School, Gravesend

Qualifications: 5 O-levels, 1 A-level

Cricketing superstitions or habits: Put gear on in set order

Overseas teams played for: Pirates, Johannesburg, 1981–82; University of
Tasmania, 1983–86

Cricketers particularly learnt from: 'Learnt from my father and members of
local club, Gravesend.'

Cricketers particularly admired: 'Admire Clive Loyd's style and power and
anyone who has proved themselves over a long period.'

Other sports played: Most ball games

Relaxations: TV, music, papers, books

Opinions on cricket: 'More should be done by administrators to help players
find employment during the off-season. Too many players rely on coaching
jobs abroad. Less travelling. Two one-day games at weekend and 16 three-
day games midweek.'

Best batting performance: 131 Kent v Hampshire, Canterbury 1986

Best bowling performance: 1-10 Kent v Oxford Unversity, Oxford 1986

LAST SEASON: BATTING

	I.	N.O.	R.	H.S.	AV.
TEST					
1ST-CLASS	33	2	992	112	32.00
INT					
RAL	12	0	175	64	14.58
NAT.W.	1	0	0		0.00
B & H	6	0	252	85	42.00

CAREER: BATTING

	I.	N.O.	R.	H.S.	AV.
TEST					
1ST-CLASS	147	8	3914	131	28.15
INT					
RAL	45	2	867	99	20.16
NAT.W.	5	0	188	95	37.60
B & H	18	0	487	85	27.05

LAST SEASON: BOWLING

	O.	M.	R.	W.	AV.
TEST					
1ST-CLASS	17	2	73	0	–
INT					
RAL	7	0	52	1	52.00
NAT.W.					
B & H	27	0	144	3	48.00

CAREER: BOWLING

	O.	M.	R.	W.	AV.
TEST					
1ST-CLASS	75.4	9	261	4	65.25
INT					
RAL	25	1	139	4	34.75
NAT.W.					
B & H	41	0	198	5	39.60

89. What was unusual about S. M. J. Woods playing for England v
South Africa in the First Test in 1896?

HODGSON, G. D.   Warwickshire

Full Name: Geoffrey Dean
Hodgson
Role: Right-hand bat
Born: 22 October 1966, Carlisle
Height: 6' 1" **Weight:** 12st
Nickname: Deano
County debut: 1987
Parents: John Geoffrey and
Dorothy Elizabeth
Marital status: Single
Education: Nelson Thomlinson
Comprehensive, Wigton, Cumbria;
Loughborough University
Education: 10 O-levels, 4 A-levels,
BSc Hons Human Biological Sciences
Off-season 1987–88: Finishing
degree at Loughborough
Cricketing superstitions or habits:
Left pad, gloves and boot on
first. Wear a gumshield
Overseas tours: England Youth XI to Bermuda 1985
Cricketers particularly learnt from: Dennis Amiss, Richard Hadlee
Cricketers particularly admired: Dennis Amiss, Viv Richards, Ian Botham,
Geoff Boycott, Richard Hadlee
Other sports played: Football, tennis
Other sports followed: Most sports
Injuries 1987: Damaged shoulder tendon and bruised foot
Relaxations: Music, books, films
Extras: Played one match in the Refuge Assurance Sunday League 1987

LAST SEASON: BATTING

	I.	N.O.	R.	H.S.	AV.
TEST					
1ST-CLASS					
INT					
RAL	1	0	12	12	12.00
NAT.W.					
B & H					

CAREER: BATTING

	I.	N.O.	R.	H.S.	AV.
TEST					
1ST-CLASS					
INT					
RAL	1	0	12	12	12.00
NAT.W.					
B & H					

HOLDING, M. A.   Derbyshire

Full Name: Michael Anthony Holding
Role: Right-hand bat, right-arm fast bowler
Born: 16 February 1954, Kingston, Jamaica
County debut: 1981 (Lancashire), 1983 (Derbyshire)
County cap: 1983 (Derbyshire)
Test debut: 1975–76
No. of Tests: 60
No. of One-Day Internationals: 102
50 wickets in a season: 2
1st-Class 50s scored: 14
1st-Class 5 w. in innings: 35
1st-Class 10 w. in match: 4
One-Day 50s: 6
Place in batting averages: 198th

av. 17.37 (1986 204th av. 16.38)
Place in bowling averages: 28th av. 24.36 (1986 8th av. 20.09)
Strike rate 1987: 47.91 (career 45.37)
1st-Class catches 1987: 10 (career 89)
Overseas tours: With West Indies to Australia 1975–86, 1981–82; to England 1976, 1980, 1984; to India 1983–84; International team to Pakistan 1981–82
Overseas teams played for: Jamaica, Tasmania
Extras: Played for Lancashire in 1981. Moved to Derbyshire in 1983. Has 'deepest voice in county cricket'. Retired from Test cricket in 1987

LAST SEASON: BATTING

	I.	N.O.	R.	H.S.	AV.
TEST					
1ST-CLASS	18	2	278	63*	17.37
INT					
RAL	14	1	183	54	14.07
NAT.W.	2	0	30	21	15.00
B & H	3	1	46	22	23.00

CAREER: BATTING

	I.	N.O.	R.	H.S.	AV.
TEST	76	10	910	73	13.78
1ST-CLASS	162	21	2308	80	16.36
INT	42	11	282	64	9.09
RAL	38	4	507	58	14.91
NAT.W.	6	1	69	27	13.80
B & H	10	2	182	69	22.75

LAST SEASON: BOWLING

	O.	M.	R.	W.	AV.
TEST					
1ST-CLASS	391.2	72	1194	49	24.36
INT					
RAL	98.4	5	397	21	18.90
NAT.W.	33.3	8	81	6	13.50
B & H	44	4	137	3	45.66

CAREER: BOWLING

	O.	M.	R.	W.	AV.
TEST	140.5 1925.5	15 395	5898	249	23.68
1ST-CLASS	56 2954.5	5 745	9765	431	22.65
INT	912.1	100	3034	142	21.36
RAL	354.2	37	1395	68	20.51
NAT.W.	99.3	18	270	13	20.76
B & H	137	21	407	14	29.07

Best batting performance: 80 Derbyshire v Yorkshire, Chesterfield 1985
Best bowling performance: 8-92 West Indies v England, The Oval 1976

HOLMES, G. C. Glamorgan

Full Name: Geoffrey Clark Holmes
Role: Right-hand bat, right-arm
medium bowler, cover fielder
Born: 16 September 1958,
Newcastle-on-Tyne
Height: 5′ 10″ **Weight:** 10st 10lbs
County debut: 1978
County cap: 1985
1000 runs in a season: 3
1st-Class 50s scored: 27
1st-Class 100s scored: 4
1st-Class 5 w. in innings: 1
One-Day 50s: 11
Place in batting averages: 146th
av. 24.91 (1986 121st av. 28.35)
Place in bowling averages: —
(1986 112th av. 45.36)
1st-Class catches 1987: 9 (career 67)
Parents: George and Rita
Wife: Christine
Family links with cricket: Father played in the Northumberland League
Education: West Denton High School
Qualifications: 6 O-levels, 2 A-levels; Advanced Cricket Coach
Jobs outside cricket: Trainee estimator; has worked as milkman

LAST SEASON: BATTING

	I.	N.O.	R.	H.S.	AV.
TEST					
1ST-CLASS	43	6	922	95	24.91
INT			-		
RAL	12	3	306	51	34.00
NAT.W.	2	0	57	57	28.50
B & H	3	0	104	56	34.66

CAREER: BATTING

	I.	N.O.	R.	H.S.	AV.
TEST					
1ST-CLASS	249	38	5592	112	26.50
INT					
RAL	82	16	1575	73	23.86
NAT.W.	9	0	163	57	18.11
B & H	17	2	388	70	25.86

LAST SEASON: BOWLING

	O.	M.	R.	W.	AV.
TEST					
1ST-CLASS	103.4	19	363	2	181.50
INT					
RAL	82.1	2	454	22	20.63
NAT.W.	11	4	25	0	—
B & H	23	2	97	5	19.40

CAREER: BOWLING

	O.	M.	R.	W.	AV.
TEST					
1ST-CLASS	920.2	185	3191	69	46.24
INT					
RAL	385.4	12	2034	84	24.21
NAT.W.	73	15	181	9	20.11
B & H	120.2	13	490	21	23.33

Overseas teams played for: Villa CC, Antigua, 1980–81; Bathurst RUCC, New South Wales, 1983–84; Fish Hoek, South Africa, 1984–85
Cricketers particularly learnt from: Javed Miandad
Other sports played: Soccer, snooker
Relaxations: Reading (especially cricket books), TV, sport
Best batting performance: 112 Glamorgan v Leicestershire, Leicester 1985
Best bowling performance: 5-86 Glamorgan v Surrey, The Oval 1980

HOPKINS, J. A.   Glamorgan

Full Name: John Anthony Hopkins
Role: Right-hand bat, occasional wicket-keeper
Born: 16 June 1953, Maesteg
Nickname: Ponty
County debut: 1970
County cap: 1977
Benefit: 1986
1000 runs in a season: 7
1st-Class 50s scored: 60
1st-Class 100s scored: 18
1st-Class 200s scored: 1
One-Day 50s: 28
One-Day 100s: 2
Place in batting averages: 216th av. 15.45 (1986 120th av. 28.38)
1st-Class catches 1987: 13 (career 204 + 1 stumping)
Family links with cricket: Younger brother of J. D. Hopkins

LAST SEASON: BATTING

	I.	N.O.	R.	H.S.	AV.
TEST					
1ST-CLASS	26	2	371	39*	15.45
INT					
RAL	10	0	359	68	35.90
NAT.W.	1	0	33	33	33.00
B & H	4	0	26	25	6.50

CAREER: BATTING

	I.	N.O.	R.	H.S.	AV.
TEST					
1ST-CLASS	512	31	13208	230	27.45
INT					
RAL	167	13	3618	130*	23.49
NAT.W.	19	0	394	63	20.73
B & H	44	2	1072	103*	25.52

LAST SEASON: BOWLING

	O.	M.	R.	W.	AV.
TEST					
1ST-CLASS					
INT					
RAL					
NAT.W.					
B & H					

CAREER: BOWLING

	O.	M.	R.	W.	AV.
TEST					
1ST-CLASS	21.2	2	102	0	–
INT					
RAL					
NAT.W.					
B & H					

who appeared for Middlesex CCC and formerly on Glamorgan staff
Education: Trinity College of Education, Carmarthen
Qualifications: Trained as a teacher
Jobs outside cricket: Teacher
Extras: Known as fine baritone singer and raconteur in the Glamorgan 'cabaret' act
Best batting performance: 230 Glamorgan v Worcestershire, Worcester 1977

HUGHES, D. P. Lancashire

Full Name: David Paul Hughes
Role: Right-hand bat, slow left-arm bowler
Born: 13 May 1947, Newton-le-Willows
Height: 5′ 11″ **Weight:** 12st
Nickname: Yozzer
County debut: 1967
County cap: 1970
Testimonial: 1981
1000 runs in a season: 2
50 wickets in a season: 2
1st-Class 50s scored: 39
1st-Class 100s scored: 8
1st-Class 5 w. in innings: 20
1st-Class 10 w. in match: 2
One-Day 50s: 10
Place in batting averages: 199th av. 17.34
1st-Class catches 1987: 20 (career 263)
Parents: Both deceased
Wife and date of marriage: Christine, March 1973
Children: James, July 1975
Family links with cricket: Father, Lloyd, a professional with Bolton League club Walkden, before and after Second World War
Education: Newton-le-Willows Grammar School
Qualifications: NCA Coaching Certificate
Overseas tours: With Derrick Robins XI to South Africa 1972–73; England Counties side to West Indies 1974–75
Overseas teams played for: Tasmania while coaching there in 1975–76 and 1976–77
Cricketers particularly learnt from: 'At the start of my career I spoke to all the leading left-arm spin bowlers in the game for help.'
Relaxations: Golf

Extras: Coached in South Africa 1977–78; coached in Tasmania 1978–79 and 1979–80. Gillette Cup 'specialist'. Hit 24 runs off John Mortimer v Gloucestershire in penultimate over in Gillette semi-final in 1972. Hit 26 runs off last over of innings v Northamptonshire in Gillette Final at Lord's, 1976. Bowled 13 consecutive maiden overs v Gloucestershire at Bristol, 1980. John Player League 9th wicket partnership of 86 with P. Lever v Essex, Leyton 1973. Appointed Lancashire captain for 1987

Best batting performance: 153 Lancashire v Glamorgan, Old Trafford 1983
Best bowling performance: 7-24 Lancashire v Oxford University, Oxford 1970

LAST SEASON: BATTING

	I.	N.O.	R.	H.S.	AV.
TEST					
1ST-CLASS	35	6	503	81	17.34
INT					
RAL	11	1	192	72	19.20
NAT.W.	1	0	1	1	1.00
B & H	3	0	47	28	15.66

LAST SEASON: BOWLING

	O.	M.	R.	W.	AV.
TEST					
1ST-CLASS	28	6	99	3	33.00
INT					
RAL	19	0	152	8	19.00
NAT.W.					
B & H	6	0	20	0	–

CAREER: BATTING

	I.	N.O.	R.	H.S.	AV.
TEST					
1ST-CLASS	500	90	9121	153	22.24
INT					
RAL	191	43	2748	92	18.56
NAT.W.	35	15	760	71	38.00
B & H	50	13	907	52	24.51

CAREER: BOWLING

	O.	M.	R.	W.	AV.
TEST					
1ST-CLASS	23 6748.1	3 2090	18392	614	29.95
INT					
RAL	809.1	62	3568	169	21.11
NAT.W.	300.2	29	1166	44	26.50
B & H	235.2	40	746	29	25.72

HUGHES, S. P.   Middlesex

Full Name: Simon Peter Hughes
Role: Right-hand bat, right-arm fast-medium bowler
Born: 20 December 1959, Kingston, Surrey
Height: 5′ 10″ **Weight:** 11st 7lbs
Nickname: Yozzer, Spam, Yule
County debut: 1980
County cap: 1981
50 wickets in a season: 1
1st-Class 5 w. in innings: 8
Place in batting averages: 227th av. 13.92 (1986 229th av. 12.33)
Place in bowling averages: 117th av. 40.24 (1986 34th av. 26.22)
Strike rate 1987: 74.06 (career 53.43)
1st-Class catches 1987: 6 (career 31)
Parents: Peter and Erica

Marital status: Single

Family links with cricket: Father very keen coach and player who owned indoor cricket school. 'Uncle once hit a ball over the school pavilion!'

Education: Latymer Upper School, Hammersmith; Durham University

Qualifications: 10 O-levels, 4 A-levels, BA General Studies

Jobs outside cricket: Writes regular sports column in local weekly paper, and monthly for *The Cricketer*. Also contributes a weekly cricket column to *The Independent*

Off-season 1987–88: Freelancing

Overseas tours: Personal overseas spell playing in Sri Lanka 1979; Middlesex CCC tour to Zimbabwe winter 1980; with Overseas XI (captained by J. M. Brearley) to Calcutta (v Indian XI) 1980–81; International Ambassadors tour to India 1985

Overseas teams played for: Colts CC, Colombo, Sri Lanka, and Sri Lanka Board President's XI; Northern Transvaal 1982–83; Grosvenor-Fynaland 1983–84; Auckland University 1984–85; Freemantle CC (Perth) 1985–86

Cricketers particularly learnt from: Father, Jack Robertson, Mike Brearley, Mike Selvey, Gubby Allen

Cricketers particularly admired: John Emburey, Clive Radley, Malcolm Marshall, Richard Hadlee

Other sports played: Soccer (for university), tennis, golf

Relaxations: Travelling, slapstick films, jazz and blues piano, eating curry, broadcasting and journalism

Extras: Took 4-82 v Kent on Championship debut, plus played in County Championship and Gillette Cup winning sides (Lord's Final) in 1980 in first season. Selected for England U-25 XI v Sri Lanka (Trent Bridge) July 1981. Awarded cap after only 20 matches. Middlesex/Austin Reed Player of the Year 1986. Won a free holiday as Middlesex leading wicket-taker 1986

Opinions on cricket: 'For several years I suggested uncovered wickets were essential for more variety, but 1987 proved that utterly wrong. The problem is either in the soil or my head. With declining public interest in county cricket,

LAST SEASON: BATTING

	I.	N.O.	R.	H.S.	AV.
TEST					
1ST-CLASS	20	7	181	26*	13.92
INT					
RAL	4	2	24	13*	12.00
NAT.W.	1	0	1	1	1.00
B & H	3	3	8	6*	–

CAREER: BATTING

	I.	N.O.	R.	H.S.	AV.
TEST					
1ST-CLASS	121	44	845	47	10.97
INT					
RAL	21	9	143	22*	11.91
NAT.W.	6	2	13	6	3.25
B & H	7	5	24	8*	12.00

LAST SEASON: BOWLING

	O.	M.	R.	W.	AV.
TEST					
1ST-CLASS	358	55	1167	29	40.24
INT					
RAL	75.4	3	326	11	29.63
NAT.W.	12	1	41	1	41.00
B & H	22.1	1	101	6	16.83

CAREER: BOWLING

	O.	M.	R.	W.	AV.
TEST					
1ST-CLASS	2671.4	507	8740	300	29.13
INT					
RAL	349.5	8	1662	56	29.67
NAT.W.	128.2	17	486	20	24.30
B & H	79.1	8	306	12	25.50

it is time players adjusted their attitudes towards leaving the field for bad light, and umpires to take a stronger line on intimidatory bowling.'

Best batting performance: 47 Middlesex v Warwickshire, Uxbridge 1986
Best bowling performance: 7-35 Middlesex v Surrey, The Oval 1986

HUMPAGE, G. W.   Warwickshire

Full Name: Geoffrey William Humpage
Role: Right-hand bat, wicket-keeper; can also bowl right-arm medium
Born: 24 April 1954, Birmingham
Height: 5′ 9″ **Weight:** 12st 7lbs
Nickname: Farsley
County debut: 1974
County cap: 1976
Benefit: 1987
No. of One-Day Internationals: 3
1000 runs in a season: 10
1st-Class 50s scored: 84
1st-Class 100s scored: 26
1st-Class 200s scored: 2
One-Day 50s: 31
One-Day 100s: 3
Place in batting averages: 34th
av. 41.18 (1986 57th av. 38.47)
Parents: Ernest and Mabel
Wife and date of marriage: Valerie Anne, 14 September 1983 (2nd marriage)
Children: Philip Andrew Guy, 16 November 1977
Education: Golden Hillock Comprehensive School, Birmingham
Jobs outside cricket: Former police cadet, then police constable, Birmingham City Police. Coach, Scarborough CC, Western Australia, 1978–79. Sports executive for Pace Insurance Consultants, Birmingham
Other sports played: Soccer, squash, tennis, swimming, golf, snooker, table tennis
Relaxations: Reading, listening to E.L.O.
Extras: Good impressionist, particularly of Frankie Howerd. Took part in record Warwickshire and English first-class 4th wicket partnership of 470 v Lancashire at Southport, July 1982, with Kallicharran (230*). Humpage made 254* including 13 sixes. Previous 4th wicket record was 448 for Surrey at The Oval v Yorkshire in 1899, by R. Abel and T. W. Hayward. Joined England Rebels in South Africa in 1982
Best batting performance: 254 Warwickshire v Lancashire, Southport 1982
Best bowling performance: 2-13 Warwickshire v Gloucestershire, Edgbaston 1980

LAST SEASON: BATTING

	I.	N.O.	R.	H.S.	AV.
TEST					
1ST-CLASS	41	9	1318	99*	41.18
INT					
RAL	11	3	288	47	36.00
NAT.W.	3	0	120	76	40.00
B & H	3	0	45	25	15.00

CAREER: BATTING

	I.	N.O.	R.	H.S.	AV.
TEST					
1ST-CLASS	492	64	16018	254	37.42
INT	2	0	11	6	5.50
RAL	159	24	3475	109*	25.74
NAT.W.	29	4	720	77	28.80
B & H	51	7	1257	100*	28.56

LAST SEASON: WICKET KEEPING

	C.	ST.			
TEST					
1ST-CLASS	31	3			
INT					
RAL	8	1			
NAT.W.	2	–			
B & H	2	1			

LAST SEASON: BOWLING

	O.	M.	R.	W.	AV.
TEST					
1ST-CLASS	2	0	8	0	–
INT					
RAL	3	0	29	0	–
NAT.W.					
B & H					

CAREER: BOWLING

	O.	M.	R.	W.	AV.
TEST					
1ST-CLASS	132.1	17	452	10	45.20
INT					
RAL	97.5	2	556	15	37.06
NAT.W.					
B & H					

CAREER: WICKET KEEPING

	C.	ST.			
TEST					
1ST-CLASS	545	67			
INT	2	–			
RAL	107	20			
NAT.W.	32	6			
B & H	61	3			

HUSSAIN, N.   Essex

Full Name: Nasser Hussain
Role: Right-hand bat
Born: 28 March 1968, Madras, India
Height: 6′ 1″
Nickname: Bunny
County debut: 1987
1st-Class catches 1987: 2 (career 2)
Parents: Jainad and Shireen
Marital status: Single
Family links with cricket: Father
played for Madras in Ranji
Trophy 1966–67. Uncle played
for Combined Indian Universities.
Brother Amel on Hampshire staff
in 1983 and 1984. Brother Abbas
played for Essex 2nd XI
Education: Forest School;
Durham University

Qualifications: 9 O-levels, 3 A-levels; NCA Cricket Coaching Award
Jobs outside cricket: Worked at Morgan Guaranty Bank during holidays
Off-season 1987–88: Studying at Durham University, touring with Young
England and playing golf

210

Overseas teams played for: Madras 1986–87
Cricketers particularly learnt from: Father, Ray East (Essex coach)
Other sports played: Golf, football
Other sports followed: Golf, football, American football
Relaxations: Music
Extras: Played for England Schools U-15 for two years (one as captain). Youngest player to play for Essex Schools U-11 at the age of 8 and U-15 at the age of 12. At 15, was considered the best young leg-spin bowler in the country
Best batting performance: 18 Essex v Lancashire, Chelmsford 1987

LAST SEASON: BATTING

	I.	N.O.	R.	H.S.	AV.
TEST					
1ST-CLASS	3	0	32	18	10.66
INT					
RAL	4	1	91	30	30.33
NAT.W.					
B & H					

CAREER: BATTING

	I.	N.O.	R.	H.S.	AV.
TEST					
1ST-CLASS	3	0	32	18	10.66
INT					
RAL	4	1	91	30	30.33
NAT.W.					
B & H					

HUTCHINSON I. J. F.   Middlesex

Full Name: Ian James Frederick Hutchinson
Role: Right-hand bat, right-arm medium pace bowler
Born: 31 October 1964, Welshpool
Height: 6′ 1″
County debut: 1987
Education: Shrewsbury School
Extras: Played for Shropshire 1984–85. On MCC groundstaff 1984–86. Was substitute fielder for England v New Zealand at Lord's 1986. Played one Refuge Assurance Sunday League match 1987

LAST SEASON: BATTING

	I.	N.O.	R.	H.S.	AV.
TEST					
1ST-CLASS					
INT					
RAL	1	1	22	22*	–
NAT.W.					
B & H					

CAREER: BATTING

	I.	N.O.	R.	H.S.	AV.
TEST					
1ST-CLASS					
INT					
RAL	1	1	22	22*	–
NAT.W.					
B & H					

IBADULLA, K. B. K.   Gloucestershire

Full Name: Kassim Ben
Khalid Ibadulla
Role: Right-hand bat,
off-break bowler
Born: 13 October 1964,
Birmingham
County debut: 1987
1st-Class 5 w. in innings: 1
Place in batting averages: 169th
av. 20.57
1st-Class catches 1987: 2 (career 5)
Family links with cricket: Father
Khalid 'Billy' Ibadulla played
for Warwickshire and Pakistan
Extras: Played for
Warwickshire 2nd XI 1981–84
and for Otago in New Zealand
1982–86

Best batting performance: 46*
Gloucestershire v Lancashire, Old Trafford 1987
Best bowling performance: 5-22 Otago v Canterbury, Invercargill 1982–83

LAST SEASON: BATTING

	I.	N.O.	R.	H.S.	AV.
TEST					
1ST-CLASS	8	1	144	46*	20.57
INT					
RAL	1	0	12	12	12.00
NAT.W.					
B & H					

LAST SEASON: BOWLING

	O.	M.	R.	W.	AV.
TEST					
1ST-CLASS	54	8	156	4	39.00
INT					
RAL					
NAT.W.					
B & H					

CAREER: BATTING

	I.	N.O.	R.	H.S.	AV.
TEST					
1ST-CLASS	12	3	189	46*	21.00
INT					
RAL	1	0	12	12	12.00
NAT.W.					
B & H					

CAREER: BOWLING

	O.	M.	R.	W.	AV.
TEST					
1ST-CLASS	145.2	30	390	13	30.00
INT					
RAL					
NAT.W.					
B & H					

90. Which wicket-keeper has the most Test dismissals, and how
many?

IGGLESDEN, A. P.　　　　　　　Kent

Full Name: Alan Paul Igglesden
Role: Right-hand bat, right-arm
fast bowler, outfielder
Born: 8 October 1964,
Farnborough, Kent
Height: 6′ 6″ **Weight:** 14st 4lbs
Nickname: Iggy
County debut: 1986
1st-Class 5 w. in innings: 3
Place in bowling averages: 43rd
av. 25.98
Strike rate 1987: 44.13 (career 48.33)
1st-Class catches 1987: 3 (career 5)
Parents: Alan Trevor and Gillian
Catherine
Marital status: Single
Family links with cricket: Brother
Kevin plays for same Kent
League club
Education: St Mary's Primary School, Westerham; Hosey School, Westerham; Churchill Secondary School, Westerham
Qualifications: 9 CSEs
Jobs outside cricket: 'Since I left school I have had a few jobs just to fit in with my cricket at Kent.'
Off-season 1987–88: Playing and coaching for Bob Woolmer's multi-racial club, Avendale in Cape Town
Cricketing superstitions or habits: Like to be at the ground early. Try to keep to the same match build-up if things are going well.
Overseas teams played for: Avendale 1985–86, 1986–87, 1987–88
Cricketers particularly learnt from: Terry Alderman, Bob Woolmer, Colin Page, Stuart Leary and senior players at Kent
Cricketers particularly admired: Terry Alderman, Dennis Lillee, Ian Botham, Imran Khan
Other sports played: Golf, football, snooker
Other sports followed: Football (follows Crystal Palace)
Injuries 1987: Torn ligaments in left ankle (3 weeks) and thigh strain (2 weeks)
Relaxations: Listening to music (especially Simple Minds, U2, Kate Bush), sleeping, watching sport on TV, crosswords
Extras: 'I didn't play any schools representative cricket.'
Opinions on cricket: 'I just feel sorry for the cricketers of South Africa, past and present. They surely would have been a tremendous force in Test cricket today. 110 overs in a day is too many. Fines system for over rates should be

abolished. If you bowl your 110 overs by 6.30 you still get fined. No sense in that to me!'

Best batting performance: 30 Kent v Sussex, Hove 1987
Best bowling performance: 5-45 Kent v Glamorgan, Canterbury 1987

LAST SEASON: BATTING

	I.	N.O.	R.	H.S.	AV.
TEST					
1ST-CLASS	15	4	89	30	8.09
INT					
RAL	3	1	25	13*	12.50
NAT.W.					
B & H	1	1	5	5*	–

CAREER: BATTING

	I.	N.O.	R.	H.S.	AV.
TEST					
1ST-CLASS	20	6	111	30	7.92
INT					
RAL	3	1	25	13*	12.50
NAT.W.					
B & H	1	1	5	5*	–

LAST SEASON: BOWLING

	O.	M.	R.	W.	AV.
TEST					
1ST-CLASS	382.3	54	1351	52	25.98
INT					
RAL	53.5	5	217	9	24.11
NAT.W.	19	5	60	4	15.00
B & H	23	2	92	2	46.00

CAREER: BOWLING

	O.	M.	R.	W.	AV.
TEST					
1ST-CLASS	507.3	79	1723	63	27.34
INT					
RAL	53.5	5	217	9	24.11
NAT.W.	19	5	60	4	15.00
B & H	23	2	92	2	46.00

ILLINGWORTH, R. K.   Worcestershire

Full Name: Richard Keith Illingworth
Role: Right-hand bat, slow left-arm bowler
Born: 23 August 1963, Bradford
Height: 6′ **Weight:** 12st
Nickname: Illy, Lucy, Harry
County debut: 1982
County cap: 1986
50 wickets in a season: 1
1st-Class 100s scored: 1
1st-Class 50s scored: 1
1st-Class 5 w. in innings: 6
1st-Class 10 w. in match: 1
Place in batting averages: 5th av. 56.00 (1986 196th av. 17.36)
Place in bowling averages: 122nd av. 42.15 (1986 116th av. 48.60)
Strike rate 1987: 86.96 (career 84.67)
1st-Class catches 1987: 8 (career 48)
Parents: Keith and Margaret
Wife and date of marriage: Anne, 20 September 1985

214

Family links with cricket: Father plays Bradford League cricket. Mother secretary Yorkshire CA Centre of Excellence nets
Education: Wrose Brow Middle; Salts Grammar School
Qualifications: 6 O-levels, senior coaching award holder
Jobs outside cricket: Civil servant
Overseas tours: Denmark Youth Tournament NAYC 1981; Whitbread scholarship playing for Colts CC, Brisbane 1982–83; Wisden Cricket XI, Barbados 1983
Cricketers particularly learnt from: Father
Other sports played: Golf, football
Other sports followed: Football (follows Leeds United and Bradford City)
Relaxations: 'Listening to music, watching sport on TV, sampling my wife's wonderful cooking.'
Extras: Had a better batting average in 1987 than G. A. Hick
Best batting performance: 120* Worcestershire v Warwickshire, Worcester 1987
Best bowling performance: 7-50 Worcestershire v Oxford University, Oxford 1985

LAST SEASON: BATTING

	I.	N.O.	R.	H.S.	AV.
TEST					
1ST-CLASS	19	11	448	120*	56.00
INT					
RAL	3	1	3	2	1.50
NAT.W.	1	0	1	1	1.00
B & H					

CAREER: BATTING

	I.	N.O.	R.	H.S.	AV.
TEST					
1ST-CLASS	125	40	1614	120*	18.98
INT					
RAL	32	16	131	21	8.18
NAT.W.	4	0	39	22	9.75
B & H	7	4	52	17*	17.33

LAST SEASON: BOWLING

	O.	M.	R.	W.	AV.
TEST					
1ST-CLASS	478.2	116	1391	33	42.15
INT					
RAL	53.1	1	333	12	27.75
NAT.W.	8	2	20	4	5.00
B & H	10	1	33	2	16.50

CAREER: BOWLING

	O.	M.	R.	W.	AV.
TEST					
1ST-CLASS	3119	869	8311	221	37.60
INT					
RAL	330.1	19	1567	73	21.46
NAT.W.	67.1	11	199	7	28.42
B & H	137	18	495	19	26.05

91. Which wicket-keeper has most dismissals in one Test?
92. Who took the most catches in first-class cricket in 1987, and how many?

JAMES, K. D.   Hampshire

Full Name: Kevan David James
Role: Left-hand bat, left-arm
fast-medium bowler; fields
'anywhere but short leg'
Born: 18 March 1961, Lambeth,
South London
Height: 6′ 0½″ **Weight:** 12st 6lbs
Nickname: Jambo, Jaimo
County debut: 1980 (Middlesex),
1985 (Hampshire)

1st-Class 50s scored: 3
1st-Class 100s scored: 3
1st-Class 5 w. in innings: 4
One-Day 50s: 1
Place in batting averages: 3rd
av. 62.00 (1986 147th av. 25.00)
Place in bowling averages: 113th
av. 39.84 (1986 70th av. 32.95)
Strike rate 1987: 65.10 (career 63.85)
1st-Class catches 1987: 5 (career 19)
Parents: David and Helen
Wife and date of marriage: Debbie, October 1987
Family links with cricket: Late father played club cricket in North London
Education: Edmonton County High School
Qualifications: 5 O-levels; qualified coach
Off-season 1987–88: Playing for Eden-Roskill in Auckland, New Zealand
Overseas tours: Young England tour of Australia, 1978–79; Young England
tour of West Indies, 1979–80
Overseas teams played for: Canterbury Province U-23, New Zealand, 1980;
Sydenham CC, Christchurch, New Zealand, 1980–81; Wellington, New
Zealand, 1982–83, 1984–85; Eden-Roskill, Auckland 1987–88
Cricketers particularly learnt from: Don Bennett (Middlesex coach)
Other sports played: Soccer
Other sports followed: Watches American football, follows Spurs
Injuries 1987: Side strain for one month
Relaxations: DIY and making money. Writes two columns, one in *The Club
Cricketer*, the other in a local Southampton paper. 'It would be nice just to
have time to relax.'
Extras: Released by Middlesex at end of 1984 season and joined Hampshire
Best batting performance: 142* Hampshire v Nottinghamshire, Bournemouth
1987
Best bowling performance: 6-22 Hampshire v Australia, Southampton 1985

LAST SEASON: BATTING

	I.	N.O.*	R.	H.S.	AV.
TEST					
1ST-CLASS	16	6	620	142*	62.00
INT					
RAL	10	3	185	37	26.42
NAT.W.	1	0	10	10	10.00
B & H	4	0	46	29	11.50

LAST SEASON: BOWLING

	O.	M.	R.	W.	AV.
TEST					
1ST-CLASS	206.1	36	757	19	39.84
INT					
RAL	74.4	3	394	8	49.25
NAT.W.	19.4	2	101	4	25.25
B & H	43.5	0	198	5	39.60

CAREER: BATTING

	I.	N.O.	R.	H.S.	AV.
TEST					
1ST-CLASS	62	18	1500	142*	34.09
INT					
RAL	23	10	394	54*	30.30
NAT.W.	3	1	46	19	23.00
B & H	10	0	112	29	11.20

CAREER: BOWLING

	O.	M.	R.	W.	AV.
TEST					
1ST-CLASS	968.3	231	3034	91	33.34
INT					
RAL	305	15	1375	36	38.19
NAT.W.	48.4	3	223	7	31.85
B & H	120.5	11	459	14	32.78

JAMES, S. P. Glamorgan

Full Name: Stephen Peter James
Role: Right-hand opening bat
Born: 7 September 1967, Lydney
Height: 6′ **Weight:** 12st 10lbs
Nickname: Jamer, Pedro
County debut: 1985
1st-Class 100s scored: 1
1st-Class catches 1987: 4 (career 4)
Parents: Peter and Margaret
Marital status: Single
Family links with cricket: Father played for Gloucestershire 2nd XI and for Lydney CC for many years
Education: Monmouth School; Swansea University
Qualifications: 10 O-levels, 3-A levels
Off-season 1987–88: Finishing Classics degree at Swansea University
Overseas tours: Welsh Schools U-17 tour to Barbados (as captain); Monmouth School tour to Sri Lanka (as captain)
Cricketers particularly learnt from: 'Sonny' Avery, Graham Burgess, Alan Jones
Cricketers particularly admired: Geoffrey Boycott, Adrian Knox (Lydney CC)
Other sports played: Rugby Union, squash

Injuries 1987: Damaged knee ligaments (one month), virus (three weeks)
Relaxations: Listening to music, sociable pint at the pub
Extras: Averaged 107 for Lydney CC in Three Counties League 1987. Did not get onto field on debut v Sussex because of rain, in 1985, eventually played v Sussex in 1987 after 1st day had been washed out. Scored 43*. Followed up with 106 v Oxford University in second 1st-Class innings. Plays regularly for Lydney RFC. Has also represented Gloucestershire and South West of England at U-21 level in rugby union
Best batting performance: 106 Glamorgan v Oxford University, Oxford 1987

LAST SEASON: BATTING

	I.	N.O.	R.	H.S.	AV.
TEST					
1ST-CLASS	13	1	246	106	20.50
INT					
RAL					
NAT.W.	2	0	32	26	16.00
B & H					

CAREER: BATTING

	I.	N.O.	R.	H.S.	AV.
TEST					
1ST-CLASS	13	1	246	106	20.50
INT					
RAL					
NAT.W.	2	0	32	26	16.00
B & H					

JARVIS, K. B. S.   Gloucestershire

Full Name: Kevin Bertram Sidney Jarvis
Role: Right-hand bat, right-arm fast-medium bowler
Born: 23 April 1953, Dartford, Kent
Height: 6' 3" **Weight:** 13st
Nickname: Jarvo, Ferret, KJ
County debut: 1975 (Kent)
County cap: 1977 (Kent)
Benefit: 1987
50 wickets in a season: 7
1st-Class 5 w. in innings: 19
1st-Class 10 w. in match: 3
Place in batting averages: 245th av. 11.00
Place in bowling averages: 81st av. 31.57 (1986 99th av. 40.58)
Strike rate 1987: 53.85 (career 56.17)
1st-Class catches 1987: 0 (career 56)
Parents: Herbert John and Margaret Elsie
Wife and date of marriage: Margaret Anne, 16 September 1978
Children: Simon Martin, 16 April 1985

Family links with cricket: Son very keen; father played club cricket; Simon Hinks is a distant relative
Education: Springhead School, Northfleet, Kent; Thames Polytechnic
Qualifications: 6 O-levels, 3 A-levels, NCA coach, ISMA, MAMSA
Jobs outside cricket: Accountancy, insurance, clerical
Off-season 1987–88: Looking for winter employment
Cricketing superstitions or habits: 'I never hook before October and have a habit of not getting any runs.'
Overseas tours: Derrick Robins' XI to Far East 1977; Jamaica 1982
Overseas teams played for: Played and coached for South Melbourne, 1979 and 1981; Tooronga, 1978
Cricketers particularly learnt from: Derek Underwood, Bob Woolmer
Cricketers particularly admired: Richard Hadlee, Dennis Lillee
Other sports played: Squash, badminton, tennis, football, hockey, darts
Other sports followed: 'Watch everything except synchronised swimming.'
Injuries 1987: Pulled calf muscle
Extras: Released by Kent at end of 1987 season. Joined Gloucestershire on a two-year contract in 1988
Opinions on cricket: 'Play more one-day cricket and more exciting three-day cricket. Play on uncovered pitches (so D. Underwood can play forever!); four-day cricket will kill the Championship as a spectator sport.'
Best batting performance: 19 Kent v Derbyshire, Maidstone 1984
Best bowling performance: 8-97 Kent v Worcestershire, Worcester 1978

LAST SEASON: BATTING

	I.	N.O.	R.	H.S.	AV.
TEST					
1ST-CLASS	8	7	11	4*	11.00
INT					
RAL	2	1	0	–	0.00
NAT.W.					
B & H					

LAST SEASON: BOWLING

	O.	M.	R.	W.	AV.
TEST					
1ST-CLASS	251.2	41	884	28	31.57
INT				.	
RAL	47.4	2	239	5	47.80
NAT.W.					
B & H	7	0	27	0	–

CAREER: BATTING

	I.	N.O.	R.	H.S.	AV.
TEST					
1ST-CLASS	182	81	336	19	3.32
INT					
RAL	48	29	58	8*	3.05
NAT.W.	11	5	16	5*	2.66
B & H	24	15	16	4*	1.77

CAREER: BOWLING

	O.	M.	R.	W.	AV.
TEST					
1ST-CLASS	5936.2	1302	18763	634	29.59
INT					
RAL	980.5	81	4106	175	23.46
NAT.W.	236.5	29	874	37	23.62
B & H	533.2	82	1885	86	21.91

93. Who took the first hat-trick in Test cricket?

94. England and Australia were the first two Test countries. Who was the third?

JARVIS, P. W.   Yorkshire

Full Name: Paul William Jarvis
Role: Right-hand bat, right-arm
fast-medium bowler
Born: 29 June 1965, Redcar,
North Yorkshire
Height: 5′ 11″ **Weight:** 12st 5lbs
Nickname: Jarv, Beaver,
Gnasher
County debut: 1981
County cap: 1986
50 wickets in a season: 2
1st-Class 5 w. in innings: 12
1st-Class 10 w. in match: 2
Place in batting averages: 208th
av. 16.30 (1986 191st av. 18.30)
Place in bowling averages: 30th
av. 24.58 (1986 10th av. 22.20)
Strike rate 1987: 47.71 (career 50.59)
1st-Class catches 1987: 6 (career 29)
Parents: Malcolm and Marjorie
Marital status: Single
Family links with cricket: Father has played league cricket for 30 years with
Marske CC; brother, Andrew, played for English Schools U-15s, and also had
trials for Northamptonshire and Derbyshire
Education: Bydales Comprehensive School, Marske
Qualifications: 4 O-levels
Jobs outside cricket: Trainee groundsman, Marske Cricket Club
Off-season 1987–88: Touring with England
Cricketing superstitions: The number 111
Overseas tours: Channel Islands April 1986 and Ireland June 1986 with
Yorkshire; St Lucia and Barbados, 1987, with Yorkshire; with England to
World Cup, Pakistan, Australia and New Zealand 1987–88
Overseas teams played for: Mosman Middle Harbour CC, Sydney, 1984–85;
Avendale CC, Cape Town 1985–86
Cricketers particularly learnt from: Maurice Hill, Phil Carrick, Geoff
Boycott, Albert Padmore
Cricketers particularly admired: Dennis Lillee, Richard Hadlee
Other sports played: Football, running and fitness, golf, squash
Other sports followed: Most sports
Relaxations: Fishing, music, cooking
Extras: Youngest player ever to play for Yorkshire 1st XI in John Player
League and County Championships (16 years, 2 months, 1 day in John Player
League; 16 years, 2 months, 13 days for County Championship). Youngest

player to do hat-trick in JPL and Championship. Played for Young England v West Indies 1982 and Australia 1983. Selected for TCCB XI v New Zealand 1986

Opinions on cricket: 'Only people actually born in England should be permitted to play for England. The English first-class season should be changed to 16 four-day matches.'

Best batting performance: 47 Yorkshire v Essex, Chelmsford 1986
Best bowling performance: 7-55 Yorkshire v Surrey, Leeds 1986

LAST SEASON: BATTING

	I.	N.O.	R.	H.S.	AV.
TEST					
1ST-CLASS	24	11	212	32	16.30
INT					
RAL	6	3	41	29*	13.66
NAT.W.	1	0	0	–	0.00
B & H	1	0	11	11	11.00

LAST SEASON: BOWLING

	O.	M.	R.	W.	AV.
TEST					
1ST-CLASS	644.1	148	1991	81	24.58
INT					
RAL	90	8	427	18	23.72
NAT.W.	25.2	3	77	7	11.00
B & H	62	15	193	11	17.54

CAREER: BATTING

	I.	N.O.	R.	H.S.	AV.
TEST					
1ST-CLASS	80	29	733	47	14.37
INT					
RAL	24	12	120	29*	10.00
NAT.W.	4	1	35	16	11.66
B & H	5	1	40	20	10.00

CAREER: BOWLING

	O.	M.	R.	W.	AV.
TEST					
1ST-CLASS	1964.4	378	6499	233	27.89
INT					
RAL	351.5	22	1580	76	20.78
NAT.W.	93.5	12	346	13	26.61
B & H	143	25	463	25	18.52

JEAN-JACQUES, M.   Derbyshire

Full Name: Martin Jean-Jacques
Role: Right-hand bat, right-arm medium pace bowler
Born: 2 July 1960, Dominica
County debut: 1986
1st-Class 50s scored: 1
1st-Class 5 w. in innings: 1
1st-Class 10 w. in match: 1
Place in batting averages: 239th av. 12.00 (1986 164th av. 23.11)
Place in bowling averages: 111th av. 39.55 (1986 41st av. 27.22)
Strike rate 1987: 77.22 (career 59.26)
1st-Class catches 1987: 6 (career 7)
Extras: Played Minor Counties cricket for Buckinghamshire since 1983. Formerly played for Shepherds Bush CC. On debut for Derbyshire (v Yorkshire) put on 132 with A. Hill for the 10th wicket – a new Derbyshire record

Best batting performance: 73 Derbyshire v Yorkshire, Sheffield 1986
Best bowling performance: 8-77 Derbyshire v Kent, Derby 1986

LAST SEASON: BATTING

	I.	N.O.	R.	H.S.	AV.
TEST					
1ST-CLASS	20	4	192	47	12.00
INT					
RAL	8	1	48	15	6.85
NAT.W.	2	1	11	10*	11.00
B & H	2	1	4	2*	4.00

CAREER: BATTING

	I.	N.O.	R.	H.S.	AV.
TEST					
1ST-CLASS	32	7	400	73	16.00
INT					
RAL	10	1	49	15	5.44
NAT.W.	5	2	28	16	9.33
B & H	2	1	4	2*	4.00

LAST SEASON: BOWLING

	O.	M.	R.	W.	AV.
TEST					
1ST-CLASS	325	59	1068	27	39.55
INT					
RAL	78	2	410	14	29.29
NAT.W.	30	3	149	7	21.28
B & H	30	0	164	5	32.80

CAREER: BOWLING

	O.	M.	R.	W.	AV.
TEST					
1ST-CLASS	484	75	1667	49	34.02
INT					
RAL	108	2	580	19	30.52
NAT.W.	64	7	254	12	21.16
B & H	30	0	164	5	32.80

JESTY, T. E. Surrey

Full Name: Trevor Edward Jesty
Role: Right-hand bat, right-arm
medium bowler
Born: 2 June 1948, Gosport,
Hampshire
Height: 5′ 9″ **Weight:** 11st 10lbs
Nickname: Jets
County debut: 1966 (Hampshire),
1985 (Surrey)
County cap: 1971 (Hampshire),
1985 (Surrey)
Benefit: 1982
No. of One-Day Internationals: 10
1000 runs in a season: 9
50 wickets in a season: 2
1st-Class 50s scored: 92
1st-Class 100s scored: 32
1st-Class 200s scored: 2
1st-Class 5 w. in innings: 19
One-Day 50s: 41
One-Day 100s: 7

Place in batting averages: 75th av. 34.64 (1986 75th av. 34.41)
Place in bowling averages: 12th av. 21.20
Strike rate 1987: 43.60 (career 62.67)
1st-Class catches 1987: 8 (career 250 + 1 stumping)

Parents: Aubrey Edward and Sophia

Wife and date of marriage: Jacqueline, 12 September 1970

Children: Graeme Barry, 27 September 1972; Lorna Samantha, 7 November 1976

Family links with cricket: Brother, Aubrey Jesty, wicket-keeper and left-hand bat, could have joined Hampshire staff, but decided to continue with his apprenticeship

Education: Privet County Secondary Modern, Gosport

Jobs outside cricket: Cricket coach in South Africa and New Zealand. Representative for wine company

Overseas teams played for: Border in 1973–74, and Griqualand West in 1974–75 and 1975–76 in the Currie Cup Competition, South Africa

Cricketers particularly learnt from: Barry Richards

Other sports played: Soccer, golf

Relaxations: Watching soccer, gardening

Extras: Took him 10 years to score maiden first-class century. Missed most of 1980 season through injury. Made vice-captain of Hampshire in 1981. Considered to be most unlucky not to be chosen for England tour of Australia 1982–83 after brilliant 1982 season, then was called in as a replacement. Left Hampshire at end of 1984 when not appointed captain. Took over captaincy of Surrey in 1985. Replaced as captain in 1986. Released by Surrey at end of 1987 season

Best batting performance: 248 Hampshire v Cambridge University, Cambridge 1984

Best bowling performance: 7-75 Hampshire v Worcestershire, Southampton 1976

LAST SEASON: BATTING

	I.	N.O.	R.	H.S.	AV.
TEST					
1ST-CLASS	36	5	1074	124*	34.64
INT					
RAL	11	2	225	77*	25.00
NAT.W.	1	0	35	35	35.00
B & H	6	2	166	85*	41.50

CAREER: BATTING

	I.	N.O.	R.	H.S.	AV.
TEST					
1ST-CLASS	686	89	19258	248	32.25
INT	10	4	127	52*	21.17
RAL	238	33	5151	166*	25.12
NAT.W.	31	2	920	118	31.72
B & H	66	10	2016	105	36.00

LAST SEASON: BOWLING

	O.	M.	R.	W.	AV.
TEST					
1ST-CLASS	72.4	11	212	10	21.20
INT					
RAL	9	0	63	0	–
NAT.W.	4	1	6	1	6.00
B & H	30	2	102	3	34.00

CAREER: BOWLING

	O.	M.	R.	W.	AV.
TEST					
1ST-CLASS	6100.1	1622	15949	584	27.30
INT	18	0	93	1	93.00
RAL	1296.3	76	6090	248	24.55
NAT.W.	303	51	990	39	25.38
B & H	503.4	62	1751	69	25.37

JOHNSON, P.   Nottinghamshire

Full Name: Paul Johnson
Role: Right-hand bat, right-arm
occasional bowler
Born: 24 April 1965, Newark
Height: 5′ 8″ **Weight:** 11st 7lbs
Nickname: Johno, Dwarf, Gus,
Ledge
County debut: 1982
County cap: 1986
1000 runs in a season: 2
1st-Class 50s scored: 23
1st-Class 100s scored: 10
One-Day 50s: 8
One-Day 100s: 1
Place in batting averages: 65th
av. 35.91 (1986 53rd av. 39.06)
1st-Class catches 1987: 20
(career 73 + 1 stumping)
Parents: Donald Edward and Joyce
Wife and date of marriage: Hazel, 17 October 1987
Family links with cricket: Father played local cricket and is a qualified coach
Education: Grove Comprehensive School, Newark
Qualifications: 9 CSEs, senior coaching certificate
Off-season 1987–88: Working and coaching in Nottingham
Cricketing superstitions or habits: Left pad on first
Cricketers particularly learnt from: Most of Nottinghamshire staff
Cricketers particularly admired: Richard Hadlee, Ian Botham, Dennis
Lillee, Derek Underwood, Graeme Pollock
Other sports played: Football referee, golf (14 handicap)
Other sports followed: Watches ice-hockey (Nottingham Panthers), football
(Forest and County)
Relaxations: Good films, good music, reading (Tom Sharpe) and cricket
books
Extras: Played for English Schools cricket in 1980–81 season. Youngest
member ever to join the Nottinghamshire CCC staff. Hit 16 sixes in School
County Cup game v Joseph Whittaker, scoring 195*. Played for Young
England U-19, 1982 and 1983. Made 235 for Nottinghamshire 2nd XI, July
1982, aged 17. Won man of match award in first NatWest game (101* v
Staffordshire); missed 1985 final due to appendicitis
Opinions on cricket: 'Counties should make more effort to play 2nd XI games
on first-class standard wickets. White balls should be given a trial in Sunday
games as they are easier to see not only for the players but also for the crowd.'
Best batting performance: 133 Nottinghamshire v Kent, Folkestone 1984

	I.	N.O.	R.	H.S.	AV.
TEST					
1ST-CLASS	39	4	1257	125	35.91
INT					
RAL	12	2	289	63	28.90
NAT.W.	5	1	73	41	18.25
B & H	4	1	58	49	19.33

LAST SEASON: BOWLING

	O.	M.	R.	W.	AV.
TEST					
1ST-CLASS	6	0	64	0	–
INT					
RAL					
NAT.W.					
B & H					

CAREER: BATTING

	I.	N.O.	R.	H.S.	AV.
TEST					
1ST-CLASS	159	17	4789	133	33.72
INT					
RAL	56	7	1109	90	22.63
NAT.W.	12	2	241	101*	24.10
B & H	14	1	149	49	11.46

CAREER: BOWLING

	O.	M.	R.	W.	AV.
TEST					
1ST-CLASS	55	6	352	3	117.33
INT					
RAL					
NAT.W.	1	0	5	0	–
B & H					

JONES, A. N. Somerset

Full Name: Adrian Nicholas Jones
Role: Left-hand bat, right-arm
fast bowler, outfielder
Born: 22 July 1961, Woking
Height: 6′ 2″ **Weight:** 13st 10lbs
Nickname: Quincy, Jonah
County debut: 1981 (Sussex),
1987 (Somerset)
County cap: 1986 (Sussex),
1987 (Somerset)
1st-Class 5 w. in innings: 5
1st-Class 10 w. in match: 1
Place in bowling averages: 58th
av. 28.57 (1986 59th av. 29.52)
Strike rate 1987: 49.25 (career 51.55)
1st-Class catches 1987: 8 (career 18)
Parents: William Albert and Emily
Doris
Family links with cricket: Father
and brother, Glynne, both fine
club cricketers
Education: Forest Grange Preparatory School; Seaford College
Qualifications: 8 O-levels, 2 A-levels, NCA coaching qualification, consumer
credit licence
Jobs outside cricket: Financial consultant/advisor
Cricketing superstitions or habits: 'Always salute a magpie.'
Overseas teams played for: Old Selbournians and Bohemians, South Africa,

1981–82; Border 1981–82; Red and White CC, Haarlem, Holland, 1980; Orange Free State, 1986

Cricketers particularly learnt from: Geoff Arnold, Imran Khan, Garth le Roux

Cricketers particularly admired: Imran Khan, Geoff Arnold, Richard Hadlee, Ian Botham, Garth le Roux, Sylvester Clarke, Steve Waugh

Other sports played: 'Golf badly; hockey slightly better; rugby like an animal.'

Relaxations: 'UB40, watching Laurel and Hardy films, walking, eating, good wine and port.'

Extras: Played for Young England in 1981. Left Sussex to join Somerset at end of 1986 season

Opinions on cricket: 'There should be an alternative system for the awarding of a benefit than the present haphazard method. Perhaps an endowment scheme taken out when the player is capped.'

Best batting performance: 35 Sussex v Middlesex, Hove 1984

Best bowling performance: 7-85 Somerset v Nottinghamshire, Trent Bridge 1987

LAST SEASON: BATTING

	I.	N.O.	R.	H.S.	AV.
TEST					
1ST-CLASS	21	8	114	15	8.76
INT					
RAL	4	3	22	11*	22.00
NAT.W.	1	1	1	1*	–
B & H	4	2	14	8	7.00

CAREER: BATTING

	I.	N.O.	R.	H.S.	AV.
TEST					
1ST-CLASS	67	28	398	35	10.20
INT					
RAL	9	8	56	17*	56.00
NAT.W.	2	2	4	3*	–
B & H	8	3	41	20	8.20

LAST SEASON: BOWLING

	O.	M.	R.	W.	AV.
TEST					
1ST-CLASS	517.1	85	1800	63	28.57
INT					
RAL	82.2	3	379	19	19.94
NAT.W.	12	3	38	2	19.00
B & H	45.2	6	193	9	21.44

CAREER: BOWLING

	O.	M.	R.	W.	AV.
TEST					
1ST-CLASS	1357.3	221	4753	158	30.08
INT					
RAL	251.4	14	1149	67	17.14
NAT.W.	52	7	186	9	20.66
B & H	87.4	9	386	19	20.31

95. Who took the first hat-trick in any World Cup game?

96. Who batted number three for England in the First Test v South Africa in 1913–14, opened in the Second, number eight in the Third, number nine in the Fourth, and number eleven in the Fifth?

KELLEHER, D. J. M.   Kent

Full Name: Daniel John
Michael Kelleher
Role: Right-hand bat, right-arm
medium bowler, outfielder
Born: 5 May 1966, London
Height: 6′ **Weight:** 12st 13lbs
Nickname: Donk, Shots
County debut: 1987
1st-Class 5 w. in innings: 2
Place in bowling averages: 38th
av. 25.82
Strike rate 1987: 53.11 (career 53.11)
1st-Class catches 1987: 1 (career 1)
Parents: John and Joan
Marital status: Single
Family links with cricket: Uncle
played county cricket for Surrey
and Northants. Father played
club cricket

Education: St Mary's Grammar School, Sidcup; Erith College of Technology
Qualifications: O-levels
Jobs outside cricket: Gardener
Off-season 1987–88: Playing Grade cricket in Perth, Australia
Cricketing superstitions or habits: Always put gear on in set order
Overseas tours: Kent Schools U-17 to Vancouver and Victoria, Canada, 1984;
UK Upsetters to Trinidad and Tobago, 1986
Overseas teams played for: Doncaster CC Melbourne, 1984–85; Avendale
CC, Cape Town, 1986–87

LAST SEASON: BATTING

	I.	N.O.	R.	H.S.	AV.
TEST					
1ST-CLASS	12	1	81	20	7.36
INT					
RAL	4	0	19	19	4.75
NAT.W.	1	1	0	0*	–
B & H	1	1	0	0*	–

CAREER: BATTING

	I.	N.O.	R.	H.S.	AV.
TEST					
1ST-CLASS	12	1	81	20	7.36
INT					
RAL	4	0	19	19	4.75
NAT.W.	1	1	0	0*	–
B & H	1	1	0	0*	–

LAST SEASON: BOWLING

	O.	M.	R.	W.	AV.
TEST					
1ST-CLASS	301	72	878	34	25.82
INT					
RAL	44	1	176	5	35.20
NAT.W.	17.2	2	79	2	39.50
B & H	33	1	113	2	56.50

CAREER: BOWLING

	O.	M.	R.	W.	AV.
TEST					
1ST-CLASS	301	72	878	34	25.82
INT					
RAL	44	1	176	5	35.20
NAT.W.	17.2	2	79	2	39.50
B & H	33	1	113	2	56.50

Cricketers particularly learnt from: My father, Claude Lewis, Alan Spencer, Colin Page
Cricketers particularly admired: Ian Botham, David Gower, Richard Davis, David Sabine
Other sports played: Golf, skiing
Other sports followed: Rugby, American football, women's tennis
Injuries 1987: Various finger injuries, knee injury
Relaxations: Watching TV, music, watching Richard Davis bat
Extras: Played for Kent Schools from U-11 to U-19. At school played rugby and cricket for Kent
Opinions on cricket: 'Too much cricket played.'
Best batting performance: 20 Kent v Surrey, Tunbridge Wells 1987
Best bowling performance: 6-109 Kent v Somerset, Bath 1987

KIMBER, S. J. S. Sussex

Full Name: Simon Julian Spencer Kimber
Role: Right-hand bat, right-arm fast-medium bowler
Born: 6 October 1983, Ormskirk Lancashire
Height: 6' 2" **Weight:** 13st
Nickname: Que, Kipper
County debut: 1985 (Worcestershire), 1987 (Sussex)
1st-Class 50s scored: 1
Place in batting averages: 131st av. 26.83
Place in bowling averages: 139th av. 53.25
Strike rate 1987: 76.00 (career 62.79)
1st-Class catches 1987: 2 (career 3)
Parents: Ron and Joan
Marital status: Single

Family links with cricket: Father played good standard of club cricket in England and West Indies (Jamaica) for 3 years
Education: Thomas More School, South Africa
Qualifications: School matriculation
Jobs outside cricket: Insurance broker
Off-season 1987–88: Working for an insurance broker and playing cricket for Durban Collegians in South Africa
Overseas teams played for: Durban Collegians, South Africa, 1984–85 and 1987–88; Natal B 1986–87

Cricketers particularly learnt from: Father, various others
Cricketers particularly admired: Richard Hadlee, Martin Crowe
Other sports played: Soccer, rugby, tennis, squash, golf
Other sports followed: Soccer, rugby, tennis, athletics
Relaxations: Music, watching sport and films, eating out
Best batting performance: 54 Sussex v Nottinghamshire, Eastbourne 1987
Best bowling performance: 4-76 Natal B v Eastern Province B, Uitenhage 1986–87

LAST SEASON: BATTING

	I.	N.O.	R.	H.S.	AV.
TEST					
1ST-CLASS	9	3	161	54	26.83
INT					
RAL	2	0	5	3	2.50
NAT.W.					
B & H					

LAST SEASON: BOWLING

	O.	M.	R.	W.	AV.
TEST					
1ST-CLASS	152	21	639	12	53.25
INT					
RAL	13	0	82	0	–
NAT.W.					
B & H					

CAREER: BATTING

	I.	N.O.	R.	H.S.	AV.
TEST					
1ST-CLASS	12	4	212	54	26.50
INT					
RAL	2	0	5	3	2.50
NAT.W.					
B & H					

CAREER: BOWLING

	O.	M.	R.	W.	AV.
TEST					
1ST-CLASS	251.1	36	919	24	38.29
INT					
RAL	13	0	82	0	–
NAT.W.					
B & H					

KRIKKEN, K. M.   Derbyshire

Full Name: Karl Matthew Krikken
Role: Right-hand bat, wicket-keeper
Born: 9 April 1969, Bolton
Height: 5′ 9½″ **Weight:** 11st 4lbs
Nickname: Krikk
County debut: 1987
Parents: Brian Egbert and Irene Ida
Marital status: Single
Family links with cricket: Father played county cricket for Lancashire and Worcestershire
Education: Horwich Parish Church School; Rivington and Blackrod High School
Qualifications: 6 O-levels, 3 A-levels
Off-season 1987–88: Staying at home, coaching at local clubs

Cricketers particularly learnt from: Father, Keith Eccleshare, Phil Russell, Alan Hill

Cricketers particularly admired: Bob Taylor, Alan Knott

Other sports played: Golf, squash

Other sports followed: Wigan Athletic FC

Relaxations: Listening to music, jogging

Extras: Played for England Schoolboys U-15. Captained North of England NCA U-19 side in the International Youth Tournament. Played in one Refuge Assurance Sunday League match v Sussex, Hove 1987

LAST SEASON: WICKET KEEPING

	C.	ST.			
TEST					
1ST-CLASS					
INT					
RAL	1	–			
NAT.W.					
B & H					

CAREER: WICKET KEEPING

	C.	ST.			
TEST					
1ST-CLASS					
INT					
RAL	1	–			
NAT.W.					
B & H					

LAMB, A. J. Northamptonshire

Full Name: Allan Joseph Lamb

Role: Right-hand bat, right-arm medium bowler

Born: 20 June 1954, Langebaanweg, Cape Province, South Africa

Height: 5′ 8″ **Weight:** 12st 12lbs

Nickname: Lambie, Legger, Lambo

County debut: 1978

County cap: 1978

Benefit: 1988

Test debut: 1982

No. of Tests: 51

No. of One-Day Internationals: 68

1000 runs in a season: 7

1st-Class 50s scored: 110

1st-Class 100s scored: 47

One-Day 50s: 52

One-Day 100s: 12

Place in batting averages: 90th av. 32.73 (1986 4th av. 59.08)

1st-Class catches 1987: 19 (career 233)

Parents: Michael and Joan

Wife and date of marriage: Lindsay St Leger, 8 December 1979

Family links with cricket: Father played in the Boland League. Brother played for Western Province B. Brother-in-law, Tony Bucknall, won 10 caps for England at rugger

Education: Wynberg Boys' High School; Abbotts College

Qualifications: Matriculation

Jobs outside cricket: Timber representative. Promotions and selling

Off-season 1987–88: Touring with England for World Cup and playing in South Africa

Cricketing superstitions or habits: 'Try to use the same batting shirt which I have scored runs in.'

Overseas tours: With England to Australia and New Zealand 1982–83; New Zealand and Pakistan 1983–84; India and Australia 1984–85; West Indies 1986; World Cup 1987

Overseas teams played for: Western Province in Currie Cup Competition, 1972–81

Cricketers particularly learnt from: 'Everyone.'

Other sports played: Squash, golf. Rode in a British bobsled at Cervinia (Italy) in 1985

Other sports followed: Most sports

Relaxations: Shooting, fishing

Extras: Made first-class debut for Western Province in 1972–73 Currie Cup. Applied to be registered as English in 1980 but application deferred. Was top of batting averages 1980. Was primarily a bowler when first played schoolboy cricket in South Africa. Missed two years of first-class cricket because of military training. Qualified to play for England 1982

Best batting performance: 178 Northamptonshire v Leicestershire, Leicester 1979

Best bowling performance: 1-1 Northamptonshire v Derbyshire, Derby 1978

LAST SEASON: BATTING

	I.	N.O.	R.	H.S.	AV.
TEST					
1ST-CLASS	34	4	982	101*	32.73
INT	3	0	101	61	33.66
RAL	11	0	311	68	28.27
NAT.W.	5	0	230	88	46.00
B & H	7	2	398	126*	79.60

CAREER: BATTING

	I.	N.O.	R.	H.S.	AV.
TEST	88	7	2644	137*	32.64
1ST-CLASS	421	73	17071	178	49.05
INT	67	11	2315	118	41.33
RAL	110	17	3610	132*	38.81
NAT.W.	27	1	988	101	38.00
B & H	43	7	1736	126*	48.22

LAST SEASON: BOWLING

	O.	M.	R.	W.	AV.
TEST					
1ST-CLASS	2	0	18	1	18.00
INT					
RAL					
NAT.W.					
B & H					

CAREER: BOWLING

	O.	M.	R.	W.	AV.
TEST	4	1	23	1	23.00
1ST-CLASS	33.2	9	118	5	23.60
INT					
RAL					
NAT.W.	1.2	0	12	1	12.00
B & H					

LAMPITT, S. R. — Worcestershire

Full Name: Stuart Richard Lampitt
Role: Right-hand bat, right-arm
medium pace bowler, slip fielder
Born: 29 July 1966, Wolverhampton
Height: 5′ 10″ **Weight:** 13st 6lbs
Nickname: Louie
County debut: 1985
Place in batting averages: 250th
av. 10.09
1st-Class catches 1987: 6 (career 6)
Parents: Joseph Charles and
Muriel-Ann
Marital status: Single
Education: Kingswinford School;
Dudley College of Technology
Qualifications: 7 O-levels
Jobs outside cricket: Steel
shearers' mate
Off-season 1987–88: Playing
and coaching in Auckland, New Zealand

Cricketing superstitions or habits: Always check guard when new bowler
comes on
Overseas tours: NCA tour to Bermuda with England South, 1985
Overseas teams played for: Mangere CC, South Auckland 1986–87
Cricketers particularly learnt from: Ron Headley, Basil D'Oliveira
Cricketers particularly admired: Viv Richards, Ian Botham
Other sports played: Football, golf, snooker
Other sports followed: Every sport
Relaxations: Sleeping, listening to music, watching TV

LAST SEASON: BATTING

	I.	N.O.	R.	H.S.	AV.
TEST					
1ST-CLASS	14	3	111	24	10.09
INT					
RAL	2	1	15	12*	15.00
NAT.W.					
B & H					

LAST SEASON: BOWLING

	O.	M.	R.	W.	AV.
TEST					
1ST-CLASS	79.2	11	273	3	91.00
INT					
RAL	20	1	117	4	29.25
NAT.W.					
B & H					

CAREER: BATTING

	I.	N.O.	R.	H.S.	AV.
TEST					
1ST-CLASS	16	4	122	24	10.16
INT					
RAL	2	1	15	12*	15.00
NAT.W.					
B & H					

CAREER: BOWLING

	O.	M.	R.	W.	AV.
TEST					
1ST-CLASS	87.2	12	295	3	98.33
INT					
RAL	20	1	117	4	29.25
NAT.W.					
B & H					

Extras: Took five wickets in first appearance at Lord's, helping club side Stourbridge to win National Club Knockout in 1986
Opinions on cricket: 'Politics should not enter into cricket or any sport.'
Best batting performance: 24 Worcestershire v Hampshire, Worcester 1987
Best bowling performance: 2-37 Worcestershire v Middlesex, Lord's 1987

LARKINS, W.   Northamptonshire

Full Name: Wayne Larkins
Role: Right-hand bat, right-arm medium bowler
Born: 22 November 1953
Height: 5′ 11″ **Weight:** 12st
Nickname: Ned
County debut: 1972
County cap: 1976
Benefit: 1986
Test debut: 1979–80
No. of Tests: 6
No. of One-Day Internationals: 6
1000 runs in a season: 9
1st-Class 50s scored: 72
1st-Class 100s scored: 38
1st-Class 200s scored: 2
1st-Class 5 w. in innings: 1
One-Day 50s: 41
One-Day 100s: 11
Place in batting averages: 72nd av. 34.97 (1986 134th av. 26.56)
1st-Class catches 1987: 17 (career 178)
Parents: Mavis (father deceased)
Wife and date of marriage: Jane Elaine, 22 March 1975
Children: Philippa Jane, 30 May 1981
Family links with cricket: Father was umpire. Brother, Melvin, played for Bedford Town for many years
Education: Bushmead, Eaton Socon, Huntingdon
Jobs outside cricket: Farming
Overseas tours: England to Australia and India 1979–80
Cricketers particularly learnt from: Mushtaq Mohammad
Other sports played: Golf, football (currently with Buckingham and was on Notts County's books), squash
Relaxations: Gardening
Extras: With Peter Willey, received 2016 pints of beer (seven barrels) from a Northampton brewery as a reward for their efforts in Australia in 1979–80. Hat-trick for Northamptonshire v Combined Universities, Benson & Hedges

Cup, 1980. Banned from English Test Cricket for three years for joining rebel tour of South Africa in 1982. Recalled to Test team 1986 but withdrew due to thumb injury. Missed another Test recall in 1987 due to injury sustained whilst playing football

Best batting performance: 252 Northamptonshire v Glamorgan, Cardiff 1983
Best bowling performance: 5-59 Northamptonshire v Worcestershire, Worcester 1984

LAST SEASON: BATTING

	I.	N.O.	R.	H.S.	AV.
TEST					
1ST-CLASS	43	4	1364	120	34.97
INT					
RAL	11	0	356	91	32.36
NAT.W.	5	1	294	121*	73.50
B & H	7	0	112	38	16.00

LAST SEASON: BOWLING

	O.	M.	R.	W.	AV.
TEST					
1ST-CLASS	16.2	4	51	0	–
INT					
RAL	4	0	25	0	–
NAT.W.					
B & H					

CAREER: BATTING

	I.	N.O.	R.	H.S.	AV.
TEST	11	0	176	34	16.00
1ST-CLASS	555	35	18066	252	34.74
INT	6	0	84	34	14.00
RAL	185	13	4817	172*	28.00
NAT.W.	33	3	1230	121*	41.00
B & H	55	3	1683	132	32.36

CAREER: BOWLING

	O.	M.	R.	W.	AV.
TEST					
1ST-CLASS	504.1	99	1695	39	43.46
INT	2	0	21	0	–
RAL	309.5	9	1530	54	28.33
NAT.W.	73.5	9	248	4	62.00
B & H	105.3	14	413	16	25.81

LAWRENCE, D. V.   Gloucestershire

Full Name: David Valentine Lawrence
Role: Right-hand bat, right-arm fast bowler, slip fielder
Born: 28 January 1964, Gloucester
Height: 6′ 3″ **Weight:** 15st 7lbs
Nickname: Syd, Bruno
County debut: 1981
County cap: 1985
1st-Class 50s scored: 1
1st-Class 5 w. in innings: 10
Place in bowling averages: 104th av. 37.10 (1986 85th av. 36.49)
Strike rate 1987: 55.23 (career 55.49)
1st-Class catches 1987: 2 (career 23)
Parents: Joseph and Joyce
Education: Linden School, Gloucester
Qualifications: 3 CSEs
Overseas tours: England B to Sri Lanka 1986
Overseas teams played for: Scarborough CC, Perth, Western Australia

Cricketers particularly learnt from: Michael Holding, Richard Hadlee, Dennis Lillee
Cricketers particularly admired: Viv Richards
Other sports played: Rugby football. 'Was offered terms to play professional rugby league winter 1985–86, but turned them down.'
Relaxations: 'Like listening to jazz, funk and dancing.'
Best batting performance: 65* Gloucestershire v Glamorgan, Swansea 1987
Best bowling performance: 7-48 Gloucestershire v Sussex, Hove, 1985

LAST SEASON: BATTING

	I.	N.O.	R.	H.S.	AV.
TEST					
1ST-CLASS	19	4	138	65*	9.20
INT					
RAL	3	0	4	3	1.33
NAT.W.					
B & H	1	1	1	1*	—

LAST SEASON: BOWLING

	O.	M.	R.	W.	AV.
TEST					
1ST-CLASS	349.5	44	1410	38	37.10
INT					
RAL	77	0	369	9	41.00
NAT.W.	30.2	2	141	5	28.20
B & H	48	0	245	5	49.00

CAREER: BATTING

	I.	N.O.	R.	H.S.	AV.
TEST					
1ST-CLASS	110	23	815	65*	9.36
INT					
RAL	12	5	79	21*	11.28
NAT.W.	6	2	2	1*	0.50
B & H	7	5	37	22*	18.50

CAREER: BOWLING

	O.	M.	R.	W.	AV.
TEST					
1ST-CLASS	2284.3	325	8711	247	35.26
INT					
RAL	276	2	1484	47	31.57
NAT.W.	118.4	10	539	18	29.94
B & H	144	4	638	22	29.00

LENHAM, N. J. Sussex

Full Name: Neil John Lenham
Role: Right-hand bat, right-arm medium bowler
Born: 17 December 1965, Worthing
Height: 5′ 11″ **Weight:** 10st 7lbs
Nickname: Archie, Pin
County debut: 1984
1st-Class 50s scored: 6
1st-Class 100s scored: 1
One-Day 50s: 1
Place in batting averages: — (1986 176th av. 21.36)
1st-Class catches 1987: 2 (career 13)
Parents: Leslie John and Valerie Anne
Marital status: Single
Family links with cricket: Father ex-Sussex county cricketer and now NCA National Coach

Education: Broadwater Manor House Prep School; Brighton College
Qualifications: 5 O-levels, 2 A-levels, Advanced Cricket Coach
Jobs outside cricket: Teacher, grease monkey in a garage
Cricketing superstitions or habits: Adjusting all equipment to obtain comfort
Overseas tours: 1981 tour to Barbados with Sussex U-16; 1982 tour to Barbados with Sussex Young Cricketers; 1985 England Young Cricketers tour to West Indies (as captain)
Cricketers particularly learnt from: Father, John Spencer, Ralph Dellor
Cricketers particularly admired: Ken McEwan, Barry Richards
Other sports played: Hockey, squash, golf, snooker
Relaxations: Music (Van Morrison and Fleetwood Mac), reading
Extras: Made debut for Young England 1983. Broke record for number of runs scored in season at a public school in 1984 (1534 av. 80.74). Youngest player to appear for County 2nd XI at 14 years old
Opinions on cricket: 'Over-rate fines should be looked into so they don't end up punishing attacking cricket.'
Best batting performance: 104* Sussex v Pakistanis, Hove 1987
Best bowling performance: 4-88 Sussex v Leicestershire, Leicester 1986

LAST SEASON: BATTING

	I.	N.O.	R.	H.S.	AV.
TEST					
1ST-CLASS	5	4	126	104*	126.00
INT					
RAL	2	1	29	22	29.00
NAT.W.					
B & H	2	1	18	18*	18.00

LAST SEASON: BOWLING

	O.	M.	R.	W.	AV.
TEST					
1ST-CLASS					
INT					
RAL					
NAT.W.					
B & H					

CAREER: BATTING

	I.	N.O.	R.	H.S.	AV.
TEST					
1ST-CLASS	51	10	1174	104*	28.63
INT					
RAL	4	3	37	22	37.00
NAT.W.	1	0	6	6	6.00
B & H	5	1	139	82	34.75

CAREER: BOWLING

	O.	M.	R.	W.	AV.
TEST					
1ST-CLASS	131	26	409	9	45.44
INT					
RAL	8	0	40	0	–
NAT.W.	9	0	48	1	48.00
B & H					

97. Who captained Australia in the first ever Test?
98. Who captained England in the first ever Test?
99. Who faced the first ball in Test cricket?

LE ROUX, G. S.

Sussex

Full Name: Garth Sterling Le Roux
Role: Right-hand bat, right-arm
fast bowler, slip fielder
Born: 4 September 1955, Cape
Town, South Africa
Height: 6′ 3″ **Weight:** 15st 5lbs
Nickname: Rocky, Grumps
County debut: 1978
County cap: 1981
50 wickets in a season: 3
1st-Class 50s scored: 26
1st-Class 5 w. in innings: 35
1st-Class 10 w. in match: 3
One-Day 50s: 8
Place in batting averages: 55th
av. 37.50 (1986 105th av. 29.80)
Place in bowling averages: 22nd
av. 22.00 (1986 81st av. 35.69)
Strike rate 1987: 50.03 (career 48.16)
1st-Class catches 1987: 3 (career 78)

Parents: Pierre and Audrey
Wife and date of marriage: Martine, 19 February 1986
Education: Wynberg Boys' High School; Stellenbosch University
Qualifications: BA Physical Education
Off-season 1987–88: Playing in South Africa
Overseas tours: World XI in World Series Cricket Tour 1978–79
Overseas teams played for: Western Province; South African XI
Cricketers particularly learnt from: Hylton Ackerman, Eddie Barlow
Cricketers particularly admired: Dennis Lillee, Graeme Pollock

LAST SEASON: BATTING

	I.	N.O.	R.	H.S.	AV.
TEST					
1ST-CLASS	15	5	375	73	37.50
INT					
RAL	9	4	354	83*	70.80
NAT.W.	1	0	8	8	8.00
B & H	4	0	49	19	12.25

CAREER: BATTING

	I.	N.O.	R.	H.S.	AV.
TEST					
1ST-CLASS	278	76	5287	86	26.17
INT					
RAL	68	17	1445	88	28.33
NAT.W.	12	3	127	39*	14.11
B & H	26	6	425	50	21.25

LAST SEASON: BOWLING

	O.	M.	R.	W.	AV.
TEST					
1ST-CLASS	266.5	54	768	32	24.00
INT					
RAL	63	3	272	11	24.72
NAT.W.	24	4	49	3	16.33
B & H	30.4	3	126	4	31.50

CAREER: BOWLING

	O.	M.	R.	W.	AV.
TEST					
1ST-CLASS	6502.5	1436	17173	810	21.20
INT					
RAL	591.5	30	2504	118	21.22
NAT.W.	169.5	29	440	32	13.75
B & H	287.3	30	1140	46	31.66

Other sports played: Golf, tennis, fishing
Relaxations: Cooking, sailing, reading
Extras: Played for Packer's World Series Cricket, 1978–79 in Australia. First player to get a hat-trick in the Rebel Series in South Africa (1985–86)
Opinions on cricket: 'Too much travelling and playing on the county circuit.'
Best batting performance: 86 Western Province v Border, Cape Town 1985–86
Best bowling performance: 8-107 Sussex v Somerset, Taunton 1981

LEVER, J. K.   Essex

Full Name: John Kenneth Lever
Role: Right-hand bat, left-arm fast-medium bowler
Born: 24 February 1949, Stepney
Height: 6′ 0″ **Weight:** 13st
Nickname: Jake, JK, Stanley
County debut: 1967
County cap: 1970
Benefit: 1980 (£66,250)
Test debut: 1976–77
No. of Tests: 21
No. of One-Day Internationals: 22
50 wickets in a season: 16
1st-Class 50s scored: 3
1st-Class 5 w. in innings: 84
1st-Class 10 w. in match: 12
Place in bowling averages: 82nd av. 31.73 (1986 53rd av. 28.42)
Strike rate 1987: 69.88 (career 52.69)
1st-Class catches 1987: 4 (career 182)
Parents: Ken and Doris
Wife and date of marriage: Chris, 30 July 1983
Children: Jocelyn Jennifer, 9 January 1985
Education: Highlands Junior; Dane County Secondary School
Qualifications: 3 O-levels, 3 RSAs
Jobs outside cricket: Clerk with Access Social Club; Byron Shipping; Dominion Insurance
Cricketing superstitions or habits: 'Too many to mention.'
Overseas tours: India, Sri Lanka and Australia, 1976–77; Pakistan and New Zealand, 1977–78; Australia, 1978–79 and 1979–80
Cricketers particularly learnt from: 'The Essex team.'
Cricketers particularly admired: Sir Gary Sobers

Other sports played: Football, golf
Injuries 1987: 'Groin strain and old age!'
Relaxations: Indian food, real ale
Extras: Took 10 wickets on his Test debut in 1976 v India at Delhi. Took 106 wickets at an average of 15.80 in 1978, and 106 wickets at an average of 17.30 in 1979, and 106 wickets at an average of 16.28 in 1983. President of Blythswood CC. Member of Ilford CC since the age of 14. Another of the renowned Essex comedians. Has reputation of 'not breaking down'. On the executive of the Cricketers' Association. Banned from Test Cricket for three years for joining rebel tour of South Africa in 1982. Recalled to England side in 1986 after four-year absence
Opinions on cricket: 'Uncovered wickets did not work!'
Best batting performance: 91 Essex v Glamorgan, Cardiff 1970
Best bowling performance: 8-37 Essex v Gloucestershire, Bristol 1984

LAST SEASON: BATTING

	I.	N.O.	R.	H.S.	AV.
TEST					
1ST-CLASS	9	2	60	18	8.57
INT					
RAL	5	3	8	6*	4.00
NAT.W.	1	1	3	3*	–
B & H	1	1	10	10*	–

LAST SEASON: BOWLING

	O.	M.	R.	W.	AV.
TEST					
1ST-CLASS	396	99	1079	34	31.73
INT					
RAL	77.2	8	383	13	29.46
NAT.W.	20	6	58	5	11.60
B & H	30	4	102	5	20.40

CAREER: BATTING

	I.	N.O.	R.	H.S.	AV.
TEST	31	5	306	53	11.76
1ST-CLASS	487	186	3263	91	10.84
INT	11	4	56	27*	8.00
RAL	106	65	390	23	9.51
NAT.W.	25	17	93	15*	11.62
B & H	26	18	104	13	13.00

CAREER: BOWLING

	O.	M.	R.	W.	AV.
TEST	166.7 / 516.2	27 / 113	1951	73	26.72
1ST-CLASS	210.4 / 13498.4	40 / 3026	37945	1580	24.01
INT	33 / 148	5 / 15	713	24	29.70
RAL	1837.4	208	6813	357	19.08
NAT.W.	427.3	99	1145	67	17.08
B & H	789.5	151	2392	137	17.45

100. Who has bowled the most balls in one Test, and how many?

101. Who has scored 100 and taken 5 wickets in a Test innings most often, and how many times has he done it?

LEWIS, C. C. Leicestershire

Full Name: Christopher Clairmonte Lewis
Role: Right-hand bat, right-arm medium bowler
Born: 14 February 1968, Georgetown, Guyana
Height: 6′ 2½″ **Weight:** 13st
Nickname: Carl
County debut: 1987
1st-Class catches 1987: 1 (career 1)
Parents: Philip and Patricia
Marital status: Single
Education: Willesden High School
Qualifications: 2 O-levels
Off-season 1987–88: On tour
Overseas tours: Young England to Australia 1987
Cricketers particularly learned from: Ted Jackson, Paddy Clift
Cricketers particularly admired: Richard Hadlee
Other sports played: Snooker, football
Other sports followed: Snooker, football, darts, American football
Injuries 1987: Side strain
Relaxations: Music, sleeping
Best batting performance: 42 Leicestershire v Nottinghamshire, Leicester 1987
Best bowling performance: 2-26 Leicestershire v Middlesex, Leicester 1987

LAST SEASON: BATTING

	I.	N.O.	R.	H.S.	AV.
TEST					
1ST-CLASS	4	0	53	42	13.25
INT					
RAL	4	4	35	23*	–
NAT.W.	2	0	33	18	16.50
B & H					

CAREER: BATTING

	I.	N.O.	R.	H.S.	AV.
TEST					
1ST-CLASS	4	0	53	42	13.25
INT					
RAL	4	4	35	23*	–
NAT.W.	2	0	33	18	16.50
B & H					

LAST SEASON: BOWLING

	O.	M.	R.	W.	AV.
TEST					
1ST-CLASS	63	9	167	5	33.40
INT					
RAL	31	1	159	3	53.00
NAT.W.	27	2	103	2	51.50
B & H					

CAREER: BOWLING

	O.	M.	R.	W.	AV.
TEST					
1ST-CLASS	63	9	167	5	33.40
INT					
RAL	31	1	159	3	53.00
NAT.W.	27	2	103	2	51.50
B & H					

LILLEY, A. W. Essex

Full Name: Alan William Lilley
Role: Right-hand bat, right-arm
medium bowler, cover fielder
Born: 8 May 1959, Ilford, Essex
Height: 6′ 2″ **Weight:** 14st
Nickname: Lil
County debut: 1978
County cap: 1986
1st-Class 50s scored: 17
1st-Class 100s scored: 2
One-Day 50s: 7
One-Day 100s: 2
Place in batting averages: 99th
av. 31.32 (1986 146th av. 25.16)
1st-Class catches 1987: 11 (career 40)
Parents: Min and Ron
Wife and date of marriage: Helen,
6 October 1984
Family links with cricket: Father
played for Osborne CC as a bowler for 18 years

Education: Caterham High School, Ilford
Off-season 1987–88: Working in a shipping office
Jobs outside cricket: Shipping broker
Overseas teams played for: Perth CC, Western Australia, 1979–80
Cricketers particularly learnt from: Stuart Turner, Bill Morris
Other sports played: Most
Injuries 1987: Broken finger
Extras: Was on MCC Young Pro staff at Lord's one season after leaving
school. Scored century in second innings of debut v Nottinghamshire

LAST SEASON: BATTING

	I.	N.O.	R.	H.S.	AV.
TEST					
1ST-CLASS	29	4	783	102	31.32
INT					
RAL	10	0	138	55	13.80
NAT.W.	3	0	36	19	12.00
B & H	3	0	28	24	9.33

LAST SEASON: BOWLING

	O.	M.	R.	W.	AV.
TEST					
1ST-CLASS	12	1	77	0	–
INT					
RAL					
NAT.W.					
B & H					

CAREER: BATTING

	I.	N.O.	R.	H.S.	AV.
TEST					
1ST-CLASS	129	10	3078	102	25.86
INT					
RAL	90	7	1287	60	15.50
NAT.W.	13	2	344	113	31.27
B & H	25	2	469	119	20.39

CAREER: BOWLING

	O.	M.	R.	W.	AV.
TEST					
1ST-CLASS	68.3	4	386	7	55.14
INT					
RAL	3.3	0	20	3	6.66
NAT.W.	8	3	33	2	16.50
B & H	1	0	4	1	4.00

Best batting performance: 102 Essex v Middlesex, Chelmsford 1987
Best bowling performance: 3-116 Essex v Glamorgan, Swansea 1985

LLOYD, T. A.   Warwickshire

Full Name: Timothy Andrew Lloyd
Role: Left-hand bat, off-break bowler
Born: 5 November 1956, Oswestry
Height: 5′ 11″ **Weight:** 11st 10lbs
Nickname: Teflon
County debut: 1977
County cap: 1980
Test debut: 1984
No. of Tests: 1
No. of One-Day Internationals: 3
1000 runs in a season: 6
1st-Class 50s scored: 62
1st-Class 100s scored: 20
1st-Class 200s scored: 1
One-Day 50s: 39
One-Day 100s: 1
Place in batting averages: 73rd
av. 34.95 (1986 122nd av. 28.32)
1st-Class catches 1987: 11 (career 109)
Marital status: Single
Children: Sophie, Georgia
Education: Oswestry Boys' High School; Dorset College of Higher Education
Qualifications: O-levels, A-levels, HND Tourism, NCA Advanced Coach
Jobs outside cricket: Agent for Italian colour printer, book publishing, lorry driver, sports promotions agent
Off-season 1987–88: Working with Elite Promotions
Overseas tours: Derrick Robins' XI to South America 1979; Warwickshire CCC to Zambia 1977; Warwickshire Wanderers to Barbados 1978
Overseas teams played for: Orange Free State, Zingari CC, Waverley CC
Cricketers particularly learnt from: Dennis Amiss
Cricketers particularly admired: Gary Sobers
Other sports: Soccer, golf, tennis, table tennis, squash
Other sports followed: Most sports
Relaxations: 'Enjoying my home, drinking good wine and beer, eating various cuisine.'
Extras: Scored 202* for Shropshire Schools v Worcestershire. Played for

Shropshire and Warwickshire 2nd XI, both in 1975. Appointed captain of Warwickshire for 1988 season

Opinions on cricket: 'Toss should be awarded to visiting captain in Championship cricket in an attempt to prevent home sides preparing pitches geared to their advantage.'

Best batting performance: 208* Warwickshire v Gloucestershire, Edgbaston 1983

Best bowling performance: 3-62 Warwickshire v Surrey, Edgbaston 1985

LAST SEASON: BATTING

	I.	N.O.	R.	H.S.	AV.
TEST					
1ST-CLASS	46	3	1503	162	34.95
INT					
RAL	12	1	302	57*	27.45
NAT.W.	3	0	165	71	55.50
B & H	3	0	88	67	29.33

LAST SEASON: BOWLING

	O.	M.	R.	W.	AV.
TEST					
1ST-CLASS	1	0	1	0	–
INT					
RAL					
NAT.W.					
B & H					

CAREER: BATTING

	I.	N.O.	R.	H.S.	AV.
TEST	1	1	10	10*	–
1ST-CLASS	367	34	11938	208*	35.84
INT	3	0	101	49	33.66
RAL	109	12	2968	90	30.59
NAT.W.	21	3	738	81	41.00
B & H	32	3	905	137*	31.20

CAREER: BOWLING

	O.	M.	R.	W.	AV.
TEST					
1ST-CLASS	233	41	981	13	75.46
INT					
RAL	23.1	0	149	1	149.00
NAT.W.	9	1	47	2	23.50
B & H	15	1	76	0	–

LLOYDS, J. W.　　　Gloucestershire

Full Name: Jeremy William Lloyds
Role: Left-hand bat, off-break bowler, close fielder
Born: 17 November 1954, Penang, Malaya
Height: 5′ 11″ **Weight:** 12st
Nickname: Jo'burg, JJ or Jerry
County debut: 1979 (Somerset), 1985 (Gloucestershire)
County cap: 1982 (Somerset), 1985 (Gloucestershire)
1000 runs in a season: 2
1st-Class 50s scored: 43
1st-Class 100s scored: 9
1st-Class 5 w. in innings: 11
1st-Class 10 w. in match: 1
One-Day 50s: 2
Place in batting averages: 25th av. 43.32 (1986 37th av. 43.16)

Place in bowling averages: 118th av. 40.72 (1986 72nd av. 33.00)
Strike rate 1987: 67.22 (career 64.32)
1st-Class catches 1987: 16 (career 148)
Parents: Edwin William and Grace Cicely
Marital status: Single
Family links with cricket: Father played Blundell's 1st XI 1932–35, selected for Public Schools Rest v Lord's Schools at Lord's 1935. Played Inter-State cricket in Malaya and Singapore 1950–55. Brother, Christopher Edwin Lloyds, played for Blundell's 1st XI 1964–66 and Somerset 2nd XI in 1966
Education: St Dunstan's Prep School; Blundell's School
Qualifications: 10 O-levels, NCA Advanced Coach
Jobs outside cricket: Lloyds Bank, Taunton, for 1½ years. MCC Young Professionals at Lord's 1975 for four years
Off-season 1987–88: Playing for Orange Free State in South Africa
Overseas tours: With Somerset to Antigua, 1981; with Gloucestershire to Barbados, 1985; Sri Lanka 1987
Overseas teams played for: St Stithian's Old Boys, Johannesburg, 1978–80; Toombul DCC, Brisbane, 1980–82; North Sydney District 1982–83; Orange Free State 1983–84; Preston (Victoria) 1986
Cricketers particularly learnt from: Don Wilson, Derek Taylor, Brian Davison
Cricketers particularly admired: John Hampshire, Graeme Pollock, Viv Richards, Ian Botham, Derek Underwood, Brian Davison
Other sports played: Golf, swimming, windsurfing
Other sports followed: Watches motor racing and tennis
Injuries 1987: Chipped bone in left hand
Relaxations: Music, cinema, driving, reading
Extras: Scored 132* and 102* for Somerset in same Championship match, June 1982. Took 30 catches in 1982 season for Somerset. Moved to Gloucestershire for 1985 season

LAST SEASON: BATTING

	I.	N.O.	R.	H.S.	AV.
TEST					
1ST-CLASS	32	4	1213	130	43.32
INT					
RAL	14	1	260	57	20.00
NAT.W.	4	1	35	15	11.66
B & H	2	0	63	36	31.50

CAREER: BATTING

	I.	N.O.	R.	H.S.	AV.
TEST					
1ST-CLASS	269	40	7382	132*	32.23
INT					
RAL	64	11	737	57	13.96
NAT.W.	13	3	181	40	18.10
B & H	15	0	225	51	15.00

LAST SEASON: BOWLING

	O.	M.	R.	W.	AV.
TEST					
1ST-CLASS	403.2	63	1466	36	40.72
INT					
RAL	36.3	3	189	5	37.80
NAT.W.	18	0	67	1	67.00
B & H	8	0	42	0	—

CAREER: BOWLING

	O.	M.	R.	W.	AV.
TEST					
1ST-CLASS	2455	532	7955	229	34.73
INT					
RAL	92.2	6	461	11	41.90
NAT.W.	38.3	4	120	3	40.00
B & H	29.2	2	97	4	24.25

Opinions on cricket: '1 Coloured clothing worn for all one-day cricket. 2 Covered wickets at all times. 3 If another TV channel wants to cover full Sunday cricket and one-day games, let them.'
Best batting performance: 132* Somerset v Northamptonshire, Northampton 1982
Best bowling performance: 7-88 Somerset v Essex, Chelmsford 1982

LORD, G. J. Worcestershire

Full Name: Gordon John Lord
Role: Left-hand bat, slow left-arm bowler
Born: 25 April 1961, Birmingham
Height: 5′ 10″ **Weight:** 12st 7lbs
Nickname: Jazz Hat
County debut: 1983 (Warwickshire), 1987 (Worcestershire)
1st-Class 50s scored: 4
1st-Class 100s scored: 1
One-Day 50s: 1
One-Day 100s: 1
Place in batting averages: 168th av. 20.76
1st-Class catches 1987: 3 (career 9)
Parents: Michael David and Christine Frances
Marital status: Single
Family links with cricket: Uncle Charlie Watts played for Leicestershire
Education: Warwick School; Durham University
Qualifications: 7 O-levels, 4 A-levels, BA General Studies, NCA Coaching Award
Jobs outside cricket: Personnel trainee, Lucas Engineering and Systems
Off-season 1987–88: Coaching

LAST SEASON: BATTING

	I.	N.O.	R.	H.S.	AV.
TEST					
1ST-CLASS	19	2	353	66	20.76
INT					
RAL	1	0	6	6	6.00
NAT.W.					
B & H					

CAREER: BATTING

	I.	N.O.	R.	H.S.	AV.
TEST					
1ST-CLASS	45	4	861	199	21.00
INT					
RAL	13	1	249	103	20.75
NAT.W.					
B & H	1	0	0	–	0.00

Overseas tours: England U-19 tour Australia 1978–79 and West Indies 1979–80

Cricketers particularly learnt from: Allan Wilkins (school coach), Neal Abberley (2nd XI coach), Norman Graham (University coach), Peter Stringer, Tim Curtis

Cricketers particularly admired: Dennis Amiss, Andy Moles

Other sports played: Squash

Other sports followed: Watches rugby, squash, snooker

Relaxations: All forms of music, particularly church organ music; astronomy, reading, people

Extras: Released by Warwickshire at end of 1986 season. Joined Worcestershire for 1987

Best batting performance: 199 Warwickshire v Yorkshire, Edgbaston 1985

LOVE, J. D. Yorkshire

Full Name: James Derek Love
Role: Right-hand bat, right-arm medium bowler
Born: 22 April 1955, Leeds
Height: 6′ 2″ **Weight:** 14st
Nickname: Jim
County debut: 1975
County cap: 1980
No. of One-Day Internationals: 3
1000 runs in a season: 2
1st-Class 50s scored: 49
1st-Class 100s scored: 13
One-Day 50s: 16
One-Day 100s: 4
Place in batting averages: 123rd
av. 27.78 (1986 74th av. 34.62)
1st-Class catches 1987: 7 (career 107)
Parents: Derek Oliver and Betty
Wife and date of marriage: Janice,
28 February 1986

Family links with cricket: Father played local cricket; brother Robert plays for Tadcaster CC in Yorkshire League

Education: Brudenell County Secondary, Leeds

Jobs outside cricket: Civil servant for three years until left to become professional cricketer

Overseas teams played for: Whitbread Scholarship to Mosman Middle Harbour and District CC in 1977–78; Scarborough CC, Perth, Western Australia, 1978–79; Mosman Middle Harbour and District CC 1982–83, 1984–85

Cricketers particularly learnt from: Doug Padgett (county coach)
Other sports played: Local football, golf
Injuries 1987: Broken finger
Relaxations: Shooting
Extras: Man of the Match in Yorkshire's victory in B & H Cup Final 1987
Opinions on cricket: 'I wish employment could be found for more cricketers when the season ends.'
Best batting performance: 170* Yorkshire v Worcestershire, Worcester 1979
Best bowling performance: 2-0 Yorkshire v Windward Islands, Castries 1986–87

LAST SEASON: BATTING

	I.	N.O.	R.	H.S.	AV.
TEST					
1ST-CLASS	30	7	639	79*	27.78
INT					
RAL	13	2	307	118*	27.90
NAT.W.	2	0	77	62	38.50
B & H	3	3	162	75*	–

LAST SEASON: BOWLING

	O.	M.	R.	W.	AV.
TEST					
1ST-CLASS	115.2	14	394	5	78.80
INT					
RAL	10	1	31	2	15.50
NAT.W.	12	3	39	2	19.50
B & H	1	0	7	0	–

CAREER: BATTING

	I.	N.O.	R.	H.S.	AV.
TEST					
1ST-CLASS	348	55	9312	170*	31.78
INT	3	0	61	43	20.33
RAL	127	15	2628	118*	23.46
NAT.W.	16	3	191	62	14.69
B & H	32	10	1003	118*	45.59

CAREER: BOWLING

	O.	M.	R.	W.	AV.
TEST					
1ST-CLASS	229	37	804	9	89.33
INT					
RAL	18	1	69	3	23.00
NAT.W.	12	3	39	2	19.50
B & H	1	0	7	0	–

---

102. What have Maurice Tate, Intikhab Alam, and G. G. Macaulay got in common?

103. Who has taken the most Test wickets for England?

104. Who has taken the most Test wickets for Australia?

LYNCH, M. A.   Surrey

Full Name: Monte Allan Lynch
Role: Right-hand bat, right-arm
medium and off-break bowler
Born: 21 May 1958, Georgetown,
Guyana
Weight: 12st
Nickname: Mont
County debut: 1977
County cap: 1982
1000 runs in a season: 6
1st-Class 50s scored: 50
1st-Class 100s scored: 26
One-Day 50s: 24
One-Day 100s: 4
Place in batting averages: 86th
av. 33.14 (1986 76th av. 34.27)
1st-Class catches 1987: 24
(career 198)
Parents: Lawrence and Doreen
Austin
Marital status: Single
Family links with cricket: 'Father and most of family played at some time or
another.'
Education: Ryden's School, Walton-on-Thames
Other sports: Football, table tennis
Extras: Hitting 141* for Surrey v Glamorgan at Guildford in August 1982, off
78 balls in 88 minutes, one six hit his captain's, Roger Knight's, car, denting it.
Repeated trick in 1983 v Worcestershire in John Player Special League.

LAST SEASON: BATTING

	I.	N.O.	R.	H.S.	AV.
TEST					
1ST-CLASS	39	5	1127	128*	33.14
INT					
RAL	11	2	214	53	23.77
NAT.W.	2	1	54	53*	54.00
B & H	5	1	157	112*	39.25

CAREER: BATTING

	I.	N.O.	R.	H.S.	AV.
TEST					
1ST-CLASS	356	40	10964	152	34.69
INT					
RAL	121	15	2912	136	27.47
NAT.W.	20	4	456	129	28.50
B & H	34	2	843	112*	26.34

LAST SEASON: BOWLING

	O.	M.	R.	W.	AV.
TEST					
1ST-CLASS	61.3	13	200	3	66.66
INT					
RAL	6.2	0	42	5	8.40
NAT.W.	4	1	11	1	11.00
B & H					

CAREER: BOWLING

	O.	M.	R.	W.	AV.
TEST					
1ST-CLASS	265.3	47	1028	20	51.40
INT					
RAL	10.5	0	83	5	16.60
NAT.W.	16	6	42	2	21.00
B & H					

Joined West Indies Rebels in South Africa 1983–84, although qualified for England
Best batting performance: 152 Surrey v Nottinghamshire, The Oval 1986
Best bowling performance: 3-6 Surrey v Glamorgan, Swansea 1981

MAHER, B. J. M.   Derbyshire

Full Name: Bernard Joseph Michael Maher
Role: Right-hand bat, wicket-keeper
Born: 11 February 1958, Hillingdon
Height: 5' 10" **Weight:** 11st 7lbs
Nickname: 'Tends to vary but all derogatory!'
County debut: 1981
County cap: 1987
1st-Class 50s scored: 9
1st-Class 100s scored: 3
One-Day 50s: 2
Place in batting averages: 164th av. 21.38 (1986 50th av. 39.57)
Parents: Francis J. and Mary Ann
Marital status: Single
Family links with cricket: Brother kept wicket for school; father followed Derbyshire CCC quite closely
Education: Abbotsfield Comprehensive; Bishopsmalt Grammar; Harrow College; Loughborough University
Qualifications: 10 O-levels, 3 A-levels, BSc Hons in Economics and Accountancy. NCA Coaching Award. Gave up accountancy studies to play cricket
Jobs outside cricket: Accountant
Off-season 1987–88: Playing and coaching in Whangarei, New Zealand
Overseas tours: With the Middlesex Cricket League touring team to Trinidad and Tobago, 1978; Amsterdam with Loughborough University 1981
Overseas teams played for: Ellerslie CC, Auckland, New Zealand 1984–85; Kamo CC & Northland, New Zealand 1985–86; Northern Districts B 1986–87
Cricketers particularly learnt from: Bob Taylor, Alan Knott
Cricketers particularly admired: Malcolm Marshall, Richard Hadlee, Gordon Greenidge
Other sports played: Badminton, rugby union (for Old Abbotsonians)
Other sports followed: Athletics, rugby, tennis, boxing
Injuries 1987: Missed one Sunday game with damaged ankle

Relaxations: Scuba-diving, fishing, fell-walking

Extras: Caught five catches in innings on debut v Gloucestershire. Topped wicket-keepers' dismissals list in 1987 with 76 victims

Opinions on cricket: 'i) The game of cricket is not marketed well at all. It seems that the 'armchair' traditionalists will not allow the game to change with the times. The game needs one-day competitions at the weekends throughout the season with a three- or four-day County Championship during the week. The Refuge Assurance game should use the gimmicks of coloured clothing and a white ball. If we don't change the media coverage will gradually decline and with it sponsorship. ii) I would like to see a "transfer system" operate as with football. This will enable players and clubs to make more money. It will also indirectly improve the scouting system for young players. iii) A national coaching scheme for young players should be introduced. Most English children haven't picked up a bat until they are twelve-years-old. In South Africa, Australia and New Zealand, children receive formal coaching by English pro's at the age of eight upwards. This will do a lot to improve the standard of English cricket. iv) English county clubs should be encouraged to produce fast pitches of consistent bounce to encourage English fast bowlers.'

Best batting performance: 126 Derbyshire v New Zealand, Derby 1986

Best bowling performance: 2-69 Derbyshire v Glamorgan, Abergavenney 1986

LAST SEASON: BATTING

	I.	N.O.	R.	H.S.	AV.
TEST					
1ST-CLASS	41	2	834	105	21.38
INT					
RAL	13	0	248	78	19.07
NAT.W.	3	0	13	11	4.33
B & H	4	0	133	50	33.25

LAST SEASON: BOWLING

	O.	M.	R.	W.	AV.
TEST					
1ST-CLASS					
INT					
RAL					
NAT.W.					
B & H					

CAREER: BATTING

	I.	N.O.	R.	H.S.	AV.
TEST					
1ST-CLASS	120	23	2087	126	21.51
INT					
RAL	35	4	438	78	14.12
NAT.W.	4	0	13	11	3.25
B & H	6	1	135	50	27.00

CAREER: BOWLING

	O.	M.	R.	W.	AV.
TEST					
1ST-CLASS	33	2	151	3	50.33
INT					
RAL					
NAT.W.					
B & H					

LAST SEASON: WICKET KEEPING

	C.	ST.	
TEST			
1ST-CLASS	72	4	
INT			
RAL	10	1	
NAT.W.	5	–	
B & H	6	–	

CAREER: WICKET KEEPING

	C.	ST.	
TEST			
1ST-CLASS	163	11	
INT			
RAL	27	7	
NAT.W.	5	–	
B & H	9	1	

MALCOLM, D. E. Derbyshire

Full Name: Devon Eugene Malcolm
Role: Right-hand bat, right-arm
fast bowler
Born: 22 February 1963, Kingston,
Jamaica
Height: 6′ 3″ **Weight:** 14st 7lbs
Nickname: Dude
County debut: 1984
1st-Class 5 w. in innings: 1
Place in bowling averages: 95th
av 34.53 (1986 43rd av. 27.34)
Strike rate 1987: 58.84 (career 52.37)
1st-Class catches 1987: 5 (career 11)
Parents: Albert and Brendalee
(deceased)
Marital status: Single
Education: St Elizabeth Technical
High School; Richmond College
Qualifications: College certificates, O-levels, coaching certificate
Jobs outside cricket: Coaching
Overseas teams played for: Ellerslie CC, New Zealand 1985–86
Cricketers particularly admired: Michael Holding, Richard Hadlee
Other sports played: Football
Other sports followed: Football, table tennis
Relaxations: Reggae, funk and soul music
Best batting performance: 29* Derbyshire v Gloucestershire, Gloucester 1986
Best bowling performance: 5-42 Derbyshire v Gloucestershire, Gloucester
1986

LAST SEASON: BATTING

	I.	N.O.	R.	H.S.	AV.
TEST					
1ST-CLASS	16	4	43	9*	3.58
INT					
RAL					
NAT.W.	1	0	1	1	1.00
B & H					

LAST SEASON: BOWLING

	O.	M.	R.	W.	AV.
TEST					
1ST-CLASS	255	45	898	26	34.53
INT					
RAL					
NAT.W.	11	0	53	1	53.00
B & H					

CAREER: BATTING

	I.	N.O.	R.	H.S.	AV.
TEST					
1ST-CLASS	23	8	80	29*	5.33
INT					
RAL	1	0	16	16	16.00
NAT.W.	1	0	1	1	1.00
B & H					

CAREER: BOWLING

	O.	M.	R.	W.	AV.
TEST					
1ST-CLASS	471.2	83	1663	54	30.79
INT					
RAL	16	0	87	3	29.00
NAT.W.	11	0	53	1	53.00
B & H					

MALLENDER, N. A.   Somerset

Full Name: Neil Alan Mallender
Role: Right-hand bat, right-arm
fast-medium bowler
Born: 13 August 1961, Kirk
Sandall, Nr Doncaster
Height: 6′ 1″ **Weight:** 13st
Nickname: Ghostie
County debut: 1980
(Northamptonshire), 1987
(Somerset)
County cap: 1984
(Northamptonshire), 1987
(Somerset)
50 wickets in a season: 2
1st-Class 50s scored: 4
1st-Class 5 w. in innings: 10
1st-Class 10 w. in match: 1
Place in batting averages: 206th
av. 16.37 (1986 232nd av. 11.90)
Place in bowling averages: 29th av. 24.54 (1986 83rd av. 36.02)
Strike rate 1987: 45.78 (career 58.95)
1st-Class catches 1987: 6 (career 62)
Parents: Ron and Jean
Wife and date of marriage: Caroline, 1 October 1983
Family links with cricket: Brother, Graham, used to play good representative
cricket before joining the RAF
Education: Beverley Grammar School, East Yorkshire
Qualifications: 7 O-levels
Off-season 1987–88: Playing and coaching for Kaikorai CC and Otago CC in
New Zealand
Cricketing superstitions or habits: Left boot on first
Overseas tours: Young England tour to West Indies, 1980
Overseas teams played for: Belmont DCC, NSW, 1980–81; Bathurst, NSW,
1982–83; Otago and Kaikorai CC, New Zealand, 1983–87
Cricketers particularly learnt from: Peter Willey, Warren Lees, Martin
Crowe
Cricketers particularly admired: Richard Hadlee, Dennis Lillee
Other sports played: Golf
Other sports followed: Rugby league (especially Hull RFC), most sports
Injuries 1987: Back muscle
Relaxations: Pop/modern music, golf
Extras: Signed a 3-year contract to play for Somerset in 1987. Took hat-trick
in first round of 1987 B & H Cup v Combined Universities

Best batting performance: 88 Otago v Central Districts, Oamaru 1984–85
Best bowling performance: 7-27 Otago v Auckland, Auckland 1984–85

LAST SEASON: BATTING

	I.	N.O.	R.	H.S.	AV.
TEST					
1ST-CLASS	17	9	131	20*	16.37
INT					
RAL	5	4	26	9*	26.00
NAT.W.	1	0	6	6	6.00
B & H	2	0	1	1	0.50

LAST SEASON: BOWLING

	O.	M.	R.	W.	AV.
TEST					
1ST-CLASS	351	61	1129	46	24.54
INT					
RAL	71	3	274	10	27.40
NAT.W.	12	1	27	2	13.50
B & H	52.2	6	220	10	22.00

CAREER: BATTING

	I.	N.O.	R.	H.S.	AV.
TEST					
1ST-CLASS	203	65	1898	88	13.75
INT					
RAL	36	19	178	22	10.47
NAT.W.	9	3	45	11*	7.50
B & H	10	3	24	7	3.42

CAREER: BOWLING

	O.	M.	R.	W.	AV.
TEST					
1ST-CLASS	4411.3	969	13090	449	29.15
INT					
RAL	605.5	37	2786	109	25.55
NAT.W.	176.4	27	499	28	17.82
B & H	254.2	30	957	37	25.86

MARKS, V. J. Somerset

Full Name: Victor James Marks
Role: Right-hand bat, off-break bowler
Born: 25 June 1955, Middle Chinnock, Somerset
Height: 5′ 9″ **Weight:** 11st 8lbs
Nickname: Vic
County debut: 1975
County cap: 1979
Benefit: 1988
Test debut: 1982
No. of Tests: 6
No. of One-Day Internationals: 33
1000 runs in a season: 2
50 wickets in a season: 7
1st-Class 50s scored: 66
1st-Class 100s scored: 5
1st-Class 5 w. in innings: 34
1st-Class 10 w. in match: 4
One-Day 50s: 12
Place in batting averages: 142nd av 25.40 (1986 30th av. 44.04)
Place in bowling averages: 73rd av. 30.78 (1986 82nd av. 35.94)
Strike rate 1987: 66.75 (career 71.18)
1st-Class catches 1987: 9 (career 128)
Parents: Harold and Joan

Wife and date of marriage: Anna, 9 September 1978
Children: Amy, 27 November 1979
Family links with cricket: 'Father a dangerous village cricketer.'
Education: Blundell's School; Oxford University
Qualifications: MA Classics
Jobs outside cricket: Teaching – but not since March 1981
Overseas tours: Derrick Robins' XI to Canada 1977; England to Australia and New Zealand 1982–83, New Zealand and Pakistan 1983–84, India and Australia 1984–85; Christians in Sport to India 1985
Overseas teams played for: Grade cricket with Bayswater Morley CC in Perth, Western Australia, 1981–82, Western Australia 1986–87
Cricketers particularly learnt from: Tom Cartwright, Arthur Milton
Cricketers particularly admired: Colin Dredge
Other sports played: Squash, golf
Extras: Half-blue for rugby fives at Oxford University. Debut for Oxford University CC 1975. Blue 1975–76–77–78. Captain 1976–77. Somerset vice-captain 1984. Author of *Somerset County Cricket Scrapbook* (1984), *Marks Out of XI* (1985) and *TCCB Guide to Better Cricket* (1987)
Opinions on cricket: 'We play too much.'
Best batting performance: 134 Somerset v Worcestershire, Weston-super-Mare 1984
Best bowling performance: 8-17 Somerset v Lancashire, Bath 1985

LAST SEASON – BATTING

	I.	N.O.	R.	H.S.	AV.
TEST					
1ST-CLASS	31	6	635	63*	25.40
INT					
RAL	10	1	173	61	19.22
NAT.W.	1	0	14	14	14.00
B & H	4	0	172	70	43.00

LAST SEASON: BOWLING

	O.	M.	R.	W.	AV.
TEST					
1ST-CLASS	778.5	203	2155	70	30.78
INT					
RAL	81	4	363	10	36.30
NAT.W.	12	7	10	1	10.00
B & H	49	8	189	6	31.50

CAREER: BATTING

	I.	N.O.	R.	H.S.	AV.
TEST	10	1	249	83	27.66
1ST-CLASS	427	75	10629	134	30.19
INT	24	3	285	44	13.57
RAL	109	27	1789	72	21.81
NAT.W.	21	6	406	55	27.06
B & H	42	8	928	81*	27.29

CAREER: BOWLING

	O.	M.	R.	W.	AV.
TEST	180.2	54	484	11	44.00
1ST-CLASS	8652.3	2389	23641	725	32.60
INT	295.2	28	1076	44	24.45
RAL	745.4	45	3014	113	26.67
NAT.W.	202.1	35	630	20	31.50
B & H	457.5	80	1383	46	30.06

105. Who has taken the most Test wickets for South Africa?
106. Who has taken the most Test wickets for West Indies?

MARSH, S. A.   Kent

Full Name: Steven Andrew Marsh
Role: Right-hand bat, wicket-keeper
Born: 27 January 1961, Westminster
Height: 6′ **Weight:** 12st
County debut: 1982
Nickname: Marshy
1st-Class 50s scored: 8
Place in batting averages: 185th
av. 18.68 (1986 100th av. 30.60)
Parents: Melvyn Graham and Valerie
Ann
Wife and date of marriage: Julie,
27 September 1986
Family links with cricket: Father
played local cricket for Lordswood.
Father-in-law, Bob Wilson, played
for Kent 1954–66
Education: Walderslade Secondary
School for Boys; Mid-Kent College
of Higher and Further Education
Qualifications: 6 O-levels, 2 A-levels, OND in Business Studies
Off-season 1987–88: 'Working for my car sponsor, Swale Motors.'
Jobs outside cricket: Office clerk, cricket coach
Cricketing superstitions or habits: 'When batting, getting into double figures.'
Overseas tours: Lordswood CC, Kent to Barbados 1979
Overseas teams played for: Avendale CC, South Africa 1985–86
Cricketers particularly learnt from: Alan Igglesden ('I have learnt to keep to
leg-side bowling!'), Bob Woolmer
Cricketers particularly admired: Gary Sobers, Alan Knott

LAST SEASON: BATTING

	I.	N.O.	R.	H.S.	AV.		
TEST							
1ST-CLASS	27	5	411	72*	18.68		
INT							
RAL	9	3	118	36	19.66		
NAT.W.							
B & H	5	0	17	6	3.40		

CAREER: BATTING

	I.	N.O.	R.	H.S.	AV.		
TEST							
1ST-CLASS	77	16	1448	72*	23.73		
INT							
RAL	21	6	194	36	12.93		
NAT.W.	1	0	1	1	1.00		
B & H	8	2	49	15	8.16		

LAST SEASON: WICKET KEEPING

	C.	ST.			
TEST					
1ST-CLASS	39	2			
INT					
RAL	17	2			
NAT.W.					
B & H	5	1			

CAREER: WICKET KEEPING

	C.	ST.			
TEST					
1ST-CLASS	113	8			
INT					
RAL	34	2			
NAT.W.	2	–			
B & H	15	1			

Other sports played: Golf, snooker, soccer, horse riding
Relaxations: Horse racing, eating and sleeping
Best batting performance: 72* Kent v Glamorgan, Canterbury 1987

MARSHALL, M. D.   Hampshire

Full Name: Malcolm Denzil
Marshall
Role: Right-hand bat, right-arm
fast bowler
Born: 18 April 1958, Barbados
Height: 5' 11" **Weight:** 12st 8lbs
Nickname: Macko
County debut: 1979
County cap: 1981
Benefit: 1987
Test debut: 1978–79
No. of Tests: 51
No. of One-Day Internationals: 86
50 wickets in a season: 7
1st-Class 50s scored: 28
1st-Class 100s scored: 4
1st-Class 5 w. in innings: 64
1st-Class 10 w. in match: 9
One-Day 50s: 3
Place in batting averages: 66th av. 35.88 (1986 228th av. 12.52)
Place in bowling averages: 8th av. 19.84 (1986 1st av. 15.08)
Strike rate 1987: 46.90 (career 32.09)
1st-Class catches 1987: 7 (career 99)
Parents: Mrs Eleanor Inniss
Children: Shelly, 24 November 1984
Family links with cricket: Cousin plays for Texaco as a fast bowler
Education: Parkinson Comprehensive School, Barbados
Jobs outside cricket: Promoter of bank's products
Overseas tours: With West Indies to India and Sri Lanka 1978–79; Australia
1979–80, 1981–82, 1984–85; Pakistan 1980–81; India 1983–84; England 1980
and 1984; Zimbabwe 1981; New Zealand 1979–80
Overseas teams played for: Barbados (debut 1977–78)
Cricketers particularly learnt from: 'The West Indies team.'
Other sports played: Tennis, darts, pool, golf
Relaxations: Soul-music, reggae
Extras: Took nine wickets in debut match v Glamorgan in May 1979. Scored
his first first-class century (109) in Zimbabwe, October 1981, for the West
Indies against Zimbabwe. Most wickets in the Shell Shield Competition (25)

by a Barbadian. Broke record of number of wickets taken in 22-match season (i.e. since 1969) with 133. Published autobiography *Marshall Arts* (1987)
Best batting performance: 116* Hamsphire v Lancashire, Southampton 1982
Best bowling performance: 8-71 Hampshire v Worcestershire, Southampton 1982

LAST SEASON: BATTING

	I.	N.O.	R.	H.S.	AV.
TEST					
1ST-CLASS	22	5	610	99	35.88
INT					
RAL	10	3	124	41*	17.71
NAT.W.	1	0	51	51	51.00
B & H	4	0	76	34	19.00

CAREER: BATTING

	I.	N.O.	R.	H.S.	AV.
TEST	62	5	1068	92	18.73
1ST-CLASS	257	34	5215	116*	23.38
INT	45	15	501	66	16.70
RAL	59	16	742	46	17.25
NAT.W.	13	7	194	51	32.33
B & H	23	1	285	34	12.95

LAST SEASON: BOWLING

	O.	M.	R.	W.	AV.
TEST					
1ST-CLASS	594.1	152	1508	76	19.84
INT					
RAL	89.5	3	309	18	17.16
NAT.W.	17	3	41	2	20.50
B & H	46.1	5	136	6	22.66

CAREER: BOWLING

	O.	M.	R.	W.	AV.
TEST	1879.4	397	5194	240	21.64
1ST-CLASS	6024.5	1708	15158	886	17.10
INT	758.5	86	2530	111	22.79
RAL	698.4	68	2404	104	23.11
NAT.W.	190.4	36	495	18	27.50
B & H	265.1	51	737	37	19.91

MARTINDALE, D. J. R.
Nottinghamshire

Full Name: Duncan John Richardson Martindale
Role: Right-hand bat, cover fielder
Born: 13 December 1963, Harrogate
Height: 5′ 11½″ **Weight:** 12st
Nickname: Bloers, BC
County debut: 1985
1st-Class 50s scored: 2
1st-Class 100s scored: 2
Place in batting averages: 196th av. 17.45
1st-Class catches 1987: 3 (career 9)
Parents: Don and Isabel
Marital status: Single
Family links with cricket: Father and grandfather played club cricket in Nottingham; great uncle played for Nottinghamshire 2nd XI
Education: Lymm Grammar School; Trent Polytechnic

Qualifications: 9 O-levels, 2 A-levels, HND Business Studies, NCA Coaching Award

Off-season 1987–88: 'Working in Nottingham, expanding my extra-cricketing interest, as well as training for 1988 season.'

Overseas tours: International Ambassadors XI to India, 1985

Overseas teams played for: Prospect and District CC, Adelaide, 1985–86, 1986–87

Cricketers particularly learnt from: 'All professional cricketers'

Cricketers particularly admired: Richard Hadlee, Clive Rice, Vic Marks

Other sports played: All sports, particularly long-distance running, squash and golf

Relaxations: Reading, listening to all types of music, meeting people, good food, travelling

Extras: Scored century (104*) in fifth first-class innings. First one-day match was 1985 NatWest final. Member of Christians in Sport

Opinions on cricket: '1) The reintroduction of uncovered pitches wasn't practical and didn't produce the results expected, i.e. spinners were *more* redundant, valuable time was wasted; seam bowlers *over-encouraged* by dry approaches and wet wickets. 2) Groundsmen should strive to prepare "result" wickets, so increasing spectator interest and improving skills, e.g. Ron Allsop at Trent Bridge – his efforts have encouraged positive cricket. 3) County clubs should liase with potential employers to guarantee off-season employment to its players – be it at home or overseas – hence having the finger on the pulse of "player-development" both in and outside the game.'

Best batting performance: 104* Nottinghamshire v Lancashire, Old Trafford 1985

LAST SEASON: BATTING

	I.	N.O.	R.	H.S.	AV.
TEST					
1ST-CLASS	13	2	192	103	17.45
INT					
RAL	1	0	1	1	1.00
NAT.W.					
B & H					

CAREER: BATTING

	I.	N.O.	R.	H.S.	AV.
TEST					
1ST-CLASS	31	5	624	104*	24.00
INT					
RAL	4	0	45	33	11.25
NAT.W.	1	1	20	20*	–
B & H					

107. Who has taken the most Test wickets for New Zealand?

108. Who has taken the most Test wickets for India?

MARU, R. J. G. Hampshire

Full Name: Rajesh Jamandass
Govind Maru
Role: Right-hand bat, slow left-
arm bowler, close fielder
Born: 28 October 1962, Nairobi
Height: 5′ 6″ **Weight:** 10st 7lbs
Nickname: Raj
County debut: 1980 (Middlesex),
1984 (Hampshire)
County cap: 1986 (Hampshire)
50 wickets in a season: 1
1st-Class 50s scored: 1
1st-Class 5 w. in innings: 9
Place in batting averages: — (1986
113th av. 29.00)
Place in bowling averages: 60th
av. 29.02 (1986 51st av. 27.83)
Strike rate 1987: 67.83 (career 64.90)
1st-Class catches 1987: 24

(career 88)
Parents: Jamandass and Prabhavati
Family links with cricket: Brother has played for Middlesex 2nd XI and in
Middlesex League
Education: Harrow College
Qualifications: Cricket coach
Jobs outside cricket: Cricket coach
Off-season 1987–88: Coaching in Blenheim, New Zealand
Cricketing superstitions or habits: Nelsons: 111, 222 and 333
Overseas tours: Young England tour of West Indies 1980; NCA tour of

LAST SEASON: BATTING

	I.	N.O.	R.	H.S.	AV.
TEST					
1ST-CLASS	14	3	92	15	8.36
INT					
RAL	2	2	6	6*	—
NAT.W.					
B & H					

CAREER: BATTING

	I.	N.O.	R.	H.S.	AV.
TEST					
1ST-CLASS	79	25	828	62	15.33
INT					
RAL	3	3	9	6*	—
NAT.W.					
B & H					

LAST SEASON: BOWLING

	O.	M.	R.	W.	AV.
TEST					
1ST-CLASS	802.4	229	2061	71	29.02
INT					
RAL	37	3	172	4	43.00
NAT.W.	2	0	5	2	2.50
B & H					

CAREER: BOWLING

	O.	M.	R.	W.	AV.
TEST					
1ST-CLASS	2834	782	7750	262	29.58
INT					
RAL	52	3	258	6	43.00
NAT.W.	2	0	5	2	2.50
B & H					

Canada; Barbican International XI to Dubai; Middlesex to Zimbabwe
1980–81
Overseas teams played for: Blenheim CC, New Zealand, 1985–86
Cricketers particularly learnt from: Jack Robertson, Derek Underwood,
David Graveney, Malcolm Marshall, Peter Sainsbury, Don Bennett
Cricketers admired: Malcolm Marshall, Mike Gatting, Derek Underwood
Other sports played: Badminton, table tennis, squash, swimming
Other sports followed: Football, rugby union
Relaxations: Music, reading, TV
Extras: Played for Middlesex 1980–83. Joined Hampshire in 1984
Best batting performance: 62 Hamsphire v Sussex, Portsmouth 1985
Best bowling performance: 7-79 Hampshire v Middlesex, Bournemouth 1984

MAYNARD, M. P. Glamorgan

Full Name: Matthew Peter Maynard
Role: Right-hand bat, right-arm
medium bowler, slip fielder
Born: 21 March 1966, Oldham
Height: 5′ 10½″ **Weight:** 12st 3lbs
Nickname: Walter
County debut: 1985
County cap: 1987
1000 runs in a season: 2
1st-Class 50s scored: 19
1st-Class 100s scored: 5
One-Day 50s: 2
Place in batting averages: 38th
av. 40.65 (1986 85th av. 33.40)
1st-Class catches 1987: 30
(career 44)
Parents: Pat and Ken (deceased)
Wife and date of marriage: Susan,
27 September 1986

Family links with cricket: Father pro'd for Duckinfield. Brother played club
cricket. Brother, Charles, started playing again for St Fagans
Education: Ysgol David Hughes, Anglesey
Jobs outside cricket: Sales rep for Bangor City FC; barman
Off-season 1987–88: Playing and coaching for St Joseph's CC, Whakatane,
New Zealand
Cricketing superstitions or habits: 'Nothing if things are going well. Every-
thing if they aren't!'
Overseas tours: Barbados with North Wales XI, 1982
Overseas teams played for: St Josephs, Whakatane, 1986–87, 1987–88

Cricketers particularly learnt from: Father, Colin Page, Bill Clutterbuck, John Steele and 'everyone at Glamorgan'
Cricketers particularly admired: Richard Hadlee, Ian Botham, Imran Khan
Other sports played: Football, rugby, golf, snooker, squash
Relaxations: Listening to Lionel Ritchie and George Benson, decorating
Extras: Scored century on debut v Yorkshire at Swansea. Also youngest centurion for Glamorgan. Scored 1000 runs in first full season. Fastest ever 50 for Glamorgan (14 mins) v Yorkshire. Youngest player to be awarded Glamorgan cap. Fastest TV 50 in Refuge Assurance League 1987. Leading 6-hitter in Championship in 1987
Opinions: 'Go back to covered wickets, especially now we are going to play four-day matches.'
Best batting performance: 160 Glamorgan v Somerset, Weston-super-Mare 1987
Best bowling performance: 3-21 Glamorgan v Oxford University, Oxford 1987

LAST SEASON: BATTING

	I.	N.O.	R.	H.S.	AV.
TEST					
1ST-CLASS	45	5	1626	160	40.65
INT					
RAL	14	1	311	66	23.92
NAT.W.	2	0	16	10	8.00
B & H	4	2	101	41*	50.50

CAREER: BATTING

	I.	N.O.	R.	H.S.	AV.
TEST					
1ST-CLASS	82	9	2826	160	38.71
INT					
RAL	30	1	539	66	18.58
NAT.W.	4	0	32	10	8.00
B & H	5	2	101	41*	33.66

LAST SEASON: BOWLING

	O.	M.	R.	W.	AV.
TEST					
1ST-CLASS	27	4	89	4	22.25
INT					
RAL					
NAT.W.					
B & H					

CAREER: BOWLING

	O.	M.	R.	W.	AV.
TEST					
1ST-CLASS	31.1	4	106	4	26.50
INT					
RAL					
NAT.W.					
B & H					

109. Who has taken the most Test wickets for Pakistan?

110. Which batsman scored the most Test runs in one day, and how many?

MAYS, C. S.   Surrey

Full Name: Christopher Sean Mays
Role: Right-hand bat, off-break
bowler
Born: 11 May 1966, Brighton
Height: 5′ 9″
County debut: 1986 (Sussex),
1987 (Surrey)
Place in bowling averages: — (1986
123rd av. 54.30)
1st-Class catches 1987: 1 (career 3)
Education: Lancing College
Overseas tours: To Holland with
NAYC 1983; West Indies with
Young England 1985
Off-season 1987–88: On five-
year course at Middlesex
Hospital Medical School
Extras: Has represented
England Schools and MCC Schools.
Left Sussex at end of 1986 season and joined Surrey
Best batting performance: 8* Sussex v Gloucestershire, Bristol 1986
Best bowling performance: 3-77 Sussex v New Zealand, Hove 1986

LAST SEASON: BATTING

	I.	N.O.	R.	H.S.	AV.
TEST					
1ST-CLASS	2	1	7	5*	7.00
INT					
RAL					
NAT.W.					
B & H					

LAST SEASON: BOWLING

	O.	M.	R.	W.	AV.
TEST					
1ST-CLASS	56	7	201	2	100.50
INT					
RAL					
NAT.W.					
B & H					

CAREER: BATTING

	I.	N.O.	R.	H.S.	AV.
TEST					
1ST-CLASS	8	3	26	8*	5.20
INT					
RAL					
NAT.W.					
B & H					

CAREER: BOWLING

	O.	M.	R.	W.	AV.
TEST					
1ST-CLASS	268.5	52	907	15	60.46
INT					
RAL					
NAT.W.					
B & H					

111. Who took the most wickets in one Test innings, when and where?

McEWAN, S. M.   Worcestershire

Full Name: Steven Michael McEwan
Role: Right-hand bat, right-arm fast-medium bowler, slip fielder
Born: 5 May 1962, Worcester
Height: 6' 1" **Weight:** 13st 5lbs
Nickname: Mac, Maciz, Freddy
County debut: 1985
Place in bowling averages: 98th av. 39.87 (1986 102nd av. 39.69)
1st-Class catches 1987: 0 (career 8)
Parents: Michael James and Valerie Jeanette
Marital status: Single
Family links with cricket: Father and uncle played club cricket
Education: Worcester Royal Grammar School
Qualifications: 6 O-levels, 3 A-levels. Technician's certificate in building
Jobs outside cricket: Assistant buyer, building trade; cricket coach
Off-season 1987–88: Coaching in New Zealand
Overseas teams played for: Birkenhead City, Auckland, 1985–88
Cricketers particularly learnt from: Dipak Patel, Basil D'Oliveira, Kapil Dev
Cricketers particularly admired: Richard Hadlee, Malcolm Marshall
Other sports played: Soccer
Other sports followed: American football
Injuries 1987: Cut finger while fielding that needed stitches
Relaxations: TV, reading

LAST SEASON: BATTING

	I.	N.O.	R.	H.S.	AV.
TEST					
1ST-CLASS	1	0	1	1	1.00
INT					
RAL					
NAT.W.					
B & H					

LAST SEASON: BOWLING

	O.	M.	R.	W.	AV.
TEST					
1ST-CLASS	87.4	12	298	9	33.11
INT					
RAL	15	0	85	2	42.50
NAT.W.					
B & H					

CAREER: BATTING

	I.	N.O.	R.	H.S.	AV.
TEST					
1ST-CLASS	12	7	39	13*	7.80
INT					
RAL	3	2	13	7*	13.00
NAT.W.					
B & H					

CAREER: BOWLING

	O.	M.	R.	W.	AV.
TEST					
1ST-CLASS	444.5	72	1571	41	38.31
INT					
RAL	89	2	470	15	31.33
NAT.W.					
B & H					

Extras: Took 10 wickets for 13 runs in an innings in 1983 for Worcester Nomads against Moreton-in-Marsh. Also broke school bowling record, 60 wickets, at WRGS, 1982
Best batting performance: 13* Worcestershire v Oxford University, Oxford 1985
Best bowling performance: 3-29 Worcestershire v Warwickshire, Edgbaston 1987

McLEOD, K. W.   Lancashire

Full Name: Kenneth Walcott McLeod
Role: Right-hand bat, left-arm fast-medium bowler
Born: 18 March 1964, St Elizabeth, Jamaica
Height: 6′ 2″
County debut: 1987
1st-Class 5 w. in innings: 2
Place in bowling averages: 23rd av. 24.05
Strike rate 1987: 44.70 (career 50.82)
Extras: Played for Jamaica in Shell Shield 1984–87. Took 5-94 v Glamorgan and 5-8 v Leicestershire in his second and third matches for Lancashire

Best batting performance: 31 Lancashire v Worcestershire, Old Trafford 1987
Best bowling performance: 5–8 Lancashire v Leicestershire, Leicester 1987

LAST SEASON: BATTING

	I.	N.O.	R.	H.S.	AV.
TEST					
1ST-CLASS	6	0	92	31	15.33
INT					
RAL	1	0	1	1	1.00
NAT.W.					
B & H	2	1	9	5*	9.00

CAREER: BATTING

	I.	N.O.	R.	H.S.	AV.
TEST					
1ST-CLASS	14	0	120	31	8.57
INT					
RAL	1	0	1	1	1.00
NAT.W.					
B & H	2	1	9	5*	9.00

LAST SEASON: BOWLING

	O.	M.	R.	W.	AV.
TEST					
1ST-CLASS	126.4	24	409	17	24.05
INT					
RAL	11	1	39	1	39.00
NAT.W.					
B & H	28	1	139	1	139.00

CAREER: BOWLING

	O.	M.	R.	W.	AV.
TEST					
1ST-CLASS	237.1	47	748	28	26.71
INT					
RAL	11	1	39	1	39.00
NAT.W.					
B & H	28	1	139	1	139.00

MEDLYCOTT, K. T. Surrey

Full Name: Keith Thomas Medlycott
Role: Right-hand bat, slow left-arm bowler, short-leg fielder
Born: 12 May 1965, Whitechapel
Height: 5′ 11″ **Weight:** 12st 3lbs
Nickname: Medders
County debut: 1984
1st-Class 50s scored: 6
1st-Class 100s scored: 2
1st-Class 5 w. in innings: 4
1st-Class 10 w. in match: 1
Place in batting averages: 113th
av. 29.36 (1986 214th av. 14.07)
Place in bowling averages: 110th
av. 39.04 (1986 55th av. 29.15)
Strike rate 1987: 78.09 (career 68.33)
1st-Class catches 1987: 13 (career 22)
Parents: Thomas Alfred and June
Elizabeth

Marital status: Single
Family links with cricket: 'Father plays club cricket (getting better). Brother, Paul, played one game and scored one more than me!'
Education: Parmiters Grammar School; Wandsworth Comprehensive
Qualifications: 2 O-levels
Jobs outside cricket: Coaching in South Africa for Waterkloof House Prep. School
Cricketing superstitions or habits: 'Bad habit of talking rubbish before batting, which definitely annoys the coach!'
Off-season 1987–88: Coaching in South Africa

LAST SEASON: BATTING

	I.	N.O.	R.	H.S.	AV.
TEST					
1ST-CLASS	30	5	734	153	29.36
INT					
RAL	3	0	11	10	3.66
NAT.W.					
B & H					

LAST SEASON: BOWLING

	O.	M.	R.	W.	AV.
TEST					
1ST-CLASS	546.4	148	1640	42	39.04
INT					
RAL	4	0	39	1	39.00
NAT.W.					
B & H					

CAREER: BATTING

	I.	N.O.	R.	H.S.	AV.
TEST					
1ST-CLASS	54	13	1070	153	26.09
INT					
RAL	4	0	11	10	2.75
NAT.W.					
B & H					

CAREER: BOWLING

	O.	M.	R.	W.	AV.
TEST					
1ST-CLASS	1025	280	3031	90	33.67
INT					
RAL	6	0	60	1	60.00
NAT.W.					
B & H					

Overseas teams played for: Oostelikes CC 1983–88; Harlequins CC 1984–85
Cricketers particularly learnt from: Geoff Arnold, T. Sheppard, Chris Waller
Cricketers particularly admired: Bishan Bedi, David Ward
Other sports played: Football
Relaxations: 'Sleeping!'
Extras: Scored 100 on debut (117* v Cambridge University) in 1984
Opinions on cricket: 'Four-day cricket, as long as the wickets are prepared properly, must come in, as it is the best thing for Test cricket in England.'
Best batting performance: 153 Surrey v Kent, The Oval 1987
Best bowling performance: 6-63 Surrey v Kent, The Oval 1986

MENDIS, G. D. Lancashire

Full Name: Gehan Dixon Mendis
Role: Right-hand opening bat
Born: 24 April 1955, Colombo, Sri Lanka
Height: 5' 8" **Weight:** 10st 7lbs
Nickname: Mendo, Dix
County debut: 1974 (Sussex), 1986 (Lancashire)
County cap: 1980 (Sussex), 1986 (Lancashire)
1000 runs in a season: 8
1st-Class 50s scored: 71
1st-Class 100s scored: 25
1st-Class 200s scored: 3
One-Day 50s: 24
One-Day 100s: 6
Place in batting averages: 49th av. 38.61 (1986 48th av. 40.08)
1st-Class catches 1987: 6
(career 100 + 1 stumping)

Parents: Sam Dixon Charles and Sonia Marcelle
Children: Hayley, 11 December 1982
Education: St Thomas College, Mount Lavinia, Sri Lanka; Brighton, Hove & Sussex Grammar School; Bede College, Durham University
Qualifications: BEd Mathematics, Durham; NCA coaching certificate
Jobs outside cricket: Teacher at Rosemead School, Littlehampton, Sussex; Richard Ellis, Perth, Western Australia; City Sales & Marketing Ltd, London
Overseas tours: Maharaja Organisation XI to India 1980; Rohan Kanhai's Invitation XI to Pakistan 1981; numerous international teams to West Indies
Overseas teams played for: Maharaja Organisation XI in Sri Lanka 1980–81;

Colombo CC; Sebastianites CC, and Mount Lawley CC, Western Australia; Nedlands CC, Perth

Cricketers particularly admired: Barry Richards, Richard Hadlee

Other sports played: Table tennis for Sussex at junior level

Other sports followed: Formula One motor racing

Relaxations: Music, cinema and wine bars

Extras: Played for TCCB XI in 1981. Has twice turned down invitations to play for Sri Lanka in order to be free to be chosen for England. Left Sussex at end of 1985 to join Lancashire

Opinions on cricket: 'Championship to be 16 four-day games Tuesday–Friday. B & H/NatWest to be played Sat/Mon. Sunday League to remain the same.'

Best batting performance: 209* Sussex v Somerset, Hove 1984

Best bowling performance: 1-65 Sussex v Yorkshire, Hove 1985

LAST SEASON: BATTING

	I.	N.O.	R.	H.S.	AV.
TEST					
1ST-CLASS	42	6	1390	203*	38.61
INT					
RAL	11	2	286	48	31.77
NAT.W.	1	0	11	11	11.00
B & H	4	0	79	29	19.75

LAST SEASON: BOWLING

	O.	M.	R.	W.	AV.
TEST					
1ST-CLASS	10	1	33	0	–
INT					
RAL					
NAT.W.					
B & H					

CAREER: BATTING

	I.	N.O.	R.	H.S.	AV.
TEST					
1ST-CLASS	444	42	14400	209*	35.82
INT					
RAL	135	14	3475	125*	28.71
NAT.W.	28	2	883	141*	33.96
B & H	45	1	1153	109	26.20

CAREER: BOWLING

	O.	M.	R.	W.	AV.
TEST					
1ST-CLASS	15.3	1	109	1	109.00
INT					
RAL					
NAT.W.					
B & H					

112. Who scored the fastest triple century in Test cricket?

113. Who scored the fastest double century in Test cricket?

114. Who scored the fastest century in Test cricket?

MERRICK, A. T.   Warwickshire

Full Name: Anthony Tyrone
Merrick
Role: Right-hand bat, right-arm
fast-medium bowler
Born: 10 June 1963, Antigua
Height: 6′
County debut: 1987
1st-Class 50s scored: 2
1st-Class 5 w. in innings: 8
1st-Class 10 w. in match: 1
One-Day 50s: 1
Place in batting averages: 212th
av. 15.71
Place in bowling averages: 32nd
av. 25.24
Strike rate 1987: 45.63 (career 42.88)
1st-Class catches 1987: 6 (career 18)
Children: Anthea, 6 January
1987

Education: All Saints Primary and Secondary Schools
Jobs outside cricket: Physical Education Teacher
Overseas tours: West Indies Youth Team to England 1982; West Indies B to
Zimbabwe 1986
Overseas teams played for: Leeward Islands
Cricketers particularly learnt from: Andy Roberts, Eldine Baptiste
Other sports followed: Soccer, lawn tennis
Injuries 1987: Back injury
Relaxations: Listening to music
Extras: Played for Rawtenstall in Lancashire League 1985 and 1986

LAST SEASON: BATTING

	I.	N.O.	R.	H.S.	AV.
TEST					
1ST-CLASS	19	5	220	74*	15.71
INT					
RAL	4	1	76	59	25.33
NAT.W.					
B & H	1	1	13	13*	–

LAST SEASON: BOWLING

	O.	M.	R.	W.	AV.
TEST					
1ST-CLASS	433.3	71	1439	57	25.24
INT					
RAL	53.2	7	226	9	25.11
NAT.W.					
B & H	11	1	32	0	–

CAREER: BATTING

	I.	N.O.	R.	H.S.	AV.
TEST					
1ST-CLASS	50	10	618	74*	15.45
INT					
RAL	4	1	76	59	25.33
NAT.W.					
B & H	1	1	13	13*	–

CAREER: BOWLING

	O.	M.	R.	W.	AV.
TEST					
1ST-CLASS	1072.1	73	3608	150	24.05
INT					
RAL	53.2	7	226	9	25.11
NAT.W.					
B & H	11	1	32	0	–

Best batting performance: 74* Warwickshire v Gloucestershire, Edgbaston 1987
Best bowling performance: 7-45 Warwickshire v Lancashire, Edgbaston 1987

METCALFE, A. A. Yorkshire

Full Name: Ashley Anthony Metcalfe
Role: Right-hand bat, off-break bowler
Born: 25 December 1963, Horsforth, Leeds
Height: 5′ 9½″ **Weight:** 11st 7lbs
County debut: 1983
County cap: 1986
1000 runs in a season: 2
1st-Class 50s scored: 17
1st-Class 100s scored: 10
One-Day 50s: 14
One-Day 100s: 1
Place in batting averages: 101st av. 31.00 (1986 26th av. 45.07)
1st-Class catches 1987: 8 (career 25)
Wife and date of marriage: Diane, 20 April 1986
Parents: Tony and Ann
Family links with cricket: Father played in local league; father-in-law Ray Illingworth (Yorkshire and England)
Education: Ladderbanks Middle School; Bradford Grammar School; University College, London
Qualifications: 9 O-levels, 3 A-levels, NCA Coaching Certificate
Jobs outside cricket: Worked for Grattan Mail Order Co, Paul Madeley's DIY
Off-season 1987–88: Working in England
Overseas tours: NCA tour of Denmark 1981
Overseas teams played for: Ringwood CC, Melbourne 1985–87
Cricketers particularly learnt from: Doug Padgett, Ray Illingworth, Don Wilson
Cricketers particularly admired: Barry Richards
Other sports played: Golf
Other sports followed: Most
Injuries 1987: Missed first match with hip injury
Relaxations: 'Relaxing at home with my wife.'
Extras: 'I made 122 on my debut for Yorkshire against Nottinghamshire at

Park Avenue in 1983. I was the youngest ever Yorkshire player to do so and it was the highest ever score by a Yorkshireman on debut.'

Opinions on cricket: 'Politics should not interfere with sport – South Africa should be eligible for Test cricket.'

Best batting performance: 152 Yorkshire v MCC, Scarborough 1987

Best bowling performance: 2-18 Yorkshire v Warwickshire, Scarborough 1987

LAST SEASON: BATTING

	I.	N.O.	R.	H.S.	AV.
TEST					
1ST-CLASS	42	4	1178	152	31.00
INT					
RAL	14	0	467	96	33.35
NAT.W.	3	0	183	85	61.00
B & H	7	2	445	94*	89.00

CAREER: BATTING

	I.	N.O.	R.	H.S.	AV.
TEST					
1ST-CLASS	112	5	3594	152	33.58
INT					
RAL	47	2	1256	115*	27.91
NAT.W.	8	0	245	85	30.62
B & H	9	2	487	94*	69.57

LAST SEASON: BOWLING

	O.	M.	R.	W.	AV.
TEST					
1ST-CLASS	12.2	1	62	3	20.66
INT					
RAL					
NAT.W.	7	0	44	2	22.00
B & H					

CAREER: BOWLING

	O.	M.	R.	W.	AV.
TEST					
1ST-CLASS	35.3	5	147	3	49.00
INT					
RAL					
NAT.W.	7	0	44	2	22.00
B & H					

METSON, C. P. Glamorgan

Full Name: Colin Peter Metson
Role: Right-hand bat, wicket-keeper
Born: 2 July 1963, Cuffley, Hertfordshire
Height: 5′ 7″ **Weight:** 10st 8lbs
Nickname: Dempster, Reggie, Jazzer
County debut: 1981 (Middlesex), 1987 (Glamorgan)
County cap: 1987 (Glamorgan)
1st-Class 50s scored: 3
Place in batting averages: 205th av. 16.43
Parents: Denis Alwyn and Jean Mary
Marital status: Single
Family links with cricket: Father played good club cricket and for MCC; brother plays club cricket

Education: Stanborough School, Welwyn Garden City; Enfield Grammar School; Durham University

Qualifications: 10 O-levels, 5 A-levels, BA Hons Economic History, NCA Senior Coaching Award

Jobs outside cricket: Trainee accounts clerk

Off-season 1987–88: 'Joining the rush-hour commuters'

Cricketing superstitions or habits: 'Always put right pad on before left; try to use the same equipment right through the season if possible, especially wicket-keeping gloves. Try not to watch the cricket as a wicket always falls when I do.'

Overseas team played for: Payeham CC, Adelaide 1985–86

Cricketers particularly learnt from: Jack Robertson, Bob Taylor, Father, Don Bennett

Cricketers particularly admired: Bob Taylor, Mike Brearley

Other sports played: Football, golf

Other sports followed: American football

Relaxations: Computers, sleeping

Extras: Young Wicket-keeper of the Year 1981. Three Young England Tests v India 1981. Captain Durham University 1984, losing finalists in UAU competition. Beat Cambridge University twice. Middlesex 2nd XI Player of the Year 1984. Left Middlesex in March 1987 to replace Terry Davies at Glamorgan

Opinions on cricket: 'Cricket must find ways to market itself better, and in finding the sponsors, must give them value for money.'

Best batting performance: 96 Middlesex v Gloucestershire, Uxbridge 1984

LAST SEASON: BATTING

	I.	N.O.	R.	H.S.	AV.
TEST					
1ST-CLASS	37	7	493	81	16.43
INT					
RAL	10	5	96	23*	19.20
NAT.W.	2	1	4	4*	4.00
B & H	2	0	7	7	3.50

LAST SEASON: WICKET KEEPING

	C.	ST.			
TEST					
1ST-CLASS	47	6			
INT					
RAL	16	6			
NAT.W.	2	–			
B & H	2	1			

CAREER: BATTING

	I.	N.O.	R.	H.S.	AV.
TEST					
1ST-CLASS	68	16	919	96	17.67
INT					
RAL	18	10	149	23*	18.62
NAT.W.	2	1	4	4*	4.00
B & H	2	0	7	7	3.50

CAREER: WICKET KEEPING

	C.	ST.			
TEST					
1ST-CLASS	97	8			
INT					
RAL	26	9			
NAT.W.	2	–			
B & H	2	1			

115. Who has the highest Test batting average of all time, and how much?

Full Name: Tony Charles Middleton
Role: Right-hand bat, slow left-arm bowler
Born: 1 February 1964, Winchester
Height 5′ 11″ Weight: 11 st
Nickname: Roo, Midders, TC
County debut: 1984
1st-Class 50s scored: 1
Place in batting averages: — (1986 119th av. 28.72)
1st-Class catches 1987: 1 (career 8)
Parents: Peter and Molly
Marital status: Single
Family links with cricket: Brother plays local club cricket in Hampshire
Education: Weeke Infants and Junior Schools; Montgomery of Alamein Comprehensive, Winchester; Peter Symonds Sixth Form College, Winchester
Qualifications: 1 A-level, 5 O-levels
Jobs outside cricket: Worked for two winters as an electrical engineer
Off-season 1987–88: Playing club cricket in Newcastle, New South Wales
Cricketing superstitions or habits: Always wear spikes to bat in
Overseas teams played for: Club cricket for Durban Police, South Africa, 1984–85 and 1985–86
Cricketers particularly learnt from: 'Too many to name.'
Cricketers particularly admired: Barry Richards, Gordon Greenidge

LAST SEASON: BATTING

	I.	N.O.	R.	H.S.	AV.
TEST					
1ST-CLASS	1	0	7	7	7.00
INT					
RAL					
NAT.W.					
B & H					

LAST SEASON: BOWLING

	O.	M.	R.	W.	AV.
TEST					
1ST-CLASS					
INT					
RAL					
NAT.W.					
B & H					

CAREER: BATTING

	I.	N.O.	R.	H.S.	AV.
TEST					
1ST-CLASS	17	3	338	68*	24.14
INT					
RAL					
NAT.W.					
B & H					

CAREER: BOWLING

	O.	M.	R.	W.	AV.
TEST					
1ST-CLASS	8	1	39	1	39.00
INT					
RAL					
NAT.W.					
B & H					

Other sports played: Squash, football, badminton
Other sports followed: Football, rugby union
Relaxations: Watching and playing other sports
Extras: Played for England Schools 1982
Opinions on cricket: 'Sunday League should be increased to 50 overs with normal run ups and only one knock-out cup plus play-offs for top Sunday League sides. Hopefully the introduction of a full four-day Championship in the near future will put an end to contrived results and "result" wickets.'
Best batting performance: 68* Hampshire v Somerset, Taunton 1986
Best bowling performance: 1-13 Hampshire v Middlesex, Lord's 1986

MILBURN, E. T. Warwickshire

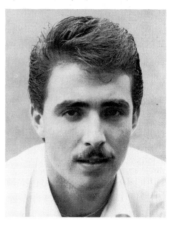

Full Name: Edward Thomas Milburn
Role: Right-hand bat, right-arm medium bowler
Born: 15 September 1967, Nuneaton
Height 6′ 2″ **Weight:** 12 st
Nickname: Rohan, Ed
County debut: 1987
1st-Class catches 1987: 2 (career 2)
Marital status: Single
Family links with cricket: 'My Father has always loved the game (hence my own interest) and has played against a team of Aborigines in Bundeburg (just outside Sydney). That's the highest standard he reached.'
Education: Chilvers Coton First School; Coventry Preparatory School; Bablake School, Coventry; King Edward VI College, Nuneaton
Qualifications: 1 A-level, 8 O-levels
Jobs outside cricket: Popcorn making in Sydney last winter while playing for Waverley District CC
Off-season 1987–88: Playing and coaching in South Africa
Cricketing superstitions or habits: 'Humming current hits in between overs and at the non-strikers end. Always walking back to my mark to the right of the run-up disc.'
Overseas teams played for: Waverley District CC Sydney, 1986–87; Virginia CC, Bloemfontein, South Africa, 1987–88

Cricketers particularly learnt from: Staff at Warwickshire CC
Cricketers particularly admired: Richard Hadlee
Other sports played: Golf, squash
Relaxations: Reading science fiction novels
Best batting performance: 24 Warwickshire v Hampshire, Edgbaston 1987
Best bowling performance: 1-26 Warwickshire v Somerset, Edgbaston 1987

LAST SEASON: BATTING

	I.	N.O.	R.	H.S.	AV.
TEST					
1ST-CLASS	4	2	37	24	18.50
INT					
RAL					
NAT.W.					
B & H					

LAST SEASON: BOWLING

	O.	M.	R.	W.	AV.
TEST					
1ST-CLASS	36	6	128	2	64.00
INT					
RAL					
NAT.W.					
B & H					

CAREER: BATTING

	I.	N.O.	R.	H.S.	AV.
TEST					
1ST-CLASS	4	2	37	24	18.50
INT					
RAL					
NAT.W.					
B & H					

CAREER: BOWLING

	O.	M.	R.	W.	AV.
TEST					
1ST-CLASS	36	6	128	2	64.00
INT					
RAL					
NAT.W.					
B & H					

MILLER, A. J. T. Middlesex

Full Name: Andrew John Trevor Miller
Role: Left-hand opening bat, right-arm medium bowler, short-leg fielder
Born: 30 May 1963, Chesham
Height: 5′ 11″ **Weight:** 12st
Nickname: Dusty, Wino
County debut: 1983
1st-Class 50s scored: 18
1st-Class 100s scored: 3
One-Day 50s: 3
One-Day 100s: 1
Place in batting averages: 109th av. 29.76 (1986 98th av. 31.06)
1st-Class catches 1987: 1 (career 20)
Parents: John Innes and Sheila Mary
Wife and date of marriage: Philippa Jane, 26 September 1987
Education: Belmont School; Haileybury; Oxford University
Qualifications: 10 O-levels, 3 A-levels; BA Hons Biochemistry

Jobs outside cricket: Stockbroker
Off-season 1987–88: Stockbroking
Cricketing superstitions or habits: 'I have a fixed order for putting on gear, which changes after failure.'
Overseas tours: Australia with Oxford and Cambridge Combined Universities 1985–86
Overseas teams played for: Adelaide University 1986
Other sports played: Squash
Other sports followed: Rugby union
Relaxations: 'Drinking; sports of many kinds; playing brag and taking money off Andrew Needham.'
Extras: First Oxonian since 1975 to score a century in the Varsity Match. First century by Combined Universities batsman in Benson and Hedges competition. Captain of Oxford University 1985. Scored 231 v Combined Services 1984
Opinions on cricket: 'Too much cricket played. Four-day cricket will be a good experiment. Wickets should be covered.'
Best batting performance: 128* Oxford University v Cambridge University, Lord's 1984
Best bowling performance: 1–4 Oxford University v Somerset, Oxford 1984

LAST SEASON: BATTING

	I.	N.O.	R.	H.S.	AV.
TEST					
1ST-CLASS	15	2	387	97	29.76
INT					
RAL					
NAT.W.					
B & H	1	0	1	1	1.00

CAREER: BATTING

	I.	N.O.	R.	H.S.	AV.
TEST					
1ST-CLASS	113	14	3131	128*	31.62
INT					
RAL	8	1	276	69	39.42
NAT.W.	3	0	69	35	23.00
B & H	11	0	403	101	36.63

LAST SEASON: BOWLING

	O.	M.	R.	W.	AV.
TEST					
1ST-CLASS	1	0	4	0	–
INT					
RAL					
NAT.W.					
B & H					

CAREER: BOWLING

	O.	M.	R.	W.	AV.
TEST					
1ST-CLASS	4	0	14	1	14.00
INT					
RAL					
NAT.W.					
B & H	1	0	7	0	–

116. Which Englishman has the highest Test batting average, and how much?

MILLER, G. Essex

Full Name: Geoffrey Miller
Role: Right-hand bat, off-break bowler
Born: 8 September 1952, Chesterfield
Height: 6′ 2″ **Weight:** 11st 6lbs
Nickname: Dusty
County debut: 1973 (Derbyshire), 1987 (Essex)
County cap: 1976 (Derbyshire)
Benefit: 1985
Test debut: 1976
No. of Tests: 34
No. of One-Day Internationals: 25
50 wickets in a season: 4
1st-Class 50s scored: 68
1st-Class 100s scored: 2
1st-Class 5 w. in innings: 37
1st-Class 10 w. in match: 7
One-Day 50s: 17
Place in batting averages: 221st av. 14.84 (1986 179th av. 20.48)
Place in bowling averages: 76th av. 31.09 (1986 103rd av. 41.80)
Strike rate 1987: 71.15 (career 65.55)
1st-Class catches 1987: 28 (career 272)
Parents: Gwen and Keith
Wife: Carol
Children: Helen Jane; Anna Louise; James Daniel
Family links with cricket: Father played local cricket in Chesterfield. Brother plays for Chesterfield CC
Education: Chesterfield Grammar School
Overseas tours: With England Young Cricketers to India 1970–71 and West Indies 1972; toured with England to India, Sri Lanka, Australia 1976–77; Pakistan and New Zealand 1977–78; Australia 1978–79 and 1979–80 but had to return December 1979 through injury; West Indies 1981; Australia and New Zealand 1982–83
Cricketers particularly learnt from: Eddie Barlow, Ray Illingworth, Fred Titmus
Other sports played: Golf, table tennis, football
Relaxations: Crosswords, reading, television, family life. Watching Chesterfield FC particularly, and all sports in general
Extras: Became captain of Derbyshire half-way through 1979 season, but relinquished it half-way through 1981 season in favour of Barry Wood. Declined to sign for Derbyshire for 1982 season, and was released. Negoti-

ated with several other counties, but signed again. Eventually left at end of 1986 season and joined Essex for 1987
Best batting performance: 130 Derbyshire v Lancashire, Old Trafford 1984
Best bowling performance: 8-70 Derbyshire v Leicestershire, Coalville 1982

LAST SEASON: BATTING

	I.	N.O.	R.	H.S.	AV.
TEST					
1ST-CLASS	30	5	371	33*	14.84
INT					
RAL	8	1	143	38	20.42
NAT.W.	2	0	28	21	14.00
B & H	3	0	28	19	9.33

LAST SEASON: BOWLING

	O.	M.	R.	W.	AV.
TEST					
1ST-CLASS	379.3	84	995	32	31.09
INT					
RAL	45.2	2	153	8	19.12
NAT.W.	12	1	46	0	–
B & H	22	4	61	5	12.20

CAREER: BATTING

	I.	N.O.	R.	H.S.	AV.
TEST	51	4	1213	98*	25.80
1ST-CLASS	448	75	9858	130	26.42
INT	18	2	136	46	8.50
RAL	145	29	2368	84	20.41
NAT.W.	18	4	333	59*	23.78
B & H	50	10	1006	88*	25.15

CAREER: BOWLING

	O.	M.	R.	W.	AV.
TEST	280.1 484.4	79 140	1859	60	30.98
1ST-CLASS	256.2 7584.2	48 2148	20046	744	26.94
INT	13 194	1 19	813	25	32.52
RAL	854.3	58	3588	125	28.70
NAT.W.	206	48	553	18	30.72
B & H	488	96	1381	58	23.81

MOLES, A. J. Warwickshire

Full Name: Andrew James Moles
Role: Right-hand opening bat, right-arm medium bowler
Born: 12 February 1961, Solihull
Height: 5' 10" **Weight:** 13½st
Nickname: Molar
County debut: 1986
County cap: 1987
1st-Class 50s scored: 9
1st-Class 100s scored: 6
One-Day 50s: 4
One-Day 100s: 1
Place in batting averages: 85th av. 33.27 (1986 14th av. 49.20)
Place in bowling averages: 124th av. 42.75
1st-Class catches 1987: 24 (career 28)
Parents: Stuart Francis and Gillian Margaret
Marital status: Single
Family links with cricket: Brother plays for Solihull in the Midland Championship

Education: Finham Park Comprehensive, Coventry; Henley College of Further Education; Butts College of Further Education
Qualifications: 3 O-levels, 4 CSEs, Toolmaker/Standard Room Inspector City & Guilds 205 Pts I, II, III
Jobs outside cricket: Standard Room Inspector
Off-season 1987–88: Playing and coaching cricket in South Africa
Cricketing superstitions or habits: Put left pad on first. Never look back at stumps after being bowled
Overseas team: Griqualand West Cricket Union, South Africa 1985–86
Cricketers particularly learnt from: Dennis Amiss, Fred Gardner
Cricketers particularly admired: Dennis Amiss, Martin Crowe
Other sports played: Football
Relaxations: Listening to music or a meal with friends
Best batting performance: 174 Griqualand West v Transvaal B, Kimberley 1986–87
Best bowling performance: 3-21 Warwickshire v Oxford University, Oxford 1987

LAST SEASON: BATTING

	I.	N.O.	R.	H.S.	AV.
TEST					
1ST-CLASS	46	3	1431	151	33.27
INT					
RAL	12	0	268	83	22.33
NAT.W.	3	0	140	127	46.66
B & H	3	0	80	72	26.66

CAREER: BATTING

	I.	N.O.	R.	H.S.	AV.
TEST					
1ST-CLASS	76	7	2874	174	41.65
INT					
RAL	20	2	410	85	22.77
NAT.W.	4	0	154	127	38.50
B & H	3	0	80	72	26.66

LAST SEASON: BOWLING

	O.	M.	R.	W.	AV.
TEST					
1ST-CLASS	182.3	46	513	12	42.75
INT					
RAL	43	0	219	6	36.50
NAT.W.	9	0	54	0	–
B & H	18	0	84	1	84.00

CAREER: BOWLING

	O.	M.	R.	W.	AV.
TEST					
1ST-CLASS	342	80	989	23	43.00
INT					
RAL	59	0	326	7	46.57
NAT.W.	15	0	81	0	–
B & H	18	0	84	1	84.00

117. Who scored the most centuries for England: Hammond, Cowdrey, or Boycott?

118. Who had a higher batting average for England: Hobbs or Hutton?

MONKHOUSE, S. Glamorgan

Full Name: Steven Monkhouse
Role: Right-hand bat, left-arm
fast-medium bowler, outfielder
Born: 24 November 1962, Bury
Height: 6′ 3″ **Weight:** 13st 7lbs
Nickname: Bob, Millstone,
Monky
County debut: 1985 (Warwickshire),
1987 (Glamorgan)
1st-Class catches 1987: 2 (career 2)
Parents: Harold and May
Marital status: Single
Family links with cricket: Father
played in the Lancashire League
for Ramsbottom CC
Education: Derby Technical
Grammar School; Peel College
Qualifications: 7 O-levels,
BEC National Business Studies
Cert, NCA Coaching Certificate

Off-season 1987–88: 'Having a break from cricket and working for a local company.'
Overseas teams played for: Newtown District, Tasmania 1985–86, 1986–87
Cricketing superstitions or habits: 'I try to avoid them if I can!'
Cricketers particularly learnt from: Murray Bennett, Anton Ferreira
Cricketers particularly admired: Michael Holding, Ian Botham
Other sports played: 'Golf, snooker and a few others, but not seriously.'
Relaxations: 'Music, TV, and a few drinks with the lads.'
Extras: Signed for Glamorgan at end of 1986 season

LAST SEASON: BATTING

	I.	N.O.	R.	H.S.	AV.
TEST					
1ST-CLASS	8	3	23	15	4.60
INT					
RAL	1	0	0	–	0.00
NAT.W.					
B & H					

LAST SEASON: BOWLING

	O.	M.	R.	W.	AV.
TEST					
1ST-CLASS	82	7	326	11	29.63
INT					
RAL	16	5	61	3	20.33
NAT.W.	12	3	32	5	6.40
B & H					

CAREER: BATTING

	I.	N.O.	R.	H.S.	AV.
TEST					
1ST-CLASS	11	4	30	15	4.28
INT					
RAL	1	0	0	–	0.00
NAT.W.					
B & H					

CAREER: BOWLING

	O.	M.	R.	W.	AV.
TEST					
1ST-CLASS	109	13	421	13	32.38
INT					
RAL	16	5	61	3	20.33
NAT.W.	12	3	32	5	6.40
B & H					

Opinions on cricket: '2nd XI's don't play enough games on county grounds but play nearly every game on club grounds, where the wickets are not good enough.'

Best batting performance: 15 Glamorgan v Northamptonshire, Swansea 1987

Best bowling performance: 2-21 Glamorgan v Oxford University, Oxford 1987

MOORES, P.   Sussex

Full Name: Peter Moores
Role: Right-hand bat, wicket-keeper
Born: 18 December 1962, Macclesfield, Cheshire
Height: 6' **Weight:** 12st 11lbs
Nickname: Stos, Stumper, Moorsey
County debut: 1983 (Worcestershire), 1985 (Sussex)
1st-Class 50s scored: 2
Place in batting averages: 195th av. 17.50
Parents: Bernard and Winifred
Marital status: Single
Family links with cricket: Three brothers, Anthony, Stephen and Robert all play local cricket
Education: King Edward VI School, Macclesfield

Qualifications: 7 O-levels, 3 A-levels. Senior NCA Coaching Award
Off-season 1987–88: Coaching in Orange Free State in South Africa
Overseas teams played for: Harare Sports Club, Zimbabwe 1984–85
Cricketers particularly learnt from: Don Wilson, Basil D'Oliveira
Cricketers particularly admired: Bob Taylor, Clive Lloyd, Alan Knott
Other sports played: Squash, football, swimming and most ball games
Other sports followed: Football, hockey
Relaxations: Old films, music, photography
Extras: On the MCC groundstaff in 1982 before joining Worcestershire in latter half of 1982 season. Joined Sussex in 1985
Opinions on cricket: 'I feel four-day cricket will be a good thing in that it will allow more genuine results and should also give more opportunities to younger players in the side.'
Best batting performance: 55 Sussex v Northamptonshire, Eastbourne 1987

LAST SEASON: BATTING

	I.	N.O.	R.	H.S.	AV.
TEST					
1ST-CLASS	24	2	385	55	17.50
INT					
RAL	6	3	14	6*	4.66
NAT.W.	1	1	3	3*	–
B & H					

LAST SEASON: WICKET KEEPING

	C.	ST.			
TEST					
1ST-CLASS	19	–			
INT					
RAL	11	1			
NAT.W.	1	–			
B & H	1	–			

CAREER: BATTING

	I.	N.O.	R.	H.S.	AV.
TEST					
1ST-CLASS	39	5	600	55	17.64
INT					
RAL	10	7	39	14*	13.00
NAT.W.	1	1	3	3*	–
B & H					

CAREER: WICKET KEEPING

	C.	ST.			
TEST					
1ST-CLASS	38	6			
INT					
RAL	18	3			
NAT.W.	2	–			
B & H	1	–			

MORRIS, H. Glamorgan

Full Name: Hugh Morris
Role: Left-hand bat, right-arm medium bowler
Born: 5 October 1963, Cardiff
Height: 5′ 8″ **Weight:** 12st
Nickname: 'H', Banacek
County debut: 1981
County cap: 1986
1000 runs in a season: 2
1st-Class 50s scored: 26
1st-Class 100s scored: 6
One-Day 50s: 10
One-Day 100s: 2
Place in batting averages: 121st
av. 28.34 (1986 68th av. 36.23)
1st-Class catches 1987: 15 (career 38)
Parents: Roger and Anne
Marital status: Single
Family links with cricket: Brother
played for Wales U-19 and Glamorgan U-19. Father played league cricket
Education: Blundell's School; South Glamorgan Institute
Qualifications: 8 O-levels, 3 A-levels, 1 AO-level, BA Physical Education, NCA Coaching Award
Off-season 1987–88: Working on Glamorgan CCC centenary programme
Cricketing superstitions or habits: Getting off 111. Put right pad on first
Overseas tours: With English Public Schoolboy tour to West Indies, 1980–81; to Sri Lanka 1982–83; to USA (Los Angeles) with Haverfordwest CC, 1984

Cricketers particularly learnt from: Alan Jones, Tom Cartwright, Kevin Lyons

Cricketers admired: Ian Botham, Javed Miandad

Other sports played: Rugby, squash, golf

Other sports followed: Most sports

Relaxations: Music, watching movies, having a few quiet pints

Extras: Highest schoolboy cricket average in 1979 (89.71), 1981 (184.6) and 1982 (149.2). Captain of England U-19 Schoolboys in 1981 and 1982. Played for Young England v Young West Indies 1982, and captained Young England v Australia. Won Gray-Nicholls 'Most Promising Schoolboy' Award 1981, and Young Cricketer of 1982. Played first-class rugby for Aberavon 1984–85 and South Glamorgan Institute scoring over 150 points. Appointed Glamorgan captain 1986 – the youngest ever for county. Scored most runs in Sunday League by a Glamorgan player – 586

Best batting performance: 143 Glamorgan v Oxford University, Oxford 1987

Best bowling performance: 1-6 Glamorgan v Oxford University, Oxford 1987

LAST SEASON: BATTING

	I.	N.O.	R.	H.S.	AV.
TEST					
1ST-CLASS	48	2	1304	143	28.34
INT					
RAL	13	1	229	89	19.08
NAT.W.	2	0	29	16	14.50
B & H	4	0	153	115	38.25

LAST SEASON: BOWLING

	O.	M.	R.	W.	AV.
TEST					
1ST-CLASS	7	1	26	1	26.00
INT					
RAL					
NAT.W.					
B & H					

CAREER: BATTING

	I.	N.O.	R.	H.S.	AV.
TEST					
1ST-CLASS	152	18	4205	143	31.38
INT					
RAL	42	4	1183	100	31.13
NAT.W.	7	0	221	75	31.57
B & H	9	1	242	115	30.25

CAREER: BOWLING

	O.	M.	R.	W.	AV.
TEST					
1ST-CLASS	33.5	6	170	2	85.00
INT					
RAL					
NAT.W.					
B & H					

119. Who has scored the most runs ever in a Test series, and how many?

MORRIS, J. E.   Derbyshire

Full Name: John Edward Morris
Role: Right-hand bat,
right-arm medium bowler
Born: 1 April 1964, Crewe
Height: 5′ 10½″ **Weight:** 13st 6lbs
Nickname: Animal
County debut: 1982
County cap: 1986
1000 runs in a season: 2
1st-Class 50s scored: 23
1st-Class 100s scored: 11
One-Day 50s: 9
One-Day 100s: 1
Place in batting averages: 76th
av. 34.43 (1986 23rd av. 47.00)
1st-Class catches 1987: 13 (career 34)
Parents: George (Eddie) and Jean
Marital status: Single
Family links with cricket: Father

played for Crewe CC for many years as an opening bowler
Education: Shavington Comprehensive School; Dane Bank College of
Further Education
Qualifications: O-levels
Jobs outside cricket: Worked as a carpet fitter. PR officer for indoor cricket
centre
Overseas teams played for: Subiaco Floreat CC, Perth, Western Australia,
1986–87
Cricketers particularly learnt from: Tony Borrington, Phil Russell, Father
Other sports played: Football, basketball, snooker

LAST SEASON: BATTING

	I.	N.O.	R.	H.S.	AV.
TEST					
1ST-CLASS	40	1	1343	162	34.43
INT					
RAL	14	0	315	81	22.50
NAT.W.	3	0	39	16	13.00
B & H	4	1	115	36	38.33

CAREER: BATTING

	I.	N.O.	R.	H.S.	AV.
TEST					
1ST-CLASS	157	7	5131	191	34.20
INT					
RAL	60	4	1370	104	24.46
NAT.W.	8	1	78	16	11.14
B & H	16	1	303	65	20.20

LAST SEASON: BOWLING

	O.	M.	R.	W.	AV.
TEST					
1ST-CLASS	5.3	0	61	1	61.00
INT					
RAL					
NAT.W.					
B & H					

CAREER: BOWLING

	O.	M.	R.	W.	AV.
TEST					
1ST-CLASS	68.2	7	434	3	144.66
INT					
RAL					
NAT.W.					
B & H					

Other sports followed: Watching athletics and motor racing
Relaxations: Movies, music, good food
Best batting performance: 191 Derbyshire v Kent, Derby 1986

MORTENSEN, O. H. Derbyshire

Full Name: Ole Henrik Mortensen
Role: Right-hand bat, right-arm
fast-medium bowler
Born: 29 January 1958, Vejle,
Denmark
Height: 6' 4" **Weight:** 14st 2lbs
Nickname: Stan (coined by Bob
Taylor after England footballer
Stan Mortenson), Blood-Axe
County debut: 1983
County cap: 1986
1st-Class 50s scored: 1
50 wickets in a season: 2
1st-Class 5 w. in innings: 7
1st-Class 10 w. in match: 1
Place in batting averages:
238th av. 12.00
Place in bowling averages: 7th
av. 19.70 (1986 23rd av. 23.52)
Strike rate 1987: 47.21 (career 52.84)
1st-Class catches 1987: 2 (career 16)
Parents: Will Ernst and Inge Wicka
Wife: Jette Jepmond
Children: Julie Jepmond, 30 August 1982
Family links with cricket: 'My small brother, Michael, used to play cricket. He is now a professional tennis player, and has played in Davis Cup for Denmark.'
Education: Brondbyoster School; Avedore School
Jobs outside cricket: Worked as a tax assistant in Denmark
Off-season 1987–88: Coaching and playing in Australia
Overseas tours: East Africa in 1976 with the Danish national side, and Scotland, Wales, Ireland and Holland
Overseas teams played for: Ellerslie, Auckland, New Zealand, 1983–84; Brighton CC, Melbourne 1985–86; Svanholm CC, Denmark
Cricketers particularly learnt from: Torben Jensen, Jorgen Janson, Peter Hargreaves and many others
Cricketers particularly admired: Dennis Lillee, Bob Taylor
Other sports played: Tennis, golf, football

Relaxations: Music, books, movies
Extras: *Derbyshire's Dane* by Peter Hargreaves, published 1984. Has played for Denmark. Only Dane to play first-class cricket
Opinions on cricket: 'Too much cricket; seam bowlers turn into robots by August.'
Best batting performance: 74* Derbyshire v Yorkshire, Chesterfield 1987
Best bowling performance: 6-27 Derbyshire v Yorkshire, Sheffield 1983

LAST SEASON: BATTING

	I.	N.O.	R.	H.S.	AV.
TEST					
1ST-CLASS	24	10	168	74*	12.00
INT					
RAL	6	5	13	5*	13.00
NAT.W.	2	1	2	1*	2.00
B & H	2	1	3	3*	3.00

CAREER: BATTING

	I.	N.O.	R.	H.S.	AV.
TEST					
1ST-CLASS	87	45	415	74*	9.88
INT					
RAL	24	19	32	5*	6.40
NAT.W.	5	3	19	11	9.50
B & H	3	1	5	3*	2.50

LAST SEASON: BOWLING

	O.	M.	R.	W.	AV.
TEST					
1ST-CLASS	432.5	111	1084	55	19.70
INT					
RAL	97.5	12	334	10	33.40
NAT.W.	32	7	78	2	39.00
B & H	44	8	129	8	16.12

CAREER: BOWLING

	O.	M.	R.	W.	AV.
TEST					
1ST-CLASS	1920.1	460	5367	218	24.61
INT					
RAL	444.3	41	1756	62	28.32
NAT.W.	76.4	17	229	8	28.62
B & H	135.2	20	391	25	15.64

MOXON, M. D. Yorkshire

Full Name: Martyn Douglas Moxon
Role: Right-hand bat, right-arm medium bowler, slip fielder
Born: 4 May 1960, Barnsley
Height: 6' 1" **Weight:** 13st 7lbs
Nickname: Frog
County debut: 1981
County cap: 1984
Test debut: 1986
No. of Tests: 3
No. of One-Day Internationals: 5
1000 runs in a season: 3
1st-Class 50s scored: 38
1st-Class 100s scored: 17
One-Day 50s: 18
One-Day 100s: 1
Place in batting averages: 43rd av. 40.03 (1986 82nd av. 33.86)
1st-Class catches 1987: 26 (career 94)
Parents: Audrey and Derek (deceased)

Wife and date of marriage: Sue, October 1985
Family links with cricket: Father and grandfather played local league cricket. Father was coach to Wombwell Cricket Lovers' Society
Education: Holgate Grammar School, Barnsley
Qualifications: 8 O-levels, 3 A-levels, HNC in Business Studies, NCA Coaching Award
Off-season 1987–88: Touring with England
Jobs outside cricket: Bank clerk with Barclays Bank for two years before turning professional full-time
Cricketing superstitions or habits: Always put left pad on first
Overseas tours: Captain of North of England U-19 tour of Canada, 1979; with England to India and Australia 1984–85, England B tour to Sri Lanka 1986; England to Pakistan and New Zealand 1987–88
Overseas teams played for: Griqualand West, South Africa 1982–83 and 1983–84
Cricketers particularly learnt from: Doug Padgett, Phil Carrick, Steve Oldham
Cricketers particularly admired: Viv Richards
Other sports played: Football in the local league in the winter and golf
Other sports followed: 'Am a keen supporter of Barnsley FC.'
Relaxations: Listening to most types of music, having a drink with friends
Extras: Captained Yorkshire Schools U-15s and North of England U-15s. Played for Yorkshire Cricket Federation U-19s. Captained Yorkshire Senior Schools. Like Yorkshire colleagues, G. Stevenson and A. Sidebottom, he played for Wombwell Cricket Lovers' Society U-18 side which competes in the Joe Lumb U-18 Competition. At the time, made the highest score by a player on his Yorkshire debut – 116 v Essex (since overtaken by Ashley Metcalfe). First Yorkshire player to make centuries on his first two Championship games in Yorkshire: 116 v Essex at Headingley and 111 v Derbyshire at Sheffield. Changed from spectacles to contact lenses in 1981. Scored 153 in first 'Roses' innings. Picked for Lord's Test of 1984 v West Indies, but had to withdraw through injury and had to wait until 1986 to make Test debut

LAST SEASON: BATTING

	I.	N.O.	R.	H.S.	AV.
TEST	2	0	23	15	11.50
1ST-CLASS	35	4	1298	130	41.87
INT					
RAL	6	0	159	64	26.50
NAT.W.	3	1	135	74	67.50
B & H	7	1	289	97	48.16

LAST SEASON: BOWLING

	O.	M.	R.	W.	AV.
TEST	6	2	27	0	–
1ST-CLASS	29	7	78	1	78.00
INT					
RAL	9	2	33	0	–
NAT.W.	4	0	15	0	–
B & H	7	0	34	0	–

CAREER: BATTING

	I.	N.O.	R.	H.S.	AV.
TEST	6	0	134	74	22.33
1ST-CLASS	207	13	7272	168	37.48
INT	5	0	132	70	26.40
RAL	44	5	1103	74	28.28
NAT.W.	11	3	458	82*	57.25
B & H	22	2	882	106*	44.10

CAREER: BOWLING

	O.	M.	R.	W.	AV.
TEST	6	2	27	0	–
1ST-CLASS	296.4	49	1050	18	58.33
INT					
RAL	40	2	230	3	76.66
NAT.W.	8	0	32	1	32.00
B & H	32	0	145	2	72.50

Best batting performance: 168 Yorkshire v Worcestershire, Worcester 1985
Best bowling performance: 3-26 D. B. Close's XI v Sri Lankans, Scarborough 1985

MUNTON, T. A. Warwickshire

Full Name: Timothy Alan Munton
Role: Right-hand bat, right-arm
fast-medium bowler
Born: 30 July 1965, Melton
Mowbray
Height: 6′ 6″ **Weight:** 14st
County debut: 1985
Nickname: Tiny, Herman
1st-Class 5 w. in innings: 2
Place in batting averages: 247th
av. 10.54
Place in bowling averages: 33rd
av. 25.43 (1986 52nd av. 28.28)
Strike rate 1987: 52.48 (career 54.74)
1st-Class catches 1987: 3 (career 4)
Parents names: Alan and Brenda
Wife and date of marriage: Helen,
20 September 1986
Education: Sarson High School,
King Edward VII Upper School
Qualifications: 8 O-levels, 1 A-level; cricket coach
Overseas teams played for: Victoria University, Wellington, New Zealand
1985–86; Witswatersrand University, Johannesburg, 1986–87
Cricketers particularly learnt from: Ken Hughes

LAST SEASON: BATTING

	I.	N.O.	R.	H.S.	AV.
TEST					
1ST-CLASS	16	5	116	38	10.54
INT					
RAL	3	2	7	7*	7.00
NAT.W.					
B & H	1	1	1	6*	–

CAREER: BATTING

	I.	N.O.	R.	H.S.	AV.
TEST					
1ST-CLASS	31	11	174	38	8.70
INT					
RAL	6	4	17	7*	8.50
NAT.W.					
B & H	3	3	6	6*	–

LAST SEASON: BOWLING

	O.	M.	R.	W.	AV.
TEST					
1ST-CLASS	341.1	72	992	39	25.43
INT					
RAL	73	1	380	11	34.54
NAT.W.	6	0	22	2	11.00
B & H	21	2	73	2	36.50

CAREER: BOWLING

	O.	M.	R.	W.	AV.
TEST					
1ST-CLASS	647.5	140	1932	71	27.21
INT					
RAL	135	5	689	21	32.80
NAT.W.	6	0	22	2	11.00
B & H	53	5	175	6	29.16

Cricketers particularly admired: Bob Willis, Clive Rice, Richard Hadlee
Other sports played: Basketball, soccer
Injuries 1987: Broken nose, groin strain
Relaxations: Listening to music
Extras: Appeared for Leicestershire 2nd XI 1982–84
Best batting performance: 38 Warwickshire v Yorkshire, Scarborough 1987
Best bowling performance: 6-69 Warwickshire v Nottinghamshire, Edgbaston 1987

MURPHY, A. J.   Lancashire

Full Name: Anthony John Murphy
Role: Right-hand bat,
right-arm medium bowler
Born: 6 August 1962, Manchester
Height: 6′ 0″ **Weight:** 13½st
Nickname: Audi, Headless,
Tramp, Compo
County debut: 1985
1st-Class catches 1987: 1 (career 3)
Parents: John Desmond and
Elizabeth Catherine
Marital status: Single
Family links with cricket: Brother
plays club cricket for Cheadle
Education: Xaverian College,
Manchester; Swansea University
Qualifications: 9 O-levels, 4 A-levels
Jobs outside cricket: Computer
operator for Barclays Bank. Part-time store detective

LAST SEASON: BATTING

	I.	N.O.	R.	H.S.	AV.
TEST					
1ST-CLASS	1	0	5	5	5.00
INT					
RAL					
NAT.W.					
B & H					

LAST SEASON: BOWLING

	O.	M.	R.	W.	AV.
TEST					
1ST-CLASS	36	5	133	4	33.25
INT					
RAL					
NAT.W.					
B & H					

CAREER: BATTING

	I.	N.O.	R.	H.S.	AV.
TEST					
1ST-CLASS	15	7	22	6	2.75
INT					
RAL	1	1	2	2*	–
NAT.W.					
B & H					

CAREER: BOWLING

	O.	M.	R.	W.	AV.
TEST					
1ST-CLASS	263.2	55	873	27	32.33
INT					
RAL	6	0	33	1	33.00
NAT.W.					
B & H					

Off-season 1987–88: Playing and coaching for Taradale CC in New Zealand
Overseas tours: Minor Counties U-25s to Kenya 1986
Overseas teams played for: Central Districts & Taradale CC, New Zealand, 1985–86
Cricketers particularly learnt from: Søren Henriksen, Mark Chadwick, David Varey, Ian Davidson
Cricketers particularly admired: Steve O'Shaughnessy, Ken McLeod
Other sports played: Boat racing
Other sports followed: American football, dog and horse racing
Relaxations: 'Flapping when raining during a game. Helping Chris Maynard back to fitness.'
Best batting performance: 6 Minor Counties v New Zealanders, Lakenham 1986
Best bowling performance: 4-115 Lancashire v Somerset, Taunton 1987

MYLES, S. D. Sussex

Full Name: Simon David Myles
Role: Right-hand bat,
right-arm medium bowler
Born: 2 June 1966, Mansfield
Height: 5′ 10″ **Weight:** 13st
Nickname: Slopey, Phoey
County debut: 1987
1st-Class catches 1987: 1 (career 1)
Parents: David Wilson and
Carolyn Margaret
Marital status: Single
Family links with cricket: Both
younger brothers are keen
players and followers of
the game
Education: King George V School,
Hong Kong
Qualifications: 9 O-levels, 1 A-level,
NCA Coaching Certificate

Jobs outside cricket: Selling and surveying tennis courts in Hong Kong. Bicycle courier in Perth, Western Australia
Off-season 1987–88: Playing and coaching in Perth
Cricketing superstitions or habits: 'Regularly – if I'm in for long enough – marking and remarking my guard.'
Overseas tours: Hong Kong to Singapore and Malaysia 1983; to Bangladesh for South East Asian Cup 1984; to England for ICC Trophy 1986

Overseas team played for: Hong Kong domestic sides; Mount Lawley, Perth 1986–87
Cricketers particularly learnt from: David Clinton, Geoff Boycott, Paul Parker
Cricketers particularly admired: Geoff Boycott, Richard Hadlee, Bob Taylor
Other sports played: All ball sports but particularly football
Other sports followed: Football (Derby County FC), most other sports
Injuries 1987: Dislocated finger
Relaxations: 'Golf, listening to music, watching a good film or just sleeping.'
Extras: Hong Kong Sportsboy of the Year 1984. Record ICC Trophy score of 172 in 1986. Released by Sussex at end of 1987 season
Opinions on cricket: 'I feel a fairer Championship would be a round-robin league. Obviously finances are limited but perhaps opponents could play the host in alternate seasons. I think our climate and uncovered wickets will defeat the purpose of four-day cricket.'
Best batting performance: 18* Sussex v Hampshire, Horsham 1987

LAST SEASON: BATTING

	I.	N.O.	R.	H.S.	AV.
TEST					
1ST-CLASS	3	1	19	18*	9.50
INT					
RAL	4	0	24	15	6.00
NAT.W.					
B & H					

LAST SEASON: BOWLING

	O.	M.	R.	W.	AV.
TEST					
1ST-CLASS	4	0	28	0	–
INT					
RAL	2	0	20	0	–
NAT.W.	4	0	11	0	–
B & H					

CAREER: BATTING

	I.	N.O.	R.	H.S.	AV.
TEST					
1ST-CLASS	3	1	19	18*	9.50
INT					
RAL	4	0	24	15	6.00
NAT.W.					
B & H					

CAREER: BOWLING

	O.	M.	R.	W.	AV.
TEST					
1ST-CLASS	4	0	28	0	–
INT					
RAL	2	0	20	0	–
NAT.W.	4	0	11	0	–
B & H					

120. Is it true or false that Richard Hadlee took a wicket in his last over for Notts?

121. Which family had three brothers appearing in the same Test, two for England and one for South Africa, and when?

NEALE, P. A.   Worcestershire

Full Name: Phillip Anthony Neale
Role: Right-hand bat, cover fielder
Born: 5 June 1954, Scunthorpe
Height: 5′ 11″ **Weight:** 11st 11lbs
County debut: 1975
County cap: 1978
Benefit: 1988
1000 runs in a season: 7
1st-Class 50s scored: 74
1st-Class 100s scored: 22
One-Day 50s: 25
One-Day 100s: 2
Place in batting averages: 62nd
av. 36.81 (1986 66th av. 36.55)
1st-Class catches 1987: 10
(career 102)
Parents: Geoff and Margaret
Wife and date of marriage: Christine,
26 September 1976

Children: Kelly Joanne, 9 November 1979; Craig Andrew, 11 February 1982
Education: Frederick Gough Grammar School, Scunthorpe; John Leggot Sixth Form College, Scunthorpe; Leeds University
Qualifications: 10 O-levels, 2 A-levels, BA Hons Russian. Preliminary football and cricket coaching awards
Jobs outside cricket: Teacher, footballer
Cricketing superstitions or habits: Left pad on first
Cricketers particularly learnt from: 'Most county players – you learn by watching'.

LAST SEASON: BATTING

	I.	N.O.	R.	H.S.	AV.
TEST					
1ST-CLASS	34	7	994	103*	36.81
INT					
RAL	12	5	150	27*	20.57
NAT.W.	2	1	39	27	39.00
B & H	5	0	117	52	23.40

CAREER: BATTING

	I.	N.O.	R.	H.S.	AV.
TEST					
1ST-CLASS	451	65	13906	163*	36.02
INT					
RAL	160	33	3573	102	28.13
NAT.W.	21	1	599	81	29.95
B & H	47	6	1252	128	30.53

LAST SEASON: BOWLING

	O.	M.	R.	W.	AV.
TEST					
1ST-CLASS	3.1	0	12	0	–
INT					
RAL					
NAT.W.					
B & H					

CAREER: BOWLING

	O.	M.	R.	W.	AV.
TEST					
1ST-CLASS	45.5	3	213	1	213.00
INT					
RAL	8.2	0	50	2	25.00
NAT.W.					
B & H					

Cricketers particularly admired: Basil D'Oliveira, Norman Gifford, Alan Ormrod

Other sports played: Squash, golf ('very badly')

Other sports followed: Most sports – mainly via TV

Relaxations: Reading, spending time with my family

Extras: Played for Lincolnshire 1973–74. Scored 100 runs before lunch v Warwickshire at Worcester, 1979. Captain 1983–. Testimonial season with Lincoln City 1984–85. Now retired from full-time football

Best batting performance: 163* Worcestershire v Nottinghamshire, Worcester 1979

Best bowling performance: 1-15 Worcestershire v Derbyshire, Worcester 1976

NEEDHAM, A. Middlesex

Full Name: Andrew Needham

Role: Right-hand bat, off-break bowler

Born: 23 March 1957, Calow, Derbyshire

Height: 5′ 10″ **Weight:** 10st 7lbs

Nickname: Needers

County debut: 1977 (Surrey), 1987 (Middlesex)

County cap: 1985 (Surrey)

1000 runs in a season: 1

1st-Class 50s scored: 10

1st-Class 100s scored: 4

1st-Class 5 w. in innings: 5

One-Day 50s: 3

Place in batting averages: 190th av. 18.22 (1986 199th av. 17.06)

Place in bowling averages: 129th av. 45.41

Strike rate 1987: 89.50 (career 86.71)

1st-Class catches 1987: 3 (career 45)

Parents: Thomas Robin and Peggy

Wife and date of marriage: Jane Marion, 1 November 1984

Education: Ecclesbourne Grammar School, Derbyshire; Paisley Grammar School, Scotland; Watford Grammar School

Qualifications: 6 O-levels

Off-season 1987–88: Working with my father for Needham and Needham Ltd

Cricketing superstitions or habits: Always put left pad on first

Overseas tours: Antigua with Surrey Young Cricketers 1977–78; Hong

Kong, Singapore and Bangkok with Surrey 1979–80; Bangladesh with MCC 1980–81; UAE with Barbican Touring Side 1983; South Africa with Alfred McAlpine 1983–84

Overseas teams played for: Glenwood Old Boys, Durban 1979–80 and 1984
Cricketers particularly learnt from: Fred Titmus
Cricketers particularly admired: Barry Richards
Other sports played: Squash and snooker
Other sports followed: Watches Chesterfield (football), horse racing and American football
Relaxations: Horses, cards, music, learning about wines
Extras: Left Surrey after 1986 season to join Middlesex
Best batting performance: 138 Surrey v Warwickshire, The Oval 1985
Best bowling performance: 6-30 Surrey v Oxford University, The Oval 1983

LAST SEASON: BATTING

	I.	N.O.	R.	H.S.	AV.
TEST					
1ST-CLASS	12	3	164	33	18.22
INT					
RAL	6	0	84	29	14.00
NAT.W.	1	0	11	11	11.00
B & H	1	0	5	5	5.00

LAST SEASON: BOWLING

	O.	M.	R.	W.	AV.
TEST					
1ST-CLASS	179	34	545	12	45.41
INT					
RAL	44.4	2	199	7	28.42
NAT.W.	21	2	74	2	37.00
B & H	11	0	38	0	–

CAREER: BATTING

	I.	N.O.	R.	H.S.	AV.
TEST					
1ST-CLASS	144	20	2784	138	22.45
INT					
RAL	45	8	678	55	18.32
NAT.W.	4	0	54	26	13.50
B & H	7	1	111	30	18.50

CAREER: BOWLING

	O.	M.	R.	W.	AV.
TEST					
1ST-CLASS	1676.3	408	4974	116	42.87
INT					
RAL	179.1	9	896	29	30.89
NAT.W.	48	5	173	9	19.22
B & H	30	3	99	0	–

122. Who were the last two brothers to play in the same Test for England?

NEWELL, M. — Nottinghamshire

Full Name: Michael Newell
Role: Right-hand opening bat, leg-break bowler, occasional wicket-keeper
Born: 25 February 1965, Blackburn
Height: 5′ 8″ **Weight:** 11st 3lbs
Nickname: Sam, Mugly, Tricky
County debut: 1984
County cap: 1987
1000 runs in a season: 1
1st-Class 50s scored: 9
1st-Class 100s scored: 3
1st-Class 200s scored: 1
One-Day 50s: 1
Place in batting averages: 46th av. 39.03 (1986 43rd av. 41.04)
1st-Class catches 1987: 15 (career 40 + 1 stumping)
Parents: Barry and Janet
Marital status: Single
Family links with cricket: Father chairman of Notts Unity CC. Brother Paul plays for Loughborough University
Education: West Bridgford Comprehensive
Qualifications: 8 O-levels, 3 A-levels. Qualified coach
Jobs outside cricket: Part-time barman; has worked in children's home; packer at Gunn and Moore
Off-season 1987–88: Working as a coach at Trent Bridge
Cricketing superstitions or habits: 'Always put right pad on first; always bat in short sweater and long-sleeved shirt. Wear the same whites if I am in form.'

LAST SEASON: BATTING

	I.	N.O.	R.	H.S.	AV.
TEST					
1ST-CLASS	34	7	1054	203*	39.03
INT					
RAL	2	1	40	28*	40.00
NAT.W.	2	0	62	60	31.00
B & H	2	0	52	27	26.00

LAST SEASON: BOWLING

	O.	M.	R.	W.	AV.
TEST					
1ST-CLASS	8.3	0	45	2	22.50
INT					
RAL					
NAT.W.					
B & H					

CAREER: BATTING

	I.	N.O.	R.	H.S.	AV.
TEST					
1ST-CLASS	84	17	2334	203*	34.83
INT					
RAL	2	1	40	28*	–
NAT.W.	2	0	62	60	31.00
B & H	2	0	52	27	26.00

CAREER: BOWLING

	O.	M.	R.	W.	AV.
TEST					
1ST-CLASS	26.3	2	140	3	46.66
INT					
RAL					
NAT.W.					
B & H					

Overseas tours: NCA U-19 tour to Holland 1983
Overseas teams played for: Nedland CC, Perth 1985–86
Cricketers particularly learnt from: All the batsmen at Nottinghamshire, Mike Bore and Bob White
Cricketers particularly admired: Richard Hadlee, Peter Willey
Other sports played: Football ('of a low standard'), indoor cricket
Other sports followed: Watches rugby union and football, horse racing
Relaxations: Good films, music and drinking at the Trent Bridge Inn
Opinions on cricket: 'Four-day cricket will hopefully put an end to the large amount of contrived finishes.'
Best batting performance: 203* Nottinghamshire v Derbyshire, Derby 1987
Best bowling performance: 1-0 Nottinghamshire v Worcestershire, Trent Bridge 1987

NEWMAN, P. G.   Derbyshire

Full Name: Paul Geoffrey Newman
Role: Right-hand bat, right-arm fast-medium bowler
Born: 10 January 1959, Leicester
Height: 6' 2" **Weight:** 14st
Nickname: Judge
County debut: 1980
County cap: 1986
50 wickets in a season: 1
1st-Class 50s scored: 3
1st-Class 100s scored: 1
1st-Class 5 w. in innings: 4
One-Day 50s: 2
Place in batting averages: 191st av. 17.94
Place in bowling averages: 26th av. 24.28
Strike rate 1987: 48.53 (career 55.60)
1st-Class catches 1987: 5 (career 24)
Marital status: Single
Education: Alderman Newton's Grammar School, Leicester
Qualifications: 6 O-levels
Jobs outside cricket: Various temporary jobs
Off-season 1987–88: In Cape Town, South Africa
Cricketing superstitions or habits: Always wears wrist bands to bowl. Puts left pad on first
Overseas tours: English Counties XI to Zimbabwe 1985

Overseas teams played for: Queensland Cricket Association Colts XI, 1981–82; Old Collegians and Pietermaritzburg, South Africa, 1983–84 and 1985–86

Cricketers admired: John Snow, Richard Hadlee, Dennis Lillee

Other sports played: Golf, football, snooker, pool

Injuries 1987: Out for one month with back injury

Relaxations: Crosswords, music, watching Leicester FC, keeping up scrapbooks, eating, socialising

Extras: Played for Leicestershire 2nd XI in 1978 and 1979, but was released. As a schoolboy, was a wicket-keeper. Took 50 wickets in his first season with Derbyshire. Won Commercial Union U-23 Bowling Award for 1981. Won Whitbread Scholarship to Brisbane, Australia 1981–82

Opinions on cricket: 'Having to listen to our wicket-keepers' opinions all season, most of us never have time to form any of our own.'

Best batting performance: 115 Derbyshire v Leicestershire, Chesterfield 1985

Best bowling performance: 7-104 Derbyshire v Surrey, The Oval 1984

LAST SEASON: BATTING

	I.	N.O.	R.	H.S.	AV.
TEST					
1ST-CLASS	24	5	341	42	17.94
INT					
RAL	12	4	171	52*	21.37
NAT.W.	2	1	21	11	21.00
B & H	4	1	38	27	12.66

CAREER: BATTING

	I.	N.O.	R.	H.S.	AV.
TEST					
1ST-CLASS	126	23	1656	115	16.07
INT					
RAL	41	11	425	52*	14.16
NAT.W.	6	2	90	35	22.50
B & H	16	7	183	56*	20.33

LAST SEASON: BOWLING

	O.	M.	R.	W.	AV.
TEST					
1ST-CLASS	364	75	1093	45	24.28
INT					
RAL	91.2	4	441	10	44.10
NAT.W.	19	3	58	5	11.60
B & H	44	5	172	4	43.00

CAREER: BOWLING

	O.	M.	R.	W.	AV.
TEST					
1ST-CLASS	2317	426	7772	250	31.08
INT					
RAL	485.2	27	2175	73	29.79
NAT.W.	100.4	12	316	14	22.57
B & H	223.1	27	860	29	29.65

123. Which of the two Chappell brothers, G. S. and I. M., took most catches for Australia, and how many?

NEWPORT, P. J.   Worcestershire

Full Name: Philip John Newport
Role: Right-hand bat, right-arm
fast-medium bowler, outfielder
Born: 11 October 1962, High
Wycombe
Height: 6′ 2″ **Weight:** 13st 7lbs
Nickname: Newps, Spike, Schnozz
County debut: 1982
County cap: 1986
50 wickets in a season: 1
1st-Class 50s scored: 4
1st-Class 5 w. in innings: 9
1st-Class 10 w. in match: 1
Place in batting averages: 35th
av. 41.09 (1986 174th av. 21.92)
Place in bowling averages: 126th
av. 43.78 (1986 30th av. 25.24)
Strike rate 1987: 78.50 (career 52.96)
1st-Class catches 1987: 8 (career 21)

Parents: John and Sheila Diana
Wife and date of marriage: Christine, 26 October 1985
Family links with cricket: 'Father is a good club cricketer, my younger brother
Stewart plays for High Wycombe CC.'
Education: Royal Grammar School, High Wycombe; Portsmouth
Polytechnic
Qualifications: 8 O-levels, 3 A-levels, BA (Hons) Geography, basic coaching
qualification
Jobs outside cricket: Schoolmaster at Worcester Royal Grammar School
1985–86

LAST SEASON: BATTING

	I.	N.O.	R.	H.S.	AV.
TEST					
1ST-CLASS	25	12	534	64*	41.07
INT					
RAL	5	4	38	26*	38.00
NAT.W.	1	0	1	1	1.00
B & H	3	2	6	3*	6.00

LAST SEASON: BOWLING

	O.	M.	R.	W.	AV.
TEST					
1ST-CLASS	504.3	79	1839	42	43.78
INT					
RAL	87	2	385	17	22.64
NAT.W.	17	3	27	3	9.00
B & H	50	5	156	14	11.14

CAREER: BATTING

	I.	N.O.	R.	H.S.	AV.
TEST					
1ST-CLASS	88	33	1454	68	26.43
INT					
RAL	20	9	166	26*	15.09
NAT.W.	4	1	45	25	15.00
B & H	5	2	26	15	8.66

CAREER: BOWLING

	O.	M.	R.	W.	AV.
TEST					
1ST-CLASS	1792	260	6244	203	30.75
INT					
RAL	237	3	1144	35	32.68
NAT.W.	80.2	10	254	8	31.75
B & H	76	5	247	15	16.46

Cricketing superstitions or habits: 'Always put a 10p piece in left pocket when batting.'
Overseas tours: With NCA to Denmark 1981
Cricketers particularly admired: Richard Hadlee
Other sports played: Soccer, rugby union
Other sports followed: American football, golf, athletics
Relaxations: Listening to music, reading; in New Zealand surfing, water-skiing, horse riding
Extras: Had trial as schoolboy for Southampton FC. Played cricket for NAYC England Schoolboys 1981. Also for Buckinghamshire in Minor Counties in 1981. Took part in Minor Counties final 1982. Wears contact lens in left eye only
Opinions on cricket: 'Sponsored incentive schemes such as Webster's Yorkshire Bitter scheme for fast bowlers certainly add to a player's determination to do well. Schemes for run-scoring, boundary hitting, catches, etc., etc. are a great idea and I hope to see more introduced.'
Best batting performance: 68 Worcestershire v Derbyshire, Derby 1986
Best bowling performance: 6-48 Worcestershire v Hampshire, Worcester 1986

NICHOLAS, M. C. J. Hampshire

Full Name: Mark Charles Jefford Nicholas
Role: Right-hand bat, right-arm medium bowler, slip fielder
Born: 29 September 1957, London
Height: 5′ 11½″ **Weight:** 12st 7lbs
Nickname: Skip, Cappy, Leader, Busby
County debut: 1978
County cap: 1982
1000 runs in a season: 5
1st-Class 50s scored: 40
1st-Class 100s scored: 20
1st-Class 200s scored: 1
1st-Class 5 w. in innings: 1
One-Day 50s: 20
One-Day 100s: 1
Place in batting averages: 37th av. 40.79 (1986 188th av. 18.80)
1st-Class catches 1987: 12 (career 127)
Parents: Anne
Marital status: Single

Family links with cricket: Grandfather (F.W.H.) played for Essex as batsman and wicket-keeper and toured with MCC

Education: Fernden Prep School; Bradfield College

Qualifications: 9 O-levels, 3 A-levels

Jobs outside cricket: Worked in Classified Advertising for *The Observer*. Selling for agencies. Writing for papers and magazines

Cricketing superstitions or habits: 'Kit must fit.'

Overseas tours: Toured South Africa with Dragons (Public Schools team) 1976–77 as captain; with MCC to Bangladesh, February 1981; and to East and Central Africa, October 1981; Dubai with *Cricketer* International XI, November 1981; Dubai and Bahrain with 'England XI', March 1981; Sri Lanka with England B 1986 as captain

Overseas teams played for: Captain of Southern Lakes in Australia 1978–79 and Grosvenor/Fynnland, Durban, 1982–83, 1983–84

Cricketers particularly learnt from: Barry Richards, Mike Brearley, Graham Gooch

Other sports played: Regular football with Old Bradfieldians (Arthurian League)

Relaxations: Bruce Springsteen concerts

Extras: Appointed captain 1985

Opinions on cricket: 'Heavens above – do we have all night?!'

Best batting performance: 206* Hampshire v Oxford University, Oxford 1982

Best bowling performance: 5-45 Hampshire v Worcestershire, Southampton 1983

LAST SEASON: BATTING

	I.	N.O.	R.	H.S.	AV.
TEST					
1ST-CLASS	38	9	1183	147	40.79
INT					
RAL	13	1	315	79*	26.25
NAT.W.	2	0	110	60	55.00
B & H	5	1	119	59*	29.75

LAST SEASON: BOWLING

	O.	M.	R.	W.	AV.
TEST					
1ST-CLASS	6.5	0	31	0	
INT					
RAL	10	0	66	1	66.00
NAT.W.	5	0	24	0	–
B & H	13	0	90	0	–

CAREER: BATTING

	I.	N.O.	R.	H.S.	AV.
TEST					
1ST-CLASS	331	42	9480	206*	32.80
INT					
RAL	99	16	2305	108	27.77
NAT.W.	21	1	501	63	25.05
B & H	32	2	673	74	22.43

CAREER: BOWLING

	O.	M.	R.	W.	AV.
TEST					
1ST-CLASS	647.3	140	2044	48	42.58
INT					
RAL	257	2	1420	50	28.40
NAT.W.	75.2	8	312	9	34.66
B & H	144	9	641	19	33.73

NORTH, P. D. — Glamorgan

Full Name: Philip David North
Role: Right-hand bat, slow
left-arm bowler
Born: 16 May 1965, Newport,
Gwent
Height: 5′ 6″ **Weight:** 9st 7lbs
Nickname: Knobhead, Philthy
County debut: 1986
1st-Class catches 1987: 2 (career 2)
Parents: Arthur and Audrey
Marital status: Single
Family links with cricket: Father
and uncles played club cricket
Education: St Julian's
Comprehensive; Nash College of
Further Education
Qualifications: 5 O-levels, TEC
Mechanical Engineering, qualified
toolmaker.

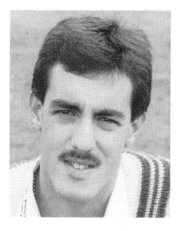

Jobs outside cricket: Toolmaker with brake manufacturer (Lucas Girling in
Cwmbran). Gardener and window cleaner in Australia
Off-season 1987–88: Playing in Australia for Penrith CC, Sydney
Overseas teams played for: Southport CC, Brisbane 1985–86; Penrith CC,
Sydney, 1986–87, 1987–88
Cricketers particularly learnt from: Alan Jones, Tom Cartwright
Cricketers particularly admired: Jim Pressdee, Richard Hadlee
Other sports played: Golf
Other sports followed: Soccer, golf
Relaxations: Films, socialising, eating out, driving, quiet drinking

LAST SEASON: BATTING

	I.	N.O.	R.	H.S.	AV.
TEST					
1ST-CLASS	7	1	39	15	6.50
INT					
RAL	1	0	0		0.00
NAT.W.					
B & H					

LAST SEASON: BOWLING

	O.	M.	R.	W.	AV.
TEST					
1ST-CLASS	103.5	27	242	7	34.57
INT					
RAL	16	1	81	2	40.50
NAT.W.					
B & H					

CAREER: BATTING

	I.	N.O.	R.	H.S.	AV.
TEST					
1ST-CLASS	13	4	61	17*	6.77
INT					
RAL	1	0	0		0.00
NAT.W.					
B & H					

CAREER: BOWLING

	O.	M.	R.	W.	AV.
TEST					
1ST-CLASS	190.1	47	451	12	37.58
INT					
RAL	16	1	81	2	40.50
NAT.W.					
B & H					

Injuries 1987: 'Mild schizophrenia diagnosed but both of us recovered quickly.'
Extras: 'Nothing to do with cricket but when I was an apprentice with Lucas Girling, I machined three or four disc brakes that were on Richard Noble's "Thrust II" world land speed record-breaking car.'
Opinions on cricket: 'Too much travelling involved in a season. Maybe fixtures should be better arranged.'
Best batting performance: 17* Glamorgan v Lancashire, Lytham 1986
Best bowling performance: 4-43 Glamorgan v Worcestershire, Neath 1987

O'GORMAN, T. J. G.   Derbyshire

Full Name: Timothy Joseph Gerard O'Gorman
Role: Right-hand bat
Born: 15 May 1967, Woking
Height: 6′ 2″ **Weight:** 11st 7lbs
County debut: 1987
1st-Class catches 1987: 2 (career 2)
Parents: Brian and Kathleen
Marital status: Single
Family links with cricket:
Grandfather played for Surrey;
father played for Nigeria
Education: St George's College,
Weybridge, Surrey; Durham
University
Qualifications: 12 O-levels,
3 A-levels
Jobs outside cricket: Working
in solicitors' office during holidays
Off-season 1987–88: Studying as a law student
Overseas tours: St George's College to Zimbabwe 1984; Troubadours to Argentina 1987
Cricketers particularly learnt from: Father, Mike Edwards (Surrey)
Cricketers particularly admired: David Gower, Greg Chappell, Richard Hadlee
Other sports played: Hockey (England Schools U-16s and U-18s trialist), rugby (England Schools U-18 final trialist)
Other sports followed: Tennis, football, golf
Injuries 1987: Dislocated shoulder
Relaxations: Arts, theatre, music, movies

Extras: Surrey Young Cricketer of the Year 1984. Captained Surrey Young Cricketers for three years (1986 winners of Hilda Overy Trophy)
Best batting performance: 11* Derbyshire v Glamorgan, Cardiff 1987

LAST SEASON: BATTING

	I.	N.O.	R.	H.S.	AV.
TEST					
1ST-CLASS	4	1	19	11*	6.33
INT					
RAL					
NAT.W.					
B & H					

CAREER: BATTING

	I.	N.O.	R.	H.S.	AV.
TEST					
1ST-CLASS	4	1	19	11*	6.33
INT					
RAL					
NAT.W.					
B & H					

ONTONG, R. C. Glamorgan

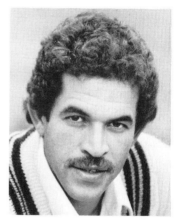

Full Name: Rodney Craig Ontong
Role: Right-hand bat,
off-break bowler
Born: 9 September 1955,
Johannesburg
County debut: 1975
County cap: 1979
1000 runs in a season: 5
50 wickets in a season: 5
1st-Class 50s scored: 70
1st-Class 100s scored: 19
1st-Class 200s scored: 1
1st-Class 5 w. in innings: 31
1st-Class 10 w. in match: 4
One-Day 50s: 17
One-Day 100s: 1
Place in batting averages: 97th
av. 31.57 (1986 171st av. 22.54)
Place in bowling averages: 93rd
av. 34.39 (1986 48th av. 27.71)
Strike rate 1987: 68.73 (career 61.76)
1st-Class catches 1987: 13 (career 163)
Education: Selbourne College, East London, South Africa
Overseas teams played for: Made debut in 1972–73 for Border in Currie Cup Competition. Transferred to Transvaal for 1976–77 season, before returning to Border
Extras: Took over Glamorgan captaincy during 1984, but resigned during 1986
Best batting performance: 204* Glamorgan v Middlesex, Swansea 1984

Best bowling performance: 8-67 Glamorgan v Nottinghamshire, Trent Bridge 1985

LAST SEASON: BATTING

	I.	N.O.	R.	H.S.	AV.
TEST					
1ST-CLASS	27	8	600	100	31.57
INT					
RAL	8	3	209	69*	41.80
NAT.W.					
B & H	4	1	210	77*	70.00

CAREER: BATTING

	I.	N.O.	R.	H.S.	AV.
TEST					
1ST-CLASS	547	75	13893	204*	29.43
INT					
RAL	129	19	2677	100	24.33
NAT.W.	15	3	480	64	40.00
B & H	35	5	829	81	27.63

LAST SEASON: BOWLING

	O.	M.	R.	W.	AV.
TEST					
1ST-CLASS	469.4	89	1410	41	34.39
INT					
RAL	63	3	277	4	69.25
NAT.W.					
B & H	43	2	187	3	62.33

CAREER: BOWLING

	O.	M.	R.	W.	AV.
TEST					
1ST-CLASS	8050	1863	23451	782	29.98
INT					
RAL	859	45	3907	123	31.76
NAT.W.	141	24	548	12	45.66
B & H	328.4	55	1063	45	23.62

O'SHAUGHNESSY, S. J.   Lancashire

Full Name: Steven Joseph O'Shaughnessy
Role: Right-hand bat, right-arm medium bowler
Born: 9 September 1961, Bury
Height: 5' 10½"
County debut: 1980
County cap: 1985
1000 runs in a season: 1
1st-Class 50s scored: 16
1st-Class 100s scored: 5
One-Day 50s: 11
One-Day 100s: 1
Place in batting averages: 155th av. 22.91 (1986 136th av. 26.45)
1st-Class catches 1987: 15 (career 52)
Education: Harper Green Secondary School, Farnworth, Lancashire
Overseas tours: Canada 1979 with NCA U-19 XI; West Indies 1980 with England Young Cricketers
Relaxations: Snooker
Extras: Scored 100 in 35 minutes v Leicestershire, 11 September 1983 to equal fastest first-class century scored by Percy Fender in 1920. Released at end of 1987 season

Best batting performance: 159* Lancashire v Somerset, Bath 1984
Best bowling performance: 4-66 Lancashire v Nottinghamshire, Trent Bridge 1982

LAST SEASON: BATTING

	I.	N.O.	R.	H.S.	AV.
TEST					
1ST-CLASS	16	4	275	61*	22.91
INT					
RAL	9	3	169	33	28.16
NAT.W.					
B & H	4	1	99	69*	33.00

LAST SEASON: BOWLING

	O.	M.	R.	W.	AV.
TEST					
1ST-CLASS	131	35	355	7	50.71
INT					
RAL	60	1	340	9	37.77
NAT.W.					
B & H	26	3	119	1	119.00

CAREER: BATTING

	I.	N.O.	R.	H.S.	AV.
TEST					
1ST-CLASS	161	27	3567	159*	26.61
INT					
RAL	71	14	1334	101*	23.40
NAT.W.	14	4	264	62	26.40
B & H	24	1	576	90	25.04

CAREER: BOWLING

	O.	M.	R.	W.	AV.
TEST					
1ST-CLASS	1161.3	217	3947	110	35.88
INT					
RAL	451.1	14	2261	57	39.66
NAT.W.	135	13	563	13	43.30
B & H	183	32	667	25	26.68

PAGE, H. A. Essex

Full Name: Hugh Ashton Page
Role: Left-hand bat, right-arm fast-medium bowler
Born: 3 August 1962, Harare, Zimbabwe
County debut: 1987
1st-Class 50s scored: 3
1st-Class 5 w. in innings: 4
Place in batting averages: 203rd av. 16.62
Place in bowling averages: 89th av. 33.48
Strike rate 1987: 58.34 (career 48.26)
1st-Class catches 1987: 5 (career 19)
Education: King Edward VII School, Johannesburg
Overseas teams played for: Transvaal, 1981–

Extras: Played for Staffordshire 1985. Also played for Warwickshire 2nd XI and Nottinghamshire 2nd XI
Best batting performance: 57 Transvaal B v Natal B, Johannesburg 1984–85
Best bowling performance: 5-26 Essex v Cambridge University, Cambridge 1987

LAST SEASON: BATTING

	I.	N.O.	R.	H.S.	AV.
TEST					
1ST-CLASS	20	4	266	60	16.62
INT					
RAL	6	1	92	39	18.40
NAT.W.	1	0	7	7	7.00
B & H	2	0	23	23	11.50

LAST SEASON: BOWLING

	O.	M.	R.	W.	AV.
TEST					
1ST-CLASS	340.2	52	1172	35	33.48
INT					
RAL	55	5	256	10	25.60
NAT.W.	12	4	10	2	5.00
B & H	26.4	4	100	4	25.00

CAREER: BATTING

	I.	N.O.	R.	H.S.	AV.
TEST					
1ST-CLASS	82	19	1153	60	18.30
INT					
RAL	6	1	92	39	18.40
NAT.W.	1	0	7	7	7.00
B & H	2	0	23	23	11.50

CAREER: BOWLING

	O.	M.	R.	W.	AV.
TEST					
1ST-CLASS	1608.5	266	4738	200	23.69
INT					
RAL	55	5	256	10	25.60
NAT.W.	12	4	10	2	5.00
B & H	26.4	4	100	4	25.00

PALMER, G. V. — Somerset

Full Name: Gary Vincent Palmer
Role: Right-hand bat, right-arm fast-medium bowler
Born: 1 November 1965, Taunton
Height: 6' 1" **Weight:** 11st 7lbs
Nickname: Pedlar
County debut: 1982
1st-Class 50s scored: 3
1st-Class 5 w. in innings: 1
One-Day 50s: 1
Place in batting averages: 182nd av. 19.50
Place in bowling averages: 116th av. 40.06
Strike rate 1987: 65.37 (career 73.18)
1st-Class catches 1987: 4 (career 30)
Parents: Kenneth Ernest and Joy Valerie
Marital status: Single
Family links with cricket: Father, K. E. Palmer, played for Somerset and England. Toured Pakistan with Commonwealth team, 1963. Test Umpire. Coach at Somerset CCC in winter. Grandfather did the double for 13 consecutive seasons in club cricket, and scored 25 centuries for Devizes CC
Education: North Town Junior School; Queen's College, Junior and Senior
Qualifications: SRA Part 1 Squash Coaching Certificate, NCA Cricket Coaching Award, GCEs
Jobs outside cricket: Squash coaching

Overseas tours: English Schools U-19 to Zimbabwe 1982–83; England Young Cricketers to West Indies 1984–85
Cricketers particularly learnt from: 'Learnt from my father from an early age.'
Cricketers particularly admired: Viv Richards, Joel Garner, Ian Botham
Other sports played: Squash
Relaxations: 'Listening to music – the up-to-date variety.'
Extras: Somerset U-19 Squash champion. Youngest professional ever; had summer contract with Somerset at 14. Captain of England U-15. English Schools U-16 Cricketer of the Year. Possibly youngest cricketer to play for England U-19. Made debut for Somerset 1st XI at 16. Opened his first-class career v Leicestershire by bowling two maidens
Best batting performance: 78 Somerset v Gloucestershire, Bristol 1983
Best bowling performance: 5-38 Somerset v Warwickshire, Taunton 1983

LAST SEASON: BATTING

	I.	N.O.	R.	H.S.	AV.
TEST					
1ST-CLASS	16	4	234	68	19.50
INT					
RAL	6	2	41	12*	10.25
NAT.W.					
B & H	1	0	4	4	4.00

LAST SEASON: BOWLING

	O.	M.	R.	W.	AV.
TEST					
1ST-CLASS	316	54	1162	29	40.06
INT					
RAL	74.2	0	359	17	21.11
NAT.W.					
B & H	10	0	58	1	58.00

CAREER: BATTING

	I.	N.O.	R.	H.S.	AV.
TEST					
1ST-CLASS	68	11	880	78	15.43
INT					
RAL	24	11	220	33	16.92
NAT.W.					
B & H	6	1	81	53	16.20

CAREER: BOWLING

	O.	M.	R.	W.	AV.
TEST					
1ST-CLASS	1110	180	4053	91	44.53
INT					
RAL	244	1	1281	46	27.84
NAT.W.	20	0	102	1	102.00
B & H	67	4	318	8	39.75

124. Is it true or false that Clive Rice took a wicket with his last ball for Notts?

PARKER, P. W. G.　　　　　Sussex

Full Name: Paul William Giles Parker
Role: Right-hand bat, leg-break bowler, cover fielder
Born: 15 January 1956, Bulawayo, Rhodesia
Height: 5' 10½" **Weight:** 12st
Nickname: Porky, Polly
County debut: 1976
County cap: 1979
Benefit: 1988
Test debut: 1981
1000 runs in a season: 7
1st-Class 50s scored: 59
1st-Class 100s scored: 30
1st-Class 200s scored: 1
One-Day 50s: 33
One-Day 100s: 5
Place in batting averages: 174th
av. 20.17 (1986 29th av. 44.30)
1st-Class catches 1987: 16 (career 182)
Parents: Anthony John and Margaret Edna
Wife and date of marriage: Teresa, 25 January 1980
Children: James William Ralph, 6 November 1980; Jocelyn Elizabeth, 10 September 1984
Family links with cricket: Father played for Essex 2nd XI. Uncle, David Green, played for Northamptonshire and Worcestershire. Two brothers, Guy and Rupert, 'very keen and active cricketers'. Father wrote *The Village Cricket Match* and was sports editor of ITN
Education: Collyer's Grammar School; St Catharine's College, Cambridge
Qualifications: MA (Cantab.)
Jobs outside cricket: Winter employment with Messrs Laing & Cruickshank (Stockbrokers), London
Overseas tours: Combined Oxford & Cambridge XI tour of Australia 1979–80
Overseas teams played for: Sturt CC, Adelaide, Australia, 1979–80; Natal, South Africa, 1980–81
Cricketers particularly learnt from: J. Denman, Sussex CCC
Other sports played: Most ball games
Relaxations: Reading, crosswords, bridge, music
Extras: Was selected for Cambridge for Varsity rugby match in 1977 but had to withdraw through injury. Was first reserve for England on Australia tour 1979–80. Appointed captain of Sussex for 1988

Best batting performance: 215 Cambridge University v Essex, Cambridge 1976
Best bowling performance: 2-21 Sussex v Surrey, Guildford 1984

LAST SEASON: BATTING

	I.	N.O.	R.	H.S.	AV.
TEST					
1ST-CLASS	32	4	565	85	20.17
INT					
RAL	6	2	280	106*	70.00
NAT.W.	1	0	0		0.00
B & H	4	0	63	31	15.75

LAST SEASON: BOWLING

	O.	M.	R.	W.	AV.
TEST					
1ST-CLASS	2.2	0	15	0	–
INT					
RAL	0.2	0	4	0	–
NAT.W.					
B & H	1	0	3	2	1.50

CAREER: BATTING

	I.	N.O.	R.	H.S.	AV.
TEST	2	0	13	13	6.50
1ST-CLASS	444	63	13216	215	34.68
INT					
RAL	138	22	3527	121*	30.40
NAT.W.	30	4	900	109	34.61
B & H	49	4	1115	77	24.77

CAREER: BOWLING

	O.	M.	R.	W.	AV.
TEST					
1ST-CLASS	142.5	24	581	10	58.10
INT					
RAL	5.2	0	24	2	12.00
NAT.W.	2	0	17	1	17.00
B & H	1	0	3	2	1.50

PARKS, R. J. Hampshire

Full Name: Robert James Parks
Role: Right-hand bat, wicket-keeper
Born: 15 June 1959, Cuckfield, Sussex
Height: 5′ 7½″ **Weight:** 10st 7lbs
Nickname: Bobby
County debut: 1980
County cap: 1982
1st-Class 50s scored: 13
Place in batting averages: 80th av. 33.63 (1986 162nd av. 23.33)
Parents: James and Irene
Wife and date of marriage: Amanda, 30 January 1982
Family links with cricket: Father, Jim Parks, played for Sussex and England, as did his grandfather, J. H. Parks. Uncle, H. W. Parks, also played for Sussex
Education: Eastbourne Grammar School; Southampton Institute of Technology
Qualifications: 9 O-levels, 1 A-level, OND and HND in Business Studies
Jobs outside cricket: Training in accountancy, working for Jardine Air Cargo
Off-season 1987–88: Working for LEP International

Cricketing superstitions or habits: Left pad on first

Overseas tours: English Counties XI to Zimbabwe 1985

Cricketers particularly learnt from: Alan Knott, John Rice

Cricketers particularly admired: Bob Taylor, Nick Pocock

Other sports played: Squash, football

Injuries 1987: Missed first match for seven years because of a broken finger

Relaxations: Stamp collecting, crosswords

Extras: Broke the Hampshire record for the number of dismissals in a match, v Derbyshire, 1982 (10 catches). Took over from Bob Taylor as stand-in wicket-keeper for England v New Zealand at Lord's after injury to Bruce French

Opinions on cricket: 'There is a serious danger that cricketers representing their countries are playing far too much international cricket which is proving detrimental to their fitness and performance at county level.'

Best batting performance: 89 Hampshire v Cambridge University, Cambridge 1984

LAST SEASON: BATTING

	I.	N.O.	R.	H.S.	AV.
TEST					
1ST-CLASS	19	8	370	62*	33.63
INT					
RAL	7	5	112	38*	56.00
NAT.W.	1	0	3	3	3.00
B & H	3	1	18	15*	9.00

LAST SEASON: WICKET KEEPING

	C.	ST.			
TEST					
1ST-CLASS	56	5			
INT					
RAL	14	2			
NAT.W.	1	–			
B & H	4	–			

CAREER: BATTING

	I.	N.O.	R.	H.S.	AV.
TEST					
1ST-CLASS	189	49	2712	89	19.37
INT					
RAL	38	22	402	38*	25.12
NAT.W.	9	3	70	25	11.66
B & H	21	7	127	16	9.07

CAREER: WICKET KEEPING

	C.	ST.			
TEST					
1ST-CLASS	438	52			
INT					
RAL	112	24			
NAT.W.	22	5			
B & H	38	5			

125. When Worcestershire won the Refuge Assurance League last season, how many years was it since they had won any title?

PARSONS, G. J.   Warwickshire

Full Name: Gordon James Parsons
Role: Left-hand bat, right-arm
medium bowler, outfielder
Born: 17 October 1959, Slough
Height: 6′ 1″ **Weight:** 13st 7lbs
Nickname: Bullhead, Triangle,
Vicar
County debut: 1978 (Leicestershire),
1986 (Warwickshire)
County cap: 1984 (Leicestershire),
1987 (Warwickshire)
50 wickets in a season: 2
1st-Class 50s scored: 18
1st-Class 5 w. in innings: 10
1st-Class 10 w. in match: 1
Place in batting averages: 147th
av. 24.82 (1986 201st av. 16.94)
Place in bowling averages: 100th
av. 36.14 (1986 93rd av. 38.03)

Strike rate 1987: 73.91 (career 59.08)
1st-Class catches 1987: 6 (career 55)
Parents: Dave and Evelyn
Marital status: 'Still deciding.'
Family links with cricket: Father played club cricket
Education: Woodside County Secondary School, Slough
Qualifications: 5 O-levels
Jobs outside cricket: Worked as clerk at T. L. Bennett, Ratby, Leicester
Off-season 1987–88: Coaching in South Africa
Overseas tours: Australasia with Derrick Robins' U-23 XI 1979–80; ESCA
tour to India 1977–78; Zimbabwe with Leicestershire 1981
Overseas teams played for: Maharaja in Sri Lanka, 1979, 1981–82, 1982–83;
Boland, South Africa, 1983–84
Cricketers particularly learnt from: 'Alf Gover, Ken Higgs, Roger Tolchard
and Andy Roberts have given me plenty of good advice plus too many to
mention – particularly in the team.'
Cricketers particularly admired: Jonathan Agnew, Mike Garnham, David
Allett
Other sports played: Golf, squash
Injuries 1987: 'Broken bone in right foot caused me to miss half the season.'
Extras: Played for Leicester 2nd XI since 1976 and also for Buckinghamshire
in 1977. Left Leicestershire after 1985 season and joined Warwickshire.
Capped by Warwickshire while in plaster and on crutches

Best batting performance: 76 Boland v Western Province B, Cape Town 1984–85
Best bowling performance: 9-72 Boland v Transvaal B, Johannesburg 1984–85

LAST SEASON: BATTING

	I.	N.O.	R.	H.S.	AV.
TEST					
1ST-CLASS	19	2	422	67*	24.82
INT					
RAL	7	2	88	26*	17.60
NAT.W.	2	1	21	19	10.50
B & H	3	1	15	8	7.50

LAST SEASON: BOWLING

	O.	M.	R.	W.	AV.
TEST					
1ST-CLASS	418.5	82	1229	34	36.14
INT					
RAL	72	2	296	9	32.88
NAT.W.	30.2	4	100	2	50.00
B & H	32	7	110	1	110.00

CAREER: BATTING

	I.	N.O.	R.	H.S.	AV.
TEST					
1ST-CLASS	229	48	3473	76	19.18
INT					
RAL	54	16	404	26*	10.63
NAT.W.	10	1	90	23	10.00
B & H	18	8	186	29*	18.60

CAREER: BOWLING

	O.	M.	R.	W.	AV.
TEST					
1ST-CLASS	4086.4	847	12915	415	31.12
INT					
RAL	663.2	32	2913	99	29.42
NAT.W.	163.1	24	602	14	43.00
B & H	309.3	37	1093	39	28.02

PATTERSON, B. P.　　　　Lancashire

Full Name: Balfour Patrick Patterson
Role: Right-hand bat, right-arm fast bowler, outfielder
Born: 15 September 1961, Portland, Jamaica
Height: 6′ 2½″ **Weight:** 14st
Nickname: Balf, Pato
County debut: 1984
County cap: 1987
Test debut: 1985–86
No. of Tests: 6
No. of One-Day Internationals: 9
1st-Class 5 w. in innings: 12
1st-Class 10 w. in match: 2
Place in bowling averages: 44th av. 26.13 (1986 42nd av. 27.27)
Strike rate 1987: 48.36 (career 50.07)
1st-Class catches 1987: 1 (career 18)
Parents: Maurice and Emelda
Marital status: Single
Family links with cricket: Father and grandfather played for parish in Jamaica
Education: Happy Grove High School; Wolmers High School for Boys

Qualifications: Jamaica School Certificates, O-levels
Jobs outside cricket: Accounts clerk
Off-season 1987–88: Playing for West Indies
Overseas teams played for: Tasmania 1984–85
Cricketers particularly learnt from: Anderson Roberts
Cricketers particularly admired: Present West Indian team, Dennis Lillee
Other sports played: Basketball, football, squash and table tennis for fitness and pleasure
Other sports followed: Watches football
Relaxations: Swimming, listening to music, watching television
Best batting performance: 29 Lancashire v Northamptonshire, Northampton 1987
Best bowling performance: 7-24 Jamaica v Guyana, Kingston 1985–86

LAST SEASON: BATTING

	I.	N.O.	R.	H.S.	AV.
TEST					
1ST-CLASS	16	8	65	29	812
INT					
RAL	1	1	2	2*	–
NAT.W.	1	1	0	0*	–
B & H					

CAREER: BATTING

	I.	N.O.	R.	H.S.	AV.
TEST	7	4	18	9	6.00
1ST-CLASS	71	24	220	29	4.68
INT	1	1	0	0*	–
RAL	2	2	5	3*	–
NAT.W.	2	1	4	4	4.00
B & H	2	2	18	15*	–

LAST SEASON: BOWLING

	O.	M.	R.	W.	AV.
TEST					
1ST-CLASS	419.1	61	1359	52	26.13
INT					
RAL	21	0	92	5	18.40
NAT.W.	12	1	51	0	–
B & H					

CAREER: BOWLING

	O.	M.	R.	W.	AV.
TEST	149.1	22	527	22	23.95
1ST-CLASS	1787	284	5931	210	28.24
INT	72.5	8	303	9	33.66
RAL	22.2	0	98	5	19.60
NAT.W.	24	1	120	1	120.00
B & H	31	4	108	4	27.00

126. For which Lancashire League club did Ray Lindwall play?

PENN, C.   Kent

Full Name: Christopher Penn
Role: Left-hand bat, right-arm
medium bowler
Born: 19 June 1963, Dover
Height: 6′ **Weight:** 14st 3lbs
Nickname: Penny, Cliff
County debut: 1982
County cap: 1987
1st-Class 50s scored: 4
1st-Class 100s scored: 1
1st-Class 5 w. in innings: 3
Place in batting averages: 222nd
av. 14.81
Place in bowling averages: 71st
av. 30.60
Strike rate 1987: 54.89 (career 62.38)
1st-Class catches 1987: 7 (career 31)
Parents: Reg and Brenda
Wife and date of marriage: Caroline,
22 March 1986
Family links with cricket: Father played club cricket for Dover CC for 26 years
Education: Dover Grammar School
Qualifications: 8 O-levels, 2 A-levels
Jobs outside cricket: Farm worker, car cleaner for hire company, financial
consultant
Off-season 1987–88: Working as a financial consultant
Overseas tours: NCA tour of Denmark 1981; Whitbread Scholarship to
Australia 1982–83
Overseas teams played for: Koohinore Crescents, Johannesburg, 1981–82
and 1983–84; West Perth 1982–83; Johannesburg Municipals 1983–84; Wits
University 1984–85
Cricketers particularly learnt from: 'My father, Colin Page, Brian Luckhurst,
Barney Lock and many others.'
Cricketers particularly admired: Alan Knott, Dennis Lillee, Cliff Jamieson
Other sports played: Rugby, football, golf, squash
Other sports followed: All sports
Relaxations: Music, art and art history, Indian food
Extras: Played for Young England and England Schools. Took hat-trick in
first 2nd XI match v Middlesex when 16 years old
Opinions on cricket: 'Possibly too much car travel which could lead to a
serious accident.'

313

Best batting performance: 115 Kent v Lancashire, Old Trafford 1984
Best bowling performance: 5-52 Kent v Lancashire, Maidstone 1987

LAST SEASON: BATTING

	I.	N.O.	R.	H.S.	AV.
TEST					
1ST-CLASS	18	2	237	53	14.81
INT					
RAL	5	1	32	8	8.00
NAT.W.					
B & H	3	1	2	2*	1.00

CAREER: BATTING

	I.	N.O.	R.	H.S.	AV.
TEST					
1ST-CLASS	56	12	829	115	18.84
INT					
RAL	24	5	151	40	7.94
NAT.W.	1	0	5	5	5.00
B & H	8	3	38	17	7.60

LAST SEASON: BOWLING

	O.	M.	R.	W.	AV.
TEST					
1ST-CLASS	439.1	78	1469	48	30.60
INT					
RAL	65	2	343	13	26.38
NAT.W.					
B & H	61.4	2	284	9	31.55

CAREER: BOWLING

	O.	M.	R.	W.	AV.
TEST					
1ST-CLASS	967	169	3276	93	35.22
INT					
RAL	241	9	1208	41	29.46
NAT.W.	12	1	34	1	34.00
B & H	104.4	6	431	15	28.73

PICK, R. A.   Nottinghamshire

Full Name: Robert Andrew Pick
Role: Left-hand bat, right-arm
fast-medium bowler
Born: 19 November 1963,
Nottingham
Height: 5′ 10″ **Weight:** 13st
Nickname: Dad, Picky
County debut: 1983
County cap: 1987
50 wickets in a season: 1
1st-Class 50s scored: 2
1st-Class 5 w. in innings: 3
1st-Class 10 w. in match: 1
Place in batting averages: 118th
av. 15.40 (1986 222nd av. 12.87)
Place in bowling averages: 74th
av. 30.92 (1986 65th av. 31.40)
Strike rate 1987: 55.64 (career 61.19)
1st-Class catches 1987: 1 (career 12)
Parents: Bob and Lillian
Marital status: Engaged
Family links with cricket: Father, uncles and cousins all play local cricket for
Thrumpton CC
Jobs outside cricket: Labourer

Off-season 1987–88: Coaching and playing in New Zealand with Taita District CC
Education: Alderman Derbyshire Comprehensive; High Pavement College
Qualifications: 6 O-levels, 1 A-level, coaching qualification
Overseas tours: Barbados with Keith Pont Benefit 1986
Overseas teams played for: Upper Hutt CC, New Zealand 1984–85; Taita CC, New Zealand 1986–87
Cricketers particularly admired: Bob White, Mike Hendrick, Mike Harris
Other sports played: Football, fishing
Other sports followed: Ice-hockey
Relaxations: 'As much fishing as possible and listening to a wide range of music; eating and drinking.'
Extras: Played three Tests for Young England v Young Australia 1983
Injuries 1987: Aggravation of old stress fracture in back, and sprained ankle
Opinions on cricket: 'Coloured clothing should be introduced for all one-day cricket.'
Best batting performance: 63 Nottinghamshire v Warwickshire, Nuneaton 1983
Best bowling performance: 6-68 Nottinghamshire v Yorkshire, Worksop 1986

LAST SEASON: BATTING

	I.	N.O.	R.	H.S.	AV.
TEST					
1ST-CLASS	15	5	154	42*	15.40
INT					
RAL	3	1	19	12	9.50
NAT.W.	3	2	6	6*	6.00
B & H	3	1	7	4	3.50

LAST SEASON: BOWLING

	O.	M.	R.	W.	AV.
TEST					
1ST-CLASS	361.4	74	1206	39	30.92
INT					
RAL	77	8	380	18	21.11
NAT.W.	43.1	3	141	9	15.66
B & H	37.5	5	153	8	19.12

CAREER: BATTING

	I.	N.O.	R.	H.S.	AV.
TEST					
1ST-CLASS	65	18	790	63	16.80
INT					
RAL	17	7	110	24	11.00
NAT.W.	8	6	63	34*	31.50
B & H	6	3	13	4	4.33

CAREER: BOWLING

	O.	M.	R.	W.	AV.
TEST					
1ST-CLASS	1499.2	282	5145	147	35.00
INT					
RAL	328.2	12	1718	57	30.14
NAT.W.	156.1	17	572	22	26.00
B & H	113.5	9	463	16	28.93

127. Who resigned as captain of Essex at the end of 1987?

PICKLES, C. S.   Yorkshire

Full Name: Christopher Stephen
Pickles
Role: Right-hand bat, right-arm
medium bowler
Born: 30 January 1966, Cleckheaton
Height: 6' 1" **Weight:** 13st
Nickname: Pick, Piccolo
County debut: 1985
1st-Class catches 1987: 0 (career 3)
Parents: Ronald Albert and
Christine Mary
Marital status: Single
Family links with cricket: Father
and brother both play local league
cricket
Education: Whitcliffe Mount School
Qualifications: Qualified cricket
coach

Jobs outside cricket: Work in textiles
Overseas tours: NCA U-19 to Bermuda 1985
Cricketers particularly learnt from: Ian Steen, Doug Padgett, Steve Oldham
Cricketers particularly admired: Geoff Boycott, Richard Hadlee
Other sports played: Rugby union
Relaxations: 'Going out for a pint and then having some fish and chips.'
Best batting performance: 31* Yorkshire v Leicestershire, Bradford 1985
Best bowling performance: 2-31 Yorkshire v Kent, Scarborough 1985

LAST SEASON: BATTING

	I.	N.O.	R.	H.S.	AV.
TEST					
1ST-CLASS					
INT					
RAL					
NAT.W.					
B & H	1	1	13	13*	–

LAST SEASON: BOWLING

	O.	M.	R.	W.	AV.
TEST					
1ST-CLASS					
INT					
RAL					
NAT.W.					
B & H	11	3	28	0	–

CAREER: BATTING

	I.	N.O.	R.	H.S.	AV.
TEST					
1ST-CLASS	3	1	52	31*	26.00
INT					
RAL	7	4	48	16*	16.00
NAT.W.					
B & H	1	1	13	13*	–

CAREER: BOWLING

	O.	M.	R.	W.	AV.
TEST					
1ST-CLASS	126.3	13	385	6	64.16
INT					
RAL	72	4	339	8	42.37
NAT.W.					
B & H	11	3	28	0	–

PIENAAR, R. F.   Kent

Full Name: Roy Francois Pienaar
Role: Right-hand opening bat,
right-arm fast-medium bowler
Born: 17 July 1961,
Johannesburg
Height: 6′ 2″ **Weight:** 13st 6lbs
Nickname: Vitas
County debut: 1987
1st-Class 50s scored: 23
1st-Class 100s scored: 4
1st-Class 5 w. in innings: 1
Place in batting averages: 36th
av. 40.87
1st-Class catches 1987: 2 (career 37)
Parents: Ron and Heather
Marital status: Single
Education: St Stithian's
College, Johannesburg
Qualifications: Matriculation
(Higher Grade); Bachelor of Commerce, University of Cape Town
Off-season 1987–88: Playing in South Africa
Cricketing superstitions or habits: Puts left pad on first
Overseas tours: Wanderers' Club to England 1977
Overseas teams played for: Transvaal, Western Province, Northern Transvaal, South Africa
Cricketers particularly learnt from: Peter Stringer
Cricketers particularly admired: Barry Richards, Graeme Pollock
Other sports followed: Tennis, golf, rugby
Relaxations: Keeping fit, music, movies, wildlife

LAST SEASON: BATTING

	I.	N.O.	R.	H.S.	AV.
TEST					
1ST-CLASS	8	0	327	153	40.87
INT					
RAL	2	0	28	15	14.00
NAT.W.					
B & H					

CAREER: BATTING

	I.	N.O.	R.	H.S.	AV.
TEST					
1ST-CLASS	132	7	3647	153	29.17
INT					
RAL	2	0	28	15	14.00
NAT.W.					
B & H					

LAST SEASON: BOWLING

	O.	M.	R.	W.	AV.
TEST					
1ST-CLASS	135.4	27	427	15	28.46
INT					
RAL	18	0	90	3	30.00
NAT.W.	6	2	14	1	14.00
B & H					

CAREER: BOWLING

	O.	M.	R.	W.	AV.
TEST					
1ST-CLASS			3036	94	32.29
INT					
RAL	18	0	90	3	30.00
NAT.W.	6	2	14	1	14.00
B & H					

Extras: South African Cricketer of the Year 1983. Shared in record One-Day opening stand for South Africa v Australia of 154 with Jimmy Cook. Played for Worcestershire 2nd XI and Kidderminster in Birmingham League. Joined Kent mid-season as their overseas player in place of the injured Eldine Baptiste
Best batting performance: 153 Kent v Derbyshire, Derby 1987
Best bowling performance: 5-24 Western Province v Natal, Durban 1981–82

PIERSON, A. R. K. Warwickshire

Full Name: Adrian Roger Kirshaw Pierson
Role: Right-hand bat, off-break bowler
Born: 21 July 1963, Enfield, Middlesex
Height: 6′ 4″ **Weight:** 12st
Nickname: Skirlog, Stick
County debut: 1985
1st-Class catches 1987: 3 (career 6)
Parents: Patrick Blake Kirshaw and Patricia Margaret
Marital status: Single
Education: Lochinver House Primary; Kent College, Canterbury; Hatfield Polytechnic
Qualifications: 2 A-levels, Advanced Coaching Certificate
Jobs outside cricket: Worked on light aircraft at Elstree Aerodrome, 1982
Off-season 1987–88: Coaching cricket
Cricketing superstitions or habits: Always put left pad on first
Overseas tours: Barbados 1985 with Dennis Amiss Testimonial XI
Cricketers particularly learnt from: Don Wilson and Warwickshire staff
Cricketers particularly admired: John Emburey, Phil Edmonds, Tony Greig
Other sports played: Hockey, golf
Other sports followed: All sports
Relaxations: Music, driving
Extras: On Lord's groundstaff 1984–85
Opinions on cricket: 'One-day cricket could be played in coloured clothing with each team having its own strip. One-day games to be fitted in at weekends.'
Best batting performance: 42* Warwickshire v Northamptonshire, Northampton 1986

Best bowling performance: 3-92 Warwickshire v Oxford University, Oxford 1985

LAST SEASON: BATTING

	I.	N.O.	R.	H.S.	AV.
TEST					
1ST-CLASS	1	0	0		0.00
INT					
RAL	4	2	31	21*	15.50
NAT.W.					
B & H					

CAREER: BATTING

	I.	N.O.	R.	H.S.	AV.
TEST					
1ST-CLASS	17	9	132	42*	16.50
INT					
RAL	8	3	43	21*	8.60
NAT.W.	1	1	1	1*	
B & H					

LAST SEASON: BOWLING

	O.	M.	R.	W.	AV.
TEST					
1ST-CLASS	50	11	161	5	32.20
INT					
RAL	35	1	175	5	35.00
NAT.W.	12	3	24	0	–
B & H					

CAREER: BOWLING

	O.	M.	R.	W.	AV.
TEST					
1ST-CLASS	241	46	881	15	58.73
INT					
RAL	85	4	407	7	58.14
NAT.W.	24	5	56	0	–
B & H					

PIGOTT, A. C. S. Sussex

Full Name: Anthony Charles Shackleton Pigott
Role: Right-hand bat, right-arm fast bowler, slip fielder
Born: 4 June 1958, London
Height: 6′ 1″ **Weight:** 12st 6lbs
Nickname: Lester
County debut: 1978
County cap: 1982
Test debut: 1983–84
No. of Tests: 1
50 wickets in a season: 2
1st-Class 50s scored: 8
1st-Class 100s scored: 1
1st-Class 5 w. in innings: 16
1st-Class 10 w. in match: 1
Place in batting averages: 177th av. 19.82 (1986 22nd av. 47.66)
Place in bowling averages: 84th av. 32.06 (1986 50th av. 27.81)
Strike rate 1987: 60.71 (career 51.18)
1st-Class catches 1987: 12 (career 58)
Parents: Tom and Juliet
Marital status: Divorced

Children: Elliott, 15 March 1983
Family links with cricket: Father captained club side
Education: Harrow School
Qualifications: 5 O-levels, Junior Coaching Certificate
Jobs outside cricket: Sportsmaster at Claremont Prep School, Hastings. Owner of squash club
Off-season 1987–88: Looking after the squash courts. Short tour of Barbados
Overseas tours: With Derrick Robins' XI to Australasia 1980; part of England tour to New Zealand 1983–84
Overseas teams played for: Waverley CC, Sydney, Australia, 1976–77, 1977–78, 1979–80; Wellington, New Zealand, 1982–83 and 1983–84; Claremont, Cape Town, 1980–81, 1981–82
Cricketers particularly learnt from: Geoff Arnold, Imran Khan
Cricketers particularly admired: Ian Botham, Imran Khan
Other sports played: Squash, raquets, football, tennis, rugger
Injuries 1987: Small back injury
Relaxations: 'My son. Re-building my house.'
Extras: Public Schools Raquets Champion 1975. Had operation on back, April 1981, missing most of season, and was told by a specialist he would never play cricket again. First three wickets in first-class cricket were a hat-trick. Postponed wedding to make Test debut when called into England party on tour of New Zealand. Originally going to Somerset for 1984 season, but then remained with Sussex
Opinions on cricket: 'Four-day cricket. It will be interesting if it works this season. I think it will. I also believe that until we play 16 four-day matches against every other team, we will not see the best team winning the Championship.'
Best batting performance: 104* Sussex v Warwickshire, Edgbaston 1986
Best bowling performance: 7-74 Sussex v Northamptonshire, Eastbourne 1982

LAST SEASON: BATTING

	I.	N.O.	R.	H.S.	AV.
TEST					
1ST-CLASS	27	4	456	62	19.82
INT					
RAL	4	1	24	10*	8.00
NAT.W.	1	0	11	11	11.00
B & H	2	1	12	12	12.00

CAREER: BATTING

	I.	N.O.	R.	H.S.	AV.
TEST	2	1	12	8*	12.00
1ST-CLASS	149	32	2254	104*	19.26
INT					
RAL	35	14	259	49	12.33
NAT.W.	5	0	81	30	16.20
B & H	14	5	60	21	6.66

LAST SEASON: BOWLING

	O.	M.	R.	W.	AV.
TEST					
1ST-CLASS	455.2	86	1443	45	32.06
INT					
RAL	62	1	341	15	22.73
NAT.W.	24	5	61	5	12.20
B & H					

CAREER: BOWLING

	O.	M.	R.	W.	AV.
TEST	17	7	75	2	37.50
1ST-CLASS	2909.1	517	9727	341	28.52
INT					
RAL	520.1	18	2520	118	21.35
NAT.W.	101.4	15	330	16	20.62
B & H					

POLLARD, P.   Nottinghamshire

Full Name: Paul Pollard
Role: Left-hand bat, right-arm medium bowler
Born: 24 September 1968, Carlton, Nottinghamshire
County debut: 1987
1st-Class 50s scored: 1
1st-Class catches 1987: 4 (career 4)
Extras: Made debut for Nottinghamshire 2nd XI in 1985
Best batting performance: 59 Nottinghamshire v Lancashire, Old Trafford 1987

LAST SEASON: BATTING

	I.	N.O.	R.	H.S.	AV.
TEST					
1ST-CLASS	7	0	132	59	18.85
INT					
RAL					
NAT.W.					
B & H					

CAREER: BATTING

	zi.	n.o.	r.	h.s.	av.
TEST					
1ST-CLASS	7	0	132	59	18.85
INT					
RAL					
NAT.W.					
B & H					

---

128. Who captained South Africa in the unofficial Tests against Australia in 1987?

129. Which two brothers both scored centuries in both innings in the same match for Worcestershire v Hampshire, and when?

130. Who is the only man to captain England before even playing for his county?

131. Who is the only Middlesex player to have played for England before he had played for Middlesex?

PONT, I. L. Essex

Full Name: Ian Leslie Pont
Role: Right-hand bat, right-arm
fast-medium bowler, outfielder
Born: 28 August 1961, Brentwood
Height: 6' 3" **Weight:** 14st
Nickname: Pud, Puck, Pike, Ponty
County debut: 1982 (Nottinghamshire),
1985 (Essex)
1st-Class 5 w. in innings: 2
Places in bowling averages: 97th
av. 35.31
Strike rate 1987: 57.78 (career 57.78)
1st-Class catches 1987: 1 (career 3)
Parents: Duncan and Eileen
Marital status: Single
Family links with cricket: Brother
Keith retired from Essex CCC in
1986 after 16 years. Brother
Kelvin on Lord's ground-staff

Education: Brentwood School, Essex
Qualifications: 7 O-levels, 3 A-levels, NCA Cricket Coach, qualified art
historian
Jobs outside cricket: Sales executive for American Lettering Systems Co
Off-season 1987–88: Playing for Cambeltown, New South Wales
Overseas tours: Public Schools to India 1978–79 and Australia 1979–80; NCA
Young Cricketers to Canada 1980
Overseas teams played for: Bellville, Cape Town, 1981–82; Durban 1985–87;
Natal A, 1985–86
Cricketers particularly learnt from: Richard Hadlee, Bob White, John Lever,
Mike Bore
Cricketers particularly admired: Richard Hadlee, Wayne Daniel
Other sports played: Hockey, darts, javelin, baseball
Other sports followed: Watches golf, athletics, Manchester United FC
Relaxations: Impressionist paintings, particularly Monet, Manet, and Seurat
Extras: Spent time on Nottinghamshire staff before joining Essex. Also
appeared for Buckinghamshire. Took hat-trick in 2nd XI match v Gloucester-
shire, 1985. Has come close to breaking world record for throwing the cricket
ball. Took up the javelin with coaching from Fatima Whitbread's mother. Has
also had trials as a pitcher with New York Yankees baseball team
Opinions on cricket: 'Four-day cricket will prove to be a waste of time. Not
enough county wickets will be able to last four days – most wickets are
"result" wickets. The fourth day may prove to be a loss for the sponsors.

Sunday League or a new Saturday competition would or should be played in coloured clothing. Covered wickets ought to return.'

Best batting performance: 43 Essex v New Zealand, Chelmsford 1986
Best bowling performance: 5-103 Essex v Somerset, Taunton 1985

LAST SEASON: BATTING

	I.	N.O.	R.	H.S.	AV.
TEST					
1ST-CLASS	7	2	86	39	17.20
INT					
RAL	2	2	13	12*	–
NAT.W.					
B & H					

LAST SEASON: BOWLING

	O.	M.	R.	W.	AV.
TEST					
1ST-CLASS	183	19	671	19	35.31
INT					
RAL	21	1	53	3	17.66
NAT.W.					
B & H					

CAREER: BATTING

	I.	N.O.	R.	H.S.	AV.
TEST					
1ST-CLASS	27	8	255	43	13.42
INT					
RAL	2	2	13	12*	–
NAT.W.	1	1	7	7*	–
B & H	2	1	18	13*	18.00

CAREER: BOWLING

	O.	M.	R.	W.	AV.
TEST					
1ST-CLASS	443	56	1710	46	37.17
INT					
RAL	70	1	275	10	27.50
NAT.W.	21	2	79	1	79.00
B & H	26.5	6	101	1	101.00

POTTER, L.   Leicestershire

Full Name: Laurie Potter
Role: Right-hand bat, slow left-arm bowler, slip fielder
Born: 7 November 1962, Bexleyheath, Kent
Height: 6' 1" **Weight:** 13½st
Nickname: Potts, Liz, Lounge
County debut: 1981 (Kent), 1986 (Leicestershire)
1st-Class 50s scored: 20
1st-Class 100s scored: 4
One-Day 50s: 7
One-Day 100s: 2
Place in batting averages: 144th av. 25.06 (1986 183rd av. 20.18)
Place in bowling averages: —
(1986 66th av. 31.80)
1st-Class catches 1987: 22 (career 85)
Parents: Ronald Henry Ernest and Audrey Megan
Wife and date of marriage: Diana Frances, 28 September 1985
Family links with cricket: Father-in-law Kent 2nd XI scorer

Education: Kelmscott Senior High School, Perth, Western Australia
Qualifications: Australian leaving exams
Off-season 1987–88: Playing and coaching for Harmony CC, South Africa
Overseas tours: With Australian U-19 team to Pakistan 1981
Overseas teams played for: Australia U-19 team, West Perth CC, 1977–82; Griqualand West, 1984–85 and 1985–86 as captain; Harmony CC, South Africa 1987–88
Cricketers particularly learnt from: Norman O'Neill, Alan Beukas (Griqualand West), majority of senior players
Cricketers particularly admired: Derek Underwood, Alan Knott
Other sports played: Australian rules football, soccer, squash
Relaxations: Music, watching movies (cinema), reading, following sports
Extras: Captained Australia U-19 team to Pakistan 1981. Played for Young England v Young India 1981. Parents emigrated to Australia when he was 4. His mother wrote to Kent in 1978 asking for trial for him. Captained Young Australia as well as Young England. Decided to leave Kent after 1985 season and joined Leicestershire
Best batting performance: 165* Griqualand West v Border, East London 1984–85
Best bowling performance: 4-52 Griqualand West v Boland, Stellenbosch 1985–86

LAST SEASON: BATTING

	I.	N.O.	R.	H.S.	AV.
TEST					
1ST-CLASS	20	4	401	68	25.06
INT					
RAL	9	2	241	76	34.42
NAT.W.					
B & H	4	0	40	21	10.00

LAST SEASON: BOWLING

	O.	M.	R.	W.	AV.
TEST					
1ST-CLASS	53	9	186	5	37.20
INT					
RAL					
NAT.W.					
B & H	7	0	34	1	34.00

CAREER: BATTING

	I.	N.O.	R.	H.S.	AV.
TEST					
1ST-CLASS	151	15	3660	165*	26.91
INT					
RAL	53	4	1340	105	27.34
NAT.W.	5	0	122	45	24.40
B & H	11	0	275	112	25.00

CAREER: BOWLING

	O.	M.	R.	W.	AV.
TEST					
1ST-CLASS	806.3	202	2261	67	33.74
INT					
RAL	93.5	4	424	19	22.31
NAT.W.	14	3	35	1	35.00
B & H	32	2	179	3	59.66

132. In 1947, when Compton and Edrich scored 7355 runs during the English season, how many wickets did each take?

PRICHARD, P. J.   Essex

Full Name: Paul John Prichard
Role: Right-hand bat,
cover/mid-wicket fielder
Born: 7 January 1965, Brentwood
Height: 5' 10" **Weight:** 11st 7lbs
Nickname: Prich, Dilch,
Ditch, Pablo, Pilch
County debut: 1984
County cap: 1986
1000 runs in a season: 1
1st-Class 50s scored: 24
1st-Class 100s scored: 2
One-Day 50s: 4
One-Day 100s: 1
Place in batting averages: 84th
av. 33.38 (1986 91st av. 32.73)
1st-Class catches 1987: 3 (career 46)
Parents: Margaret and John
Wife: Alicia
Family links with cricket: Father played club cricket in Essex
Education: Brentwood County High School
Qualifications: NCA Senior Coaching Award
Jobs outside cricket: Worked for shipping company
Off-season 1987–88: Playing and coaching in Sydney
Overseas tours: Kingfishers tour of South Africa 1981
Overseas teams played for: VOB Cavaliers, Cape Town, 1981–82; Sutherland
CC, Sydney 1985–86, 1987–88
Cricketers particularly learnt from: All at Essex
Cricketers particularly admired: 'Too many to mention.'
Other sports played: Golf
Other sports followed: American football
Injuries 1987: Badly broken finger
Relaxations: 'Sailing my boat, listening to music.'
Best batting performance: 147* Essex v Nottinghamshire, Chelmsford 1986

LAST SEASON: BATTING

	I.	N.O.	R.	H.S.	AV.
TEST					
1ST-CLASS	16	3	434	72	33.38
INT					
RAL	3	0	6	4	2.00
NAT.W.					
B & H					

CAREER: BATTING

	I.	N.O.	R.	H.S.	AV.
TEST					
1ST-CLASS	123	12	3443	147*	31.01
INT					
RAL	23	3	569	103*	28.45
NAT.W.	6	0	173	94	28.83
B & H	9	1	203	52	25.37

PRIDGEON, A. P. — Worcestershire

Full Name: Alan Paul Pridgeon
Role: Right-hand bat, right-arm
medium bowler
Born: 22 February 1954, Wall
Heath, Staffordshire
Height: 6′ 3″ **Weight:** 13st 2lbs
Nickname: Pridge
County debut: 1972
County cap: 1980
50 wickets in a season: 6
1st-Class 50s scored: 1
1st-Class 5 w. in innings: 10
1st-Class 10 w. in match: 1
Place in bowling averages: 86th
av. 32.85 (1986 24th av. 23.66)
Strike rate 1987: 73.71 (career 67.54)
1st-Class catches 1987: 7 (career 79)
Parents: Albert Ernest and Sybil
Ruby
Wife and date of marriage: Jane, 7 October 1978
Children: Laura, 8 August 1983
Education: Summerhill Secondary Modern, Kingswinford, West Midlands
Qualifications: 6 CSEs, Qualified FA Coach, Qualified NCA Coach
Jobs outside cricket: Semi-professional footballer, salesman; has worked for
Manpower Commission
Cricketing superstitions or habits: 'Hate batting while Sylvester Clarke is
bowling.'
Overseas tours: Worcestershire CC to Barbados 1980
Overseas teams played for: Howick and Pakuranga, New Zealand, 1983–84

LAST SEASON: BATTING

	I.	N.O.	R.	H.S.	AV.
TEST					
1ST-CLASS	10	2	57	19	7.12
INT					
RAL					
NAT.W.	1	1	0	0*	
B & H	1	1	4	4*	

CAREER: BATTING

	I.	N.O.	R.	H.S.	AV.
TEST					
1ST-CLASS	205	80	1133	67	9.06
INT					
RAL	49	27	142	17	6.45
NAT.W.	10	7	38	13*	12.66
B & H	18	10	75	13*	9.37

LAST SEASON: BOWLING

	O.	M.	R.	W.	AV.
TEST					
1ST-CLASS	344	80	920	28	32.85
INT					
RAL	91	5	330	10	33.00
NAT.W.	17	5	41	4	10.25
B & H	32	4	100	2	50.00

CAREER: BOWLING

	O.	M.	R.	W.	AV.
TEST					
1ST-CLASS	5685.1	1176	16556	505	32.78
INT					
RAL	968.2	47	4360	134	32.53
NAT.W.	165.2	30	482	15	32.13
B & H	383.2	42	1504	32	47.00

Cricketers particularly learnt from: Viv Richards, Dennis Lillee, Norman Gifford

Cricketers particularly admired: Steve Perryman

Other sports played: Semi-professional footballer for Dudley Town FC, West Midlands League; golf, snooker, tennis

Other sports followed: Horse racing

Relaxations: Horse racing, taking dog (Muffin) for walks

Best batting performance: 67 Worcestershire v Warwickshire, Worcester 1984

Best bowling performance: 7-35 Worcestershire v Oxford University, Oxford 1976

PRINGLE, D. R. Essex

Full Name: Derek Raymond Pringle

Role: Right-hand bat, right-arm fast-medium bowler, 1st slip fielder

Born: 18 September 1958, Nairobi

Height: 6′ 5″ **Weight:** 15¾st

Nickname: Ignell, Suggs

County debut: 1978

County cap: 1982

Test debut: 1982

No. of Tests: 14

No. of One-Day Internationals: 13

50 wickets in a season: 4

1st-Class 50s scored: 29

1st-Class 100s scored: 7

1st-Class 5 w. in innings: 12

1st-Class 10 w. in match: 1

One-Day 50s: 19

Place in batting averages: 112th av. 29.37 (1986 175th av. 21.82)

Place in bowling averages: 46th av. 26.45 (1986 28th av. 24.07)

Strike rate 1987: 65.41 (career 60.87)

1st-Class catches 1987: 15 (career 106)

Parents: Donald James (deceased) and Doris May

Marital status: Single

Family links with cricket: Father represented Kenya and East Africa (played in World Cup 1975)

Education: St Mary's School, Nairobi; Felsted School, Essex; Cambridge University (Fitzwilliam College)

Qualifications: 8 O-levels, 3 A-levels, MA Cantab.

Jobs outside cricket: T-shirt designer

Off-season 1987–88: With England in World Cup. Cultural tour to Peru, Ecuador and Venezuela

Cricketing superstitions or habits: 'None now; too many ducks have seen to that.'

Overseas tours: With England Schools to India 1978–79; Oxbridge tour of Australia 1979–80; England to Australia and New Zealand 1982–83; England B tour to Sri Lanka 1986

Cricketers particularly learnt from: My father, Gordon Barker, 'Tonker' Taylor, Keith Fletcher

Cricketers particularly admired: 'Neil Foster for his flexible philosophy about bowling and life.'

Other sports played: Squash, golf

Other sports followed: Watches rugby union

Relaxations: 'Modern music, especially The Smiths, New Order, Billy Bragg and The The, photography, conchology, pub discussions over a pint of Adnams. Good novels: Kunderg, Naipaul, Garcia Marquez etc.'

Injuries 1987: Back injury and Achilles tendon strain

Extras: 'Took all ten wickets for Nairobi Schools U-13½ v Up Country Schools U-13½. Captain of Cambridge 1982 season. Extra in *Chariots of Fire*. Once went shark hunting with Chris Smith of Hampshire (a recklessly brave fellow) in the Maldive Islands.'

Opinions on cricket: 'If four-day cricket will allow more days off in order to mentally prepare oneself for each match, then I'm all for it. Uncovered wickets don't suit our batsmen so scrap that idea. Our spinners have also bowled far less than normal, so wet wickets don't always equal more spin. Inception of up-to-date technologies in order to reduce umpiring errors, as there is too much at stake (particularly at international level) to merely grin and accept bad decisions, i.e. off-the-field panel of 3 watching replays, electrode implants in ball, pads, bat etc, anything to aid the umpires who are now in a very high-pressure situation.'

Best batting performance: 127* Cambridge University v Worcestershire, Cambridge 1981

Best bowling performance: 7-32 Essex v Middlesex, Chelmsford 1983

LAST SEASON: BATTING

	I.	N.O.	R.	H.S.	AV.
TEST					
1ST-CLASS	33	9	705	84*	29.37
INT					
RAL	11	1	148	40*	14.80
NAT.W.	3	1	81	63*	40.50
B & H	3	0	42	37	14.00

LAST SEASON: BOWLING

	O.	M.	R.	W.	AV.
TEST					
1ST-CLASS	599.4	155	1457	55	26.49
INT					
RAL	75.2	5	372	12	31.00
NAT.W.	26	2	85	1	85.00
B & H	36.5	3	127	4	31.75

CAREER: BATTING

	I.	N.O.	R.	H.S.	AV.
TEST	25	3	413	63	18.77
1ST-CLASS	247	52	5627	127*	28.85
INT	11	4	183	49*	26.14
RAL	63	16	1339	81*	28.48
NAT.W.	18	4	339	63*	24.21
B & H	39	7	977	68	30.53

CAREER: BOWLING

	O.	M.	R.	W.	AV.
TEST	401.5	85	1128	29	38.89
1ST-CLASS	4021.4	990	10818	407	26.57
INT	120.2	11	575	13	44.23
RAL	542.2	25	2586	85	30.42
NAT.W.	190.3	37	579	24	24.12
B & H	396.2	45	1405	56	25.08

Full Name: Meyrick Wayne Pringle
Role: Right-hand bat, right-arm
fast bowler, all rounder
Born: 22 June 1966, Adelaide,
South Africa
Height: 6′ 4″ **Weight:** 13st 4lbs
Nickname: Perky, Magnum
County debut: 1987
1st-Class catches 1987: 0 (career 1)
Parents: Errol and Sheila
Marital status: Single
Education: Dale College; Kingswood
College, South Africa
Qualifications: Matriculation
Jobs outside cricket: Professional
cricket coach
Off-season 1987–88: Playing
cricket in South Africa
Cricketing superstitions or habits: Left
pad on first, Nelsons 111, 222 etc
Overseas tours: Kingswood College to England, Holland and Channel Islands
1984
Overseas teams played for: Orange Free State 1986–87
Cricketers particularly learnt from: Percy Davis
Cricketers particularly admired: Imran Khan, Richard Hadlee, Malcolm
Marshall
Other sports played: Rugby, squash
Other sports followed: Rugby, tennis, golf
Injuries 1987: Shin strains

LAST SEASON: BATTING

	I.	N.O.	R.	H.S.	AV.
TEST					
1ST-CLASS	1	0	12	12	12.00
INT					
RAL					
NAT.W.					
B & H					

LAST SEASON: BOWLING

	O.	M.	R.	W.	AV.
TEST					
1ST-CLASS	16	4	45	2	22.50
INT					
RAL					
NAT.W.					
B & H					

CAREER: BATTING

	I.	N.O.	R.	H.S.	AV.
TEST					
1ST-CLASS	4	1	41	26	13.66
INT					
RAL					
NAT.W.					
B & H					

CAREER: BOWLING

	O.	M.	R.	W.	AV.
TEST					
1ST-CLASS	49.4	6	180	4	45.00
INT					
RAL					
NAT.W.					
B & H					

Relaxations: Fishing, stamp collecting, watching videos, music
Extras: Opened bowling for South African Schools 1983 and 1984; opened bowling for Orange Free State in Currie Cup Competition 1986–87
Opinions on cricket: 'Sportsmanship.'
Best batting performance: 26 Orange Free State v Northern Transvaal, Bloemfontein 1985–86
Best bowling performance: 2-45 Sussex v Pakistanis, Hove 1987

PRINGLE, N. J. Somerset

Full Name: Nicholas John Pringle
Role: Right-hand bat, right-arm medium bowler, cover fielder
Born: 20 September 1966, Weymouth, Dorset
Height: 5′ 11″ **Weight:** 12st
Nickname: Pring
County debut: 1986
1st-Class 50s scored: 2
Place in batting averages: 172nd av. 20.41
1st-Class catches 1987: 1 (career 1)
Parents: Marion and Guy Pease
Marital status: Single
Education: Priorswood Comprehensive, Taunton; Taunton School
Qualifications: 8 O-levels, 1 A-level. NCA Coaching Award
Off-season 1987–88: In New Zealand
Overseas tours: Taunton School to Sri Lanka 1983
Overseas teams played for: Mossman CC, Sydney, 1986–87
Cricketers particularly learnt from: Martin Crowe, Don Wilson, John Jameson
Cricketers particularly admired: Martin Crowe, Richard Hadlee, Viv Richards, Greg Chappell
Other sports played: Football
Other sports followed: Rugby, American football, anything except horse racing
Relaxations: Gardeners Arms, Taunton, reading, watching videos and sport
Injuries 1987: Dislocated shoulder
Extras: On Lord's ground staff 1986. Called up from there by Somerset for his debut
Opinions on cricket: 'I think that there should be cricket apprenticeships,

similar to that of the Lord's groundstaff around the counties. This way young cricketers learn about other aspects of the game and perform duties that in years to come they can look back at, and not take things for granted, which these days, with all the money and sponsorship involved in cricket, is very easy to do. I would like to see four-day cricket, 16 games a year, on uncovered wickets without the bowlers run-ups being covered.'

Best batting performance: 79 Somerset v Warwickshire, Edgbaston 1987
Best bowling performance: 2-35 Somerset v Glamorgan, Weston-super-Mare 1987

LAST SEASON: BATTING

	I.	N.O.	R.	H.S.	AV.
TEST					
1ST-CLASS	18	1	347	79	20.41
INT					
RAL	3	1	37	22	18.50
NAT.W.					
B & H					

LAST SEASON: BOWLING

	O.	M.	R.	W.	AV.
TEST					
1ST-CLASS	93	14	341	4	85.25
INT					
RAL	3	0	18	0	–
NAT.W.					
B & H					

CAREER: BATTING

	I.	N.O.	R.	H.S.	AV.
TEST					
1ST-CLASS	20	1	368	79	19.36
INT					
RAL	3	1	37	22	18.50
NAT.W.					
B & H					

CAREER: BOWLING

	O.	M.	R.	W.	AV.
TEST					
1ST-CLASS	103	14	389	4	97.25
INT					
RAL	3	0	18	0	–
NAT.W.					
B & H					

RADFORD, N. V.   Worcestershire

Full Name: Neal Victor Radford
Role: Right-hand bat, right-arm fast-medium bowler, gully fielder
Born: 7 June 1957, Luanshya, Zambia
Height: 5′ 11″ **Weight:** 12st 4lbs
Nickname: Radiz, Vic
County debut: 1980 (Lancashire), 1985 (Worcestershire)
County cap: 1985 (Worcestershire)
Test debut: 1986
No. of Tests: 2
50 wickets in a season: 2
1st-Class 50s scored: 3
1st-Class 5 w. in innings: 29
1st-Class 10 w. in match: 5
Place in batting averages: 243rd av. 11.58 (1986 217th av. 13.69)

Place in bowling averages: 10th av. 20.81 (1986 37th av. 26.71)
Strike rate 1987: 40.83 (career 48.94)
1st-Class catches 1987: 14 (career 74)
Parents: Edith Joyce and Victor Reginald
Wife: Lynne
Family links with cricket: Brother Wayne pro for Gowerton (SWCA) and Glamorgan 2nd XI. Also played for Orange Free State in Currie Cup
Education: Athlone Boys High School, Johannesburg
Qualifications: Matriculation and university entrance. NCA Advanced Coach
Jobs outside cricket: Auditor
Off-season 1987–88: Three months in South Africa playing for Transvaal, and three months with England in New Zealand and Australia
Cricketing superstitions or habits: 'Nelson and left pad on first.'
Overseas teams played for: Transvaal 1979–87; South African Schools XI; South African Army
Overseas tours: With England to New Zealand and Australia 1988
Cricketers particularly admired: Vincent van der Bijl
Other sports played: Golf, squash
Other sports followed: 'All sports.'
Relaxations: Music, TV, films
Extras: Only bowler to take 100 first-class wickets in 1985. First player to 100 wickets in 1987. Took most first-class wickets in 1987 with 109
Opinions on cricket: 'Play too much cricket! A cut down will result in better standard all round. Have a day off for travelling as the majority of injuries and stiffness are caused by travelling hundreds of miles immediately after matches.'
Best batting performance: 76* Lancashire v Derbyshire, Blackpool 1981
Best bowling performance: 9-70 Worcestershire v Somerset, Worcester 1986

LAST SEASON: BATTING

	I.	N.O.	R.	H.S.	AV.
TEST					
1ST-CLASS	21	4	197	31	11.58
INT					
RAL	5	1	62	41*	15.50
NAT.W.	1	0	37	37	37.00
B & H	3	1	18	9*	9.00

CAREER: BATTING

	I.	N.O.	R.	H.S.	AV.
TEST	3	1	13	12*	6.50
1ST-CLASS	160	38	1970	76*	16.14
INT					
RAL	41	20	409	48*	19.47
NAT.W.	7	2	82	37	16.40
B & H	12	4	95	29*	11.87

LAST SEASON: BOWLING

	O.	M.	R.	W.	AV.
TEST					
1ST-CLASS	741.5	125	2269	109	20.81
INT					
RAL	115.4	3	534	25	21.36
NAT.W.	15	0	67	3	22.33
B & H	49.4	5	148	8	18.50

CAREER: BOWLING

	O.	M.	R.	W.	AV.
TEST	63	7	219	3	73.00
1ST-CLASS	4513.1	879	14271	558	25.57
INT					
RAL	444	22	2005	89	22.52
NAT.W.	136.3	20	426	23	18.52
B & H	173	22	613	19	32.26

RADLEY, C. T. — Middlesex

Full Name: Clive Thornton Radley
Role: Right-hand bat, leg-break bowler
Born: 13 May 1944, Hertford
Height: 5′ 10″ **Weight:** 12st
Nickname: Radders
County debut: 1964
County cap: 1967
Benefit: 1977 (£26,000)
Testimonial: 1987
Test debut: 1977–78
No. of Tests: 8
No. of One-Day Internationals: 4
1000 runs in a season: 16
1st-Class 50s scored: 139
1st-Class 100s scored: 45
1st-Class 200s scored: 1
One-Day 50s: 57
One-Day 100s: 7
Place in batting averages: 58th av. 37.30 (1986 109th av. 29.33)
1st-Class catches 1987: 4 (career 517)
Parents: Laura and Arthur (deceased)
Wife and date of marriage: Linda, 22 September 1973
Children: Louise, 18 September 1978; Paul Craig Thornton, 26 July 1980
Family links with cricket: Father played club cricket
Education: King Edward VI Grammar School, Norwich
Jobs outside cricket: Has coached in South Africa and Australia
Overseas tours: England to Pakistan and New Zealand 1977–78; Australia 1978–79

LAST SEASON: BATTING

	I.	N.O.	R.	H.S.	AV.
TEST					
1ST-CLASS	13	3	373	72	37.30
INT					
RAL	5	0	114	56	22.80
NAT.W.	2	0	59	31	29.50
B & H	3	0	33	30	11.00

LAST SEASON: BOWLING

	O.	M.	R.	W.	AV.
TEST					
1ST-CLASS					
INT					
RAL					
NAT.W.					
B & H	0.3	0	1	0	–

CAREER: BATTING

	I.	N.O.	R.	H.S.	AV.
TEST	10	0	481	158	48.10
1ST-CLASS	870	134	25960	200	35.27
INT	4	1	250	117*	83.33
RAL	251	26	6650	133*	29.55
NAT.W.	56	6	1573	105*	31.46
B & H	71	14	1858	121*	32.59

CAREER: BOWLING

	O.	M.	R.	W.	AV.
TEST					
1ST-CLASS	1 44	0 10	160	8	20.00
INT					
RAL	3.4	1	17	1	17.00
NAT.W.					
B & H	0.3	0	1	0	–

Cricketers particularly learnt from: Ken Barrington
Cricketers particularly admired: Bob Willis
Other sports: Squash, golf
Extras: Played for Norfolk under former Middlesex and England player W. J. Edrich, who eased his way to Middlesex. Shared in the 6th wicket partnership record for Middlesex, 227 with F. Titmus v South Africans at Lord's in 1965. First fielder to hold 50 catches in JPL. Gold Award winner in 1983 Benson and Hedges Final. Retired at end of 1987 season
Best batting performance: 200 Middlesex v Northamptonshire, Uxbridge 1985
Best bowling performance: 2-38 Middlesex v Glamorgan, Cardiff 1985

RAMPRAKASH, M.   Middlesex

Full Name: Mark Ramprakash
Role: Right-hand bat
Born: 5 September 1969, Bushey, Herts
Height: 5′ 9″ **Weight:** 11½st
Nickname: Ramps
County debut: 1987
1st-Class 50s scored: 2
One-Day 50s: 1
1st-Class catches 1987: 6 (career 6)
Parents: Jennifer and Deo
Marital status: Single
Family links with cricket: Father played club cricket in Guyana
Education: Gayton High School; Harrow Weald College
Qualifications: 5 O-levels
Off-season 1987–88: Studying at college
Cricketing superstitions or habits: Left pad on first
Overseas tours: England U-19s to Sri Lanka 1987
Cricketers particularly learnt from: Jack Robertson, Don Bennett
Cricketers particularly admired: All the great all-rounders
Other sports played: Football
Other sports followed: Snooker, tennis
Injuries 1987: Elbow of throwing arm
Relaxations: Watching good comedy films and westerns
Extras: Won Best U-15 Schoolboy of 1985 by Cricket Society. Won Gray Nicholls Award for Best Young Cricketer 1986

Opinions on cricket: 'Wickets should be covered at all times.'
Best batting performance: 71 Middlesex v Essex, Chelmsford 1987

LAST SEASON: BATTING

	I.	N.O.	R.	H.S.	AV.
TEST					
1ST-CLASS	14	3	321	71	29.18
INT					
RAL	7	1	139	82*	23.16
NAT.W.					
B & H					

CAREER: BATTING

	I.	N.O.	R.	H.S.	AV.
TEST					
1ST-CLASS	14	3	321	71	29.18
INT					
RAL	7	1	139	82*	23.16
NAT.W.					
B & H					

RANDALL, D. W.   Nottinghamshire

Full Name: Derek William Randall
Role: Right-hand bat, cover fielder
Born: 24 February 1951, Retford, Nottinghamshire
Height: 5′ 8½″ **Weight:** 11st
Nickname: Arkle, Rags
County debut: 1972
County cap: 1973
Benefit: 1983 (£42,000)
Test debut: 1976–77
No. of Tests: 47
No. of One-Day Internationals: 49
1000 runs in a season: 10
1st-Class 50s scored: 127
1st-Class 100s scored: 37
1st-Class 200s scored: 2
One-Day 50s: 49
One-Day 100s: 5
Place in batting averages: 71st
av. 35.00 (1986 161st av. 23.47)
1st-Class catches 1987: 18 (career 292)
Parents: Frederick and Mavis
Wife and date of marriage: Elizabeth, September 1973
Children: Simon, June 1977
Family links with cricket: Father played local cricket – 'tried to bowl fast off a long run and off the wrong foot too!'
Education: Sir Frederick Milner Secondary Modern School, Retford
Qualifications: ONC mechanical engineering, mechanical draughtsman
Jobs outside cricket: Coaching
Overseas tours: India, Sri Lanka and Australia 1976–77; Pakistan and New

Zealand 1977–78; Australia 1978–79, Australia and India 1979–80; Australia and New Zealand 1982–83; New Zealand and Pakistan 1983–84
Overseas teams played for: North Perth, Australia
Cricketers particularly learnt from: Sir Gary Sobers, Tom Graveney (boyhood idol), Reg Simpson
Other sports played: Football, squash, golf
Relaxations: Listening to varied selection of tapes. Family man
Extras: Played in one John Player League match in 1971 for Nottinghamshire. Before joining Nottinghamshire staff, played for Retford CC in the Bassetlaw League, and helped in Championship wins of 1968 and 1969. One of the finest fielders in cricket. Scored 174 in Centenary Test v Australia 1977. Renowned for his untidiness in the dressing room. Drinks endless cups of coffee during a game
Best batting performance: 209 Nottinghamshire v Middlesex, Trent Bridge 1979
Best bowling performance: 3-15 Nottinghamshire v MCC, Lord's 1982

LAST SEASON: BATTING

	I.	N.O.	R.	H.S.	AV.
TEST					
1ST-CLASS	20	1	665	133	35.00
INT					
RAL	8	3	418	123	83.60
NAT.W.	3	1	50	22	25.00
B & H	4	1	115	45	38.33

LAST SEASON: BOWLING

	O.	M.	R.	W.	AV.
TEST					
1ST-CLASS					
INT					
RAL					
NAT.W.					
B & H					

CAREER: BATTING

	I.	N.O.	R.	H.S.	AV.
TEST	79	5	2470	174	33.37
1ST-CLASS	567	53	19499	209	37.93
INT	45	5	1067	88	26.68
RAL	179	25	4883	123	31.70
NAT.W.	32	3	705	75	24.31
B & H	70	11	2047	103*	34.69

CAREER: BOWLING

	O.	M.	R.	W.	AV.
TEST	2	0	3	0	–
1ST-CLASS	69.5	5	380	12	31.66
INT	0.2	0	2	1	2.00
RAL	0.5	0	9	0	–
NAT.W.	1.	0	3	0	–
B & H	2.5	0	5	0	–

133. Who captained the South African tourists to England in 1947?

134. How many Tests did Michael Holding play: 49, 60 or 93?

135. What is the commonest English surname for Test cricketers after Smith?

REDPATH, I. Essex

Full Name: Ian Redpath
Role: Right-hand bat, right-arm
medium bowler, cover fielder
Born: 12 September 1965, Basildon
Height: 5′ 9″ **Weight:** 11st 7lbs
Nickname: Redders, Frosty
County debut: 1987
Place in batting averages: 242nd
av. 11.63
1st-Class catches 1987: 2 (career 2)
Parents: Bill and Sheila
Marital status: Single
Family links with cricket: Father
was a useful club player
Education: Woodlands School,
Basildon; Bastable Sixth Form
Qualifications: 6 O-levels,
1 A-level, NCA Senior Coaching
Award

Jobs outside cricket: Worked for Nat West Bank during one winter
Off-season 1987: Playing club cricket in Melbourne
Overseas tours: NCA U-19 International competition in Holland 1983
Overseas teams played for: Penrith CC, Sydney 1985–86 and 1986–87
Cricketers particularly learnt from: Keith Fletcher, John Lever and all at
Essex
Cricketers particularly admired: Graham Gooch, Imran Khan
Other sports played: Squash, football and most others
Other sports followed: Football
Injuries 1987: Split webbing between fingers
Relaxations: Music, films, sleeping and listening to wise words from Don
Topley
Extras: Awarded 2nd XI cap in 1986. Essex U-25 captain 1987. Young Player
of the Year 1986. Won Len Newbury–Gray Nicolls Most Improved Player
Award 1984. Played for England Schools U-15 and U-19

LAST SEASON: BATTING

	I.	N.O.	R.	H.S.	AV.
TEST					
1ST-CLASS	12	1	128	46	11.63
INT					
RAL	1	1	11	11*	–
NAT.W.					
B & H					

CAREER: BATTING

	I.	N.O.	R.	H.S.	AV.
TEST					
1ST-CLASS	12	1	128	46	11.63
INT					
RAL	1	1	11	11*	–
NAT.W.					
B & H					

Opinions on circket: 'Believe 1st XI and 2nd XI Championships can be altered so that the format is more suitable for players, officials and spectators.'
Best batting performance: 46 Essex v Northamptonshire, Ilford 1987

REEVE, D. A. Sussex

Full Name: Dermot Alexander Reeve
Role: Right-hand bat, right-arm fast-medium bowler
Born: 2 April 1963, Hong Kong
Height: 6′ 0″ **Weight:** 11st 7lbs
Nickname: Ears
County debut: 1983
County cap: 1986
50 wickets in a season: 2
1st-Class 50s scored: 11
1st-Class 100s scored: 1
1st-Class 5 w. in innings: 5
Place in batting averages: 39th av. 40.40 (1986 141st av. 25.58)
Place in bowling averages: 67th av. 29.52 (1986 40th av. 27.13)
Strike rate 1987: 64.28 (career 62.67)
1st-Class catches 1987: 14 (career 51)
Parents: Monica and Alexander James
Wife and date of marriage: Julie, 20 December 1986
Family links with cricket: Father captain of school XI, brother Mark an improving club cricketer
Education: King George V School, Kowloon, Hong Kong
Qualifications: 7 O-levels
Overseas tours: Hong Kong tour to Malaysia and Singapore 1980; Hong Kong British Forces tour to Malaysia 1982; MCC tour to Holland and Denmark 1983
Overseas teams played for: Claremont-Cottesloe CC, Western Australia, 1982–83; Mount Lawley CC, Perth, 1985–86
Cricketers particularly learnt from: Don Wilson, David Clinton
Cricketers particularly admired: Ian Botham, Peter Willey, Paul Parker, J. Middleton (ex-Hong Kong pace bowler)
Other sports played: Golf, volleyball
Other sports followed: Football and most sports
Relaxations: Music, movies, sleeping in
Extras: Formerly on Lord's groundstaff. Represented Hong Kong in the ICC Trophy competition June 1982. Hong Kong Cricketer of the Year 1980–81.

Hong Kong's Cricket Sports Personality of the Year 1981. Man of the Match in 1986 NatWest final

Opinions on cricket: 'Four-day cricket on covered wickets, 100 overs a day, 16 matches. More one-day internationals in England.'

Best batting performance: 119 Sussex v Surrey, Guildford 1984

Best bowling performance: 7-37 Sussex v Lancashire, Lytham 1987

LAST SEASON) BATTING

	I.	N.O.	R.	H.S.	AV.
TEST					
1ST-CLASS	23	8	606	87*	40.40
INT					
RAL	7	0	62	21	8.85
NAT.W.	1	1	26	26*	
B & H	3	3	38	30*	

LAST SEASON: BOWLING

	O.	M.	R.	W.	AV.
TEST					
1ST-CLASS	450	108	1240	42	29.52
INT					
RAL	73.5	1	357	6	59.50
NAT.W.	23	3	89	1	89.00
B & H	19	3	79	5	15.80

CAREER: BATTING

	I.	N.O.	R.	H.S.	AV.
TEST					
1ST-CLASS	101	31	1761	119	25.15
INT					
RAL	28	10	180	21	10.00
NAT.W.	7	5	63	26*	31.50
B & H	10	4	103	30*	17.16

CAREER: BOWLING

	O.	M.	R.	W.	AV.
TEST					
1ST-CLASS	2496.3	648	6728	239	28.15
INT					
RAL	393	11	1855	69	26.88
NAT.W.	123.5	27	621	16	38.81
B & H	127.4	14	569	16	35.56

RHODES, S. J.   Worcestershire

Full Name: Steven John Rhodes
Role: Right-hand bat, wicket-keeper
Born: 17 June 1964, Bradford
Height: 5′ 8″ **Weight:** 11st 9lbs
Nickname: Wilf, Bumpy
County debut: 1981 (Yorkshire), 1985 (Worcestershire)
1st-Class 50s scored: 9
One-Day 50s: 1
Place in batting averages: 158th av. 22.66 (1986 105th av. 29.94)
Parents: Bill and Norma
Marital status: Single
Family links with cricket: Father played for Nottinghamshire 1961–64
Education: Bradford Moor Junior School; Lapage St Middle; Carlton-Bolling Comprehensive
Qualifications: 4 O-levels, cricket coaching certificate

Jobs outside cricket: Trainee manager in sports retailer in winters of 1980–81 and 1981–82. Cucumber picker in Queensland
Off-season 1987–88: Coaching and playing overseas
Cricketing superstitions or habits: 'I like to make sure I am not last out of the changing room when fielding.'
Overseas teams played for: Past Brothers Cricket Club, Bundaberg, Queensland, Australia, 1982–83 and 1983–84, and Bundaberg Cricket Association
Cricketers particularly learnt from: 'Phil Carrick, Doug Padgett, Kapil Dev and my father.'
Cricketers particularly admired: Alan Knott ('seemed to have lots of time with his keeping')
Other sports played: Golf
Other sports followed: Rugby league (Bradford Northern)
Extras: Played for Young England v Young Australia in 1983. Youngest wicket-keeper to play for Yorkshire. Holds record for most victims in an innings for Young England. Played for England Schools U-15s. Released by Yorkshire to join Worcestershire at end of 1984 season
Opinions on cricket: 'I think that there is too much cricket in the English cricket season and it should be reduced. I also don't agree with uncovered wickets. Also keepers shouldn't have to carry the batsman's helmet between overs.'
Best batting performance: 80 Worcestershire v Leicestershire, Worcester 1987

LAST SEASON: BATTING

	I.	N.O.	R.	H.S.	AV.
TEST					
1ST-CLASS	31	7	544	80	22.66
INT					
RAL	9	4	156	39	31.20
NAT.W.	1	0	1	1	1.00
B & H	4	1	98	51*	32.66

LAST SEASON: WICKET KEEPING

	C.	ST.		
TEST				
1ST-CLASS	51	6		
INT				
RAL	20	4		
NAT.W.	4	1		
B & H	11	–		

CAREER: BATTING

	I.	N.O.	R.	H.S.	AV.
TEST					
1ST-CLASS	104	35	1924	80	27.88
INT					
RAL	37	9	674	46	24.07
NAT.W.	7	4	68	32*	22.66
B & H	12	3	165	51*	18.33

CAREER: WICKET KEEPING

	C.	ST.		
TEST				
1ST-CLASS	175	20		
INT				
RAL	45	12		
NAT.W.	13	2		
B & H	22	4		

136. Who was the first man to score 10,000 Test runs?

RICE, C. E. B.   Nottinghamshire

Full Name: Clive Edward Butler Rice
Role: Right-hand bat, right-arm fast-medium bowler, slip fielder
Born: 23 July 1949, Johannesburg, South Africa
Height: 6' 0" **Weight:** 13st 3lbs
Nickname: Ricey
County debut: 1975
County cap: 1975
Benefit: 1982 (South Africa), 1985 (England)
1000 runs in a season: 13
50 wickets in a season: 4
1st-Class 50s scored: 126
1st-Class 100s scored: 42
1st-Class 200s scored: 3
1st-Class 5 w. in innings: 20
1st-Class 10 w. in match: 1
One-Day 50s: 59
One-Day 100s: 7

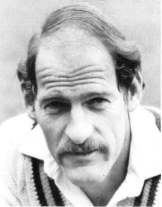

Place in batting averages: 18th av. 45.95 (1986 27th av. 44.72)
Place in bowling averages: 57th av. 28.57 (1986 31st av. 25.25)
Strike rate 1987: 66.10 (career 51.22)
1st-Class catches 1987: 26 (career 372 + 1 stumping)
Parents: Patrick and Angela
Wife and date of marriage: Susan Elizabeth, 28 February 1975
Children: Jackie Elizabeth, 27 June 1981; Mark Richard, 11 August 1983
Family links with cricket: Grandfather, Phillip Syndercombe Bower, played for Repton and Oxford University. Brother, Richard Patrick Butler Rice, selected for Transvaal B but unavailable because of university exams. Brother, John Cromwell Rice, captain of school 1st XI
Education: St John's College and Damelin College, Johannesburg; Natal University, Pietermaritzburg
Jobs outside cricket: Director of companies
Off-season 1987–88: Playing in South Africa for Transvaal
Cricketing superstitions or habits: '111, 222 or 333 on scoreboard.'
Overseas tours: World Team in World Series Cricket, Australia 1978–79
Overseas teams played for: World Series Cricket; Transvaal; Bedfordview CC, Johannesburg
Cricketers particularly learnt from: Don Mackay-Coghill, Ali Bacher, Graeme Pollock

Cricketers particularly admired: Mike Procter, Graeme Pollock, Richard Hadlee, Dennis Lillee

Other sports followed: English football, rugby, motor racing

Injuries 1987: 'Old age'

Relaxations: Reading, listening to music, studying stock markets

Extras: Writes for local South African newspapers. Captain of Bedfordview CC, Johannesburg. Made debut for Transvaal in 1969. Professional for Ramsbottom in Lancashire League, 1973. Originally appointed captain of Nottinghamshire in 1978 but was at first relieved of his appointment after signing for World Series Cricket. Reappointed for 1979. Played three 'Super-tests' for WSC. Was sponsored at 5 rands (£2.77) a run, 50 rands (£27) a wicket and 100 rands (£55) a catch in the 1980–81 Currie Cup competition in South Africa. Wisden Cricketer of the Year 1981. South African Players' Player 1985–86. Most runs in John Player League in a season: 814 in 1977 and equalled bowling record with 34 wickets. Highest score for Transvaal in Datsun Shield, 169 v Griqualand West. Highest score for Nottinghamshire in John Player League, 120 v Glamorgan. Winner of Silk Cut Challenge all-rounders competition 1984, 1985 and 1987. Hat-trick for South Africa v Australians 1985–86. Led Nottinghamshire to County Championship and NatWest Trophy in 1987. Played for MCC in Bicentenary Test and won the fielding award. Retired at the end of 1987 season

Opinions on cricket: 'We need quality cricket and not quantity for England to perform better. Uncovered wickets are a waste of time, and don't help develop cricketers in any way.'

Best batting performance: 246 Nottinghamshire v Sussex, Hove 1976

Best bowling performance: 7-62 Transvaal v Western Province, Johannesburg 1975–76

LAST SEASON: BATTING

	I.	N.O.	R.	H.S.	AV.
TEST					
1ST-CLASS	32	8	1103	138	45.95
INT					
RAL	11	3	329	84	42.12
NAT.W.	4	0	129	63	32.25
B & H	4	0	76	64	19.00

LAST SEASON: BOWLING

	O.	M.	R.	W.	AV.
TEST					
1ST-CLASS	308.3	90	800	28	28.57
INT					
RAL	72.3	1	351	14	25.07
NAT.W.	47	13	152	7	21.71
B & H	28.5	2	124	1	124.00

CAREER: BATTING

	I.	N.O.	R.	H.S.	AV.
TEST					
1ST-CLASS	697	112	24067	246	30.65
INT					
RAL	180	32	6265	120*	42.33
NAT.W.	28	2	580	71	22.30
B & H	58	7	1761	130*	34.52

CAREER: BOWLING

	O.	M.	R.	W.	AV.
TEST					
1ST-CLASS	7274.3	1946	19072	852	22.38
INT					
RAL	934	52	4215	184	22.90
NAT.W.	227	36	772	33	23.39
B & H	458.1	60	1590	74	21.48

RICHARDS, C. J. Surrey

Full Name: Clifton James Richards
Role: Right-hand bat, wicket-keeper
Born: 10 August 1958, Penzance
Height: 5′ 11″ **Weight:** 11st 8lbs
Nickname: Jack
County debut: 1976
County cap: 1978
Benefit: 1988
Test debut: 1986–87
No. of Tests: 6
No. of One-Day Internationals: 21
1000 runs in a season: 1
1st-Class 50s scored: 31
1st-Class 100s scored: 7
One-Day 50s: 5
One-Day 100s: 2
Place in batting averages: 61st
av. 36.90 (1986 46th av. 40.24)
Parents: Clifton and Elizabeth June
Wife: Birgitta, 27 September 1980
Family links with cricket: Father a member of Penzance CC and Surrey CCC
Education: Humphrey Davy Grammar School, Penzance

LAST SEASON: BATTING

	I.	N.O.	R.	H.S.	AV.
TEST	2	0	8	6	4.00
1ST-CLASS	24	6	730	172*	40.55
INT	2	0	16	16	8.00
RAL	10	0	378	113	37.80
NAT.W.	1	0	27	27	27.00
B & H	5	2	63	28*	21.00

CAREER: BATTING

	I.	N.O.	R.	H.S.	AV.
TEST	9	0	272	133	30.22
1ST-CLASS	334	82	6836	172*	27.12
INT	15	2	140	50	10.76
RAL	102	24	1491	113	19.11
NAT.W.	17	5	335	105*	27.91
B & H	33	9	349	45	14.54

LAST SEASON: BOWLING

	O.	M.	R.	W.	AV.
TEST					
1ST-CLASS					
INT					
RAL					
NAT.W.					
B & H					

CAREER: BOWLING

	O.	M.	R.	W.	AV.
TEST					
1ST-CLASS	43	3	198	5	39.60
INT					
RAL					
NAT.W.					
B & H					

LAST SEASON: WICKET KEEPING

	C.	ST.			
TEST	2	–			
1ST-CLASS	66	7			
INT	2	–			
RAL	8	3			
NAT.W.	1	–			
B & H	6	–			

CAREER: WICKET KEEPING

	C.	ST.			
TEST	17	1			
1ST-CLASS	509	71			
INT	16	1			
RAL	86	36			
NAT.W.	30	5			
B & H	45	5			

Qualifications: 7 O-levels
Jobs outside cricket: Trainee electrical engineer, apprentice draughtsman
Off-season 1987–88: Touring with England in New Zealand and Australia
Cricketing superstitions or habits: Always last out of the dressing room when fielding
Overseas tours: Australia with Derrick Robins' U-23 XI in 1979–80; Far East with Surrey CCC in 1978–79; England to India 1981–82; New Zealand and Australia 1988
Overseas teams played for: Klaas Vervelde XI, 1981
Other sports played: Tennis, golf, rugby, skiing, ice-skating, sailing
Other sports followed: Most sports, especially American and other foreign sports
Relaxations: Reading, television, driving
Best batting performance: 172* Surrey v Kent, The Oval 1987
Best bowling performance: 2-42 Surrey v Somerset, The Oval 1985

RICKETTS, C. I. O. Sussex

Full Name: Courtney Ian Oswald Ricketts
Role: Right-hand bat, slow left-arm bowler
Born: 26 April 1965, Kennington
County debut: 1987
1st-Class catches 1987: 1 (career 1)
Education: St Andrews Technical College
Extras: Recruited from Harringey Cricket College. Released by Sussex at end of 1987 season
Best batting performance: 29 Sussex v Worcestershire, Worcester 1987
Best bowling performance: 2-40 Sussex v Worcestershire, Worcester 1987

LAST SEASON: BATTING

	I.	N.O.	R.	H.S.	AV.
TEST					
1ST-CLASS	1	0	29	29	29.00
INT					
RAL	2	0	10	9	5.00
NAT.W.					
B & H					

LAST SEASON: BOWLING

	O.	M.	R.	W.	AV.
TEST					
1ST-CLASS	71.4	8	253	5	50.60
INT					
RAL	11	0	74	1	74.00
NAT.W.	4	1	11	0	–
B & H	22	2	67	2	33.50

CAREER: BATTING

	I.	N.O.	R.	H.S.	AV.
TEST					
1ST-CLASS	1	0	29	29	29.00
INT					
RAL	2	0	10	9	5.00
NAT.W.					
B & H					

CAREER: BOWLING

	O.	M.	R.	W.	AV.
TEST					
1ST-CLASS	71.4	8	253	5	50.60
INT					
RAL	11	0	74	1	74.00
NAT.W.	4	1	11	0	–
B & H	22	2	67	2	33.50

RIPLEY, D.   Northamptonshire

Full Name: David Ripley
Role: Right-hand bat, wicket-keeper
Born: 13 September 1966, Leeds
Height: 5′ 11″ **Weight:** 11st
Nickname: Rippers, Rips, Spud
County debut: 1984
County cap: 1987
1st-Class 50s scored: 2
1st-Class 100s scored: 2
Place in batting averages: 145th
av. 24.94 (1986 104th av. 30.10)
Parents: Arthur and Brenda
Marital status: Single
Education: Woodlesford Primary
and Royds High, Leeds
Qualifications: 5 O-levels, NCA
Coaching Certificate
Family links with cricket: 'My Mum
once made the teas at Farsley CC.'
Jobs outside cricket: 'Any odds
and ends jobs I can find.'
Cricketing superstitions or habits: 'If having a good run will not have my hair
cut; left pad on first. Like to be last out of changing room. The number 111.'
Overseas tours: To West Indies with England Young Cricketers 1984–85
Overseas teams played for: Poverty Bay Cricket Association, New Zealand,
1985–86

Cricketers particularly learnt from: Brian Reynolds, Jim Yardley, Ian Stein, Billy Rhodes, Roy Wills
Cricketers particularly admired: Alan Knott, Bob Taylor, Roy Fredericks
Other sports played: Soccer, golf, pool
Other sports followed: Soccer (Leeds United) and rugby league (Castleford)
Relaxations: Music, eating out
Best batting performance: 134* Northamptonshire v Yorkshire, Scarborough 1986
Best bowling performance: 2-89 Northamptonshire v Essex, Ilford 1987

LAST SEASON: BATTING

	I.	N.O.	R.	H.S.	AV.
TEST					
1ST-CLASS	24	5	474	125*	24.94
INT					
RAL	6	4	61	33*	30.50
NAT.W.	2	1	3	2*	3.00
B & H	5	1	87	33	21.75

CAREER: BATTING

	I.	N.O.	R.	H.S.	AV.
TEST					
1ST-CLASS	74	17	1139	134*	19.98
INT					
RAL	20	10	191	36*	19.10
NAT.W.	5	2	43	27*	14.33
B & H	7	1	113	33	18.83

LAST SEASON: WICKET KEEPING

	C.	ST.			
TEST					
1ST-CLASS	40	9			
INT					
RAL	4	–			
NAT.W.	3	1			
B & H	8	1			

LAST SEASON: BOWLING

	O.	M.	R.	W.	AV.
TEST					
1ST-CLASS	9	0	89	2	44.50
INT					
RAL					
NAT.W.					
B & H					

CAREER: BOWLING

	O.	M.	R.	W.	AV.
TEST					
1ST-CLASS	9	0	89	2	44.50
INT					
RAL					
NAT.W.					
B & H					

CAREER: WICKET KEEPING

	C.	ST.			
TEST					
1ST-CLASS	99	29			
INT					
RAL	16	6			
NAT.W.	11	2			
B & H	11	2			

137. For which Lancashire League club did Viv Richards play last season?

138. Who does Martin Crowe play for in New Zealand?

ROBERTS, B.   Derbyshire

Full Name: Bruce Roberts
Role: Right-hand bat, right-arm
medium bowler, slip fielder,
occasional wicket-keeper
Born: 30 May 1962, Lusaka,
Zambia
Height: 6′ 1½″ **Weight:** 14st
County debut: 1984
County cap: 1986
1000 runs in a season: 2
1st-Class 50s scored: 26
1st-Class 100s scored: 8
One-Day 100s: 2
One-Day 50s: 11
Place in batting averages: 26th
av. 43.23 (1986 170th av. 22.70)
1st-Class catches 1987: 22 (career
94 + 1 stumping)
Parents: Arthur William and Sara
Ann
Marital status: Single
Family links with cricket: Father played for Orange Free State

LAST SEASON: BATTING

	I.	N.O.	R.	H.S.	AV.
TEST					
1ST-CLASS	41	3	1643	184	43.23
INT					
RAL	14	3	405	101*	36.81
NAT.W.	3	0	103	60	34.33
B & H	4	0	167	100	41.75

LAST SEASON: BOWLING

	O.	M.	R.	W.	AV.
TEST					
1ST-CLASS	71.2	14	202	8	25.25
INT					
RAL	8	0	44	3	14.66
NAT.W.	4	1	15	0	
B & H					

CAREER: BATTING

	I.	N.O.	R.	H.S.	AV.
TEST					
1ST-CLASS	200	18	5697	184	31.30
INT					
RAL	50	9	1346	101*	32.82
NAT.W.	7	1	133	60	22.16
B & H	16	3	501	100	38.53

CAREER: BOWLING

	O.	M.	R.	W.	AV.
TEST					
1ST-CLASS	732.1	134	2520	76	33.15
INT					
RAL	101.4	1	635	27	23.51
NAT.W.	20	2	99	2	49.50
B & H	30	2	151	4	37.75

LAST SEASON: WICKET KEEPING

	C.	ST.
TEST		
1ST-CLASS		
INT		
RAL		
NAT.W.		
B & H	1	1

CAREER: WICKET KEEPING

	C.	ST.
TEST		
1ST-CLASS	2	1
INT		
RAL	5	–
NAT.W.	2	–
B & H	8	1

Education: Ruzawi, Peterhouse; Prince Edward, Zimbabwe
Qualifications: O-levels, Coaching qualifications
Off-season 1987–88: Playing for Transvaal in South Africa
Overseas teams played for: Transvaal B 1982–88
Cricketers particularly learnt from: 'My father and Ali Bacher.'
Cricketers particularly admired: Imran Khan, Michael Holding
Other sports played: Swimming, squash, jogging
Other sports followed: Rugby, athletics, golf
Relaxations: Family, music, TV
Best batting performance: 184 Derbyshire v Sussex, Chesterfield 1987
Best bowling performance: 5-68 Transvaal B v Northern Transvaal B, Johannesburg 1986–87

ROBERTS, M. L. Glamorgan

Full Name: Martin Leonard Roberts
Role: Right-hand bat, wicket-keeper
Born: 12 April 1966, Mullion, Cornwall
Height: 6' 1" **Weight:** 11st 7lbs
Nickname: Mert
County debut: 1985
Parents: Len and Marian
Wife and date of marriage: Sue, 20 September 1986
Family links with cricket: Father and brother both play club cricket in Cornwall. Brother played for Cornwall Colts 1982
Education: Helston Comprehensive School
Qualifications: 4 O-levels, 6 CSEs, qualified coach
Jobs outside cricket: Working at W. H. Smiths and helping out PE staff at Helston Comprehensive School. Administrative assistant at Cardiff Crown Court
Cricketing superstitions or habits: Always put left pad on first. Always use same pair of gloves all season, if possible
Overseas tours: Holland with Young England amateur side, 1983
Cricketers particularly learnt from: Bob Taylor, Andy Brassington, Terry Davies, David Evans, Alan Jones
Cricketers particularly admired: Bob Taylor, Alan Knott, Richard Hadlee
Other sport played: Football, volleyball, golf

Other sports followed: Rugby

Injuries 1987: 'Pulled a hamstring at the beginning of the season which kept me out of the first two matches.'

Relaxations: Playing golf, watching films, going for the occasional dance and meal

Extras: England Schools U-19s 1983–1984. Played for Cornwall in Minor Counties. 42 dismissals in 13 games in 2nd XI Championship 1987

Opinions on cricket: 'I think fines in limited-overs cricket should not be allowed. How is a captain able to set the correct field nearing the end of a game, when one man in the wrong position could be the losing of the match, if he is rushing through the overs so as not to be fined?'

Best batting performance: 8 Glamorgan v Northamptonshire, Northampton 1986

LAST SEASON: BATTING

	I.	N.O.	R.	H.S.	AV.
TEST					
1ST-CLASS	1	0	6	6	6.00
INT					
RAL					
NAT.W.					
B & H					

LAST SEASON: WICKET KEEPING

	C.	ST.			
TEST					
1ST-CLASS	2	–			
INT					
RAL					
NAT.W.					
B & H					

CAREER: BATTING

	I.	N.O.	R.	H.S.	AV.
TEST					
1ST-CLASS	3	0	14	8	4.66
INT					
RAL	1	1	6	6*	–
NAT.W.					
B & H					

CAREER: WICKET KEEPING

	C.	ST.			
TEST					
1ST-CLASS	4	1			
INT					
RAL	1	–			
NAT.W.					
B & H					

---

139. How many did West Indies make in the first innings in the Third Test v New Zealand in March 1987: 100, 398 for 2 declared, or 601?

ROBINSON, M. A.   Northamptonshire

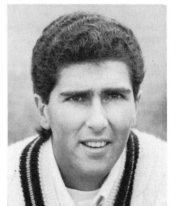

Full Name: Mark Andrew Robinson
Role: Right-hand bat, right-arm
fast-medium bowler
Born: 23 November 1966, Hull
Height: 6′ 3″ **Weight:** 12½st
Nickname: Smokey, Coddy, Robbo
County debut: 1987
1st-Class catches 1987: 1 (career 1)
Parents: Joan Margaret and Malcolm
Marital status: Single
Family links with cricket: Maternal
grandfather an established local
cricketer
Education: Fifth Avenue Primary;
Endike Junior High; Hull Grammar
School
Qualifications: 6 O-levels,
2 A-levels, 1st NCA Cricket
Coaching Award
Jobs outside cricket: Jeweller, sports shop assistant, employee at Hull indoor
cricket stadium
Off-season 1987–88: Playing for East Christchurch-Shirley CC
Cricketing superstitions or habits: Refuse to walk on the pitch sixth in line
Overseas tours: North of England U-19s to Bermuda 1985
Cricketers particularly learnt from: Fred Cowell, Ken Lake, Doug Ferguson,
Dave Rees, Bob Carter
Cricketers particularly admired: Dennis Lillee, Richard Hadlee, Duncan
Wild
Other sport played: Football (Hull Schools and Humberside U-19), indoor
cricket (National League)
Other sports followed: Hull City FC
Injuries 1987: Fractured left wrist. Side strain last game of season
Relaxations: Movies, soap operas, reading, music
Extras: Took part in Leeds to London relay run around all county headquar-
ters, in aid of Leukaemia Research. Took hat-trick with first three balls of
innings in Yorkshire League, playing for Hull v Doncaster. First time this has
been done for 71 years. First player to win Yorkshire U-19s Bowler of the
Season Award in two successive years
Opinions on cricket: 'Politics and sport should not mix. Cricketers should
have freedom of movement to be able to earn their living where they wish.
More 2nd XI games should be played on frequently used first-class grounds,
as too many are played on pitches which are not realistic to county cricket, i.e.
they are too slow and low, suiting neither batsman nor bowler.'

Best batting performance: 2 Northamptonshire v Middlesex, Wellingborough 1987
Best bowling performance: 3-45 Northamptonshire v Sussex, Hove 1987

LAST SEASON: BATTING

	I.	N.O.	R.	H.S.	AV.
TEST					
1ST-CLASS	6	2	4	2	1.00
INT					
RAL	2	1	1	1	1.00
NAT.W.					
B & H					

LAST SEASON: BOWLING

	O.	M.	R.	W.	AV.
TEST					
1ST-CLASS	150	25	501	13	38.53
INT					
RAL	33.3	1	167	1	167.00
NAT.W.					
B & H					

CAREER: BATTING

	I.	N.O.	R.	H.S.	AV.
TEST					
1ST-CLASS	6	2	4	2	1.00
INT					
RAL	2	1	1	1	1.00
NAT.W.					
B & H					

CAREER: BOWLING

	O.	M.	R.	W.	AV.
TEST					
1ST-CLASS	150	25	501	13	38.53
INT					
RAL	33.3	1	167	1	167.00
NAT.W.					
B & H					

ROBINSON, P. E.   Yorkshire

Full Name: Phillip Edward Robinson
Role: Right-hand bat, slip or cover fielder
Born: 3 August 1963, Keighley
Height: 5′ 10″ **Weight:** 12½st
Nickname: Red Robbo, Billy
County debut: 1984
1st-Class 50s scored: 15
1st-Class 100s scored: 1
One-Day 50s: 6
Place in batting averages: 51st
av. 38.27 (1986 70th av. 35.63)
1st-Class catches 1987: 8 (career 24)
Parents: Keith and Margaret Lesley
Wife: Jane
Family links with cricket: Father and brothers played in Bradford League
Education: Long Lee Primary; Hartington Middle; Greenhead Grammar
Qualifications: 2 O-levels
Off-season 1987–88: Coaching in New Zealand
Cricketing superstitions or habits: 'Always put my left sock on first.'
Cricketers particularly learnt from: 'I learn from all cricketers.'

Cricketers particularly admired: Gary Sobers, Viv Richards
Other sports played: Football, golf, squash – I'll have a go at all sports
Other sports followed: Manchester United FC and Meadowbank FC
Relaxations: Watching TV, having a drink
Extras: Scored the highest score by a Yorkshire 2nd XI player of 233 in 1983 v Kent at Canterbury
Best batting performance: 104* Yorkshire v Kent, Scarborough 1986

LAST SEASON: BATTING

	I.	N.O.	R.	H.S.	AV.
TEST					
1ST-CLASS	13	2	421	95	38.27
INT					
RAL	12	1	260	41	23.63
NAT.W.					
B & H					

CAREER: BATTING

	I.	N.O.	R.	H.S.	AV.
TEST					
1ST-CLASS	66	10	2019	104*	36.05
INT					
RAL	41	3	982	78*	25.84
NAT.W.	3	0	66	66	22.00
B & H	3	0	59	42	19.66

ROBINSON, R. T.   Nottinghamshire

Full Name: Robert Timothy Robinson
Role: Right-hand opening bat, cover fielder
Born: 21 November 1958, Sutton-in-Ashfield, Nottinghamshire
Height: 6′ **Weight:** 12st 4lbs
Nickname: Robbo, Chop
County debut: 1978
County cap: 1983
Test debut: 1984–85
No. of Tests: 21
No. of One-Day Internationals: 13
1000 runs in a season: 5
1st-Class 50s scored: 61
1st-Class 100s scored: 25
1st-Class 200s scored: 1
One-Day 50s: 29
One-Day 100s: 2
Place in batting averages: 45th av. 39.06 (1986 18th av. 48.20)
1st-Class catches 1987: 14 (career 102)
Parents: Eddy and Christine
Wife and date of marriage: Trisha, 2 November 1985
Family links with cricket: Father, uncle, cousin and brother all played local cricket. Brother played for Nottinghamshire Schoolboys
Education: Dunstable Grammar School; High Pavement College, Nottingham; Sheffield University

Qualifications: Honorary degree in Accounting and Financial Management
Jobs outside cricket: Trainee accountant. Working in Commercial Department, Nottinghamshire CCC
Off-season 1987–88: On tour with England
Cricketing superstitions or habits: Always put left pad on first
Overseas tours: NCA U-19 tour 1976; England to India and Australia 1984–85 and West Indies 1986; World Cup, Pakistan, New Zealand and Australia 1987–88
Overseas teams played for: Durban Collegians, South Africa, 1980–81
Cricketers particularly learnt from: Clive Rice, Eddie Hemmings, Mike Harris
Cricketers particularly admired: Geoff Boycott, Clive Rice, Richard Hadlee
Other sports played: Soccer, golf, squash
Other sports followed: Soccer
Relaxations: Driving, listening to all music, films, doing nothing, spending time with the family
Extras: Played for Northants 2nd XI in 1974–75 and for Nottinghamshire 2nd XI in 1977. Had soccer trials with Portsmouth, Chelsea and QPR. Plays in contact lenses
Opinions on cricket: 'I would like to see the opinions of people who actually play the game taken more seriously by the TCCB cricket committee.'
Best batting performance: 207 Nottinghamshire v Warwickshire, Trent Bridge 1983
Best bowling performance: 1-22 Nottinghamshire v Northamptonshire, Northampton 1982

LAST SEASON: BATTING

	I.	N.O.	R.	H.S.	AV.
TEST	8	0	299	166	37.37
1ST-CLASS	28	4	951	137	39.62
INT					
RAL	9	1	295	78	36.87
NAT.W.	5	0	158	79	31.60
B & H	4	0	204	89	51.00

LAST SEASON: BOWLING

	O.	M.	R.	W.	AV.
TEST					
1ST-CLASS					
INT					
RAL					
NAT.W.					
B & H					

CAREER: BATTING

	I.	N.O.	R.	H.S.	AV.
TEST	36	3	1351	175	40.93
1ST-CLASS	290	37	10253	207	40.52
INT	13	0	297	83	22.84
RAL	92	9	2450	97*	29.51
NAT.W.	21	2	852	139	44.84
B & H	35	3	1034	120	32.31

CAREER: BOWLING

	O.	M.	R.	W.	AV.
TEST	1	1	0	0	–
1ST-CLASS	18	0	120	2	6.00
INT					
RAL					
NAT.W.					
B & H					

ROEBUCK, P. M.   Somerset

Full Name: Peter Michael Roebuck
Role: Right-hand bat, right-arm
leg-break bowler, slip fielder
Born: 6 March 1956, Oxford
Height: 6′ 0″ **Weight:** 13st 5lbs
Nickname: Professor
County debut: 1974
County cap: 1978
1000 runs in a season: 7
1st-Class 50s scored: 75
1st-Class 100s scored: 23
1st-Class 200s scored: 1
1st-Class 5 w. in innings: 1
One-Day 50s: 26
One-Day 100s: 3
Place in batting averages: 10th
av. 49.95 (1986 21st av. 47.70)
1st-Class catches 1987: 15 (career 138)
Parents: James and Elizabeth
Marital status: Single
Family links with cricket: Mother and sister both played for Oxford University Ladies. Younger brother, Paul, played for ESCA U-15 and now Gloucestershire
Education: Park School, Bath; Millfield School; Emmanuel College, Cambridge University
Qualifications: 1st Class Hons degree in law
Jobs outside cricket: Teacher, author and freelance journalist
Off-season 1987–88: Working as a journalist
Cricketing superstitions or habits: 'Just about conquered all of these now (I am over 30!).'
Overseas tours: Toured in Australia with Combined Oxford & Cambridge XI 1979–80. Christians in Sport tour to India 1985
Overseas teams played for: Played in Perth, Australia, 1979–80; also in Corfu, Sydney and Fiji
Cricketers particularly learnt from: Viv Richards, Martin Crowe
Cricketers particularly admired: R. J. O. Meyer, Keith Fletcher
Other sports played: Tennis
Other sports followed: Anything except American sports ('They shriek too much!')
Injuries 1987: Broken finger
Relaxations: 'Reading, music, sitting in a bath, telephone calls.'
Extras: Cambridge blue 1975–76–77. Plays in spectacles. Youngest Minor County cricketer, playing for Somerset 2nd XI at age of 13. Shared in 4th

wicket partnership record for county of 251 with I. V. A. Richards v Surrey at Weston-super-Mare in 1977. Books: *Slice of Cricket, It Never Rains* and *It Sort of Clicks*. Articles in *Sunday Times*, *Independent*, *Guardian*, 'and anyone else who asks'. Founder member of campaign for fair play. Appointed captain in 1986

Opinions on cricket: 'People seem to have forgotten that this is, above all else, an aesthetic game.'

Best batting performance: 221* Somerset v Nottinghamshire, Trent Bridge 1986

Best bowling performance: 6-50 Cambridge University v Kent, Canterbury 1977

LAST SEASON: BATTING

	I.	N.O.	R.	H.S.	AV.
TEST					
1ST-CLASS	29	5	1199	165*	49.95
INT					
RAL	9	0	363	82	40.33
NAT.W.	1	0	2	2	2.00
B & H	4	1	283	110*	94.33

LAST SEASON: BOWLING

	O.	M.	R.	W.	AV.
TEST					
1ST-CLASS	13	1	54	0	–
INT					
RAL					
NAT.W.					
B & H					

CAREER: BATTING

	I.	N.O.	R.	H.S.	AV.
TEST					
1ST-CLASS	439	67	13732	221*	36.91
INT					
RAL	127	22	3324	105	31.65
NAT.W.	29	2	736	98	27.25
B & H	48	6	1156	120	27.52

CAREER: BOWLING

	O.	M.	R.	W.	AV.
TEST					
1ST-CLASS	785.3	201	2243	43	51.16
INT					
RAL	12.3	0	65	2	32.50
NAT.W.					
B & H	8.2	1	23	2	11.50

---

140. Who said 'The first time I saw Plum Warner bat, he made one. The second time, he was not as successful'?

141. Which county cricket club was founded first: Sussex or Notts, and when?

142. Which legendary England player took 2068 first-class wickets, 1017 catches and scored 58,969 runs?

143. Who is Ashley Metcalfe's father-in-law?

ROMAINES, P. W.   Gloucestershire

Full Name: Paul William Romaines
Role: Right-hand opening bat, off-break bowler
Born: 25 December 1955, Bishop Auckland, Co Durham
Height: 6' 0" **Weight:** 12st 8lbs
Nickname: Canny, Human
County debut: 1975 (Northampton-shire), 1982 (Gloucestershire)
County cap: 1983 (Gloucestershire)
1000 runs in a season: 3
1st-Class 50s scored: 30
1st-Class 100s scored: 12
One-Day 50s: 17
One-Day 100s: 2
Place in batting averages: 119th av. 28.60 (1986 178th av. 20.69)
1st-Class catches 1987: 7 (career 49)
Parents: George and Freda
Wife and date of marriage: Julie Anne, 1979
Children: Claire Louise
Family links with cricket: Father played local cricket and is still an avid watcher. Grandfather, W. R. Romaines, represented Durham in Minor Counties cricket, and played v Australia in 1926
Education: Leeholme School, Bishop Auckland
Qualifications: 8 O-levels, NCA Qualified Coach
Jobs outside cricket: Sales representative
Off-season 1987–88: Working for Bioglan Laboratories Ltd
Overseas teams played for: Griqualand West 1984–85; De Beers CC 1984–85; Gordon CC, Sydney 1981–2, 1982–3
Cricketers particularly learnt from: Peter Willey, Barry Dudleston, David Graveney
Cricketers particularly admired: Zaheer Abbas, Graham Gooch, Clive Radley, Gordon Greenidge
Other sports played: Squash, golf, soccer
Other sports followed: Athletics
Relaxations: 'Listening to music, having a good pint, antiques, people, writing letters, good conversation.'
Extras: Debut for Northamptonshire 1975. Played Minor County cricket with Durham 1977–1981. Joined Gloucestershire in 1982
Best batting performance: 186 Gloucestershire v Warwickshire, Nuneaton 1982
Best bowling performance: 3-42 Gloucestershire v Surrey, The Oval, 1985

	I.	N.O.	R.	H.S.	AV.
TEST					
1ST-CLASS	42	2	1144	119	28.60
INT					
RAL	11	2	187	33	20.77
NAT.W.					
B & H	3	0	24	11	8.00

LAST SEASON: BOWLING

	O.	M.	R.	W.	AV.
TEST					
1ST-CLASS					
INT					
RAL					
NAT.W.					
B & H					

CAREER: BATTING

	I.	N.O.	R.	H.S.	AV.
TEST					
1ST-CLASS	243	18	6615	186	29.40
INT					
RAL	67	5	1832	105	29.54
NAT.W.	12	1	324	82	29.45
B & H	16	1	554	125	36.93

CAREER: BOWLING

	O.	M.	R.	W.	AV.
TEST					
1ST-CLASS	36.4	2	211	3	70.33
INT					
RAL					
NAT.W.					
B & H					

ROSE, B. C. Somerset

Full Name: Brian Charles Rose
Role: Left-hand bat
Born: 4 June 1950, Dartford, Kent
Height: 6′ 1″ **Weight:** 13st 8lbs
Nickname: Harry
County debut: 1969
County cap: 1975
Benefit: 1983 (£71,863)
Test debut: 1977–78
No. of Tests: 9
No. of One-Day Internationals: 2
1000 runs in a season: 8
1st-Class 50s scored: 53
1st-Class 100s scored: 23
1st-Class 200s scored: 2
One-Day 50s: 29
One-Day 100s: 3
Place in batting averages: — (1986
34th av. 43.55)
1st-Class catches 1987: 1 (career 124)
Parents: Jean and Charles
Wife and date of marriage: Stevie, 16 March 1978
Children: Stuart Charles, 19 March 1979; Jamie Joseph, 14 December 1981
Education: Weston-super-Mare Grammar School; Borough Road College, Isleworth
Jobs outside cricket: Teacher
Overseas tours: Pakistan, New Zealand 1977–78; West Indies 1981
Overseas teams played for: Claremont-Cottesloe, Western Australia 1979–80

Other sports played: Golf, squash
Relaxations: Gardening
Extras: Played for English Schools Cricket Association at Lord's in 1968. Plays in spectacles. Captain of Somerset 1978–83
Opinions on cricket: 'There should be a 16-match Championship.'
Best batting performance: 205 Somerset v Northamptonshire, Weston 1977
Best bowling performance: 3-9 Somerset v Gloucestershire, Taunton 1975

LAST SEASON: BATTING

	I.	N.O.	R.	H.S.	AV.
TEST					
1ST-CLASS	4	0	60	31	15.00
INT					
RAL	1	0	3	3	3.00
NAT.W.					
B & H	1	0	0		0.00

LAST SEASON: BOWLING

	O.	M.	R.	W.	AV.
TEST					
1ST-CLASS					
INT					
RAL					
NAT.W.					
B & H					

CAREER: BATTING

	I.	N.O.	R.	H.S.	AV.
TEST	16	2	358	70	25.57
1ST-CLASS	432	48	12878	205	33.53
INT	2	0	99	54	49.50
RAL	161	21	3609	112*	25.77
NAT.W.	25	5	757	128	37.85
B & H	51	7	1342	137*	30.50

CAREER: BOWLING

	O.	M.	R.	W.	AV.
TEST					
1ST-CLASS	70.1	6	289	8	36.12
INT					
RAL	34	0	152	7	21.71
NAT.W.					
B & H					

ROSE, G. D. Somerset

Full Name: Graham David Rose
Role: Right-hand bat, right-arm fast-medium bowler
Born: 12 April 1964, Tottenham
Height: 6′ 4″ **Weight:** 14st 9lbs
Nickname: Rosie
County debut: 1985 (Middlesex), 1987 (Somerset)
1st-Class 50s scored: 2
1st-Class 5 w. in innings: 2
One-Day 50s: 1
Place in batting averages: 146th av. 24.73
Place in bowling averages: 36th av. 25.68
Strike rate 1987: 49.68 (career 47.09)
1st-Class catches 1987: 10 (career 10)
Parents: William and Edna
Wife and date of marriage: Teresa Julie, 19 September 1987

Family links with cricket: Father and brother played club cricket in North London

Education: Northumberland Park School, Tottenham

Qualifications: 6 O-levels, 4 A-levels. NCA Coaching Certificate

Jobs outside cricket: 'Many and various – for example, bricklayer's mate, tele-researcher, wool sampler.'

Overseas tours: ESCA U-19 to Zimbabwe; Haringey Cricket College to West Indies 1986; NCA South to Holland 1983

Overseas teams played for: Carey Park, Western Australia, 1984–85; Fremantle, Perth, 1986–87

Cricketers particularly learnt from: Jack Robertson, Ted Jackson, Father, Graeme Porter

Cricketers particularly admired: Dennis Lillee, Richard Hadlee

Other sports: Golf, squash

Other sports followed: 'Follow Spurs for my sins.'

Injuries 1987: Severe back strain and strained rib muscles

Relaxations: Music – Dire Straits, Beatles, Pink Floyd, U2

Extras: Played for Young England v Young Australia 1983. Took 6 wickets for 41 on Middlesex debut. Joined Somerset for 1987 season and scored 95 on debut

Opinions on cricket: 'i) I would like to see 16 four-day county games with B&H/NatWest fixtures on Saturdays and the Sunday game to remain. One-day cricket could be played in coloured clothing similar to that in Australia. ii) It would be interesting to see one-day games played without leg-byes and no-balls/wides bringing a penalty of two runs instead of one. iii) The standard of covering varies far too much from county to county; I would like to see TCCB setting up some sort of fund so that covers and other wet weather equipment could be of a uniform standard throughout the country. iv) I do not think that playing on partially covered pitches is a good idea. As it stands, the quicker bowlers will do all the bowling as their run-ups and footholds will remain dry. Instead of helping spinners, it will push them further into the background. I feel that spinners will play a greater part in

LAST SEASON: BATTING

	I.	N.O.	R.	H.S.	AV.
TEST					
1ST-CLASS	23	4	470	95	24.73
INT					
RAL	6	1	134	50	26.80
NAT.W.	1	0	26	26	26.00
B & H	4	0	57	42	14.25

CAREER: BATTING

	I.	N.O.	R.	H.S.	AV.
TEST					
1ST-CLASS	31	5	563	95	21.65
INT					
RAL	15	2	238	50	18.30
NAT.W.	1	0	26	26	26.00
B & H	5	0	60	42	12.00

LAST SEASON: BOWLING

	O.	M.	R.	W.	AV.
TEST					
1ST-CLASS	314.4	56	976	38	25.68
INT					
RAL	67.3	6	246	11	22.36
NAT.W.	11.5	4	30	2	15.00
B & H	50	4	210	9	23.33

CAREER: BOWLING

	O.	M.	R.	W.	AV.
TEST					
1ST-CLASS	423.5	74	1395	54	25.83
INT					
RAL	164.3	10	671	16	41.93
NAT.W.	11.5	4	30	2	15.00
B & H	54	4	225	9	25.00

four-day cricket, especially on the fourth day. v) Now that we are entering the era of "result" pitches where the home side produces either "green" or "turning" pitches, it might be a good idea to give the choice of who bats first to the visiting captain.'

Best batting performance: 95 Somerset v Lancashire, Taunton 1987
Best bowling performance: 6-41 Middlesex v Worcestershire, Worcester 1985

ROSEBERRY, M. A. Middlesex

Full Name: Michael Anthony Roseberry
Role: Right-hand bat, right-arm slow-medium bowler, slip and silly point fielder
Born: 28 November 1966, Sunderland
Height: 6′ 0″ **Weight:** 14st
Nickname: Zorro
County debut: 1985
1st-Class 50s scored: 3
Place in batting averages: 148th av. 24.54 (1986 151st av. 24.85)
1st-Class catches 1987: 7 (career 8)
Parents: Matthew and Jean
Marital status: Single
Family links with cricket: Uncle, Peter Wyness, played for Royal Navy
Education: Durham School
Qualifications: 5 O-levels, 1 A-level
Cricketing superstitions or habits: 'Tend to put my front batting pad on first.'
Overseas tours: Durham School 1st XI to Barbados, 1983; Young England to West Indies, 1985
Cricketers particularly learnt from: Alec Coxon (ex-England and Yorkshire bowler), Don Wilson and Gordon Jenkins (MCC Indoor School)
Cricketers particularly admired: Ian Botham, Geoff Boycott
Other sports played: 'Rugby, squash, snooker and whatever takes my fancy.'
Other sports followed: Rugby, basketball, football
Relaxations: Snooker, music, watching movies
Extras: Won Lord's Taverners/MCC Cricketer of the Year 1983. Won Sunday Sun/Dixon Sport Cricketer of the Year 1983. Won Cricket Societies' Wetherall Award 1983, 1984. Won Cricket Societies' Award for Best Young Cricketer of the Year 1984 and Frank Morris Memorial Award 1984
Best batting performance: 70* Middlesex v Northamptonshire, Northampton 1986

	I.	N.O.	R.	H.S.	AV.
TEST					
1ST-CLASS	14	3	270	52	24.54
INT					
RAL	4	0	94	27	23.50
NAT.W.					
B & H	2	0	8	6	4.00

	I.	N.O.	R.	H.S.	AV.
TEST					
1ST-CLASS	22	4	444	70*	24.66
INT					
RAL	7	0	154	27	22.00
NAT.W.					
B & H	2	0	8	6	4.00

RUDD, C. F. B. P. Derbyshire

Full Name: Christopher Francis Baines Paul Rudd
Role: Right-hand bat, right-arm slow seam bowler
Born: 9 December 1963, Sutton Coldfield
Height: 5′ 10½″ **Weight:** 11st 12lbs
Nickname: Ruddy
County debut: 1986
Parents: Christopher Michael and Christine Ann
Marital status: Single
Education: St Richards Prep School, Herefordshire; Douai School, Berkshire
Qualifications: 5 O-levels, cricket coach, qualified ambulance driver
Jobs outside cricket: Ambulance driver
Off-season 1987–88: Driving ambulances
Overseas tours: Minor Counties U-25 to Kenya 1986
Overseas teams played for: Newcastle University, Newcastle District, Australia
Cricketers particularly learnt from: Phil Russell, Bob Taylor, Bernie Maher
Cricketers particularly admired: Dennis Amiss, Viv Richards, Bernie Maher
Other sports played: Show-jumping and wrestling (at school)
Relaxations: Golf, music, meeting friends/people, night-clubs ('especially with Paul Newman, my drinking partner')
Extras: Captain Devon U-19 1983. Played for Devon (Minor Counties) 1984–86. 'Started as an off-spinner, but with encouragement from Reg Sharma, turned myself into an away-swing bowler.'
Opinions on cricket: 'i) There should be four-day cricket. ii) I think spinners should have to bowl forty per cent of the overs bowled in a day (in four-day competition). iii) I think young players like myself should be paid. iv) There

should be special coaching clinics set up to enable spin bowlers to spin the ball.
v) I think a sponsorship scheme should be set up to send young players
abroad.'
Best batting performance: 9 Derbyshire v Yorkshire, Harrogate 1987
Best bowling performance: 3-27 Derbyshire v Cambridge University,
Cambridge 1987

LAST SEASON: BATTING

	I.	N.O.	R.	H.S.	AV.
TEST					
1ST-CLASS	4	1	13	9	4.33
INT					
RAL	3	1	10	7*	5.00
NAT.W.					
B & H					

LAST SEASON: BOWLING

	O.	M.	R.	W.	AV.
TEST					
1ST-CLASS	46	13	159	5	31.80
INT					
RAL	16	0	71	1	71.00
NAT.W.					
B & H					

CAREER: BATTING

	I.	N.O.	R.	H.S.	AV.
TEST					
1ST-CLASS	5	1	14	9	3.50
INT					
RAL	3	1	10	7*	5.00
NAT.W.	2	0	41	30	20.50
B & H					

CAREER: BOWLING

	O.	M.	R.	W.	AV.
TEST					
1ST-CLASS	74.3	20	249	5	49.80
INT					
RAL	16	0	71	1	71.00
NAT.W.	22	0	86	1	86.00
B & H					

RUSSELL, R. C.   Gloucestershire

Full Name: Robert Charles Russell
Role: Left-hand bat, wicket-keeper
Born: 15 August 1963, Stroud
Height: 5′ 8½″ **Weight:** 9st 8lbs
Nickname: Jack
County debut: 1981
County cap: 1985
1st-Class 50s scored: 10
One-Day 50s: 3
One-Day 100s: 1
Place in batting averages: 127th
av. 27.51 (1986 133rd av. 26.59)
Parents: Derek John and Jennifer
Mary Anne
Wife and date of marriage: Aileen
Ann, 6 March 1985
Children: Stepson, Marcus Anthony
Family links with cricket: Keen
sporting family
Education: Archway Comprehensive School
Qualifications: 6 O-levels, 2 A-levels

Jobs outside cricket: Carpet fitter
Off-season 1987–88: On tour with England
Cricketing superstitions or habits: 'The numbers 37 and 87. In general try to make clothing and equipment last as long as possible.'
Overseas tours: Denmark with NCA Young Cricketers 1981; with Gloucestershire to Barbados 1985; Mendip Acorns Pacific tour 1984; England to Pakistan 1987
Overseas teams played for: Takapuna CC, New Zealand, 1983–85
Cricketers particularly learnt from: Alan Knott, Bob Taylor, Andy Brassington
Other sports played: Squash, snooker, darts
Other sports followed: Football, snooker
Relaxations: Watching cricket videos, oil painting, sketching, films and comedy
Extras: Record for most dismissals in a match for first-class debut: 8 (7 caught, 1 stumped) for Gloucestershire v Sri Lanka at Bristol, 1981. Youngest wicket-keeper for Gloucestershire (17 years 307 days). Represented Young England v Young West Indies in the Agatha Christie 'Test Match' series, 1982. Played for Duchess of Norfolk's XI v West Indies at Arundel in 1984. Joint holder of world record for hat-trick of catches (v Surrey at The Oval 1986). Youngest wicket-keeper to score Sunday League hundred (v Worcestershire at Hereford 1986)
Best batting performance: 71 Gloucestershire v Surrey, The Oval 1986

LAST SEASON: BATTING

	I.	N.O.	R.	H.S.	AV.
TEST					
1ST-CLASS	38	9	798	57*	27.51
INT					
RAL	13	2	290	72*	26.36
NAT.W.	2	1	41	27*	41.00
B & H	4	1	36	11	12.00

CAREER: BATTING

	I.	N.O.	R.	H.S.	AV.
TEST					
1ST-CLASS	160	40	2789	71	23.24
INT					
RAL	42	15	725	108	26.85
NAT.W.	10	3	142	39	20.28
B & H	13	3	115	36*	11.50

LAST SEASON: WICKET KEEPING

	C.	ST.			
TEST					
1ST-CLASS	54	10			
INT					
RAL	15	5			
NAT.W.	5	1			
B & H	5	1			

CAREER: WICKET KEEPING

	C.	ST.			
TEST					
1ST-CLASS	253	50			
INT					
RAL	43	14			
NAT.W.	13	5			
B & H	21	7			

SADIQ, Z. A.　　　　　　　　　　　Surrey

Full Name: Zahid Asa Sadiq
Role: Right-hand bat
Born: 6 May 1965, Nairobi
Height: 5′ 11″ **Weight:** 11st 2lbs
Nickname: Zeidi, Munch, Shag
Parents: Mohammed Sadiq
Marital status: Single
Education: Rutlish School
Qualifications: 2 O-levels
Off-season 1987–88: Playing
cricket in Australia
Cricketing superstitions or habits:
Right pad on first
Overseas teams played for:
Claremont CC, Australia, 1986–87;
Wembley CC, Australia 1987–88
Cricketers particularly learnt from:
Monte Lynch, Chris Waller,
Geoff Arnold

Cricketers particularly admired: Viv Richards, Zaheer Abbas
Other sports played: Squash, rugby
Relaxations: Listening to music
Extras: Played in one Sunday League match 1987

LAST SEASON: BATTING

	I.	N.O.	R.	H.S.	AV.
TEST					
1ST-CLASS					
INT					
RAL	1	0	0		0.00
NAT.W.					
B & H					

CAREER: BATTING

	O.	M.	R.	W.	AV.
TEST					
1ST-CLASS					
INT					
RAL	1	0	0		0.00
NAT.W.					
B & H					

144. Was Frank Woolley, Woolley (F. E.) or F. E. Woolley?

SAINSBURY, G. E. Gloucestershire

Full Name: Gary Edward Sainsbury
Role: Right-hand bat, left-arm medium bowler
Born: 17 January 1958, Wanstead, Essex
Height: 6′ 3″ **Weight:** 12st
Nickname: Sains, Noddy
County debut: 1979 (Essex), 1983 (Gloucestershire)
County cap: 1987
50 wickets in a season: 1
1st-Class 5 w. in innings: 7
Place in bowling averages: 137th av. 48.52
Strike rate 1987: 108.73 (career 68.66)
1st-Class catches 1987: 4 (career 15)
Parents: Gordon and Muriel
Wife and date of marriage: Karen Frances, 24 December 1985
Education: Beal Grammar School; Bath University
Qualifications: 11 O-levels, 3 A-levels, BSc (Hons) Statistics. First stage of the NCA Coaching Award
Jobs outside cricket: Computer programmer, C. E. Heath & Co Ltd. Assistant in Finance Section of Tower Hamlets Council's Social Services Department. Assistant in Research Department, Mortgages Services Department and Dealing Room for Bristol and West Building Society
Overseas teams played for: Hamilton-Wickham CC, Newcastle, New South Wales, 1981–82
Cricketers particularly learnt from: Bill Morris (Ilford Cricket School), John Gray (Wanstead CC), Mike Denness, John Lever
Cricketers particularly admired: 'First childhood hero was Clive Lloyd; have since admired many cricketers.'
Other sports played: Squash, badminton, golf
Other sports followed: Casual interest in most sports
Relaxations: Music (Todd Rundgren, Hall and Oates, Judy Tzuke, Phil Collins), walking the dog, TV, reading (Tolkien, Donaldson, Forsyth), eating out ('when I can afford it')
Extras: 'Played for Essex CCC 1977–1982. First-class appearances limited to three matches. In my last season with them I was named Young Player of the Year. I believe my claim to fame is taking the first 1st-Class wicket in England this decade (Essex v MCC).'
Opinions on cricket: 'County cricket clubs should be adopting a more professional approach to attracting sponsors. Cricket should be cashing in

365

now on potential sponsors' current disenchantment with football. At the same time, all professional cricketers should recognise their responsibilities towards maintaining cricket's favourable image and keeping existing sponsors happy.'

Best batting performance: 14* Gloucestershire v Yorkshire, Bristol 1986
Best bowling performance: 7-38 Gloucestershire v Northamptonshire, Northampton 1985

LAST SEASON: BATTING

	I.	N.O.	R.	H.S.	AV.
TEST					
1ST-CLASS	16	8	16	5	2.00
INT					
RAL	5	2	8	5	2.66
NAT.W.	1	0	2	2	2.00
B & H					

LAST SEASON: BOWLING

	O.	M.	R.	W.	AV.
TEST					
1ST-CLASS	344.2	78	992	19	48.52
INT					
RAL	81	4	332	12	27.66
NAT.W.	24	4	59	3	19.66
B & H					

CAREER: BATTING

	I.	N.O.	R.	H.S.	AV.
TEST					
1ST-CLASS	70	38	179	14*	5.59
INT					
RAL	17	8	36	7*	4.00
NAT.W.	3	1	7	3	3.50
B & H	4	2	6	4	3.00

CAREER: BOWLING

	O.	M.	R.	W.	AV.
TEST					
1ST-CLASS	1968.3	489	5717	172	33.23
INT					
RAL	415.5	25	1835	55	33.36
NAT.W.	78	18	239	9	26.55
B & H	75	12	237	12	19.75

SAXELBY, K.   Nottinghamshire

Full Name: Kevin Saxelby
Role: Right-hand bat, right-arm fast medium bowler
Born: 23 February 1959, Worksop
Height: 6′ 2″ **Weight:** 14st
Nickname: Sax, Sacko, Nasty
County debut: 1978
County cap: 1984
50 wickets in a season: 1
1st-Class 50s scored: 1
1st-Class 5 w. in innings: 6
1st-Class 10 w. in match: 1
Place in batting averages: — (1986 47th av. 41.33)
Place in bowling averages: 49th av. 27.19 (1986 77th av. 33.51)
Strike rate 1987: 57.72 (career 58.90)
1st-Class catches 1987: 5 (career 20)
Parents: George Kenneth and Hilda Margaret

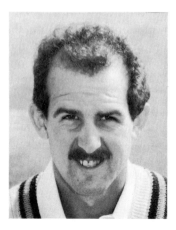

Wife: Peta Jean Wendy
Children: Craig Robert, 6 June 1985
Family links with cricket: Father played in local league cricket. Brother played for NAYC and Nottinghamshire 2nd XI
Education: Magnus Grammar School, Newark
Qualifications: 10 O-levels, 4 A-levels
Jobs outside cricket: Farmer
Off-season 1987–88: Working on family farm
Overseas teams played for: North Perth, Australia 1979–80; Durban Collegians, South Africa 1980–81; Alma-Marist, Cape Town 1982–83
Other sports played: Rugby union
Other sports followed: 'Most sports except soccer and anything to do with horses.'
Relaxations: Gardening, DIY
Best batting performance: 59* Nottinghamshire v Derbyshire, Chesterfield 1982
Best bowling performance: 6-49 Nottinghamshire v Sussex, Trent Bridge 1987

LAST SEASON: BATTING

	I.	N.O.	R.	H.S.	AV.
TEST					
1ST-CLASS	15	6	69	14	7.66
INT					
RAL	3	2	13	9*	13.00
NAT.W.	1	1	0	0*	–
B & H	1	0	1	1	1.00

CAREER: BATTING

	I.	N.O.	R.	H.S.	AV.
TEST					
1ST-CLASS	107	34	942	59*	12.90
INT					
RAL	29	19	134	23*	13.40
NAT.W.	4	3	25	12	25.00
B & H	11	7	52	13*	13.00

LAST SEASON: BOWLING

	O.	M.	R.	W.	AV.
TEST					
1ST-CLASS	452.1	121	1278	47	27.19
INT					
RAL	85.2	10	362	22	16.45
NAT.W.	50.2	4	220	7	31.42
B & H	33.2	2	135	7	19.28

CAREER: BOWLING

	O.	M.	R.	W.	AV.
TEST					
1ST-CLASS	2533	608	7791	258	30.19
INT					
RAL	535.2	23	2607	102	25.55
NAT.W.	159.1	22	567	25	22.68
B & H	247.4	27	938	36	26.05

145. What age was Graeme Pollock when he first played for South Africa?

SCOTT, C. W.　　　Nottinghamshire

Full Name: Christopher Wilmot Scott
Role: Right-hand bat, wicket-keeper
Born: 23 January 1964, Lincoln
Height: 5′ 9″ **Weight:** 11st
Nickname: George, Ginge
County debut: 1981
1st-Class 50s scored: 2
Place in batting averages: 193rd av. 17.85 (1986 31st av. 44.00)
Parents: Kenneth and Kathleen
Marital status: Single
Family links with cricket: Father and brothers play for Collingham CC. Younger brother plays for Lincolnshire U-19s
Education: Robert Pattinson Comprehensive School
Qualifications: 4 O-levels, 2 CSEs, cricket coach

Jobs outside cricket: Farming
Off-season 1987–88: Playing for Queensland University, Brisbane
Cricketing superstitions or habits: 'Don't like anyone touching my bat before I go in.'
Overseas teams played for: Poverty Bay CC, New Zealand 1983–84; Queensland University, 1985–88
Cricketers particularly learnt from: Bruce French, Pasty Harris, Bob White
Other sports played: Rugby union, skiing
Relaxations: Watching films, listening to records

LAST SEASON: BATTING

	I.	N.O.	R.	H.S.	AV.
TEST					
1ST-CLASS	15	1	250	45	17.85
INT					
RAL	3	1	41	26	20.50
NAT.W.					
B & H					

LAST SEASON: WICKET KEEPING

	C.	ST.			
TEST					
1ST-CLASS	27	2			
INT					
RAL	5	–			
NAT.W.	1	–			
B & H					

CAREER: BATTING

	I.	N.O.	R.	H.S.	AV.
TEST					
1ST-CLASS	32	7	660	78	26.40
INT					
RAL	5	1	60	26	15.00
NAT.W.					
B & H					

CAREER: WICKET KEEPING

	C.	ST.			
TEST					
1ST-CLASS	67	5			
INT					
RAL	10	1			
NAT.W.	1	–			
B & H					

Extras: One of the youngest players to play for Nottinghamshire in County Championship team – made debut at 17 years 157 days
Best batting performance: 78 Nottinghamshire v Cambridge University, Cambridge 1983

SCOTT, R. J. Hampshire

Full Name: Richard James Scott
Role: Left-hand bat, right-arm medium pace bowler
Born: 2 November 1963, Poole, Dorset
County debut: 1985
Education: Queen Elizabeth School, Wimborne
Extras: Played Minor Counties Cricket for Dorset since 1981. Represented Minor Counties Cricket Association in 1985

LAST SEASON: BATTING

	I.	N.O.	R.	H.S.	AV.
TEST					
1ST-CLASS					
INT					
RAL	3	0	71	48	23.66
NAT.W.					
B & H					

CAREER: BATTING

	I.	N.O.	R.	H.S.	AV.
TEST					
1ST-CLASS					
INT					
RAL	4	1	79	48	26.33
NAT.W.	1	0	0	–	0.00
B & H					

---

146. What age was Graeme Pollock when he played his last game for South Africa in 1987?

SHARMA, R.   Derbyshire

Full Name: Rajesh Sharma
Role: Right-hand bat, off-break
bowler, slip or short-leg
fielder
Born: 27 June 1962, Kenya
Height: 6′ 3″ **Weight:** 13st
Nickname: Reg
County debut: 1985
1st-Class 50s scored: 5
1st-Class 100s scored: 1
1st-Class 5 w. in innings: 1
Place in batting averages: 137th
av. 25.91 (1986 109th av. 29.18)
Place in bowling averages: 123rd
av. 42.66 (1986 88th av. 37.00)
Strike rate 1987: 82.40 (career 80.03)
1st-Class catches 1987: 19 (career 39)
Parents: M. R. and R. D.
Marital status: Single

Family links with cricket: Younger brother has played 2nd XI cricket for Kent
Education: Parkland School for Boys
Qualifications: CSEs and O-levels
Jobs outside cricket: Family business (retail trade)
Overseas teams played for: Mudgreeba, Queensland 1982–83; Helensvale, Queensland 1983–84
Cricketers particularly learnt from: Ron Harland (played for Bexley CC)
Cricketers particularly admired: Viv Richards
Other sports played: Snooker and golf
Other sports followed: Football and snooker

LAST SEASON: BATTING

	I.	N.O.	R.	H.S.	AV.
TEST					
1ST-CLASS	27	4	596	111	25.91
INT					
RAL	5	2	73	19*	24.33
NAT.W.	2	0	26	21	13.00
B & H					

CAREER: BATTING

	I.	N.O.	R.	H.S.	AV.
TEST					
1ST-CLASS	56	12	1126	111	25.59
INT					
RAL	15	5	182	37	18.20
NAT.W.	4	0	46	21	11.50
B & H	1	0	2	2	2.00

LAST SEASON: BOWLING

	O.	M.	R.	W.	AV.
TEST					
1ST-CLASS	206	46	640	15	42.66
INT					
RAL	15	3	72	3	24.00
NAT.W.	13	1	61	0	
B & H					

CAREER: BOWLING

	O.	M.	R.	W.	AV.
TEST					
1ST-CLASS	346.5	79	1047	26	40.26
INT					
RAL	53	5	275	4	68.75
NAT.W.	33	5	113	4	28.25
B & H					

Relaxations: 'Spending lots of time with my dogs, Simba, Sable and Bruno.'
Opinions on cricket: 'I believe that overseas players have improved the standard of county cricket and their experience has helped younger players. However, I fail to understand the fairness of one county being allowed to have more overseas players than others. When each county is allowed an equal number of overseas players the standards will improve even more.'
Best batting performance: 111 Derbyshire v Yorkshire, Chesterfield 1987
Best bowling performance: 6-80 Derbyshire v Gloucestershire, Bristol 1987

SHARP, K. Yorkshire

Full Name: Kevin Sharp
Role: Left-hand bat, off-break bowler
Born: 6 April 1959, Leeds
Height: 5' 10" **Weight:** 12st 9lbs
Nickname: Lambsy, Poodle
County debut: 1976
County cap: 1982
1000 runs in a season: 1
1st-Class 50s scored: 40
1st-Class 100s scored: 13
One-Day 50s: 20
One-Day 100s: 3
Place in batting averages: 132nd av. 26.75 (1986 58th av. 38.32)
1st-Class catches 1987: 6 (career 88)
Parents: Joyce and Gordon
Wife and date of marriage: Karen, 1 October 1983
Children: Amy Lauren, 28 December 1985
Family links with cricket: Father played with Woodhouse in Leeds League for many years. Young brother, David, now playing local cricket
Education: Abbey Grange C of E High School, Leeds
Qualifications: CSE Grade I Religious Education. Coaching award
Jobs outside cricket: Plasterer's labourer, warehouseman, driver for film company
Off-season 1987–88: Coaching at home
Overseas tours: Derrick Robins' XI to Australasia 1980
Overseas teams played for: Subiaco Floreat CC, Perth, Australia; De Beers CC, Griqualand West, 1981–82
Cricketers particularly learnt from: Doug Padgett, Geoff Boycott, Phil Carrick
Cricketers particularly admired: Richard Hadlee, Malcolm Marshall

Other sports played: Golf, squash
Other sports followed: Snooker, soccer
Relaxations: Decorating and maintaining the house
Extras: 260* v Young West Indies 1977. Rested during latter part of 1980 season on medical advice. Captain of England U-19 v West Indies U-19 1978 at Worcester. Winston Churchill Travelling Fellowship to Australia for two months, 1978. 'I took the first wicket of my career in 1984 – a feat I never thought possible.'
Opinions on cricket: 'Would like to see more Englishmen playing for England. Would like to see Graham Gooch and company left alone because of their contact with South Africa. Why should English players be made scapegoats when South Africans are left well alone?'
Best batting performance: 181 Yorkshire v Gloucestershire, Harrogate 1986
Best bowling performance: 2-13 Yorkshire v Glamorgan, Bradford 1984

LAST SEASON: BATTING

	I.	N.O.	R.	H.S.	AV.
TEST					
1ST-CLASS	32	4	749	79*	26.75
INT					
RAL	10	2	299	70*	37.37
NAT.W.	2	0	63	50	31.50
B & H	5	1	125	64*	31.25

CAREER: BATTING

	I.	N.O.	R.	H.S.	AV.
TEST					
1ST-CLASS	310	29	8702	181	30.96
INT					
RAL	108	11	2543	114	26.21
NAT.W.	11	2	192	50	21.33
B & H	37	3	993	118*	45.59

LAST SEASON: BOWLING

	O.	M.	R.	W.	AV.
TEST					
1ST-CLASS	37.1	6	189	1	189.00
INT					
RAL					
NAT.W.	9	0	40	4	10.00
B & H					

CAREER: BOWLING

	O.	M.	R.	W.	AV.
TEST					
1ST-CLASS	195.2	43	791	12	65.91
INT					
RAL	0.1	0	1	0	–
NAT.W.	10	0	47	4	11.75
B & H					

147. What was remarkable about Graeme Pollock's last innings for South Africa in 1987?

SHASTRI, R.　　　　　　　　　Glamorgan

Full Name: Ravishankar Shastri
Role: Right-hand bat, slow
left-arm bowler, close fielder
Born: 27 May 1962, Bombay
Height: 6′ 3½″ **Weight:** 13st 1lb
Nickname: Shas
County debut: 1987
Test debut: 1980–81
No. of Tests: 54
No. of One-Day Internationals: 83
1st-Class 50s scored: 34
1st-Class 100s scored: 14
1st-Class 200s scored: 1
1st-Class 5 w. in innings: 13
1st-Class 10 w. in match: 2
One-Day 50s: 12
One-Day 100s: 2
1st-Class catches 1987: 7 (career 74)

Parents: Jayadritha and Lakshmi
Marital status: Single
Qualifications: Bachelor of Commerce, Bombay University
Jobs outside cricket: Public relations executive
Off-season 1987–88: Playing for India in World Cup and for Bombay
Cricketing superstitions or habits: Left pad and left boot on first
Overseas tours: Young India to Sri Lanka 1980 and England 1981; India to England 1982, 1983, 1986; to West Indies 1983; to New Zealand 1981; to Australia 1985, 1986; to Pakistan 1982, 1983, 1984; to Sri Lanka 1985; to Zimbabwe 1984
Overseas teams played for: Bombay 1979–88

LAST SEASON: BATTING

	I.	N.O.	R.	H.S.	AV.
TEST					
1ST-CLASS	22	3	765	103	40.26
INT					
RAL	12	1	249	46	22.63
NAT.W.	2	0	37	37	18.50
B & H	3	0	50	28	16.66

LAST SEASON: BOWLING

	O.	M.	R.	W.	AV.
TEST					
1ST-CLASS	461.1	100	1181	37	31.91
INT					
RAL	84	4	321	6	53.50
NAT.W.	3.1	1	5	1	5.00
B & H	33	2	117	1	117.00

CAREER: BATTING

	I.	N.O.	R.	H.S.	AV.
TEST	79	11	2463	142	36.22
1ST-CLASS	105	19	3867	200*	44.96
INT	66	15	1690	102	33.13
RAL	12	1	249	46	22.63
NAT.W.	2	0	37	37	18.50
B & H	3	0	50	28	16.66

CAREER: BOWLING

	O.	M.	R.	W.	AV.
TEST	2087.4	557	4683	119	39.35
1ST-CLASS			6209	224	27.71
INT	651	42	2661	82	32.45
RAL	84	4	321	6	53.50
NAT.W.	3.1	1	5	1	5.00
B & H	33	2	117	1	117.00

Cricketers particularly learnt from: Chandu Borde, Sunil Gavaskar, Gary Sobers
Cricketers particularly admired: Imran Khan, Viv Richards, Richard Hadlee, Gundappa Vishwanath, Gary Sobers, Gordon Greenidge
Other sports played: Swimming, tennis, chess
Other sports followed: Tennis, athletics
Injuries 1987: Split webbing between fingers twice and trapped ligaments between shoulder blades
Relaxations: Watching sports, films, listening to music
Extras: Has batted at every number for India except No. 11. Hit six sixes in an over off Tank Raj for Bombay v Baroda at Bombay 1984–85 on the way to highest first-class score of 200*. Played in MCC Bicentenary Test
Opinions on cricket: 'We must have neutral umpires.'
Best batting performance: 200* Bombay v Baroda, Bombay 1984–85
Best bowling performance: 9-101 Bombay v Rest of India, Indore 1981–82

SHAW, C. Yorkshire

Full Name: Christopher Shaw
Role: Right-hand bat, right-arm fast-medium bowler
Born: 17 February 1964, Hemsworth
Height: 6′ **Weight:** 12st 7lbs
Nickname: Sandie
County debut: 1984
1st-Class 5 w. in innings: 3
Place in bowling averages: — (1986 44th av. 27.35)
1st-Class catches 1987: 0 (career 7)
Parents: Brian and Betty
Marital status: Single
Family links with cricket: Father good local league cricketer
Education: Crofton High School
Qualifications: 5 CSEs, Qualified Cricket Coach
Jobs outside cricket: Electrician
Overseas tours: Holland with NCA U-19s (North of England) 1983; Barbados with Yorkshire Cricket Association 1984
Overseas teams played for: Epuni-Cambridge CC, New Zealand 1985–86
Cricketers particularly learnt from: Father, Doug Padgett, Steve Oldham, J. Lawrence
Cricketers particularly admired: Dennis Lillee, Michael Holding

Other sports played: Golf
Other sports followed: Likes watching all sports; keen supporter of Feather-stone Rovers RLFC
Relaxations: Playing golf, listening to music
Extras: 'On debut at Lord's took 4-68 v Middlesex. Took 5-41 in my second JPL match v Hampshire at Bournemouth.'
Best batting performance: 22* Yorkshire v Somerset, Taunton 1987
Best bowling performance: 6-64 Yorkshire v Lancashire, Leeds 1987

LAST SEASON: BATTING

	I.	N.O.	R.	H.S.	AV.
TEST					
1ST-CLASS	5	4	24	22*	24.00
INT					
RAL					
NAT.W.	1	1	1	1*	–
B & H					

LAST SEASON: BOWLING

	O.	M.	R.	W.	AV.
TEST					
1ST-CLASS	95.2	21	268	9	29.77
INT					
RAL	10	1	35	1	35.00
NAT.W.	8	1	41	1	41.00
B & H					

CAREER: BATTING

	I.	N.O.	R.	H.S.	AV.
TEST					
1ST-CLASS	33	15	170	22*	9.44
INT					
RAL	11	4	85	26	12.14
NAT.W.	3	1	8	6*	4.00
B & H					

CAREER: BOWLING

	O.	M.	R.	W.	AV.
TEST					
1ST-CLASS	866.1	185	2579	77	33.49
INT					
RAL	147.3	5	732	26	28.15
NAT.W.	42.1	8	145	6	24.16
B & H					

SHEPHERD, J. N.　　　Gloucestershire

Full Name: John Neil Shepherd
Role: Right-hand bat, right-arm medium bowler
Born: 9 November 1943, St Andrews, Barbados
Height: 5′ 10½″ **Weight:** 12st 11lbs
Nickname: Shep, Walter
County debut: 1966 (Kent), 1982 (Gloucestershire)
County cap: 1967 (Kent), 1983 (Gloucestershire)
Benefit: 1979 (£58,537)
Test debut: 1969
No. of Tests: 5
1000 runs in a season: 2
50 wickets in a season: 65
1st-Class 100s scored: 10
1st-Class 5 w. in innings: 54

1st-Class 10 w. in match: 2
One-Day 50s scored: 13
One-Day 100s scored: 1
1st-Class catches 1987: 2 (career 292)
Parents: Ollie and Kathleen
Wife and date of marriage: Terri, 14 December 1968
Children: Caroline, 31 May 1976; Jacqueline, 21 September 1978; David, 19 January 1982
Family links with cricket: Grandfather and two younger brothers all played
Education: St Andrew's Boys Primary; Alleyn's School, Barbados
Off-season 1987–88: Coaching in county
Cricketing superstitions or habits: 'Always clean my boots and pads before batting. When fielding, try to be last man on field. Never like being on 22 or 33, or facing the last over before any interval.'
Overseas tours: Derrick Robins' XI to South Africa 1973 (being first black cricketer to tour there)
Overseas teams played for: Barbados 1965; Rhodesia in 1975–76 Currie Cup
Cricketers particularly learnt from: Charlie Griffiths, Everton Weekes, Colin Cowdrey, John Snow
Other sports followed: Most sports
Relaxations: Music, golf, squash
Extras: Never played Test cricket again for West Indies after playing for Rhodesia. Played for Kent 1966 to 1981. Introduced to Kent by Colin Cowdrey. Joined Gloucestershire in 1982
Opinions on cricket: 'I would like to see youngsters appear to enjoy the game a bit more, bring back some fun into it.'
Best batting performance: 170 Kent v Northamptonshire, Folkestone 1968
Best bowling performance: 8-40 West Indies v Gloucestershire, Bristol 1969

LAST SEASON: BATTING

	I.	N.O.	R.	H.S.	AV.
TEST					
1ST-CLASS	2	0	6	5	3.00
INT					
RAL	1	0	1	1	1.00
NAT.W.					
B & H					

LAST SEASON: BOWLING

	O.	M.	R.	W.	AV.
TEST					
1ST-CLASS	28	9	92	2	46.00
INT					
RAL	12	1	60	2	30.00
NAT.W.					
B & H					

CAREER: BATTING

	I.	N.O.	R.	H.S.	AV.
TEST	8	0	77	32	9.62
1ST-CLASS	605	106	13282	170	26.61
INT					
RAL	174	48	2953	94	23.43
NAT.W.	32	3	517	101	17.82
B & H	52	7	761	96	16.91

CAREER: BOWLING

	O.	M.	R.	W.	AV.
TEST	240.5	70	479	19	25.21
1ST-CLASS	12303.5	3270	31589	1138	27.75
INT					
RAL	1444.1	108	5732	267	21.46
NAT.W.	443.4	80	1388	60	23.13
B & H	649.1	86	2116	102	20.74

SIDEBOTTOM, A. Yorkshire

Full Name: Arnold Sidebottom
Role: Right-hand bat, right-arm
fast-medium bowler, outfielder
Born: 1 April 1954, Barnsley
Height: 6′ 2″ **Weight:** 13st 10lbs
Nickname: Woofer, Red Setter, Arnie
County debut: 1973
County cap: 1980
Benefit: 1988
Test debut: 1985
No. of Tests: 1
50 wickets in a season: 2
1st-Class 50s scored: 11
1st-Class 100s scored: 1
1st-Class 5 w. in innings: 15
1st-Class 10 w. in match: 2
One-Day 50s: 1
Place in batting averages: 207th
av. 16.31
Place in bowling averages: 65th
av. 29.32 (1986 39th av. 26.84)
Strike rate 1987: 62.34 (career 51.43)
1st-Class catches 1987: 5 (career 46)
Parents: Jack and Florence
Wife and date of marriage: Gillian, 17 June 1977
Children: Ryan Jay, 1978; Dale, 1980
Family links with cricket: Father good cricketer
Education: Barnsley Broadway Grammar School
Jobs outside cricket: Professional footballer with Manchester United for five years, Huddersfield Town for two years and Halifax Town
Overseas tours: Rebel England team to South Africa 1982
Cricketers particularly learnt from: Father, Doug Padgett, Geoff Boycott
Cricketers particularly admired: Steve Oldham, David Bairstow, Graham Stevenson
Other sports played: Professional football, tennis, table tennis, badminton
Other sports followed: Most sports
Relaxations: Watching television, horse racing, playing with sons
Extras: Banned from Test cricket for three years for joining rebel team to South Africa in 1982. Injured toe during Test debut in 1985 and not picked for England again
Best batting performance: 124 Yorkshire v Glamorgan, Cardiff 1977
Best bowling performance: 8-72 Yorkshire v Leicestershire, Middlesbrough 1986

	I.	N.O.	R.	H.S.	AV.
TEST					
1ST-CLASS	22	6	261	33	16.31
INT					
RAL	6	1	84	37	16.80
NAT.W.	1	1	1	1*	–
B & H	3	1	2	2*	1.00

CAREER: BATTING

	I.	N.O.	R.	H.S.	AV.
TEST	1	0	2	2	2.00
1ST-CLASS	209	51	3523	124	22.29
INT					
RAL	65	22	718	52*	16.69
NAT.W.	12	5	173	45	24.71
B & H	24	8	233	32	14.56

LAST SEASON: BOWLING

	O.	M.	R.	W.	AV.
TEST					
1ST-CLASS	446.5	83	1261	43	29.32
INT					
RAL	84	7	354	13	27.23
NAT.W.	13	5	30	5	6.00
B & H	58.4	12	168	12	14.00

CAREER: BOWLING

	O.	M.	R.	W.	AV.
TEST	18.4	3	65	1	65.00
1ST-CLASS	3925	844	11384	459	24.80
INT					
RAL	805.5	36	3486	121	28.80
NAT.W.	174.2	23	507	31	16.35
B & H	403.4	63	1317	65	20.26

SIMMONS, J.   Lancashire

Full Name: Jack Simmons
Role: Right-hand bat, off-break bowler, slip fielder
Born: 28 March 1941, Clayton-le-Moors, nr Accrington
Height: 6′ 2′ **Weight:** 15st
Nickname: Simmo, Flat Jack
County debut: 1968
County cap: 1971
Benefit: 1980 (£128,000)
50 wickets in a season: 8
1st-Class 50s scored: 38
1st-Class 100s scored: 6
1st-Class 5 w. in innings: 39
1st-Class 10 w. in match: 6
One-Day 50s: 6
Place in batting averages: 233rd av. 13.26 (1986 148th av. 25.00)
Place in bowling averages: 13th av. 21.26 (1986 9th av. 21.16)
Strike rate 1987: 57.35 (career 64.56)
1st-Class catches 1987: 16 (career 325)
Parents: Ada and Robert
Wife and date of marriage: Jacqueline, 23 March 1963
Children: Kelly Louise, 28 January 1979
Family links with cricket: Father, Robert, played for Enfield in Lancashire League. Grandfather, Robert, also played for Enfield from 1887, giving 92 years' association with the same club

Education: Accrington Technical School; Blackburn Technical College
Qualifications: 5 O-levels, ONC, City & Guilds in Quantities
Jobs outside cricket: Draughtsman with Accrington Brick & Tile Co Ltd, and Lancashire County Surveyors' Department. Partnership with Clive Lloyd as agents for cricketers; also partnership with Pat Pocock in managing cricket matches for club cricketers at La Manga in Spain. Director of Leisure Centre called 'Bowlers', the largest indoor cricket and bowls centre in the world, situated in Trafford Park, Manchester
Off-season 1987–88: Working at 'Bowlers' plus tour of Bermuda with MCC, and visiting Australia and New Zealand to watch England and take in a tour
Cricketing superstitions or habits: 'I always like to be last on the field. To do the same things again if successful once, i.e. clothes or eating habits.'
Overseas tours: Zimbabwe and South Africa with Whitbread Wanderers 1975; Mike Brearley Invitation XI to Calcutta 1981; New York 1985 with C. Lloyd Lancashire XI
Overseas teams played for: Tasmania 1972–79 (where he is 'a bit of a folk hero'). Captained Tasmania to Gillette Cup for first time in 1979, and when they first entered Sheffield Shield (1978)
Cricketers particularly learnt from: 'Coached by Clyde Walcott when I was a youngster. Learnt from Clive Lloyd with Lancashire. Jack Bond, Ray Illingworth, plus many more off-spinners.'
Cricketers particularly admired: 'Clive Lloyd (great team man), Viv Richards, Chappell brothers and great bowlers, Dennis Lillee and Michael Holding.'
Injuries 1987: Index fingers and thumbs
Relaxations: Soccer, golf, horse racing, eating, playing cards, watching television and going on holiday
Extras: 'I didn't play for a couple of years because I broke my leg three times in ten months and the previous year broke my arm quite badly, all playing soccer – except one broken leg, which was broken going down to the football ground just after I had it out of plaster for the first time.' Made debut for 2nd

LAST SEASON: BATTING

	I.	N.O.	R.	H.S.	AV.
TEST					
1ST-CLASS	24	5	252	64	13.26
INT					
RAL	3	0	26	21	8.66
NAT.W.	1	0	12	12	12.00
B & H	3	1	25	24	12.50

LAST SEASON: BOWLING

	O.	M.	R.	W.	AV.
TEST					
1ST-CLASS	640.3	196	1425	67	21.26
INT					
RAL	72	2	390	14	27.85
NAT.W.	12	0	39	3	13.00
B & H	33	4	134	4	33.50

CAREER: BATTING

	I.	N.O.	R.	H.S.	AV.
TEST					
1ST-CLASS	525	131	8990	112	22.81
INT					
RAL	171	50	1891	65	15.62
NAT.W.	34	14	454	54*	22.70
B & H	50	19	626	64	20.19

CAREER: BOWLING

	O.	M.	R.	W.	AV.
TEST					
1ST-CLASS	446.2 9756.4	94 2284	26096	962	27.12
INT					
RAL	1729.2	132	7189	275	26.14
NAT.W.	567.5	103	1665	74	22.50
B & H	639.2	128	1811	72	25.15

XI in 1959. Hat-trick v Nottinghamshire, Liverpool 1977. Director of Burnley FC. Published autobiography *Flat Jack* in 1986

Opinions on cricket: 'Cricket fines for over rates getting ridiculous. Lbw law should be rethought out by authorities and umpires, especially with regard to batsmen not attempting to play the ball, or a shot at all. I look forward to four-day cricket. It should eventually help young spinners with pitches being covered.'

Best batting performance: 112 Lancashire v Sussex, Hove 1970

Best bowling performance: 7-59 Tasmania v Queensland, Brisbane 1978–79

SLACK, W. N.   Middlesex

Full Name: Wilfred Norris Slack
Role: Left-hand opening bat, right-arm medium bowler, short-leg fielder
Born: 12 December 1954, Troumaca, St Vincent, West Indies
Height: 6′ **Weight:** 13st
Nickname: Slacky, Bishop, Tutu
County debut: 1977
County cap: 1981
Test debut: 1985–86
No. of Tests: 3
No. of One-Day Internationals: 2
1000 runs in a season: 7
1st-Class 50s scored: 69
1st-Class 100s scored: 19
1st-Class 200s scored: 3
One-Day 50s: 24
One-Day 100s: 2
Place in batting averages: 47th av. 38.95 (1986 59th av. 38.25)
1st-Class catches 1987: 14 (career 163)
Parents: Grafton and Doreen
Education: Wellesbourne Secondary, High Wycombe
Qualifications: City & Guilds in Radio and TV mechanics, NCA Advanced Coach
Jobs outside cricket: Digital electronics test engineer
Off-season 1987–88: 'Enjoying life'
Overseas tours: To Pakistan with Rohan Kanhai's World XI 1981; England B to Sri Lanka 1986 and then joined England tour of West Indies 1986; England to Australia 1986–87
Overseas teams played for: Played in Auckland, New Zealand, 1979–80; World XI in Pakistan 1981; Windward Islands in Shell Shield 1981–83

Cricketers particularly learnt from: Don Bennett, Clive Radley
Other sports played: Basketball for Bucks and Wycombe Pirates; tennis, squash, badminton, football, athletics
Injuries 1987: 'Too many to mention'
Relaxations: Building electronic projects. Relaxing in a sauna. Travelling
Extras: Played for Buckinghamshire in 1976. At 16 played for Wycombe Colts. Played for Freith in Haigh Village Cricket Competition. Then joined High Wycombe; then Buckinghamshire in 1976; then Middlesex in 1977. Qualified to play for both West Indies and England
Best batting performance: 248* Middlesex v Worcestershire, Lord's 1981
Best bowling performance: 3-17 Middlesex v Leicestershire, Uxbridge 1982

LAST SEASON: BATTING

	I.	N.O.	R.	H.S.	AV.
TEST					
1ST-CLASS	42	0	1636	173	38.95
INT					
RAL	9	1	173	49	21.62
NAT.W.	2	0	71	45	35.50
B & H	4	1	148	110	49.33

CAREER: BATTING

	I.	N.O.	R.	H.S.	AV.
TEST	6	0	81	52	13.50
1ST-CLASS	360	35	12641	248*	38.89
INT	2	0	43	34	21.50
RAL	84	10	2033	101*	27.47
NAT.W.	21	1	751	98	37.55
B & H	32	4	801	110	28.60

LAST SEASON: BOWLING

	O.	M.	R.	W.	AV.
TEST					
1ST-CLASS	33	9	93	2	46.50
INT					
RAL	15	0	74	3	24.66
NAT.W.	3	0	27	0	–
B & H					

CAREER: BOWLING

	O.	M.	R.	W.	AV.
TEST					
1ST-CLASS	232.5	43	674	21	32.09
INT					
RAL	173.4	1	853	34	25.08
NAT.W.	84	6	317	8	39.62
B & H	7	0	34	0	–

148. What make of bat does Ian Botham use?
149. What make of bat does Mike Gatting use?

SMALL, G. C.   Warwickshire

Full Name: Gladstone Cleophas Small
Role: Right-hand bat, right-arm fast-medium bowler
Born: 18 October 1961, St George, Barbados
Height: 5′ 11″ **Weight:** 12st
Nickname: Gladys
County debut: 1980
County cap: 1982
Test debut: 1986
No. of One-Day Internationals: 13
No. of Tests: 4
50 wickets in a season: 4
1st-Class 50s scored: 1
1st-Class 5 w. in innings: 16
Place in batting averages: 209th av. 16.06 (1986 205th av. 16.00)
Place in bowling averages: 79th av. 31.38 (1986 17th av. 23.12)
Strike rate 1987: 61.76 (career 55.34)
1st-Class catches 1987: 4 (career 46)

Parents: Chelston and Gladys
Marital status: Married
Family links with cricket: Cousin, Milton Small, toured England with West Indies in 1984
Education: Mosely School; Hall Green Technical College, Birmingham
Qualifications: 2 O-levels
Off-season 1987–88: Touring with England
Overseas tours: With Young England to New Zealand 1979–80; Derrick Robins' XI tour of Australia, Tasmania and New Zealand 1980; Rohan Kanhai International XI tour of Pakistan 1981; England to Australia, 1986–87; World Cup 1987; England to Pakistan, Australia and New Zealand 1987–88
Overseas teams played for: Balwyn CC, Melbourne 1982–83, 1984–85; South Australia and West Torrens, Adelaide 1985–86
Cricketers particularly learnt from: David Brown (manager at Warwickshire)
Cricketers particularly admired: Dennis Lillee, Malcolm Marshall, Richard Hadlee, Bob Willis
Other sports played: Golf, tennis
Other sports followed: Athletics, golf, tennis, soccer
Relaxations: 'Playing a round of golf really relaxes me; listening to music and relaxing with my wife.'

Extras: In 1980, became youngest bowler to take five JPL wickets in one innings. Was called up for England Test squad v Pakistan at Edgbaston, July 1982, but did not play. Bowled 18-ball over v Middlesex in August 1982, with 11 no balls

Opinions on cricket: 'The introduction of four-day Championship cricket will improve the first-class game in that teams would have to bowl out the opposition twice instead of relying on contrived results. For four-day cricket to be successful, clubs must be made to produce good, hard cricketing wickets that would be beneficial to both batsmen and bowlers.'

Best batting performance: 57* Warwickshire v Oxford University, Oxford 1982

Best bowling performance: 7-42 South Australia v New South Wales, Adelaide 1985–86

LAST SEASON: BATTING

	I.	N.O.	R.	H.S.	AV.
TEST					
1ST-CLASS	20	4	257	42	16.06
INT					
RAL	2	1	1	1*	–
NAT.W.	1	1	5	5*	–
B & H	1	0	0	0	0.00

LAST SEASON: BOWLING

	O.	M.	R.	W.	AV.
TEST					
1ST-CLASS	350	71	1067	34	31.38
INT					
RAL	23	4	70	3	23.33
NAT.W.	12	1	53	1	53.00
B & H	14	1	52	2	26.00

CAREER: BATTING

	I.	N.O.	R.	H.S.	AV.
TEST	5	2	49	21*	16.33
1ST-CLASS	206	48	2128	57*	13.52
INT	6	3	23	8*	7.66
RAL	41	15	217	40*	8.34
NAT.W.	11	5	104	33	17.33
B & H	17	5	76	19*	6.33

CAREER: BOWLING

	O.	M.	R.	W.	AV.
TEST	142.5	43	314	16	19.62
1ST-CLASS	4155.4	815	13220	450	29.37
INT	128	9	490	12	40.83
RAL	600.3	43	2761	125	22.08
NAT.W.	178.1	34	605	23	26.30
B & H	258.2	44	974	34	28.64

150. What make of bat does David Gower use?

151. What make of bat does Viv Richards endorse?

SMITH, C. L. Hampshire

Full Name: Christopher Lyall Smith
Role: Right-hand bat
Born: 15 October 1958, Durban, South Africa
Height: 5′ 11″ **Weight:** 13st 10lbs
Nickname: Kippy
County debut: 1979 (Glamorgan), 1980 (Hampshire)
County cap: 1981 (Hampshire)
Test debut: 1983
No. of Tests: 8
No. of One-Day Internationals: 4
1000 runs in a season: 6
1st-Class 50s scored: 55
1st-Class 100s scored: 31
1st-Class 200s scored: 1
One-Day 50s: 28
One-Day 100s: 2

Place in batting averages: 17th
av. 46.03 (1986 17th av. 48.22)
1st-Class catches 1987: 26 (career 124)
Parents: John Arnold and Elaine Jessie
Marital status: Single
Family links with cricket: Grandfather, Vernon Lyall Shearer, played for Natal; brother, Robin, also plays for Hampshire
Education: Northlands High School, Durban, South Africa
Qualifications: Matriculation (2 A-level equivalents)
Jobs outside cricket: 'Running Chris Smith Sports Entertainment which specialises in corporate entertaining. Also run a travel business and am involved with Car Phone Group's activities around Hampshire.'
Overseas tours: Toured UK with Kingsmead Mynahs (Natal U-25s under another name) 1976; with England to New Zealand and Pakistan 1983–84; England B to Sri Lanka 1986
Overseas teams played for: Kingsmead Mynahs; Natal Schools 1975; South African Schools 1976; Natal B (debut 1978)
Cricketers particularly admired: Barry Richards, Grayson Heath (coach in South Africa)
Other sports played: League squash, golf (15 handicap)
Other sports followed: Watches football (Southampton FC)
Relaxations: Walking in the countryside with my dog or lying on the beach, swimming, listening to music
Extras: Made debut for Glamorgan in 1979. Played for Gorseinon in South

Wales League in 1979. Made Hampshire debut 1980. Captained Hampshire 2nd XI in 1981. Became eligible to play for England in 1983

Opinions on cricket: 'Still feel the game is undersold and that too few clubs employ successful, proven, get-up-and-go marketing managers. Welcome four-day cricket as it should help to produce more potential Test players.'

Best batting performance: 217 Hampshire v Warwickshire, Edgbaston 1987

Best bowling performance: 3-35 Hampshire v Glamorgan, Southampton 1983

LAST SEASON: BATTING

	I.	N.O.	R.	H.S.	AV.
TEST					
1ST-CLASS	42	9	1519	217	46.03
INT					
RAL	14	4	476	76*	47.60
NAT.W.	2	1	180	140*	180.00
B & H	3	0	30	26	10.00

LAST SEASON: BOWLING

	O.	M.	R.	W.	AV.
TEST					
1ST-CLASS	25	5	75	1	75.00
INT					
RAL					
NAT.W.					
B & H					

CAREER: BATTING

	I.	N.O.	R.	H.S.	AV.
TEST	14	1	392	91	30.15
1ST-CLASS	311	42	11531	217	42.86
INT	4	0	109	70	27.25
RAL	74	13	2513	95	41.19
NAT.W.	16	3	488	140*	37.53
B & H	18	2	446	82*	27.87

CAREER: BOWLING

	O.	M.	R.	W.	AV.
TEST	17	4	39	3	13.00
1ST-CLASS	592.5	114	2243	35	64.08
INT	6	0	28	2	14.00
RAL	3.3	1	10	2	5.00
NAT.W.	12	3	32	3	10.66
B & H					

SMITH, D. M. Surrey

Full Name: David Mark Smith
Role: Left-hand bat, right-arm fast-medium bowler
Born: 9 January 1956, Balham
Height: 6′ 4″ **Weight:** 15st
Nickname: Smudger, Tom
County debut: 1973 (Surrey), 1984 (Worcestershire)
County cap: 1980 (Surrey), 1984 (Worcestershire)
Test debut: 1985–86
No. of Tests: 2
No. of One-Day Internationals: 1
1000 runs in a season: 4
1st-Class 50s scored: 47
1st-Class 100s scored: 17
One-Day 50s: 22
One-Day 100s: 4
Place in batting averages: 53rd av. 37.95 (1986 36th av. 43.37)

1st-Class catches 1987: 10 (career 139)
Parents: Dennis Henry and Tina
Wife and date of marriage: Jacqui, 7 January 1977
Children: Sarah Jane Louise, 4 April 1982
Family links with cricket: Father plays cricket for the BBC
Education: Battersea Grammar School
Qualifications: 3 O-levels
Jobs outside cricket: Two years with insurance company, one year with Harrods, one year spent in Zimbabwe, two years with building firm. Contracts manager, painting and decorating firm
Cricketing superstitions or habits: 'No room for them all.'
Overseas tours: West Indies with England 1986
Overseas teams played for: Sydney University, Australia, 1980–81, 1982–83
Cricketers particularly learnt from: Mickey Stewart, Graham Roope
Cricketers particularly admired: Graham Gooch, Malcolm Marshall, Ian Botham
Other sports played: Football, motor racing
Relaxations: 'I own my own racing car.'
Extras: Played for Surrey 2nd XI in 1972. Was not retained after 1977 but was reinstated in 1978. Top of Surrey first-class batting averages in 1982. Sacked by Surrey during 1983 season. Joined Worcestershire in 1984. Rejoined Surrey in 1987. Has a cocker spaniel called Winston
Best batting performance: 189* Worcestershire v Kent, Worcester, 1984
Best bowling performance: 3-40 Surrey v Sussex, The Oval 1976

LAST SEASON: BATTING

	I.	N.O.	R.	H.S.	AV.
TEST					
1ST-CLASS	27	4	873	121*	37.95
INT					
RAL	8	2	272	72*	45.33
NAT.W.	2	0	36	35	18.00
B & H	6	2	254	110*	63.50

CAREER: BATTING

	I.	N.O.	R.	H.S.	AV.
TEST	4	0	80	47	20.00
1ST-CLASS	335	66	9455	189*	35.14
INT	1	1	10	10*	–
RAL	115	26	2426	87*	27.25
NAT.W.	25	5	978	109	48.90
B & H	46	9	1363	126	36.83

LAST SEASON: BOWLING

	O.	M.	R.	W.	AV.
TEST					
1ST-CLASS					
INT					
RAL					
NAT.W.					
B & H					

CAREER: BOWLING

	O.	M.	R.	W.	AV.
TEST					
1ST-CLASS	456	96	1520	30	50.66
INT					
RAL	124.5	6	606	12	50.50
NAT.W.	31	6	118	4	29.50
B & H	56	4	266	8	33.25

SMITH, G.   Northamptonshire

Full Name: Gareth Smith
Role: Right-hand bat, left-arm
fast-medium bowler, mid-off
or cover fielder
Born: 20 July 1966, Jarrow
Height: 6′ 1″ **Weight:** 12st
Nickname: 'Quite a few actually! –
Happy, Hippy, Bob, Oz, Gelders,
Smudger.'
County debut: 1986
1st-Class 5 w. in innings: 1
1st-Class catches 1987: 1 (career 2)
Parents: John and Patricia
Marital status: Single
Family links with cricket: Father
– 'a fantastic back-garden
all-rounder' – is on selection
committee at Boldon CC
Education: Boldon Comprehensive
School; South Tyneside College
Qualifications: 6 O-levels. B/Tec ONC and OND in computer studies
Jobs outside cricket: Worked in sports shop in Newcastle
Cricketing superstitions or habits: If there is one, it is putting left pad on first
Cricketers particularly learnt from: Bob Carter (Northamptonshire CCC),
Bob Cottam, Keith Judd
Cricketers particularly admired: Michael Holding
Other sports played: Football, squash, golf, badminton
Other sports followed: Follows Sunderland FC
Injuries 1987: Slight back and groin strains
Relaxations: Listening to music, watching TV, reading, go out for a pint to the
local with team-mates
Extras: 'With only my 2nd ball in first-class cricket got the wicket of S. M.
Gavaskar (v Indian tourists, 1986). Was part of a team of runners who ran 759
miles in a relay run from Headingley, via all the other first-class county
grounds to The Oval to raise money for Leukaemia Research.'
Opinions on cricket: 'At times I wish the stumps were twice the normal size
(when bowling of course!). County clubs should do more to find or help find
employment for players who stay at home as opposed to playing cricket
abroad. Uncovered wickets should be outlawed and full covering restored.'
Best batting performance: 29* Northamptonshire v Lancashire, Old Trafford
1987
Best bowling performance: 6-72 Northamptonshire v Sussex, Hove 1987

	I.	N.O.	R.	H.S.	AV.
TEST					
1ST-CLASS	5	1	47	29*	11.75
INT					
RAL					
NAT.W.					
B & H					

LAST SEASON: BOWLING

	O.	M.	R.	W.	AV.
TEST					
1ST-CLASS	81	10	308	13	23.69
INT					
RAL	4	0	17	0	–
NAT.W.					
B & H					

CAREER: BATTING

	I.	N.O.	R.	H.S.	AV.
TEST					
1ST-CLASS	7	1	54	29*	9.00
INT					
RAL					
NAT.W.					
B & H					

CAREER: BOWLING

	O.	M.	R.	W.	AV.
TEST					
1ST-CLASS	121	18	440	15	29.33
INT					
RAL	4	0	17	0	–
NAT.W.					
B & H					

SMITH, I.   Glamorgan

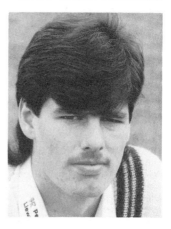

Full Name: Ian Smith
Role: Right-hand bat, right-arm medium bowler, slip fielder, all-rounder
Born: 11 March 1967, Consett
Height: 6′ 3″ **Weight:** 13st
Nickname: Smudger
County debut: 1985
Place in batting averages: 210th av. 16.00
Place in bowling averages: 115th av. 39.84
Strike rate 1987: 66.78 (career 80.04)
1st-Class catches 1987: 6 (career 8)
Parents: Jim and Mary
Marital status: Single
Family links with cricket: Father NCA staff coach, brother plays league cricket
Education: Ryton Comprehensive School
Qualifications: 2 O-levels, CSE
Jobs outside cricket: Coach
Off-season 1987–88: Playing in New Zealand
Cricketing superstitions or habits: Never walk onto the field third
Overseas tours: England Young Cricketers to West Indies 1985
Overseas teams played for: Belgrano CC, Buenos Aires 1986; Papatoetoe, New Zealand 1986–7, 1987–88
Cricketers particularly learnt from: Tom Cartwright, Alan Jones

Cricketers particularly admired: Ian Botham
Other sports played: Football
Other sports followed: All sports
Injuries 1987: Groin strains
Relaxations: Music, fishing
Extras: Played for Young England v Sri Lanka 1986. Represented county at football. Offered terms by Southampton, York City and Carlisle United. Now plays for Blyth Spartans
Best batting performance: 45 Glamorgan v Derbyshire, Cardiff 1987
Best bowling performance: 3-65 Glamorgan v Gloucestershire, Swansea 1987

LAST SEASON: BATTING

	I.	N.O.	R.	H.S.	AV.
TEST					
1ST-CLASS	23	5	288	45	16.00
INT					
RAL	9	3	106	34	17.66
NAT.W.	1	0	5	5	5.00
B & H	1	0	0		0.00

LAST SEASON: BOWLING

	O.	M.	R.	W.	AV.
TEST					
1ST-CLASS	211.3	40	757	19	39.84
INT					
RAL	59	3	264	8	33.00
NAT.W.	4	0	18	1	18.00
B & H	7	0	37	1	37.00

CAREER: BATTING

	I.	N.O.	R.	H.S.	AV.
TEST					
1ST-CLASS	30	5	315	45	12.60
INT					
RAL	13	4	114	34	12.66
NAT.W.	1	0	5	5	5.00
B & H	2	0	6	6	3.00

CAREER: BOWLING

	O.	M.	R.	W.	AV.
TEST					
1ST-CLASS	280.1	54	1022	21	48.66
INT					
RAL	59	3	264	8	33.00
NAT.W.	4	0	18	1	18.00
B & H	14	0	69	1	69.00

152. What make of bat does Graham Gooch use?

153. Who had a higher batting average for Worcestershire last season than Graeme Hick?

SMITH, L. K.   Worcestershire

Full Name: Lawrence Kilner Smith
Role: Right-hand opening bat,
occasional wicket-keeper
Born: 6 January 1964, Mirfield,
Spen Valley, Yorkshire
Height: 5' 8" **Weight:** 9st
Nickname: Smithy, Smudge
County debut: 1985
1st-Class catches 1987: 1 (career 2)
Parents: David Henry Kilner and
Christine Sonia
Marital status: Single
Family links with cricket: Father
played for Derbyshire and Orange
Free State
Education: Stancliffe Hall,
Derbyshire; CBC and St Andrew's,
Welkom, South Africa; KES
Johannesburg; Beachwood, Durban
Jobs outside cricket: Worked as a video electrician for a company operating
video games
Overseas teams played for: Lived and played in South Africa for seven years.
Played in Durban, Natal for Durban Collegians winning batting trophy in
1984–85 season
Cricketers particularly learnt from: 'My father particularly and since coming
to Worcester, Basil D'Oliveira.'
Cricketers particularly admired: Geoff Boycott, David Gower
Other sports played: Squash, golf
Other sports followed: Motor sport and golf

LAST SEASON: BATTING

	I.	N.O.	R.	H.S.	AV.
TEST					
1ST-CLASS	4	1	30	20*	10.00
INT					
RAL					
NAT.W.					
B & H					

LAST SEASON: BOWLING

	O.	M.	R.	W.	AV.
TEST					
1ST-CLASS	7	2	20	1	20.00
INT					
RAL					
NAT.W.					
B & H					

CAREER: BATTING

	I.	N.O.	R.	H.S.	AV.
TEST					
1ST-CLASS	7	1	62	28	10.33
INT					
RAL	1	0	3	3	3.00
NAT.W.					
B & H					

CAREER: BOWLING

	O.	M.	R.	W.	AV.
TEST					
1ST-CLASS	7	2	20	1	20.00
INT					
RAL					
NAT.W.					
B & H					

Relaxations: Music, movies
Extras: Broke batting record for most runs in a season at Stancliffe Hall 1977. First ever honours for cricket at St Andrew's Welkom. OFS schools side
Best batting performance: 28 Worcestershire v Cambridge University, Cambridge 1985
Best bowling performance: 1-20 Worcestershire v Warwickshire, Worcester 1987

SMITH, N. M. K. Warwickshire

Full Name: Neil Michael Knight Smith
Role: Right-hand bat, off-break bowler, slip fielder
Born: 27 July 1967, Birmingham
Height: 6′ 1″ **Weight:** 12½st
Nickname: Smudge, Kit
County debut: 1987
1st-Class catches 1987: 1 (career 1)
Parents: Mike (M.J.K.) and Diana
Marital status: Single
Family links with cricket: Father played for Warwickshire and England
Education: Warwick School
Qualifications: 3 O-levels
Off-season 1987: 'Staying at home and getting a job.'
Cricketing superstitions or habits: 'I always say see you in a minute when leaving the pavilion to go out to bat.'

LAST SEASON: BATTING

	I.	N.O.	R.	H.S.	AV.
TEST					
1ST-CLASS	4	1	56	23	18.66
INT					
RAL	1	0	22	22	22.00
NAT.W.					
B & H					

LAST SEASON: BOWLING

	O.	M.	R.	W.	AV.
TEST					
1ST-CLASS	42	6	152	4	38.00
INT					
RAL	7	0	45	1	45.00
NAT.W.					
B & H					

CAREER: BATTING

	I.	N.O.	R.	H.S.	AV.
TEST					
1ST-CLASS	4	1	56	23	18.66
INT					
RAL	1	0	22	22	22.00
NAT.W.					
B & H					

CAREER: BOWLING

	O.	M.	R.	W.	AV.
TEST					
1ST-CLASS	42	6	152	4	38.00
INT					
RAL	7	0	45	1	45.00
NAT.W.					
B & H					

Overseas tours: South America 1987
Cricketers particularly learnt from: Father, John Emburey
Cricketers particularly admired: David Gower, Derek Randall
Other sports played: Rugby, squash, golf
Other sports followed: Rugby, football, squash, golf
Relaxations: Music and sport
Best batting performance: 23 Warwickshire v Lancashire, Southport 1987
23 Warwickshire v Nottinghamshire, Worksop 1987
Best bowling performance: 2-73 Warwickshire v Lancashire, Southport 1987

SMITH, O. C. K. Gloucestershire

Full Name: Oliver Charles Kennedy Smith
Role: Left-hand bat, off-break bowler
Born: 29 October 1967, Birmingham
Height: 6′ 0″ **Weight:** 11st 12lbs
Nickname: Ollie, Tonto
County debut: 1987
Parents: Anthony Charles and Alison
Marital status: Single
Family links with cricket: Maternal grandfather played for Nottinghamshire Club and Ground
Education: Cotham Grammar School, Bristol; York University
Qualifications: 3 A-levels
Off-season 1987: Studying French at York University
Overseas tours: NCA U-19 to Bermuda 1985; Young England to Sri Lanka 1987
Cricketers particularly learnt from: Graham Wiltshire, John Shepherd, Jim Andrew
Cricketers particularly admired: David Gower, Alec Backhouse (York CC)

LAST SEASON: BATTING	I.	N.O.	R.	H.S.	AV.
TEST					
1ST-CLASS	2	0	15	14	7.50
INT					
RAL					
NAT.W.					
B & H					

CAREER: BATTING	I.	N.O.	R.	H.S.	AV.
TEST					
1ST-CLASS	2	0	15	14	7.50
INT					
RAL					
NAT.W.					
B & H					

Other sports played: Football, badminton
Other sports followed: Almost all sports
Relaxations: Films, music, all sports

SMITH, P. A. Warwickshire

Full Name: Paul Andrew Smith
Role: Right-hand bat, right-arm fast-medium bowler, cover fielder
Born: 15 April 1964, Newcastle
Height: 6′ 2″ **Weight:** 12st
Nickname: Moonman, Smithy
County debut: 1982
County cap: 1986
1000 runs in a season: 2
1st-Class 50s scored: 33
1st-Class 100s scored: 2
One-Day 50s: 4
Place in batting averages: 183rd av. 19.46 (1986 63rd av. 37.70)
Place in bowling averages: 133rd av. 46.05 (1986 124th av. 57.15)
Strike rate 1987: 62.76 (career 62.96)
1st-Class catches 1987: 1 (career 35)
Parents: Kenneth and Joy
Wife and date of marriage: Caroline, 31 July 1987
Family links with cricket: Father played for Leicestershire and Northumberland. Both brothers played for Warwickshire
Education: Heaton Grammar School
Qualifications: 5 O-levels
Jobs outside cricket: Warehouseman 1985–86. Worked for Birmingham Post and Mail
Off-season 1987–88: Working for Birmingham Post and Mail
Cricketing superstitions or habits: 'They all went after last season.'
Overseas teams played for: Florida, Johannesburg, 1982–83; Belgrano CC, Argentina 1983–84; Carlton, Melbourne, 1984–85
Cricketers particularly learnt from: Dennis Amiss, David Brown, Bob Willis
Cricketers particularly admired: Father, K. D. Smith, Ian Botham, David (Vic) Thorne
Other sports played: Occasional squash
Other sports followed: Just cricket
Injuries 1987: Stitches in head, hamstring, cracked hand, back injury
Relaxations: Listening to music, reading music and cricket books, and drinking the odd pint

Extras: Along with Andy Moles set a new world record for most consecutive 50+ partnerships in first 12 innings together. 'In the past 2 years I have had more new helmets than bats.'

Opinions on cricket: 'I think we play far too much cricket and with the amount of time spent on motorways players are very tired before they bowl a ball or take guard. If Sunday matches become 50 overs it will make matters worse.'

Best batting performance: 119 Warwickshire v Worcestershire, Edgbaston 1986

Best bowling performance: 4-25 Warwickshire v Lancashire, Edgbaston 1985

LAST SEASON: BATTING

	I.	N.O.	R.	H.S.	AV.
TEST					
1ST-CLASS	31	5	506	89	19.46
INT					
RAL	6	1	124	56	24.80
NAT.W.	3	0	39	19	13.00
B & H	2	0	18	13	9.00

CAREER: BATTING

	I.	N.O.	R.	H.S.	AV.
TEST					
1ST-CLASS	186	20	4710	119	28.37
INT					
RAL	58	17	914	56	22.29
NAT.W.	12	2	259	79	25.90
B & H	16	3	223	37	17.15

LAST SEASON: BOWLING

	O.	M.	R.	W.	AV.
TEST					
1ST-CLASS	177.5	21	783	17	46.05
INT					
RAL	42	1	235	8	29.37
NAT.W.	18	2	55	2	27.50
B & H	19	3	75	5	15.00

CAREER: BOWLING

	O.	M.	R.	W.	AV.
TEST					
1ST-CLASS	1122.5	139	4888	107	45.68
INT					
RAL	256.1	5	1419	42	33.78
NAT.W.	61.4	3	244	9	27.11
B & H	57.1	4	259	10	25.90

154. Which current county wicket-keeper played soccer for Tottenham Hotspur as a junior?

155. To which county did Yorkshire and England all-rounder Graham Stevenson go when he left Yorkshire?

SMITH, R. A.   Hampshire

Full Name: Robin Arnold Smith
Role: Right-hand bat
Born: 13 September 1963,
Durban, South Africa
Height: 5′ 11½″ **Weight:** 15st
Nickname: Judge
County debut: 1982
County cap: 1985
1000 runs in a season: 2
1st-Class 50s scored: 31
1st-Class 100s scored: 10
1st-Class 200s scored: 1
One-Day 50s: 12
One-Day 100s: 3
Place in batting averages: 13th
av. 48.27 (1986 41st av. 41.23)
1st-Class catches 1987: 18 (career 72)
Parents: John Arnold and Elaine
Jessie

Family links with cricket: Grandfather played for Natal in Currie Cup.
Brother Chris plays for Hampshire, Natal and England
Education: Northlands Boys High, Durban
Qualifications: 'Highly qualified with regard to my educational studies.'
Cricketing superstitions or habits: 'Always have a big night out before a game.'
Overseas teams played for: Natal B, 1980–81; Natal A, 1981–82
Cricketers particularly admired: Barry Richards, Viv Richards, Graeme Pollock, Malcolm Marshall

LAST SEASON: BATTING

	I.	N.O.	R.	H.S.	AV.
TEST					
1ST-CLASS	25	7	869	209*	48.27
INT					
RAL	9	0	174	52	19.33
NAT.W.	1	0	49	49	49.00
B & H	1	0	4	4	4.00

CAREER: BATTING

	I.	N.O.	R.	H.S.	AV.
TEST					
1ST-CLASS	186	34	5977	209*	39.32
INT					
RAL	42	9	1415	104	42.87
NAT.W.	7	1	301	110	50.16
B & H	11	1	324	81	32.40

LAST SEASON: BOWLING

	O.	M.	R.	W.	AV.
TEST					
1ST-CLASS	12	0	88	2	44.00
INT					
RAL					
NAT.W.					
B & H	1	0	2	0	–

CAREER: BOWLING

	O.	M.	R.	W.	AV.
TEST					
1ST-CLASS	94.2	14	408	9	45.33
INT					
RAL					
NAT.W.	2.5	0	13	2	6.50
B & H	1	0	2	0	–

Other sports played: Rugby, squash, golf
Other sports followed: Soccer, athletics
Relaxations: Backgammon, fishing, music and 'siestas'
Extras: Played rugby for Natal Schools, 1980. South Africa Schools Cricket, 1979–80. Still holds South African shot-putt and hurdles U-19 records
Opinions on cricket: 'I am looking forward to seeing the four-day game introduced into English county cricket.'
Best batting performance: 209* Hampshire v Essex, Southampton 1987
Best bowling performance: 2-11 Hampshire v Surrey, Southampton 1985

SPEAK, N. J. Lancashire

Full Name: Nicholas Jason Speak
Role: Right-hand opening bat, off-break bowler, slip fielder
Born: 21 October 1966, Manchester
Height: 6′ 0″ **Weight:** 11st
Nickname: Speaky
County debut: 1987
Parents: John and Irene
Marital status: Single
Family links with cricket: Father was league professional in Lancashire and Yorkshire
Education: Parrswood High School and Sixth Form College
Qualifications: 5 O-levels; NCA Coaching Certificate
Jobs outside cricket: YTS with Lancashire CCC (1986)

Off-season 1987–88: Coaching and playing cricket in New Zealand
Cricketing superstitions or habits: 'Still practising with my local club during the week.'
Overseas tours: NAYC North (for International Youth Competition) to Bermuda 1985; Lancashire CCC pre-season tour to Jamaica 1987
Overseas teams played for: Taradale CC, Napier, New Zealand 1985; Napier Old Boys CC (contracted player), New Zealand 1986 and 1987
Cricketers particularly learned from: Harry Pilling, Alan Ormrod, David Hughes
Cricketers particularly admired: Clive Lloyd, Geoff Boycott, Richard Hadlee, Martin Crowe, Ian Botham
Other sports played: Football, lacrosse, golf
Other sports followed: Golf, tennis, American football

Relaxations: General interest in all sports, music, reading
Opinions on cricket: 'One overseas player per county, with a minimum of a five-year contract. The return of spin bowlers to county and Test cricket. To have more U-25 matches at county level. To see return of South Africa to Test cricket. To see Holland reach Test level, along with Zimbabwe.'
Best batting performance: 4 Lancashire v Jamaica, Sabina Park 1986–87

LAST SEASON: BATTING

	I.	N.O.	R.	H.S.	AV.
TEST					
1ST-CLASS					
INT					
RAL	1	0	13	13	13.00
NAT.W.					
B & H					

CAREER: BATTING

	I.	N.O.	R.	H.S.	AV.
TEST					
1ST-CLASS	2	0	4	4	2.00
INT					
RAL	1	0	13	13	13.00
NAT.W.					
B & H					

STANDING, D. K. — Sussex

Full Name: David Kevin Standing
Role: Right-hand bat, off-break bowler
Born: 21 October 1963, Brighton
Height: 5′ 7″ **Weight:** 11st
Nickname: Uppers, Theo, Gummy
County debut: 1983
1st-Class 50s scored: 5
Place in batting averages: 201st av. 17.03 (1986 193rd av. 17.91)
1st-Class catches 1987: 5 (career 17)
Parents: David Eric and Valerie Mavis
Marital status: Single
Family links with cricket: Father was good local cricketer
Education: Tideway School, Newhaven; Brighton and Hove VI Form
Qualifications: 9 O-levels, 1 A-level, coaching certificate
Jobs outside cricket: Crown Financial Management
Off-season 1987–88: 'Making money!'
Overseas tours: Sussex Young Cricketers to West Indies (as captain) 1983
Cricketers particularly learnt from: Paul Parker
Cricketers particularly admired: Greg Chappell
Other sports played: Golf (as much as possible)
Injuries 1987: Right index finger

Relaxations: Reading, music, drinking – anything other than cricket
Extras: Captained England Schools U-15. Played for England Schools U-19
Opinions on cricket: 'Too much cricket played. Welcome four-day county cricket. Uncovered pitches have caused more hours spent in the pavilion and have done nothing to encourage young spinners as fast bowlers can still stand up.'
Best batting performance: 65 Sussex v Warwickshire, Edgbaston 1986
Best bowling performance: 2-28 Sussex v New Zealand, Hove 1986

LAST SEASON: BATTING

	I.	N.O.	R.	H.S.	AV.
TEST					
1ST-CLASS	29	3	443	56	17.03
INT					
RAL					
NAT.W.					
B & H					

LAST SEASON: BOWLING

	O.	M.	R.	W.	AV.
TEST					
1ST-CLASS	31.2	5	157	2	78.50
INT					
RAL	17	0	85	4	21.25
NAT.W.					
B & H	1	0	7	0	–

CAREER: BATTING

	I.	N.O.	R.	H.S.	AV.
TEST					
1ST-CLASS	67	10	1117	65	19.59
INT					
RAL	2	1	12	8*	12.00
NAT.W.	2	2	1	1*	–
B & H					

CAREER: BOWLING

	O.	M.	R.	W.	AV.
TEST					
1ST-CLASS	230.5	42	725	6	120.83
INT					
RAL	37.1	1	176	7	25.14
NAT.W.	17	3	54	2	27.00
B & H	1	0	7	0	–

STANWORTH, J.   Lancashire

Full Name: John Stanworth
Role: Right-hand bat, wicket-keeper
Born: 30 September 1960, Oldham
Height: 5' 10" **Weight:** 10st 7lbs
Nickname: Stick
County debut: 1983
1st-Class 50s scored: 1
Parents: Robert and Freda
Wife and date of marriage: Dianne, 22 March 1986
Education: Chadderton Grammar School; North Cheshire College, Warrington
Qualifications: 8 O-levels, 1 A-level, BEd Physical Education
Jobs outside cricket: Health and fitness programmer, PE teacher

Off-season 1987–88: Teaching PE

Overseas tours: Australia 1978, playing and coaching in Grade cricket; West Indies 1981 with British Colleges Sports Association

Cricketers particularly learnt from: 'Bob Blair (ex-New Zealand and Wellington) gave me a kick up the pants in my formative years.'

Cricketers particularly admired: Alan Knott for his dedication, Bob Taylor for his 'ease' behind the wicket

Other sports played: Rugby

Relaxations: Car mechanics, TV, music and films

Extras: Instigated pre-season training for the squad

Opinions on cricket: 'The view of the county cricketer should be given more importance in the making of decisions which directly affects his job.'

Best batting performance: 50* Lancashire v Gloucestershire, Bristol 1985

LAST SEASON: BATTING

	I.	N.O.	R.	H.S.	AV.
TEST					
1ST-CLASS	10	3	45	14*	6.42
INT					
RAL	2	2	5	4*	–
NAT.W.	1	0	0	–	–
B & H	2	1	9	7*	9.00

CAREER: BATTING

	I.	N.O.	R.	H.S.	AV.
TEST					
1ST-CLASS	38	11	236	50*	8.74
INT					
RAL	4	2	7	4*	3.50
NAT.W.					
B & H	3	2	17	8*	17.00

LAST SEASON: WICKET KEEPING

	C.	ST.			
TEST					
1ST-CLASS	21	4			
INT					
RAL	2	1			
NAT.W.		1			
B & H	3	–			

CAREER: WICKET KEEPING

	C.	ST.			
TEST					
1ST-CLASS	49	8			
INT					
RAL	10	1			
NAT.W.	6	1			
B & H	4	–			

STEPHENSON, J. P. — Essex

Full Name: John Patrick Stephenson
Role: Right-hand opening bat,
right-arm medium bowler
Born: 14 March 1965, Stebbing
Height: 6′ 1″ **Weight:** 12½st
Nickname: Stanley, DD
County debut: 1985
1st-Class 50s scored: 6
One-Day 50s: 2
Place in batting averages: 130th
av. 27.10 (1986 131st av. 26.95)
1st-Class catches 1987: 10 (career 17)
Parents: Patrick and Eve
Marital status: Single

Family links with cricket: 'Father
member of Rugby Meteors Cricketer
Cup winning side in 1973. Three
brothers in Felstead 1st XI.
Guy played for Essex 2nd XI
and Paul terrorised me in back garden with short-pitched bowling. Mum does
my whites!'
Education: Felstead Prep School; Felstead Senior School; Durham
University
Qualifications: 7 O-levels, 3 A-levels, NCA Coaching Award
Off-season 1987–88: Working at Melbourne CEGS and playing for Fitzroy-
Doncaster CC
Cricketing superstitions or habits: 'They change with my form.'

LAST SEASON: BATTING

	I.	N.O.	R.	H.S.	AV.
TEST					
1ST-CLASS	22	3	515	67*	27.10
INT					
RAL	8	1	123	40*	17.57
NAT.W.	2	0	6	6	3.00
B & H	3	0	119	75	39.66

LAST SEASON: BOWLING

	O.	M.	R.	W.	AV.
TEST					
1ST-CLASS	25.1	3	94	1	94.00
INT					
RAL					
NAT.W.					
B & H	16	0	75	2	37.50

CAREER: BATTING

	I.	N.O.	R.	H.S.	AV.
TEST					
1ST-CLASS	49	4	1176	85	26.13
INT					
RAL	11	2	216	45	24.00
NAT.W.	3	0	61	55	20.33
B & H	3	0	119	75	39.66

CAREER: BOWLING

	O.	M.	R.	W.	AV.
TEST					
1ST-CLASS	27.1	3	99	1	99.00
INT					
RAL					
NAT.W.					
B & H	16	0	75	2	37.50

Overseas tours: Zimbabwe 1982–83 with ESCA U-19s; Barbados with Keith Pont Benefit 1986

Overseas teams played for: Fitzroy CC, Melbourne 1983–84

Cricketers particularly learnt from: Gordon Barker, Ray East

Other sports played: Squash, football, hockey, snooker, golf

Injuries 1987: Recurring problem with right shoulder dislocation

Relaxations: 'Music, keep fit, running, the odd pint, cleaning my car.'

Extras: Awarded 2nd XI cap in 1984 when leading run-scorer with Essex 2nd XI. Young Player of the Year 1985 for Essex CCC. Captained Durham University to victory in UAU Competition 1986. Captain of Combined Universities team 1987 in the first year that it was drawn from all universities

Opinions on cricket: 'Maybe I will be in a position to have some in a couple of years.'

Best batting performance: 85 Essex v Worcestershire, Southend 1986

Best bowling performance: 1-20 Essex v Worcestershire, Colchester 1987

---

156. What is David Bairstow's nickname?

157. Who is captain of Derbyshire?

158. Who is captain of Worcestershire?

159. Who is captain of Northamptonshire?

160. Which county had the least England Test cricketers playing for them last season?

STEVENSON, G. B.   Northamptonshire

Full Name: Graham Barry
Stevenson
Role: Right-hand bat, right-arm
fast-medium bowler
Born: 16 December 1955,
Hemsworth, Yorkshire
Height: 6' **Weight:** 13st
Nickname: Moonbeam
County debut: 1973 (Yorkshire),
1987 (Northamptonshire)
County cap: 1978 (Yorkshire)
Test debut: 1979–80
No. of Tests: 2
No. of One-Day Internationals: 4
50 wickets in a season: 5
1st-Class 50s scored: 16
1st-Class 100s scored: 2
1st-Class 5 w. in innings: 18
1st-Class 10 w. in match: 2
One-Day 50s: 2
1st-Class catches 1987: 0 (career 73)
Wife and date of marriage: Angela, 29 October 1977
Children: Christopher George, 9 January 1982
Family links with cricket: Two uncles, Keith and Jack Stevenson, both played
local league cricket
Education: Minsthorpe High School (where they did not play cricket)
Jobs outside cricket: Clerk at Foster Wheeler Power Products Ltd, Snaith
Overseas tours: England to Australia 1979–80; West Indies 1981
Cricketers particularly learnt from: Geoff Boycott

LAST SEASON: BATTING

	I.	N.O.	R.	H.S.	AV.
TEST					
1ST-CLASS	2	0	2	2	1.00
INT					
RAL	1	0	21	21	21.00
NAT.W.					
B & H					

LAST SEASON: BOWLING

	O.	M.	R.	W.	AV.
TEST					
1ST-CLASS	19.1	3	67	2	33.50
INT					
RAL	8	0	55	4	13.75
NAT.W.					
B & H					

CAREER: BATTING

	I.	N.O.	R.	H.S.	AV.
TEST	2	1	28	27*	28.00
1ST-CLASS	227	33	3937	115*	20.29
INT	4	3	43	28*	43.00
RAL	117	16	1296	81*	12.83
NAT.W.	13	1	190	34	15.83
B & H	28	6	234	36	10.63

CAREER: BOWLING

	O.	M.	R.	W.	AV.
TEST	52	7	183	5	36.60
1ST-CLASS	4394.4	981	13892	483	28.76
INT	32	3	125	7	17.86
RAL	1031.1	76	4696	190	24.71
NAT.W.	193.3	36	612	30	20.40
B & H	413.3	55	1567	74	21.17

Other sports played: Member of local club snooker team, golf
Relaxations: Watching Sheffield Wednesday FC
Extras: Toured Australia with England 1979–80, being called in after return
to England through injury of Mike Hendrick. Vice-President Townville CC.
Steve Oldham was his best man. Batting No. 11 made 115* in a record stand of
149 for Yorkshire v Warwickshire, May 1982, with Geoff Boycott, beating
previous Yorkshire record for last wicket by one run, set by Lord Hawke and
David Hunter in 1898. Released by Yorkshire at end of 1986. Joined
Northamptonshire in 1987. Released at end of 1987 season
Best batting performance: 115* Yorkshire v Warwickshire, Edgbaston 1982
Best bowling performance: 8-57 Yorkshire v Northamptonshire, Leeds 1980

STEWART, A. J. Surrey

Full Name: Alec James Stewart
Role: Right-hand bat, right-arm
medium bowler, occasional
wicket-keeper
Born: 8 April 1963, Wimbledon
Nickname: Stewie
Height: 5′ 11″ Weight: 12st
County debut: 1981
County cap: 1985
1000 runs in a season: 3
1st-Class 50s scored: 33
1st-Class 100s scored: 8
One-Day 50s: 7
Place in batting averages: 52nd
av. 38.09 (1986 24th av. 46.25)
1st-Class catches 1987: 20 (career 100
+ 2 stumpings)
Parents: Michael James and Sheila
Marie Macdonald

Marital status: Single
Family links with cricket: Father played for England (1962–64) and Surrey
(1954–72). Brother Neil plays club cricket and Surrey 2nd XI; sister, Judy,
plays for Malden Wanderers Ladies XI
Education: Tiffin Grammar School
Qualifications: 4 O-levels
Off-season 1987–88: Playing for Midland-Guildford CC in Australia
Overseas tours: 1980–81 tour of Australia with Surrey U-19
Overseas teams played for: Midland-Guildford CC, Western Australia
1981–88

Cricketers particularly learnt from: Geoff Arnold, Mickey Stewart, Kevin Gartrell
Cricketers particularly admired: Geoff Boycott, Tony Mann
Other sports played: 'All sports, especially football.'
Relaxations: 'Music, Perth beaches, eating out, driving.'
Opinions on cricket: 'Sixteen four-day matches and completely covered pitches, both matters meaning all players would be better prepared for Test match cricket.'
Best batting performance: 166 Surrey v Kent, The Oval 1986

LAST SEASON: BATTING

	I.	N.O.	R.	H.S.	AV.
TEST					
1ST-CLASS	34	2	1219	132	38.09
INT					
RAL	8	1	126	52	18.00
NAT.W.	2	1	110	66*	110.00
B & H	2	0	9	9	4.50

CAREER: BATTING

	I.	N.O.	R.	H.S.	AV.
TEST					
1ST-CLASS	151	16	5023	166	37.20
INT					
RAL	52	7	925	86	20.55
NAT.W.	7	1	206	66*	34.33
B & H	12	1	168	63*	15.27

STORIE, A. C. Warwickshire

Full Name: Alastair Caleb Storie
Role: Right-hand bat, right-arm medium bowler
Born: 25 July 1965, Glasgow
Height: 5' 8" **Weight:** 9st 11lbs
Nickname: Ally, Wolf, Archie
County debut: 1985 (Northamptonshire), 1987 (Warwickshire)
1st-Class 50s scored: 4
1st-Class 100s scored: 1
One-Day 50s: 3
Place in batting averages: 156th av. 22.77 (1986 208th av. 15.54)
1st-Class catches 1987: 16 (career 22)
Parents: Hank and Jenny
Marital status: Single
Family links with cricket: Father played club cricket in Glasgow and Johannesburg

Education: St Stithians College, Johannesburg; UNISA Correspondence University
Qualifications: JMB Matriculation
Off-season 1987–88: Coaching abroad

Cricketing superstitions or habits: Always put left pad on first
Overseas teams played for: Transvaal Schools 1978–83; Transvaal B 1985
Cricketers particularly learnt from: Willie Watson, Peter Stringer, Richard Lumb
Cricketers particularly admired: Clive Rice, Dennis Amiss, Wayne Larkins
Other sports played: Represented South Africa U-19 hockey team 1982–83
Other sports followed: Football, rugby union, hockey
Injuries 1987: Broken finger
Relaxations: Music, reading magazines
Extras: First Northamptonshire batsman to score a 100 on first-class debut. Left to join Warwickshire for 1987 season. Scored 50s on both B & H and Sunday League debuts
Opinions on cricket: '2nd XI wickets and umpiring are generally of a low standard and thus do not simulate conditions in first-class cricket.'
Best batting performance: 106 Northamptonshire v Hampshire, Northampton 1985

LAST SEASON: BATTING

	I.	N.O.	R.	H.S.	AV.
TEST					
1ST-CLASS	26	8	410	66*	22.77
INT					
RAL	4	0	86	55	21.50
NAT.W.	2	2	40	24*	–
B & H	3	0	142	66	47.33

CAREER: BATTING

	I.	N.O.	R.	H.S.	AV.
TEST					
1ST-CLASS	49	10	988	106	25.33
INT					
RAL	4	0	86	55	21.50
NAT.W.	2	2	40	24*	–
B & H	3	0	142	66	47.33

---

161. Who is captain of Glamorgan?

162. What have Doug Padgett, Basil D'Oliveira, and Bob Woolmer got in common?

STOVOLD, A. W.   Gloucestershire

Full Name: Andrew Willis-Stovold
Role: Right-hand bat, wicket-keeper
Born: 19 March 1953, Bristol
Height: 5′ 7″ **Weight:** 12st 4lbs
Nickname: Stumper, Squeak, Stov,
Stovers, Stubble
County debut: 1973
County cap: 1976
Benefit: 1987
1000 runs in a season: 7
1st-Class 50s scored: 90
1st-Class 100s scored: 17
1st-Class 200s scored: 1
One-Day 50s: 33
One-Day 100s: 3
Place in batting averages: 152nd
av. 24.09 (1986 116th av. 28.79)
1st-Class catches 1987: 3 (career 270)
Parents: Lancelot Walter and
Dorothy Patricia
Wife and date of marriage: Kay Elizabeth, 30 September 1978
Children: Nicholas, 18 June 1981; Neil, 24 February 1983

LAST SEASON: BATTING

	I.	N.O.	R.	H.S.	AV.
TEST					
1ST-CLASS	43	2	988	88	24.09
INT					
RAL	8	0	180	45	22.50
NAT.W.	4	0	218	94	54.50
B & H	5	1	135	101*	33.75

CAREER: BATTING

	I.	N.O.	R.	H.S.	AV.
TEST					
1ST-CLASS	574	33	16121	212*	29.79
INT					
RAL	164	20	3473	98*	24.11
NAT.W.	29	2	926	94	34.29
B & H	56	8	1804	123	37.58

LAST SEASON: WICKET KEEPING

	C.	ST.			
TEST					
1ST-CLASS	3	–			
INT					
RAL	2	–			
NAT.W.					
B & H	1	–			

LAST SEASON: BOWLING

	O.	M.	R.	W.	AV.
TEST					
1ST-CLASS					
INT					
RAL					
NAT.W.					
B & H					

CAREER: BOWLING

	O.	M.	R.	W.	AV.
TEST					
1ST-CLASS	52.3	8	218	4	54.50
INT					
RAL					
NAT.W.					
B & H					

CAREER: WICKET KEEPING

	C.	ST.			
TEST					
1ST-CLASS	270	45			
INT					
RAL	80	13			
NAT.W.	17	5			
B & H	37	4			

Family links with cricket: Father played local club cricket for Old Down CC. Brother, Martin, also played county cricket for Gloucestershire
Education: Filton High School; Loughborough College of Education
Qualifications: Certificate of Education
Jobs outside cricket: Teacher at Tockington Manor Prep School
Cricketing superstitions or habits: 'Keeping the same routine until I have a bad run, then trying something else. Always prepare for batting in the same order.'
Overseas tours: England Schools to India 1970–71; England Young Cricketers to West Indies 1972
Overseas teams played for: Orange Free State 1974–76
Cricketers particularly admired: Mike Procter, Barry Richards, Richard Hadlee
Other sports played: Football, golf
Other sports followed: Rugby, hunting, horse racing
Relaxations: Gardening, walking
Extras: Writes a weekly article for *Gloucestershire Echo*
Opinions on cricket: 'Worried about the sudden increase in player "transfers". We must not let it get too much like football.'
Best batting performance: 212* Gloucestershire v Northamptonshire, Northampton 1982
Best bowling performance: 1-0 Gloucestershire v Derbyshire, Bristol 1976

SUCH, P. M. — Leicestershire

Full Name: Peter Mark Such
Role: Right-hand bat, off-break bowler
Born: 12 June 1964, Helensburgh, Scotland
Height: 6' 1" **Weight:** 11st 7lbs
Nickname: Suchy
County debut: 1982 (Nottinghamshire), 1987 (Leicestershire)
1st-Class 5 w. in innings: 6
Place in bowling averages: 72nd av. 30.63 (1986 32nd av. 25.72)
Strike rate 1987: 71.73 (career 62.59)
1st-Class catches 1987: 8 (career 37)
Parents: John and Margaret
Marital status: Single
Family links with cricket: Father and brother village cricketers

Education: Harry Carlton Comprehensive
Qualifications: 9 O-levels, 3 A-levels. Qualified Cricket Coach (Senior)
Jobs outside cricket: Van driver
Off-season 1987–88: Working in England
Overseas teams played for: Kempton Park CC, South Africa 1982–83; Bathurst CC, New South Wales 1985–86
Cricketers particularly learnt from: Bob White, Eddie Hemmings
Cricketers particularly admired: Richard Hadlee
Other sports played: Hockey, golf
Other sports followed: American football
Relaxations: Music, TV, films, playing golf
Extras: Played for Young England v Young Australia in three 'Tests' in 1983. Represented TCCB v New Zealand 1986. Left Nottinghamshire at end of 1986 season. Joined Leicestershire for 1987
Best batting performance: 16 Nottinghamshire v Middlesex, Lord's 1984
Best bowling performance: 6-123 Nottinghamshire v Kent, Trent Bridge 1983

LAST SEASON: BATTING

	I.	N.O.	R.	H.S.	AV.
TEST					
1ST-CLASS	17	9	28	12	3.50
INT					
RAL					
NAT.W.					
B & H					

CAREER: BATTING

	I.	N.O.	R.	H.S.	AV.
TEST					
1ST-CLASS	67	26	100	16	2.43
INT					
RAL	1	1	0	0*	–
NAT.W.					
B & H					

LAST SEASON: BOWLING

	O.	M.	R.	W.	AV.
TEST					
1ST-CLASS	490.1	142	1256	41	30.63
INT					
RAL	20	1	105	1	105.00
NAT.W.					
B & H					

CAREER: BOWLING

	O.	M.	R.	W.	AV.
TEST					
1ST-CLASS	1898.5	527	5415	182	29.75
INT					
RAL	35	1	221	3	73.66
NAT.W.					
B & H	33	1	151	4	37.75

163. Which county had the most Test players playing for them last season?

SWALLOW, I. G. — Yorkshire

Full Name: Ian Geoffrey Swallow
Role: Right-hand bat, off-break bowler, cover or slip fielder
Born: 18 December 1962, Barnsley
Height: 5′ 7″ **Weight:** 10st
Nickname: Chicken or Swal
County debut: 1983
1st-Class 50s scored: 1
1st-Class 100s scored: 1
1st-Class 5 w. in innings: 1
Place in batting averages: 67th av. 35.57 (1986 144th av. 25.33)
1st-Class catches 1987: 4 (career 18)
Parents: Joyce and Geoffrey
Marital status: Single
Family links with cricket: Father and brother both played for Elsecar Village CC
Education: Hayland Kirk, Balk, Comprehensive School; Barnsley Technical College
Qualifications: 3 O-levels
Jobs outside cricket: Storeman
Off-season 1987–88: Working in England
Cricketing superstitions or habits: Always put left pad on first
Overseas teams played for: Sunshine CC, Melbourne 1985–86, 1986–87
Cricketers particularly learnt from: Doug Padgett, Phil Carrick, Steve Oldham
Cricketers particularly admired: Viv Richards, John Emburey

LAST SEASON: BATTING

	I.	N.O.	R.	H.S.	AV.
TEST					
1ST-CLASS	9	2	249	114	35.57
INT					
RAL					
NAT.W.					
B & H					

CAREER: BATTING

	I.	N.O.	R.	H.S.	AV.
TEST					
1ST-CLASS	43	14	657	114	22.65
INT					
RAL	1	0	2	2	2.00
NAT.W.					
B & H	3	2	18	10*	18.00

LAST SEASON: BOWLING

	O.	M.	R.	W.	AV.
TEST					
1ST-CLASS	111	25	349	11	31.72
INT					
RAL					
NAT.W.					
B & H					

CAREER: BOWLING

	O.	M.	R.	W.	AV.
TEST					
1ST-CLASS	767.5	178	2231	46	48.50
INT					
RAL	4	0	31	0	–
NAT.W.					
B & H	36	4	151	2	75.50

Other sports played: Football and most sports for fun
Other sports followed: Barnsley FC, all sports
Relaxations: Sport in general
Extras: Took hat-trick v Warwickshire 2nd XI 1984. Figures: 4-3-2-4
Best batting performance: 114 Yorkshire v MCC, Scarborough 1987
Best bowling performance: 7-95 Yorkshire v Nottinghamshire, Trent Bridge
1987

SYKES, J. F.   Middlesex

Full Name: James Frederick Sykes
Role: Right-hand bat, off-break
bowler, slip or gully fielder
Born: 30 December 1965,
Shoreditch
Height: 6′ 2″ **Weight:** 13st 7lbs
Nickname: Eric, Sykesy
County debut: 1983
1st-Class 50s scored: 1
1st-Class 100s scored: 1
1st-Class catches 1987: 2 (career 12)
Parents: James and Kathleen
Education: Bow Comprehensive
Qualifications: 1 O-level
Jobs outside cricket: Coaching
in South Africa for 2 weeks
Off-season 1987–88: Training
hard for 1988 season

Cricketing superstitions or habits: 49, 99

LAST SEASON: BATTING

	I.	N.O.	R.	H.S.	AV.
TEST					
1ST-CLASS	3	1	21	10	10.50
INT					
RAL	2	0	16	11	8.00
NAT.W.					
B & H					

LAST SEASON: BOWLING

	O.	M.	R.	W.	AV.
TEST					
1ST-CLASS	50	16	115	6	19.16
INT					
RAL	30	0	128	6	21.33
NAT.W.					
B & H					

CAREER: BATTING

	I.	N.O.	R.	H.S.	AV.
TEST					
1ST-CLASS	21	5	363	126	22.68
INT					
RAL	8	1	65	25	9.28
NAT.W.					
B & H					

CAREER: BOWLING

	O.	M.	R.	W.	AV.
TEST					
1ST-CLASS	306.2	69	905	25	36.20
INT					
RAL	86	1	342	12	28.50
NAT.W.					
B & H					

Overseas tours: England U-19 to West Indies 1984–85
Cricketers particularly learnt from: John Emburey, Don Bennett, Graham Barlow, Wayne Daniel
Cricketers particularly admired: Clive Radley, Neil Williams
Other sports played: Squash, football
Injuries 1987: Shoulder injury
Best batting performance: 126 Middlesex v Cambridge University, Cambridge 1985
Best bowling performance: 4-49 Middlesex v Glamorgan, Cardiff 1987

TAVARÉ, C. J. Kent

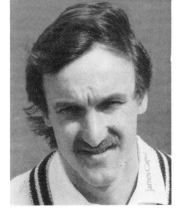

Full Name: Christopher James Tavaré
Role: Right-hand bat, off-break bowler, slip fielder
Born: 27 October 1954, Orpington
Height: 6′ 1½″ **Weight:** 12st 12lbs
Nickname: Tav, Rowdy
County debut: 1974
County cap: 1978
Benefit: 1988
Test debut: 1980
No. of Tests: 30
No. of One-Day Internationals: 29
1000 runs in a season: 11
1st-Class 50s scored: 98
1st-Class 100s scored: 31
One-Day 50s: 43
One-Day 100s: 8
Place in batting averages: 87th
av. 33.05 (1986 86th av. 33.34)
1st-Class catches 1987: 29 (career 299)
Parents: Andrew and June
Wife and date of marriage: Vanessa, 22 March 1980
Family links with cricket: Father, uncle Jack Tavaré, and uncle, Derrick Attwood, all played school and club cricket, father and Uncle Jack at Chatham House, father and Uncle Derrick at Bickley Park CC. Elder brother, Stephen, and younger brother, Jeremy, both play cricket
Education: Sevenoaks School; Oxford University
Qualifications: Zoology degree
Jobs outside cricket: Consultant, N. M. Schroder Financial Management Ltd
Off-season 1987–88: Working for Schroders

Overseas tours: England to India and Sri Lanka 1981–82; England to Australia and New Zealand 1982–83; England to New Zealand and Pakistan 1983–84

Overseas teams played for: University of Western Australia, Perth, 1977–78; West Perth CC for half a season 1978–79

Other sports followed: 'Take an interest in most sports, especially American football in winter.'

Relaxations: Music, zoology, films, gardening, woodwork, golf

Extras: Played for England Schools v All-India Schools at Birmingham in 1973, scoring 124*. Oxford University cricket blue 1975–76–77. Whitbread Scholarship to Perth, Australia, 1978–79. Suffers from asthma and hay-fever. Was top-scorer with 82* and Man of the Match, on debut for England in 55-over match v West Indies at Headingley, May 1980. Captain of Kent 1983–84

Best batting performance: 168* Kent v Essex, Chelmsford 1982
Best bowling performance: 1-3 Kent v Hampshire, Canterbury 1986

LAST SEASON: BATTING

	I.	N.O.	R.	H.S.	AV.
TEST					
1ST-CLASS	42	7	1157	152	33.05
INT					
RAL	14	0	389	90	27.78
NAT.W.	2	0	0		0.00
B & H	6	1	246	78	49.20

CAREER: BATTING

	I.	N.O.	R.	H.S.	AV.
TEST	55	2	1753	149	33.07
1ST-CLASS	461	55	15356	168*	37.82
INT	28	2	720	83*	27.69
RAL	143	19	4001	136*	32.26
NAT.W.	26	3	871	118*	37.86
B & H	66	4	1790	143	28.87

LAST SEASON: BOWLING

	O.	M.	R.	W.	AV.
TEST					
1ST-CLASS	30.1	5	125	1	125.00
INT					
RAL					
NAT.W.					
B & H					

CAREER: BOWLING

	O.	M.	R.	W.	AV.
TEST	6	3	11	0	–
1ST-CLASS	102.5	15	514	5	102.80
INT					
RAL					
NAT.W.					
B & H					

164. Who won the World Cup in 1987?

TAYLOR, L. B. Leicestershire

Full Name: Leslie Brian Taylor
Role: Right-hand bat, right-arm
fast-medium bowler
Born: 25 October 1953, Earl Shilton,
Leicestershire
Height: 6′ 3½″ **Weight:** 14st 7lbs
Nickname: Les
County debut: 1977
County cap: 1981
Test debut: 1985
No. of Tests: 2
No. of One-Day Internationals: 2
50 wickets in a season: 4
1st-Class 5 w. in innings: 17
1st-Class 10 w. in match: 1
Place in bowling averages: 42nd
av. 25.95 (1986 62nd av. 29.96)

Strike rate 1987: 44.19 (career 51.88)
1st-Class catches 1987: 0 (career 44)
Parents: Peggy and Cyril
Wife and date of marriage: Susan, 12 July 1973
Children: Jamie, 24 June 1976; Donna, 10 November 1978; Suzy, 3 June 1981
Family links with cricket: Relation of the late Sam Coe, holder of highest
individual score for Leicestershire, 252* v Northamptonshire at Leicester in
1914
Education: Heathfield High School, Earl Shilton
Qualifications: Qualified carpenter and joiner
Overseas tours: South America with Derrick Robins' XI in 1978–79; West
Indies with England 1986

LAST SEASON: BATTING

	I.	N.O.	R.	H.S.	AV.
TEST					
1ST-CLASS	9	3	66	16	11.00
INT					
RAL	3	2	8	5*	8.00
NAT.W.					
B & H	3	2	7	4*	7.00

LAST SEASON: BOWLING

	O.	M.	R.	W.	AV.
TEST					
1ST-CLASS	154.4	20	545	21	25.95
INT					
RAL	36.2	1	204	4	51.00
NAT.W.					
B & H	29.4	4	99	6	16.50

CAREER: BATTING

	I.	N.O.	R.	H.S.	AV.
TEST	1	1	1	1*	–
1ST-CLASS	164	71	889	47	9.55
INT	1	1	1	1*	–
RAL	29	22	99	15*	14.14
NAT.W.	6	5	18	6*	18.00
B & H	10	5	18	5	3.60

CAREER: BOWLING

	O.	M.	R.	W.	AV.
TEST	63.3	11	178	4	44.50
1ST-CLASS	4479.4	1102	12598	518	24.32
INT	14	3	47	0	–
RAL	731	58	3164	150	21.09
NAT.W.	146.1	23	496	30	16.53
B & H	297	57	961	50	19.22

Overseas teams played for: Natal 1982–84
Other sports: Swimming and football
Relaxations: Game-shooting and fox-hunting with the Atherstone Hunt
Extras: Was banned from Test cricket for three years for joining rebel England tour of South Africa in 1982
Opinions on cricket: 'Should not be subjected to over-rate fines in one-day cricket.'
Best batting performance: 47 Leicestershire v Derbyshire, Derby 1983
Best bowling performance: 7-28 Leicestershire v Derbyshire, Leicester 1981

TAYLOR, N. R.   Kent

Full Name: Neil Royston Taylor
Role: Right-hand bat, off-break bowler, outfielder
Born: 21 July 1959, Farnborough, Kent
Height: 6′ 1″ **Weight:** 13st 10lbs
Nickname: Map
County debut: 1979
County cap: 1982
1000 runs in a season: 5
1st-Class 50s scored: 35
1st-Class 100s scored: 18
One-Day 50s: 10
One-Day 100s: 3
Place in batting averages: 60th av. 37.14 (1986 97th av. 31.10)
1st-Class catches 1987: 14 (career 84)
Parents: Leonard and Audrey
Wife and date of marriage: Jane Claire, 25 September 1982
Children: Amy Louise, 7 November 1985
Family links with cricket: Brother Colin played for Kent U-19s. Father played club cricket
Education: Cray Valley Technical High School
Qualifications: 8 O-levels, 2 A-levels, NCA Coaching Certificate
Jobs outside cricket: Insurance broker, and working in Civil Service
Off-season 1987–88: Working for Mildon & Co, financial consultants, Canterbury
Cricketing superstitions or habits: Always put batting gear on in same order
Overseas tours: With England Schools Team to India 1977–78; Kent to Vancouver 1979

Overseas teams played for: Randburg, Johannesburg, South Africa, 1980–86; Coach at St Stithians College 1981–86

Cricketers particularly learnt from: Bob Woolmer, Mark Benson

Cricketers particularly admired: Alan Knott

Other sports played: Rugby (played for Kent U-21 XV), golf

Injuries 1987: Badly bruised left hand

Relaxations: Listening to records, reading autobiographies, lying in bed reading the Sunday newspapers

Extras: Made 110 on debut for Kent CCC v Sri Lanka, 1979. Won four Man of the Match awards in first five matches. Scored highest score by Kent player in Benson and Hedges cricket: 121 v Sussex and Somerset

Opinions on cricket: 'Have uncovered wickets worked? If the aim of uncovering was to aid the spinners, there seems to be very few in the first-class averages. And you can't get a much wetter summer. The faster bowlers are the only one's benefiting.'

Best batting performance: 155* Kent v Glamorgan, Cardiff 1983

Best bowling performance: 2-20 Kent v Somerset, Canterbury 1985

LAST SEASON: BATTING

	I.	N.O.	R.	H.S.	AV.
TEST					
1ST-CLASS	38	3	1300	142*	37.14
INT					
RAL	6	2	64	26*	16.00
NAT.W.	1	0	85	85	85.00
B & H	1	0	15	15	15.00

LAST SEASON: BOWLING

	O.	M.	R.	W.	AV.
TEST					
1ST-CLASS	7	0	28	0	–
INT					
RAL					
NAT.W.					
B & H	2	1	5	0	–

CAREER: BATTING

	I.	N.O.	R.	H.S.	AV.
TEST					
1ST-CLASS	264	36	7909	155*	34.68
INT					
RAL	56	6	1282	75*	25.64
NAT.W.	11	0	318	85	28.90
B & H	21	1	801	121	40.05

CAREER: BOWLING

	O.	M.	R.	W.	AV.
TEST					
1ST-CLASS	228.3	37	788	14	56.28
INT					
RAL					
NAT.W.	9	3	19	0	–
B & H	2	1	5	0	–

165. Who was beaten in the 1987 World Cup Final, and by how many runs?

166. On what ground was the 1987 World Cup Final played?

TEDSTONE, G. A.   Warwickshire

Full Name: Geoffrey Alan Tedstone
Role: Right-hand bat, wicket-keeper
Born: 19 January 1961, Southport
Height: 5′ 6½″ **Weight:** 10½st
Nickname: Ted
County debut: 1982
1st-Class 50s scored: 2
One-Day 50s: 1
Place in batting averages:
229th av. 13.84
Parents: Ken and Win
Marital status: Single
Family links with cricket:
Sister, Janet Aspinall, plays for
England Ladies. Father played club
cricket for Leamington. Brother
Roger plays for Leamington
Education: Warwick School;
St Pauls College, Cheltenham

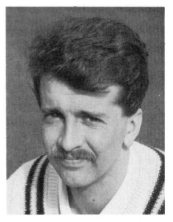

Qualifications: 6 O-levels, 4 A-levels, BEd degree, qualified teacher, FA coach
Jobs outside cricket: PE teacher
Off-season 1987–88: Teaching at Westhouse School in Edgbaston
Overseas tours: Young England to West Indies 1980; British Colleges to West Indies 1981; Dennis Amiss XI to Barbados 1985
Overseas teams played for: Union High School, South Africa 1982–83
Cricketers particularly admired: Dennis Amiss, Bob Taylor
Other sports played: Hockey for Coventry and Warwickshire

LAST SEASON: BATTING

	I.	N.O.	R.	H.S.	AV.
TEST					
1ST-CLASS	14	1	180	51	13.84
INT					
RAL	3	2	49	31*	49.00
NAT.W.	1	1	55	55*	
B & H					

LAST SEASON: WICKET KEEPING

	C.	ST.			
TEST					
1ST-CLASS	13	2			
INT					
RAL	6	–			
NAT.W.					
B & H					

CAREER: BATTING

	I.	N.O.	R.	H.S.	AV.
TEST					
1ST-CLASS	37	7	490	67*	16.33
INT					
RAL	5	2	74	31*	24.66
NAT.W.	1	1	55	55*	
B & H					

CAREER: WICKET KEEPING

	C.	ST.			
TEST					
1ST-CLASS	42	9			
INT					
RAL	8	–			
NAT.W.	–	–			
B & H					

Other sports followed: Soccer (Wolverhampton Wanderers FC)
Relaxations: Playing or watching most sports, listening to music, watching films and socialising
Extras: 'Changed last season from being a tireless medium pace net bowler into a tiresome non-turning off-spin net bowler.'
Best batting performance: 67* Warwickshire v Cambridge University, Cambridge 1983

TENNANT, L.   Leicestershire

Full Name: Lloyd Tennant
Role: Right-hand bat, right-arm medium bowler, outfielder
Born: 9 April 1968, Walsall
Height: 5′ 11″ **Weight:** 12st 7lbs
Nickname: Charmaine (after the Tennent Lager advert)
County debut: 1986
1st-Class catches 1987: 1 career (1)
Parents: Jean and Dennis Tennant
Marital status: Single
Family links with cricket:
Father played local club cricket as opening bowler
Education: Shellfield Comprehensive School
Qualifications: 8 CSEs
Jobs outside cricket:
Fencing and bricklaying
Off-season 1987–88:
Working for GBG Fencing Ltd

LAST SEASON: BATTING

	I.	N.O.	R.	H.S.	AV.
TEST					
1ST-CLASS					
INT					
RAL					
NAT.W.					
B & H					

CAREER: BATTING

	I.	N.O.	R.	H.S.	AV.
TEST					
1ST-CLASS	2	1	13	12*	13.00
INT					
RAL	1	1	2	2*	–
NAT.W.					
B & H					

LAST SEASON: BOWLING

	O.	M.	R.	W.	AV.
TEST					
1ST-CLASS	19	3	56	2	28.00
INT					
RAL					
NAT.W.					
B & H					

CAREER: BOWLING

	O.	M.	R.	W.	AV.
TEST					
1ST-CLASS	27	4	91	2	45.50
INT					
RAL	33	2	145	6	24.16
NAT.W.					
B & H					

Cricketing superstitions or habits: Wearing favourite gear
Overseas tours: England U-19 to Sri Lanka 1986–87
Cricketers particularly learnt from: Ken Higgs, Alan Townsend
Cricketers particularly admired: Ian Botham, Dennis Lillee
Other sports played: Football
Relaxations: Listening to music, watching TV
Best batting performance: 12* Leicestershire v Sussex, Leicester 1986
Best bowling performance: 1-15 Leicestershire v Cambridge University, Cambridge 1987

TERRY, V. P.   Hampshire

Full Name: Vivian Paul Terry
Role: Right-hand bat, right-arm medium bowler, slip or cover fielder
Born: 14 January 1959, Osnabruck, West Germany
Height: 6′ 0″ **Weight:** 13st
County debut: 1978
County cap: 1983
Test debut: 1984
No. of Tests: 2
1000 runs in a season: 4
1st-Class 50s scored: 40
1st-Class 100s scored: 13
One-Day 50s: 16
One-Day 100s: 5
Place in batting averages: 27th av. 43.18 (1986 124th av. 28.00)
1st-Class catches 1987: 29 (career 123)

Parents: Michael and Patricia
Wife and date of marriage: Bernadette, 4 June 1986
Education: Durlston Court, Barton-on-Sea, Hampshire; Millfield School, Somerset
Qualifications: 8 O-levels, 1 A-level, cricket coach
Jobs outside cricket: Worked in a fish factory, apple picker, estate agent
Off-season 1987–88: Playing in Perth
Overseas tours: ESCA tour to India 1977–78; Gordon Greenidge benefit tour to Paris and Isle of Wight; English Counties tour to Zimbabwe 1985
Overseas teams played for: Sydney 1978–79; in New Zealand 1980–81; Durban Collegians 1982–83
Cricketers particularly learnt from: Chris Smith

Cricketers particularly admired: Gordon Greenidge, Chris Smith, Viv and Barry Richards, Malcolm Marshall, Gary Sobers
Other sports played: Golf, squash, soccer
Injuries 1987: 'Being dropped was the biggest injury.'
Relaxations: Music, sport
Best batting performance: 175* Hampshire v Gloucestershire, Bristol 1984

LAST SEASON: BATTING

	I.	N.O.	R.	H.S.	AV.
TEST					
1ST-CLASS	37	5	1382	122	43.18
INT					
RAL	13	1	467	80	38.91
NAT.W.					
B & H	5	1	228	67*	57.00

CAREER: BATTING

	I.	N.O.	R.	H.S.	AV.
TEST	3	0	16	3	5.33
1ST-CLASS	205	25	6496	175*	36.08
INT					
RAL	86	14	2315	142	32.15
NAT.W.	13	1	440	165*	36.66
B & H	25	1	690	72	28.75

THOMAS, D. J. Gloucestershire

Full Name: David James Thomas
Role: Left-hand bat, left-arm fast-medium bowler
Born: 30 June 1959, Solihull, Warwickshire
Height: 6' 0" **Weight:** 13st 6lbs
Nickname: Teddy
County debut: 1977 (Surrey)
County cap: 1982 (Surrey)
50 wickets in a season: 2
1st-Class 50s scored: 7
1st-Class 100s scored: 2
1st-Class 5 w. in innings: 7
1st-Class 10 w. in match: 1
One-Day 50s: 6
Place in batting averages: 184th av. 18.69 (1986 125th av. 27.75)
Place in bowling averages: 105th av. 37.27 (1986 117th av. 49.00)
Strike rate 1987: 64.90 (career 64.08)
1st-Class catches 1987: 5 (career 49)
Parents: Howard James and Heather
Wife and date of marriage: Miranda, 20 February 1982
Children: Christopher James Owen, 4 May 1986
Family links with cricket: Father played for RAF. Brother, Howard, played for Bucks U-19 and now club cricket
Education: Licensed Victuallers' School, Slough

Jobs outside cricket: Salesman for Securicor Communications and PR for Europa Communications

Off-season 1987–88: Working for own sports promotion company, Thomas Promotions

Overseas tours: Surrey CCC tour of the Far East and Antigua; *Cricketer* International to Dubai; Whitbread Scholarship in Australia 1982–83

Overseas teams played for: Northern Transvaal 1980–81; Natal 1983–84

Cricketers particularly admired: Mike Procter, Robin Jackman, Imran Khan, Graham Monkhouse

Other sports played: Golf, squash

Injuries 1987: Groin strain, torn calf muscle, shoulder strain

Relaxations: Theatre, pubs, watching Chelsea FC

Extras: Played for England U-19 v West Indies U-19, and for Derrick Robins' XI v New Zealand U-25 XI. Released by Surrey at end of 1987 season and joined Gloucestershire on a two-year contract in 1988

Best batting performance: 119 Surrey v Nottinghamshire, The Oval 1983

Best bowling performance: 6-36 Surrey v Somerset, The Oval 1984

LAST SEASON: BATTING

	I.	N.O.	R.	H.S.	AV.
TEST					
1ST-CLASS	17	4	243	49	18.69
INT					
RAL	3	1	41	24	20.50
NAT.W.					
B & H	3	1	33	22	16.50

CAREER: BATTING

	I.	N.O.	R.	H.S.	AV.
TEST					
1ST-CLASS	189	40	2967	119	19.91
INT					
RAL	70	15	1056	72	19.20
NAT.W.	16	5	279	65	25.36
B & H	14	2	108	22	9.00

LAST SEASON: BOWLING

	O.	M.	R.	W.	AV.
TEST					
1ST-CLASS	357	61	1230	33	37.27
INT					
RAL	44	2	232	7	33.14
NAT.W.	12	2	34	2	17.00
B & H	53	5	225	3	75.00

CAREER: BOWLING

	O.	M.	R.	W.	AV.
TEST					
1ST-CLASS	3513.5	741	11241	329	34.16
INT					
RAL	628.5	37	2952	90	32.80
NAT.W.	201.5	24	737	23	32.04
B & H	196.3	29	735	16	45.93

167. Who is the only man to have hit a ball over the pavilion at Lords, and when?

THOMAS, J. G. Glamorgan

Full Name: John Gregory Thomas
Role: Right-hand bat, right-arm
fast bowler
Born: 12 August 1960, Trebanos,
Swansea
Height: 6′ 3″ **Weight:** 14st
Nickname: Blodwen
County debut: 1979
County cap: 1986
Test debut: 1985–86
No. of Tests: 5
No. of One-Day Internationals: 3
1st-Class 50s scored: 5
1st-Class 5 w. in innings: 8
1st-Class 10 w. in match: 1
Place in batting averages: 119th
av. 15.38 (1986 150th av. 24.90)
Place in bowling averages: 63rd
av. 29.16 (1986 95th av. 38.80)
Strike rate 1987: 49.10 (career 51.49)
1st-Class catches 1987: 3 (career 47)
Parents: Illtyd and Margaret
Marital status: Single
Family links with cricket: Father played village cricket
Education: Cwmtawe Comprehensive School; South Glamorgan Institute of
Higher Education
Qualifications: Qualified teacher, advanced cricket coach
Cricketing superstitions or habits: The number 111

LAST SEASON: BATTING

	I.	N.O.	R.	H.S.	AV.
TEST					
1ST-CLASS	15	2	200	48	15.38
RAL	1	1	1	1*	
RAL	6	0	38	13	6.33
NAT.W.	2	0	67	34	33.50
B & H	4	1	57	32	19.00

CAREER: BATTING

	I.	N.O.	R.	H.S.	AV.
TEST	10	4	83	31*	13.83
1ST-CLASS	135	23	1874	84	16.73
INT	3	2	1	1*	1.00
RAL	52	11	521	37	12.70
NAT.W.	7	1	128	34	21.33
B & H	14	1	107	32	8.23

LAST SEASON: BOWLING

	O.	M.	R.	W.	AV.
TEST					
1ST-CLASS	245.3	48	875	30	29.16
RAL	11	0	59	2	29.50
RAL	43.3	2	209	5	41.80
NAT.W.	12	0	32	1	32.00
B & H	40.5	3	202	3	67.33

CAREER: BOWLING

	O.	M.	R.	W.	AV.
TEST	129	18	504	10	50.40
1ST-CLASS	2317.2	434	8286	270	30.68
INT	26	2	144	3	48.00
RAL	383.4	23	1894	72	26.30
NAT.W.	51	5	195	6	32.50
B & H	139.2	17	580	18	32.22

Overseas tours: West Indies with British Colleges 1982; West Indies with England 1986
Overseas teams played for: Border Cricket Union, South Africa
Other sports followed: Watches rugby
Relaxations: Any sport, music
Extras: Bowling award for 4 wickets or more most times in 1983
Best batting performance: 84 Glamorgan v Surrey, Guildford 1982
Best bowling performance: 6-109 Glamorgan v Warwickshire, Cardiff 1987

THORNE, D. A. Warwickshire

Full Name: David Anthony Thorne
Role: Right-hand bat, left-arm medium bowler
Born: 12 December 1964, Coventry
Height: 5′ 11″ **Weight:** 12st
Nickname: Strop, Thorney
County debut: 1983
1st-Class 50s scored: 12
1st-Class 100s scored: 2
1st-Class 5 w. in innings: 1
Place in batting averages: —
(1986 115th av. 28.82)
Place in bowling averages: —
(1986 122nd av. 53.72)
1st-Class catches 1987: 10 (career 32)
Parents: Dennis and Barbara
Marital status: Single
Family links with cricket:
Father is a qualified coach in
Warwickshire area, and was a very good club player. Brothers, Robert and Philip, both played for Warwickshire Schools. Mother played for Hinckley Ladies
Education: Bablake School, Coventry; Keble College, Oxford
Qualifications: 10 O-levels, 3 A-levels, BA (2.1) in Modern History
Jobs outside cricket: Components packager for Quinton Hazell car components. Worked as a labourer on building site pre-season 1983
Off-season 1987–88: 'Forgetting the 1987 season.'
Cricketing superstitions or habits: 'Always left pad on first. If I get runs I try to wear the same shirt and trousers no matter how dirty until I fail again.'
Overseas tours: Oxbridge to Hong Kong and Australia 1985–86
Cricketers particularly learnt from: 'Dennis Amiss, Paul Smith and above all my Father.'
Cricketers particularly admired: Rob Weir

Other sports played: Rugby, golf
Other sports followed: 'Football, any sports except horse racing.'
Injuries 1987: Broken index finger in May, appendicitis in July
Relaxations: Listening to music, reading
Extras: 'Hit for 26 in 3rd over in first John Player League game by Trevor Jesty. Was out first ball on first-class debut v Oxford University. Once took 7 for 7 in a school's first XI match including a hat-trick and all 7 bowled. Secretary OUCC 1985, captain 1986. Scored unbeaten 100 in 1986 Varsity Match only to lose off last ball to a leg-bye. Suspended for one match in mid-July
Opinions: 'The format of the season is wrong. The Benson and Hedges Cup is spread over too long a time and is too early in the season. Teams can have a Benson and Hedges game on a Saturday and nothing for a week. Early season is precisely when Championship cricket is needed. The qualifying system should be played over a week at the most, eg. Saturday, Tuesday, Thursday, Saturday, leaving more time to fit in a three- or four-day game early season. It works out that some teams have played three or more Championship games than others by June and that is unfair.'
Best batting performance: 124 Oxford University v Zimbabwe, Oxford 1985
Best bowling performance: 5-39 Oxford University v Cambridge University, Lord's 1984

LAST SEASON: BATTING

	I.	N.O.	R.	H.S.	AV.
TEST					
1ST-CLASS	14	1	116	43	8.92
INT					
RAL	5	2	29	14	9.66
NAT.W.					
B & H	3	1	47		23.50

CAREER: BATTING

	I.	N.O.	R.	H.S.	AV.
TEST					
1ST-CLASS	78	14	1823	124	28.48
INT					
RAL	21	6	218	42	14.53
NAT.W.	3	0	50	21	16.66
B & H	15	3	204	36*	17.00

LAST SEASON: BOWLING

	O.	M.	R.	W.	AV.
TEST					
1ST-CLASS	13	2	45	0	–
INT					
RAL	4	0	32	2	16.00
NAT.W.					
B & H	4	0	21	0	–

CAREER: BOWLING

	O.	M.	R.	W.	AV.
TEST					
1ST-CLASS	696.5	154	2054	41	50.09
INT					
RAL	95.5	1	580	13	44.61
NAT.W.	1	0	4	0	–
B & H	60.3	4	251	1	251.00

168. True or false: in the 1930 Test series v England, Bradman hit 974 runs but not a single six?

TODD, P. A.   Glamorgan

Full Name: Paul Adrian Todd
Role: Right-hand bat
Born: 12 March 1953, Morton, Nottinghamshire
Height: 6′ 1″ **Weight:** 13st 9lbs
Nickname: Toddy
County debut:
1972 (Nottinghamshire),
1987 (Glamorgan)
County cap: 1977 (Nottinghamshire)
1000 runs in a season: 3
1st-Class 50s scored: 41
1st-Class 100s scored: 9
One-Day 50s: 4
One-Day 100s: 1
Place in batting averages: 190th
av. 19.58
1st-Class catches 1987: 13 (career 118)

Parents: Tom and Joan
Marital status: Single
Family links with cricket: Brother played for Nottinghamshire Colts and Nottinghamshire 2nd XI
Education: Edward Cludd, Southwell
Jobs outside cricket: Process worker for British Sugar
Off-season 1987–88: Working for British Sugar
Overseas teams played for: Woodridge College, Port Elizabeth, South Africa 1964–65; Nedlands CC, Perth, Western Australia 1978–79; Avendale CC, Cape Town, South Africa 1981–82
Cricketers particularly admired: Richard Hadlee
Other sports played: Football, golf
Other sports followed: All sports
Relaxations: Stamp collecting
Extras: Left Nottinghamshire in 1982. Played for Lincolnshire 1985–87. Joined Glamorgan during 1987 season
Best batting performance: 178 Nottinghamshire v Gloucestershire, Trent Bridge 1975

LAST SEASON: BATTING

	I.	N.O.	R.	H.S.	AV.
TEST					
1ST-CLASS	24	0	470	135	19.58
INT					
RAL	8	0	109	33	13.62
NAT.W.	1	0	1	1	1.00
B & H	4	0	199	107	49.75

CAREER: BATTING

	I.	N.O.	R.	H.S.	AV.
TEST					
1ST-CLASS	300	16	7638	178	26.89
INT					
RAL	94	1	1588	79	17.07
NAT.W.	10	0	345	105	34.50
B & H	36	1	709	59	20.25

424

TOMLINS, K. P.   Gloucestershire

Full Name: Keith Patrick Tomlins
Role: Right-hand bat, short-leg
fielder
Born: 23 October 1957, Kingston-
upon-Thames
Height: 5' 9½" **Weight:** 11st 9lbs
Nickname: Tommo
County debut: 1977 (Middlesex),
1986 (Gloucestershire)
County cap: 1983 (Middlesex)
1st-Class 50s scored: 18
1st-Class 100s scored: 5
One-Day 50s: 6
Place in batting averages: 139th
av. 25.87 (1986 114th av. 29.00)
1st-Class catches 1987: 1 (career 66)
Parents: Royston John and Joan
Muriel

Marital status: Single
Family links with cricket: Father and two brothers play for Wycombe House CC in Osterley, Middlesex
Education: St Benedict's School, Ealing; College of St Hilda and St Bede, Durham University
Qualifications: 5 O-levels, 3 A-levels
Jobs outside cricket: Stage-hand at Richmond Theatre. Sports and music management with Williams Maloney Associates. Ship hand with BP on survey ship
Off-season 1987–88: Studying at Gloucester College of Landscape Architecture
Overseas tours: South America with Derrick Robins' XI in 1983; West Indies with British Colleges 1978 and Ealing CC 1982; Zimbabwe with Middlesex CCC 1984
Overseas teams played for: Greenpoint CC, Cape Town, 1979–80, 1983–84; Merewether DCC, Newcastle, New South Wales, 1981–82; Parnell CC, Auckland 1985–86
Cricketers particularly learnt from: Mike Brearley
Cricketers particularly admired: Graham Gooch, John Emburey
Other sports played: Golf, fly fishing
Other sports followed: Rugby, American football
Injuries 1987: Bruised fingers, slightly chipped finger-nail
Relaxations: Reading, gardening, crosswords, fly fishing
Extras: Left Middlesex after 1985 season and joined Gloucestershire
Opinions on cricket: 'Over-rate fines wrong, particularly in one-day cricket

when the setting of fields is so vital and bound to be a bit time consuming. I don't think spectators feel cheated by below normal over rates in these circumstances. It is an unavoidable part of the game. Certain respected umpires should be on the England selection panel as these people are "closer to the pulse" of the current form and abilities of the players. Team should be announced the evening prior to the game, to allow for social activities.'

Best batting performance: 146 Middlesex v Oxford University, Oxford 1982
Best bowling performance: 2-28 Middlesex v Kent, Lord's 1982

LAST SEASON: BATTING

	I.	N.O.	R.	H.S.	AV.
TEST					
1ST-CLASS	9	1	207	100	25.87
INT					
RAL	2	0	21	11	10.50
NAT.W.					
B & H					

LAST SEASON: BOWLING

	O.	M.	R.	W.	AV.
TEST					
1ST-CLASS					
INT					
RAL	9	0	39	2	19.50
NAT.W.					
B & H					

CAREER: BATTING

	I.	N.O.	R.	H.S.	AV.
TEST					
1ST-CLASS	163	20	3880	146	27.13
INT					
RAL	56	11	845	59	18.77
NAT.W.	6	0	201	80	33.50
B & H	7	0	104	40	14.86

CAREER: BOWLING

	O.	M.	R.	W.	AV.
TEST					
1ST-CLASS	102.3	21	360	4	90.00
INT					
RAL	76	2	376	13	28.92
NAT.W.	1	0	10	0	–
B & H					

TOPLEY, T. D. Essex

Full Name: Thomas Donald Topley
Role: Right-hand bat, right-arm fast-medium bowler
Born: 25 February 1964, Canterbury
Height: 6′ 3″ **Weight:** 13st 8lbs
Nickname: Toppers
County debut: 1985 (Surrey), 1985 (Essex)
1st-class 50s scored: 1
1st-Class 5 w. in innings: 2
Place in batting averages: 167th av. 21.00 (1986 127th av. 12.55)
Place in bowling averages: 51st av. 28.00 (1986 20th av. 23.25)
Strike rate 1987: 60.06 (career 54.01)
1st-Class catches 1987: 2 (career 12)
Parents: Tom and Rhoda
Marital status: Single

Family links with cricket: Brother, Peter, played for Kent (1972–75). Father played for Royal Navy
Education: Royal Hospital School, Holbrook, Suffolk
Qualifications: 6 O-levels, NCA Senior Coach
Jobs outside cricket: Cricket coach; exporting to the Gulf States
Off-season 1987–88: Playing for Guiqualand West, South Africa
Overseas tours: Keith Pont Benefit Tour to Barbados 1986
Overseas teams played for: Natal Midlands & Noodsburg, South Africa 1985–86; Griqualand West, South Africa 1987–88
Cricketers particularly learnt from: Don Wilson, Geoff Arnold, and all at Essex
Cricketers particularly admired: John Lever, Richard Hadlee, Imran Khan and anyone who gives 100 per cent
Other sports played: Rugby, football, badminton and all ball sports
Injuries 1987: Operation on shins, faciotomy on calf-muscle
Relaxations: Photography, food
Extras: Spent three years prior to joining Essex on the MCC Young Professionals at Lord's. As 12th man held famous Test match 'catch' for England v West Indies at Lord's. Also appeared for Surrey during 1985
Opinions on cricket: 'Abolish over rate during three-day cricket.'
Best batting performance: 66 Essex v Yorkshire, Leeds 1987
Best bowling performance: 5-52 Essex v Sussex, Ilford 1986

LAST SEASON: BATTING

	I.	N.O.	R.	H.S.	AV.
TEST					
1ST-CLASS	15	4	231	66	21.00
INT					
RAL	5	2	26	7	8.66
NAT.W.	1	1	15	15*	–
B & H	1	1	3	3*	

LAST SEASON: BOWLING

	O.	M.	R.	W.	AV.
TEST					
1ST-CLASS	300.2	66	840	30	28.00
INT					
RAL	78	8	280	10	28.00
NAT.W.	29.2	7	90	8	11.25
B & H	21	7	48	4	12.00

CAREER: BATTING

	I.	N.O.	R.	H.S.	AV.
TEST					
1ST-CLASS	30	8	359	66	16.31
INT					
RAL	7	4	34	8*	11.33
NAT.W.	3	1	25	15*	12.50
B & H	1	1	3	3*	–

CAREER: BOWLING

	O.	M.	R.	W.	AV.
TEST					
1ST-CLASS	711.1	148	2048	79	25.92
INT					
RAL	138	11	541	21	25.76
NAT.W.	52.2	8	171	11	15.54
B & H	43	10	122	6	20.33

169. What was the title of Malcolm Marshall's autobiography, published last season?

TREMLETT, T. M.   Hampshire

Full Name: Timothy Maurice
Tremlett
Role: Right-hand bat, right-arm
medium bowler
Born: 26 July 1956, Wellington,
Somerset
Height: 6′ 2″ **Weight:** 13st 7lbs
Nickname: Hurricane, Trooper, R2
County debut: 1976
County cap: 1983
50 wickets in a season: 4
1st-Class 50s scored: 17
1st-Class 100s scored: 1
1st-Class 5 w. in innings: 11
Place in batting averages: 231st
av. 13.41 (1986 110th av. 29.27)
Place in bowling averages: 6th
av. 19.54 (1986 58th av. 29.37)
Strike rate 1987: 45.58 (career 58.76)

1st-Class catches 1987: 7 (career 69)
Parents: Maurice Fletcher and Melina May
Wife and date of marriage: Carolyn Patricia, 28 September 1979
Children: Christopher Timothy, 2 September 1981; Alastair Jonathan, 1 February 1983; Benjamin Paul, 2 May 1984
Family links with cricket: Father played for Somerset and for England against West Indies in the West Indies 1947–48. Captained Somerset 1958–60. Younger brother plays local club cricket for Deanery CC
Education: Bellemoor Secondary Modern; Richard Taunton Sixth-Form College
Qualifications: 5 O-levels, 1 A-level. Advanced Coaching Certificate
Jobs outside cricket: One winter spent labouring on building site for muscle-building ('did not seem to work'). Furrier in father-in-law's business
Off-season 1987–88: Coaching administrator for Hampshire plus part-time employment through an agency for IBM
Cricketing superstitions or habits: 'I always like to be the last to leave the dressing room when taking the field plus always walk round the large table on the right-hand side in our dressing room before taking the field. This has replaced leaving the dressing room last as most of our players rarely get out on time!'
Overseas tours: English Counties tour to Zimbabwe 1985; England B to Sri Lanka 1986

Overseas teams played for: Oudtshoorn Teachers' Training College, Western Cape, South Africa 1978–79

Cricketers particularly learnt from: 'My father, and in general watching and listening to other cricketers, first-class or club players.'

Cricketers particularly admired: Vincent van der Bijl, Mike Hendrick, Malcolm Marshall, Richard Hadlee

Other sports played: Golf (7 handicap), table tennis, squash, swimming and badminton

Relaxations: Collecting cricket books and records, gardening, cinema

Extras: Member of local cricket club, Deanery. Batted in almost every position for Hants in batting order from 1 to 11 in 1979. Captained both his school and sixth-form college at cricket

Opinions on cricket: 'With ever increasing numbers of top-class cricketers withdrawing from international fixtures, the cricketing authorities will hopefully begin to reduce the amount of cricket played in this country, especially one-day cricket. With the emphasis still geared towards one-day matches, specialists are still outnumbered heavily by bits-and-pieces performers, with young spin-bowlers particularly at a disadvantage. To ensure that the highest standards are maintained, the structure of English first-class cricket is in further need of streamlining.'

Best batting performance: 102* Hampshire v Somerset, Taunton 1985

Best bowling performance: 6-53 Hampshire v Somerset, Weston-super-Mare 1987

LAST SEASON: BATTING

	I.	N.O.	R.	H.S.	AV.
TEST					
1ST-CLASS	17	5	161	42	13.41
INT					
RAL	7	4	21	12	7.00
NAT.W.	1	1	43	43*	–
B & H	4	2	22	10	11.00

LAST SEASON: BOWLING

	O.	M.	R.	W.	AV.
TEST					
1ST-CLASS	547	153	1407	72	19.54
INT					
RAL	103.1	3	487	20	24.35
NAT.W.	20	2	110	5	22.00
B & H	51	9	163	6	27.16

CAREER: BATTING

	I.	N.O.	R.	H.S.	AV.
TEST					
1ST-CLASS	226	57	3498	102*	20.69
INT					
RAL	53	24	306	35	10.55
NAT.W.	13	4	142	43*	15.77
B & H	25	10	213	36*	14.20

CAREER: BOWLING

	O.	M.	R.	W.	AV.
TEST					
1ST-CLASS	4006	1155	9684	409	23.67
INT					
RAL	849.4	36	3940	155	25.41
NAT.W.	213.2	37	697	28	24.89
B & H	325.5	50	1063	46	23.10

170. Who succeeded Colin Cowdrey as President of the M.C.C?

171. Can you get back editions of the *Cricketers' Who's Who*?

TUFNELL, P. C. R.   Middlesex

Full Name: Philip Clive Roderick Tufnell
Role: Right-hand bat, slow left-arm spinner
Born: 29 April 1966, Hadley Wood, Hertfordshire
Height: 6′ 0″ **Weight:** 11st 8lbs
Nickname: Tuffers, Brucie
County debut: 1986
1st-Class 5 w. in innings: 1
Place in bowling averages: 68th av. 29.81
Strike rate 1987: 60.96 (career 76.31)
1st-Class catches 1987: 5 (career 6)
Parents: Sylvia and Alan
Wife and date of marriage: Alison Jane, 5 October 1986
Education: Highgate School; Southgate School
Qualifications: O-level in Art; City & Guilds Silversmithing
Jobs outside cricket: Silversmith, mini cabbing
Off-season 1987–88: In Brisbane, Australia
Overseas tours: Young England tour to the West Indies 1985
Cricketers particularly learnt from: Jack Robertson, Gordon Jenkins, Don Wilson
Cricketers particularly admired: Clive Radley, Derek Underwood
Other sports played: Snooker, hack around at golf

LAST SEASON: BATTING

	I.	N.O.	R.	H.S.	AV.
TEST					
1ST-CLASS	8	4	21	12*	5.25
INT					
RAL					
NAT.W.					
B & H					

CAREER: BATTING

	I.	N.O.	R.	H.S.	AV.
TEST					
1ST-CLASS	15	5	53	12*	5.30
INT					
RAL					
NAT.W.					
B & H					

LAST SEASON: BOWLING

	O.	M.	R.	W.	AV.
TEST					
1ST-CLASS	335.2	75	984	33	29.81
INT					
RAL					
NAT.W.					
B & H					

CAREER: BOWLING

	O.	M.	R.	W.	AV.
TEST					
1ST-CLASS	483.2	107	1463	38	38.50
INT					
RAL					
NAT.W.					
B & H					

Other sports followed: American football
Relaxations: 'Taking Alison and her friend Elaine shopping. Finding excuses to get out of buying a round.'
Extras: MCC Young Cricketer of the Year 1984. Middlesex uncapped Bowler of the Year 1987
Opinions on cricket: 'Tea should be longer. Keep uncovered wickets.'
Best batting performance: 12* Middlesex v Sussex, Uxbridge 1987
Best bowling performance: 6-60 Middlesex v Kent, Canterbury 1987

TURNER, D. R.   Hampshire

Full Name: David Roy Turner
Role: Left-hand bat, right-arm medium bowler, cover fielder
Born: 5 February 1949, Corsham, nr Chippenham, Wiltshire
Height: 5' 6" **Weight:** 11st 8lbs
Nickname: Birdy, Fossil
County debut: 1966
County cap: 1970
Benefit: 1981 (£23,011)
1000 runs in a season: 8
1st-Class 50s scored: 81
1st-Class 100s scored: 26
One-Day 50s: 55
One-Day 100s: 4
Place in batting averages: 12th av. 49.18 (1986 67th av. 36.30)
1st-Class catches 1987: 8 (career 184)
Parents: Robert Edward and Evelyn Peggy
Wife and date of marriage: Henriette, 18 February 1977
Children: Nicola Marianna, 15 March 1984
Education: Chippenham Boys' High School
Qualifications: 5 O-levels
Off-season 1987–88: Becoming involved in the shoe business
Overseas tours: With Derrick Robins' XI to South Africa 1972–73
Overseas teams played for: Western Province in the winning 1977–78 Currie Cup Competition side. Player-coach for Paarl Cricket Club, South Africa 1972–80, 1982–85
Cricketers particularly learnt from: Roy Marshall
Cricketers particularly admired: Mike Procter
Cricket records: Shared in an unbeaten partnership of 283 with C. G.

431

Greenidge, a record in any one-day competition, in Benson & Hedges Cup, Hampshire v Minor Counties South at Amersham in 1973

Other sports played: Golf, football, athletics

Relaxations: Chess, gardening, reading, television, watching war films

Extras: Played for Wiltshire in 1965. Took a hat-trick in a Lambert & Butler 7-a-side floodlit tournament at Ashton Gate, Bristol on 17 September 1981 v Glamorgan. Captained school at soccer, rugger and cricket. Also ran for school in cross-country and athletics. Scored a career best 184* v Gloucestershire in 1987, 18 years since previous best Championship score

Opinions on cricket: 'I would like the cricket authorities to try for one season, 16 four-day Championship matches, coupled with a Saturday 60-overs limited cricket league, along with the usual Sunday League. There should be tighter controls on overseas players.'

Best batting performance: 184* Hampshire v Gloucestershire, Gloucester 1987

Best bowling performance: 2-7 Hampshire v Glamorgan, Bournemouth 1981

LAST SEASON: BATTING

	I.	N.O.	R.	H.S.	AV.
TEST					
1ST-CLASS	35	8	1328	184*	49.18
INT					
RAL	10	0	199	60	19.90
NAT.W.	2	1	118	100*	118.00
B & H	4	0	160	93	40.00

LAST SEASON: BOWLING

	O.	M.	R.	W.	AV.
TEST					
1ST-CLASS					
INT					
RAL					
NAT.W.					
B & H					

CAREER: BATTING

	I.	N.O.	R.	H.S.	AV.
TEST					
1ST-CLASS	639	64	17437	184*	30.32
INT					
RAL	224	20	5856	114	28.70
NAT.W.	33	4	921	100*	31.75
B & H	66	10	1988	123*	35.50

CAREER: BOWLING

	O.	M.	R.	W.	AV.
TEST					
1ST-CLASS	99.4	27	338	9	37.55
INT					
RAL	1.3	0	11	0	–
NAT.W.	1	0	4	0	–
B & H	0.2	0	4	0	–

172. What is Allan Lamb's middle name?

173. Name the missing player in this famous Test duo: Lillee and . . . ?

UNDERWOOD, D. L. — Kent

Full Name: Derek Leslie Underwood
Role: Right-hand bat, slow left-arm bowler
Born: 8 June 1945, Bromley, Kent
Height: 5′ 11″ **Weight:** 12st
Nickname: Deadly, Unders
County debut: 1963
County cap: 1964
Benefit: 1975 (£24,114) 1986
Test debut: 1966
No. of Tests: 86
No. of One-Day Internationals: 26
50 wickets in a season: 22
1st-Class 50s scored: 2
1st-Class 100s scored: 1
1st-Class 5 w. in innings: 153
1st-Class 10 w. in match: 47
Place in batting averages:
220th av. 15.27 (1986 235th av. 11.57)
Place in bowling averages: 59th av. 28.77 (1986 35th av. 26.36)
Strike rate 1987: 81.53 (career 56.86)
1st-Class catches 1987: 3 (career 261)
Parents: Leslie (deceased) and Evelyn
Wife and date of marriage: Dawn, 6 October 1973
Children: Heather, 7 February 1976; Fiona, 22 November 1977
Education: Beckenham & Penge Grammar School
Jobs outside cricket: Company representative, cricket coach, PE schoolmaster. Director of company of Law Stationers
Family links with cricket: 'I played with my father and brother for a local village team, Farnborough. I played for Beckenham with my brother until I played for the Kent 1st XI. My brother now plays for Orpington CC.'
Overseas tours: Pakistan 1966–67; Sri Lanka and Pakistan 1968–69; Australia and New Zealand 1970–71 and 1974–75; India, Sri Lanka and Pakistan 1972–73; West Indies 1973–74; India, Sri Lanka and Australia 1976–77; Australia and India 1979–80
Other sports played: Occasional golf
Relaxations: Photography, philately, coarse fishing, gardening
Extras: Second youngest player to receive county cap. Played World Series Cricket 1978–79. Youngest player ever to take 100 wickets in debut season. Banned from Test cricket for three years for joining rebel team from England to South Africa. Writes articles for *Cricketer International* magazine. Top of Kent first-class bowling averages in 1982, 1983 and 1984. Awarded MBE.

Scored maiden century in 1984 in 618th first-class innings. Retired at end of 1987 season
Best batting performance: 111 Kent v Sussex, Hastings 1984
Best bowling performance: 9-28 Kent v Sussex, Hastings 1964

LAST SEASON: BATTING

	I.	N.O.	R.	H.S.	AV.
TEST					
1ST-CLASS	20	9	168	29*	15.27
INT					
RAL	2	1	2	1*	2.00
NAT.W.					
B & H	2	2	7	4*	–

CAREER: BATTING

	I.	N.O.	R.	H.S.	AV.
TEST	116	35	937	45	11.56
1ST-CLASS	594	165	4228	111	9.85
INT	13	4	53	17	5.89
RAL	100	42	384	22	6.62
NAT.W.	33	12	156	28	7.42
B & H	46	21	197	17	7.88

LAST SEASON: BOWLING

	O.	M.	R.	W.	AV.
TEST					
1ST-CLASS	611.3	211	1295	45	28.77
INT					
RAL	15	0	67	2	33.50
NAT.W.	23.1	6	52	10	5.20
B & H	57.2	3	256	10	25.60

CAREER: BOWLING

	O.	M.	R.	W.	AV.
TEST	542.2 2920.4	142 1097	7674	297	25.84
1ST-CLASS	390.5 19198.4	85 7627	42319	2168	19.51
INT	6 205	0 26	734	32	22.93
RAL	1574.3	197	5846	346	16.89
NAT.W.	582.4	155	1711	77	22.22
B & H	834.4	170	2435	107	22.75

VAN ZYL, C. J. P. G.   Glamorgan

Full Name: Cornelius Johannes Petrus Gerhardus van Zyl
Role: Right-hand bat, right-arm fast-medium bowler
Born: 1 October 1961, Bloemfontein, South Africa
Nickname: Cornie
County debut: 1987
1st-Class 5 w. in innings: 9
1st-Class 10 w. in match: 2
1st-Class catches 1987: 0 (career 11)
Education: University of Orange Free State
Overseas teams played for: Orange Free State 1981–
Best batting performance: 49 Orange Free State v Natal B, Bloemfontein 1984–85
Best bowling performance: 8-84 Orange Free State v Northern Transvaal B, Bloemfontein 1984–85

	I.	N.O.	R.	H.S.	AV.
TEST					
1ST-CLASS	5	0	85	35	17.00
INT					
RAL					
NAT.W.					
B & H	1	0	5	5	5.00

LAST SEASON: BOWLING

	O.	M.	R.	W.	AV.
TEST					
1ST-CLASS	172	37	511	14	36.50
INT					
RAL					
NAT.W.					
B & H	11	2	45	1	45.00

CAREER: BATTING

	I.	N.O.	R.	H.S.	AV.
TEST					
1ST-CLASS	56	9	591	49	12.57
INT					
RAL					
NAT.W.					
B & H	1	0	5	5	5.00

CAREER: BOWLING

	O.	M.	R.	W.	AV.
TEST					
1ST-CLASS	1136.1	276	3579	176	20.33
INT					
RAL					
NAT.W.					
B & H	11	2	45	1	45.00

VAREY, D. W.   Lancashire

Full Name: David William Varey
Role: Right-hand opening bat,
occasional off-break bowler
Born: 15 October 1961, Darlington
Height: 6′ 2″ **Weight:** 13st
Nickname: Wilbur, D-Dubs, Dubsy,
Hoorah Henry
County debut: 1984
1st-Class 50s scored: 11
1st-Class 100s scored: 2
Place in batting averages: 150th
av. 24.44 (1986 81st av. 33.87)
1st-Class catches 1987: 0
(career 24 + 1 stumping)
Parents: Bill (deceased) and
Monica
Marital status: Single
Family links with cricket:
Brother, John, is an Oxford Blue
Education: Birkenhead School; Pembroke College, Cambridge
Qualifications: BA Hons French and German
Overseas teams played for: South Hobart CC, Tasmania, 1984–86
Cricketers particularly learnt from: Peter Lever, Mick Bowyer, Mike Fell,
Dave Ewing
Cricketers particularly admired: Clive Lloyd, Viv Richards, Ian Botham
Other sports played: Rugby, snooker
Other sports followed: Rugby, soccer (Everton FC)
Relaxations: Disco dancing, body-popping, reading, watching TV, music

Extras: Played for Cheshire 1977. Lancashire 2nd XI debut 1980. Blues in 1982 and 1983. Secretary CUCC 1983
Best batting performance: 156* Cambridge University v Northamptonshire, Cambridge 1982

	I.	N.O.	R.	H.S.	AV.
TEST					
1ST-CLASS	10	1	220	59	24.44
INT					
RAL	2	0	23	15	11.50
NAT.W.					
B & H	1	0	27	27	27.00

	I.	N.O.	R.	H.S.	AV.
TEST					
1ST-CLASS	112	12	2723	156*	27.23
INT					
RAL	3	0	26	15	8.66
NAT.W.					
B & H	6	0	85	27	14.16

WAKEFIELD, M.   Derbyshire

Full Name: Mark Wakefield
Role: Right-hand bat,
slow left-arm bowler
Born: 17 November 1968, Rochdale
Height: 5′ 7″ **Weight:** 11st
Nickname: Wakey, Trowel
County debut: 1987
Parents: Brian and Sheila
Marital status: Single
Family links with cricket:
Father played as a professional
in the Lancashire leagues for a
few years
Education: Bishop Henshaw RC
Upper School, Rochdale
Jobs outside cricket: Painter
Off-season 1987–88: Carpet fitting
Cricketing superstitions or habits:
Always put right pad on first
Cricketers particularly learnt from: Father, D. Bloodworth (Derbyshire coach)
Cricketers particularly admired: Phil Edmonds, David Gower
Other sports played: Golf, squash
Other sports followed: Football, golf, snooker
Relaxations: Watching TV, reading, papers
Best batting performance: 4 Derbyshire v Cambridge University, Cambridge 1987
Best bowling performance: 1-30 Derbyshire v Cambridge University, Cambridge 1987

	I.	N.O.	R.	H.S.	AV.
TEST					
1ST-CLASS	1	0	4	4	4.00
INT					
RAL					
NAT.W.					
B & H					

LAST SEASON: BOWLING

	O.	M.	R.	W.	AV.
TEST					
1ST-CLASS	12	5	30	1	30.00
INT					
RAL					
NAT.W.					
B & H					

CAREER: BATTING

	I.	N.O.	R.	H.S.	AV.
TEST					
1ST-CLASS	1	0	4	4	4.00
INT					
RAL					
NAT.W.					
B & H					

CAREER: BOWLING

	O.	M.	R.	W.	AV.
TEST					
1ST-CLASS	12	5	30	1	30.00
INT					
RAL					
NAT.W.					
B & H					

WALKER, A.   Northamptonshire

Full Name: Alan Walker
Role: Left-hand bat, right-arm fast-medium bowler, outfielder
Born: 7 July 1962, Emley, nr Huddersfield
Height: 5′ 11″ **Weight:** 12st 7lbs
Nickname: Walks, Wacky
County debut: 1983
County cap: 1987
1st-Class 5 w. in innings: 1
Place in batting averages: 214th av. 15.60 (1986 194th av. 17.40)
Place in bowling averages: 11th av. 21.06 (1986 97th av. 39.81)
Strike rate 1987: 49.79 (career 60.33)
1st-Class catches 1987: 6 (career 25)
Parents: Malcolm and Enid
Wife and date of marriage: Janice, 17 September 1983
Education: Emley Junior School; Kirkburton Middle School; Shelley High School
Qualifications: 2 O-levels, 4 CSEs, qualified coal-face worker
Jobs outside cricket: Miner
Off-season 1987–88: Playing for Uitenhage, South Africa
Cricketing superstitions or habits: Put left boot on first, right pad on first, wears the same thing next day if successful the day before
Overseas tours: Denmark with NCA U-19s (North of England) 1980
Overseas teams played for: Uitenhage, South Africa 1984–85, 1986–88

Cricketers particularly learnt from: David Steele, Nick Cook, Winston Davis
Cricketers particularly admired: Dennis Lillee, Richard Hadlee
Other sports played: Football
Other sports followed: Rugby league (Wakefield Trinity), football (Huddersfield Town)
Relaxations: 'Watching TV, listening to music, DIY, having a pint.'
Extras: Took part in a sponsored drive to every first-class headquarters, including Oxford, Cambridge and Arundel, in one day, with four other members of the club, raising money for Cat-scan appeal and the cricket club
Best batting performance: 41* Northamptonshire v Warwickshire, Edgbaston 1987
Best bowling performance: 6-50 Northamptonshire v Lancashire, Northampton 1986

LAST SEASON: BATTING

	I.	N.O.	R.	H.S.	AV.
TEST					
1ST-CLASS	10	5	78	41*	15.60
INT					
RAL					
NAT.W.	1	0	1	1	1.00
B & H	4	3	27	15*	27.00

CAREER: BATTING

	I.	N.O.	R.	H.S.	AV.
TEST					
1ST-CLASS	58	30	330	41*	11.78
INT					
RAL	7	3	41	13	10.25
NAT.W.	2	1	4	3*	4.00
B & H	5	4	30	15*	30.00

LAST SEASON: BOWLING

	O.	M.	R.	W.	AV.
TEST					
1ST-CLASS	390.2	104	1011	48	21.06
INT					
RAL	51	5	217	9	24.11
NAT.W.	40	8	118	8	14.75
B & H	72	5	330	8	41.25

CAREER: BOWLING

	O.	M.	R.	W.	AV.
TEST					
1ST-CLASS	1538.3	313	4807	153	31.41
INT					
RAL	342.4	19	1552	63	24.63
NAT.W.	88.5	13	316	13	24.30
B & H	147.5	9	676	17	39.76

174. Name the missing player in this famous Test duo: Trueman and . . . ?

WALSH, C. A.   Gloucestershire

Full Name: Courtney Andrew Walsh
Role: Right-hand bat, right-arm
fast bowler
Born: 30 October 1962, Kingston,
Jamaica
Height: 6′ 5½″ **Weight:** 13st 7lbs
Nickname: Mark, Walshy
County debut: 1984
County cap: 1985
Test debut: 1984–85
No. of Tests: 13
No. of One-Day Internationals: 34
50 wickets in a season: 3
1st-Class 50s scored: 1
1st-Class 5 w. in innings: 29
1st-Class 10 w. in match: 6
Place in batting averages: —
(1986 230th av. 12.27)
Place in bowling averages: 34th
av. 25.53 (1986 5th av. 18.17)
Strike rate 1987: 49.95 (career 44.68)
1st-Class catches 1987: 9 (career 40)
Parents: Joan Wollaston and Erick
Marital status: Single
Education: Excelsior High School
Qualifications: GCE and CXL
Off-season 1987–88: Touring with West Indies
Overseas tours: West Indies Young Cricketers to Zimbabwe 1983; West Indies to England 1984; to Australia 1984–85; to Pakistan 1986; World Cup 1987
Overseas teams played for: Jamaica
Cricketers particularly learnt from: Michael Holding, Andy Roberts, Malcolm Marshall, George Headley
Cricketers particularly admired: Michael Holding, Viv Richards, Lawrence Rowe
Other sports played: Football
Other sports followed: Basketball, track and field events
Injuries 1987: Groin, knee and back strains
Relaxations: Music, reading, watching TV
Extras: Took record 10-43 in Jamaican school cricket in 1979. Played in MCC Bicentenary Test 1987
Best batting performance: 52 Gloucestershire v Yorkshire, Bristol 1986
Best bowling performance: 9-72 Gloucestershire v Somerset, Bristol 1986

LAST SEASON: BATTING

	I.	N.O.	R.	H.S.	AV.
TEST					
1ST-CLASS	23	2	190	27	9.04
INT					
RAL	8	2	83	33	13.83
NAT.W.	2	0	13	7	6.50
B & H	4	2	20	7*	10.00

CAREER: BATTING

	I.	N.O.	R.	H.S.	AV.
TEST	16	7	82	18*	9.11
INT	127	31	977	52	36.11
INT	9	4	27	7*	5.40
RAL	21	4	148	35	8.70
NAT.W.	6	2	47	25*	11.75
B & H	6	3	30	8	10.00

LAST SEASON: BOWLING

	O.	M.	R.	W.	AV.
TEST					
1ST-CLASS	524.3	108	1609	63	25.53
INT					
RAL	90.2	6	311	25	12.44
NAT.W.	46	5	160	8	20.00
B & H	53	5	183	6	30.50

CAREER: BOWLING

	O.	M.	R.	W.	AV.
TEST	422.1	95	1111	45	24.68
INT	3256.4	542	10043	449	22.36
INT	291.3	24	1136	43	26.41
RAL	272.5	20	1121	53	21.15
NAT.W.	93	11	318	14	22.71
B & H	114.3	13	407	14	29.07

WARD, D. M. Surrey

Full Name: David Mark Ward
Role: Right-hand bat,
off-break bowler, gully fielder
Born: 10 February 1961, Croydon
Height: 6' **Weight:** 13st 2lbs
Nickname: Cocker, Wardy, Jaws,
Gnasher, Chad, Pianoman
County debut: 1985
1st-Class 100s scored: 1
One-Day 50s: 3
Place in batting averages: 194th
av. 17.80
1st-Class catches 1987: 7 (career 10)
Parents: Dora Kathleen and Thomas
Marital status: Single
Family links with cricket:
'Grandad played for the
Tamworth Arms, Croydon.'
Education: Haling Manor High
School; Croydon Technical College

Qualifications: 2 O-levels, Advanced City and Guilds in Carpentry and Joinery
Jobs outside cricket: Carpenter. Working in Chinese take-away
Off-season 1987–88: Playing in Australia
Cricketing superstitions or habits: Marks across corner of non-striking crease with bat
Overseas tours: Barbados 1985 with Surrey

Overseas teams played for: Caulfield CC, Australia 1984–85, 1985–86 and 1986–87; Sunshine CC, Australia 1987–88
Cricketers particularly learnt from: Geoff Arnold, Graham Clinton, Geoff Howarth, Monte Lynch, Chris Walker, Mickey Stewart, Trevor Jesty
Cricketers particularly admired: Graham Gooch, Ian Botham, Viv Richards, John Goodey (Banstead CC), Geoff Howarth, Keith Ebdon (Chipstead and Coulsdon CC)
Other sports played: Football, snooker, table tennis
Relaxations: Eating out, watching TV, movies, jazz
Opinions on cricket: 'Avoid the politics and get on with the game!'
Best batting performance: 143 Surrey v Derbyshire, Derby 1985

LAST SEASON: BATTING

	I.	N.O.	R.	H.S.	AV.
TEST					
1ST-CLASS	10	0	178	44	17.80
INT					
RAL	10	1	206	73*	22.88
NAT.W.					
B & H					

CAREER: BATTING

	I.	N.O.	R.	H.S.	AV.
TEST					
1ST-CLASS	26	4	557	143	25.31
INT					
RAL	24	5	449	73*	23.63
NAT.W.					
B & H					

WARD, T. R. Kent

Full Name: Trevor Robert Ward
Role: Right-hand opening bat
Born: 18 January 1968, Farningham, Kent
Height: 5′ 11″ **Weight:** 12st 11lbs
Nickname: Zippy
County debut: 1986
Parents: Robert Henry and Hazel Ann
Marital status: Single
Family links with cricket: Father played a little village cricket with Farningham
Education: Anthony Roper County Primary; Hextable Comprehensive
Qualifications: 7 O-levels
Jobs outside cricket: Worked in building trade

Off-season 1987–88: Playing in Youth World Cup
Overseas teams played for: Scarborough CC, Perth, Western Australia 1986–87

Overseas tours: NCA to Bermuda 1985; Young England to Sri Lanka 1987
Cricketers particularly learnt from: Alan Ealham, Derek Aslett, Colin Page
Cricketers particularly admired: Viv Richards, Richard Hadlee, Derek Underwood
Other sports played: Football, golf, squash
Other sports followed: American football, fishing
Injuries 1987: Cracked thumb
Relaxations: Watching films, playing golf, fishing
Opinions in cricket: 'Too much cricket played. Players need more relaxation time.'
Best batting performance: 29 Kent v Hampshire, Southampton 1986

LAST SEASON: BATTING

	I.	N.O.	R.	H.S.	AV.
TEST					
1ST-CLASS	2	1	19	13*	19.00
INT					
RAL					
NAT.W.					
B & H					

CAREER: BATTING

	I.	N.O.	R.	H.S.	AV.
TEST					
1ST-CLASS	4	1	60	29	20.00
INT					
RAL					
NAT.W.					
B & H					

WARING, I. C.   Sussex

Full Name: Ian Charles Waring
Role: Left-hand bat, right-arm fast-medium bowler
Born: 6 December 1963, Chesterfield
Height: 6' 1" **Weight:** 13st 10lbs
Nickname: Eddie
County debut: 1985
1st-Class catches 1987: 1 (career 2)
Parents: Jack and Dorothy
Marital status: Single
Education: Tupton Hall
Qualifications: 7 O-levels, NCA Coaching Certificate
Overseas tours: Sheffield Cricket Lovers to Gibraltar 1980
Overseas teams played for: Pretoria High School Old Boys 1983–84; Alma Marist, Cape Town 1984–85; Bishops School, Cape Town 1985–86

Cricketers particularly learnt from: Tony Pigott, Tony Borrington, Les Lenham

Cricketers particularly admired: Barry Richards, Imran Khan, Peter Kirsten
Other sports played: Football, swimming, baseball and anything outdoors
Other sports followed: All sports on TV
Relaxations: Listening to music, reading autobiographies and photography
Extras: Took wicket with first ball at Lord's
Best bowling performance: 2-76 Sussex v Worcestershire, Worcester 1987

LAST SEASON: BATTING

	I.	N.O.	R.	H.S.	AV.
TEST					
1ST-CLASS	3	2	0		0.00
INT					
RAL	3	1	11	8	5.50
NAT.W.					
B & H					

LAST SEASON: BOWLING

	O.	M.	R.	W.	AV.
TEST					
1ST-CLASS	50	9	172	2	86.00
INT					
RAL	56	2	280	10	28.00
NAT.W.					
B & H	11	1	55	0	–

CAREER: BATTING

	I.	N.O.	R.	H.S.	AV.
TEST					
1ST-CLASS	3	2	0		0.00
INT					
RAL					
NAT.W.					
B & H					

CAREER: BOWLING

	O.	M.	R.	W.	AV.
TEST					
1ST-CLASS	72	15	217	3	72.33
INT					
RAL	67	2	338	10	33.80
NAT.W.					
B & H	11	1	55	0	–

WARNER, A. E. Derbyshire

Full Name: Allan Esmond Warner
Role: Right-hand bat, right-arm
fast bowler, outfielder
Born: 12 May 1959, Birmingham
Height: 5′ 8″ **Weight:** 10st
Nickname: Esis
County debut: 1982 (Worcestershire),
1985 (Derbyshire)
County cap: 1987
1st-Class 50s scored: 10
1st-Class 5 w. in innings: 2
One-Day 50s: 1
Place in batting averages: 187th
av. 18.50 (1986 132nd av. 26.95)
Place in bowling averages: 64th
av. 29.31 (1986 107th av. 42.85)
Strike rate 1987: 56.37 (career 62.56)
1st-Class catches 1987: 4 (career 22)
Parents: Edgar and Sarah
Children: Alvin, 6 September 1980

Education: Tabernacle School, St Kitts, West Indies
Qualifications: CSE Maths
Jobs outside cricket: Bricklaying
Cricketers particularly learnt from: John Browny, Henry Benjamin
Cricketers particularly admired: Malcolm Marshall, Michael Holding
Other sports played: Football, table tennis
Other sports followed: Football, boxing and athletics
Relaxations: Watching movies, music (soul, reggae and calypso)
Extras: Released by Worcestershire at end of 1984 and joined Derbyshire
Best batting performance: 91 Derbyshire v Leicestershire, Chesterfield 1986
Best bowling performance: 5-27 Worcestershire v Glamorgan, Worcester 1984

LAST SEASON: BATTING

	I.	N.O.	R.	H.S.	AV.
TEST					
1ST-CLASS	28	4	444	72	18.50
INT					
RAL	10	2	184	40	23.00
NAT.W.	1	0	32	32	32.00
B & H	3	1	12	11*	6.00

LAST SEASON: BOWLING

	O.	M.	R.	W.	AV.
TEST					
1ST-CLASS	328.5	67	1026	35	29.31
INT					
RAL	69	2	386	15	25.73
NAT.W.	16	1	51	3	17.00
B & H	42	2	195	5	39.00

CAREER: BATTING

	I.	N.O.	R.	H.S.	AV.
TEST					
1ST-CLASS	115	21	1831	91	19.47
INT					
RAL	40	11	397	68	13.68
NAT.W.	4	0	57	32	14.25
B & H	13	5	85	24*	10.62

CAREER: BOWLING

	O.	M.	R.	W.	AV.
TEST					
1ST-CLASS	1543.1	280	5186	148	35.04
INT					
RAL	342.5	8	1774	65	27.29
NAT.W.	53.1	4	229	6	38.16
B & H	212.3	12	718	24	29.91

175. Name the missing player in this famous Test duo: Ramadhin and . . . ?

WATERTON, S. N. V. Northamptonshire

Full Name: Stuart Nicholas Varney Waterton
Role: Right-hand bat, wicket-keeper
Born: 6 December 1960, Dartford
Height: 5′ 11½″ **Weight:** 12st
Nickname: Buck, Twatters
County debut: 1980 (Kent), 1986 (Northamptonshire)
1st-Class 50s scored: 3
Place in batting averages: —
(1986 156th av. 24.25)
Parents: Barry and Olive
Marital status: Single
Family links with cricket:
'Father was a magnificent back garden bowler and avid watcher.'
Education: St George's Church of England School; Gravesend School for Boys; London School of Economics, London University
Qualifications: 10 O-levels, 3 A-levels, BSc Hons Economics, NCA Coaching Award
Jobs outside cricket: Civil servant, building labourer, cricket coach
Off-season 1987–88: 'Contemplating my retirement.'
Cricketing superstitions or habits: 'I always cross myself before going onto the field.'
Overseas tours: Club tour of Barbados 1986
Overseas teams played for: Goudstad Onderwyskollege, Johannesburg, 1984–85; Florida Park CC 1985
Cricketers particularly learnt from: Alan Knott, Bob Taylor, George Baker
Cricketers particularly admired: Bob Taylor, Alan Knott, Glenn Turner, Viv Richards
Other sports played: Golf, road-running, cross-country running
Other sports followed: Athletics
Relaxations: Music, TV, reading, cinema, restaurants
Extras: Second wicket-keeper from Gravesend School to play for Kent CCC – David Nicolls being the other. Record individual score for Kent Schools Player, 163 v Sussex Schools 1979. Record number of runs aggregated in a season for Gravesend School, 983 runs at average of 75 in 1979. England Young Wicket-keeper of the Year 1980. Played for UAU 1981–83 (captain 1983 but did not take the field due to bad weather). Made NatWest debut in 1984 final. Member (with Laurie Potter) of Ashford CC side which won the Courage Kent League in 1985. Batting average in 2nd XI of 59.86 in 1985.

Left Kent after 1985 season to join Northamptonshire. 'Retired from full-time cricket in 1987 due to lack of opportunities to play in 1st XI; last innings was 50* v Essex.'

Opinions on cricket: '1) Working life after cricket is not adequately allowed for by players, especially younger ones, who do not seem to be given useful advice regarding the acquisition of a trade or work experience by their clubs. 2) There should be a reduction in the amount of three-day cricket played in favour of more financially viable competitions. 3) County clubs should do more to help young cricketers to find employment in winters. 4) The reinstatement of South Africa into Test cricket is vital, and would be a positive step forward.'

Best batting performance: 58* Northamptonshire v Worcestershire, Northampton 1986

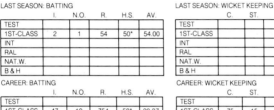

LAST SEASON: BATTING

	I.	N.O.	R.	H.S.	AV.
TEST					
1ST-CLASS	2	1	54	50*	54.00
INT					
RAL					
NAT.W.					
B & H					

LAST SEASON: WICKET KEEPING

	C.	ST.			
TEST					
1ST-CLASS					
INT					
RAL					
NAT.W.					
B & H					

CAREER: BATTING

	I.	N.O.	R.	H.S.	AV.
TEST					
1ST-CLASS	47	10	754	58*	20.37
INT					
RAL	6	3	74	13*	24.66
NAT.W.	2	1	5	4*	5.00
B & H					

CAREER: WICKET KEEPING

	C.	ST.			
TEST					
1ST-CLASS	75	15			
INT					
RAL	12	5			
NAT.W.					
B & H	2	1			

176. Name the missing player in this famous Test duo: McDonald and . . . ?

177. Name the missing player in this famous Test duo: Lindwall and . . . ?

WATKINSON, M.   Lancashire

Full Name: Michael Watkinson
Role: Right-hand bat, right-arm medium or off-break bowler
Born: 1 August 1961, Westhoughton
Height: 6′ 1½″ **Weight:** 13st
Nickname: Winker
County debut: 1982
County cap: 1987
1st-Class 50s scored: 15
1st-Class 100s scored: 1
1st-Class 5 w. in innings: 9
One-Day 50s: 2
Place in batting averages: 79th av. 33.73 (1986 287th av. 19.45)
Place in bowling averages: 18th av. 23.47 (1986 119th av. 50.08)
Strike rate 1987: 45.42 (career 64.12)
1st-Class catches 1987: 17 (career 46)
Parents: Albert and Marian
Wife and date of marriage: Susan, 12 April 1986
Education: Rivington and Blackrod High School, Horwich
Qualifications: 8 O-levels, HTC Civil Engineering
Jobs outside cricket: Draughtsman
Off-season 1987–88: Playing and coaching in Canberra, Australia
Overseas teams played for: Woder Valley CC, Canberra, 1984–85
Cricketers particularly learnt from: Paul Allott, Steve O'Shaughnessy
Cricketers particularly admired: Clive Lloyd, Imran Khan
Other sports played: Football

LAST SEASON: BATTING

	I.	N.O.	R.	H.S.	AV.
TEST					
1ST-CLASS	27	4	776	91	33.73
INT					
RAL	9	1	153	57	19.12
NAT.W.	1	0	22	22	22.00
B & H	1	1	4	4*	–

CAREER: BATTING

	I.	N.O.	R.	H.S.	AV.
TEST					
1ST-CLASS	130	19	2693	106	24.26
INT					
RAL	45	19	493	57	18.96
NAT.W.	10	3	152	56	21.71
B & H	11	2	88	34	9.77

LAST SEASON: BOWLING

	O.	M.	R.	W.	AV.
TEST					
1ST-CLASS	318	66	986	42	23.47
INT					
RAL	79	3	423	11	38.45
NAT.W.	12	0	64	3	21.33
B & H	9	2	25	1	25.00

CAREER: BOWLING

	O.	M.	R.	W.	AV.
TEST					
1ST-CLASS	1934.2	393	6170	181	34.08
INT					
RAL	423	23	1988	64	31.06
NAT.W.	143.5	12	562	12	46.83
B & H	173.1	16	715	26	27.50

Extras: Played for Cheshire CCC in Minor Counties, and NatWest Trophy (v Middlesex) 1982
Best batting performance: 106 Lancashire v Surrey, Southport 1985
Best bowling performance: 7-25 Lancashire v Sussex, Lytham 1987

WAUGH, S. R. Somerset

Full Name: Stephen Rodger Waugh
Role: Right-hand bat, right-arm medium bowler
Born: 2 June 1965, Canterbury, New South Wales
County debut: 1987
Test debut: 1985–86
No. of Tests: 13
No. of One-Day Internationals: 39
1st-Class 50s scored: 12
1st-Class 100s scored: 4
1st-Class 5 w. in innings: 1
One-Day 50s: 6
1st-Class catches 1987: 4
(career 48)
Off-season 1987–88:
Touring with Australia
Overseas tours: Young Australia to Zimbabwe; Australia to New Zealand; India 1986–87; India and Pakistan for World Cup 1987
Extras: Played for Nelson in Lancashire League 1987. Signed by Somerset during season as overseas player to cover for the injured Martin Crowe
Best batting performance: 137* Somerset v Gloucestershire, Bristol 1987
Best bowling performance: 5-69 Australia v England, Perth 1986–87

LAST SEASON: BATTING

	I.	N.O.	R.	H.S.	AV.
TEST					
1ST-CLASS	6	3	340	137*	113.33
INT					
RAL					
NAT.W.					
B & H					

LAST SEASON: BOWLING

	O.	M.	R.	W.	AV.
TEST					
1ST-CLASS	112	22	348	11	31.63
INT					
RAL					
NAT.W.					
B & H					

CAREER: BATTING

	I.	N.O.	R.	H.S.	AV.
TEST	21	4	482	79*	28.35
1ST-CLASS	41	6	1581	137*	45.17
INT	35	8	928	83*	34.37
RAL					
NAT.W.					
B & H					

CAREER: BOWLING

	O.	M.	R.	W.	AV.
TEST	197.3	45	618	19	32.52
1ST-CLASS	483.5	97	1451	43	33.74
INT	273.5	11	1215	41	29.63
RAL					
NAT.W.					
B & H					

WELLS, A. P.

Sussex

Full Name: Alan Peter Wells
Role: Right-hand bat, right-arm
medium bowler, cover fielder
Born: 2 October 1961, Newhaven
Height: 6′ 0″ **Weight:** 12st 4lbs
Nickname: Morph, Bomber
County debut: 1981
County cap: 1986
1000 runs in a season: 2
1st-Class 50s scored: 21
1st-Class 100s scored: 7
One-Day 50s: 12
Place in batting averages: 93rd
av. 32.06 (1986 89th av. 33.00)
1st-Class catches 1987: 11
(career 58)
Parents: Ernest William Charles and
Eunice Mae
Marital status: Single
Family links with cricket: Father played for many years for local club. Eldest
brother, Ray, plays club cricket. Brother of C. M. Wells of Sussex
Education: Tideway Comprehensive, Newhaven
Qualifications: 5 O-levels, NCA Coaching Certificate
Jobs outside cricket: Laboratory assistant. Coached in South Africa
Cricketing superstitions or habits: 'Have to put bat at junction of return and
popping crease at the end of each over. Never stand inside the return crease
when backing up. When repairing wicket count how many times I tap ground.
Double whirl of arms with bat when going in to bat. Plus many more.'
Overseas tours: NCA U-19 tour of Canada, 1979

LAST SEASON: BATTING

	I.	N.O.	R.	H.S.	AV.
TEST					
1ST-CLASS	37	4	1058	161*	32.06
INT					
RAL	11	1	233	52	23.30
NAT.W.	2	1	68	55	68.00
B & H	4	0	86	72	21.50

CAREER: BATTING

	I.	N.O.	R.	H.S.	AV.
TEST					
1ST-CLASS	183	32	4570	161*	30.26
INT					
RAL	71	12	1478	71*	25.05
NAT.W.	12	3	147	55	16.33
B & H	18	2	458	72	28.62

LAST SEASON: BOWLING

	O.	M.	R.	W.	AV.
TEST					
1ST-CLASS	31	1	182	3	60.66
INT					
RAL	8.1	0	53	3	17.66
NAT.W.					
B & H	6	0	40	2	20.00

CAREER: BOWLING

	O.	M.	R.	W.	AV.
TEST					
1ST-CLASS	56	4	268	4	67.00
INT					
RAL	10.2	0	69	4	17.25
NAT.W.	1	0	1	0	–
B & H	8.1	1	57	3	19.00

Cricketers particularly learnt from: Father, Chris Waller, Roger Marshall, Les Lenham
Other sports played: Table tennis, squash, darts, snooker, tennis
Relaxations: Listening to music, eating out, drinking in country pubs
Extras: Played for England Young Cricketers v India 1981
Best batting performance: 161* Sussex v Kent, Hove 1987
Best bowling performance: 3-67 Sussex v Worcestershire, Worcester 1987

WELLS, C. M. Sussex

Full Name: Colin Mark Wells
Role: Right-hand bat, right-arm medium bowler
Born: 3 March 1960, Newhaven
Height: 6′ 0″ **Weight:** 13st
Nickname: Bomber, Dougie
County debut: 1979
County cap: 1982
No. of One-Day Internationals: 2
1000 runs in a season: 5
50 wickets in a season: 2
1st-Class 50s scored: 39
1st-Class 100s scored: 16
1st-Class 200s scored: 1
1st-Class 5 w. in innings: 4
One-Day 50s: 17
One-Day 100s: 2
Place in batting averages: 19th
av. 45.50 (1986 61st av. 37.86)
Place in bowling averages: 66th av. 29.44 (1986 90th av. 37.10)
Strike rate 1987: 64.25 (career 69.11)
1st-Class catches 1987: 15 (career: 59)
Parents: Ernest William Charles and Eunice Mae
Wife and date of marriage: Celia, 25 September 1982
Family links with cricket: Father, Billy, had trials for Sussex and played for Sussex Cricket Association. Both brothers play cricket and youngest brother, Alan, plays for Sussex
Education: Tideway Comprehensive School, Newhaven
Qualifications: 9 O-levels, 2 CSEs, 1 A-level, MCC Intermediate Coaching Certificate
Jobs outside cricket: Working as a cellular telephone salesman for F. Smith & Co. of Horsham
Cricketing superstitions or habits: Left boot and left pad on first

Overseas tours: With England to Sharjah 1985
Overseas teams played for: Border, 1980–81; Western Province 1984–85
Other sports played: Football, rugby, hockey, basketball, tennis, table tennis
Relaxations: Sea-angling, philately, listening to music
Extras: Played in three John Player League matches in 1978. Was recommended to Sussex by former Sussex player, Ian Thomson. Highest 4th wicket partnership of 256 for Sussex v Glamorgan with Imran Khan
Opinions on cricket: 'Strongly believe that we cram in too much cricket, which must have a detrimental effect on all, especially the fast bowlers, particularly long term.'
Best batting performance: 203 Sussex v Hampshire, Hove 1984
Best bowling performance: 6-34 Sussex v Lancashire, Lytham 1987

LAST SEASON: BATTING

	I.	N.O.	R.	H.S.	AV.
TEST					
1ST-CLASS	39	7	1456	148*	45.50
INT					
RAL	12	0	430	70	35.83
NAT.W.	2	1	43	37*	43.00
B & H	4	1	129	101*	43.00

LAST SEASON: BOWLING

	O.	M.	R.	W.	AV.
TEST					
1ST-CLASS	546.1	98	1531	51	29.44
INT					
RAL	99.4	7	336	14	24.00
NAT.W.	21	2	84	1	84.00
B & H	35	4	120	1	120.00

CAREER: BATTING

	I.	N.O.	R.	H.S.	AV.
TEST					
1ST-CLASS	298	49	8672	203	34.82
INT	2	0	22	17	11.00
RAL	106	16	2510	104*	27.88
NAT.W.	19	3	405	76	25.31
B & H	33	4	791	101*	27.27

CAREER: BOWLING

	O.	M.	R.	W.	AV.
TEST					
1ST-CLASS	2925.5	686	8386	254	33.01
INT					
RAL	600.2	42	2236	89	25.12
NAT.W.	149.4	23	424	11	38.54
B & H	172	26	591	21	28.14

178. Name the missing player in this famous Test duo: Hobbs and . . . ?

WELLS, V. J. Kent

Full Name: Vincent John Wells
Role: Right-hand bat, right-arm
medium pace bowler, wicket-keeper
Born: 6 August 1965, Dartford
Height: 6′ 1″ **Weight:** 12st 11lbs
Nickname: Wellsy
County debut: 1987
Parents: Pat and Jack
Marital status: Single
Education: Downs School, Dartford;
Sir William Nottidge School
Qualifications: 1 O-level, 8 CSEs
Jobs outside cricket: Ex-partner of
sportshop
Off-season 1986–87: Coaching abroad
Overseas teams played for: Parnell CC,
Auckland, New Zealand 1986
Cricketers particularly learnt from:

Colin Page, Bob Woolmer, all at Kent CCC
Cricketers particularly admired: David Gower, Ian Botham
Other sports played: Football
Other sports followed: Most sports
Injuries 1987: Broken nose
Relaxations: 'Eating out with my girlfriend Debbie.'
Extras: Was a schoolboy footballer with Leyton Orient. Played in one Sunday
League match 1987

LAST SEASON: BATTING	I.	N.O.	R.	H.S.	AV.
TEST					
1ST-CLASS					
INT					
RAL	1	0	2	2	2.00
NAT.W.					
B & H					

CAREER: BATTING	I.	N.O.	R.	H.S.	AV.
TEST					
1ST-CLASS					
INT					
RAL	1	0	2	2	2.00
NAT.W.					
B & H					

---

179. Name the missing player in this famous Test duo: Compton
and . . . ?

WESTON, M. J.   Worcestershire

Full Name: Martin John Weston
Role: Right-hand bat, right-arm
medium bowler
Born: 8 April 1959, Worcester
Height: 6′ 1″ **Weight:** 14st 7lbs
Nickname: Wesso, Shag
County debut: 1979
County cap: 1986
1000 runs in season: 1
1st-Class 50s scored: 21
1st-Class 100s scored: 3
One-Day 50s: 6
One-Day 100s: 1
Place in batting averages: 160th
av. 22.42 (1986 202nd av. 16.70)
1st-Class catches 1987: 6 (career 47)
Parents: John Franklyn and Sheila
Margaret
Marital status: Single
Education: St George's C of E Junior; Samuel Southall Secondary Modern
Qualifications: City & Guilds and Advance Crafts in Bricklaying
Overseas tours: 1980 tour to Barbados with Worcestershire CCC
Cricketers particularly learnt from: Basil D'Oliveira
Other sports played: Football, squash
Relaxations: Horse racing
Best batting performance: 145* Worcestershire v Northamptonshire, Worcester 1984
Best bowling performance: 4-44 Worcestershire v Northamptonshire, Wellingborough 1984

LAST SEASON: BATTING

	I.	N.O.	R.	H.S.	AV.
TEST					
1ST-CLASS	21	2	426	54	22.42
INT					
RAL	7	1	62	44	10.33
NAT.W.					
B & H	5	0	36	18	7.20

CAREER: BATTING

	I.	N.O.	R.	H.S.	AV.
TEST					
1ST-CLASS	183	11	4202	145*	24.43
INT					
RAL	71	8	1166	109	18.50
NAT.W.	8	2	148	44*	24.66
B & H	25	0	451	56	18.04

LAST SEASON: BOWLING

	O.	M.	R.	W.	AV.
TEST					
1ST-CLASS	96	18	326	7	46.57
INT					
RAL	26.3	0	160	2	80.00
NAT.W.					
B & H	7	0	41	1	41.00

CAREER: BOWLING

	O.	M.	R.	W.	AV.
TEST					
1ST-CLASS	755.4	176	2239	53	42.24
INT					
RAL	234.3	6	1147	33	34.75
NAT.W.	47.5	7	176	5	35.20
B & H	70	7	259	9	28.77

WHITAKER, J. J. Leicestershire

Full Name: John James Whitaker
Role: Right-hand bat,
off-break bowler
Born: 5 May 1962, Skipton,
Yorkshire
Height: 6′ 0″ **Weight:** 13st
County debut: 1983
County cap: 1986
Test debut: 1986–87
No. of Tests: 1
No. of One-Day Internationals: 2
1000 runs in a season: 4
1st-Class 50s scored: 30
1st-Class 100s scored: 12
1st-Class 200s scored: 1
One-Day 50s: 8
One-Day 100s: 3
Place in batting averages: 64th
av. 36.61 (1986 2nd av. 66.34)

1st-Class catches 1987: 17 (career 67)
Parents: John and Anne
Family links with cricket: Father plays club cricket for Skipton
Education: Uppingham School
Qualifications: 7 O-levels
Jobs outside cricket: Employee of Whitakers Chocolates Ltd; groundsman, Adelaide 1982–83; cricket coach and farmer, Tasmania 1983
Overseas tours: Australia 1981–82 with Uppingham School; England to Australia 1986–87
Overseas teams played for: Glenelg CC, Adelaide 1982–83; Old Scotch CC,

LAST SEASON: BATTING

	I.	N.O.	R.	H.S.	AV.
TEST					
1ST-CLASS	39	5	1245	126	36.61
INT					
RAL	11	1	380	95	38.00
NAT.W.	4	0	155	52	38.75
B & H	3	0	59	45	19.66

LAST SEASON: BOWLING

	O.	M.	R.	W.	AV.
TEST					
1ST-CLASS	5	0	33	0	–
INT					
RAL					
NAT.W.					
B & H					

CAREER: BATTING

	I.	N.O.	R.	H.S.	AV.
TEST	1	0	11	11	11.00
1ST-CLASS	159	23	5479	200*	40.28
INT	2	1	48	44*	48.00
RAL	45	6	1380	132	35.38
NAT.W.	9	0	423	155	47.00
B & H	17	2	341	73*	22.73

CAREER: BOWLING

	O.	M.	R.	W.	AV.
TEST					
1ST-CLASS	20.2	2	168	1	168.00
INT					
RAL	0.2	0	4	0	–
NAT.W.	2	1	5	0	–
B & H					

Tasmania 1983–84; Somerset West, South Africa 1984–85
Cricketers particularly learnt from: Maurice Hallam (coach at Uppingham), Brian Davison
Cricketers particularly admired: Geoff Boycott, Dennis Amiss
Other sports played: Rugby, hockey, tennis, golf, squash
Relaxations: Discos, music, reading, eating out
Best batting performance: 200* Leicestershire v Nottinghamshire, Leicester 1986
Best bowling performance: 1-41 Leicestershire v Essex, Leicester 1986

WHITTICASE, P. Leicestershire

Full Name: Philip Whitticase
Role: Right-hand bat, wicket-keeper
Born: 15 March 1965, Birmingham
Height: 5′ 8″ **Weight:** 10st 7lbs
Nickname: Jasper, Tracy, Roland Rat
County debut: 1984
County cap: 1987
1st-Class 50s scored: 7
Place in batting averages: 226th av. 14.04 (1986 92nd av. 32.58)
Parents: Larry Gordon and Ann
Marital status: Single
Family links with cricket: Grandfather and Father club cricketers (both wicket-keepers)
Education: Buckpool Secondary; Crestwood Comprehensive
Qualifications: 5 O-levels, 4 CSEs, coaching certificate
Jobs outside cricket: Inland Revenue, Linkbronze Ltd
Overseas teams played for: South Bunbury, Western Australia 1984–86
Cricketers particularly learnt from: D. Collins (Stourbridge CC), members of Leicestershire staff
Cricketers particularly admired: Bob Taylor, Alan Knott, Philip DeFreitas, Dennis Amiss
Other sports played: Football, table tennis, golf (used to be on schoolboy forms with Birmingham City FC)
Relaxations: Football, golf, listening to music. 'I'm interested in most sports. Playing cards is amusing especially when Les Taylor and John Agnew are involved. A good night out.'
Extras: Played for MCC v Scotland 1985. Took two catches in P. Clift's

hat-trick v Derby at Chesterfield 1985. Was Derek Underwood's last first-class victim

Opinions on cricket: 'I would like to see 16 four-day games, so that you play every county just once, during the week. Have the weekends purely for one-day cricket, Refuge League on a Sunday, and have a new competition on a Saturday, possibly involving coloured clothing.'

Best batting performance: 67* Leicestershire v Somerset, Leicester 1986

LAST SEASON: BATTING

	I.	N.O.	R.	H.S.	AV.
TEST					
1ST-CLASS	31	6	351	59	14.04
INT					
RAL	3	1	11	9	5.50
NAT.W.	2	0	7	4	3.50
B & H	3	1	49	36	24.50

LAST SEASON: WICKET KEEPING

	C.	ST.		
TEST				
1ST-CLASS	67	2		
INT				
RAL	5	1		
NAT.W.	4	–		
B & H	10	–		

CAREER: BATTING

	I.	N.O.	R.	H.S.	AV.
TEST					
1ST-CLASS	66	13	1089	67*	20.54
INT					
RAL	11	4	81	29*	11.57
NAT.W.	3	0	39	32	13.00
B & H	5	2	81	36	27.00

CAREER: WICKET KEEPING

	C.	ST.		
TEST				
1ST-CLASS	117	3		
INT				
RAL	18	3		
NAT.W.	7	–		
B & H	14	–		

WILD, D. J.   Northamptonshire

Full Name: Duncan James Wild
Role: Left-hand bat, right-arm medium bowler, cover fielder
Born: 28 November 1962, Northampton
Height: 6' 0" **Weight:** 12st 7lbs
Nickname: Oscar, Wildy
County debut: 1980
County cap: 1986
1st-Class 50s scored: 11
1st-Class 100s scored: 4
One-Day 50s: 2
Place in batting averages: 110th av. 29.47 (1986 83rd av. 33.77)
Place in bowling averages: 136th av. 48.27 (1986 54th av. 28.60)
Strike rate 1987: 117.09 (career 88.14)
1st-Class catches 1987: 15 (career 30)
Parents: John and Glenys
Marital status: Single

Family links with cricket: Father played for Northamptonshire
Education: Cherry Orchard Middle; Northampton School for Boys
Qualifications: 7 O-levels. Diploma in international trade
Jobs outside cricket: Law costs draughtsman, manufacturer's agent
Off-season 1987–88: Working as manufacturer's agent
Overseas tours: England Young Cricketers to West Indies 1980
Cricketers particularly learnt from: Wayne Larkins, Bob Carter
Cricketers particularly admired: David Gower, Richard Hadlee, Geoff Cook
Other sports played: Squash, golf, snooker
Other sports followed: Rugby, rallying
Extras: Played for England Young Cricketers v Young India in 3-Test series 1981. Also for Young England v Young West Indies, 1982
Best batting performance: 144 Northamptonshire v Lancashire, Southport 1984
Best bowling performance: 4-4 Northamptonshire v Cambridge University, Cambridge 1986

LAST SEASON: BATTING

	I.	N.O.	R.	H.S.	AV.
TEST					
1ST-CLASS	23	6	501	102*	29.47
INT					
RAL	8	4	83	29*	20.75
NAT.W.	2	0	14	8	7.00
B & H	6	1	89	36	17.80

CAREER: BATTING

	I.	N.O.	R.	H.S.	AV.
TEST					
1ST-CLASS	121	20	2892	144	28.63
INT					
RAL	47	16	532	63*	17.16
NAT.W.	8	0	37	11	4.62
B & H	17	7	228	48	22.80

LAST SEASON: BOWLING

	O.	M.	R.	W.	AV.
TEST					
1ST-CLASS	214.4	68	531	11	48.27
INT					
RAL	70	1	313	9	34.77
NAT.W.	39.3	3	119	4	29.75
B & H	43.5	1	174	4	43.50

CAREER: BOWLING

	O.	M.	R.	W.	AV.
TEST					
1ST-CLASS	690.3	142	2273	47	48.36
INT					
RAL	359.1	9	1701	63	27.00
NAT.W.	113.3	12	391	13	30.07
B & H	85.5	5	332	9	36.88

180. Who opened the batting for Australia in the winning World Cup 1987 team?

181. What is the name of the famous cricket ground in Johannesburg?

WILLEY, P.   Leicestershire

Full Name: Peter Willey
Role: Right-hand bat,
off-break bowler
Born: 6 December 1949, Sedgefield,
Co Durham
Height: 6' 1" **Weight:** 13st
Nickname: Chin, Will
County debut: 1966
(Northamptonshire), 1984
(Leicestershire)
County cap: 1971
(Northamptonshire), 1984
(Leicestershire)
Benefit: 1981 (£31,400)
Test debut: 1976
No. of Tests: 25
No. of One-Day Internationals: 26
1000 runs in a season: 8
50 wickets in a season: 3
1st-Class 50s scored: 86
1st-Class 100s scored: 39
1st-Class 200s scored: 1
1st-Class 5 w. in innings: 25
1st-Class 10 w. in match: 3
One-Day 50s: 58
One-Day 100s: 9
Place in batting averages: 77th av. 33.94 (1986 28th av. 44.68)
Place in bowling averages: 90th av. 34.11
Strike rate 1987: 73.11 (career 75.15)
1st-Class catches 1987: 11 (career 197)
Parents: Oswald and Maisie
Wife and date of marriage: Charmaine, 23 September 1971
Family links with cricket: Father played local club cricket in County Durham
Education: Secondary School, Seaham, County Durham
Jobs outside cricket: Has worked as a groundsman, labourer and in a shoe factory. Coached in South Africa 1978–79
Overseas tours: Toured Australia with England 1979–80; West Indies, 1981 and 1986
Overseas teams played for: Eastern Province, South Africa
Other sports played: Golf, shooting
Other sports followed: All sports
Relaxations: Reading, taking Irish Setter for long walks and shooting
Extras: With Wayne Larkins, received 2016 pints of beer (seven barrels) from

a brewery in Northampton as a reward for their efforts in Australia with England in 1978–79. Hit a six off his first ball v Middlesex in JPL, 26 July 1981. Shared in 4th wicket partnership record for county, 370 with R. T. Virgin v Somerset at Northampton in 1976. Youngest player ever to play for Northamptonshire CCC at 16 years 180 days v Cambridge in 1966. Banned from Test cricket for three years for joining England rebel tour of South Africa in 1982. Left Northamptonshire at end of 1983 and moved to Leicestershire as vice-captain. Appointed Leicestershire captain for 1987. Resigned captaincy at end of season

Best batting performance: 227 Northamptonshire v Somerset, Northampton 1976

Best bowling performance: 7-37 Northamptonshire v Oxford University, Oxford 1975

LAST SEASON: BATTING

	I.	N.O.	R.	H.S.	AV.
TEST					
1ST-CLASS	40	3	1256	122	33.94
INT					
RAL	10	1	220	95*	24.44
NAT.W.	4	1	171	154*	57.00
B & H	4	2	151	80*	75.50

LAST SEASON: BOWLING

	O.	M.	R.	W.	AV.
TEST					
1ST-CLASS	219.2	46	614	18	34.11
INT					
RAL	46	4	219	8	27.37
NAT.W.	38	0	145	2	72.50
B & H	34	3	104	4	26.00

CAREER: BATTING

	I.	N.O.	R.	H.S.	AV.
TEST	50	6	1184	102*	26.90
1ST-CLASS	733	101	19819	227	31.35
INT	24	1	538	64	23.39
RAL	224	18	5807	107	28.18
NAT.W.	42	6	1253	154*	34.80
B & H	57	11	1478	88*	32.13

CAREER: BOWLING

	O.	M.	R.	W.	AV.
TEST	181.5	49	456	7	65.14
1ST-CLASS	32.6 8191.3	13 2256	19624	665	29.50
INT	171.5	9	659	13	50.69
RAL	1295.2	114	5249	199	26.37
NAT.W.	407.3	56	1239	31	39.96
B & H	519.4	85	1420	38	37.36

182. What is the name of the cricket ground at Pretoria?

183. What is the name of the cricket ground at Port Elizabeth?

184. What is the name of the cricket ground at Cape Town?

185. For which first-class side did Robin Smith, Collis King, Paddy Clift, and J. K. Lever all play in the same season?

WILLIAMS, N. F.   Middlesex

Full Name: Neil Fitzgerald
Williams
Role: Right-hand bat, right-arm
fast-medium bowler
Born: 2 July 1962, Hopewell,
St Vincent, West Indies
Height: 5′ 11″ **Weight:** 11st 7lbs
Nickname: Joe
County debut: 1982
County cap: 1984
50 wickets in a season: 2
1st-Class 50s scored: 5
1st-Class 5 w. in innings: 4
1st-Class 10 w. in match: 1
Place in batting averages:
235th av. 12.80
Place in bowling averages:
129th av. 44.23

Strike rate 1987: 87.53 (career 55.94)
1st-Class catches 1987: 1 (career 25)
Parents: Alexander and Aldreta
Marital status: Single
Family links with cricket: 'Uncle Joe was 12th man for St Vincent and plays 1st
Division cricket.'
Education: Cane End Primary School, St Vincent; Acland Burghley School,
Tufnell Park
Qualifications: School Leavers Certificate, 6 O-levels, 1 A-level
Overseas tours: English Counties to Zimbabwe 1985
Overseas teams played for: Windward Islands 1983; Tasmania 1983–84

LAST SEASON: BATTING

	I.	N.O.	R.	H.S.	AV.
TEST					
1ST-CLASS	9	4	64	18*	12.80
INT					
RAL	5	0	61	31	12.20
NAT.W.					
B & H	3	0	18	12	6.00

LAST SEASON: BOWLING

	O.	M.	R.	W.	AV.
TEST					
1ST-CLASS	189.4	32	575	13	44.23
INT					
RAL	70	2	305	9	33.88
NAT.W.					
B & H	25	2	93	1	93.00

CAREER: BATTING

	I.	N.O.	R.	H.S.	AV.
TEST					
1ST-CLASS	111	28	1637	67	19.72
INT					
RAL	26	8	213	31*	11.83
NAT.W.	6	2	28	10	7.00
B & H	12	3	130	29*	14.44

CAREER: BOWLING

	O.	M.	R.	W.	AV.
TEST					
1ST-CLASS	2498.5	455	8163	268	30.45
INT					
RAL	333.3	9	1505	52	28.94
NAT.W.	77	11	277	11	25.18
B & H	203.4	23	778	23	33.82

Cricketers particularly learnt from: Wilf Slack, Roland Butcher, Wayne Daniel

Cricketers particularly admired: Viv Richards, Andy Roberts, Michael Holding, Dennis Lillee, Malcolm Marshall, Lawrence Rowe

Other sports followed: Most

Relaxations: Reggae, soca, soul, cinema

Extras: Was on stand-by for England in New Zealand and Pakistan 1983–84

Best batting performance: 67 Middlesex v Cambridge University, Cambridge 1985

Best bowling performance: 7-55 English Counties XI v Zimbabwean XI, Harare 1984–85

WILLIAMS, R. G.   Northamptonshire

Full Name: Richard Grenville Williams

Role: Right-hand bat, off-break bowler

Born: 10 August 1957, Bangor, Caernarvonshire

Height: 5′ 6″ **Weight:** 12st

Nickname: Chippy

County debut: 1974

County cap: 1979

1000 runs in a season: 6

1st-Class 50s scored: 46

1st-Class 100s scored: 16

1st-Class 5 w. in innings: 8

One-Day 50s: 19

Place in batting averages: 20th av. 44.90

Place in bowling averages: 35th av. 25.65

Strike rate 1987: 55.76 (career 71.39)

1st-Class catches 1987: 5 (career 81)

Parents: Gordon and Rhianwen

Wife and date of marriage: Helen Laura, 24 April 1982

Family links with cricket: Father played for Caernarvonshire

Education: Ellesmere Port Grammar School

Jobs outside cricket: Qualified carpenter

Overseas tours: Australasia in 1980 with Derrick Robins' U-23 XI; West Indies with England Young Cricketers 1976; Zimbabwe with English Counties 1985

Overseas teams played for: Stockton CC and Belmont CC in Sydney, Australia, on Whitbread Scholarship. Also played in New Zealand

Relaxations: Fly fishing and shooting

Extras: Debut for 2nd XI in 1972 aged 14 years 11 months. Made maiden century in 1979 and then scored four centuries in five innings. Hat-trick v Gloucestershire, at Northampton 1980. Was first player to score a century against the 1980 West Indies touring team. Was stand-by for England in India 1981

Best batting performance: 175* Northamptonshire v Leicestershire, Leicester 1980

Best bowling performance: 7-73 Northamptonshire v Cambridge University, Cambridge 1980

LAST SEASON: BATTING

	I.	N.O.	R.	H.S.	AV.
TEST					
1ST-CLASS	27	7	898	104	44.90
INT					
RAL	8	2	203	63*	33.83
NAT.W.	4	1	44	30	14.66
B & H	5	0	163	72	32.60

LAST SEASON: BOWLING

	O.	M.	R.	W.	AV.
TEST					
1ST-CLASS	241.4	61	667	26	25.65
INT					
RAL	20.4	1	102	7	14.57
NAT.W.	42	6	128	7	18.28
B & H	42	2	183	9	20.33

CAREER: BATTING

	I.	N.O.	R.	H.S.	AV.
TEST					
1ST-CLASS	365	47	9990	175*	31.41
INT					
RAL	115	20	2232	82	23.49
NAT.W.	25	5	488	94	24.40
B & H	31	7	765	83	31.87

CAREER: BOWLING

	O.	M.	R.	W.	AV.
TEST					
1ST-CLASS	3593.2	926	10152	302	33.61
INT					
RAL	384.2	25	1818	65	27.96
NAT.W.	160	22	491	25	19.64
B & H	176	25	604	20	30.20

186. Who was 'The Croucher'?

187. True or False: W. G. Grace had an exceptionally deep voice?

188. Which West Indies team does Gordon Greenidge play for?

WOOLSTON, R. G.　　　　　Somerset

Full Name: Robert George
Woolston
Role: Right-hand bat, slow left-
arm bowler, cover fielder
Born: 23 May 1968, Enfield
Height: 5′ 11″ **Weight:** 12st
Nickname: Wooly
County debut: 1987
Parents: George and Patricia
Marital status: Single
Education: Enfield Grammar
School; Ware College
Qualifications: B Tech course
in graphic design
Jobs outside cricket: Sales
demonstrator, graphics sales
assistant, building worker
Off-season 1987–88: Playing
for Waverley CC, Sydney, Australia

Cricketers particularly learnt from: Ted Jackson, Don Wilson, Peter Robin-
son
Cricketers particularly admired: Phil Edmonds, Ian Botham
Other sports played: All sports
Other sports followed: All sports apart from horse racing
Relaxations: Listening to music
Extras: Played for MCC ground staff for one year
Best bowling performance: 2-70 Somerset v Derbyshire, Taunton 1987

LAST SEASON: BATTING

	I.	N.O.	R.	H.S.	AV.
TEST					
1ST-CLASS	1	0	0		0.00
INT					
RAL					
NAT.W.					
B & H					

LAST SEASON: BOWLING

	O.	M.	R.	W.	AV.
TEST					
1ST-CLASS	43	10	107	2	53.50
INT					
RAL					
NAT.W.					
B & H					

CAREER: BATTING

	I.	N.O.	R.	H.S.	AV.
TEST					
1ST-CLASS	1	0	0		0.00
INT					
RAL					
NAT.W.					
B & H					

CAREER: BOWLING

	O.	M.	R.	W.	AV.
TEST					
1ST-CLASS	43	10	107	2	53.50
INT					
RAL					
NAT.W.					
B & H					

WRIGHT, A. J.   Gloucestershire

Full Name: Anthony John Wright
Role: Right-hand bat, off-break
bowler, short-leg or slip fielder
Born: 27 July 1962, Stevenage
Height: 6′ 0″ **Weight:** 13st 7lbs
Nickname: Billy, Horace
County debut: 1980
County cap: 1987
1000 runs in a season: 1
1st-Class 50s scored: 20
1st-Class 100s scored: 2
One-Day 50s: 7
Place in batting averages: 120th
av. 28.38 (1986 163rd av. 23.19)
1st-Class catches 1987: 19
(career 55)
Parents: Michael and Patricia
Wife and date of marriage: Rachel,
21 December 1986

Education: Alleyn's School, Stevenage
Qualifications: 6 O-levels
Jobs outside cricket: Plasterer's labourer, wine waiter, working for Gray
Nicholls (Australia)
Overseas tours: Barbados 1980, 1985 and 1986 with Gloucestershire
Overseas teams played for: Port Melbourne 1981–82, 1982–83, 1984–85
Cricketers particularly learnt from: John Childs, Barry Dudleston, Andy
Brassington
Cricketers particularly admired: Zaheer Abbas, Viv Richards, Ian Botham
Other sports played: Rugby, golf, soccer
Relaxations: Eating out, drinking socially, listening to music
Opinions on cricket: 'Clubs should attempt to give assistance to players
seeking winter employment. Like to see more ex-pro's serving on committees
instead of people who know absolutely nothing about professional cricket.'
Best batting performance: 161 Gloucestershire v Glamorgan, Bristol 1987

LAST SEASON: BATTING

	I.	N.O.	R.	H.S.	AV.
TEST					
1ST-CLASS	38	2	1022	161	28.38
INT					
RAL	12	0	216	80	18.00
NAT.W.	4	0	223	88	55.75
B & H	4	0	109	58	27.25

CAREER: BATTING

	I.	N.O.	R.	H.S.	AV.
TEST					
1ST-CLASS	157	12	3631	161	25.04
INT					
RAL	38	4	439	80	12.91
NAT.W.	7	0	331	88	47.28
B & H	7	0	123	58	17.57

WRIGHT, J. G.   Derbyshire

Full Name: John Geoffrey Wright
Role: Left-hand opening bat,
right-arm medium bowler
Born: 5 July 1954, Darfield,
New Zealand
Height: 6′ 1″ **Weight:** 12st 7lbs
Nickname: Shake
County debut: 1977
County cap: 1977
Test debut: 1977–78
No. of Tests: 52
No. of One-Day Internationals: 88
1000 runs in a season: 6
1st-Class 50s scored: 98
1st-Class 100s scored: 45
One-Day 50s: 30
One-Day 100s: 4
Place in batting averages: 59th
av. 37.20 (1986 94th av. 32.47)
1st-Class catches 1987: 6 (career 157)
Parents: Geoff and Helen
Wife: Susan
Family links with cricket: Father played first-class cricket
Education: Christ's College, Christchurch, New Zealand; University of Otago, Dunedin, New Zealand
Qualifications: BSc in Biochemistry
Off-season 1987–88: Playing for New Zealand
Cricketing superstitions or habits: 'Ironed shirts are bad luck.'

LAST SEASON: BATTING

	I.	N.O.	R.	H.S.	AV.
TEST					
1ST-CLASS	17	2	558	118	37.20
INT					
RAL					
NAT.W.					
B & H					

LAST SEASON: BOWLING

	O.	M.	R.	W.	AV.
TEST					
1ST-CLASS					
INT					
RAL					
NAT.W.					
B & H					

CAREER: BATTING

	I.	N.O.	R.	H.S.	AV.
TEST	92	4	9874	141	32.65
1ST-CLASS	417	32	16486	192	42.82
INT	87	1	2166	84	25.18
RAL	91	6	2710	108	31.88
NAT.W.	12	2	555	87*	55.50
B & H	30	2	1005	102	35.89

CAREER: BOWLING

	O.	M.	R.	W.	AV.
TEST	5	1	5	0	
1ST-CLASS	48.4	5	277	2	138.50
INT	4	1	8	0	
RAL					
NAT.W.					
B & H					

Overseas tours: With New Zealand to England 1978, 1986; Australia 1980 –81; Sri Lanka and Pakistan 1984–85; West Indies 1985; World Cup 1987
Overseas teams played for: Northern Districts, Canterbury, New Zealand
Cricketers particularly learnt from: Eddie Barlow, David Steele
Cricketers particularly admired: 'Cutter' Curtayne
Other sports followed: Horse racing, tennis, rugby
Relaxations: Music
Extras: Holds record of 7 centuries for Derbyshire in a season – beating record of 6 held by Peter Kirsten in previous season, after record of 5 had stood for 49 years. Vice-captain of New Zealand 1984
Best batting performance: 192 Canterbury v Central Districts, New Plymouth 1986–87

WYATT, J. G. Somerset

Full Name: Julian George Wyatt
Role: Right-hand bat, right-arm medium bowler
Born: 19 June 1963, Paulton, Somerset
Height: 5' 10" **Weight:** 11st 10lbs
Nickname: Jules, Earp
County debut: 1983
1st-Class 50s scored: 9
1st-Class 100s scored: 3
One-day 50s: 1
Place in batting averages: 157th av. 22.72
1st-Class catches 1987: 2 (career 18)
Parents: Christopher Hedley and Dinah Ruby
Marital status: Single
Education: Wells Cathedral School, Somerset

Qualifications: 5 O-levels, NCA Senior Coaching Certificate
Jobs outside cricket: Brandon Tool Hire 1980–83
Off-season 1987–88: Playing in Australia for Manley CC
Cricketing superstitions or habits: Right pad on first
Overseas tours: Barbados with Somerset 1985
Overseas teams played for: Kew CC, Melbourne 1984–85; Manley CC, Sydney 1987–88
Cricketers particularly admired: Brian Rose, Peter Denning, Colin Dredge, Trevor Gard

Other sports played: Squash, football, tennis
Other sports followed: Rugby, soccer
Relaxations: 'Socialising at local pubs. Sport.'
Opinions on cricket: 'Over-rate rule needs reorganising. Why should a side be fined for bowling its allotted overs in a day, whether before 6.30 or later, as long as they are bowled?'
Best batting performance: 145 Somerset v Oxford University, Oxford 1985
Best bowling performance: 1-0 Somerset v Sussex, Hove 1984

LAST SEASON: BATTING

	I.	N.O.	R.	H.S.	AV.
TEST					
1ST-CLASS	13	2	250	58*	22.72
INT					
RAL	6	0	69	52	11.50
NAT.W.					
B & H					

LAST SEASON: BOWLING

	O.	M.	R.	W.	AV.
TEST					
1ST-CLASS					
INT					
RAL					
NAT.W.					
B & H					

CAREER: BATTING

	I.	N.O.	R.	H.S.	AV.
TEST					
1ST-CLASS	85	4	2165	145	26.72
INT					
RAL	15	2	211	52	16.23
NAT.W.	2	0	3	3	1.50
B & H	4	0	39	22	9.75

CAREER: BOWLING

	O.	M.	R.	W.	AV.
TEST					
1ST-CLASS	13	1	63	2	31.50
INT					
RAL					
NAT.W.					
B & H					

189. Which West Indies team does Roger Harper play for?

190. Who hit 3003 runs and took 101 wickets for Sussex in 1937?

191. Who has scored the most first-class centuries, and how many?

FIRST-CLASS COUNTY AVERAGES 1987

BATTING
(Qualification: 100 runs in 8 innings, average 10.00)

	M.	I.	N.O.	Runs	H.S.	Avge.	100s	50s
M. D. Crowe	18	29	5	1,627	206*	67.79	6	6
K. D. James	17	16	6	620	142*	62.00	2	2
M. W. Gatting	19	29	2	1,646	196	60.96	6	5
R. K. Illingworth	20	19	11	448	120*	56.00	1	1
R. J. Hadlee	21	28	7	1,111	133*	52.90	2	6
G. A. Hick	25	38	2	1,879	173	52.19	8	6
P. M. Roebuck	16	29	5	1,199	165*	49.95	5	4
C. G. Greenidge	12	18	0	899	163	49.94	3	6
D. R. Turner	25	35	8	1,328	184*	49.18	2	9
R. A. Smith	18	25	7	869	209*	48.27	1	4
R. A. Harper	7	9	5	193	127*	48.25	1	–
G. Fowler	24	43	5	1,800	169*	47.36	3	11
T. S. Curtis	25	40	6	1,601	138*	47.08	4	5
C. L. Smith	26	42	9	1,519	217	46.03	4	5
C. E. B. Rice	22	32	8	1,103	138	45.95	3	6
C. M. Wells	24	39	7	1,456	148*	45.50	5	6
R. G. Williams	22	27	7	898	104	44.90	1	5
N. E. Briers	21	32	4	1,257	104	44.89	2	9
C. W. J. Athey	21	34	5	1,295	160	44.65	6	2
D. I. Gower	20	31	4	1,197	125	44.33	2	6
M. R. Benson	24	39	0	1,725	131	44.23	5	10
J. W. Lloyds	23	32	4	1,213	130	43.32	2	9
B. Roberts	25	41	3	1,643	184	43.22	4	8
V. P. Terry	23	37	5	1,382	122	43.18	2	10
K. M. Curran	21	33	6	1,142	119	42.29	3	4
N. H. Fairbrother	21	30	6	1,014	109*	42.25	3	3
T. J. Boon	20	26	2	1,009	94	42.04	–	11
J. D. Carr	24	41	4	1,541	156	41.64	3	7
R. J. Blakey	24	38	5	1,361	204*	41.24	4	6
G. W. Humpage	24	41	9	1,318	99*	41.18	–	13
P. J. Newport	25	25	12	534	64*	41.07	–	3

	M.	I.	N.O.	Runs	H.S.	Avge.	100s	50s
R. F. Pienaar	7	8	0	327	153	40.87	1	1
M. C. J. Nicholas	25	38	9	1,183	147	40.79	4	4
M. P. Maynard	26	45	5	1,626	160	40.65	2	12
D. A. Reeve	17	23	8	606	87*	40.40	–	6
A. R. Butcher	15	27	2	1,009	135*	40.36	3	4
R. J. Shastri	13	22	3	765	103	40.26	1	6
M. D. Moxon	22	37	4	1,321	130	40.03	2	10
R. T. Robinson	21	36	4	1,250	166	39.06	3	3
M. Newell	20	34	7	1,054	203*	39.03	3	4
W. N. Slack	25	42	0	1,636	173	38.95	3	7
G. A. Gooch	24	41	6	1,361	171	38.88	3	7
G. D. Mendis	24	42	6	1,390	203*	38.61	3	7
M. A. Atherton	21	35	4	1,193	110	38.48	2	4
P. E. Robinson	7	13	2	421	95	38.27	–	3
A. J. Stewart	22	34	2	1,219	132	38.09	3	8
D. M. Smith	17	27	4	873	121*	37.95	1	7
J. Abrahams	9	15	1	525	140*	37.50	1	3
G. S. le Roux	13	15	5	375	73	37.50	–	2
R. J. Bailey	26	42	8	1,274	158	37.47	3	4
P. R. Downton	26	39	9	1,120	103*	37.33	1	9
C. T. Radley	9	13	3	373	72	37.30	–	3
J. G. Wright	10	17	2	558	118	37.20	1	3
N. R. Taylor	24	38	3	1,300	142*	37.14	3	6
C. J. Richards	20	26	6	738	172*	36.90	1	4
P. A. Neale	25	34	7	994	103*	36.81	2	5
K. J. Barnett	25	40	1	1,429	130	36.64	3	7
J. J. Whitaker	27	39	5	1,245	126	36.61	2	10
P. Johnson	25	39	4	1,257	125	35.91	3	5
M. D. Marshall	22	22	5	610	99	35.88	–	3
I. G. Swallow	5	9	2	249	114	35.57	1	1
D. J. Bicknell	12	20	3	600	105	35.29	1	4
P. Bainbridge	17	25	6	668	151	35.15	2	3
B. R. Hardie	27	43	4	1,370	143	35.12	3	8
D. W. Randall	13	20	1	665	133	35.00	1	3
W. Larkins	25	43	4	1,364	120	34.97	3	6
T. A. Lloyd	25	46	3	1,503	162	34.95	3	5
T. E. Jesty	24	36	5	1,074	124*	34.64	1	5
J. E. Morris	26	40	1	1,343	162	34.43	3	6
P. Willey	26	40	3	1,256	122	33.94	2	7
I. P. Butcher	8	12	0	407	88	33.91	–	4
M. Watkinson	19	27	4	776	91	33.73	–	6
R. J. Parks	25	19	8	370	62*	33.63	–	2
D. B. D'Oliveira	25	37	4	1,106	131*	33.51	2	5
D. L. Bairstow	20	23	1	736	128	33.45	2	2
P. J. Prichard	11	16	3	434	72	33.38	–	4
A. J. Moles	25	46	3	1,431	151	33.27	4	4

	M.	I.	N.O.	Runs	H.S.	Avge.	100s	50s
M. A. Lynch	26	39	5	1,127	128*	33.14	2	6
C. J. Tavare	26	42	7	1,157	152	33.05	1	6
I. J. Gould	21	29	5	792	111	33.00	1	4
Asif Din	23	36	4	1,056	115*	33.00	2	5
A. J. Lamb	23	34	4	982	101*	32.73	1	5
J. E. Emburey	18	26	4	710	74	32.27	–	7
B. C. Broad	15	26	4	708	80	32.18	–	6
A. P. Wells	23	37	4	1,058	161*	32.06	3	4
P. B. Clift	17	22	3	608	88	32.00	–	4
S. G. Hinks	21	33	2	992	112	32.00	2	3
R. C. Ontong	16	27	8	600	100	31.57	1	1
J. D. Birch	23	32	3	914	82	31.51	–	8
G. R. Cowdrey	5	8	1	219	68	31.28	–	3
A. A. Metcalfe	24	42	4	1,178	152	31.00	2	6
A. W. Lilley	20	29	4	773	102	30.92	1	3
C. S. Cowdrey	25	37	6	958	135	30.90	3	3
I. A. Greig	26	35	6	887	104*	30.58	1	5
G. Cook	25	41	9	969	111*	30.28	1	6
D. G. Aslett	25	40	8	969	101*	30.28	1	4
G. S. Clinton	19	30	2	848	93	30.28	–	7
D. L. Amiss	25	46	3	1,300	123	30.23	2	6
I. T. Botham	16	22	2	598	126*	29.90	1	2
A. J. T. Miller	10	15	2	387	97	29.76	–	3
D. J. Wild	22	23	6	501	102*	29.47	1	3
D. R. Pringle	22	33	9	705	84*	29.37	–	4
K. T. Medlycott	25	30	5	734	153	29.36	1	5
M. R. Ramprakash	8	14	3	321	71	29.18	–	2
R. A. Cobb	17	26	5	612	88	29.14	–	3
K. W. R. Fletcher	24	35	3	925	121	28.90	1	5
J. J. E. Hardy	24	40	2	1,089	119	28.65	1	7
P. W. Romaines	25	42	2	1,144	119	28.60	2	5
A. J. Wright	23	38	2	1,022	161	28.38	1	6
H. Morris	26	48	2	1,304	143	28.34	3	4
P. J. W. Allott	22	27	4	641	88	27.86	–	4
J. D. Love	21	30	7	639	79*	27.78	–	4
R. O. Butcher	17	22	1	580	118	27.61	1	2
K. R. Brown	15	24	3	579	70	27.57	–	5
R. C. Russell	26	38	9	798	57*	27.51	–	3
M. W. Alleyne	20	30	7	628	82*	27.30	–	5
J. P. Stephenson	13	22	3	515	67*	27.10	–	2
S. J. S. Kimber	8	9	3	161	54	26.83	–	1
K. Sharp	20	32	4	751	81*	26.82	–	6
R. J. Boyd-Moss	8	13	1	321	77	26.75	–	2
N. A. Felton	24	41	0	1,094	110	26.68	1	5
V. S. Greene	8	11	4	186	62*	26.57	–	1
C. Gladwin	10	17	2	339	77	26.07	–	2

	M.	I.	N.O.	Runs	H.S.	Avge.	100s	50s
N. D. Burns	24	35	7	729	100*	26.03	1	4
R. Sharma	17	27	4	596	111	25.91	1	3
C. K. Bullen	11	13	3	259	65	25.90	–	2
K. P. Tomlins	7	9	1	207	100	25.87	1	–
E. A. E. Baptiste	16	23	3	517	95	25.85	–	3
V. J. Marks	22	31	6	635	63*	25.40	–	2
L. Potter	14	20	4	401	68	25.06	–	1
D. Ripley	25	24	5	474	125*	24.94	1	1
G. C. Holmes	25	43	6	922	95	24.91	–	5
G. J. Parsons	16	19	2	422	67*	24.82	–	3
G. D. Rose	18	23	4	470	95	24.73	–	1
M. A. Roseberry	10	14	3	270	52	24.54	–	1
R. J. Finney	23	36	5	760	77	24.51	–	4
D. W. Varey	7	10	1	220	59	24.44	–	2
A. M. Green	20	36	2	821	115	24.14	1	3
A. W. Stovold	26	43	2	988	88	24.09	–	5
D. J. Capel	22	30	3	639	91*	23.66	–	3
R. J. Harden	19	30	6	568	59	23.66	–	2
S. J. O'Shaughnessy	9	16	4	275	61	22.91	–	1
A. C. Storie	16	26	8	410	66*	22.77	–	1
J. G. Wyatt	8	13	2	250	58*	22.72	–	1
S. J. Rhodes	25	31	7	544	80	22.66	–	3
M. J. Weston	14	21	2	426	54	22.42	–	3
W. K. Hegg	13	20	4	350	130	21.87	1	–
R. I. Alikhan	19	34	3	666	78	21.48	–	3
I. S. Anderson	15	21	2	407	87*	21.42	–	3
B. J. M. Maher	25	41	2	834	105	21.38	2	2
T. D. Topley	12	15	4	231	66	21.00	–	1
G. J. Lord	12	19	2	353	66	20.76	–	2
K. Ibadulla	5	8	1	145	46*	20.71	–	–
S. P. James	8	13	1	246	106	20.50	1	–
E. E. Hemmings	25	27	8	389	75	20.47	–	3
N. J. Pringle	10	18	1	347	79	20.41	–	2
B. N. French	18	20	2	365	70	20.27	–	2
P. W. G. Parker	19	32	4	565	85	20.17	–	2
N. A. Foster	21	23	2	419	49*	19.95	–	–
J. Derrick	18	27	7	398	57	19.90	–	1
A. C. S. Pigott	19	27	4	456	62	19.82	–	2
N. G. Cowley	10	12	2	197	96	19.70	–	1
P. A. J. DeFreitas	18	23	2	412	74	19.61	–	2
P. A. Todd	14	24	0	470	135	19.58	1	2
G. V. Palmer	14	16	4	234	68	19.50	–	1
P. A. Smith	17	31	5	506	89	19.46	–	2
D. J. Thomas	17	17	4	243	49	18.69	–	–
S. A. Marsh	21	27	5	411	72*	18.68	–	2
S. N. Hartley	10	18	2	298	63	18.62	–	2

	M.	I.	N.O.	Runs	H.S.	Avge.	100s	50s
A. E. Warner	18	28	4	444	22	18.50	–	1
P. J. Hartley	22	26	7	347	49	18.26	–	–
A. Needham	10	12	3	164	33	18.22	–	–
P. G. Newman	17	24	5	341	42	17.94	–	–
P. A. Cottey	7	10	1	161	42*	17.88	–	–
C. W. Scott	12	15	1	250	45	17.85	–	–
D. M. Ward	6	10	0	178	44	17.80	–	–
P. Moores	18	24	2	385	55	17.50	–	2
D. J. R. Martindale	9	13	2	192	103	17.45	1	–
P. Carrick	24	29	2	471	61	17.44	–	2
M. A. Holding	13	18	2	278	63*	17.37	–	1
D. P. Hughes	25	35	6	503	81	17.34	–	1
P. H. Edmonds	16	18	6	208	32	17.33	–	–
D. K. Standing	17	29	3	443	56	17.03	–	2
J. P. Agnew	25	27	4	387	90	16.82	–	1
H. A. Page	15	20	4	266	60	16.62	–	1
N. G. B. Cook	26	25	7	299	64	16.61	–	2
C. P. Metson	25	37	7	493	81	16.43	–	1
N. A. Mallender	15	17	9	131	20*	16.37	–	–
A. Sidebottom	18	22	6	261	33	16.31	–	–
P. W. Jarvis	24	24	11	212	32	16.30	–	–
G. C. Small	12	20	4	257	42	16.06	–	–
I. Smith	18	23	5	288	45	16.00	–	–
A. A. Donald	11	10	3	111	37*	15.85	–	–
T. A. Merrick	14	19	5	220	74*	15.71	–	1
D. E. East	27	32	3	449	73	15.48	–	1
J. A. Hopkins	15	26	2	371	39*	15.45	–	–
M. P. Bicknell	14	14	7	108	18	15.42	–	–
R. A. Pick	17	15	5	154	42*	15.40	–	–
J. G. Thomas	10	15	2	200	48	15.38	–	–
D. L. Underwood	23	20	9	168	29*	15.27	–	–
G. Miller	23	30	5	371	33*	14.84	–	–
C. Penn	17	18	2	237	53	14.81	–	1
I. Folley	25	31	7	355	33	14.79	–	–
M. A. Feltham	11	12	3	129	39	14.33	–	–
W. W. Davis	19	18	5	186	25*	14.30	–	–
P. Whitticase	26	31	6	351	59	14.04	–	1
S. P. Hughes	18	20	7	180	26*	14.00	–	–
G. A. Tedstone	10	14	1	180	51	13.84	–	1
T. M. Tremlett	24	17	5	161	42	13.41	–	–
J. Simmons	22	24	5	252	64	13.26	–	1
S. J. Base	8	14	4	127	38	12.70	–	–
J. H. Childs	22	22	13	113	26	12.55	–	–
M. Jean-Jacques	16	20	4	192	47	12.00	–	–
O. H. Mortensen	19	24	10	168	74*	12.00	–	1
A. R. C. Fraser	22	22	5	202	38	11.88	–	–

	M.	I.	N.O.	Runs	H.S.	Avge.	100s	50s
I. Redpath	7	12	1	128	46	11.63	–	–
N. V. Radford	23	21	4	197	31	11.58	–	–
P. A. W. Heseltine	18	18	3	172	26	11.46	–	–
T. A. Munton	16	16	5	116	38	10.54	–	–
S. R. Lampitt	12	14	3	111	24	10.09	–	–
N. Gifford	25	25	12	131	36	10.07	–	–

BOWLING
(Qualification: 10 wickets)

	O.	M.	R.	W.	Avge.	Best	5w.I.
R. J. Hadlee	591	189	1,227	97	12.64	6–20	9
A. H. Gray	291.1	59	748	48	15.58	5–46	2
K. J. Barnett	88.2	27	225	13	17.30	4–31	–
S. T. Clarke	456.4	114	1,160	67	17.31	8–62	6
N. G. Cowans	341.3	74	958	51	18.78	5–43	2
T. M. Tremlett	547	152	1,407	72	19.54	6–53	3
O. H. Mortensen	432.5	111	1,084	55	19.70	5–57	2
M. D. Marshall	594.1	152	1,508	76	19.84	5–49	1
P. J. W. Allott	535.2	166	1,222	59	20.71	7–42	1
P. J. Bakker	92.5	23	249	12	20.75	7–31	1
N. V. Radford	741.5	125	2,269	109	20.81	8–56	8
A. Walker	390.2	103	1,011	48	21.06	4–22	–
T. E. Jesty	72.4	11	212	10	21.20	6–81	1
J. Simmons	640.3	196	1,425	67	21.26	6–20	4
S. J. W. Andrew	316.1	61	1,022	48	21.29	7–92	2
G. J. F. Ferris	359.1	69	1,143	52	21.98	6–42	4
N. A. Foster	674.5	145	1,892	86	22.00	8–107	5
G. R. Dilley	265.3	52	817	35	23.34	6–43	4
M. Watkinson	318	66	986	42	23.47	7–25	4
S. J. Base	203.1	38	660	28	23.57	5–67	2
G. Smith	81	9	308	13	23.69	6–72	1
M. P. Bicknell	363.2	94	997	42	23.73	6–63	2
G. S. le Roux	266.5	55	768	32	24.00	5–64	1
K. W. McLeod	126.4	24	409	17	24.05	5–8	2
E. E. Hemmings	872.4	294	2,119	88	24.09	6–62	7
J. P. Agnew	777	144	2,451	101	24.26	7–46	9
P. G. Newman	363	75	1,093	45	24.28	5–46	1
P. B. Clift	405.1	114	900	37	24.32	6–64	2
M. A. Holding	391.2	72	1,194	49	24.36	5–41	2
N. A. Mallender	351	61	1,129	46	24.54	7–61	1
P. W. Jarvis	644.1	150	1,991	81	24.58	7–82	2
I. Folley	753.1	240	1,865	74	25.20	7–15	5
T. A. Merrick	433.3	71	1,439	57	25.24	7–45	4
T. A. Munton	341.1	72	992	39	25.43	6–69	2
C. A. Walsh	525.4	108	1,609	63	25.53	5–38	2

	O.	M.	R.	W.	Avge.	Best	5w.I.
R. G. Williams	241.4	61	667	26	25.65	5–81	1
G. D. Rose	314.4	56	976	38	25.68	5–24	1
K. E. Cooper	158.3	50	387	15	25.80	3–38	–
D. J. M. Kelleher	301	71	878	34	25.82	6–109	2
P. A. J. DeFreitas	477.2	107	1,450	56	25.89	7–85	3
A. A. Donald	301.4	36	1,012	39	25.94	6–74	2
P. Carrick	575.4	198	1,323	51	25.94	5–42	1
L. B. Taylor	154.4	20	545	21	25.95	6–47	2
A. P. Igglesden	382.3	54	1,351	52	25.98	5–45	3
B. P. Patterson	419.1	61	1,359	52	26.13	6–40	4
D. J. Capel	464.5	87	1,396	53	26.33	7–46	4
M. K. Bore	148.2	58	344	13	26.46	4–52	–
D. R. Pringle	598.5	156	1,457	55	26.49	5–70	1
E. A. E. Baptiste	519.3	118	1,495	56	26.69	8–76	2
C. K. Bullen	225.4	71	564	21	26.85	6–119	1
K. Saxelby	452.1	121	1,278	47	27.19	6–49	1
W. W. Davis	591.1	100	1,906	70	27.22	6–57	5
T. D. Topley	300.2	66	840	30	28.00	4–75	–
J. A. Afford	276.4	86	729	26	28.03	5–79	1
P. Bainbridge	288.4	62	927	33	28.09	5–70	1
S. D. Fletcher	276.3	54	903	32	28.21	4–22	–
V. S. Greene	236.5	32	819	29	28.24	7–96	1
R. F. Pienaar	135.4	27	427	15	28.46	4–66	–
A. N. Jones	517.1	85	1,800	63	28.57	7–85	3
C. E. B. Rice	308.3	91	800	28	28.57	4–42	–
D. L. Underwood	611.3	211	1,295	45	28.77	5–43	1
R. J. Maru	802.4	229	206	71	29.02	5–45	3
N. G. B. Cook	705.2	228	1,574	54	29.14	6–77	1
J. G. Thomas	245.3	48	875	30	29.16	6–109	2
A. E. Warner	328.5	67	1,026	35	29.31	4–12	–
A. Sidebottom	446.5	83	1,261	43	29.32	4–46	–
C. M. Wells	546.1	99	1,531	52	29.44	6–34	2
D. A. Reeve	450	108	1,240	42	29.52	7–37	1
S. Monkhouse	82	7	326	11	29.63	2–21	–
P. C. R. Tufnell	335.2	65	984	33	29.81	6–60	1
M. A. Feltham	412.1	101	1,201	40	30.02	4–24	–
D. A. Graveney	356.1	112	848	28	30.28	5–37	1
P. M. Such	490.1	142	1,256	41	30.60	4–14	–
C. Penn	439.1	78	1,469	48	30.60	5–52	2
V. J. Marks	778.5	203	2,155	70	30.78	5–35	2
R. A. Pick	361.4	74	1,206	29	30.92	4–75	–
R. J. Finney	275.2	57	839	27	31.07	3–39	–
G. Miller	379.3	84	995	32	31.09	7–59	1
N. Gifford	453	136	1,121	36	31.13	5–71	2
J. Derrick	321.3	70	1,064	34	31.29	5–50	1
G. C. Small	350	70	1,067	34	31.38	4–80	–

	O.	M.	R.	W.	Avge.	Best	5w.I.
R. A. Harper	256	56	662	21	31.52	5–28	2
K. B. S. Jarvis	251.2	41	884	28	31.57	5–48	1
S. R. Waugh	112	18	348	11	31.63	3–48	–
I. G. Swallow	111	25	349	11	31.72	7–95	1
J. K. Lever	398	94	1,079	34	31.73	5–59	2
R. J. Shastri	460.1	99	1,181	37	31.91	5–100	1
A. C. S. Pigott	455.2	87	1,443	45	32.06	5–32	3
G. A. Gooch	250.3	64	687	21	32.71	4–42	–
A. P. Pridgeon	344	80	920	28	32.85	7–44	1
C. A. Connor	397	87	1,061	32	33.15	4–26	–
J. H. Childs	479.3	143	1,228	37	33.18	5–40	2
H. A. Page	339	52	1,172	35	33.48	5–26	1
P. Willey	219.2	46	614	18	34.11	4–32	–
P. H. Edmonds	481.5	160	1,094	32	34.18	4–34	–
A. R. C. Fraser	569.1	143	1,506	44	34.22	4–50	–
R. C. Ontong	469.4	89	1,410	41	34.39	6–91	2
N. G. Cowley	250.1	57	689	20	34.45	4–35	–
W. K. M. Benjamin	207.2	54	525	15	35.00	5–50	1
I. L. Pont	183	19	671	19	35.31	5–73	1
P. G. Edwards	172.4	42	500	14	35.71	4–93	–
I. A. Greig	410.4	86	1,257	35	35.91	4–47	–
G. J. Parsons	418.5	82	1,229	34	36.14	5–80	1
C. J. G. P. van Zyl	172	37	511	14	36.50	3–35	–
P. J. Hartley	501	89	1,726	47	36.72	4–52	–
D. V. Lawrence	349.5	41	1,411	38	37.13	6–63	1
D. J. Thomas	357	61	1,230	33	37.27	5–73	1
J. E. Emburey	570.3	152	1,311	35	37.45	5–60	1
D. J. Foster	111.5	10	490	13	37.69	4–56	–
S. R. Barwick	602.1	120	1,799	47	38.27	4–60	–
M. A. Robinson	150	25	501	13	38.53	3–45	–
K. T. Medlycott	546.4	148	1,640	42	39.04	5–103	1
M. Jean-Jacques	325	62	1,068	27	39.55	4–39	–
W. W. Daniel	348.1	50	1,275	32	39.84	4–69	–
I. Smith	211.3	40	757	19	39.84	3–65	–
K. D. James	206.1	36	757	19	39.84	5–62	1
G. V. Palmer	316	54	1,162	29	40.06	4–63	–
S. P. Hughes	358	55	1,167	29	40.24	3–74	–
J. W. Lloyds	403.2	63	1,466	36	40.72	6–57	2
A. M. G. Scott	250.3	50	744	18	41.33	5–97	1
G. A. Hick	310.2	59	1,042	25	41.38	4–31	–
I. T. Botham	260	47	883	21	42.04	3–51	–
R. K. Illingworth	476.2	115	1,391	33	42.15	4–28	–
R. Sharma	206	46	640	15	42.66	6–80	1
A. J. Moles	182.3	46	513	12	42.75	3–21	–
A. M. Babington	248.1	44	898	21	42.76	3–44	–
P. J. Newport	504.3	80	1,839	42	43.78	4–28	–

	O.	M.	R.	W.	Avge.	Best	5w.I.
N. F. Williams	189.4	32	575	13	44.23	3–55	–
A. Needham	179	34	545	12	45.41	4–96	–
C. S. Cowdrey	278.1	64	871	19	45.84	2–30	–
P. A. W. Heseltine	316.2	75	963	21	45.85	3–33	–
M. R. Davis	151.5	25	505	11	45.90	3–43	–
P. A. Smith	177.5	21	783	17	46.05	3–31	–
R. P. Davis	153	35	473	10	47.30	3–68	–
M. Beardshall	158.2	21	572	12	47.66	4–68	–
D. J. Wild	214.4	68	531	11	48.27	2–11	–
G. E. Sainsbury	344.2	79	922	19	48.52	3–48	–
S. J. S. Kimber	152	21	639	12	53.25	2–13	–
M. W. Alleyne	172.4	35	709	11	64.45	4–128	–

WICKET-KEEPERS

76 B. J. M. Maher (72ct, 4st)
74 C. J. Richards (67ct, 7st)
69 P. Whitticase (67ct, 2st)
65 P. R. Downton (57ct, 8st)
61 D. E. East (57ct, 4st)
    R. J. Parks (56ct, 5st)

57 S. J. Rhodes (51ct, 6st)
53 C. P. Metson (47ct, 6st)
50 N. D. Burns (44ct, 6st)
49 B. N. French (45ct, 4st)
48 D. Ripley (39ct, 9st)
41 S. A. Marsh (39ct, 2st)

FIELDERS

30 M. P. Maynard
29 C. J. Tavare
    V. P. Terry
28 R. J. Blakey
    G. Miller
26 M. D. Moxon
    C. E. B. Rice

    C. L. Smith
25 D. B. D'Oliveira
    P. J. W. Allott
    M. A. Lynch
    R. J. Maru
24 A. J. Moles

BRITANNIC ASSURANCE COUNTY CHAMPIONSHIP

					Bonus pts.		
	P.	W.	L.	D.	Btg.	Blg.	Pts.
Nottinghamshire (4)	24	9	1	14	68	80	292
Lancashire (15)	24	10	4	10	55	73	288
Leicestershire (7)	24	8	3	13	57	75	260
Surrey (3)	24	7	4	13	65	73	250
Hampshire (6)	24	7	3	14	59	73	244
Derbyshire (11)	24	6	5	12	51	70	225
Northamptonshire (9)	24	7	4	13	48	68	224
Yorkshire (9)	24	7	3	14	52	58	222
Worcestershire (10)	24	5	4	15	58	68	206
Gloucestershire (2)	24	5	8	10	62	50	200
Somerset (16)	24	2	3	19	61	70	163

	P.	W.	L.	D.	Btg.	Blg.	Pts.
Essex (1)	24	2	4	18	45	77	162
Glamorgan (17)	24	3	9	12	40	70	158
Kent (8)	24	2	7	15	53	66	151
Warwickshire (12)	24	2	7	15	48	67	147
Middlesex (12)	24	2	8	14	47	60	139
Sussex (14)	24	1	8	15	47	56	119

1986 positions in brackets

Essex's record includes eight points for drawn match in which the scores finished level. Northamptonshire's record includes 12 points for win in one innings match.

REFUGE ASSURANCE SUNDAY LEAGUE

	P.	W.	L.	Tie	N.R.	Pts.
Worcestershire (16)	16	11	4	0	1	46
Nottinghamshire (3)	16	9	3	0	4	44
Gloucestershire (17)	16	9	4	1	2	42
Somerset (6)	16	8	4	0	4	40
Derbyshire (9)	16	8	4	1	3	40
Kent (6)	16	8	5	0	3	38
Hampshire (1)	16	6	6	2	2	32
Surrey (12)	16	6	6	0	4	32
Lancashire (12)	16	5	6	0	5	30
Middlesex (9)	16	5	7	0	4	28
Northamptonshire (5)	16	4	6	0	6	28
Leicestershire (16)	16	3	6	0	7	26
Yorkshire (8)	16	5	8	0	3	26
Essex (2)	16	4	8	0	4	24
Glamorgan (12)	16	5	9	0	2	24
Sussex (4)	16	4	8	0	4	24
Warwickshire (9)	16	3	9	0	4	20

1986 positions in brackets

NATWEST TROPHY
Winners: Nottinghamshire.
Runners-up: Northamptonshire.
Losing Semi-finalists: Leicestershire and Gloucestershire.

BENSON & HEDGES CUP
Winners: Yorkshire.
Runners-up: Northamptonshire.
Losing Semi-finalists: Surrey and Kent.

UMPIRES

BIRD, H. D.

Full Name: Harold Dennis Bird
Role: Right-hand opening bat
Born: 19 April 1933, Barnsley
Height: 5′ 10½″ **Weight:** 11st 6lbs
Nickname: Dickie
Counties: Yorkshire, Leicestershire
County debut: 1956 (Yorkshire),
1960 (Leicestershire)
County cap: 1960 (Leicestershire)
1000 runs in a season: 1
1st-Class 50s scored: 14
1st-Class 100s scored: 2
1st-Class catches: 20
Best batting performance: 181*
Yorkshire v Glamorgan, Bradford
1959
Appointed to 1st-Class list: 1969
Appointed to Test panel: 1972
No. of Tests umpired: 37
No. of One-Day Internationals umpired: 62
Parents: James Harold and Ethel
Marital status: Bachelor
Education: Raley School, Barnsley
Jobs outside cricket: 'Cricket is my life.'
Off-season 1987–88: Umpiring in World Cup
Other sports followed: Football
Cricketers particularly admired: Johnny Wardle, Sir Gubby Allen
Relaxations: 'Listening to Barbra Streisand and Diana Ross records.'
Opinions on cricket: 'I would like to see an experimental law where we do away with leg-byes, because it is difficult to know whether a batsman has played a genuine shot or not.'
Extras: Awarded MBE, June 1986. Only man to umpire in three World Cup

CAREER: BATTING

	I.	N.O.	R.	H.S.	AV.
TEST					
1ST-CLASS	170	10	3314	181*	20.71
INT					
JPL					
NAT.W.	2	0	9	7	4.50
B & H					

CAREER: BOWLING

	O.	M.	R.	W.	AV.
TEST					
1ST-CLASS	8	2	22	0	–
INT					
JPL					
NAT.W.					
B & H					

Finals, 1975, 1979 and 1983. Voted Yorkshire Personality of the Year, 1977. Umpired Centenary Test Match, England v Australia, 1980. Umpired Queen's Silver Jubilee Test Match, England v Australia, Lord's 1977. Author of *Not Out* (1978), *That's Out* (1985)

BIRKENSHAW, J.

Full Name: Jack Birkenshaw
Role: Left-hand bat,
off-break bowler
Born: 13 November 1940,
Rothwell, Leeds
Height: 5′ 9″ **Weight:** 11st
Nickname: Birky
Counties: Yorkshire, Leicestershire,
Worcestershire
County debut: 1958 (Yorkshire),
Leicestershire (1961),
Worcestershire (1981)
County cap: 1965 (Leicestershire)
Test debut: 1972
No. of Tests: 5
Benefit: 1974 (£13,100)
50 wickets in a season: 8
1st-Class 50s scored: 53
1st-Class 100s scored: 4
1st-Class catches: 318
1st-Class 5 w. in innings: 44
1st-Class 10 w. in match: 4
One-Day 50s: 6
One-Day 100s: 1
Best batting performance: 131 Leicestershire v Surrey, Guildford 1969
Best bowling performance: 8-94, Leicestershire v Somerset, Taunton 1972
Appointed to 1st-Class list: 1982
Appointed to Test panel: 1986
Parents: John and Edith
Wife: Gloria
Children: Mark, 9 December 1962
Education: Rothwell Grammar School
Qualifications: 5 GCEs, qualified coach
Jobs outside cricket: 'Everything from the bakehouse to promotional work, plus coaching for Leicestershire County Cricket Club.'
Off-season 1987–88: Coaching and umpiring in Australia
Overseas tours: India, Pakistan and Sri Lanka 1972–73; West Indies 1973–74

Cricket records: Shared in seventh wicket partnership record for county, 206 with B. Dudleston v Kent at Canterbury, 1969

Cricketers particularly learnt from: J. Lawrence, A. Mitchell, M. Leyland, A. Boolt

Other sports played: Squash, table tennis

Relaxations: Coaching young people, music, gardening, wine-making

Extras: Played for Yorkshire 1958–60. Joined Leicestershire in 1961. Released at end of 1980 season and joined Worcestershire

CAREER: BATTING

	I.	N.O.	R.	H.S.	AV.
TEST	7	0	148	64	21.14
1ST-CLASS	658	123	12632	131*	23.61
INT					
JPL	89	16	1344	79	18.41
NAT.W.	19	3	290	101*	18.13
B & H	17	4	197	35*	15.15

CAREER: BOWLING

	O.	M.	R.	W.	AV.
TEST	169.3	33	469	13	36.08
1ST-CLASS	11362.4	3060	28803	1060	27.18
INT					
JPL	285.4	20	1147	52	22.05
NAT.W.	106	18	335	14	23.93
B & H	166	21	574	16	35.88

CONSTANT, D. J.

Full Name: David John Constant
Role: Left-hand bat, slow left-arm bowler
Born: 9 November 1941, Bradford-on-Avon, Wiltshire
Counties: Kent 1961–63, Leicestershire 1965–68
County debut: 1961 (Kent), 1965 (Leicestershire)
1st-Class 50s scored: 6
1st-Class catches: 33
Best batting performance: 80 Leicestershire v Gloucestershire, Bristol 1966
Appointed to 1st-Class list: 1969
Appointed to Test panel: 1971
No. of Tests umpired: 34
No. of One-day Internationals umpired: 27

CAREER: BATTING

	I.	N.O.	R.	H.S.	AV.
TEST					
1ST-CLASS	93	14	1517	80	19.20
INT					
JPL					
NAT.W.	1	0	5	5	–
B & H					

CAREER: BOWLING

	O.	M.	R.	W.	AV.
TEST					
1ST-CLASS	12.3	3	36	1	–
INT					
JPL					
NAT.W.					
B & H					

DUDLESTON, B.

Full Name: Barry Dudleston
Role: Right-hand bat, slow
left-arm bowler
Born: 16 July 1945, Bebington,
Cheshire
Height: 5′ 9″ **Weight:** 11st 8lbs
Nickname: Danny
Counties: Leicestershire,
Gloucestershire
County debut: 1966 (Leicestershire),
1981 (Gloucestershire)
County cap: 1969 (Leicestershire)
Benefit: 1980 (£25,000)
1000 runs in a season: 8
1st-Class 100s scored: 31
1st-Class 200s scored: 1
1st-Class catches: 234
One-Day 50s: 21
One-Day 100s: 4
Best batting performance: 202 Leicestershire v Derbyshire, Leicester 1979
Best bowling performance: 4-6 Leicestershire v Surrey, Leicester 1972
Appointed to 1st-Class list: 1984
Parents: Percy and Dorothy Vera
Wife and date of marriage: Lindsey Vivien Stratford, 5 April 1980
Children: Sharon Louise, 29 October 1968
Education: Stockport School
Qualifications: O-levels. Junior Coaching Certificate. Shell marketing exams
Jobs outside cricket: Retail and commercial representative for Shell
Overseas tours: With Derrick Robins' XI to Rhodesia
Overseas teams played for: Rhodesia 1966–67 to 1979–80 in Currie Cup
competition
Cricketers particularly learnt from: Vinoo Mankad
Cricket records: Leicestershire CCC 1st wicket record of 390, 7th wicket
record of 206, with Jack Birkenshaw v Kent at Canterbury in 1969. Fastest to
1000 runs in Currie Cup ever for Rhodesia, 2nd fastest of all time in Currie
Cup. Highest score by overseas player on debut in South Africa, 142 v
Western Province
Relaxations: Bridge and philately, watching all sports, red wine
Extras: England Under-25. Has suffered badly from broken fingers. Broke
fingers on same hand three times in 1978. Made debut for Leicestershire in
1966, gaining county cap in 1969. Released by Leicestershire at end of 1980
season and made debut for Gloucestershire 1981
Opinions on cricket: 'Now we are playing on covered wickets I should like to

481

see a Championship programme of 16 four-day games, two one-day matches and a day off per week, which would then be a balanced programme.'

CAREER: BATTING

	I.	N.O.	R.	H.S.	AV.
TEST					
1ST-CLASS	501	47	14747	202	32.48
INT					
JPL	123	8	2490	152	24.41
NAT.W.	18	1	586	125	34.47
B & H	42	5	1171	90	31.65

CAREER: BOWLING

	O.	M.	R.	W.	AV.
TEST					
1ST-CLASS	406	87	1365	47	29.04
INT					
JPL	1	0	4	0	–
NAT.W.	3	0	14	0	–
B & H					

EELE, P. J.

Full Name: Peter James Eele
Role: Left-hand bat, wicket-keeper
Born: 27 January 1935, Taunton
Height: 5′ 6″ **Weight:** 11st
County: Somerset
County debut: 1958
Benefit: 1969 (£3,500)
1st-Class 100s scored: 1
1st-Class catches: 87 + 19 stumpings
Best batting performance: 103* Somerset v Pakistan Eaglets, Taunton 1969
Appointed to 1st-Class list: 1981
Marital status: Single
Education: Taunton School

192. What have the following got in common: M. Maynard, Rev. D. Shepherd, M. Moxon and G. H. G. Doggart?

EVANS, D. G. L.

Full Name: David Gwillim
Lloyd Evans
Role: Right-hand bat,
wicket-keeper
Born: 27 July 1933, Lambeth
County: Glamorgan
County debut: 1956
County cap: 1959
Benefit: 1969 (£3,500)
Best batting performance: 46*
Glamorgan v Oxford University,
Oxford 1961
Appointed to 1st-Class list: 1971
Appointed to Test panel: 1981

CAREER: BATTING

	I.	N.O.	R.	H.S.	AV.
TEST					
1ST-CLASS	364	91	2875	46*	10.53
INT					
JPL					
NAT.W.	2	0	9	8	4.50
B & H					

CAREER: WICKET KEEPING

	C.	ST.			
TEST					
1ST-CLASS	503	55			
INT					
JPL					
NAT.W.	4	–			
B & H					

---

193. What is the longest recorded hit of a cricket ball from hit to first
bounce?

HAMPSHIRE, J. H.

Full Name: John Harry Hampshire
Role: Right-hand bat, leg-break bowler
Born: 10 February 1941, Thurnscoe
Height: 6′ **Weight:** 13½st
Nickname: Hamps (not Jackie)
Counties: Yorkshire, Derbyshire
County debut: 1961 (Yorkshire), 1982 (Derbyshire)
County cap: 1963 (Yorkshire), 1982 (Derbyshire)
1000 runs in a season: 15
1st-Class 50s scored: 142
1st-Class 100s scored: 43
1st-Class catches: 445
1st-Class 5 w. in innings: 1
One-Day 50s: 39
One-Day 100s: 7
Test debut: 1969
No. of Tests: 8

Best batting performance: 183* Yorkshire v Sussex, 1971
Best bowling performance: 7-52 Yorkshire v Glamorgan, 1963
Appointed to 1st-Class list: 1985
Education: Oakwood Technical High School, Rotherham
Off-season 1986–87: Manager, Redball, Yorkshire Indoor Cricket Centre, Sheffield
Wife and date of marriage: Judith, 5 September 1964
Children: Ian, 6 January 1969; Paul, 12 July 1972
Family links with cricket: Father played pre-war for Yorkshire CCC
Other sports played: Golf
Relaxations: Gardening, reading
Extras: Scored 107 in his first Test Match v West Indies at Lord's

CAREER: BATTING

	I.	N.O.	R.	H.S.	AV.
TEST	16	1	403	107	26.67
1ST-CLASS	908	111	27063	183*	33.96
INT	3	1	48	25*	24.00
JPL	172	20	4994	119	32.85
NAT.W.	33	5	930	110	33.21
B & H	45	6	1091	85*	27.97

CAREER: BOWLING

	O.	M.	R.	W.	AV.
TEST					
1ST-CLASS	16.6 402.5	1 85	1637	30	54.57
INT					
JPL	4	1	22	1	–
NAT.W.	2	0	4	0	–
B & H					

HARRIS, J. H.

Full Name: John Humphrey
Harris
Role: Left-hand bat, right-arm
fast-medium bowler
Born: 13 February 1936, Taunton
County: Somerset
County debut: 1952 (at
16 years 99 days)
1st-Class catches: 6
Best batting performance: 41
Somerset v Worcestershire,
Taunton 1957
Best bowling performance: 3-29
Somerset v Worcestershire,
Bristol 1959
Appointed to 1st-Class list: 1983
Extras: Played for Suffolk
1960–62 and Devon 1975

CAREER: BATTING

	I.	N.O.	R.	H.S.	AV.
TEST					
1ST-CLASS	18	4	154	41	11.00
INT					
JPL					
NAT.W.					
B & H					

CAREER: BOWLING

	O.	M.	R.	W.	AV.
TEST					
1ST-CLASS	217.2	42	619	19	32.57
INT					
JPL					
NAT.W.					
B & H					

194. What is the longest recorded throw of a cricket ball: 101, 140, or
167 yards?

HARRIS, M. J.

Full Name: Michael John Harris
Role: Right-hand bat, wicket-keeper, leg-break bowler
Born: 25 May 1944, St Just-in-Roseland, Cornwall
Height: 6′ 1″ **Weight:** 15st
Nickname: Pasty
Counties: Middlesex, Nottinghamshire
County debut: 1964 (Middlesex), 1969 (Nottinghamshire)
County cap: 1970 (Nottinghamshire)
Benefit: 1977
1000 runs in a season: 11
1st-Class 50s scored: 98
1st-Class 100s scored: 40
1st-Class 200s scored: 1
Parents: Winnie and Dick

Wife and date of marriage: Danielle Ruth, 10 September 1969
Children: Jodene, Elizabeth, Richard
Family links with cricket: Father and uncles on both sides played top village cricket
Education: Gerrans C/P
Qualifications: MCC Advanced Coach. SRA Squash Coach
Jobs outside cricket: Squash club manager
Cricketing superstitions or habits: Left boot and pad go on first
Overseas tours: With Derrick Robins' XI to West Indies 1974; with International Wanderers to South Africa and Rhodesia in 1974
Overseas teams played for: Eastern Province in 1971–72 Currie Cup Competition; Wellington in New Zealand Shell Shield Competition 1975–76
Appointed to 1st-Class list: On reserve list
Cricket records: Scored nine centuries in 1971 to equal county record. Shared in first wicket partnership record for Middlesex, 312 with W. E. Russell v Pakistan, Lord's 1967
Cricketers particularly learnt from: Eric Russell of Middlesex

CAREER: BATTING

	I.	N.O.	R.	H.S.	AV.
TEST					
1ST-CLASS	581	58	19196	201*	36.70
INT					
JPL	139	31	3303	104*	30.58
NAT.W.	25	1	579	101	24.13
B & H	34	7	925	101	34.26

CAREER: BOWLING

	O.	M.	R.	W.	AV.
TEST					
1ST-CLASS	1047.5	229	3459	79	43.78
INT					
JPL	6.4	1	41	3	13.67
NAT.W.					
B & H	9	0	46	1	–

Other sports played: Squash, golf, football
Extras: Made debut for Middlesex in 1964. Left staff after 1968 to join Nottinghamshire in 1969. Scored 2,238 at an average of 50.86 in 1971. Scored two centuries in a match twice in 1971, 118 and 123 v Leicestershire at Leicester, and 107 and 131* v Essex at Chelmsford

HASSAN, S. B.

Full Name: Sheikh Basharat Hassan
Role: Right-hand bat, right-arm medium bowler, occasional wicket-keeper
Born: 24 March 1944, Nairobi, Kenya
Height: 5′ 11″ **Weight:** 11st
Nickname: Basher, Scooby Doo
County: Nottinghamshire
County debut: 1966
County cap: 1970
Benefit: 1978
1000 runs in a season: 5
1st-Class 50s scored: 80
1st-Class 100s scored: 15
One-Day 50s scored: 36
One-Day 100s scored: 4
1st-Class catches: 308 + 1 stumping

Parents: Haji Sarwar Hussain (deceased) and Sairan Sheikh
Wife: Dorothy Ann
Children: Jamil Hassan, 22 October 1980; Sarah Jane Hassan, 30 June 1982
Family links with cricket: Father and brothers played
Education: City High School, Nairobi; Kenya Polytechnic
Qualifications: City and Guilds in Printing; Advanced Coaching Certificate
Jobs outside cricket: Sales representative for a printing firm
Off-season 1987–88: Working for Nottinghamshire CCC in their marketing department
Cricketing superstitions or habits: 'Never take off my "necklace" which was given to me by my father.'
Overseas tours: Kenya 1967; West Indies 1974; Dubai 1982; Bermuda 1987
Overseas teams played for: Kenya 1960–66; East Africa 1961–66
Appointed to 1st-Class list: On reserve list
Cricketers particularly learnt from: M. J. K. Smith, M. Ali (Kenya), Sir Garfield Sobers, Tom Graveney
Cricketers particularly admired: Richard Hadlee, Viv Richards

Other sports played: Hockey, golf, football
Other sports followed: Athletics, golf, football
Relaxations: 'TV, gardening, going for long walks with my pet dog (Sheik) and listening to music.'
Extras: Played first Test for Kenya at age of 15½, the youngest in the country. Made debut for East Africa Invitation XI v MCC 1963–64. Played for Kenya against touring sides. Scored a century with the aid of a runner v Kent at Canterbury in 1977. Best sprinter at Nottinghamshire. Short-listed for Kenyan Olympic team in 1960. Announced retirement in 1985 while fielding substitute for England in Trent Bridge Test v Australia
Best batting performance: 182* Nottinghamshire v Gloucestershire, Trent Bridge 1977
Best bowling performance: 3-33 Nottinghamshire v Lancashire, Old Trafford 1976

CAREER: BATTING

	I.	N.O.	R.	H.S.	AV.
TEST					
1ST-CLASS	549	54	14394	182*	29.07
INT					
JPL	196	21	5168	120*	29.53
NAT.W.	27	1	568	79	21.85
B & H	48	7	1070	99*	26.09

CAREER: BOWLING

	O.	M.	R.	W.	AV.
TEST					
1ST-CLASS	141.2	35	407	6	67.83
INT					
JPL	16.3	0	131	2	65.50
NAT.W.	7.1	2	20	3	6.66
B & H					

HOLDER, J. W.

Full Name: John Wakefield Holder
Role: Right-arm fast bowler
Born: 19 March 1945, Barbados
Height: 6' **Weight:** 13½st
Nickname: Benson, Hod
County: Hampshire
County debut: 1968
50 wickets in a season: 1
1st-Class 5 w. in innings: 5
1st-Class 10 w. in match: 1
1st-Class catches: 12
Best batting performance: 33 Hampshire v Sussex, Hove 1971
Best bowling performance: 6-49 and 7-79 (in same match) Hampshire v Gloucestershire, Gloucester 1972
Appointed to 1st-Class list: 1983
Parents: Charles and Carnetta
Wife: Glenda
Children: Christopher, 1968; Nigel, 1970

Family links with cricket: 'Both my sons play for Royston in the Central Lancashire League. They want to play county cricket. Father taught me to play.'

Education: St Giles Boys School; Combermere High School, Barbados

Qualifications: 3 O-levels. MCC Advanced Coach

Jobs outside cricket: Part-time cricket coach

Off-season 1987–88: Coaching cricket in Kalgoorlie, Western Australia

Cricketers particularly learnt from: Wes Hall, Everton Weekes

Cricketers particularly admired: Sir Garfield Sobers, Dennis Lillee

Other sports played: Weight-training in winter

Other sports followed: Manchester United FC, boxing

Relaxations: Watching documentaries about wildlife. Would like to become an accomplished after-dinner speaker

Extras: Holds best bowling performance ever for Rothmans International Cavaliers cricket matches. Playing for Hampshire Cavaliers, took 6-7 at Tichbourne Park, 1968. Would love to spend a winter in Australia, coaching and playing. Between 1974 and 1982, played professional league cricket in Lancashire and Yorkshire. One first-class hat-trick, Hampshire v Kent, 1972

Opinions on cricket: 'Until pitches and interest at school and club level improves, England will not produce enough top-class young players. Coaching in comprehensive schools is poor or non-existent. At club level and higher, coaches must not stick too rigidly to the coaching book. After all, it is only a guideline.'

CAREER: BATTING

	I.	N.O.	R.	H.S.	AV.
TEST					
1ST-CLASS	49	14	374	33	10.68
INT					
JPL	21	7	87	25	6.21
NAT.W.	2	0	4	3	2.00
B & H	3	1	23	14	11.50

CAREER: BOWLING

	O.	M.	R.	W.	AV.
TEST					
1ST-CLASS	1183	229	3415	139	24.56
INT					
JPL	237	14	984	38	25.89
NAT.W.	47	10	144	5	28.80
B & H	26	4	85	3	28.33

195. What is the highest individual batsman's score in a public schools match?

JAMESON, J. A.

Full Name: John Alexander Jameson
Role: Right-hand bat, occasional
off-break bowler
Born: 30 June 1941, Bombay
Height: 6′ **Weight:** 15½st
Nickname: Tub
County: Warwickshire
County debut: 1960
County cap: 1964
1000 runs in a season: 11
1st-Class 50s scored: 90
1st-Class 100s scored: 31
1st-Class 200s scored: 2
1st-Class catches: 255
One-Day 50s: 20
One-Day 100s: 6
Test debut: 1971
No. of Tests: 4
No. of One-Day Internationals: 3
Best batting performance: 240* Warwickshire v Gloucestershire, 1974
Best bowling performance: 4-22 Warwickshire v Oxford University, 1971
Appointed to 1st-Class list: 1984
Parents: John James and Florence Sylvia
Education: Cathedral School Bombay; Sherwood College, Naini Tal; Taunton School, Taunton
Qualifications: 6 O-levels
Wife and date of marriage: Angela, 1967
Children: Alexandra, 1974; Victoria, 1977
Family links with cricket: Father played for Bombay State Police
Other sports played: Hockey, rugby
Relaxations: Watching all sports, photography
Extras: Holds world record for 2nd wicket partnership of 465 (unbroken) with Rohan Kanhai, Warwickshire v Gloucestershire, Edgbaston 1974. Achieved first-class hat-trick v Gloucestershire, 1965. Appointed Sussex coach for 1988

CAREER: BATTING

	I.	N.O.	R.	H.S.	AV.
TEST	8	0	214	82	26.75
1ST-CLASS	603	43	18727	240*	33.44
INT	3	0	60	28	20.00
JPL	108	6	3077	123*	30.17
NAT.W.	31	2	758	100*	26.13
B & H	25	0	580	94	23.20

CAREER: BOWLING

	O.	M.	R.	W.	AV.
TEST	7	2	17	1	–
1ST-CLASS	1208.3	251	3765	88	42.78
INT	2	0	3	0	–
JPL	80.3	4	477	24	19.87
NAT.W.	36.1	5	138	6	23.00
B & H	46	9	135	6	22.50

JONES, A. A.

Full Name: Allan Arthur Jones
Role: Left-arm fast bowler
Born: 9 December 1947, Horley,
Surrey
Height: 6′ 3½″ **Weight:** 14st
Nickname: Jonah, Buckets
Counties: Sussex, Somerset,
Middlesex, Glamorgan
County debut: 1966 (Sussex),
1970 (Somerset), 1976 (Middlesex),
1980 (Glamorgan)
County cap: 1972 (Somerset),
1976 (Middlesex)
50 wickets in a season: 4
1st-Class 5 w. in innings: 23
1st-Class 10 w. in match: 3
1st-Class catches: 50
Best batting performance: 33
Middlesex v Kent, Canterbury 1978
Best bowling performance: 9-51 Somerset v Sussex, Hove 1976
Appointed to 1st-Class list: 1985
Parents: Leslie and Hazel
Wife and date of marriage: Marilyn, 1979
Children: Clare Michelle, 4 July 1979
Education: St John's College, Horsham
Qualifications: 5 O-levels. MCC 'A' coach, NCA staff coach
Jobs outside cricket: None at present
Off-season 1987–88: 'Playing lots of golf.'
Cricketers particularly learnt from: Brian Close, Mike Brearley, Tom Cartwright
Cricketers particularly admired: Brian Close, Barry Richards, John Snow
Other sports followed: 'All sports.'
Relaxations: Horse racing, cinema, reading
Opinions on cricket: 'I think there is too much one-day cricket played at present. Although it has its place and has brought money into the game, one-day cricket has undoubtedly lowered the standard of cricket as a whole. Also I am of the opinion that overseas players should be banned completely, or only allowed to play one-day cricket. That way we might be able to find more than just a dozen decent players in this country. As for cricket correspondents, most of them should take a look at their own knowledge of the game, and be seen to be watching, rather than just copying the scorecards. Also it might be good if they stuck to writing about cricket, and not cricketers. I think last year's attempt to uncover wickets was irrelevant, and basically a

waste of time, especially as this year four-day cricket is being introduced. I am not in favour of four-day cricket in this country, as it won't work, and I think it will lose an already dwindling Championship audience.'

CAREER: BATTING

	I.	N.O.	R.	H.S.	AV.
TEST					
1ST-CLASS	216	68	799	33	5.40
INT					
JPL	56	27	90	18*	3.10
NAT.W.	9	6	13	5*	4.33
B & H	18	8	51	14	5.10

CAREER: BOWLING

	O.	M.	R.	W.	AV.
TEST					
1ST-CLASS	4994.1	997	15414	549	28.08
INT					
JPL	952.1	99	3995	187	21.36
NAT.W.	167	14	658	29	22.68
B & H	352.2	60	1115	65	17.15

JULIAN, R.

Full Name: Raymond Julian
Role: Right-hand bat, wicket-keeper
Born: 23 August 1936, Cosby, Leicestershire
Height: 5′ 11″ **Weight:** 11st 4lbs
Nickname: Julie
County: Leicestershire
County debut: 1953
County cap: 1961
1st-Class 50s scored: 2
1st-Class catches: 382
Best batting performance: 51 Leicestershire v Worcestershire, Worcester 1962
Parents: George Ernest and Doris
Wife and date of marriage: Ruth Ann, 30 April 1958
Children: Peter, 1 February 1958; John, 13 October 1960; David, 15 October 1963; Paul, 22 September 1967
Family links with cricket: Father and 2 brothers all played local club cricket
Education: Wigston Secondary Modern School
Jobs outside cricket: Painter and decorator, cricket kit salesman
Off-season 1987–88: Cricket coaching. Painting and decorating
Cricketers particularly learnt from: Keith Andrew
Cricketers particularly admired: Gary Sobers, Richard Hadlee, Clive Rice
Other sports played: Ex-1st-Class football referee (local), linesman on Southern League for four seasons, refereed one FA Cup match
Relaxations: Gardening, listening to Johnny Mathis records

Extras: Youngest player to make debut (age 15) for Leicestershire v Gloucestershire, Bristol 1953. Gave 8 lbw decisions on the trot, Glamorgan v Sussex, Cardiff 1986. Played for Army 1955–57. Three Benson & Hedges semi-finals, one Gillette Cup semi-final
Opinions on cricket: 'In favour of four-day cricket.'

CAREER: BATTING

	I.	N.O.	R.	H.S.	AV.
TEST					
1ST-CLASS	288	23	2581	51	9.73
INT					
JPL					
NAT.W.	3	0	6	4	2.00
B & H					

CAREER: WICKET KEEPING

	C.	ST.			
TEST					
1ST-CLASS	381	40			
INT					
JPL					
NAT.W.	–	–			
B & H					

KITCHEN, M. J.

Full Name: Mervyn John Kitchen
Role: Left-hand bat, right-arm medium bowler
Born: 1 August 1940, Nailsea, Somerset
County: Somerset
County debut: 1960
County cap: 1966
Benefit: 1973 (£6000)
1000 runs in a season: 7
1st-Class 50s scored: 68
1st-Class 100s scored: 17
One-Day 50s: 22
One-Day 100s: 1
1st-Class catches: 157
Best batting performance: 189 Somerset v Pakistan, Taunton 1967
Appointed to 1st-Class list: 1982
Education: Backwell Secondary Modern, Nailsea

CAREER: BATTING

	I.	N.O.	R.	H.S.	AV.
TEST					
1ST-CLASS	612	32	15230	189	26.25
INT					
JPL	111	10	2069	82	20.48
NAT.W.	27	1	815	116	31.34
B & H	25	1	504	70	21.00

CAREER: BOWLING

	O.	M.	R.	W.	AV.
TEST					
1ST-CLASS	30.1	7	109	2	54.50
INT					
JPL	17.5	0	89	4	22.25
NAT.W.	3	2	8	1	–
B & H					

LEADBEATER, B.

Full Name: Barrie Leadbeater
Role: Right-hand opening bat,
right-arm medium bowler,
slip fielder
Born: 14 August 1943, Leeds
Height: 6′ **Weight:** 13st
Nickname: Leady
County: Yorkshire
County debut: 1966
County cap: 1969
Benefit: 1980 (£33,846 shared
with G. A. Cope)
1st-Class 50s scored: 27
1st-Class 100s scored: 1
One-Day 50s: 11
1st-Class catches: 82
Best batting performance: 140*
Yorkshire v Hampshire, Portsmouth
1976
Appointed to 1st-Class list: 1981
Parents: Ronnie (deceased) and Nellie
Wife and date of marriage: Jacqueline, 18 September 1971
Children: Richard Barrie, 23 November 1972; Michael Spencer, 21 March
1976; Daniel Mark Ronnie, 19 June 1981
Family links with cricket: Father played works cricket
Education: Brownhill County Primary; Harehills Secondary Modern, Leeds
Qualifications: 2 O-levels
Jobs outside cricket: Coach, driver
Close season 1987–88: Driver for Supercook Group
Cricketing superstitions or habits: 'As a player always touched down behind
my crease at the end of an over.'
Overseas tours: Duke of Norfolk's XI to West Indies 1970
Overseas teams played for: Johannesburg Municipals 1978–79
Cricketers particularly learnt from: Brian Close, Willie Watson, Arthur
Mitchell

CAREER: BATTING

	I.	N.O.	R.	H.S.	AV.
TEST					
1ST-CLASS	241	29	5373	140*	25.34
INT					
JPL	68	14	1423	86*	26.35
NAT.W.	9	0	155	76	17.22
B & H	21	5	601	90	37.56

CAREER: BOWLING

	O.	M.	R.	W.	AV.
TEST					
1ST-CLASS	5	1	5	1	5.00
INT					
JPL	8.5	0	38	2	19.00
NAT.W.					
B & H					

Cricketers particularly admired: Colin Cowdrey, Clive Rice, Richard Hadlee, Mike Procter, Gary Sobers
Other sports played: Golf, table tennis, snooker
Other sports followed: Rugby union, most other sports
Relaxations: Family, car maintenance, music, DIY
Opinions on cricket: 'Disappointed in players who lack self-control and set bad examples to young players and public alike.'

LLOYD, D.

Full Name: David Lloyd
Role: Left-hand opening bat
Born: 18 March 1947, Accrington, Lancashire
Height: 6' **Weight:** 12½st
Nickname: Bumble
County: Lancashire
County debut: 1965
County cap: 1968
Test debut: 1974
No. of Tests: 9
No. of One-Day Internationals: 8
1000 runs in a season: 11
1st-Class 50s scored: 93
1st-Class 100s scored: 37
1st-Class 200s scored: 1
1st-Class 5 w. in innings: 5
1st-Class 10 w. in match: 1
One-Day 50s: 41
One-Day 100s: 7
1st-Class catches: 334
Best batting performance: 214* England v India, Edgbaston 1974
Best bowling performance: 7-38 Lancashire v Gloucestershire, Lydney 1966
Appointed to 1st-Class list: 1987
Parents: David and Mary
Wife and date of marriage: Susan, 30 March 1968
Children: Graham, 1969; Sarah, 1971; Steven, 1980; Ben, 1984
Education: Accrington Secondary Technical School
Cricketers particularly admired: 'Here's a few: Cowdrey, Fowler, Marks, Hadlee, Marshall, Greenidge, Botham, Hick, Arnold, Underwood, Ian and Tony Greig, Gavaskar, Fletcher – they're all good lads!'
Other sports played: Soccer ('just hung up my boots – the linesman keeps passing me!'), bad golf
Relaxations: Fly fishing, antiques

Extras: Played for Cumberland in Minor Counties. Son Graham is on Lancashire staff
Opinions on cricket: 'Glad to be a part of it.'

CAREER: BATTING

	I.	N.O.	R.	H.S.	AV.
TEST	15	2	552	214*	42.46
1ST-CLASS	637	72	18717	195	33.12
INT	8	1	285	116*	40.72
JPL	171	27	4653	103*	32.31
NAT.W.	42	7	1207	121*	34.49
B & H	48	3	1474	113	32.76

CAREER: BOWLING

	O.	M.	R.	W.	AV.
TEST	4	0	17	0	–
1ST-CLASS	2584.1	719	9155	237	30.19
INT	2	1	3	1	–
JPL	77	2	420	17	24.70
NAT.W.	48.5	5	155	3	51.66
B & H	63.2	10	220	13	16.93

LYONS, K. J.

Full Name: Kevin James Lyons
Role: Right-hand bat, right-arm medium bowler
Born: 18 December 1946, Cardiff
County: Glamorgan
County debut: 1967
1st-Class 50s scored: 8
1st-Class catches: 27
Best batting performance: 92 Glamorgan v Cambridge University, Cambridge 1976
Appointed to 1st-Class list: 1985
Education: Lady Mary's High School, Cardiff

CAREER: BATTING

	I.	N.O.	R.	H.S.	AV.
TEST					
1ST-CLASS	99	14	1673	92	19.68
INT					
JPL	24	3	205	56	9.76
NAT.W.	3	1	29	16	14.50
B & H	5	1	102	40	25.50

CAREER: BOWLING

	O.	M.	R.	W.	AV.
TEST					
1ST-CLASS	69	10	252	2	126.00
INT					
JPL	14	0	94	2	47.00
NAT.W.					
B & H	23.5	0	104	7	14.85

MEYER, B. J.

Full Name: Barrie John Meyer
Role: Right-hand bat, wicket-keeper
Born: 21 August 1932, Bournemouth
Height: 5′ 10½″ **Weight:** 12st 7lbs
Nickname: BJ
County: Gloucestershire
County debut: 1957
County cap: 1958
1st-Class 50s scored: 11
Best batting performance: 63
Gloucestershire v Indians, 1959;
Gloucestershire v Oxford University,
1962; Gloucestershire v Sussex, 1964
Appointed to 1st-Class list: 1973
Appointed to Test panel: 1978
No. of Tests umpired: 20
**No. of One-Day Internationals
umpired:** 17
Wife and date of marriage: Gillian,
4 September 1965

Children: Stephen, Christopher, Adrian
Education: Boscombe Secondary, Bournemouth
Jobs outside cricket: Salesman
Off-season 1987–88: Working overseas
Overseas tours: Gloucestershire to Bermuda 1960
Cricketers particularly learnt from: Andy Wilson
Cricketers particularly admired: Keith Andrew, Bob Taylor
Other sports played: Ex-professional footballer, golf (7 handicap)
Relaxations: Music, reading

CAREER: BATTING

	I.	N.O.	R.	H.S.	AV.
TEST					
1ST-CLASS	569	190	5367	63	14.16
INT					
JPL	16	3	65	15	5.00
NAT.W.	9	2	69	21	9.86
B & H					

CAREER: BOWLING

	O.	M.	R.	W.	AV.
TEST					
1ST-CLASS	5	1	28	0	–
INT					
JPL					
NAT.W.					
B & H					

CAREER: WICKET-KEEPING

	C.	ST.
TEST		
1ST-CLASS	708	117
INT		
JPL	31	2
NAT.W.	16	3
B & H		

OSLEAR, D. O.

Full Name: Donald Osmund Oslear
Born: 3 March 1929, Cleethorpes
Height: 5' 11" **Weight:** 13st 6lbs
Appointed to 1st-Class list: 1975
Appointed to Test panel: 1980
No. of Tests umpired: 5
No. of One-Day Internationals umpired: 9
Parents: John Osmund and Violet Maude
Marital status: Divorced
Children: Sara Elizabeth, 25 February 1970
Family links with cricket: Father and brother very good club cricketers
Education: Elliston Street Secondary School

Qualifications: Member of General Council ACU. Training Officer of ACU. Member of TCCB Electronic Aids Committee
Jobs outside cricket: Fishing Industry in Grimsby. Lecturing to umpires overseas
Other sports followed: Anything which England are engaged in
Relaxations: The study of cricket law and the changes in the laws over the years. Reading cricket books
Extras: The only English umpire to have 'stood' in Test Matches, who has not played county cricket. Played soccer for Grimsby and ice-hockey for Grimsby and an England Select side

196. What have the following got in common: A. N. Hornby, S. M. J. Woods, C. B. van Ryneveld, and M. J. K. Smith?

197. Where was the first Test Match played?

PALMER, K. E.

Full Name: Kenneth Ernest Palmer
Role: Right-hand bat, right-arm
fast-medium bowler, all-rounder
Born: 22 April 1937, Winchester
Height: 5′ 10″ **Weight:** 13st
Nickname: Pedlar
County: Somerset
County debut: 1955
County cap: 1958
Test debut: 1965
No. of Tests: 1
1000 runs in a season: 1
50 wickets in a season: 6
1st-Class 50s scored: 27
1st-Class 100s scored: 2
1st-Class 5 w. in innings: 46
1st-Class 10 w. in match: 5
1st-Class catches: 156
Best batting performance: 125*
Somerset v Northamptonshire, Northampton 1961
Best bowling performance: 9-57 Somerset v Nottinghamshire, Trent Bridge
1963
Appointed to 1st-Class list: 1972
Appointed to Test panel: 1978
No. of Tests umpired: 16
No. of One-Day Internationals umpired: 8
Parents: Harry and Cecilia
Wife and date of marriage: Joy Valerie, 6 September 1962
Children: Gary, 1 November 1965
Family links with cricket: Son Gary professional cricketer with Somerset.
Brother umpire on first-class list and also played for Somerset
Jobs outside cricket: Coached cricket for Somerset for some time
Other sports played: Squash
Relaxations: 'I enjoy watching my son play cricket on the rare occasions that I
get the opportunity.'

CAREER: BATTING

	I.	N.O.	R.	H.S.	AV.
TEST	1	0	10	10	–
1ST-CLASS	480	105	7751	125*	20.66
INT					
JPL	6	1	28	14	5.60
NAT.W.	13	4	109	35	12.11
B & H					

CAREER: BOWLING

	O.	M.	R.	W.	AV.
TEST	63	7	189	1	–
1ST-CLASS	7260.4	1767	18304	865	21.16
INT					
JPL	59	6	282	11	25.64
NAT.W.	163.3	35	451	23	19.60
B & H					

Extras: Toured with Commonwealth side to Pakistan, 1962. Toured West Indies with Denis Compton's team January 1963. 'I had the opportunity to see him score 100 in great style with a straw hat on!' Umpired in two Benson & Hedges Finals and two NatWest Finals. Also twice on World Cup panel in England. Won Carling Single Wicket Competition in 1961. Did the 'double' in 1961: 114 wickets and 1036 runs. Batting with former Australia and Somerset cricketer (and former Test umpire) Bill Alley, holds 6th wicket partnership record for Somerset. Wife, Joy, is a PE teacher

PALMER, R.

Full Name: Roy Palmer
Role: Right-hand bat, right-arm fast-medium bowler
Born: 12 July 1942, Devizes, Wiltshire
County: Somerset
County debut: 1965
50 wickets in a season: 1
1st-Class 50s scored: 1
1st-Class 5 w. in innings: 4
1st-Class catches: 25
Best batting performance: 84 Somerset v Leicestershire, Taunton 1967
Best bowling performance: 6-45 Somerset v Middlesex, Lord's 1967
Appointed to 1st-Class list: 1980
Education: Southbroom Secondary Modern

Extras: Brother Ken played for Somerset and is also a first-class umpire

CAREER: BATTING

	I.	N.O.	R.	H.S.	AV.
TEST					
1ST-CLASS	110	32	1037	84	13.29
INT					
JPL	19	2	168	25	9.88
NAT.W.	9	2	30	11	4.28
B & H					

CAREER: BOWLING

	O.	M.	R.	W.	AV.
TEST					
1ST-CLASS	1697.1	336	5439	172	31.62
INT					
JPL	220	14	963	37	26.03
NAT.W.	148.1	19	532	30	17.73
B & H					

PLEWS, N. T.

Full Name: Nigel Trevor Plews
Born: 5 September 1934, Nottingham
Height: 6′ 6½″ **Weight:** 16st 12lbs
Appointed to 1st-Class list: 1982
Appointed to Test panel: 1986
(one-day panel)
**No. of One-Day Internationals
umpired:** 1
Wife and date of marriage: Margaret,
1956
Children: Elaine, 1961; Douglas,
1964
Education: Mundella Grammar
School, Nottingham
Qualifications: School Certificate,
Royal Society Arts in Book-keeping
Jobs outside cricket: Nottingham City
Police for 25 years as a Det. Sgt in
Fraud Squad

Off-season 1987–88: Employed off season by international chartered accountants Spicer and Pegler in insolvency work
Other sports played: Table tennis, swimming
Other sports followed: Rugby
Relaxations: Hill walking, reading, travel
Extras: Did not play first-class cricket

198. Who was the last man to play for England at both cricket and
soccer?

RHODES, H. J.

Full Name: Harold James Rhodes
Role: Right-hand bat, right-arm
fast bowler
Born: 22 July 1936, Hadfield,
Derbyshire
Height: 6' 2" **Weight:** 14st
Nickname: Dusty
County: Derbyshire
County debut: 1953
County cap: 1958
Test debut: 1959
No. of Tests: 2
50 wickets in a season: 11
1st-Class 5 w. in innings: 42
1st-Class 10 w. in match: 4
1st-Class catches: 86
Best batting performance: 48
Derbyshire v Middlesex,
Chesterfield 1958

Best bowling performance: 7-38 Derbyshire v Warwickshire, Edgbaston 1965
Appointed to 1st-Class list: On reserve list 1985 and 1986
Parents: Bert and Vera
Wife and date of marriage: Barbara 17 September 1960
Children: Marcus, 31 May 1961; Julie, 26 September 1962; Simon, 9 March
1968; Jonathan, 24 August 1969
Family links with cricket: Father was first-class and Test umpire
Education: Vernon High School, Derby
Jobs outside cricket: Mortgage manager, Abbey Life Assurance Co.
Off-season 1987–88: Mortgage manager full-time
Overseas tours: South Africa 1959 with Denis Compton's Commonwealth
team; Round the World 1960, with R. Benaud's Commonwealth team; to
West Indies with E. W. Swanton's Commonwealth team; Round the World
1967 with Mickey Stewart's Commonwealth team; MCC to Far East 1983
Cricketers particularly learnt from: Les Jackson, Cliff Gladwin
Cricketers particularly admired: Brian Statham, Richard Hadlee

CAREER: BATTING

	I.	N.O.	R.	H.S.	AV.
TEST	1	1	0	0*	–
1ST-CLASS	398	142	2427	48	9.48
INT					
JPL	11	5	23	6*	3.83
NAT.W.	10	6	84	26*	21.00
B & H	5	2	17	8*	5.66

CAREER: BOWLING

	O.	M.	R.	W.	AV.
TEST	74.5	10	244	9	27.11
1ST-CLASS	9128.4	2425	20901	1064	19.64
INT					
JPL	242.4	32	933	38	24.55
NAT.W.	173.4	41	435	22	19.77
B & H	98	18	302	11	27.45

Other sports followed: Rugby, soccer
Relaxations: Reading, gardening
Extras: Top of first-class bowling averages 1965 – 119 wickets, av. 11.09. Test career ruined by throwing controversy, cleared 1968 after eight years of deliberations. Autobiography published March 1987. Senior cricket coach at Lord's Indoor School

SHEPHERD, D. R.

Full Name: David Robert Shepherd
Role: Right-hand bat, right-arm medium bowler
Born: 27 December 1940, Bideford, Devon
County: Gloucestershire
County debut: 1965
County cap: 1969
Benefit: 1978 (shared with J. Davey)
1000 runs in a season: 2
1st-Class 50s scored: 55
1st-Class 100s scored: 12
One-Day 50s: 18
One-Day 100s: 2
1st-Class catches: 95
Best batting performance: 153 Gloucestershire v Middlesex, Bristol 1968
Appointed to 1st-Class list: 1981
Appointed to Test panel: 1985
Education: Barnstaple GS; St Luke College, Exeter
Extras: Superstitious enough to stand on one leg when the score is on a 'Nelson'. Only Gloucester player to score a hundred on first-class debut

CAREER: BATTING

	I.	N.O.	R.	H.S.	AV.
TEST					
1ST-CLASS	476	40	10672	153	24.47
INT					
JPL	118	9	2274	100	20.86
NAT.W.	24	3	457	72*	21.76
B & H	30	5	580	81	23.20

CAREER: BOWLING

	O.	M.	R.	W.	AV.
TEST					
1ST-CLASS	32.4	4	106	2	53.00
INT					
JPL	1	0	6	0	–
NAT.W.	0.2	0	4	0	–
B & H					

THOMPSETT, D. S.

Full Name: Donald Stanley Thompsett
Born: 8 April 1935, Piltdown,
Sussex
Height: 6′ 1″ **Weight:** 13st
Appointed to 1st-Class list: On
reserve list since 1985
Parents: John and Dorothy
Wife and date of marriage: Valerie,
10 October 1957
Children: Glen, Clifford, Steven,
Debbie and Linzie
Family links with cricket: Sons Cliff
and Steve play club cricket for
Chippenham in Western League
Education: Secondary
Jobs outside cricket: Poultry
farmer
Other sports played: Bowls,
football

Relaxations: Walking, gardening and reading
Extras: No first-class playing experience. Played local club cricket from the
age of 11 years. Umpired at club level since 1974. Appointed to Minor
Counties umpires list in 1978. Appointed to 1st-Class reserve list 1985.
Umpired 2nd XI 1st-Class Championship matches since 1979. Debut in
1st-Class Championship Essex v Derbyshire, Colchester 1985
Opinions on cricket: 'Like many people I do feel that we have opened the
floodgates for too many overseas players, therefore depriving us of some 25 or
30 places for youngsters coming into the game throughout the country.'

---

199. Who are the only three brothers to have played for England in
the same Test?

WHITE, R. A.

Full Name: Robert Arthur White
Role: Left-hand bat, off-break
bowler
Born: 6 October 1936, Fulham
Height: 5′ 9½″ **Weight:** 12st 4lbs
Nickname: Knocker
Counties: Middlesex, Nottinghamshire
County debut: 1958 (Middlesex),
1966 (Nottinghamshire)
County cap: 1963 (Middlesex),
1966 (Nottinghamshire)
1000 runs in a season: 1
50 wickets in a season: 2
1st-Class 50s scored: 50
1st-Class 100s scored: 5
1st-Class 5 w. in innings: 28
1st-Class 10 w. in match: 4
1st-Class catches: 190

Best batting performance: 116*
Nottinghamshire v Surrey, The Oval 1967
Best bowling performance: 7-41 Nottinghamshire v Derbyshire, Ilkeston 1971
Appointed to 1st-Class list: 1982
Wife: Janice
Children: Robin, Vanessa
Education: Chiswick Grammar School
Jobs outside cricket: Self employed agent
Cricketers particularly admired: 'Garfield Sobers more than anyone.'
Other sports followed: All sports, soccer and ice-hockey in particular
Relaxations: Theatre goer
Opinions on cricket: 'Too controversial to go into print.'

CAREER: BATTING

	I.	N.O.	R.	H.S.	AV.
TEST					
1ST-CLASS	642	105	12452	116*	23.19
INT					
JPL	78	28	844	86*	16.88
NAT.W.	20	1	284	39	14.95
B & H	21	9	251	52*	20.92

CAREER: BOWLING

	O.	M.	R.	W.	AV.
TEST					
1ST-CLASS	7946	2219	21138	693	30.50
INT					
JPL	607	54	2448	103	23.76
NAT.W.	147	15	488	14	34.86
B & H	234.5	32	800	19	42.11

WHITEHEAD, A. G. T.

Full Name: Alan Geoffrey
Thomas Whitehead
Role: Left-hand bat, slow
left-arm bowler
Born: 28 October 1940, Butleigh,
Somerset
County: Somerset
County debut: 1957
1st-Class 5 w. in innings: 3
1st-Class catches: 20
Best batting performance: 15
Somerset v Hampshire,
Southampton 1959
Best bowling performance: 6-74
Somerset v Sussex, Eastbourne 1959
Appointed to 1st-Class list: 1970
Appointed to Test panel: 1982
No. of Tests umpired: 4

CAREER: BATTING

	I.	N.O.	R.	H.S.	AV.
TEST					
1ST-CLASS	49	25	137	15	5.71
INT					
JPL					
NAT.W.					
B & H					

CAREER: BOWLING

	O.	M.	R.	W.	AV.
TEST					
1ST-CLASS	846.4	250	2306	67	34.42
INT					
JPL					
NAT.W.					
B & H					

200. How many pairs of fathers and sons have played for England,
and who were they?

WIGHT, P. B.

Full Name: Peter Bernard Wight
Role: Right-hand bat, off-break bowler
Born: 25 June 1930, Georgetown, British Guyana
County: Somerset
County debut: 1953
County cap: 1954
Benefit: 1963 (£5000)
1000 runs in a season: 10
1st-Class 50s scored: 207
1st-Class 100s scored: 26
1st-Class 200s scored: 2
1st-Class 5 w. in innings: 1
1st-Class catches: 204
Best batting performance: 222*
Somerset v Kent, Taunton 1959
Best bowling performance: 6-29
Somerset v Derbyshire, Chesterfield 1957
Appointed to 1st-Class list: 1966
Family links with cricket: Brother G. L. played for West Indies. Brothers H. A. and N. played for British Guyana

CAREER: BATTING

	I.	N.O.	R.	H.S.	AV.
TEST					
1ST-CLASS	590	53	17773	222*	33.10
INT					
JPL					
NAT.W.	6	0	56	38	9.33
B & H					

CAREER: BOWLING

	O.	M.	R.	W.	AV.
TEST					
1ST-CLASS	789.1	224	2262	68	33.26
INT					
JPL					
NAT.W.					
B & H					

ANSWERS

Q. 1. Tom Richardson.

Q. 2. Lord (Victor) Rothschild of Northamptonshire.

Q. 3. The Gabba, Brisbane.

Q. 4. The WACA, Perth.

Q. 5. Chris Broad and Jack Richards. Bill Athey.

Q. 6. Greg Matthews.

Q. 7. Sir Leonard Hutton on Sonny Ramadhin.

Q. 8. Gus Logie of West Indies.

Q. 9. Chris Broad, 69.57.

Q. 10. Dean Jones, 56.77.

Q. 11. Gladstone Small, 12 for 180 at 15.

Q. 12. John Emburey, 18.

Q. 13. In both innings Gooch made 51 and was l.b.w. to Holding both times.

Q. 14. He passed Ian Botham's total of runs for Somerset in one-day games.

Q. 15. Dean Jones of Australia.

Q. 16. It was his first at Lord's (for Rest of the World v MCC, August 1987).

Q. 17. Rex Alston.

Q. 18. S. F. Barnes, 49 at 10.93 in 4 Tests v South Africa in 1913–14.

Q. 19. He had over 200 runs (217) hit off him for the first time in an innings.

Q. 20. 708.

Q. 21. Javed Miandad, 260.

Q. 22. Phil Edmonds of Middlesex and England.

Q. 23. Tony Lewis.

Q. 24. 5′ 6¾″.

Q. 25. Allan Border.

Q. 26. Qadir had to set a field to stop Greenidge getting so many runs from his reverse sweep.

Q. 27. Rajesh Maru, 802.

Q. 28. 16.

Q. 29. True.

Q. 30. W. G. Grace.

Q. 31. £700,000.

Q. 32. 1963 and 1987.

Q. 33. True.

Q. 34. Vic Marks.

Q. 35. Alex Skelding of Leicestershire.

Q. 36. M. K. Elgie.

Q. 37. Kapil Dev.

Q. 38. D. B. Vengsarkar.

Q. 39. Javed Miandad.

Q. 40. J. J. Crowe.

Q. 41. J. G. Wright.

Q. 42. L. R. D. Mendis.

Q. 43. I. V. A. Richards.

Q. 44. A. J. Traicos.

Q. 45. Bill Athey.

Q. 46. Northants capped them all on the same day, 20 August 1987.

Q. 47. John Emburey.

Q. 48. Dennis Amiss.

Q. 49. 18.

Q. 50. G. R. Marsh.

Q. 51. Haseeb Ahsan.

Q. 52. Imran Khan.

Q. 53. The Lord's Test.

Q. 54. Richard Blakey of Yorkshire.

Q. 55. David Acfield of Essex.

Q. 56. Yorkshire.

Q. 57. Northants.

Q. 58. Andy Lloyd of England and Warwickshire.

Q. 59. John Jameson of England and Warwickshire.

Q. 60. Graeme Hick and Ian Botham.

Q. 61. 204.

Q. 62. 60%.

Q. 63. Michael Holding.

Q. 64. Frank Chester.

Q. 65. They all – and nobody else – made centuries in the MCC Bicentenary Test.

Q. 66. Scored 100 before lunch.

Q. 67. A. G. Chipperfield v England in 1934.

Q. 68. Lancashire.

Q. 69. Nottinghamshire.

Q. 70. David Gower – but he did make 40.

Q. 71. Geoff Hurst.

Q. 72. M. J. K. Smith.

Q. 73. R. E. Foster.

Q. 74. He always signed the 'Bill' in inverted commas.

Q. 75. Bill Athey.

Q. 76. Winker.

Q. 77. Peshawar and Bangalore.

Q. 78. Graeme Hick, 1879.

Q. 79. Neal Radford, 109.

Q. 80. One only, Mike Gatting.

Q. 81. Martin Crowe.

Q. 82. Kevan James.

Q. 83. Richard Hadlee.

Q. 84. Kim Barnett.

Q. 85. B. J. M. Maher, 76.

Q. 86. John Emburey.

Q. 87. West Indies, between 1959 and 1966. 13 Tests.

Q. 88. Australia beat England, March 1877.

Q. 89. It was his first Test for England after playing 3 times for Australia.

Q. 90. R. W. Marsh, Australia, 355.

Q. 91. R. W. Taylor, England, 10 (all caught) v India 1979–80.

Q. 92. C. Maynard, 30.

Q. 93. F. R. Spofforth, Australia v England, 1878–79.

Q. 94. South Africa.

Q. 95. Chetan Sharma, for India v New Zealand, 1987.

Q. 96. A. E. Relf of Sussex.

Q. 97. D. W. Gregory.

Q. 98. James Lillywhite.

Q. 99. Charles Bannerman of Australia.

Q. 100. Sonny Ramadhin, 774 balls v England, 1957.

Q. 101. Ian Botham, 5 times.

Q. 102. They all took a wicket with their first ball in Test cricket.

Q. 103. Ian Botham.

Q. 104. D. K. Lillee.

Q. 105. H. J. Tayfield.

Q. 106. L. R. Gibbs.

Q. 107. R. J. Hadlee.

Q. 108. Kapil Dev.

Q. 109. Imran Khan.

Q. 110. Sir Donald Bradman, Australia v England, 1930: 300.

Q. 111. J. C. Laker, 10 for 53, England v Australia, Old Trafford, 1956.

Q. 112. W. R. Hammond, 288 mins. England v New

Zealand, Auckland
1932–33.

Q. 113. Sir Donald Bradman, 214 mins. Australia v England, Leeds, 1930.

Q. 114. J. M. Gregory, 70 mins, Australia v South Africa, Johannesburg 1921–22.

Q. 115. Sir Donald Bradman: 99.94.

Q. 116. H. Sutcliffe, 60.73.

Q. 117. Each scored 22.

Q. 118. Hobbs, 56.94; Hutton 56.67.

Q. 119. Sir Donald Bradman, 974, v England, 1930.

Q. 120. True. Nottinghamshire v Surrey, Refuge Assurance League.

Q. 121. A. and G. G. Hearne for England and F. for South Africa in 1891–92.

Q. 122. D. W. and P. E. Richardson, 1957.

Q. 123. G. S. caught 122 and I. M. caught 105.

Q. 124. Sort of true. He was bowling against Surrey in the Refuge Assurance League. He fielded off his own bowling, and ran the batsman out.

Q. 125. 13 years.

Q. 126. Nelson.

Q. 127. G. Gooch.

Q. 128. Clive Rice.

Q. 129. R. E. Foster, 134 and 101 not out, and W. L. Foster, 140 and 172 not out, in 1899.

Q. 130. R. T. Stanyforth.

Q. 131. Ian Peebles.

Q. 132. Compton took 57 and Edrich took 47.

Q. 133. Alan Melville.

Q. 134. 60.

Q. 135. Taylor.

Q. 136. Sunil Gavaskar.

Q. 137. Rishton.

Q. 138. Central Districts.

Q. 139. 100.

Q. 140. J. M. Barrie, author of *Peter Pan*.

Q. 141. Sussex, 1839.

Q. 142. F. E. Woolley of Kent.

Q. 143. Ray Illingworth of Yorkshire and England.

Q. 144. Woolley (F. E.).

Q. 145. 19.

Q. 146. 42 years and 11 months.

Q. 147. He scored 144 v an Australian XI.

Q. 148. Duncan Fearnley.

Q. 149. Gunn and Moore.

Q. 150. Gray-Nicolls.

Q. 151. Slazenger.

Q. 152. Stuart Surridge.

Q. 153. Richard Illingworth.

Q. 154. Neil Burns of Somerset.

Q. 155. Northamptonshire.

Q. 156. Bluey.

Q. 157. Kim Barnett.

Q. 158. P. A. Neale.

Q. 159. Geoff Cook.

Q. 160. Gloucestershire. One. Bill Athey.

Q. 161. H. Morris.

Q. 162. They are all ex-England Test players who are now their county coaches.

Q. 163. Middlesex. Nine.

Q. 164. Australia.

Q. 165. England, by 7 runs.

Q. 166. Eden Gardens, Calcutta.

Q. 167. Albert Trott in 1899.

Q. 168. True.

Q. 169. *Marshall Arts*.

Q. 170. J. J. Warr of Middlesex and England.

Q. 171. Yes: Write to Iain Sproat at the address at the front of this book.

Q. 172. Joseph.
Q. 173. Thomson.
Q. 174. Statham.
Q. 175. Valentine.
Q. 176. Gregory.
Q. 177. Miller.
Q. 178. Sutcliffe.
Q. 179. Edrich.
Q. 180. Boon and Marsh.
Q. 181. Wanderers.
Q. 182. Berea Park.
Q. 183. St George's Park.
Q. 184. Newlands.
Q. 185. Natal.
Q. 186. Gilbert Jessop of Gloucestershire and England.
Q. 187. False: it was surprisingly high-pitched.
Q. 188. Barbados.
Q. 189. Guyana.

Q. 190. J. H. Parks.
Q. 191. J. B. Hobbs of Surrey and England, 197.
Q. 192. They all scored 100 on their first-class debut.
Q. 193. 175 yards by the Rev. W. Fellows, at Oxford, 1856.
Q. 194. 140 yards and 2 feet.
Q. 195. 278 by J. L. Guise for Winchester v Eton, 1921.
Q. 196. They were all both Test cricketers and rugger internationals.
Q. 197. Melbourne.
Q. 198. C. A. Milton.
Q. 199. W. G., E. M., and G. F. Grace, in 1880.
Q. 200. Seven: Cowdrey, Hutton, Hardstaff, Mann, Townsend, Parks, and Tate.